Memories of State

The publisher gratefully acknowledges the generous contribution to this book provided by the General Endowment Fund of the University of California Press Associates.

Memories of State

Politics, History, and
Collective Identity in Modern Iraq

ERIC DAVIS

University of California Press
BERKELEY   LOS ANGELES   LONDON

University of California Press
Berkeley and Los Angeles, California

University of California Press, Ltd.
London, England

© 2005 by the Regents of the University of California

Library of Congress Cataloging-in-Publication Data

Davis, Eric, 1946–.
    Memories of state : politics, history, and collective identity in modern
Iraq / Eric Davis.
        p.   cm.
    Includes bibliographical references and index.
    ISBN 0-520-23545-2 (cloth : alk. paper) — ISBN 0-520-23546-0 (pbk. :
alk. paper)
        1. Iraq—Politics and government—1958–.   2. Historiography—Iraq.
3. Politics and culture—Iraq.   4. Political culture—Iraq.   5. Politics and
literature—Iraq.   6. Arab nationalism—Iraq.   I. Title.

JQ1849.A91D38   2005
306.2'09567—dc22

                                                                2003024809

Manufactured in the United States of America

14   13   12   11   10   09   08   07   06   05
10   9   8   7   6   5   4   3   2   1

Printed on Ecobook 50 containing a minimum 50% post-consumer
waste, processed chlorine free. The balance contains virgin pulp,
including 25% Forest Stewardship Council Certified for no old growth
tree cutting, processed either TCF or ECF. The sheet is acid-free and meets
the minimum requirements of ANSI/NISO Z39.48-1992 (R 1997)
(Permanence of Paper).♾

For Donna, Colin, and Simon
who have given me so many wonderful memories

Contents

Illustrations

Preface

This study's genesis is a research project on social change in Arab oil-producing countries that I directed at the Social Science Research Council during the 1980s. The goal of the project, which focused on the political and sociocultural impact of oil wealth, was to reveal how political elites attempted to use such wealth to strengthen the state, particularly through efforts to appropriate understandings of the past and cultural production more broadly defined.[1] Through visits to Iraq and extensive contact with Iraqi intellectuals, it became clear that no other Arab oil state was devoting as much of its resources to this process. Indeed, Saddam Husayn headed an official project called the Project for the Rewriting of History (Mashruʿ Iʿadat Kitabat al-Tarikh).[2] Influenced by Gramscian notions of hegemony, I questioned why the Baʿthist regime felt such a strong need to rewrite the nation's history and reinterpret its cultural heritage, especially when it seemed to have eliminated all serious domestic opposition. Why were so many resources being devoted to publishing books and articles, reviving the study of folklore, increasing archaeological research, building monuments and commissioning sculpture, organizing international conferences on Iraq's civilizational heritage, and promoting historical and cultural organizations that recruited intellectuals from throughout the Arab world?

Among Arab oil-producing states, Iraq was the most significant example of a core phenomenon examined in the SSRC project, namely, how historical memory is used to constitute a nation-state and the mechanisms the state deploys in attempting to control historical memory. The carnage and disastrous consequences of the 1980–88 Iran-Iraq War and 1991 Gulf War, the February–March 1991 Iraqi uprising *(al-Intifada)*, and the brutal repression of the uprising led me to broaden the question of how state power was related to historical memory. How had Iraq, which just prior to the

Iran-Iraq War had achieved significant social and economic development, arrived at such a sorry state after the Gulf War? Why were Saddam and the Baʿth still in power? What factors helped explain how a country with substantial oil wealth, a rich civilizational past, a developed agricultural base, and a highly educated populace—all important prerequisites for and characteristics of stable democratic regimes—found itself instead subject to despotic rule and severe material deprivation? What could be learned about nation building and how authoritarian rule constitutes and sustains itself from an examination of the Iraqi state's efforts to appropriate understandings of the past? Did the state's successful efforts to mobilize Iraqis behind two disastrous wars indicate the successful imposition of hegemonic thinking on the populace? Or had the Baʿthist regime's efforts to structure collective memory merely suppressed competing visions of political community and blinded the state, allowing it to be seduced by its own rhetoric of "invented tradition"? Placing these questions in a broader perspective, what could be said about the relationship between the formation of the modern nations-state, the political uses of historical memory and the persistence of authoritarian rule, until its collapse in 2003?

I owe a debt of gratitude to many colleagues and institutions, ranging from Leonard Binder and members of the former Committee on New Nations at the University of Chicago to my colleagues in comparative politics and political economy at Rutgers University. Funds from the Iraqi Ministry of Culture and Information supported my first trip to Iraq during the spring of 1980. A grant from the Joint Committee on the Near and Middle East of the Social Science Research Council (SSRC) supported a trip to Iraq in 1984, and SSRC funds obtained through grants from the National Endowment for the Humanities and the Ford Foundation allowed me to hold conferences on Arab oil-producing countries at Rutgers University during November 1984 and August 1985. A 1985 IREX Fellowship to the former German Democratic Republic allowed me to begin interviewing Iraqi expatriates. A 1988 Summer Faculty Fellowship from the National Endowment for the Humanities, a fellowship from the Shelby Cullom Davis Center for Historical Studies at Princeton University in 1990–91, research support during the early 1990s from the Rutgers University Office of Research and Sponsored Programs, and a grant from the Rutgers Center for Historical Analysis during 1999–2000 enabled me to pursue further research in the United States, Europe, and the Middle East and allowed me to complete the manuscript.
To the many Iraqis who helped me with this study, I cannot convey my

gratitude in words. Dr. Jassim Muhammad Jirjis, Dr. Muhsin Jasim al-Musawi, Dr. Mohammed Baqir Alwan, Mr. Rifat Chadirji, Dr. Salih Altoma, Dr. Ra'id Fahmi, Dr. ʿAziz al-Hajj Haydar, Dr. Salih Ahmad al-ʿAli, Mr. Ghanem Hamdun, Ms. Zahida Ibrahim, Dr. Muddaffar al-Amin, Dr. ʿIsam al-Khafaji, Dr. Wadood Hamad, Dr. Wamidh ʿUmar al-Nazmi, Dr. Matti Moosa, Mr. Faris Couri, the late Dr. ʿAbd al-Hamid al-ʿAlwaji, and the late Dr. Wadia Juwaidah were particularly helpful.

Many colleagues have read this study. The comments of Robert Tignor and Tareq Ismail were especially beneficial. The late Lawrence Stone, Zachary Lockman, Ian Lustick, Peter Gran, Anne Norton, Myron Aronoff, Richard Wilson, Jan Kubik, and Daniel Tichenor also offered important comments on portions of this study. Michael Rossi, Sheila Friedlander, James Chou, and Matthew Derriso provided important editorial assistance for the study. Needless to say, responsibility for its contents is completely my own.

Highland Park, New Jersey
March 2003

1 Introduction

Men make their own history, but they do not make it just as they please; they do not make it under circumstances chosen by themselves, but under circumstances directly found, given and transmitted from the past. The tradition of all dead generations weighs like a nightmare on the brain of the living. And just when they seem engaged in revolutionising themselves and things, in creating something entirely new, precisely in such epochs of revolutionary crisis they anxiously conjure up the spirits of the past to their service and borrow from their names, battle slogans and costumes in order to present the new scene of world history in this time-honoured disguise and this borrowed language.

KARL MARX, *The Eighteenth Brumaire of Louis Bonaparte*

What impels us to tamper with the past? . . . We alter the past to become part of it as well as to make it our own. . . . Most of all, we alter the past to "improve" it—exaggerating aspects we find successful, virtuous, or beautiful, celebrating what we take pride in, playing down the ignoble, the ugly, the shameful.

RICHARD LOWENTHAL, *The Past is a Foreign Country*

Nothing is more important for the future of Iraq than a clearheaded understanding of its past.

KANAN MAKIYA, *Cruelty and Silence:
War, Tyranny, Uprising, and the Arab World*

Naksib al-shabab, naksib al-mustaqbal. (If we can capture Iraqi youth, then we can capture the future.)   SADDAM HUSAYN

What is the relationship between state power and historical memory? What can we learn about nation building and the ability of states to elicit the consent of the governed from the study of this relationship? Although many Arab societies trace their origins to ancient civilizations, they are ruled by states created relatively recently, often by colonial powers. In this context, historical memory becomes an important tool for political elites to enhance their legitimacy and control. As Saddam Husayn's quote above indicates, a state can more easily impose its rule if it can convince the populace, especially impressionable youth, to subscribe to its vision of society. A state's ability to achieve consensus on its view of the past facilitates the establishment of a set of foundational myths that is critical to the sense of collective identity that all nation-states must possess. If a modern state is seen as embodying the past, and especially as carrying on the legacy of a golden age, it will enjoy much greater latitude in implementing its goals. In short, public memory can become an effective tool in the state's arsenal of social control. Conversely, a state that ignores historical memory, especially during periods of rapid social change, does so at its own peril.

This study examines the processes of nation building and state formation in modern Iraq, processes that are ongoing and incomplete because Iraqis have yet to agree upon a commonly accepted model of political community. In the course of nation building, two competing models of political community, one Iraqist and one Pan-Arab, have struggled to become hegemonic. This study argues that the inability of Iraqis to construct a viable model of political community explains to a large degree the country's political and social instability. The absence of a commonly accepted model of political community is related to the problem of collective identity and foundational myths. Is Iraq's collective identity based on Arabism and being part of a larger Pan-Arab state? Or is Iraq's Arab heritage only a part—albeit a very significant part—of the multiple cultural traditions of a nation-state whose identity is based upon a cultural pluralism that valorizes the country's ethnic diversity?

Following the Italian theorist Antonio Gramsci, the concept of hegemony is understood as the attempt of political elites to generalize their interests to the populace at large. Hegemony involves not only an effort to elicit the consent of subaltern groups through encouraging them to internalize the ruling elite's norms and values, but also an effort to generate a set of foundational myths that define and institutionalize a particular nationalist imaginary. For Gramsci, hegemony is not synonymous with ideology. Hegemony is achieved when large segments of the populace not only agree upon particular understandings of political community and societal organization, but also accept these understandings as commonsensical or the natural order of things. Hegemony involves acceptance of a comprehensive worldview linked to the state, encompassing philosophy, morality, and ethics as well. For Gramsci, hegemony involves not only domination but also "intellectual and moral leadership."[1]

The goal of hegemony is not only to manipulate the populace into thinking in prescribed ways, but also to place boundaries on its thought processes, thereby minimizing counterhegemonic ideologies. In striving to achieve hegemony, the state employs "organic intellectuals" to promote a worldview designed to delegitimate and marginalize alternative and competing political frameworks by stigmatizing their core assumptions. Reacting to the successful appeals to popular sentiment by the Roman Catholic Church, and nationalist ideologies of the right such as fascism, Gramsci recognized the importance of affect in political struggle and the need to go beyond rationalist appeals to meet society's emotional needs. For Gramsci, hegemony is promoted not only through formal institutions of the state, but also through the agencies of civil society such as the church and educational institutions, which frequently transmit core ideas of the past. Clearly, historical memory is intrinsic to any attempt to achieve hegemony.

Reflecting the influence of Max Weber, most studies of nation building have focused on the state's repressive apparatus, and particularly on its control of the use of force.[2] This study is less concerned with the institutions of overt repression under authoritarian regimes than with the state's efforts to use culture and mass psychology to elicit consent. Only when citizens have internalized both fear of a regime and a level of self-discipline that results in obedience to its dictates can that regime hope to exercise meaningful control over society. In Iraq, the state's manipulation of culture by controlling historical memory represents the state's attempt to skew the balance between external repression and self-imposed compliance in favor of the latter.

Historical memory has its own memory. We need to examine the processes whereby an increased interest in the past became a key component of nationalist political discourse, why historical memory assumed specific forms at particular points in the Iraqi nation-state's constitution, and why some political forces exploited it while others tended to ignore it. The Ba'thist regime that seized power in 1968 did not initiate the reexamination of the past, nor was it the first to attempt to mobilize historical memory to elicit consent.[3] Rather, the post-1968 Ba'thist regime, which I call the Takriti Ba'th because its cadres were largely recruited from the area around Saddam's hometown of Takrit, attempted to appropriate the process of reinterpreting the past begun by the 'Abd al-Karim Qasim regime (1958–63) and to negate that effort. The Ba'thist regime politicized historical memory far more than any prior regime, using its access to massive oil revenues during the 1970s and early 1980s to engage in the rewriting of history on a scale never seen before in Iraq or anywhere else in the Arab world.

The "imagined community" fashioned by the Takriti Ba'th entailed greater reliance on a historical imaginary than on an ideological formulation of the contours of the contemporary nation-state. This imaginary, which has always focused on an Arab Golden Age situated in the 'Abbasid Empire (750–1258 C.E.), is intended not only to suggest parallels between past greatness and the greatness that Iraq will supposedly achieve under Ba'thist rule, but also to promote distrust among Iraq's main ethnic groups. One strategy to accomplish the latter is to argue implicitly that the *al-shu'ubiyun*, the Arabized Persian Shi'a who formed the core of the 'Abbasid bureaucracy, worked to undermine the empire from within, ultimately causing its downfall. The regime's message to Iraq's Sunni Arab minority was that the Shi'a, who were untrustworthy and duplicitous under the 'Abbasids, were suspect in the modern era as well. The state's message to the Shi'a was that only by renouncing their cultural heritage could they enjoy benefits distributed by the state. Indeed, only Shi'is who made such a renunciation and subscribed to Pan-Arabism achieved any political prominence under the Ba'th.

"Historical memory" may be defined as the collective understandings that a specific group shares about events in the past that it perceives to have shaped its current economic, social, cultural, and political status and identity.[4] Although "collective memory" and "social memory" have been used in place of "historical memory," the former evokes Jungian ideas of a collective consciousness that do not inform this study, while the latter does not convey the historical depth that the Ba'thist state sought to convey in its political uses of the past. Despite commemorating relatively recent events, such as the May 1941 Movement, the 1948 Arab-Israeli War, and its own July 15–30, 1968, "Revolution," the Ba'thist state focused primarily on the premodern era, especially the 'Abbasid Empire, ancient Mesopotamia, and Arab society during the *al-Jahiliya* or pre-Islamic period.

Another reason that historical memory cannot be subsumed under the notion of either collective or social memory is because, as an integral component of any hegemonic project, it must be understood politically. Although, as Richard Lowenthal notes, memory is everywhere, there is still a need to differentiate analytically between different forms of memory. I distinguish between a socially defined historical memory that represents society's understandings of the past and that develops outside the state—usually more self-consciously articulated during periods of rapid social change—and an analytically different form of memory that is used by hegemonic or counterhegemonic elites. This latter form of historical memory, which I call politicized or politically inscribed historical memory, is conceptually different from socially defined historical memory, which, although it often contains embedded political meanings, does not necessarily serve political ends. Politicized historical memory is much more instrumental than socially defined historical memory and is mobilized by both states and oppositional forces in their efforts to impose ideological hegemony and influence the distribution of power in society.[5]

Politically inscribed historical memory has been theorized within the context of state-sponsored commemorations of the past. Studies of commemoration have, for the most part, viewed such events as part of an effort to shape and solidify national collective identities rather than attempts by states to enhance their power at the expense of certain societal groups. The emphasis on commemoration, while critical to any study of politically inscribed historical memory, cannot adequately conceptualize much of the Ba'th Party's efforts to attack its enemies through subtle forms of manipulating historical memory, such as embedding coded political messages in selected historical narratives and folkloric publications.

State-sponsored historical memory differs from social memory in another crucial way. Frequently, the transgression of state-defined memory results in sanctions for citizens who refuse to toe the official line. Although sanctions may also be imposed on those who deny social memory, or those who fail to valorize a group's historical self-conception, these sanctions, such as the ostracism of the guilty party, differ dramatically from the imprisonment, exile, or even execution that awaits those whose conception of the past challenges that of the state.[6] The state possesses not only the institutionalized means for promoting particular understandings of the past, but also the legally sanctioned means for punishing those who disagree with its views.

Politicized historical memory can be conceptualized in terms of content, audience, and goals. Politically inscribed historical memory will resonate with a wider audience if it addresses the material realities of a society and tries to engage the tensions or contradictions that those realities embody. In Iraq, these contradictions are based on two fundamental cleavages. One is the persistence of a set of sharply drawn political cleavages based on ethnic and social class differentiation that reflect deeper unresolved issues of cultural pluralism and social equity. The other issue is the Iraqi populace's desire for social and political stability after a long period of rapid and disruptive social and cultural change that began during the late nineteenth century, and their desire for the resolution of the political instability that has plagued the nation-state since the 1920s.

Intellectuals play a critical role in the production of state-sponsored historical memory, either through their own cultural production or through the codification in politically desirable ways of extant cultural production. Ruling elites or political groups always emphasize a reading of history that demonstrates their cultural and national "authenticity." Political elites claim that they embody cultural continuity by asserting an isomorphism between their own norms, values, and traditions and those of a prior Golden Age during which society purportedly reached its apogee. For nationalist forces, a concern with historical memory often reflects a reaction to discontinuity or rupture. Here political elites use historical memory to portray themselves as *reestablishing* society's links to a glorious past that have been ruptured by "reactionary" and culturally inauthentic forces such as corrupt domestic elites, colonialists, and unpatriotic minorities.

State-sponsored history writing and cultural production complement the state's use of violence in many important ways. Through the content of politicized historical memory, dominant elites seek to privilege those groups that support them while marginalizing those considered actual or potential opponents. This process of marginalization can assume at least three forms. First, the state attempts to stigmatize the historical experiences of those groups it finds threatening by explicitly or implicitly arguing that they contradict the authentic traditions of the nation-state and its "historical mission." Second, the state can ostensibly valorize the cultural heritage of groups it seeks to marginalize while simultaneously arguing that their traditions, such as forms of dress or religious practices, are at variance with modernity and hence should not be a part of daily life but rather confined to specific holidays or festivals or placed on display in museums.[7] Third, the state can also attempt to eliminate knowledge of historical events that it finds subversive by excluding references to them in public documents or oral pronouncements by government officials. All of these policies seek to undermine the ability of subaltern groups to think in counterhegemonic ways that might contest the state's concept of political community and the underlying interests subsumed therein.

In authoritarian states, political elites use state-sponsored historical memory to foster feelings of paranoia, xenophobia, and distrust. In Iraq, the Ba'th Party promoted these feelings through a transhistorical model of society that portrayed Iraq as continuously victimized throughout its history by internal and external conspiracies. This perspective serves multiple purposes. First, by blaming Iraq's internal and external enemies, who are purportedly envious of the country's great civilizational heritage and covet dominance of the country, the state is absolved of responsibility for society's ills. Second, by promoting notions of conspiracy and victimization, the state seeks to reduce Iraqis' incentive to develop an understanding of other societies' cultural experiences and traditions. Paranoia, xenophobia, distrust, and feelings of victimization not only undermine cross-cultural contact, but they also help to atomize a nation-state's citizenry. Privileged groups have little incentive to interact with stigmatized groups because such groups are viewed as having nothing "modern" or "progressive" to contribute to society, and because associating with them can draw the state's opprobrium. This process of marginalization thus promotes society's atomization, as different ethnic groups view one other with mistrust and the populace is encouraged to be constantly vigilant for "traitors."

Politicized historical memory is intended to promote the cohesion of the political elite. Politically inscribed historical memory becomes part of a strategy to promote a corporatist identity that unites elites and their supporters along vertical rather than horizontal lines. The intent is likewise to reduce the possibility that the elite's supporters will be mobilized by oppositional forces. Although ideology often functions as the central mechanism in promoting corporatist solidarity, ideological pronouncements will tend to be more effective in societies that are ethnically homogeneous. Because ideology is invariably overt and Manichaean in its delineation of good and evil, patriots and enemies, its messages can be counterproductive when an elite striving for hegemony is drawn from an ethnic minority and the boundary that separates privileged from marginalized groups in a society correlates with ethnic cleavages. In Iraq, where the Sunni Arab minority has dominated the state, historical memory became a more effective means for the Ba'th to promote group solidarity because it relied on subtle messages embedded in historical and historical-cultural narratives that were designed to avoid attacking directly and hence alienating hostile or potentially hostile ethnic groups such as the Shi'a and the Kurds.[8]

The Ba'thist state's efforts to rewrite the past were directed first and foremost at the regime's power base, which consisted of a loose alliance of tribal groupings located in the so-called Sunni Arab triangle that extends north of Baghdad to Ramadi and Mosul. Here historical memory reinforced the Ba'th Party's vague and ill-defined ideology. Pan-Arabism, the core of Ba'thist ideology (although after the 1970s no longer as central as when the Takriti Ba'th seized power in 1968), depends upon on a particular form of historical memory rooted in an Arab Golden Age tied to the Baghdad-based 'Abbasid Empire. Ideologically, Pan-Arabism offers the Sunni Arab minority the possibility of majority status in a unitary Pan-Arab nation (*al-watan al-'Arabi*), which is especially attractive to those who still adhere to tribal identities and who have dominated the state apparatus.

Historical memory provided the elite's social base with not only a sense of corporate identity, but also the cues necessary for upward mobility in the political and socioeconomic hierarchy of Ba'thist society. As fashioned by the Ba'th, historical memory promoted an insular and xenophobic under-standing of political community. It is not important whether Ba'thists, or candidates for party membership, actually believed the historical narratives of state-sponsored texts. Acceptance of these narratives, and the values they promote, constituted symbolic support for the Ba'thist worldview and rejec-tion of a political community based on political participation and cultural pluralism. If the state could convince its supporters that it constantly faced conspiracies intended to undermine it, then all must remain constantly vig-ilant and united against ever-present enemies. Here historical memory re-inforced a siegelike mentality that fostered elite cohesion while legitimating the Ba'thist regime's extensive security apparatus used to suppress real and imagined enemies. For both the elite's inner circle and the party's mass base, the manner in which state intellectuals conceived of the past provided a set of indirect cues that helped define how they should view contemporary so-ciety.

Historical memory served the state in its interactions with subaltern groups and commercial or religious elites outside the state in several ways. The responses of these groups to the state's messages may not have been as positive as the responses of the privileged elite. However, subaltern groups, if they were politically savvy, studied these messages to ascertain what *not* to say about the past to avoid antagonizing those who controlled the state. Further, when non-elite members of society sought privileges such as posi-tions in the state bureaucracy, public entitlements, or state contracts, they often made an attempt to accept particular "memories of state," at least par-tially, as a means of ingratiating themselves with bureaucrats and powerful political actors. Here state-sponsored understandings of the past informed Iraqis outside the corridors of power how they needed to conceptualize Iraqi history and cultural heritage in order to navigate the pathways of everyday life.

State-sponsored understandings of the past were also designed to under-mine subaltern groups' ability to develop a viable civil society and inclu-sionary political community. By questioning the loyalty of the non-Sunni Arab population, especially the Shi'a, the Ba'thist view of the past under-mined trust between Iraq's different ethnic groups. Although pre-1958 his-torical narratives were said to have been dominated by a colonially inspired "divide and conquer" mentality, Ba'thist historiography fostered the very mistrust and hostility among ethnic groups of which it accused "reactionary elements."

State-sponsored historical memory was directed at other Arab states and hence intended to serve the Ba'thist regime's regional objectives. No Arab state promoted the fiction of Pan-Arab unity as stridently as Baʿthist Iraq, which portrayed Iraq as a region *(qutr)* of a larger Arab nation. Linking Pan-Arabism to the history of the ʿAbbasid Empire has always provided a cover for various Iraqi regimes in their desire to assert a central role in inter-Arab politics. The history of Iraq, the longest-lasting Arab empire and a nation with an extraordinarily rich cultural heritage, provides it with a strong cachet for assuming the role of *primus inter pares* among its fellow Arab states. Further, the Baʿth's emphasis on its Mesopotamian heritage, reflected, for example, in efforts to resurrect ancient Babylon and in its naming an elite Special Republican Guard armored unit the Hammurabi Brigade, complemented rather than countered its Pan-Arab emphasis, as some observers have argued.[9] As the country with the world's oldest civilizational heritage, Iraq has the greatest historical and cultural traditions of any Arab state, except perhaps Egypt. Because the Baʿth argued that the ancient Mesopotamians were, in fact, Semitic peoples, from the Baʿth perspective there was no necessary ethnic contradiction between Iraq's Islamic and pre-Islamic civilizations.[10]

In a democratic society in which historical memory is designed to promote cultural inclusion and participatory politics, the state's interpretation of the past need not involve denigrating other nation-states to strengthen its rule. However, where authoritarian rule prevails, historical memory is invariably manipulated to vilify nation-states perceived as threatening and to sharpen the cultural boundaries between the domestic populace and the "Other" for purposes of social control. Encouraging an inward-looking culture and view of the past denies the need for cross-cultural borrowing and synthesis. The vilification of Iran, Israel, and, until the late 1990s, Syria, which the Baʿth Party considered Iraq's main external enemies, is an example of the manner in which foreign "Others" were used in the service of domestic politics.[11] Iran became a metaphor for disloyal Shiʿis and minorities, Israel a metaphor for the continuous efforts of Western imperialism to thwart Iraq's regional leadership role, and Syria a metaphor for treasonous forces working to subvert the Arabs' "historical destiny" of creating a Pan-Arab state.[12]

The impact of historical memory is often difficult to demarcate clearly in causal terms. First, understandings of the past are often neither linear nor discrete in the perceiver's mind.[13] Because memory can be very fluid, an individual or group may perceive a particular historical event in a disjointed rather than structured and temporally sequential manner and conflate one event with another. Second, the ability to internalize state-sponsored historical memory requires a certain level of literacy and formal education. Although television and other forms of visual imagery can partially transcend illiteracy in communicating political messages, a message's ability to acquire meaning requires the recipient to have at least some familiarity with the historical event in question, usually through reading texts. Even visual imagery that relates to the past requires the same minimal level of familiarity.[14] Thus, state-sponsored historical memory is most directly experienced by the educated classes.

The impact of historical memory will depend on the extent to which target audiences accept the state's political and cultural hierarchizing of society. If that memory deviates significantly from the structural realities of society, it will fail to resonate with large segments of the populace. Ba'thist historical memory was most attractive to intellectuals and members of the lower middle classes who originated in the so-called Sunni Arab triangle because it provided justification for an existing configuration of political power and distribution of wealth and privilege that favored Iraq's Sunni Arab minority. Conversely, forms of historical memory that privileged the ruling Ba'th Party's social base offered little to those who support Iraqist nationalism and whose understandings of the past stress a culturally inclusive and politically participatory society.

Rather than the result of linear processes of cause and effect, politically inscribed historical memory represents a domain of struggle in which political coalitions conduct their respective "wars of position" as they attempt to achieve hegemony. Although historical memory cannot be reduced, in some positivist sense, to a set of "independent" and "dependent" variables, it can assume causal properties. For example, historical memory helped legitimate existing hierarchies of power by providing justifications for the continued domination of the Iraqi state by a tribally based minority of the Sunni Arab community through invalidating the history and culture of non-elite groups. Alternatively, historical memory has been mobilized by counter-hegemonic forces that envision the sharing of power by all groups in society. In the former model, historical memory undermines interethnic contact and understanding by fostering suspicion of one ethnic group by another. The Ba'thist state was the beneficiary of this distrust. In the latter model, historical memory promotes interethnic solidarity. Clearly, historical memory must be viewed dialectically. For every memory promoted by the state there will be a countermemory—frequently masked by subaltern groups in their own coded historical texts or oral discourse—that challenges the state's interpretation of the past.

The state's uses of historical memory provide an indicator of struggle and change. First, it highlights the state's vulnerability by pointing to those social and political forces that it finds threatening. In authoritarian societies in which political decision making is shrouded in secrecy, studying the state's efforts to restructure historical memory provides a window through which to gain insights into its internal political struggles. A careful examination of the state's attempts to suppress those aspects of the past that challenge its political agenda and privilege those that support it helps us grasp the contours of the struggle over defining political community and the central issues of who is considered a worthy citizen, whose cultural norms are seen as contributing to society's ends, and who should be politically and socially privileged as a result.

Studying the state's efforts to control historical memory helps identify those groups that oppose the state. Not even the most authoritarian state has been able to impose its ideological vision on the populace as a whole. Paraphrasing Gramsci, memory implies countermemory. To identify what the state seeks to repress likewise indicates the counterhegemonic policies and values that those forces that oppose the state would foreground and legitimate in the public eye. Many Iraqi intellectuals have attempted to subvert the state's efforts to appropriate their services to develop officially sanctioned understandings of the past. Thus studying the struggle over historical memory reveals not only broad indicators of political conflict, but also more narrowly defined indicators of how at least some intellectuals strive to maintain a modicum of professional integrity under repressive political conditions. Studying how intellectuals subvert the state's goals by incorporating multiple levels of meanings into their texts can provide important microanalytic insights into processes of political struggle that complement the macroanalytic understandings gained from studying the state's overall program for restructuring the past.

One reason for focusing on historical memory and collective identity is to better understand why Iraq, unlike any other Arab country, has had such a turbulent experience of modern nation building and state formation. Since its founding in 1921, the nation-state has been plagued by political instability and violence, including, in 1936, the Arab world's first military coup. Although human rights abuses existed under the monarchy and, to a limited degree, the first postmonarchy regime of Brigadier ʿAbd al-Karim Qasim, these pale in significance with the savagery of the Baʿthist regime under Saddam Husayn al-Takriti. The extensive state security apparatus policy of arbitrary arrests and widespread use of torture and execution led to Iraq's characterization as a "republic of fear."[15] Having held power from 1968 until 2003, Saddam was not only Iraq's longest ruling head of state, but the longest ruling Arab leader as well.

Although the repression experienced in everyday life under the Takriti Ba‘th suggested a rigidity and fixity in Iraqi politics, a rich and diverse cultural life prior to Ba‘thist rule belied the regime's authoritarian and exclusionist practices while suggesting the need to reexamine many of the assumptions about nation building in modern Iraq. A systematic historical perspective suggests that Ba‘thist brutality does not reflect some fundamental or primordial quality of the Iraqi body politic. Rather than the "natural" condition of a polity plagued by a lack of collective identity, political instability, and a tendency toward violence, Ba‘thist rule was the result of a particular conjuncture of historical events whose roots can be traced to the late nineteenth century. Having seized power in 1968 by manipulating a power vacuum and political crisis caused by the June 1967 Arab-Israeli War, the Ba‘th failed to fulfill any of its promises, which ultimately led to its demise.

Clearly, nation building, authoritarian rule, and the state's promotion of particular forms of historical memory are interdependent. Authoritarian rule is both a cause and effect of the particular lineages of Iraq's turbulent process of nation building. It is a consequence of the inability of Iraq's ethnic groups to transcend a particular historical configuration of power in which sectors of the Sunni Arab minority have dominated the state and have been unwilling to share political power, particularly with the country's Shi‘i majority. Political repression is meant to prevent the issues of political participation and definition of political community from being placed on the nation's political agenda. Historically, the lack of trust among Iraq's ethnic groups has been due in large measure to a dearth of institutions, economic, political, and cultural, through which these groups could develop meaningful social intercourse. Ottoman and British exploitation of ethnic divisions only exacerbated this lack of trust, further undermining the development of any shared sense of collective identity and political community.

Authoritarianism is not just an outcome of the nation-building process, but also one of its causes. Under the Hashimite Monarchy, and especially under the 1963 and post-1968 Ba‘thist regimes, authoritarian rule seriously undermined if not destroyed the institutions of civil society by atomizing the nation's populace and forcing associational activity underground or, more recently, to reconstitute itself beyond Iraq's boundaries. Authoritarianism was most sharply highlighted by the Ba‘thist state's violence against its own citizenry, the decisions to attack Iran in 1980 and to seize Kuwait ten years later, and the "cultural violence" directed against ethnic groups whose heritage it has sought to extirpate from the historical record. All of these policies were enacted by Saddam Husayn and a small inner circle of Ba‘th Party members.

Political instability and authoritarian rule in Iraq trace their origins to a fundamental disagreement over the nature of political community in the modern nation-state. Historically, two competing visions of Iraqi society developed. First, a Pan-Arab definition of Iraq arose in the wake of the 1914–18 Arab Revolt and the Ottoman Empire's collapse following World War I. This vision of political community dates the origins of modern Iraq to its Semitic past, namely the Arabs of the pre-Islamic period and the ʿAbbasid Empire. According to this vision, because the Iraqi people achieved greatness during periods of Arab unity, then such unity is a prerequisite for progress in the modern era. A second or Iraqist nationalist vision, associated with opposition to the British following their 1914 invasion of Iraq and during the June–October 1920 Revolution, looks for its foundational myths to Iraq's ancient civilizations as well as to its Arab heritage, but without privileging the latter. Emphasizing the glory of the ancient Sumerian, Babylonian, and Assyrian civilizations challenges the Pan-Arabist assertion that Iraq is but a region *(qutr)* of a larger Arab nation by reducing Arabism to one among many influences in Iraq's historical and cultural development. Both Sunni and Shiʿi Arabs, as well as other minority groups, may participate in this particular form of historical memory.[16]

Throughout the twentieth century, the left has emphasized Iraq's Mesopotamian heritage because it is more representative of Iraq's ethnic diversity, especially important to groups that have historically been excluded from power, such as the Shiʿa, Kurds, and ethnic minorities. In the modern period, Iraqist nationalists have commemorated the inclusionary vision of mass-based uprisings such as the 1920 Revolution, the 1931 General Strike, the 1948 Wathba, 1952 Intifada, and the 1958 Revolution. Support for the Pan-Arab vision has tended to come from the minority Sunni Arab community, which has viewed Iraq's inclusion in a larger Arab nation as a means of transforming its minority status to that of a majority given Sunni Islam's preponderance in the larger Arab world. Unlike Iraqist nationalists, Pan-Arabists have tended to avoid questions of cultural diversity and often have downplayed equity and social justice issues in favor of cultural issues.

Each conception of Iraqi political community suffers from shortcomings. The Pan-Arabist vision of Iraq as part of a larger Sunni-dominated Arab nation *(al-watan al-ʿArabi)* has failed to recognize the right of the majority Shiʿi population and ethnic minorities to participate in national politics and cultural discourse. Iraqist nationalists, drawn heavily from the left, frequently have neglected the urban middle classes' deeply felt need for political stability and their desire to reestablish a sense of unity to offset the social and cultural fragmentation that occurred throughout much of the twentieth century. Put differently, leftist nationalists often have not been sensitive to the social and cultural unity that Pan-Arabists feel would be achieved through the creation of a supranational Arab state. The Pan-Arabists' ability to appeal to and manipulate a historical memory that has resonated more fully with the crises of dislocation that the nationalistically oriented middle classes experienced, combined with the left's relative neglect of this dimension of historical memory, constitutes a crucial element in explaining how Ba'thism was ultimately able to dominate political and cultural space in Iraq after 1968.

Gradually, the two competing visions of collective identity and political community were institutionalized in political parties and organizations. During the 1920 Revolution, the Iraqist nationalist vision was articulated by the Guardians of Independence (Haras al-Istiqlal). Later, its proponents became the National Party (al-Hizb al-Watani) and its successor organizations, the Ahali Group (Jam'iyat al-Ahali), the National Democratic Party (al-Hizb al-Watani al-Dimuqrati), and the powerful Iraqi Communist Party (al-Hizb al-Shuyu'i al-'Iraqi). The Iraqist vision of political community, which emphasized the need for social justice and cultural pluralism, attracted a large following, especially among the intelligentsia, secular Shi'is, the growing working class, and marginalized ethnic groups such as the Jews.

The Pan-Arab definition of political community was fostered during the 1920s and 1930s by the National Covenant (al-'Ahd al-Watani) and National Brotherhood (al-Ikha' al-Watani) parties, and subsequently by quasi-fascist organizations such as the al-Muthanna Club (Nadi al-Muthanna) and its al-Futuwwa youth wing, and military cliques such as the Four Colonels, which seized power and deposed the regent, 'Abd al-Ilah, in May 1941. Quickly defeated by British forces, Pan-Arabism was dealt a temporary setback as its supporters were expelled from the army and the state bureaucracy. The movement reemerged after World War II in the form of the Independence Party (Hizb al-Istiqlal) and then the Arab Socialist Ba'th Party (Hizb al-Ba'th al-'Arabi al-Ishtiraki), which was founded in Iraq in 1952. Pan-Arabism received a tremendous boost from the 1948 debacle in Palestine, partly because it was able to tar the supporters of the Iraqist vision as anti-Arab and non-patriotic due to the many Jews in their ranks, now suspected of supporting Zionism. Pan-Arabism was further strengthened during the 1950s by President Jamal 'Abd al-Nasir's perceived defeat of the Tripartite Invasion of Egypt following his nationalization of the Suez Canal in 1956 and the 1958 formation of the United Arab Republic between Egypt and Syria.

The struggle between these two visions of collective identity and politi-

cal community came to a head during the July 1958 Revolution and its turbulent aftermath. ʿAbd al-Karim Qasim's revolutionary regime, the first
Iraqi regime systematically to attempt to fashion its own "memories of
state," pursued a distinctly Iraqist model, much to the chagrin of many of
the Iraqi Free Officers and surrounding Arab states that had supported the
revolution. Although his inability to forge an effective alliance with his natural constituents in the Iraqi Communist Party (ICP) and the National
Democratic Party (NDP) was a critical reason for his regime's failure, Qasim
was also hurt by failing to recognize Pan-Arabism's symbolic meaning for
many Iraqis, especially those among the politically active middle classes. For
many urban nationalists, the attraction of Pan-Arabism was less the imminent possibility of creating a Pan-Arab state than its appeal to social and cultural unity that resonated strongly with a populace seeking relief from
decades of political, social, and economic instability. Iraqist nationalist members of the ICP and NDP largely ignored historical memory, or they promoted a historical memory that focused on the Soviet and Western experiences, with which many Iraqis could not identify.

Not all Iraqis who supported an Iraqist nationalist collective identity ignored indigenous historical memory. The group of intellectuals associated
with the state's Directorate of Antiquities and its highly respected journal,
Sumer, founded in 1945, highlighted Iraq's ancient civilizations and not just
its Arab-Islamic heritage. Qasim likewise drew upon symbols from ancient
Mesopotamia that became an integral part of the revolution's iconography,
such as the sun of Isis in the Iraqi republic's new flag. The revolutionary regime's intense focus on folklore, later copied by Saddam and the Baʿth, was
grounded in a historical memory that emphasized the continuity of
centuries-old folk traditions with which all Iraqis, especially the middle
classes, peasants, and workers, could identify. Qasim's overthrow highlights
another variable critical to the impact of historical memory. The revolutionary regime's failure to promote political institutionalization undermined its
use of historical memory as a weapon against its enemies. Despite Qasim's
creation of the Ministry of Guidance (Wizarat al-Irshad) to promote an
Iraqist collective identity, his failure to form a broad coalition of Iraqist political forces, formed especially of the ICP, NDP, and Kurdish groups, weakened the regime's ability to counter the Pan-Arab message that attracted
ever-greater support as political and social strife spread and Qasim's isolation grew.

Its many internal contradictions notwithstanding, the Iraqi Revolution
of 1958–63 fostered the continued growth of an incipient civil society that
had begun during the interwar period and spread in earnest after 1945. This

nascent civil society depended in part on new political parties that, unlike the clique-based parties that supported the monarchy, rested on significant social bases. Professional associations and their attendant clubs, in which political and civic discourse became commonplace, spread in urban areas. Large numbers of labor unions were organized throughout Iraq after World War II, often with help from the ICP. Intellectual associations concerned with literature and the arts flourished. Newspapers, magazines, and journals proliferated and, when shut down by the authorities, they quickly reappeared under different names. The coffeehouse, already a venerable institution, became associated with specific political parties and/or intellectual tendencies and an important venue for innovative cultural and political discourse. The creative character of the postwar era was evident in the Free Verse Movement—a profound innovation in poetry, the most original form of expression in Arab culture—and in new forms of sculpture, painting, and short story writing. When a temporary lapse in state repression led to relatively free parliamentary elections in 1954, Iraqist nationalists supported by moderate Pan-Arabists scored impressive victories in major urban centers.

Although the first Ba'thist regime brutally suppressed this nascent civil society in 1963, it gradually reemerged between 1964 and 1968, only to be repressed again by the second Ba'thist regime, which placed almost all private cultural expression under state control. Nevertheless, Ba'thist repression could not eliminate the historical memory of the pre-1963 era. It was firmly etched in the minds of large numbers of Iraqis that associational activity and even electoral behavior independent of state control, as well as civil discourse and cultural pluralism, could become the defining characteristics of political community.

Despite these factors, why should the ubiquitous use of violence that has characterized most Iraqi regimes not constitute the main focus in understanding the modern nation-state's formation? Am I arguing that focusing on historical memory and identity politics should replace the study of Ba'thist repression? Certainly, state-sponsored violence needs to be an integral part of any narrative of nation building in modern Iraq. Further, Ba'thist attempts to appropriate historical memory are viewed here as a form of "cultural violence" and hence as an extension of the state's physical repression. Nevertheless, a model that emphasizes historical memory and collective identity requires its own analytic autonomy and cannot be subsumed under a discourse of violence and repression. It is an axiom of political theory that no regime can rule for long without the consent of the governed. Virtually all authoritarian states, from Hitlerian Germany to Stalinist Russia, have conjoined a resort to violence with a strong emphasis on ideological persuasion. Although the Takriti Ba'thist regime's brutality was without parallel in the Arab world, its perception that it needed to structure Iraqi collective identity through influencing how Iraqis viewed the past and national cultural heritage indicates that, like other authoritarian regimes, it did not view physical coercion alone as an effective means of rule. Mao's dictum that power comes from the mouth of a gun notwithstanding, long-term political rule requires more than force to be effective.

The Ba'thist regime's massive human rights abuses have been eloquently documented in many works, most notably in those by Kanan Makiya.[17] Although these contributions are important, one shortcoming has been the lack of dynamism or change in their models in which politics is limited to the intimidation and liquidation of the Ba'th's real and perceived opponents and the regime's internal struggles. Even under the most oppressive regimes, there is always ongoing resistance by subaltern groups, even if it does not entail direct challenges to the regime's prerogatives. Moving beyond force and coercion to the struggle over history and culture reveals a contested arena in which symbols, metaphors, allusions, and double entendres belie a rich underlying debate that encompasses myriad questions concerning social equity, cultural pluralism, and political participation. The characterization of Iraq as a "republic of fear" did not capture the complexity of this realm of political discourse and its numerous "hidden texts."

Ba'thist authoritarianism forced Iraqi political discourse to assume a historical dimension. Given the danger of touching on sensitive issues, writers and artists tended to take refuge in the past to spread their message. If accused of transgressing existing political norms, they could respond that their texts or works of art concerned the past, not the present. Thus not only are Iraqis, and especially the educated middle classes, genuinely interested in historical topics, but their concern with the past has also been part of a "discourse of hidden texts," namely a methodology of resistance that uses the past as a vehicle for engaging in "safe" political discourse under authoritarian rule.

Hobsbawm argues that "invented tradition" entails formalization and ritualization.[18] Indeed, Iraq has established museums and created monuments designed to establish an institutionalized relationship to the past.[19] For example, the reconstruction of the ancient city of Babylon (for which, of course, there are no accurate visual images, but only limited archaeological plans) reflected a conscious effort to link the Ba'th to ancient Mesopotamia, as indicated by the fact that Saddam's initials were inscribed on every brick. Numerous annual festivals and holidays commemorated historical events. Saddam called for a self-conscious rewriting of history to overcome the legacy of colonial and prerevolutionary thinking on Iraqi history and national heritage *(al-turath)*. However, state-sponsored understanding of the past avoided such formalization and ritualization precisely because the Ba'thist state sought to avoid calling attention to such efforts. Historical analysis became a subtle means for attacking those groups the Ba'th viewed as threatening in the context of a nation-state in which collective identity and political community are sharply contested. Although the Ba'thist state sought to forge a master historical narrative, it could not formulate this narrative as directly and openly as have many other nation-states due to internal ethnic and political cleavages.

The realization that Iraq, unlike most European states, only became a nation-state in 1921 and independent from foreign control in 1932 (others would argue not until 1958) should temper puzzlement about why Iraq has not yet been able to establish a stable and democratic political community. Contrary to views in the West, Iraqis are strongly committed to the Iraqi nation-state. The problem is not whether there should be an Iraqi nation-state, but rather the type of political community upon which it should rest. Once Great Britain created the Iraqi state (on which it imposed British political institutions), Iraqis were forced to address a number of critical questions. What shape would Iraq's political community assume? What would constitute the new state's founding myths, and hence to what history or histories would Iraqis look? How would the state's constituent ethnic groups relate to one another? Would patterns of privilege and domination that had formerly characterized the Ottoman provinces that now comprised the new Iraqi nation-state persist or be redressed in favor of traditionally marginalized groups? How would Arab and Kurdish tribes, which had organized themselves according to regional identities, function within an institution whose raison d'être caused it to oppose local particularism?

One of the first steps by all political actors was to seek recourse to historical memory. The Hashimite Monarchy and the ex-Sharifian officers emphasized their role in the Arab Revolt (1914–18) against the Ottoman Turks in the Hijaz and the Levant. The Sunni Arab political elite focused on its historically dominant role in the state and hence its legitimacy through continuity and experience. The Shi'a stressed their role in protecting Iraq during World War I through their revolt against invading British forces. In "the production of space," the Hashimites posited a Pan-Arab political community as the highest achievement of which Iraq was but a subunit. Pursuing a slightly different tack, the traditional Sunni Arab leadership likewise stressed Arabism, but in the context of Iraq as the historical axis *(mihwar)* of the larger Pan-Arab community, derived from Baghdad's role as the 'Abbasid Empire's capital. The Shiʿa sought to privilege Iraq's Islamic character by instituting a jihad or holy war against the alien invader based on the premise that Great Britain's conquest of Iraq would corrupt both its physical and moral character. For the Shiʿi clergy who opposed the British, Iraq's political identity lay in Islam and could not be subordinated to either Arabism or "Mesopotamianism." From the founding of the modern state, historical memory was sharply contested.

The greater the degree to which a populace shares a collective memory, the less the need for the state to impose an "invented tradition" or "imagined community."[20] Thus a shared collective memory represents a critical prerequisite for effective nation building. Although a society's collective memory usually evolves over a lengthy period of time in a participatory manner through communal processes of ritualization and commemoration, such as through religion and folklore, a portion of that memory may be imposed or altered by the state. As a result, the populace may arrive at shared understandings of the past in an organic manner through processes that synthesize a variety of "subnational memories" drawn from specific ethnic communities and regions, or the state may try to use its resources to impose a certain mode of thinking on the populace. In most nation-states, both these processes operate in an interactive fashion.

Once a political elite decides to use the state to alter or add to a nation's historical memory, the intelligentsia's political significance increases because it assumes the role of transmitting the new understandings to the society at large. However, we need to be careful that this formulation does not become mechanistic and oversimplified. Nationalist thinking that precedes the formation of modern nation-states has invariably entailed a reexamination of existing descriptions and interpretations of the past by the nationalists themselves. The social change that accompanies nationalism stimulates a questioning of prevailing assumptions about the bonds that tie groups together, or what anthropologists call the "taken-for grantedness" of reality. Where colonial powers formerly ruled, there is always a call to "purify" the historical record that nationalists view as having been distorted by colonialism, often in collaboration with discredited landowning and mercantile elites. Intellectuals will only be effective in transmitting new understandings of the past if these understandings resonate with existing patterns of thought. It is therefore problematic to view the role of intellectuals as "injecting" *de novo* historical consciousness into the populace at large. Instead, their efforts should be viewed syncretically, as through them the state attempts to graft its own interpretations of the past onto changing patterns of historical consciousness.

Historical memory assumes added significance where there is a sharp disjuncture between a society's longevity and the recent establishment of the state. Iraq represents a quintessential example of the formulation "old societies and new states."[21] Mesopotamia, or the Fertile Crescent, possesses an extraordinarily rich historical past. The modern nation-state, on the other hand, was created only in 1921. The story of how the British combined the three former Ottoman provinces of Mosul (al-Mawsal), Baghdad, and Basra into a new state known as Iraq while carving Kuwait as a separate entity from the province (vilayet) of Basra is well known.[22] Although the three regions that formed the modern nation-state shared certain commonalities, they also had developed along different economic, political, and cultural trajectories. The Kurds in the northeast had, prior to World War I, possessed a relatively autarkic economy due to a rugged geography that limited their contact with the Arabic-speaking populations to the south. The Shiʿa, especially those of the holy cities of al-Najaf and Karbalaʾ in south-central Iraq, maintained close economic and cultural contacts with their confessional compatriots in neighboring Iran to the east and with the Persian Gulf to the south. The Sunni Arab population in the central and north-central areas between Baghdad and Mosul looked to the Levant and the larger Arab world for economic, political, and cultural sustenance. The Ottoman policy of favoring Arab Sunnis for state offices, combined with the tribal organization of all three communities, exacerbated these cleavages.

The working class's growth, the spread of urban bidonvilles, and the expansion of the white-collar middle class not only caused new forms of production and changes in class structure, but it also disrupted cultural norms and structures of meaning associated with traditional (village/tribal) society. Patterns of regional collective memory also were disrupted as Iraq's three ethnic groups interacted with one another in urban settings. For many urban, educated Iraqis, ethnic differentiation was part of the colonial policy of "divide and conquer."[23] The past increasingly was called upon to provide examples of social and cultural unity that would counter colonialism's fragmentary impact. For the British, the monarchy, and the traditional leadership of Iraq's three major ethnic groups, ethnic consciousness became a vehicle for reinforcing vertical ties of social solidarity that were challenged by the horizontal ties promoted by radical Iraqist nationalists, especially communists. History, or what Iraqis more often referred to as "heritage" (al-turath), became a contested domain as different ethnic groups and political tendencies sought to deploy the past to serve their own ends. Historical memory increasingly became politicized and "nationalized," that is, viewed in terms of its relationship to the nation-state as a whole rather than as the purview of specific groups or regions. The creation of a national economy, one of the main forces behind these developments, was paralleled by the rise not only of nationalism, but also of a consciously articulated Iraqi, rather than ethnic, culture. At the same time, historical memory became "ethnicized" and "tribalized" as elites within the three ethnic groups, especially the Sunni Arab elite linked to the Iraqi state, sought to use historical memory to benefit their own specific ethnic group or tribal clan. The traditional Sunni Arab leadership that supported Pan-Arabism fostered a parochial and chauvinistic historical memory to prevent cross-ethnic solidarity from threatening its historical prerogatives.

Despite efforts to impose a hegemonic understanding of political community, neither the modern Iraqi state, nor most postcolonial states, have ever achieved hegemony in the Gramscian sense of the term. Clearly, large segments of Iraqi society have not identified their interests with those of the state. The legitimacy of the regimes that have controlled the state has been questioned, if not rejected, by large sections of the Iraqi populace, either along ethnic lines (Shi'is and Kurds), along social class lines (working class, peasantry, and the Iraqi Communist Party), or along lines emphasizing liberal politics and human rights (the National Democratic Party, the Independence Party, and, during the 1990s and prior to the March–April 2003 war, by the Iraqi democratic opposition and Charter 91).

In elucidating the relationship between nation building, historical memory, and authoritarianism in modern Iraq, the concept of hegemony is nevertheless important. Frequently, hegemony is formulated as a "top-down" process along the lines of Massimo d'Azeglio's famous statement, "Fatta l'Italia bisogna fare gli Italiani" (Having made Italy we now must make Italians).[24] Although King Faysal I never stated it as succinctly, he clearly felt the need to form a common Iraqi political identity after he assumed the throne in 1921. Under the Ba'th, the attempt to achieve hegemony centered on cultural production, whether history writing, literature, folkloric studies, or art, particularly as it related to reinterpreting the past. However, cultural production often becomes an important domain of struggle, particularly when the populace does not accept the goals of the state. Far from being passive depositories of knowledge, citizens will contest historical and cultural paradigms proffered by the state if such paradigms deny them their own history and culture.[25] Whatever conceptual problems beset Gramsci's understanding of hegemony, the Iraqi case underscores his view that the concept should be seen in relational terms, as part of a dialectic emanating from the struggle between the state and subaltern groups.[26]

It is precisely the manner in which, under the Ba'th, intellectuals negotiated their relationship with the state in the context of its efforts to appropriate understandings of the past that is this volume's major focus. Some intellectuals sold their souls to the state, while others chose outright resistance leading to exile, imprisonment, or worse. The majority of Iraqi intellectuals chose neither of these two paths. Although many retreated from public life after 1968 or went into exile, others continued to write even under the severe constraints imposed by the Ba'thist state. Gramsci (and Marx) argued that it is difficult to categorize intellectuals in terms of social class. For Gramsci, an intellectual can choose to become an "organic intellectual" of either the ruling or the working class. However, Gramsci's categories offer no conceptual space for the writer or artist who attempts to maintain some measure of intellectual integrity while sustaining his or her physical existence through outwardly appearing to accommodate the existing political order. I would suggest a trichotomous distinction between support, accommodation, and resistance to characterize possible intellectual responses to the authoritarian state. In this study all three responses will be examined, but my main interest, for both theoretical and political reasons, is in intellectuals who accommodated the ruling regime. A central hypothesis of this book is that many intellectuals inside Iraq chose to ostensibly cooperate with the Ba'thist regime while simultaneously struggling in subtle ways to nurture forms of historical memory and consciousness that subverted the state's goals by pointing to a more participatory society. Such behavior has important ramifications for the idea of civil society in Iraq, a theme discussed below.

Ba'thist ideology, which has undergone numerous reformulations, is extremely abstract and strident and tells us little about the relationship of ruler to ruled. It was not taken particularly seriously by the political elite under Saddam, and very few Iraqis opted to read Ba'thist ideological tracts. That many of the party's tracts were written by non-Iraqi Ba'thists, such as Michel 'Aflaq, Iliyas Farah, and Shibli al-'Aysami, also seems to have dampened interest in such writings. Literate Iraqis have demonstrated much more interest in writings that relate to the nation's heritage *(al-turath)* or history writing. While in Iraq, I was struck by how quickly the Ministry of Culture and Information's publication, *The Journal of Popular Culture (Majallat al-Turath al-Sha'bi)*, disappeared from Baghdad kiosks. In the visual media, some of the most popular television programs during the 1980s were those relating to folk poetry and the history of popular quarters in major cities such as Baghdad, for example the program *Baghdadiyat*. It is clear that the educated middle classes' interest in historical memory or "heritage" was not imposed by the Ba'thist state. Rather, this interest reflects a deeply felt need to make sense of new environments, particularly urban areas; changing social class; ethnic and gender relations; and greater contact with foreign cultures, particularly Western culture. Historical memory is very difficult to appropriate precisely because it emanates from so many sources and because it lends itself to multiple interpretations. State efforts to control historical memory, especially in Iraq's rich historical context of a wide variety of historical memories, are extremely difficult. Many educated Iraqis purchased state-sponsored cultural and historical publications, but relatively few, I would argue, actually internalized the conclusions that the state sought to elicit by disseminating them. Those who interpreted the texts in a "politically correct" fashion were usually those who benefited most from accepting the new historical memory: Ba'th Party members, privileged bureaucrats, and military officers and security service operatives who read the texts for clues as to how they should think about the past and the implications of such thinking for their own political positions. Most adult Iraqis were aware of the subtexts of state cultural production. The extent to which young Iraqis were actually socialized into the Ba'thist state's understandings of the past is an important subject for another study.

A focus on historical memory can help transcend the static qualities of existing conceptualizations of Iraqi politics. The oldest conceptual approach that purports to explain nation building, political instability, and authoritarian rule in modern Iraq is the ethnoconfessional or communal model. It not only has attracted academic attention, but it also was ascribed to by British colonial officials, foreign diplomats, and policy makers within Iraq.[27] This model hypothesizes that authoritarian rule is the result of the innate inability of Iraq's multiple ethnic and confessional groups to cooperate in a unitary political community. According to this approach, Britain's construction of an Iraqi state from three Ottoman provinces that had never been united politically, and which were populated by different ethnic groups in which tribal loyalties and illiteracy were endemic, doomed the modern state from its founding. Further, ethnically based historical cleavages have left a legacy of distrust and hatred that cannot be transcended. Only the strong hand of an authoritarian leader offers hope of maintaining some semblance of political and social order in Iraq.

This approach to authoritarianism is problematic less because of its resort to ethnic categories than its historical determinism and static understanding of politics. To deny ethnicity's salience is to avoid a key dimension of Iraqi politics. The real problem lies with attributing to the category of ethnicity "primordial" qualities that are postulated as somehow innate to Sunni and Shi'i Arabs, Kurds, and other ethnic groups in Iraq. This study documents numerous instances of Iraqi political behavior throughout the twentieth century that have been characterized by interethnic cooperation and solidarity. As a category, ethnicity needs to be conceptualized as being constantly redefined and reconstituted, politically and socially. Consequently, this study rejects any essentialist claims regarding Iraq's ethnic diversity. There is no fundamental reason why Iraqis of different ethnic and confessional backgrounds cannot cooperate and live in the same political community. Where ethnic consciousness has become salient, it seems largely confined to segments of the middle classes. It has been largely absent among the working classes and peasantry, and, to the extent that it has appeared among the upper classes, it has often been cynically exploited for social class and political ends rather than having assumed social psychological salience.

Another model invoked to explain Iraqi politics, which acquired particular currency following the rapid rise in oil prices in the early 1970s, centers on the concept of the rentier state. The core hypothesis of this model is that "a government that can expand its services without resorting to heavy taxation acquires an independence from the people seldom found in other countries."[28] As the state's economic power becomes centralized, the traditional function of the paramount shaykh or tribal leader as distributor of benefits is now re-created at the national level.

The notion of the rentier state is intuitively appealing because the windfall profits that accrued to Arab oil-producing nations during the 1970s did dramatically increase the Iraqi state's economic and political power. Falih ʿAbd al-Jabbar argues that the wing of the Baʿth that came to power in 1968 was relatively weak and numbered only several hundred members.[29] This weakness was reflected in the alliances that the Baʿthist regime felt it needed to make in its early years with potential rivals such as the Kurdish Democratic Party and the Iraqi Communist Party. Once the state's income increased as oil prices rose dramatically, revenues were used to co-opt intellectuals and key political actors while physical repression was directed against those who would not declare loyalty to the Baʿth.

Nevertheless, the rentier state model is partial and ahistorical. Although it is true that, as oil prices and state revenues rose during the early 1970s, the Baʿthist regime was able to co-opt large segments of society, this does not explain why large numbers of Iraqis remained loyal to the Iraqi Communist Party (officially outlawed in 1979). Further, if the state had accrued so much power through its rentier status, why did it feel compelled to use a large amount of its resources to appropriate historical memory? The large working class and intelligentsia's history of struggle against the monarchy and foreign and domestic capital disputes the hypothesis that the rentier state is characterized by few social class cleavages and hence subject to little opposition from civil society.[30] It was precisely the growth of a powerful nationalist movement that created a strong political consciousness among large segments of the populace. Although oil revenues did enhance the state's authoritarian capacities, it did not remain detached from civil society. Quite the opposite was true, in fact, as the state became actively involved in all facets of economic production, strictly regulated political and associational activity, and actively sought to dominate cultural production. Finally, the rentier state thesis cannot differentiate between the brutal authoritarianism of Ba'thist Iraq and the benevolent despotism of Kuwait and other Arab Gulf states or explain the fall of the former Pahlavi state in Iran, whose historical experience provided the original stimulus for the concept.

A more recent model used to explain the prevalence of political instability, violence, and authoritarian rule in the Arab world draws upon on the concept of civil society. Although this concept has attracted many liberal thinkers, such as the Egyptian sociologist Sa'd al-Din Ibrahim, Marxist and leftist thinkers have been some of its main adherents among Iraqi intellectuals. The concern with civil society has stemmed in large measure from the state-organized violence that characterized Iraqi politics after the overthrow of the Qasim regime in 1963 and especially after the Takriti Ba'th's rise to power in July 1968. Because state-sponsored violence decimated the ranks of the Iraqi Communist Party and the leftist intelligentsia, many thinkers began to question whether their support for "revolutionary violence," such as that which overthrew the monarchy, helped pave the way for the degradation of politics under two Ba'thist regimes. Some Iraqi intellectuals also have shown increased interest in the concept of civil society as described in Western texts, particularly in the writings of Robert Putnam, whose work has strongly influenced the Civil Society and Democratic Transition in the Arab World Project of the Cairo-based Ibn Khaldun Center for Social Research.[31]

Despite producing some of the most insightful analyses of the Iraqi state, this approach suffers from many of the problems already mentioned. A variety of studies have documented what their authors see as the complete destruction of civil society in Iraq, portraying the state as omnipresent and omnipotent. Two examples are Khalil's characterization of Iraq as a "republic of fear" and 'Abd al-Jabbar's description of the Ba'thist state as a "new Leviathan."[32] Neither voluntary associations nor the market possessed the capacity to challenge the Ba'thist state. Because of the state's control of production, banking, and foreign trade, its complete regulation of political activity, the physical elimination of dissenters, and its monopoly of cultural expression, the citizen had no chance of directly challenging its power. Even the domain of religion was subordinated to the state, which, during the 1990s, assumed the role of training religious leaders and arranged assassinations of Shi'i mujtahids who failed to heed Ba'thist warnings to remove objectionable messages from their Friday sermons.

The civil society model, similar to other approaches, allows little conceptual room for change. As Diane Singerman's research in "popular" *(sha'bi)* Cairene quarters demonstrates, a rich *informal* civil society lies beyond the authoritarian edicts of the Egyptian state, which has restricted political expression through formal structures such as political parties and the media.[33] During the 1991 Intifada, it was striking how rapidly organizations sprang up throughout Iraq to challenge Ba'thist control once the opportunity to revolt presented itself.[34] This suggests the existence in Iraq, as in Egypt, of informal organizations, associations, and networks that are not under state control. Although it has not been possible to document this sector with any precision, I attempt to show that, within the cultural production of the state apparatus itself, resistance to Ba'thist efforts to appropriate the past was always present, even in studies ostensibly intended to support official perspectives on social, political, or cultural affairs.

Each of the approaches to the study of Iraqi politics mentioned above offers insights. While in power, the Ba'thist regime was able to manipulate ethnic cleavages to undermine the cohesion of opposition forces. The regime did use oil revenues very adroitly during the 1970s to strengthen its power, and it launched two major wars without consulting society at large. Through terror and co-optation, the state eliminated all overt opposition and destroyed much of civil society that had been created prior to 1968. However, the Ba'thist state never addressed the fundamental contradiction of Iraqi society, the question of social and cultural difference, which it instead chose to repress. The use of force and the attempts to appropriate historical memory do not indicate a strong state.[35] Here 'Abd al-Jabbar's insightful hypothesis about civil society is telling: Iraq's ethnic diversity has been the basis of both the populace's strength and its weakness in resisting the state.[36] Ethnic diversity represents a source of strength in that no regime has been able to dominate all elements of this diversity, nor has any regime been able to subordinate and meld it into the homogenous political and cultural system that the Ba'th under Saddam Husayn worked so hard to impose on Iraqi society. It likewise represents a source of weakness in that ethnic differences have often impeded Iraqis participating in associational behavior from achieving their ends. But the point remains: no regime can ever achieve hegemony while completely denying the fundamental characteristic of Iraqi society, namely, its ethnic and cultural diversity.

For the Ba'th, this problem was exacerbated by the regime's efforts to build a familial, tribal, and clientalistic power structure under the guise of a universalistic ideology that combined Pan-Arabism and corporatism. Within the realm of the power structure itself, that is, among those committed to the persistence of authoritarian rule, tribal groupings not privy to the core avenues of power were frequently subject to torture, incarceration, or execution due to real or imagined rebellions against Ba'thist authority.

Perhaps most significant, especially in light of the collapse of the Ba'thist state, was the state's seduction of itself through its own rhetoric. Not only did Saddam and the Ba'th deceive themselves into thinking they could avoid adhering to agreements they signed after the 1991 Gulf War, in which they agreed to dispose of all weapons of mass destruction, but self-deception also played a major role in the state's complete miscalculation in initiating the 1980 Iran-Iraq War and the seizure of Kuwait in 1990. Both events almost led to the regime's collapse and its failure to cooperate with weapon's inspections prior to the March–April 2003 war finally brought it down. Saddam's rehabilitation of King Faysal I and his predilection for parading on a white horse during official rituals demonstrated his monarchical pretensions. After numerous Ba'th Party members in the provinces were killed during the 1991 Intifada, Saddam turned to tribal shaykhs—former Ba'th Party nemeses who stood for "feudalism" and reaction—as his new minions in the countryside. The recruitment of conservative forces to buttress the state was paralleled by the elimination of all laws intended to protect urban workers and peasants from rapacious capitalists.

The Ba'thist regime ultimately devoured itself. What 'Abd al-Jabbar calls the "Ba'thization" *(al-tab'ith)* of the state and "Takritization" of the party, which led to the subsequent creation of the "Family Party," progressively narrowed the regime's power base between 1979 and 2003. The violent response to challenges to this authority increased the number of those seeking revenge for the deaths of relatives or fellow tribesmen. The Iran-Iraq and Gulf wars, which temporarily disoriented opposition forces, completely alienated members of the professional and technocratic middle classes, who frequently were forced to sell their possessions to sustain themselves. After the 1991 Intifada the regime enjoyed little support, except for that maintained by small elite that benefited from state largesse.

In this context, the efforts by expatriate Iraqis and opposition forces operating clandestinely inside Iraq to create a new democratic political culture based on a nonsectarian federated state began to attract significant support during the 1990s. Debates over historical memory following the second Gulf War demonstrated its important role in the democratic opposition's ongoing "war of position" with the Ba'thist regime.[37] Through Ba'thist policies, Iraqis became disaffected with Pan-Arabism in its romantic/proto-fascist variant, with war and foreign adventures, with violence, and with the inability to live a life devoid of any predictability or freedom of self-expression. Many Iraqis came to support the second Ba'thist regime after it seized power in 1968 based on the hope of escape from the instability that had characterized political life since the July 1958 Revolution. The destruction and instability that the Ba'th Party has inflicted on Iraqi society ultimately eliminated most of this support even among the Sunni Arab middle classes. In the end, only members of Takriti-based tribal clans who occupied high positions and the family of Saddam Husayn supported the regime. The showing on Iraq's "Youth Television" (Qanat al-Shabab), controlled by 'Uday Saddam Husayn, of a graphic video of the 1991 Intifada during the Ba'thist regime's last days was itself an indicator of the complete lack of support enjoyed by the regime at the time of its collapse. This video represented a desperate attempt to frighten Iraq's Sunni Arabs into believing that chaos and retribution awaited them if they did not help prevent the overthrow of Saddam's regime. The regime's continued glorification of its invasion of Kuwait, its deification of Saddam, and its resistance to United Nations efforts to rid Iraq of its potential to develop nuclear, biological, and chemical weapons, which exposed itself to the attack that led to its demise, demonstrates the extent to which authoritarian memories of state are ultimately self-destructive.[38]

Now that the Ba'thist regime has collapsed, one of the keys to a democratic transition will be the behavior of the democratic opposition, especially its ability to demonstrate that Sunni and Shi'i Arabs, Kurds, and other ethnic groups can work together in a broad political coalition. In light of the degradation of politics under Saddam and the Ba'th, it will not be an easy task for Iraqis from differing ideological, ethnic, and social class backgrounds to develop trust in the viability of nonauthoritarian political institutions.

2 The Formation of the Iraqi Intelligentsia and Modern Historical Memory

> In the same way that amnesia is not merely a local disturbance of the individual's memory but causes more or less serious perturbations in his personality, the absence, or voluntary or involuntary loss, of collective memory among peoples and nations can cause serious problems of collective identity.
>
> JACQUES LE GOFF, *History and Memory*

All nation-states require foundational myths that help create a sense of collective identity by explaining a society's origins. These links to the past are necessary if citizens are to enjoy political stability and development. This sense of collective identity may trace its roots to many factors, including ethnicity, religion, or a successful revolution. Without this shared sense of identity, a society lacks a fundamental tool for defining the nature of the political community in which all its members live.

Historical memory is a critical component in creating myths of origin. The evocation of the past will be most pronounced during periods of crises that challenge the "natural order of things." The central role of historical memory and collective identity in the constitution of the nation-state suggests a number of questions. Why does interest in historical memory assume greater social, cultural, and political significance in some periods compared to others? During periods of intensified interest in historical memory, why do groups choose particular moments in the past as a foundation for the present? How does an interest in the past become politicized and appropriated by those seeking to control a political system?

The role of historical memory in the formation of modern Iraq is linked to two major developments, the first, a lengthy historical process and the second, an abrupt rupture with the past. These two developments, Iraq's integration into the world market, a process that began in the mid-nineteenth century and continued well into the twentieth, and the collapse of Ottoman rule in Iraq in 1918, were defining moments in the modern political system's development. Both events forced peoples living in the three Ottoman

29

provinces that later came to constitute the Iraqi nation-state to confront, in a fundamental way, questions of collective identity and political community. Market forces and new social relations of production in late-nineteenth-century Iraq created the preconditions for the emergence of new structures of thought, particularly those that transcended regional, local, and ethnic identities. These profound changes that transformed Iraqi society were part of a multidimensional process encompassing disruption, innovation, and synthesis.

Existing narratives of Iraq's integration into the world market have largely neglected the implications of this process for historical memory and collective identity. Several developments radically altered how Iraqis viewed themselves in relation to their surrounding society. First, the sedentization of tribes during the nineteenth century and the shift to agricultural production restructured the material and cultural relationships between shaykhs and tribesmen. Through Ottoman and later British encouragement, many shaykhs became powerful landlords who exploited their erstwhile tribal brethren who were transformed into tenant farmers. Consequently, tribal shaykhs found it increasingly difficult to elicit tribal solidarity through the evocation of a historical memory based on collective myths of tribal origins.

Iraq's transformation from a largely subsistence economy to an export-oriented economy led to a growth in private landownership and a move by tribes from pastoral nomadism to agricultural pursuits as thousands of tribesmen were alienated from the land. Dispossessed from the land over which they formerly held communal rights, these tribesmen became mere tenants. Others accepted employment on the estates given by the state to *sada*[1] in an effort to erode tribal solidarity.[2] As traditional rural social structure became more rigidly hierarchical, reflecting the commercialization of agriculture, tribesmen *cum* peasants increasingly rejected the oppressive quality of rural life by migrating to urban areas.

As they prospered, many tribal shaykhs became absentee landowners and left their traditional rural domains for cities or towns, which paralleled developments elsewhere in the region such as Egypt and the Levant. Rather than maintaining their traditional ties to a shaykh, tribesmen-peasants now confronted the shaykhs' agents, the *sirkals* or lesser shaykhs, to whom they felt no allegiance. As Iraqi social structure became more hierarchical, patron-client relations were replaced by more anonymous relations based on the cash nexus.[3]

What was the legacy of Ottoman efforts to strengthen their hold over Iraq, especially as it relates to historical memory, political identity, and nationalist consciousness? Ottoman policies, which eroded the cohesion and power of the tribes, were assisted by the spread of a market economy and capitalist relations of production. The Ottomans' ability to weaken the tribes did not necessarily augment their power because the expansion of British influence filled much of the political vacuum created by the decline of tribal authority. Although unable to create a strong central state, a succession of Ottoman governors was able to weaken tribal authority, create a class of absentee shaykh-landowners, and fragment the great tribal confederations such as the Muntafiq and Shammar, which led to the proliferation of hundreds of much smaller clans *(fakdh;* pl. *afkhadh)*. Tribesmen who had become peasants became extremely resentful of the shaykhs. Their feelings were exacerbated by the memory, however idealized, of a more egalitarian era in which the tribe was constituted as a tightly knit kinship organization.

Widespread rural-urban migration was an important precondition for the development of notions of political community that transcended ethnic lines. In disrupting centuries-old regional cultures and power structures, the integration process created "crosscutting cleavages" that encouraged new forms of political behavior and thinking. Older forms of historical memory that had been used for purposes of social and political control were compromised as the ability of elites to manipulate ethnic and tribal solidarity was undermined.

Prior to the mid-nineteenth century, Iraq's inhabitants did not share a strong sense of collective identity. There was no national discourse and, to the extent that such a discourse existed, intellectual production was dominated by religious intellectuals and limited to mosques and traditional religious schools.[4] Pastoralism predominated and agriculture was unproductive, as it was largely confined to areas around major cities. Although commercial activity was more widespread than was previously believed, trade routes were insecure.[5] Cities often suffered from severe plagues that prevented an increase in population. The obverse of the weakness of Iraq's towns was the strength of its rural tribes.[6]

As in much of the Middle East, Iraq's integration into the expanding world economy led to the steady growth of foreign trade and a shift in its direction.[7] Although most of Iraq's foreign trade prior to the 1860s had been with other areas of the Middle East, by 1914 both its exports and imports were primarily oriented to the West, particularly Great Britain.[8] Not surprisingly, this dependency made the West loom ever larger in the minds of the many Iraqis affected by these new economic ties.

The development of steam transportation along the Tigris River in 1861 made the nomadic bedouin's dependence on the declining caravan trade increasingly precarious.[9] Conversely, many tribes found it profitable to turn to agriculture as river steamers assured them the ability to transport their crops to market. In southern Iraq, the rural subsistence economy had ceased to exist by the end of the nineteenth century.[10] Steam navigation also had important political ramifications, as river steamers allowed Ottoman troops to be deployed more efficiently against recalcitrant tribes.[11]

European demand for Iraqi wool, dates, and grains had a significant impact on the country's surplus of land and labor. Reminiscent of earlier developments in Tudor England,[12] the commercialization of agriculture led the rural shaykhs to view their tribesmen no longer as warriors but as peasants. This was especially true as the Ottomans attempted to extend their control over the countryside. In addition to the tradition of fostering intertribal rivalries, a more effective Ottoman policy was the manipulation of landownership. A revised land code in 1858 included a new type of tenure known as *tapu*, under which the state retained ultimate possession of the land but allowed usufruct rights to be transferred through inheritance. While the 1858 land code sought to increase state control over landownership, it also marked a step toward increasing private ownership of land.[13]

As in Europe of an earlier period, the growth of towns was a significant precondition for changing modes of political identity and particularly for the rise of nationalism. The revival of urban areas, in terms of both their population and economic activity, brought greater numbers of Iraqis into contact with one another and led to the growth of the press and an increase in education. Although the growth of these institutions was very small, even by regional standards, it nevertheless represented the awakening of an important political consciousness among the educated urban populace. The press and educational institutions brought together members of Iraq's various sects in a setting in which ethnic and confessional identities did not necessarily predominate.

A second result of Iraq's integration into the world market was the spread of ideas of European nationalism. To counter European influence, the Ottomans sought to modernize and expand the military, in part through the recruitment of Arabs. This process had an especially strong impact on Iraqis of modest social backgrounds who studied in the Ottoman military academy in Istanbul. Virtually all Iraqi army officers were Sunni Arabs, primarily drawn from the Sunni Arab triangle running from Baghdad north to Ramadi and Mosul. These recruits came into contact with the nationalist ideas that had captured the imagination of the supporters of the 1908 Young Turk Revolt. The spread of Turkish nationalism by the Committee of Union and Progress (CUP), which overthrew Sultan Abdül Hamid in 1908, stimulated young Iraqi and other Arab officers to question their own political identity, especially once it became clear that the CUP saw the Ottoman's Arab provinces as politically and culturally subordinate to the empire's Turkish core. European concepts of constitutionalism and republicanism, fostered by the Young Turks, worked at cross-purposes with an Ottoman-Islamic political identity heretofore spread by the sultan.

Although fin de siècle Ottoman efforts to confront European imperial encroachment in the empire's remaining territories were ineffectual, these reforms did stimulate a rise in an Arab or Iraqi, as opposed to Islamic or Ottoman, cultural and political identity among Iraqi military officers, which included an intensified interest in Arab history. One of the earliest Arab political organizations, al-ʿAhd (Covenant), was formed in 1912 in Istanbul by young Arab officers, the majority of whom were of Iraqi origin. Events in pre–World War I Istanbul encouraged a military-oriented political culture among the Iraqi officers who subsequently dominated not only the Iraqi army, but also the state bureaucracy until the 1958 Revolution.[14] This political acculturation promoted the Pan-Arabist sentiment that provided the support for the Hashimite-led Arab Revolt and the Pan-Arab model of political community that vied for hegemony in post-Ottoman Iraq. However, Pan-Arabism worked to divide Iraqi society because the Sunni Arab Ottoman officers rejected any political or cultural space for non–Sunni Arab members of Iraqi society. Historical memory assumed an important role in assuring Sunni Arabs' continued control of the state and the military, in which they had played a dominant role under the Ottoman Turks.

If the Young Turk Revolt spread ideas of republicanism and constitutionalism among Iraqi officers, then reform efforts in neighboring Persia during the 1906 Constitutionalist Revolt had a similar impact on the Shiʿi population of the shrine cities of al-Najaf and Karbalaʾ in south-central Iraq. Attempts to introduce constitutional reforms in Persia split the Iraqi Shiʿi clergy into pro- and antireformist factions. The Persian constitutionalist movement with its nationalist overtones likewise weakened Shiʿi ties to Persia as members of the Shiʿi clergy *(al-marjaʿiya)* began to view themselves as Iraqi, despite the fact that many had Persian ethnic origins. The British invasion of Iraq in 1914 further disrupted economic and cultural interaction between Iraq and Persia by adversely affecting trade, pilgrimages to the shrine cities, and the number of foreign students seeking to study in the great Shiʿi institutions of higher learning.

Ottoman reforms, particularly in education, reflected yet another impact of the integration process. Ottoman educational reforms sought to increase revenues through the rationalization of the taxation system and to increase the central administration's power through tighter integration of the three provinces of Baghdad, Mosul, and Basra. The first government schools, opened by the Ottoman governor *(wali)* Midhat Pasha, were intended to increase the number of Iraqis in the army and to produce technically proficient cadres for the Ottomans' modernizing projects.[15] The Ottoman *wali* also used educational reforms to reinvigorate Iraq's artisanal production by opening a vocational school.[16]

Midhat Pasha's educational reforms had a mixed impact. Since Turkish was the language of instruction, most Iraqis were excluded from the Ottoman school system. The military academy had the greatest impact, attracting Iraqis from middle- and lower-middle-class families.[17] Numbering roughly three hundred by war's end, these officers provided the core of Sharif Faysal's Arab army and support for the idea of a Pan-Arabist Iraqi state after the Ottoman collapse. Although many later became political reactionaries under the Hashimite Monarchy, the ex-Sharifian officers were radical for their times since they were highly nationalistic and hostile to British rule following World War I. Thus the continuation of Sunni Arab dominance of the lower echelons of the state was reinforced by Ottoman reforms. The tradition of Shi'i exclusion from the state, which extended back many centuries, was given new life.

An 1872 decree by the Ottoman Porte transferring a significant portion of Iraqi revenues to Istanbul undermined the ability of Midhat's immediate successors to pursue his initial reforms. The primary school system continued to be neglected by the state and left to the 'ulama' who ran the traditional *kuttab* system based on Qur'anic studies and rote memorization. Nevertheless, as Hanna Batatu notes, "the opening of two modern schools by Midhat Pasha . . . conclusively broke the 'ulama''s monopoly over education."[18] This erosion of the power of the 'ulama', particularly among the Shi'a, provided an opening for the development of secular ideologies.

As the need for a modern educational system became clearer, particularly with the increasing British colonial encroachment, the Ottoman state enacted more reforms. Educational committees, established in 1882 throughout the empire's provinces, set the stage for the founding of state schools outside Baghdad, especially three preparatory schools in Mosul and one in Basra. However, only in 1889 did the state open four elementary schools in Baghdad. At the turn of the century, these remained the only state-run elementary schools in the country.[19] These reforms were encouraged by schools developed by minority groups in Iraq such as the Chaldeans, Assyrians, Armenians, and Jews.[20] The "demonstration effect" of these schools and their links to European powers prompted the state to try and duplicate their achievements.

The 1908 Young Turk Revolt had a profound impact on the development of education in Iraq, which became the centerpiece of the Committee of Union and Progress's reformist policies. One of the CUP's first acts was to appoint a director of education for Baghdad, a post that had been vacant since 1898.[21] Elementary schools that provided education for females were established in a number of Iraqi cities and towns. A law school was opened in Baghdad in September 1908.

At the turn of the twentieth century, the most significant development encouraging the growth of Iraqi nationalism and the renewed interest in the past that accompanied it was the gathering of Iraqi intellectuals drawn from the military, the bureaucracy, and the professions to organize the first secular educational system. Their two objectives were to revive Iraq's Arab heritage and language and to examine Iraq's current political status. Two schools were established in 1908: the Freedom Memorial School (Tadhkar al-Hurriya) in Basra and the Ottoman Ja'fari Progress School (al-Taraqi al-Ja'fari) in Baghdad.[22] The former was the first school to offer instruction in Arabic.[23] However, within a year of its opening, the new Ottoman government had changed the name to the Union and Progress School and its language of instruction to Turkish.

The Ja'fari Progress School was historically significant because its founders included many prominent intellectuals such as Ja'far Abu Timman, Ra'uf al-Qattan, Mahdi al-Khayyat, and 'Ali al-Bazirgan, who maintained political and commercial interests in the school. They were interested in increasing the number of educated clerks and accountants conversant with foreign languages and modern methods of accounting.[24] The curriculum differed from Ottoman schools, which traditionally stressed the humanities. The school's founders were able to gain the support of a number of progressive religious leaders, thereby forging an important political and social alliance. Significantly, both Sunnis and Shi'is supported this project, belying the notion, commonplace even at this early stage of Iraqi political development, that the two sects were unable to cooperate in civic activity. Ja'far Abu Timman, for example, was a prominent Shi'i merchant who later headed the Baghdad Chamber of Commerce and the influential National Party (al-Hizb al-Watani).[25]

The impetus to develop an Arabic-language school system that would attract large numbers of Iraqi students was a response to the growth of Turkish nationalism. As expressed through official education committees, Iraqis who supported the new school system demanded a large number of new elementary and preparatory schools; increased emphasis on technically oriented instruction, particularly in agriculture and the industrial arts; and the imposition of Arabic as the language of instruction in the private schools run by Iraq's minority communities.[26]

Among the many important social developments set in motion by Iraq's integration into the world market was the broadening of social and political participation. Both the Young Turks and the Iraqi educational reformers were drawn largely from the urban middle classes, which were beginning to make their political impact. Significantly, several of Iraq's most important modern poets, all of whom incorporated political themes in their poetry, were products of these educational reforms. Nazik al-Mala'ika, Badr Shakir al-Sayyab, 'Abd al-Wahhab al-Bayati, Sa'di Yusif, and Lami'a 'Abbas 'Amara were all graduates of Baghdad's Higher Teaching Training College.[27]

The development of a modern educational system should not be viewed as having only a linear, progressive impact since it also planted the seeds of increased intercommunal strife. The first schools were founded in major urban centers. Most Iraqis were either too poor to take advantage of them or unable to attend because they were not conversant in Turkish. Those who were able to study at the schools were usually the sons of civil servants and were overwhelmingly Arab Sunnis, which reflected the traditional Ottoman policy of promoting the interests of fellow Sunni Muslims within the Ottoman provincial administration.[28]

As with military recruitment, educational patterns established the basis for both increased Sunni and Shi'i tension and the Shi'i community's political fragmentation. Traditionally, Iraqi Shi'is had refrained from sending their sons to the few existing government schools because the Ottomans emphasized Sunni doctrine in religious instruction. As the state educational system expanded, primarily in major urban areas, the traditional Shi'i religious schools of al-Najaf, Karbala', and al-Kathimayn remained largely insulated from these changes. Not only was a modern curriculum not introduced, but the Shi'i 'ulama' actively opposed any modern reforms. Shi'is who sought a modern curriculum that increasingly was a prerequisite for government and private employment were forced to move to urban areas.[29] Educational developments sharpened the cultural and political cleavages between older, more traditional Shi'is, on the one hand, and younger, more secular Shi'is, on the other.

The increasing divergence between religiously and secularly oriented Shi'is may explain the relative lack of emphasis on an indigenous historical memory by those who supported an Iraqist nationalist vision of political community that counted many Shi'is among its supporters. First, secular Shi'is often viewed the religious clergy as reactionary because of their immersion in a historical memory tied to the history of the Shi'ism. Second, secular Shi'is could hardly privilege their own community's historical memory given their commitment to a vision of Iraqi society that valorized the cultural contributions of all ethnic groups. Finally, the politically charged nature of all political narratives in the new Iraqi nation-state led not only secular Shi'is but also many supporters of the Iraqist vision to either focus on exogenous historical memories, such as Soviet or Western historical experiences, or to avoid the issue of historical memory altogether. This tendency to abandon historical memory to the Pan-Arabists hindered Iraqist efforts to achieve hegemony.

Despite the collapse of Ottoman rule in 1918 and the significant political mobilization of the populace both during and after the war, there was significant continuity in Iraqi society. The indigenous Sunni Arab elite that had played a significant role in the Ottoman-controlled state and bureaucracy maintained its privileges even in the face of a major uprising, the June–October 1920 Revolution, which pushed for a political community defined in pluralist terms. On the other hand, Iraqi society experienced great change. Ethnic, tribal, and regional identities were fundamentally challenged by the spread of market forces and new social relations of production. The expansion of education and increased contact with the West set the stage for new political ideologies and ways of conceptualizing the past. It was this tension between continuity and change that helps explain the rise of two competing definitions of political community, one Iraqist nationalist and one Pan-Arab, that began to vie for hegemony once it became clear that Iraqis would establish their own independent nation-state.

An increased interest in historical memory was stimulated not only by major changes in Iraq's political economy, but also by debates over the meaning of events directly related to the formation and subsequent development of the new Iraqi nation-state in 1921. The defeat of Ottoman forces in Greece, the Balkans, and Tripoli (Libya) in the early 1900s raised the question of whether Iraqis should continue to support the Ottoman Empire against European encroachments through a shared Islamic identity or adopt a political identity that rejected continued Ottoman sovereignty over Iraq. The Arab Revolt of 1914–18 challenged Iraqis, especially in light of considerable Iraqi participation in it, to consider whether they should join a Pan-Arab state should the revolt be successful. The Shi'i clergy or *al-marja'iya's* proclamation of a jihad in the wake of Great Britain's invasion of Iraq in 1914 and the Najaf Revolt of 1916 established the heretofore politically excluded Shi'i community as a major political actor in any post-Ottoman state. Through its multiethnic coalition, the 1920 Iraqi Revolution not only confirmed this role, but it also implicitly challenged the Pan-Arab vision of the Arab Revolt by demonstrating the potential of a political community defined in Iraqist nationalist terms. The British-orchestrated August 1921 referendum that established the Hashimite Monarchy and Great Britain's imprisonment and exile of Shi'i leaders who had opposed them during the war and in 1920 dealt a major blow to Iraqist nationalism. Nevertheless, the cumulative effect of these political struggles was to stimulate an intensified interest in the past, both to help contextualize it and to develop ideological weapons as competing groups sought to mobilize supporters. A variety of narratives was developed to appropriate these events for either of the two emerging definitions of political community. In light of the political rupture caused by the Ottoman state's collapse, especially the lack of any legacy of political institutionalization that could have facilitated post-Ottoman state building, and in light of the struggle between the two competing definitions of political community that crystallized after World War I, it is little wonder that the Iraqi nation-state has been plagued by the populace's inability to agree upon a set of foundational myths.[30]

The growth of an Arabic press, as well as the educational system, amplified this new sense of national identity. During the nineteenth century, only four newspapers were published in the Ottoman provinces of Iraq. Between the 1908 Young Turk Revolt and the British invasion in 1914, sixty-one newspapers published in Arabic, Arabic and Turkish, and Arabic and French were established in Baghdad, Basra, Mosul, al-Najaf, and other Iraqi cities.[31] It is highly significant that most of these newspapers were founded just after the 1908 Young Turk Revolt.[32] In their form and content, new newspapers and journals reflected the influence of the more established Egyptian press.[33] Thus the growth of the cities facilitated contact with developments elsewhere in the Middle East.

The Young Turk reforms had the unintended consequence of stimulating Iraqis to think in nationalist terms, as demonstrated by the number of indigenous political organizations that were formed after 1908. In Basra, the al-Jam'iya al-Islahiya (Reform Association) was founded under the leadership of one of most prominent of the *sada*, al-Sayyid Talib al-Naqib. Perhaps most important was the al-'Ahd, which established branches in Baghdad, Mosul, and Basra prior to World War I. The al-Hizb al-Hurr al-Mu'tadil (Moderate Liberal Party) established chapters in Baghdad and Basra in 1911, while the Hizb al-Hurriya wa-l-I'tilaf (Freedom and Entente Party) and the Jam'iyat al-Nadi al-Watani (National Club Association) were established the following year.[34] Although the goals of these organizations were often diffuse and reflected the influence of specific notables more than ideology, they were nevertheless the forerunners of political parties that would call for the establishment of an independent Iraqi state.

Under Ottoman rule, the intelligentsia was limited to two social strata: men of religion and powerful notables who, due to their wealth and religious status, played a central role in the country's political, economic, and social life. The former category included Sunni and Shi'i *ulama*', while the latter counted such families as the al-Gaylanis of Baghdad, the al-'Umaris and al-Jalilis of Mosul, and the al-Naqibs of Basra. Of course, there was also an "undocumented" oral and local culture that included street poets and other exponents of a "low culture." This latter group of intellectuals made a critical contribution to the 1920 Revolution by mobilizing the populace to action and actively opposing the monarchical state after its founding because of its close ties to Great Britain.

A national intellectual life did not exist under the Ottomans. Men of religion and prominent Arab families sustained a historical memory that was regional in character and embodied in manuscripts and oral tradition, particularly poetry. The *ulama*' played a central role in preserving a specifically Arab and Islamic historical memory through the teaching of grammar, logic, inflection *(al-sarf)*, and the Qur'an in religious schools *(al-madrasa; pl. al-madaris)*. Contrary to the argument that Iraq was a sleepy backwater under Ottoman rule, many Shi'is from outside Iraq, including from Persia and India, studied in al-Najaf with local scholars. The Najafi *ulama*' also had an important influence on *madaris* in other Shi'i centers of learning such as Karbala', al-Kathimayn, al-Hilla, and al-Samarra.[35]

Nevertheless, the Shi'i community was, for all intents and purposes, cut off from the rest of Iraq. Its primary economic ties were with Persia to the east and the Gulf to the south, and its contact with the Ottoman administration in Baghdad was kept to a minimum. The Ottoman's policy of ethnic discrimination, whereby the Shi'a were largely excluded from government posts, was exacerbated by the Shi'i *ulama*', who discouraged members of their community from formally interacting with the central state. In Gramscian terms, the Shi'i *ulama*' constituted a core of "traditional intellectuals" who, drawn from a variety of economic backgrounds, did not represent the interests of a specific social class as much as the historical memory and collective identity of the Shi'i community as a whole.[36] By refusing to recognize Ottoman rule, they passively undermined its legitimacy among the Shi'a.[37] However, by failing to press for representation in the Ottoman state, the Shi'i *ulama*' assured that their influence within the larger political community was limited.

The Sunni *ulama*' existed in a symbiotic relationship with the state in which religious and political institutions reinforced one another. They depended upon the Ottoman administration for their salaries. Furthermore, the Ottoman state exerted much more control in the areas around Baghdad and in north-central Iraq where Arab Sunnis predominated. Here, too, the Arab Sunni *'ulama'* played a key role in sustaining elements of Iraqi cultural identity. Sunni men of religion were often instrumental in organizing consent for Ottoman rule.

The intellectual played an increasingly important role during the final stages of Ottoman collapse and the process of establishing a new nation-state by posing questions related to national identity and historical memory.[38] Before 1918, intellectuals, including religious leaders, poets, journalists, and short story writers, played a central role by either supporting or criticizing Ottoman rule. Subsequently, they were critical in mobilizing support for the 1920 Revolution. During the 1920s, intellectuals acted to codify the political, social, and cultural experiences of Iraqis in the nascent state. Because most intellectuals were highly critical of the Hashimite Monarchy and actively supported opposition groups, many assumed the role of "organic intellectuals," representing not only the small and politically marginalized middle class, but also the nascent working class and the peasantry.[39] The role of the "organic intellectual" was filled primarily by religious leaders and poets in the early years of the nation-state, but it was later filled as well by journalists (e.g., Rufa'il Butti), nationalist thinkers (e.g., Sati' al-Husri, Fadil al-Jamali, and Kamil al-Chadirji), communists (e.g., Yusif Salman Yusif [Comrade Fahd]), and military officers (e.g., Salah al-Din al-Sabbagh), all of whom produced extremely influential writings. The intellectuals' role in politics was amplified by the lack of any established political institutions.

Modern Iraqi intellectual discourse was an unintended consequence of the Ottomans' development of a national education system during the late nineteenth century. I use the term "modern" advisedly to avoid the impression of a sharp discontinuity between Ottoman and British colonial rule of Iraq. As Hala Fattah has demonstrated, the Ottomans made extensive efforts to reform the Iraqi provinces and to confront the ever-increasing British influence in them.[40] "Modern" means that, for the first time, traditional intellectuals in the form of men of religion *(al-'ulama')* no longer dominated intellectual production, and that important social and political events began to be interpreted from diverse perspectives.[41] "Modern" also means that intellectual discourse began to assume a national rather than more limited regional, ethnic, or confessional character. Furthermore, intellectual production became more politically self-conscious. For example, after 1908 poetry began to express Arab nationalist themes and sharp criticism of the Ottoman government in Istanbul.[42]

One product of the Ottoman *wali* Midhat Pasha's reforms was the *effendiya,* or urban-educated civil servants who became an important component of the new intelligentsia. While many *effendiya* entered the Ottoman civil service, others became army officers. Unlike the traditional men of religion and powerful regional families who sought to maintain the status quo, the *effendiya* sought change through the social and educational reforms mentioned above. Rather than organizing consent for traditional authority, the new *effendiya* undermined it. Through agitating for greater autonomy and personal freedom for the Arab population, they eroded the central Ottoman administration's power.

The shift from an intellectual life grounded in religion, confessionalism, and traditional families to one based on education, technical expertise, and secular values had a profound impact on Iraqi society. The new intelligentsia promoted nationalism as opposed to loyalty to the Islamic *umma* (political community), secular education with an emphasis on science and technology, the education of women, and the elimination of the veil and polygamy. Differentiating itself from the Turks, the new intelligentsia sought to revive a specifically Arab-Iraqi historical memory through an emphasis on Arab heritage *(al-turath al-ʿArabi)*.[43]

These changes notwithstanding, the traditional intellectual in the form of the poet remained at the center of cultural production. Despite the assertion that pre-twentieth-century Iraqi poetry was highly traditional and lacked innovation,[44] poetry still reflected the most developed literary form in Iraqi culture. Prior to the 1908 Constitutional Revolution, poets had limited their political and social poetry to Islamic themes and praises of the Ottoman sultan and his representative in Iraq, the *wali*.[45] After the Young Turk Revolt, educated Iraqis envisioned applying the Young Turks' reforms to Iraq. Reciting their poetry in important mosques such as the Haydarkhana in Baghdad and disseminating it in the nascent press, poets articulated the urban intelligentsia's frustration at the failure of their expectation that Ottoman reforms would lead to greater freedom for Iraq. Through the Arab Revolt led by Sharif Husayn, poets tried to associate Iraq with the Arabian Peninsula during the era of the Prophet Muhammad. The poet Mahdi al-Basir, for example, sought to link the Arab Revolt with the Battle of Badr in early Islam.[46] Efforts to link Iraq to an Arab heritage were also made through the publication of medieval historical and literary texts.[47] The emphasis on secularism and an Arab rather than Islamic historical memory deepened the rift between the ʿulamaʾ and the new *effendiya*.

Much political poetry from the early twentieth century until the onset of World War I focused on rallying support for the Ottoman Empire's defense of Islam against the Christian invaders. The concretization of what was, at an abstract level, a discussion about a struggle between Islam and Christendom centered on specific territories lost by the empire. Ottoman military losses in Greece, Tripoli, and the Balkans deeply upset many Iraqis.[48] Although the poets' goal was to highlight the struggle between Islam and Western Christendom, they instead inadvertently called attention to the new ideology—nationalism—that was spreading throughout the Mediterranean basin and the larger Middle East. Unlike earlier struggles between Occident and Orient, such as the seventh-century expansion of Islam and the Crusades, in which religion constituted the dominant ideology, early-twentieth-century conflict within the Ottoman Empire was caused by the rise of nationalist identities. Notions that the Ottoman sultan was the "commander of the faithful" *(amir al-mu'minin)* and the Ottoman Empire the "abode of Islam" *(dar al-Islam)* lost their explanatory and thus emotive power as different ethnic groups within the empire, both Arabs and non-Arabs, asserted their political identity and rights to self determination within specified geographical boundaries.

Poets who portrayed the Ottoman Empire as the protector of Islam raised expectations that ultimately could not be met. Glowing and stylized descriptions of the defeats that Muslim armies would inflict upon Christian forces were not realized. Calls to Muslims to obey the Ottoman sultan and exempt him from certain dictates of Islamic law implicitly advocated an authoritarian approach to politics at a time when democratic ideas were beginning to permeate Iraqi society and the Arab east. The many poems that criticized the CUP's failure to recognize Arab desires for greater political and cultural autonomy within the Ottoman Empire were extremely bitter in tone. This was especially true of many poets, including both Sunni and Shiʿi Arabs, who heretofore had been the Ottoman Empire's most ardent defenders. It was highly significant that, in expressing similar themes that centered on the need to protect the Ottoman Empire and Iraq from European encroachment, Sunni and Shiʿi Arab poets promoted an awareness among Iraq's two main ethnic groups of their similar rather than conflicting interests.

The struggle led by intellectuals over which symbolic universe would dominate the definition of political community was more complex than a simple choice between Ottomanism and Iraqi nationalism. The Basra Reform Committee, formed in February 1913 under the leadership of the city's main notable, Sayyid Talib al-Naqib, made a distinction between the CUP, whose Turkish nationalism it rejected, and the Ottoman sultan, whose leadership of an Islamic state it supported.[49] The Basra Reform Committee's shifting policies seem to have reflected not just the machinations of al-Sayyid Talib, who sought to establish himself as a political figure of national stature, but also the confusion of many Iraqis as to what constituted an appropriate response to expanding European influence in the Ottoman provinces.

Complicating matters was the political economic overlay to what was rapidly becoming Iraq's "nationalist dilemma." As economic pressures mounted, the CUP looked to its Arab provinces for financial support. In Iraq and the Levant, proposals to auction to foreigners state-owned *saniya* lands of the former sultan Abdül Hamid brought sharp criticism from the local Arab populaces.[50] One complaint was that holding auctions in Istanbul prevented the Arab tribes along the Tigris and Euphrates rivers from purchasing their own land. CUP plans to extend concessions to foreigners, such as the proposal to give the British-owned Lynch Steamship Company a virtual monopoly on the Tigris River, and proposals for railway and customs concessions, angered many local financial and commercial interests.[51] Even before World War I, Ottoman efforts at centralization and intensified European colonial pressures had created in the minds of politically active Iraqis deep ambiguities regarding the "taken-for-grantedness" of the past. Commitment to a historical memory in which the Ottoman sultan served as paterfamilias over a unified Islamic *umma* became increasingly difficult for Iraqis to sustain. The Young Turks did not help their cause by attacking Arab heritage, including religion, language, and customs. Anti-Turkish feelings were heightened by the hanging in 1915 of thirteen Arabs in Syria by a Young Turk governor of the province.[52]

With the rise of national consciousness, Iraqi intellectuals were concerned not only with the question of political community but with social fragmentation as well given the social dislocations caused by Iraq's integration into the world market. It is important not to posit a simple inverse relationship between the decline of Ottoman power and the rise of Iraqi nationalism. A number of prominent Iraqi intellectuals did, in fact, rally around the Ottoman Empire, which they saw as the best defense against social fragmentation. Famous poets such as Maʿruf al-Rusafi (1875–1945) and Jamil Sidqi al-Zahawi (1862–1936) sought to defend the Ottoman Empire from European encroachment. Hostile to Arab nationalism, which they saw as separatist and hence damaging to Muslim unity, they evoked a historical memory of the early Arab-Islamic empires of which the Ottoman sultan was purportedly a modern representative. The ʿulamaʾ supported these efforts, especially the Shiʿa, who declared a jihad against the British in 1914. However, the Ottomans' treatment of their Iraqi subjects, their corruption and inefficacy in resisting the British, and Arab nationalist efforts to ground their own emerging ideology in the same Arab-Islamic historical memory undermined the impact of pro-Ottoman intellectuals. The shock of European military successes, such as Italy's seizure of Tripolitania, led poets to write more spontaneously, thereby breaking the tradition of linking poetry to praise of a *wali*.[53] The Ottoman defeats encouraged greater independence of thought among poets whose poetry became increasingly political in orientation.

The British invasion of Iraq, however, had the greatest impact on new poetic forms and content. The outbreak of World War I provided another shock to the Iraqi body politic by raising the issue of political loyalties. Should Iraqis rally in support of the sultan and their Ottoman coreligionists, or should they welcome the British as liberators from Ottoman oppression? The response was mixed. Many *ʿulamaʾ*, particularly Shiʿi mujtahids in al-Najaf, Karbalaʾ, and al-Kathimayn, issued *fatwas* calling for a jihad against the British.[54] Although many Iraqis, especially tribesmen closely linked to the mujtahids, heeded these calls, others remained on the sidelines, unhappy at the British invasion but equally loath to protect Ottoman interests in Iraq.

The British invasion of Iraq only temporarily slowed the movement toward secular nationalism. When the war began, many Iraqi army officers fought with the Ottomans. Following the Turkish defeat of the British at Kut in southern Iraq in 1915, many intellectuals rallied on behalf of the Ottoman Empire, as seen in the outpouring of poetry praising the sultan.[55] When, through incompetence, the Ottomans failed to capitalize on their victory and it became clear that they could not defeat the British, many Iraqis fled the country in disgust in 1916 to join Sharif Husayn and his son Faysal in the Arab Revolt against the Turks. Many of the ex-Sharifian officers were further embittered when, in 1920, the French army expelled Faysal from Damascus two years after the founding of his Arab state. The war's ultimate outcome, the Ottoman Empire's collapse, and the Arab Revolt's failure to achieve its objectives strengthened secular nationalism. With the British in control of most of Iraq at the war's end, many intellectuals expressed the hope that British promises of an independent and democratic Iraqi state would come to fruition.[56] Accordingly, many poets extolled their virtues. The entente was short-lived as it quickly became clear that the British neither intended to cede control of Iraq to an indigenous government nor planned to support Arab nationalist demands.

Initial enthusiasm for the British waned for other reasons as well. Many Iraqis who had been Ottoman civil servants were now unemployed. The oppressive taxes imposed by the British to help compensate for wartime expenditures and to pay for their colonial occupation of Iraq were seen as punitive, especially by rural tribesmen who had heretofore never been forced to meet such financial obligations.[57] The use of corvée labor further inflamed anti-British feeling. The rigid and condescending policies of the British occupation administration led by Sir Percy Cox and Col. Arnold Wilson, which was staffed by young and inexperienced civil servants who knew little of Iraqi society, irritated the populace. The success of the independent Arab state under ʿAmir Faysal in neighboring Syria highlighted the British failure to meet the expectations for Iraqi independence, which further alienated large numbers of Iraqis.[58]

The war widened the rift between many of the *ʿulamaʾ* and the new secular intelligentsia. This was especially true of *ʿulamaʾ* who had supported the Ottomans and opposed an independent Iraqi state. The war also weakened the ties to the religious community of many prominent intellectuals from prestigious families, including ʿAbd al-Rahman al-Gaylani, Iraq's first premier, ʿAbd al-Muhsin Saʿdun, and Jaʿfar Abu Timman, all of whom became secular nationalists.

Perhaps most significant for our concerns was the impact of these developments on the Shiʿi community. Although the 1920 Revolution united members of the Sunni and Shiʿi communities in a manner unprecedented in Iraqi history, the collapse of Ottoman rule and its replacement by British control further marginalized the Shiʿa. Superficially, it might appear as if the Shiʿi community had reversed its traditional position and tied its political fortunes to the Ottoman Empire during the war. The Shiʿi mujtahid Mirza Muhammad Taqi al-Shirazi, for example, issued a *fatwa* exhorting all Iraqis to rise up in a holy war against the British invasion. However, this *fatwa* represented less support for the Ottomans than an effort to prevent Iraq from falling under Western influence.

As military operations were predominantly in the south, the Iraqi Shiʿi were most profoundly affected by the war. First, the *fatwa* calling for a jihad divided the mujtahids between those who favored an activist political role and those who disdained mixing politics and religion. Second, the jihad accentuated divisions between the mujtahids and the *sada*, whose control of large landholdings made them hesitant to challenge the British, whom they perceived as the emerging economic power in Iraq. Third, the call to a jihad further weakened tribal power in the Middle Euphrates region, already eroded by Ottoman land reforms. Tribes were divided between those with close ties to politically active mujtahids who obeyed, albeit reluctantly, their call to defend the Ottomans, and those tribes that had developed close ties to the British through becoming integrated into the agricultural economy. Tribes along the Tigris whose developed system of river transportation encouraged sedentary agriculture were less inclined to revolt than those along the Euphrates, which lacked such a system.[59]

Paralleling a pattern that would recur more than seventy years later during the 1991 Intifada, tribes often supported whichever side seemed to be gaining the upper hand. Some Shi'i notable families, such as the Kamuna in Karbala' and the Zugurt and Shumurt in al-Najaf, opposed both the Turks and the British. Thus al-Najaf and Karbala' used wartime instability to throw off Turkish rule and become, in effect, independent political entities until British occupation of the cities in 1918. In al-Najaf, the Buraq quarter of the city actually promulgated a constitution to create greater cohesion among its residents.[60] Other notables, particularly merchants who sought to rejuvenate trade, supported British efforts to impose their own control over these recalcitrant cities at war's end, even to the point of betraying their fellow coreligionists.[61]

Wartime developments demonstrated that the Shi'i community did not march in lockstep. The military campaign in the south forced powerful sectors of the community to make choices. Some Shi'is supported the Turks and others the British. Thus the war promoted both the oppositional tradition among Iraqi Shi'a and a rudimentary thrust for democratic rule. Although some Shi'i intellectuals, such as the poet al-Rusafi, maintained a nostalgia for Ottoman rule after war's end and others longed for closer ties with Persia, the bulk of politically active Shi'is were avid nationalists who rallied to the postwar battle cry for al-istiqlal al-tamm (unconditional independence). Crosscutting ethnicity, social class began to assume greater salience, an important indicator of future divisions in the Shi'i community.

Unfortunately, nationalist advocacy set the Shi'i population on a collision course with the British and undermined their ability to influence not only the nascent state's newly established political institutions, but also its emerging historical memory. The Shi'i clergy's militancy—as reflected in its call for a jihad, its support of the 1918 Najaf revolt and subsequent opposition to British administration of the city, and its central role in the 1920 uprising—led the British to distrust them and expel many from the country.[62] One result was a lack of Shi'i representation in the newly formed Iraqi state. The 'ulama''s strenuous efforts to resist secularization, particularly in education, led many Shi'i youth to cut their ties to traditional elements of their community. More so than in the Sunni community, a sharp cleavage developed between religious and secular Shi'is. Of those who chose a secular political identity, particularly urban migrants, many would later embrace radical ideologies such as Marxism. Needless to say, the state was far less sympathetic to leftist radicalism than to Pan-Arabism, especially since the newly established monarchy based its legitimacy on its ties to an Arab-Islamic heritage and its leadership of the Arab Revolt. The association of many Shi'is with either religious reaction[63] or, subsequently, left-wing radicalism tarred the community in the eyes of many Sunnis. Perceptions by the state that Shi'is, of both the right and the left, contributed to social fragmentation isolated them further.

Political developments following Britain's invasion of Iraq, the Ottoman Empire's collapse, and the establishment of a nominally independent state further diminished Shi'i influence and boded ill for Iraq's future unity. However, a different scenario for the future of political community in Iraq was suggested by events during the June through October 1920 Revolution, known as the Great Iraqi Revolution (al-Thawra al-'Iraqiya al-Kubra). The revolt's impact was twofold. First, it created a sense of unified national consciousness, even if the revolt reflected a variety of motivations among its supporters. Second, it united Sunnis and Shi'is in a manner that had not been seen before in Iraqi history. This show of unity took its most pronounced form in the sharing of religious ceremonies as Shi'is participated in Sunni *mawalid* (celebrations of the birth of the Prophet) and Sunnis joined Shi'i *ta'azin* (lamentations for the deaths of the Prophet's son-in-law 'Ali and his sons Hasan and Husayn). The celebration of a *mawlid* or a *ta'ziya* reflected less a concern with its traditional religious function than an effort to utilize a popular ritual to mobilize the populace. As numerous British diplomatic and intelligence reports document, these efforts were highly effective. Far from sporadic, these events were organized by the uprising's nationalist leadership, especially the Haras al-Istiqlal (Guardians of Independence), and continued from May to mid-August 1920.[64] Reading poetry in their respective mosques, Sunni and Shi'i poets began competing to best express nationalist feelings.[65] The revolt's inclusive and ecumenical nature can be seen in the poets' call for unity among members of all Iraq's religious sects, including Christians and Jews.[66] Manifestations of Sunni-Shi'i solidarity were not limited to Baghdad and the south but also included Sunni strongholds such as Mosul.[67]

That the mosque was the primary venue of nationalist agitation, and ostensible religious rituals the mechanism for political mobilization, indicates that religion was the dominant idiom through which the populace mediated reality and the primary locus of historical memory. Underscoring religion's centrality was the role of the revolt's "organic intellectuals," the majority of whom were poets. Almost all poets were products of a religious education and expressed themselves in a classical Arabic framework closely tied to such an education. It is significant, therefore, that, despite the predominance of a religious idiom in expressing nationalist sentiments, poets emphasized unity between Sunni and Shi'i, Muslim and non-Muslim, and blamed external forces such as the Turks and British for disrupting Iraq's natural harmony.[68]

Even before the 1920 uprising, poets often facilitated political contact between urban nationalists and tribal notables. The Haras al-Istiqlal in particular contained many poets, who often acted to create alliances among important political actors for whom such cooperation had heretofore been limited. Poets also linked the populace along not just ethnic but also social class lines. During the revolt, they spread to rural areas, where they successfully agitated among the peasantry. Countless British intelligence reports documented demonstrations, processions, and political gatherings in which poets played a central role and which emphasized the unity and nonsectarian nature of Iraq's political community. Not only did Sunnis and Shi'is share religious and cultural festivals, but Iraqi Muslims welcomed public displays of Christian religious symbolism such as a Christmas processional in Baghdad, and statements were issued praising Christians and Jews as patriotic citizens.

Sunni-Shi'i cooperation was not confined to attempting to throw off British rule. Prior to the uprising, a number of prominent Sunni and Shi'i Iraqis united to form a political organization known as al-Mandubun (or delegates), which petitioned the British occupation administration for greater freedom for Iraq. In 1919 Sunnis and Shi'is formed the Haras al-Istiqlal. These broader institutional affiliations demonstrate that the two confessional groups' cooperation during the 1920 Revolution was not a historical aberration. Indeed, this political behavior during the uprising presaged subsequent more extensive and institutionalized cooperation among the country's two main sects in Iraqist nationalist organizations such as the al-Ahali Group, the Iraqi Communist Party, and numerous labor organizations.

The significance of the 1920 Revolution for modern Iraqi political development was to demonstrate that it was not preordained that Iraq should be plagued by ethnic and confessional cleavages, and that Sunnis and Shi'is should remain mutually hostile and unable to cooperate in nation building. The 1920 Revolution set a precedent for subordinating ethnic and confessional loyalties to commitment to a larger national entity. However, neither Great Britain nor the fledgling Iraqi state it formed in the wake of the revolt encouraged this spirit of cooperation. The Sunni-dominated provisional government under Sayyid Talib al-Naqib did everything possible to limit Shi'i participation in the new administration at both the national and local level.[69] British efforts to include Shi'is in the government were for the sake of appearances and did not give them any significant power. With the banishment to Persia of many Shi'i *'ulama'* who had participated in the 1918 and 1920 uprisings, and the failure to include any significant Shi'i presence in either al-Naqib's provisional administration or in King Faysal's newly formed Hashimite state, Shi'i resentment at being excluded from the reins of power increased.

The problems that developed after the 1920 Revolution and the founding of the monarchical state in 1921 were not the product of an antagonism rooted in an unchanging confessional psyche. Rather the monarchy, its supporters among the ex-Sharifian officers, who were overwhelmingly Sunni Arabs drawn from Baghdad and northern Iraq, and the British conspired to exclude the Shi'a from power. During the British mandate (1920–32), Shi'i ministerial appointments constituted only 17.7 percent of the total despite the fact that Shi'is comprised between 50 and 60 percent of the population. A Shi'i did not become prime minister until 1947.

Following the establishment of the Iraqi monarchy in August 1921, nationalist activities became more institutionally focused. One of the most important developments during the 1920s was the establishment of a large number of presses that facilitated the proliferation of newspapers and journals.[70] Between 1920 and 1929, at least 105 newspapers were founded, many of which advocated radical perspectives.[71] It is important to underscore the cooperation of different ethnic and confessional groups in producing these periodicals. For example, *al-Misbah*, whose publisher was the famous (Shi'i) short story writer Mahmud Ahmad al-Sayyid, counted a Jewish lawyer, Anwar Shawwul (Ibn Samual) as its editor.[72] In many instances periodicals were associated with nationalist political organizations such as the al-'Ahd (Covenant), the al-Ikha' al-Watani (National Brotherhood), and the al-Sha'b (People's) parties.

The radical press that developed during the 1920s called for immediate independence for Iraq, the evacuation of British troops, and the development of a democratic and participatory Iraqi state. By far the most radical Iraqi newspaper was *al-Sahifa*, which, founded in 1924, contained among its adherents the nucleus of the future Iraqi Communist Party. The newspaper was really the organ of a Marxist study group established by Husayn al-Rahhal, a law student whose studies in Germany had stimulated an interest in socialism. The group met in the Haydarkhana Mosque, which had played such a prominent role in the 1920 Revolution. The communist movement, which was to become a major force in promoting Iraqist nationalism, was thus intimately connected with the rise of a radical press.[73]

Offsetting the press's influence was the frequent censorship and closing of newspapers and journals by British mandatory officials and the monarchy, which forced many periodicals to reorganize under new titles.[74] The impact of opposition periodicals was also tempered by the support the monarchy and the British gave to officially sanctioned newspapers and journals. Semiofficial newspapers such as *al-ʿAsima, al-Liwaʾ, al-Taqaddum, Sada al-ʿAhd,* and *al-Tariq* worked to legitimize the British mandate by emphasizing a gradualist approach to Iraqi independence. Yet even these papers subscribed to the idea of Iraqi independence, and their political differences with the more radical press were more of degree than of kind.

The development of professional organizations representing the interests of teachers, lawyers, doctors, and other professionals provided another forum for the expression of nationalist sentiments. What were founded ostensibly as "fraternal" organizations frequently became platforms for political demonstrations and political parties. The formation of professional organizations was accompanied by the establishment of clubs where members could fraternize and hold meetings. Clubs such as Nadi al-Tadammun (Solidarity Club) and Nadi al-Muʿallimin (Teacher's Club) became known as forums where radical nationalists could deliver speeches.

Nadi al-Tadammun, a student organization founded by Husayn al-Rahhal in 1926, organized Iraq's first major student demonstration. The demonstration's goal was the reinstatement at the Baghdad Secondary School of Anis al-Nusuli, a Syrian teacher who had been fired for publishing a text on Umayyad history that many Iraqi Shiʿis found offensive. The club was also in the forefront of demonstrations against the visit of Sir Alfred Mond, a prominent British Zionist, to Baghdad in 1928.[75]

Nationalist sentiments also found expression in the hundreds of coffee shops that existed in major urban areas.[76] Not only could nationalists disseminate their political views through conversations with the regulars who visited such establishments, but poets could also use the coffeehouses as venues for exhorting crowds to political action. If political participation increased during the 1920s as ever-larger numbers of Iraqis became involved in politics, then ethnic tensions also intensified. However, such tensions tended to be confined to the political elite. Already in 1919, for example, members of the Iraqi wing of the al-ʿAhd Party, resentful that the Haras al-Istiqlal was attracting more public support, complained to central party headquarters in Damascus that members of the latter were working on behalf of the Turks.[77] Although the central headquarter's investigation found the accusation to be baseless, the outlines of the cleavages that were to plague Iraq under the monarchy began to become clear. Pan-Arab political organizations such as al-ʿAhd, which were largely Sunni Arab, accused Iraqist nationalists (whom they derogated as *qutri*, or regional nationalists), many of whom were Shiʿi or drawn from minority groups, of working against Arab unity. The obvious inference was that Iraqist *(qutri)* nationalists were unpatriotic since they were harming not only Pan-Arab interests but Iraqi interests as well. Although ethnic cleavages were especially noticeable among the upper echelons of Iraqi society, they were less prominent among Iraqist nationalists. The Haras leadership, which was drawn largely from wealthy landowning civil servants who had held high posts in the Ottoman administration and was Iraqist nationalist in orientation, nevertheless supported Arab nationalism.[78] Its charter emphasized that "it is incumbent on the organization to begin before all else to unify the sentiment of all Iraqis *[kalimat al-ʿIraqiyin]*, regardless of their creed or sect, and to exert the utmost effort to overcome all causes of disunity that are based on religion and religious doctrine."[79] In other words, the Haras never lost sight of the need to accommodate all Iraq's social strata in trying to achieve Arab unity. To nationalists drawn from the lower social strata, concerns with ethnicity and confessionalism were much less salient. Sunni and Shiʿi Arabs worked together in organizations such as the Sahifa Group and many other radical newspapers and journals. Opposition newspapers and journals were replete with poetry attacking British control of Iraq, which constituted the real focus of their concerns.[80]

The ex-Sharifian officers, who had provided Faysal I's base of support during the Arab Revolt and the majority of bureaucrats in the short-lived Arab state in Syria and in the fledgling Iraqi state, were overwhelmingly Sunni Arab. The same was true of the moderate nationalists upon whom Faysal relied to offset British influence in Iraq. With the British still suspicious of the Shiʿa's loyalty, and Faysal relying on the ex-Sharifians, there remained little political space for Shiʿis at the national level. Gradually the goodwill that had been engendered by Sunni-Shiʿi cooperation during the 1920 uprising began to dissipate. Although Faysal was aware of anti-Shiʿi discrimination, his struggles with the British to gain greater autonomy, and attacks from radical nationalists, both Iraqist and Pan-Arab, for not rejecting the 1922 treaty legitimizing the British mandate, left him little room for maneuver. Understandably, the state sought to protect its fragile power base rather than engage in new initiatives that might weaken it still further. Thus no significant efforts were made to incorporate Shiʿi elements into important administrative positions during Faysal's rule (1921–33).

The increasing intensity of political debate in Iraq was exacerbated during the 1920s by the persistence of British control of Iraq under its League of Nation's Mandate. Yet looming on the horizon were much more ominous problems, the most dangerous of which was the country's continued economic deterioration. Although oil had been discovered in 1907, the Iraqi government still received very little concessionary revenue during the interwar period. What came to be known in Iraq and elsewhere in the Arab world as "the social problem" (al-qadiya al-ijtima'iya) entailed the breakdown of the agrarian sector, particularly in the south, which was overwhelmingly Shi'i. The consequence was massive rural-to-urban migration, especially to Baghdad, and the development of huge squatter communities inhabited by *shurugi*, or "Easterners," around large urban areas.[81]

During the 1920s, Iraqi nationalists focused primarily on *political* change. Their main concern was ridding Iraq of the hated British mandate and Britain's indirect control over the Iraqi state through its system of British ministerial advisors.[82] Although confessional differences had begun to appear, opposition to the British was still sufficient to override them. This was evident, for example, in the opposition to the Treaty of 1922, which was brought before the Constituent Assembly for ratification in 1924. Large crowds tried to attack the Constituent Assembly, where delegates were being pressured by the palace and the British to sign the treaty.[83] Actions such as these and the constant barrage of criticism of the state for not vigorously opposing the British, such as the scorn the poet Ma'ruf al-Rusafi heaped upon the parliamentary system, undermined its legitimacy.

Despite his tenuous position, Faysal was able gradually to increase his power and to achieve an equilibrium among competing factions of the political elite. A pattern developed in which ministries were short-lived and rotated among political cliques. Because the monarchy's aim in making cabinet appointments was never to allow any politician or faction to gain substantial power, the monarchical state was characterized by indecision and inaction. The army received major support to compensate for the monarchy's institutional weakness and the political system's fractured nature, which was to create serious problems for the Iraqi state and society during the 1930s.[84]

In conclusion, what was the significance of the Ottoman Empire's collapse and the British occupation for the development of political community in Iraq? The empire's collapse created a number of voids by disrupting previously accepted patterns of authority, political and social institutions, and cultural practices. Iraqis were forced to develop new institutional structures and forms of culture to replace those that had vanished. New cultural forms entailed, among other things, redefining the role of the intellectual and looking to new forms of historical memory.

The proclamation of a jihad early during World War I was significant for many reasons, not the least of which was the Shi'i community's active involvement in national politics. The ecumenical tone of the *fatwas* issued by the Shi'i clergy offset the traditional perception of the clergy as obscurantist, parochial, and removed from worldly concerns. The autonomy of al-Najaf and Karbala' during the war likewise promoted a sense of political efficacy among Iraq's Shi'a. The crystallization of social and political solidarity among Iraq's disparate ethnic groups at war's end in the 1920 Revolution boded well for the development of a polity in which cultural diversity would be respected. The development of a genuine alliance among the (mostly Sunni Arab) Baghdadi nationalists, tribes of the Middle Euphrates, and the Shi'i clergy of the shrine cities proffered in microcosm a pattern for possible future political cooperation.

Prior to the founding of the Iraqi nation-state, all "organic intellectuals," both Sunni and Shi'i, drew upon a specifically Arab-Islamic historical memory. This historical memory was used to draw parallels between the caliphate and the Ottoman sultan, to criticize the Committee for Union and Progress for its policies toward the Arab provinces and its inability to protect them from European encroachments, and to call for a jihad against the British during World War I. The religious symbolism evoked to foster intercommunal unity during the 1920 Revolution was also replete with references to Arab heritage, such as the unity of Shi'ism and Sunnism and the centrality of Jewish and Christian profits in Islam. In other words, all efforts to mobilize the populace drew upon symbols derived from the Golden Age of the Arab-Islamic empires. Such symbolism was extremely potent, especially when wrapped in the garb of modern nationalism and emphasizing social and cultural unity. At the time of the 1920 Revolution, there was little distinction between Pan-Arabism and Iraqist nationalism as all nationalists focused on ridding Iraq of British control. During the ensuing struggle for ideological hegemony following the 1920 uprising, Iraqist nationalism failed to remain sensitive to the issue of historical memory. Perhaps one reason for this was that Iraqist nationalists were deprived of the support of nationalistically minded Shi'i clerics, who were more sensitive to history but had been either imprisoned or exiled because of their leading role in the 1920 Revolution. As such, Iraqist nationalists ceded a large part of the struggle over defining Iraq's political community to the Pan-Arabists. Although their political and social critiques were trenchant and biting, the failure of Iraqist nationalists to develop a counterhegemonic vision of a society in which the past *(al-turath)* played a central role led them to lose sight of the social-psychological dimensions involved in developing a new sense of political community. Iraqis, especially those who were politically active, were not simply responding to British colonialism and a corrupt monarchy in terms of "objective" criteria such as levels of political participation and norms of distributive justice. Given historical events, including the cultural and political divide between Sunnis and Shi'is and between town and country, and the manipulation of ethnic cleavages by local elites and foreign powers such as the Ottomans, it was critical that the regime address the issue of trust among Iraqi ethnic groups and the desire of the people not to be cut off from the past. Many Iraqis, especially the most powerful political actors, felt more comfortable holding on to the myth of recreating an Arab Golden Age than embracing materially and psychologically the idealized, but as yet untested, vision of the future based on social justice and cultural diversity proffered by Iraqist nationalists. Iraqist nationalism did attract some members of the upper middle class, but it was largely rooted in middle-class professionals, intellectuals, students from poor rural backgrounds, and members of the working class. Thus the cultural and political differences that separated the two competing views of Iraqi political community tended to have a social class division as well. How this struggle over political community played itself out leading to the turmoil that followed the 1958 Revolution and the Ba'th Party's ascendancy in 1968, and the implications of this struggle for issues of cultural inclusion and distributive justice, will occupy subsequent chapters.

3   Nationalism, Memory, and the Decline of the Monarchical State

The struggle between Iraqist and Pan-Arabist nationalism over the definition of political community intensified between 1921 and 1958. This growing polarization was exacerbated by the lack of social reforms, increased corruption within the state, and the political mobilization of ever-larger numbers of Iraqis as urban centers grew. As ideological positions hardened, historical memory assumed greater importance as a political weapon. Sensitive to the past, Pan-Arabists were more effective than Iraqist nationalists in mobilizing historical memory.[1] However, Pan-Arabism's romanticized historical memory exerted a negative influence on the development of a sense of national collective identity. Through association with control of the state by a small Sunni Arab elite, Pan-Arabism became for many Iraqis a metaphor for the political, economic, and cultural exclusion of the bulk of the populace from public life.

The increased political mobilization of the populace was accompanied by a rapid growth in political and social organizations and the development of new trends in literature and the arts. Despite the emphasis on social and political decay found in much of the literature on interwar Iraq, these developments suggest instead the growth of an incipient civil society. The proliferation of new social, cultural, and political organizations also indicates that violence, cultural intolerance, and political instability need not be the order of the day.

In charting the lineages of contemporary Iraqi politics, and particularly the lengthy rule by the Takriti Ba'th from 1968 to 2003, a number of questions deserve attention. First, what impact did the processes of state building have on civil society and understandings of collective identity after the collapse of the 1920 Revolution? Second, what impact did the increased mobilization of the populace, particularly the growing middle and working classes, have on notions of political community? Third, how did intellectuals chart the future of Iraqi society in political thought, in their use of historical memory, and in literature and the arts? Finally, how did the contours of the Iraqi political economy, and particularly the distribution of wealth, affect Iraq's social classes? In all these spheres, what role did imperial domination play? Any assessment of these four spheres—state formation, political and social mobilization, intellectual production, and political economy—must begin with an examination of a series of crises that beset the political system during the interwar years. These crises include the demonstrations against the Iraqi Constitution of 1924, the protests surrounding the Anis al-Nusuli Affair of 1927, the 1928 visit to Iraq by the British Zionist Sir Alfred Mond, the Anglo-Iraqi treaty negotiations of 1930, the 1931 General Strike, the Assyrian crisis of 1933, the tribal uprisings in the Middle and Lower Euphrates during the mid-1930s, the 1936 Bakr Sidqi coup d'état, and the denouement of the interwar years, the Anglo-Iraqi Crisis of May 1941.[2]

State formation absorbed the attention of the new political elite and their British overlords following the 1920 Revolution. Both the traditional urban Sunni Arab elite and the British were keen to eliminate the revolution's memory, which challenged their political and economic prerogatives. First, a rigged referendum in August 1921 assured the creation of the Hashimite Monarchy. Second, the Iraqi army was organized along confessional lines as it was under the Ottomans. Third, the electoral system was structured to assure domination by the wealthy, and cabinets were constructed along ethnic lines. Finally, the state bureaucracy, especially the Ministry of Education, was organized along ethnic and ideological lines.

As Hasan al-ʿAlawi has documented, all these processes were influenced by imperial and sectarian considerations as the British and their allies strove to assure that their interests would be protected.[3] Thus, the 1921 Referendum was manipulated to exclude the would-be leader of Iraq, Sayyid Talib al-Naqib, whom the British distrusted despite his Sunni confession, and to insure instead that Faysal bin Husayn was elected king. The army's new commander in chief, Jaʿfar al-ʿAskari, built the officer corps along ethnic lines dominated by Sunni Arabs. The cabinet also included only token Shiʿis. Only in the Iraqi parliament was the pattern of Sunni domination disrupted. This had less to do with sectarian criteria than with the British desire to use southern tribal shaykh-landowners, the majority of whom were Shiʿi, to offset the power of urban nationalists and the monarchy. Shiʿi presence in the Iraqi parliament was thus part of the typical colonial pattern of divide and conquer. Shiʿi mujtahids, on the other hand, were excluded from political participation by both the British and the Sunni Arab elite. Within the state bureaucracy, arguably the most important agency was the Directorate of Education, which was entrusted with the nation's educational system and the socialization of Iraqi youth. Under Khaldun Sati' al-Husari's sectarian leadership, the agency, a subunit of the Ministry of Education, vigorously promoted a Pan-Arabist understanding of Iraqi political community through an emphasis on an Arab-Islamic Golden Age. In the version of historical memory perpetuated in school textbooks, Shi'a and Kurdish heritage possessed little currency. Even though the minister of education was always a Shi'i, educational policy was effectively controlled by Sunni Arabs in the Directorate of Education.

The processes of state building, which were based on an exclusionary political system, were reinforced by a series of defining events during the interwar years. Rule by party cliques was institutionalized in the form of groups of "professional politicians" and political "parties" that were formed and disbanded to meet specific political demands. Because no clique could satisfy all political actors' demands, a discontented clique would invariably cause the government to fall, thereby creating an opening for its own political aspirations. British power, exerted directly during their mandate over Iraq and indirectly thereafter, complicated this system because the actions of both the monarchy and the parliamentary elites were shaped by their perception of the potential responses of their colonial overlords. Tribal shaykhs, who represented yet another power center, periodically engineered revolts in the Middle Euphrates region to extract concessions from the state when they felt their interests were not being addressed. Their sense of exclusion often was overlaid by sectarian feelings as Shi'i tribal leaders saw a Sunni plot behind parliamentary election results.[4]

The key variable in structuring political dynamics was the sectarianization *(tamadhhab)* of the state. The establishment of the army constituted the nascent state's most important institutional development because it assured the Hashimite Monarchy at least a modicum of social control, if only in urban areas. Although organized along sectarian lines, Sunni Arab (and, to a lesser extent, Kurdish) domination of the officer corps was also structural in that it represented a continuation of the Ottoman policy of recruiting coreligionists and the Shi'i clergy's policy of minimizing contact with the Ottoman administration. Nevertheless, because it developed in the wake of Shi'i sacrifices in the struggle against the British during the war and the 1920 Revolution, the army's formation along sectarian lines represented more than just the exclusion of the Shi'a from the military. It also represented a tacit denial of the patriotism that the Shi'a had demonstrated during two major conflicts against the British—whom most Iraqis considered an alien occupier of their country—as well as an implicit effort to erase the historical memory of Shi'i sacrifices. This pattern of exclusion, which extended not just to the military but to all aspects of public life, is one that, with the exception of 'Abd al-Karim Qasim's regime, the Iraqi state has still not addressed. Put differently, the state's cultural and political exclusion of the Shi'a was not the creation of the Takriti Ba'th Party but rather a policy with a long historical tradition or "path dependence."[5]

If the army was meant to enhance the monarchy's physical control of the newly formed Iraqi nation-state, then the state's educational policy sought to create a new generation of Iraqi youth that supported a Pan-Arabist vision of the country's future. To accomplish this end, the state attempted to inculcate Iraqi youth with a nostalgic and romanticized understanding of the past based on a historical memory tied to Sunni Arab heritage. The appointment of Khaldun Sati' al-Husari as director of education in 1921 represented a self-conscious effort to create a common Pan-Arab political identity to which all Iraqis would ascribe. In light of the Hashimites' non-Iraqi origins, it is not surprising that Faysal chose a director committed to Pan-Arabism. Had he chosen an Iraqist nationalist, the resulting educational policies could have undermined rather than enhanced the Hashimite Monarchy's legitimacy. Because Pan-Arabism was identified with the ex-Sharifian officer corps that had supported Faysal's Arab Revolt and now protected his throne, and with the majority of Arabs beyond Iraq's borders adhering to Sunnism, inevitably many Shi'is saw the state's Pan-Arabist educational policy as promoting sectarianism. Ironically, the educational policies that were intended to create a sense of national identity instead sharpened sectarian cleavages.

If the army and educational system's sectarian underpinnings undermined the state's legitimacy among large segments of the populace, then the end of Great Britain's League of Nations Mandate in 1932 ostensibly should have strengthened Iraqi state formation by promoting the perception among the Shi'a and the nation's minorities that at least one pillar of the sectarian system had been eliminated. All segments of society expected reduced British interference in Iraq's internal affairs with the mandate's end. Unfortunately, the system of British ministerial advisors remained in place, intensifying nationalist feelings and spreading cynicism in the face of failed political expectations. Sunnis saw little hope of independence, Shi'is little hope of decreased discrimination, and Kurds no hope for greater autonomy from the central government.

Faysal I's unexpected death in September 1933 left the country without a political leader of national stature. His only son and successor, King Ghazi

I, was a young and inexperienced leader. The Assyrian crisis, tribal revolts, Ghazi's inexperience, and the rising discontent of the increasingly politicized urban middle and lower classes fostered political instability and a political vacuum. These events, which drew the army into politics, set the stage for the Arab world's first military coup d'état, in 1936, and had a major impact on debates about the future of Iraqi collective identity and political community. In addition to the difficulties facing the monarchy, a classic case of immobilism beset the Iraqi polity during the 1920s and 1930s as the parliament refused to enact reformist policies. Although governments fell with great frequency, the number of politicians who occupied ministerial posts was relatively small. The only deviation from this pattern resulted from the power vacuum following Faysal's death, which forced the political elite to share power with the army between 1936 and 1941.

The most important political change occurred among middle- and lower-class organizations that represented professional, nationalist and anticolonial, literary, and educational interests. Lower-class organizations were almost totally dominated by labor and other material concerns. The populace's increased mobilization during the 1930s was accompanied by structural stasis, both organizational and ideological, among the political elite. Whereas the political elite attempted to manipulate sectarian and regional identities to maintain its power, the middle classes mounted ideologically based assaults on the political system. In this struggle, the use of historical memory benefited Pan-Arabists particularly well. For them, the creation of an "Arab nation" *(al-watan al-ʿArabi)* represented the highest political good to which all Arabs, including Iraqis, should aspire. For Pan-Arabists, a unified Arab state would overcome the deep divisions of Iraqi society. Iraqist nationalist organizations, such as the social democratic Ahali Group formed during the early 1930s, paid little attention to historical memory and focused instead on expanding civil society through enhancing democratic rights and adapting British Fabian socialism to Iraq. For the Iraqi Communist Party (ICP), the peasantry and especially the working class—which would assume its "historic role" of gathering all oppressed groups, regardless of ethnic origins, under one political umbrella—assumed center stage.

During the mid-1930s, a series of events threatened the fragile Iraqi polity with a crisis of authority. This crisis, which was compounded by the political elite's refusal to cede any privileges or address the country's growing social problems, was caused by King Ghazi's ineffectual leadership, tribal revolts, and the Assyrian crisis. Most ominous was the politicization of the army, which was deployed, under General Bakr Sidqi al-ʿAskari, to suppress

Shi'i tribal revolts in the Middle Euphrates region during the early 1930s and an uprising by Iraq's Assyrian community during the summer of 1933. In both instances, sectarian feelings among urban nationalists were intensified by their hostility toward British policies that favored minorities and rural interests. These feelings, which resulted in violent reactions to the threat presented by both the tribes but especially the Assyrians, underscored the monarchy's failure to address Iraq's ethnic and cultural diversity.

The intensity with which Shi'i tribesmen and the Assyrians were suppressed stemmed in part from resentment among army officers and urban nationalists at the British policy of favoring tribal leaders as a counterweight to urban (particularly Arab) nationalists. When the nation-state was founded, tribal leaders had been allowed to retain their arms and were given a privileged legal status, allowing them increased control over their agricultural lands and the peasant-tribesmen who worked them. As Dhu al-Nun Ayyub vividly portrayed in his 1939 novel *al-Yadd wa-l-Ard wa-l-Ma' (The Hand, Earth, and Water)*, tribal shaykhs were able to prevent the state from entering tribal domains to recruit tribesmen for the army and were given disproportionate representation in parliament.[6] British control of the army during the mandate, during which they prevented Faysal from increasing the army's size or introducing compulsory service, angered not only the king and the ex-Sharifian officers, but also urban nationalists. The army's impotence was evident in its inability to defend the country's borders against Ikhwan forces from the Najd (presently northeastern Saudi Arabia), which attacked Iraq in 1922, 1924, and 1927–28.[7]

Iraq's political insecurity and instability explain the vigor with which the army responded to tribal unrest in the Middle Euphrates during the early 1930s. Tribes were seen as preventing the army from assuming its national role and challenging the central state's authority by creating, in effect, autonomous regions in the countryside.[8] Bakr Sidqi's suppression of the tribes greatly enhanced his popularity within the officer corps and among Pan-Arabists. This was ironic because Sidqi was an Iraqi of Kurdish origins who later proved unsympathetic to Pan-Arabism. Nevertheless, Sidqi's actions were viewed as a blow to British efforts to divide and conquer Iraq by promoting rural-urban and sectarian cleavages.

Even more than the tribal revolts, the Assyrian crisis politicized the army and undermined what little institution building had taken place during Faysal's reign. The king began to lose political control as his declining health forced him to travel to Europe for rest and treatment in June 1933. Before leaving Iraq, he expressed his disgust at statements made by Pan-Arabists, including his son Ghazi, calling for the elimination of the Assyrian community. The Assyrian crisis became a bellwether for the fears of various ethnic groups trying to form a stable political community.[9]

An ancient community, the Assyrians settled in eastern Turkey, north-western Iran, and northern Iraq during the Mongol invasion.[10] During World War I, many fought with British forces against the Ottomans. The Assyrians, who became an important part of the Iraq Levies, a military unit organized within the British army that the British used to guard military fa-cilities and to control the Kurds, proved to be excellent soldiers who were feared because of their role in helping suppress the 1920 Revolution.[11] When return to Turkey became impossible after the collapse of the Ot-toman Empire, they refused to accept their new status as citizens of Iraq. The Assyrians' insularity, reinforced by the absolute authority of their spir-itual and temporal leader, the Mar Shimun, created resentment, especially after Iraq extended many benefits to them as a minority after the war. Arabs and Kurds saw the Assyrians as British protégés and beyond the state's con-trol. The Levies were also resented because their salaries were double those of Iraqi army recruits.[12]

The Assyrian demand for complete autonomy within Iraq set the stage for the August 1933 massacre. Even though the Levies had been disbanded in 1930, many Assyrians still retained their arms. The government and the army feared that an Assyrian revolt might result in an autonomous region ruled by the Mar Shimun and, given Turkish designs on the oil-rich province of Mosul, lead to Turkish military occupation of northern Iraq. Na-tionalists suspected that the British would use the Assyrians to undermine Iraq's recently achieved independence following the end of their League of Nations mandate in 1932. Thus the Assyrian issue touched on many of the problems facing Iraq: the nation-state's territorial integrity, British colonial rule, the army's efficacy, and the allegiances of minorities. When a clash oc-curred between the Iraqi army and armed Assyrians along the Iraqi-Syrian border, a panic-stricken government ordered Sidqi to throw the army's might against the Assyrians, which led to a massacre of more than three hundred men in the village of Summayl near Dohuk on August 5, 1933.

The army's return to Baghdad produced an outpouring of sympathy for the suppression of the Assyrians. What the Assyrians (and much of the world) viewed as a bloodbath, urban Iraqis, especially Sunni Arabs, saw as a triumph for Iraqi political unity. For the Kurds, the repression of the Assyr-ians eliminated a traditional enemy. The assumption that the conflict was religiously based and that Iraq's Muslims, both Arab and Kurd, were hostile to the Assyrians because they were Christians, is incorrect. The key factors in the conflict were Assyrian unwillingness to integrate into Iraqi society, their close ties to the British, and the army's desire to demonstrate that it was a force to be reckoned with.

The repression of the Middle Euphrates tribes and especially the Assyrians set in motion a train of events that undermined the development of civil society in Iraq. Violence became a substitute for the lengthy and often painstaking negotiations that were necessary to reconcile political rivals. Bakr Sidqi exploited the Assyrian massacres by parading his victorious army through the streets of Baghdad together with Crown Prince Ghazi, whose popularity had also increased due to his support of the army's actions. Ironically, Sidqi was viewed as an Arab nationalist who had rescued the population of Iraq's Sunni Arab triangle. Immensely popular, Sidqi managed to eclipse Faysal I as Iraq's most popular political leader in the summer of 1933 and to set the stage for the Arab world's first military coup d'état, which he carried out in October 1936.

The suppression of the tribes and the Assyrians highlighted the increased role of sectarianism in Iraqi politics during the 1930s. The army's 1936 coup d'état intensified the cleavage between Pan-Arabists and Iraqist nationalists, foreshadowing a similar struggle after the July 1958 Revolution. During the 1920s, this cleavage was not yet pronounced. The proposed 1924 Iraqi Constitution, the 1926 Iraqi-Turkish Petroleum Company concession, the 1927 Anis al-Nusuli Affair, the 1928 visit to Baghdad by Sir Alfred Mond, and the Anglo-Iraqi Treaty of 1930 were uniformly opposed by all Iraqi nationalists. During the early 1930s, the Hizb al-Ikha' al-Watani (National Brotherhood Party) and the al-Hizb al-Watani (National Party), which represented Pan-Arabism and Iraqist nationalism respectively, cooperated to oppose the treaty negotiations between the British and the monarchy. Faysal disrupted this alliance in 1932 by offering the Pan-Arabist Rashid ʿAli al-Gaylani presidency of the Royal Diwan, which caused the National Brotherhood Party to cease opposing the monarchy. Kamil al-Chadirji subsequently resigned from the party to join the Iraqist nationalist Ahali Group. Thus, ideological differences among Iraqi nationalists began to crystallize in 1932 and 1933. The formation in 1934 of the Iraqi Communist Party, although an anti-nationalist party, strengthened Iraqist forces seeking to blunt Pan-Arabist power and influence.

Bakr Sidqi's October 1936 coup d'état is viewed as a signal event because it constituted the first military intervention in modern Arab politics. However, the coup has yet to be analyzed for its impact on Iraqi politics both after the 1958 Revolution and during the post-1968 Baʿthist era. The coup never would have occurred without support by Iraqist nationalists such as Jaʿfar Abu Timman, head of the Baghdad Chamber of Commerce and former head of the National Party and the Ahali Group. With no institutional base beyond a small group of army officers, many of whom were Kurds, Sidqi was unwilling to engineer the coup without civilian political support or, in Gramscian terms, a set of "organic intellectuals." After seizing power, Sidqi realized even more clearly that he lacked the legitimacy and expertise to run the country, especially after the assassination of the army's popular commander in chief, Ja'far al-'Askari, by his troops. Through Hikmat Sulayman, a former minister of the interior, Sidqi offered the Ahali Group participation in a reformist government prior to the coup. Sulayman, whose Turkish ethnic origins gave him minority status like Sidqi, opportunistically embraced the Ahali Group and their concept of *al-sha'biya*[13] in plotting the coup with Sidqi.[14]

What made the coup especially significant, apart from it being led by an Iraqi of Kurdish origins, was the support of prominent intellectuals. Although the cabinet's civilian members had doubts about Sidqi's commitment to social reform, their participation reflected the Iraqi intelligentsia's frustration at its inability to bring about any meaningful change. The coup received widespread support, such as from the many Iraqi poets who sang its praises at the Haydarkhana mosque; from the communist-dominated newspaper, *al-Inqilab (The Revolt)*, edited by the famous poet Muhammad Mahdi al-Jawahiri; and from Shi'i workers in Baghdad.[15] The new cabinet heavily favored Iraqist nationalists and minorities, and included two Kurds, two ministers of Turkish extraction, two Shi'is, and two Sunni Arabs, the latter two being the least influential cabinet members. In joining the cabinet, both Abu Timman and the young members of the Ahali Group naively accepted Sulayman's assurances that Sidqi sincerely desired to implement social reforms. Ja'far Abu Timman became minister of finance, Kamil al-Chadirji, minister of economics and communications, Naji Asil (later head of the archaeological journal *Sumer*), minister of foreign affairs, and Yusif 'Izz al-Din, minister of education, while the Ahali Group supported Salih Jabr for minister of justice.[16]

Pan-Arab suspicions of the new regime were strengthened by the strong support it received from leftists and the minority communities.[17] The Hikmat Sulayman government was supported strongly by the Jewish community, which had encountered difficulties with the previous Pan-Arabist government of Yasin al-Hashimi because of support for Zionism by a number of Iraqi Jews. The 1936–39 Arab Revolt in Palestine, and strong support for the Palestinian Arabs, especially among Iraq's Sunni Arabs, also heightened Pan-Arab–Jewish antagonisms, which led to the bombings of Jewish houses and clubs and the deaths of several people.[18] Hikmat's repression of promi-

FIGURE 1. Typical *sarifa* of the 1930s and its dweller, Baghdad 1931. Rifat Chadirji, *The Photography of Kamil Chadirji: Social Life in the Middle East, 1920–1940* (Surrey: LAAM, 1991), p. 65. Used by permission of Rifat Chadirji.

nent Arab nationalists such as Fawzi al-Qawuqji and Saʿid Hajji Thabit, his Turkish extraction, and his lack of interest in Pan-Arabism further exacerbated tensions between Iraqists and Pan-Arabists.[19] The Ahali Group's participation in the Sidqi-Sulayman government proved to be a mistake. Hikmat Sulayman made little effort to implement the organization's goals. Although he promised not to interfere in politics, Sidqi gradually assumed control of the government. His alignment with conservative landowners and merchants doomed any hopes for reforms.[20] Sidqi increasingly relied upon Kurdish army officers for support. Meanwhile, Pan-Arab officers, who resented the murder of army chief of staff Jaʿfar al-ʿAskari, plotted to assassinate Sidqi.

In addition to establishing a precedent for military involvement in politics, the Sidqi coup demonstrated the extent to which ideology and sectarianism now dominated elite politics. Sidqi was able to recruit Ahali Group members by committing his government to a "reform group" of cabinet ministers that largely supported Iraqist nationalism. This policy allowed Sidqi to offset the power of Pan-Arabist officers who had provided the critical support for the deposed government of Yasin al-Hashimi.[21] One of the key motivations behind the coup was Sidqi's fear of not being promoted to army chief of staff and his realization that al-Hashimi's reliance on Pan-Arab army officers made such a promotion unlikely. The coup reflected the deepening struggle between the two primary definitions of political community, and was exacerbated by the tension between control of the state by political cliques and the efforts by leftists to enact social and economic reforms. Sidqi sought to use the coup to increase his power and that of the clique of army officers that supported him. The Ahali Group saw the coup as paving the way for extensive political and social reforms, including greater freedom of association, release of political prisoners, land distribution, elimination of corruption, and greater protection for Iraq's "racial and religious groups and minorities."[22] Hikmat Sulayman's political prominence, his promises of reform, and shared minority status also attracted the Ahali Group.[23] In addition to frustration at the lack of reforms, an additional motivation was the Ahali Group and the populace's extreme distaste with Yasin al-Hashimi's repressive government. The reformers were seduced into thinking that they could outflank the politically inexperienced Sidqi and take control of government policy.

The coalition between the army, the prime minister, and the Ahali Group, with the nascent Iraqi Communist Party's support, foreshadowed the problems that would occur after the July 1958 Revolution. In both 1936 and 1958, social reformers maintained the illusion that a military-backed regime would bring about social reforms. In both instances, their expectations were unfulfilled not only by the leaders they supported but also by Pan-Arabists who opposed these reforms. Political assassinations, the increased use of the secret police, and even, for the first time, the stripping of Iraqi citizenship from undesirable political actors by the Sidqi regime set the stage for even more repressive measures by subsequent regimes.

The period between Sidqi's assassination in 1937 and the famous 1941 coup d'état led by the four colonels known as the "Golden Square" was one of great instability. Clearly the 1936–39 Arab Revolt in Palestine, the Nazi challenge to British power in the Middle East, and King Ghazi's sudden agitation on behalf of the Palestinian uprising and his call for eliminating French influence in Syria and British influence in the Gulf further inflamed Pan-Arab and nationalist feelings.[24] Ghazi's death in an automobile accident in 1939, which many Iraqis felt had been caused by the British, further eroded political stability since Ghazi's son, Faysal II, was too young to rule. Instead, the crown was given to an ineffectual pro-British regent, Prince ʿAbd al-Ilah.

This historical context explains why the significance of the Sidqi coup for Iraqi political development extends far beyond the military's seizure of power. Abu Timman's and the Ahali Group's participation in the Sidqi cabinet was arguably the first instance in which an Iraqi regime was supported by an organized intellectual presence, a situation that was repeated during the 'Abd al-Karim Qasim and the post-1968 Ba'thist regimes. Hoping to realize the political and social goals of the 1920 Revolution, the civilian ministers in the Sidqi-Sulayman government broke decisively with the prevailing political pattern, namely the domination of cabinets by corrupt "professional politicians" who were largely Sunni Arabs.

In blocking social reforms, Sidqi feared alienating wealthy elites. After the cabinet issued its initial reformist platform, which seriously addressed the country's pressing problems, the government was accused of "communist" leanings.[25] Shortly after the coup Abu Timman, now minister of justice, listed the new regime's objectives, including the release of political prisoners, the expansion of press freedoms, and the reallocation of large land holdings, all of which attracted significant popular support. However, the twofold attack on the regime as "communist" and hostile to Pan-Arabism led Sidqi to move sharply to the right and to become much more repressive. Within a few months, Abu Timman and the Ahali Group had left the cabinet.

Sidqi's policies underscored the structural problems facing any regime that attempted to bring about social change at this point in Iraq's political development. No government could accommodate the interests of all sectors of the political elite, nor would any government want to risk being criticized as "communist." Because most cabinets enacted little or nothing in the way of public policy, personal gain and power became the order of the day. The inclusion of reformers in a government dominated by Kurdish military officers resulted in an extremely unstable coalition. Internally, Sidqi was pitted against the Ahali ministers while, externally, he faced hostile landed and monied interests and the Pan-Arabists.

The failure of the Sidqi regime also underscored the extent to which, in the struggle for hegemony, the Pan-Arabist vision of Iraqi political community had gained the upper hand. In large measure, this reflected the Pan-Arabists' greater ideological coherence, which was reflected in their formulation of a historical memory that not only posited an Arab-Islamic Golden Age, but was imbued with a strong sense of conspiracy and victimization. Although the larger and more ethnically diverse Iraqist nationalist coalition offered a more "rational" conception of Iraqi political community, its more complex and nuanced vision of the future was less easy to package politically. Unlike Pan-Arabists, Iraqist nationalists lacked a well-formulated view of the past. Further, the Pan-Arabists were able to suppress Iraqist forces, particularly the ICP and the leftist intelligentsia, through their control of the state apparatus and the military.

By the 1930s, a perverse rationality that involved a logic of rotating cabinets dominated by shifting cliques had informed Iraqi politics. Although nepotism, venality, and callous disregard of the social impact of public policy were endemic, this system indicated that the political elite, far from being in disarray, had adapted to a tripartite division of power between the monarchy, the British, and itself. Clearly the Sidqi coup threatened this pattern by disrupting the ten-year reign that Yasin al-Hashimi had disturbingly predicted with something even worse, a military dictatorship of indeterminate duration. The inspiration that Sidqi drew from Franco's overthrow of Spain's republican government, Reza Shah's coup in neighboring Iran, and Kemalism in Turkey only underscored his rivals' perception that he would not leave power any time soon. Further, the predominance of non-Sunni ministers, such as Abu Timman, in the cabinet , was viewed as an unwelcome intrusion into a political process that was heretofore dominated by a Sunni Arab elite. Thus Iraqist nationalism was tarnished by its perceived disruption of a political system that, however dysfunctional, had become institutionalized.

Intellectual support for Sidqi further harmed the Iraqist nationalist cause as social reform became identified with a regime associated with political assassination, corruption, and lax morality. Ja'far al-'Askari's assassination was followed by threats that led Yasin and his supporters to flee the country. Paralleling the behavior of Saddam Husayn and his son 'Uday at a later date, Sidqi's corruption, alcoholism, and flagrant pursuit of women, especially those who were married to other army officers, deeply offended the conservative morals of the middle classes from which many military officers were drawn.

Once the Ahali Group resigned from his cabinet, Sidqi found himself increasingly isolated. Sidqi's enemies successfully played the sectarian card by impugning his nationalist credentials. No longer seen as the "savior" of the Sunni Arab community as he was during the Assyrian crisis, he was now viewed as a Kurd who sought to separate Iraq from the Pan-Arab fold. Pan-Arabist officers deeply resented Sidqi's appointment of Kurds to important positions in the army general staff. In August 1937, Sidqi was assassinated in the lobby of the Mosul Airport as he was about to leave for a tour of Europe, auguring similar events that would happen all too frequently in the future.

Sidqi's coup not only deepened the fault lines between Iraqist and Pan-Arab nationalists, but it also left an important legacy. The Sidqi-Sulayman regime was the first to be identified with Iraqist nationalism, the first self-consciously to mobilize its own "organic intellectuals," the first to be perceived as hostile to Pan-Arabism, and the first to be accused of leftist sympathies. Even though Sulayman tried to prove that the regime was receptive to Pan-Arabism, the Sidqi interregnum cast further suspicions on the loyalty of non-Sunni Arab sectors of the population. Perhaps most important was the negative impact the failed efforts at reform had on the Iraqist nationalists themselves. First, the Ahali Group had undermined its credibility by supporting a dictator who failed to institute reforms. Second, the group engendered the hostility of Pan-Arabists. Third, cleavages between reactionaries and reformers, between Iraqist nationalists and Pan-Arabists, and between those who were sectarian and secularists committed to a more open politics pushed the political system in a more ideological direction in which intellectuals would increasingly play an important role. Following Sidqi's assassination, at least until 1941, the ascendant intellectuals were Pan-Arab, not Iraqist nationalists.

Between Sidqi's assassination and the 1941 Anglo-Iraqi War, a Pan-Arabist coalition dominated by the so-called Four Colonels, led by Salah al-Din al-Sabbagh, pushed an anti-British and vehemently Pan-Arab agenda. Pan-Arab texts increasingly stressed not only an Arab-Islamic historical memory tied to the ʿAbbasid Empire, but also a historical memory tied to a tribally based Arab historical identity and linked to a vague notion of cultural authenticity *(al-asala)*. The opening pages of al-Sabbagh's memoirs, *Fursan al-ʿUruba fi-l-ʿIraq (The Knights of Arabism in Iraq)*, are replete with assessments of the extent to which members of Iraq's political elite were culturally authentic *(asil)*. The influence of the al-Muthanna Club, dominated by Pan-Arabists such as Sami Shawkat and Yunis al-Sabʿawi, presaged the type of strident, romantic, and xenophobic nationalism that would later characterize the Baʿth Party. The issue of Palestine, intensified by the 1936–39 Arab revolt against the British and Zionist settlers, assumed a central political and symbolic role in local politics. The pragmatism of the older ex-Sharifian Pan-Arabists such as Nuri al-Saʿid and Yasin al-Hashimi gave way to interpretations of Arabism in which "ethnic purity" and "cultural authenticity" became the defining elements of political community, foreshadowing a similar construction in Baʿthist ideology.

The lessons of the 1936 military-civilian coalition were not lost on Kamil al-Chadirji and his colleagues when ʿAbd al-Karim Qasim came to power in 1958. The National Democratic Party (NDP), which al-Chadirji headed, refused to support the revolutionary regime unless it held national elections. When Qasim failed to comply, the NDP left the government, except for

Husayn Jamil, who remained as Qasim's minister of economics. However, the damage had already been done to Iraqist nationalism in 1936. The Sidqi coup created a historical memory that vilified Iraqist nationalists and played into the hands of Pan-Arabists. By 1958, many questioned the loyalty of those who, while claiming to be nationalists, failed to support Pan-Arabism. Iraqist nationalism became associated with buffoonery, authoritarian rule, inefficiency, and, above all, lack of patriotism. Indeed, Pan-Arabists used against Qasim the fact that his cousin, air force commander Muhammad 'Ali Jawad, was Sidqi's chief aide.

By the onset of World War II, the political system, overseen by a weak and politically indecisive regent, 'Abd al-Ilah, was characterized by a political elite increasingly fragmented along fault lines that represented cliques and sectarianism but also masked social class interests, namely the increasing income gap between rich and poor. As middle- and working-class Iraqis became more active politically, and institutional mechanisms to accommodate their demands for political participation failed to develop, strikes, demonstrations, and critiques of the state, disseminated in newspapers, magazines, and pamphlets, grew in number and intensity. Concerned with order, and following in Bakr Sidqi's footsteps, the army became increasingly involved in politics. Officers were evaluated according to where they stood on the important ideological issues of the day. Intensified anger at the British, strengthened by suspicions that they had orchestrated Ghazi's death because of his strong support of the Palestinian cause and his criticism of British Middle East policy, inspired the Four Colonels to flirt with the Axis powers. The Pan-Arabists' growing strength and their desire to rid Iraq of British control, combined with British fears of expanded Axis influence in the Middle East, were the main causes behind the 1941 Anglo-Iraqi War.

The Pan-Arabist regime that seized power in 1941—under the nominal leadership of Rashid 'Ali al-Gaylani, but in reality controlled by the Four Colonels—was viewed as a threat by the British, especially after the regent, 'Abd al-Ilah, fled to southern Iraq. The so-called Thirty Days War that broke out between the Iraqi army and British forces in Iraq led to a complete British victory by the end of May 1941. Shortly thereafter, the regent was returned to power and the members of the Rashid 'Ali government arrested. The four colonels as well as one of their key supporters, Yunis al-Sab'awi, were tried and executed.

The military conflict in April and May 1941 has been thoroughly analyzed elsewhere.[26] My concern is the 1941 movement's impact on Iraqi political development and historical memory. Clearly, military defeat can be turned into a political victory, as Jamal 'Abd al-Nasir demonstrated follow-

ing the Tripartite Invasion of Egypt in the wake of the Suez Canal's nationalization in 1956. Despite the Iraqi army's total defeat by British forces, the
1941 Anglo-Iraqi War quickly entered the pantheon of Pan-Arab political
memory. Defeat became martyrdom as the British seized, tried, and executed the movement's leaders. The monarchy's support of British prosecution of the movement's leaders, its removal of Pan-Arabists from the officer's corps, and its reduction of the size of the army led it to be characterized
as treasonous. As Hanna Batatu notes, the monarchy never recovered from
the events of 1941 and continued to lose legitimacy until being overthrown
in 1958.[27]

The brief Anglo-Iraqi War was followed by another event during which
sectarian politics became a substitute for a meaningful confrontation with
Iraq's ethnic and cultural diversity. The attack on Iraq's Jewish community
following the conflict further increased the political gap between Pan-
Arabists, who considered themselves culturally authentic *(asil)*, and Iraqist
nationalists. Following the defeat of Rashid ʿAli's forces at the end of May
1941, most government officials fled Baghdad. Because the regent, ʿAbd al-
Ilah, was still in the south, and British forces were on the edge of but not inside the city, there was no political authority to enforce public order. The one
member of Rashid ʿAli al-Gaylani's government who refused to leave Baghdad was Yunis al-Sabʿawi. An active member of the al-Muthanna Club,
which, under German ambassador Fritz Groba's influence developed a
youth organization, the *al-Futuwwa*, modeled on European fascist lines, al-
Sabʿawi had developed strong anti-Jewish sentiments.[28] Known in colloquial
Iraqi Arabic as the Farhud (Pogrom), a mob led by al-Muthanna Club members and its youth organization attacked the Baghdad Jewish community on
June 1 and 2, 1941, killing and wounding several Jews and destroying
considerable property.

Although Hayyim Cohen has argued that the Farhud was the only such
anti-Jewish violence to occur in Iraq, and that it was confined to Baghdad,
where the German embassy had spread Nazi influence, nevertheless the
damage was done.[29] Iraq's Jews, heretofore fully integrated into Iraqi society,
began to question their communal status. Because the attack had been led by
al-Muthanna Club members, Pan-Arabist ideology became even more
likely to be viewed as racialist and chauvinist. Although an isolated event,
the Farhud exhibited disturbing parallels to the 1933 Assyrian massacre. It
demonstrated again that political instability and frustrations could lead to
violence against minorities. The Farhud presaged later and more organized
efforts by radical Pan-Arabists in the Baʿth Party to exploit Iraq's minorities
for political ends, such as the public hangings of Jews in January 1969.

The incorporation of the 1941 movement into Iraq's collective historical memory was facilitated by its leader, Colonel Salah al-Din al-Sabbagh, who was thoroughly committed to Pan-Arabism in a selfless if obsessive manner. His sincerity and his disinterest in personal gain and cliquish opportunism set him apart from the coterie of "professional politicians." The title of his memoir, *The Knights of Arabism in Iraq*, completed shortly before his execution in 1946, points to the power of memory over his own political behavior and the manner in which romantic and idealized notions of nationalism dominated his thought. In his selfless patriotism and dignity when facing execution, al-Sabbagh became the perfect martyr. Unlike Sidqi, who, despite his many military victories, died a despised political figure who was seen as pursuing selfish interests, the Four Colonels, especially al-Sabbagh, were remembered for their selfless commitment to Pan-Arabism despite their utter military failure against the British.[30] As such, Pan-Arabists had a much more powerful legacy to draw upon when the struggle within the army between Iraqist nationalists, led by ʿAbd al-Karim Qasim, and Pan-Arabists, led by ʿAbd al-Salam ʿArif, began shortly after the Free Officer Movement seized power in 1958.

The 1941 movement's legacy reflected negatively not only on the monarchy but on the Iraqi Communist Party as well and, in a perverse way, it associated Iraqist nationalism with imperial control of Iraq. With the army greatly reduced in size, Pan-Arabists removed from the officer corps and the Ministry of Education, and al-Muthanna Club members imprisoned, Pan-Arab influence declined precipitously after 1941. During the Second World War, the ICP found a climate much more favorable to its organizational efforts, especially among labor unions. Although the ICP was officially illegal, Great Britain's alliance with the Soviet Union led the party to be treated more leniently during the war years, resulting in significant increases in its membership and influence. Pan-Arabists saw a direct correlation between their decline and Iraq's weakened military status, on the one hand, and the rise of the ICP, which was considered the archenemy of Pan-Arabism and whose membership contained many minorities, on the other. In Pan-Arab collective memory, Iraqist nationalism became even more closely associated with foreign and unpatriotic interests.

The standard approach to interwar Iraqi politics may be described as the "discourse of political decay." Such a perspective suggests a continuous trajectory of decline that ultimately led to the Baʿth Party's repressive rule. However, viewed differently, Iraqi society may be seen as experiencing positive developments during this period that reflect what Karl Deutsch referred to as "social mobilization," and what Anderson calls the positing of "imagined communities."[31] These developments included extensive rural-to-urban migration and resultant challenges to traditional rural culture, the expansion of the print media, the growth of associational life, including professional organizations, student groups, political clubs, and labor syndicates, and the emergence of new forms of cultural production such as the short story. This desire for an inclusive form of collective identity highlighted an important paradox. On the one hand, it reflected the growth of an incipient civil society. Through the establishment of organizations, the urban educated classes sought to develop new social ties and means of cultural expression. The expansion of the press reflected a desire to communicate that went beyond the extended family, the clan, or even the region. On the other hand, the inability of most Iraqis to participate in politics meant that these developments could not fulfill their potential for creating a more tolerant and open political system. Increased political mobilization, combined with the lack of institutions for expressing political views and interests, instead produced a "politics of the street." The political options facing the middle and lower classes were limited. They could choose to remain quiescent or to take to the streets, either literally or symbolically, through criticisms of the state. While focusing on the cacophony of political discontent, many observers have lost sight of the dynamic spread of new associations and cultural expression that characterized the interwar period. Despite the newness of the nation-state and the lack of a tradition of an Iraqi national consciousness, a historical memory linked to Iraq's ancient civilizations, Iraq's central role in the rise of Islam and Arab culture, and Iraqi efforts to oppose British colonialism during the 1920 Revolution provided an important set of norms and values around which Iraqis could mobilize politically and form associational ties. During the 1930s, the lower classes mobilized as well. Labor unions (niqabat ʿummaliya) proliferated. An artisans' federation, Ittihad al-Sanaʾiaʿ al-ʿIraqiya (Union of Iraqi Artisan Organizations), formed in 1930, was central in organizing the 1931 General Strike in Baghdad, which was directed against the new municipal taxes that the British had suggested be imposed on urban commerce.[32]

Considerable organizational activity also occurred in higher education. The College of Law, established in 1908 but closed during World War I, re-opened during 1920–21. To meet a serious teacher shortage, the College of Education was founded in 1923 and, having established a strong reputation, became a four-year institution in 1939. In 1927 the College of Medicine was established, followed by the College of Pharmacy in 1936. Already in 1921 the Iraqi government had begun educating teachers abroad, having realized that the Iraq's educational infrastructure could not meet the country's needs.[33] Secondary school teachers were recruited from Syria, Lebanon, and other Arab countries to improve primary and secondary school education.

The expansion of secondary and higher education stimulated the growth of nationalism and associational life, which entailed the creation of student organizations, professional associations, and political clubs. The formation of these organizations and their members' active involvement in politics were indicative of a developing civic consciousness. Although invariably urban and comprised of members with at least some formal education, these new organizations transcended sectarian boundaries as seen, for example, in the Sunni-Shi'i student coalition that opposed the Ministry of Education's attempt to remove Anis al-Nusuli from his teaching position in 1927.

The Nusuli Affair highlighted the generational cleavages between the old political-intellectual order and the new reform-oriented nationalist movement. Anis al-Nusuli, one of four American University in Beirut graduates invited to teach in the Iraqi secondary school system, published a controversial study of the Ummayad Empire in which he made disparaging remarks about the Shi'a, leading to his removal from his post. The main agitators for al-Nusuli's dismissal were prominent Shi'i 'ulama'.[34] As the minister of education was customarily a Shi'i, the educational system was one area in which the Shi'i community could exert some influence.[35] The Nusuli Affair was significant in two regards. First, the complaints of Shi'i notables contained little substance and primarily reflected an effort to use this issue to promote their interests.[36] Second, the student demonstrators, who emphasized al-Nusuli's right to free speech, included both Sunni and Shi'i youth. Although ethnic cleavages remained salient among Sunni and Shi'i elites, whether sincere or manipulated, ethnic consciousness was of negligible importance for most Iraqi students.[37] When the Shi'i clerical elite tried to mobilize Shi'i youth against al-Nusuli, they failed completely.[38] Student protests, which invoked notions of freedom of expression, ultimately forced the government to back down.

Clubs such as the Iraqi Student Organization (Jam'iyat al-Talaba al-'Iraqiya) and the Iraqi Youth Organization (Jam'iyat al-Nash' al-'Iraqi) were formed at the American University in Beirut during the 1924–25 academic year; in Baghdad, the Jam'iyat al-Ahali (Ahali Group) was founded in 1931, the Nadi Baghdad (Baghdad Club) in 1934, and the Nadi al-Tadammun (Solidarity Club) and the Nadi al-Muthanna (al-Muthanna Club) in 1935. These clubs reflected the main political tendencies that were crystallizing at this time. Nadi al-Tadammun reflected the growing interest in Marxism among the intelligentsia, Nadi al-Muthanna reflected the Pan-Arab perspective, while Nadi Baghdad provided a forum for Iraqist nationalists who supported the Western social democratic interests of the Ahali Group.[39]

During the 1930s, the three tendencies that would dominate politics until the 1963 Ba'thist coup d'état crystallized in well-defined political organizations. Three different socialist groups joined in 1934 to form the Iraqi Communist Party, the first truly ideological and mass-based political party in Iraq and, until it was suppressed in 1963, the most powerful Arab communist party. Although it refused to declare itself a political party, the Ahali Group, formed in 1931, exerted considerable influence through its newspaper, al-Ahali (The People), and its successor, Sawt al-Ahali (Voice of the People). Although it played a crucial role in the Bakr Sidqi government in 1936, only in 1946 did the Ahali Group finally divide into three distinct parties, all of which had similar political platforms.[40]

The Pan-Arabist tendency gained political currency because the Hashimite state's legitimacy was based on its Arab heritage through its lineage to the house of the Prophet Muhammad and Faysal I's leadership of the Arab Revolt. A number of ex-Sharifians incorporated Pan-Arabism into the platforms of clique-based political parties, such as Yasin al-Hashimi's National Brotherhood Party. During the 1930s, the Pan-Arabists experienced a generational divide as older ex-Sharifians such as Nuri al-Sa'id and Yasin al-Hashimi sought accommodation with the British, while younger and more radical Pan-Arabists intensified their efforts to rid Iraq of British influence. This divide was most pronounced in the al-Muthanna Club, whose members, heavily influenced by European fascism, formed the core of new radicals for the civilian-military Pan-Arab coalition led by Yunis al-Sab'awi and Salah al-Din al-Sabbagh. Although the club was disbanded after the May 1941 war and its members interred during World War II, the Pan-Arabist Hizb al-Istiqlal (Independence Party) attracted many al-Muthanna Club members when it was founded in 1946 under Muhammad Makki al-Kubba's leadership.[41]

The postwar formation of new political parties with programmatic platforms was a positive development compared to the pseudo-parties of the traditional political elite. In 1952, the Hizb al-Ba'th (later to become the Hizb al-Ba'th al-'Arabi al-Ishtiraki, or Arab Socialist Ba'th Party) joined the roster of ideological parties. The Iraqi branch of the party, which was founded by two Syrian schoolteachers during the early 1940s, was led by a Shi'i, Fu'ad al-Rikabi. Whereas the National Democratic and Independence parties were able to work together in opposing the monarchy's policies, the more rigidly ideological ICP and the Ba'th Party were unable to cooperate, except during a brief period just prior to the 1958 Revolution. These ideological tensions foreshadowed the difficulties that would plague efforts to establish a more equitable society and tolerant political culture after the overthrow of the Hashimite Monarchy.

The growth of an incipient civil society was also reflected in the expansion of the press, especially in the many newspapers and journals reflecting rising nationalist sentiment and new cultural developments that appeared during the 1920s and 1930s. The founding of *al-Sahifa* by Husayn Rahhal, Mahmud Ahmad al-Sayyid, and a group of leftist thinkers in 1924, *al-Ahali* in 1932, *Sawt al-Ahali* in 1934, and the Iraqi Communist Party's *Kifah al-Sha'b (The People's Struggle)* in 1935 created a core of nationalist newspapers.[42] Articles in the expanded nationalist press chastised British colonial rule and the monarchy's cooperation with it. The press also provided a forum for new ideas about Iraq's political and social development and an outlet for literary expression, which often itself had important political overtones. This was particularly true of the short story, a genre that began to flourish during the 1930s.[43]

The desire to communicate political and cultural views in addition to actual news indicated a new level of social interaction, even if it was limited primarily to urban areas. Urban intellectuals also began to write about rural society. These development were evidence of what Anderson calls an "imagined community," as Iraqis thought more self-consciously about the shape of Iraq's future political community. The use of the press as a vehicle of cultural expression, for example, as a venue for the publishing of poetry and the short story, was in part a function of the political economy of cultural production. Writers could not afford to publish through presses, which were, in any event, limited in number. Further, the newspaper enabled the rapid communication of ideas. Although there were many newspapers, the leftist press was not only most vigorous in its criticism of the state and British colonial control, but it was also the most innovative and experimental.

Still another indicator of a nascent civil society—what might be called the expansion of representational participation—was the transformation and growth of the museum as an important public institution. During the 1920s, Iraqi nationalists had clashed with Gertrude Bell, the alter ego of British colonial rule, over control of the Iraq Museum. Nationalists resented that the museum emphasized the nation's ancient civilizations to the exclusion of Iraq's Arab-Islamic heritage. Although Bell was able to transfer control of the museum from the nationalistically inclined Ministry of Education to the less politicized Ministry of Engineering and Public Works, the dispute demonstrated the heightened consciousness of educated Iraqis of the importance of their national heritage, especially in relation to nationalism and ideas of political community.[44]

During the 1930s additional museums such as the Costume Museum (Mathaf al-Azya') were founded and existing museums were renovated and expanded. The monarchy's sponsorship of the establishment and expansion of museums reflected its awareness of the benefits to be gained from acquiring a reputation as the protector of Iraq's national heritage. The Costume Museum was particularly important because the Hashimite Monarchy used modes of dress among Iraq's ethnic groups to demonstrate similarities between its own Hijazi tribal background and the similar tribal dress worn by all three of Iraq's main ethnic groups, the Sunnis, Shi'is, and Kurds. The ancient Khan Murjan market was reconstructed to suggest its original splendor during the 'Abbasid period. Nationalist criteria influenced the contents of the museum and presaged efforts by the state after the 1958 Revolution to use culture for political ends.

These developments suggested important changes in the structure of historical memory and its use to create political space. Only the Pan-Arabists took memory seriously, conceptually and politically. That is, Arab historical memory, which was tied to a specific geography that included important religious and cultural sites such as Makka, al-Madina, and Jerusalem, was central to their ideology. Whether King Faysal's leadership of the Arab Revolt, Sati' al-Husari's promotion of Pan-Arabism, the al-Muthanna Club's call for Arab unity, or Salah al-Din al-Sabbagh's memoirs of the 1941 uprising against the British, all evoked a common historical memory based on the glories of the Arab past, particularly the greatness of the Meccan empire's "Rightly Guided Caliphs" *(al-Khala'if al-Rashidun)* as well as the Umayyad and 'Abbasid empires. Pan-Arabism's historical narrative was always integrally linked to the Arabs' conquest of external foes, whether European Christians or Persians, and their control of a particular geographical territory. The Arabs' greatness was based on their pursuit of authenticity *(al-asala)*, namely, their adherence to a unified (political) culture. Their historical achievements were contrasted to the modern Arabs' failure to confront the European colonial powers that now occupied their lands.[45] Thus Pan-Arabists linked past, present, and future according to a historically integrated and commonsense logic.

For Pan-Arabists, the Arabs' present problems were the result of loss of control of their lands to the foreigner who had fragmented Arab culture and society. Sabbagh's memoirs, which have been read from the perspective of politics rather than cultural and historical memory, are most instructive. In his introductory section, he assesses whether Iraq's major political actors are "authentically Arab" *('Arabi asil)*, using as criteria the attitudes they hold towards the Other, that is, the British, and their ability to adhere to Arab culture and avoid the "impurities" of Westernization and neighboring Persian culture.[46] This logic leads al-Sabbagh to conclude that the Arabs will regain their former glory only if they reunite politically and "cleanse" their culture of its "nonauthentic" elements. It is little wonder that modern Ba'thist historiography begins with the 1941 Anglo-Iraqi War and Pan-Arabist efforts to evict the British, and looks to al-Sabbagh's memoirs, which reflect the type of chauvinist nationalism that the Ba'th Party perfected so well after 1968.[47]

Although Pan-Arabism had become a dominant ideology by the 1941 uprising, it was not somehow "destined" to dominate conceptions of political community in Iraq. Despite the coherence of its historical memory, the Pan-Arabist movement was by no means unified. Older Pan-Arabists gravitated to establishing a modus vivendi with the British, even while occasionally resorting to anticolonial rhetoric. A generation gap separated these Pan-Arabists from their younger co-ideologists, who would tolerate no cooperation with the British. Political factors separated the two groups as well. The radicalism of the older Pan-Arabists, who had become the new political elite, had been tempered not only by age, but also by the power they wielded through control of the state. The younger Pan-Arabists were both less powerful politically than their elders and of more modest social backgrounds. Their lack of political power, combined with Iraq's failure to become truly independent, fed their radicalism. They felt more acutely the problems affecting Iraqi society because they did not control the centers of power.

These factors explain why the younger generation of Pan-Arabists—not as widely traveled, educated, or conversant with foreign languages as the older Pan-Arabists—adopted a much more parochial view of sectarian relations in Iraq.[48] As political mobilization spread downward during the 1930s and 1940s to encompass the middle classes, workers, and peasants, and social problems intensified, ideological commitments became more sharply defined. Among some sectors of the middle classes, ethnic purity became an important political issue. It is interesting to contrast the ICP during this period with Pan-Arabists. Although the communists emphasized cross-ethnic and cross-sectarian solidarity, as seen in the party's ethnic diversity and the remarkable solidarity that workers demonstrated during strikes, Pan-Arabists focused on ethnic purity and vilification of the Other. It was among the Sunni Arab middle and lower-middle classes, especially those of rural origins, that such sectarian identities were felt most deeply.

Explaining these sentiments is critical for understanding Iraq's political development because the practical result was an unwillingness of the upper-class Sunni elite and would-be Sunni elite comprised of middle-class Pan-Arabists to accept Shi'is and Iraq's minorities as full members of Iraq's political community. Ethnic purity never became a major issue for workers and peasants whose primary struggle was (and continues to be) materially sustaining themselves and their families. Further, workers and peasants could not aspire to control of the state, except perhaps through the seizure of power by a political coalition led by the ICP, an unlikely prospect at best. The younger Pan-Arabists, unlike the communists, were not part of a broad-based mass movement. Centered around the al-Muthanna Club and a particular group of army officers, they were a secretive and conspiratorial clique that was not linked in any structured way to other ethnic groups or social classes.[49] This contrasted with workers of different ethnic backgrounds, for example, who were forced to work together in the Iraqi State Railways, the port of Basra, or the oil fields. Younger Pan-Arabists were not moved politically by the concept of social class, which reminded them of the societal fragmentation that afflicted their families and communities. The focus on ethnic purity, which was the core component of the radical Pan-Arabism that emerged during the late 1930s, was tied to a spirit or Zeitgeist that claimed to provide the cement that held societies together. This romantic concept of nationalism had much in common with the notion of the *Volk* in Pan-German thought. It is of course significant that German understandings of nationalism had pervaded Iraqi society, especially the Sunni Arab north, via the Ottomans prior to World War I.[50] Pan-Arabist nationalism was much closer to tribal understandings of society than Iraqist nationalism, which was tied to the idea of the modern nation-state. Paradoxically, Pan-Arabism was linked not to a specific territory, but rather to a vaguely defined Pan-Arab community with indeterminate borders that would recreate the early Arab-Islamic empires. Similar to tribal members who focused on blood ties rather than spatial location, the Pan-Arabists substituted ethnic purity for a more precise territorial definition of space. Because the Pan-Arab state would grow in increments as more and more "artificial states" shed their colonially defined boundaries, the state's borders could never be defined with precision. Pan-Arabism's emphasis on an Arab spirit and the recreation of a Golden Age, which was evocative of the romanticism and nostalgia that many middle-class Iraqis craved, was in sharp contrast to Iraqist nationalist thought, which sought to confront the complexities of Iraq's mounting social problems.

In contrast to the Pan-Arabists, neither faction of Iraqist nationalists—

neither the ICP nor the Ahali Group and its political offshoots—incorporated historical memory in their ideology and political platforms. The Ahali Group's proclivity for Fabian socialism seemed to dampen its interest in Arab-Iraqi culture. *al-Ahali* consistently featured reviews of Western literature while largely neglecting new trends in Iraqi literature such as the development of the short story and the Free Verse Movement in poetry. The Ahali Group's cultural policies and interests require a separate study. However, the memoirs of the organization's leader, Kamil al-Chadirji, and his artistic production indicate great interest in Western architecture, literature, and aesthetics.[51] The Ahali Group and NDP leadership failed to exert as much effort to understand the Iraqi cultural renaissance of the 1940s and 1950s as they did to study Western culture. They never played the role of "organic intellectuals" for the Iraqist nationalist movement that the al-Muthanna Club leaders and the Four Colonels did for the Pan-Arabist movement.

The ICP also made little effort to emphasize Arab culture in its political and social analysis of Iraqi society.[52] In part, communists were blinded by the Marxist aversion to "bourgeois" nationalism. The ICP continually argued for a democratic state in which all Iraq's ethnic groups would enjoy equal rights. It also argued tirelessly against imperialism, against British colonial control, and for social justice for workers and peasants. Nevertheless, the party always subordinated its ideology and domestic policies to the dictates of the Soviet Union. Paralleling the experiences of communist parties elsewhere, the party's constant shifts and turns in response to Soviet demands confused the party membership and undermined its ability to effectively challenge the Iraqi state.

It is difficult to imagine large numbers of Iraqis developing an interest in Soviet politics and culture during the 1940s and 1950s. This was a luxury reserved for a small segment of the intelligentsia such as Fahd (Yusif Salman Yusif), the ICP's leader until his execution in 1949, and Kamil al-Chadirji, leader of the Ahali Group and subsequently the NDP. Much more critical was the ICP's neglect of Iraqi culture and history, which laid it open to the charge that it represented foreign rather than Iraqi interests. Ironically, ideological roles were reversed in the cultural realm where Iraqist nationalists were internationalists, looking to cultural traditions outside Iraq, while the Pan-Arabists emphasized local Arab-Iraqi culture, particularly its Sunni Arab heritage.

The tendency of Iraqist nationalist parties to ignore indigenous culture suggests that they viewed Iraqi culture as somehow inferior to Western European and Soviet culture. This was ironic because most of the Iraqi intelli-

FIGURE 2. Typical scenery of the marshes, southern Iraq, mid-1940s. Rifat Chadirji, *The Photography of Kamil Chadirji: Social Life in the Middle East, 1920–1940* (Surrey: LAAM, 1991). Used by permission of Rifat Chadirji.

gentsia prior to the 1958 Revolution supported Iraqist nationalism and rejected the chauvinist interpretations of Iraq's heritage *(al-turath)* by Pan-Arabism. Dhu al-Nun Ayyub, Fu'ad al-Takarli, 'Abd al-Wahhab al-Bayati, Jawad Salim, Mahdi Saqr, Muhammad Mahdi al-Jawahiri, and Jamal Sidqi al-Zahawi were all leftist intellectuals whose concern with social issues shared little with the Pan-Arab Zeitgeist and its concern with ethnic purity. Iraqist nationalist interest in foreign cultures, whether European or Soviet, only fed Pan-Arabist suspicions of Iraqis of non-Arab backgrounds such as the al-Chadirji family, which claimed Persian ancestry.[53] The Ahali Group made little effort to dispel these impressions. It was not until the last year or two of the 'Abd al-Karim Qasim regime, which came to power after the 1958 Revolution, that the leftist intelligentsia seriously addressed Arab cultural issues and argued for Qasim's credentials as a leader interested in Arab affairs. Ironically, Kamil al-Chadirji, Qasim, and many other Iraqist nationalists were not opposed to inter-Arab cooperation and sympathized deeply with Arab causes such as that of the Palestinians.[54]

In avoiding active engagement of Arab culture, such as in the Ahali Group's influential newspapers *al-Ahali* and *Sawt al-Ahali*, Iraqist nationalists ceded much ideological and symbolic terrain to Pan-Arab forces. According to the logic of Western doctrines to which Iraqist nationalists adhered, social democratic reforms were critical given large inequities in income distribution and the deteriorating condition of the middle class, the small working class, and the peasantry. However, Iraqist nationalists seem not to have realized that their concern with social justice needed to be expressed in an idiom that would allow them to culturally connect with the very groups their proposed reforms were intended to help. Instead, the discourse of the Ahali Group, and its successors such as the NDP, remained largely an internal one in which members spoke more to one another and to the educated professional classes than connecting with the white-collar middle class and the poor. In Gramscian terms, the Ahali Group and the NDP failed to mount an effective "war of position."[55]

4 Memory, the Intelligentsia, and the Antinomies of Civil Society, 1945–1958

The period between 1945 and the 1958 Revolution constitutes the most active and participatory era in twentieth-century Iraqi political, social, and cultural life. Following the end of World War II, several new political parties—including the National Democratic and the Independence parties—were formed, and the Iraqi Communist Party significantly expanded its social base. In 1946, workers were given the right, soon rescinded, to organize labor unions for the first time.[1] Cultural movements proliferated. In literature, Iraq was at the forefront of innovative trends such as the Free Verse Movement, which was led by Badr Shakir al-Sayyab and Nazik al-Mala'ika. In the visual arts, the Pioneers Movement (al-Ruwwad) was stimulated by the contact of Iraqi artists with European painters who had resided in Iraq during the war. This group was followed by other artists' organizations such as the Baghdad Association of the Friends of Art (1952) and the Baghdad Association for Modern Art (1953).[2] Sculpture and architecture also witnessed important innovations.[3] The journal *Sumer*, founded in 1945, began to make important contributions in the field of archaeology, reflecting an intensified interest in Iraq's ancient, pre-Islamic civilizations.[4] Numerous archaeological excavations were sponsored by the Directorate of Antiquities, which published the findings of its research in *Sumer*. The renewed focus on antiquity coincided with the recourse to symbols drawn from ancient Mesopotamian culture by poets such as Badr Shakir al-Sayyab, ʿAbd al-Wahhab al-Bayati, and many others.[5]

The postwar period was also one of the most turbulent in modern Iraqi history. Political violence directed against the state by nationalist forces reached levels unprecedented in Iraq. Tensions between Iraqist and Pan-Arab nationalists likewise intensified, although they were partially subordinated to the desire of both groups to overthrow the existing order. Despite the level of conflict, large numbers of Iraqi intellectuals look back nostalgically to the 1950s as a modern golden age. To what degree was this period unique in Iraqi politics and cultural development, and what was its impact on state and civil society? How did the postwar period shape the contours of the 1958 Revolution and help structure the discourse about the future of political community in Iraq? How has an emerging historical memory of this era since the 1991 Intifada shaped visions of post-Ba'thist Iraq?

The period between 1946 and 1958 saw the sharpening and deepening of three cleavages in state-society relations. The first pitted the monarchy against the nationalist movement. The 1948 Wathba and Palestine debacle, the Intifada of 1952, the 1955 Baghdad Pact, and Iraq's failure to respond to the Tripartite Invasion of Egypt in 1956 leading to another *intifada* represented the main points of conflict between the state and the nationalist movement. Perhaps most importantly, the constant pressure on the state by students, intellectuals, and workers through demonstrations, critiques, and strikes paved the way for the military's overthrow of the monarchy in 1958 by eroding what little legitimacy the monarchical state still possessed.[6]

The second cleavage, the strengthening of the radical wings of both Iraqist and Pan-Arab nationalism, which first became apparent following the Bakr Sidqi coup, intensified the divisions between the two movements. The more radical exponents of both ideological perspectives were represented by the Iraqi Communist Party (ICP) and the Arab Socialist Ba'th Party, respectively. The two major groups involved in the struggle for parliamentary seats by antimonarchical forces were the National Democratic Party, headed by Kamil al-Chadirji, and the Independence Party, headed by Muhammad Mahdi al-Kubba. Although these two parties respected each other—they participated in a number of political alliances, such as the 1954 National Front—the ICP and the Ba'th Party did not demonstrate a similar tolerance.[7] Without any reformist concessions by the state, radicals within both wings of the Iraqi nationalist movement gradually assumed greater prominence, if not political dominance.

The third and most diffuse cleavage centered around historical memory, pitting intellectuals and artists against one another as they questioned the role of tradition in Iraqi society. Intellectuals demanded greater freedom of expression during the postwar era through a reduction of political repression and the removal of many of the constraints imposed in the past. Cultural production thus reflected great soul searching by intellectuals of all cultural and ideological persuasions and set "modernists" against "traditionalists." This amorphous and multifaceted cleavage, which involved debates about cultural inclusion and exclusion, the opposition of innovation to tradition, and the attitude toward reinterpretation of the past, often transcended immediate political concerns because it involved intellectuals not formally affiliated with any specific political party or organization or because it concerned abstract issues. However, discourse concerned with aesthetics, historiography, and literary forms invariably had political overtones. Calls for greater freedom of expression necessarily involved a challenge to state prerogatives. An important subtext of this cleavage was the debate, to emerge with greater vigor after the 1958 Revolution, between intellectuals committed to a pluralist vision of an Iraqi political community with permeable cultural boundaries and those who sought to ground definitions of political community in a nostalgic reading of the past and a mystical "Arab spirit."

Postwar intellectual production must be seen as an integral part of political development because it provides a broader understanding of the content and direction of change, particularly in the realm of civil society, than a focus limited to the immediate political struggles of the day. Most intellectual production during this period advocated a more cosmopolitan and participatory form of Iraqi culture and society. Hence it opened political and social space, at least conceptually, for many groups that had heretofore been marginalized, such as women, workers, peasants, and radical intellectuals.[8] Even if intellectual contributions during the postwar era did not lead to immediate political change, they provided an inspirational legacy or historical memory that democratically oriented forces could draw upon in the future.

Although "traditionalists" were often considered synonymous with the Pan-Arabists and "modernists" with the Iraqist nationalists, this was not always the case. Among Iraqist nationalists we find in the realm of poetry, for example, a split between innovators such as Badr Shakir al-Sayyab (in his early years as a communist) and traditionalists such as Muhammad Mahdi al-Jawahiri (a classicist despite the populist quality of much of his poetry). Some modernist innovators, such as Nazik al-Mala'ika, were Pan-Arabists, while others, such as al-Sayyab, changed positions from a leftist Iraqist nationalism to support for Pan-Arabism. However, even though most intellectuals were deeply concerned with the fate of Palestine and the issue of colonial control of the Middle East, few adhered to an ethnically exclusive Pan-Arabist vision such as the one articulated by Salah al-Din al-Sabbagh in *The Knights of Arabism in Iraq*. The postwar intellectuals' interest in experimentation, stemming from a dissatisfaction with the ability of past cultural forms to help them understand and interpret contemporary Iraqi society, led them to explore a myriad of historical symbols and experiences.

Although the historical memory drawn from Iraq's Arab-Islamic heritage, primarily the al-Jahili and ʿAbbasid periods, was rich and vast, intellectuals also appropriated symbols from Iraq's pre-Islamic civilizations. They also looked to authors such as T. S. Eliot for Western treatments of the relationship between tradition and innovation.[9] With the spread of communism in Iraq, symbols of social justice and equality for peasants, workers, and women also entered cultural discourse. To have accepted Pan-Arabism in its parochial form as defined by Satiʿ al-Husari, Yunis al-Sabʿawi, and Salah al-Din al-Sabbagh would have constrained the experimentation with new cultural forms that most Iraqi intellectuals so avidly pursued.

Although the first two cleavages focus more narrowly on state-society relations, the third allows us to explore broader developments in civil society. Most political studies of this period have concentrated on the first two cleavages, which, for the most part, suggest a process of decline and decay. However, a study of cultural production during the postwar period, including works on history and politics, demonstrates a vibrant intellectual life that suggested alternatives to the authoritarian politics that had dominated Iraqi political life. Fortunately, this cultural production established a historical memory to which Iraqi intellectuals can return as an inspiration for a transition to democracy.

Inherent in the emerging foundations of a nascent civil society with participatory impulses was a counterhegemonic ideology directed against the state. Intellectuals, most of whom identified with the left, defended the interests of the urban and rural poor. *Sawt al-Ahali*, the NDP's official organ, played a key role in promoting this issue. The new linkages, however tenuous, that developed after 1945 between workers and reformist elements of the middle and upper middle classes who were concerned with combating social injustice contained the ideological and institutional seeds of a new democratic and reform-minded social order. It is noteworthy that during the 1950s the vanguards of Pan-Arabism, the Independence and Baʿth parties were headed by Shiʿis. In other words, the dyads, Pan-Arabism/Sunnism and Iraqist nationalism/Shiʿism, that framed much of the politics and political discourse under the former Baʿthist regime did not conform to stereotypical understandings of Iraqi politics. It would take the February 1963 coup d'état, the Thermidor of the 1958 Revolution, to accelerate and deepen the institutionalization of sectarianism.

A number of factors contributed to the new levels of violence between the state and the nationalist movement during the late 1940s and 1950s. The continued influx of rural migrants into urban areas created large disaffected communities of semiemployed or unemployed workers. Among regularly employed workers, especially those in the growing oil industry, militancy increased, especially in response to ICP agitation. The postwar years saw the highest rate of inflation in Iraq to date, which negatively affected the salaried middle class, artisans, and workers. Civil servants, whose jobs were tenuous because of erratic pay and politically motivated dismissals caused by frequent changes in government, earned low salaries. A severe housing shortage caused by urban overcrowding added to these economic pressures. The loosening of political constraints on Iraqi communists during World War II and the brief liberalization of politics and social life immediately at war's end during Tawfiq al-Suwaydi's ministry raised expectations of a postwar era during which social reforms would finally be enacted. When the al-Suwaydi ministry was replaced by Arshad al-'Umari's highly repressive government, these hopes were dashed, convincing many nationalists that only through street demonstrations and violence could meaningful change be achieved.

Two events in 1948 exacerbated the hostility between the state and the nationalist movement. The first was the Iraqi government's efforts under Prime Minister Salih Jabr to renegotiate the 1930 Anglo-Iraqi Treaty in Portsmouth, England. News of these negotiations, which suggested that the British presence in Iraq would be extended, produced a violent reaction. Huge demonstrations in Baghdad and other cities ensued, leading to street battles between demonstrators and the police. Dozens of protesters were killed. Dubbed the Wathba, or "Great Leap," this event more than any other symbolized the revulsion that the nationalist movement felt toward the monarchy. The Wathba increased the strength of the ICP, which used popular sentiment and police violence to mobilize new cadres. Despite efforts by some Pan-Arabists to entice Independence Party members to leave street demonstrations, in which many communists and leftists participated, political solidarity of all the ideological tendencies within the nationalist movement was the uprising's hallmark.[10]

The Wathba's legacy did not end with the violence of January 1948 but continued with a series of militant strikes. This militancy was particularly evident among strikes by oil workers, among the highest-paid members of the working class. British labor advisors noted that these strikes were political in nature and seem to have been inspired, if not organized, by the ICP.[11] When labor unrest failed to subside, the government imposed martial law. The martial law regime, which continued until the following fall, allowed the government not only to repress communists, workers, and nationalists, but also to stir up animosity against the Iraqi Jewish community over the unrest in Palestine in an attempt to divert attention away from domestic social problems.

It is instructive to examine the political elite's perceptions of the proposed treaty as a measure of changes in political power that had occurred both within Iraq and regionally between 1930 and 1948. Correspondence between the regent ʿAbd al-Ilah and Salih Jabr indicated that, whereas the regent sought to extend the 1930 Anglo-Iraqi Treaty in largely the same format, Jabr warned him that political conditions had changed and that the treaty would have to correspond with similar treaties between neighboring Arab countries and the British.[12] The regent, still thankful that the British had restored him to power in 1941, was keen to please his colonial overlords. Although equally pro-British, Jabr was much more attuned to political realities and threatened to resign as prime minister if Iraq were not allowed to assume control of the two strategic air bases used by the RAF, al-Habbaniya and al-Shuʿayba.[13] This correspondence is an indicator of the power that had accrued to the Iraqist and Pan-Arabist nationalist movements by 1948. No longer could political elites act with impunity in concluding treaties with Western powers.[14] Increasingly, the sentiments of the politically mobilized middle classes and workers provided a backdrop against which elites were forced to structure their behavior.

The maneuvering around the proposed Portsmouth treaty shed important light on the Iraqi political elite and its relationship to the larger nationalist movement. When Nuri al-Saʿid brought a broad spectrum of the political elite to England to debate the treaty during the fall of 1947, the details of the treaty had already been worked out between the British, the regent, Jabr, and Nuri.[15] However, the fact that Nuri felt compelled to have all sectors of the Iraqi political elite endorse the treaty was another indication that the leaders of the state recognized that they needed broad social support for their actions, especially those relating to the British. In other words, the invitation of a large delegation to come to London was both a tacit recognition that the political elite no longer marched in lockstep with Nuri and the monarchy, and a recognition of the nationalist movement's strength. The delegation's extensive interrogation of Nuri and ʿAbd al-Ilah indicated that the Iraqi political elite was beginning to question, if only in a preliminary way, many of the assumptions underlying the traditional political system. It also indicated that the elite was losing its cohesiveness and self-confidence, thereby paving the way for its eventual overthrow in 1958.[16]

The Wathba is extremely significant in yet another regard. Although Iraqi Pan-Arabists have identified the origins of the July 1958 Revolution in the 1941 uprising and the 1948 Arab defeat in Palestine, it was in fact the

Wathba that stimulated the Iraqi Free Officers Movement (known prior to the 1952 Egyptian Revolution as the Nationalist Officers)[17] to consider overthrowing the monarchy.[18] Learning of serious opposition to the Portsmouth negotiations, Salih Jabr returned to Iraq in January 1948 to explain the treaty's objectives and have it ratified by the Iraqi parliament. Instead, his efforts only intensified the scope and violence of nationalist demonstrations, forcing him to resign and flee Baghdad. Having brought down an Iraqi government for the first time not only encouraged the nationalist movement, but it also provided nationalist army officers with a model for replacing the hated monarchy. If unarmed citizens could, through street demonstrations, cause a ministry to fall, then the army could likewise intervene to bring about political change.

Coming on the heels of the Wathba, the Iraqi army's unsuccessful campaign against Zionist forces in Palestine during the spring and summer of 1948 exacerbated antipathy toward the state. The realization that the Arab defeat resulted from poor preparation and collusion between Arab politicians and Great Britain deeply angered the officer corps, especially Iraqi and Egyptian officers.[19] The Iraqi army lacked arms and had to hire private vehicles because there were not even sufficient government trucks to transport troops and supplies from Iraq to Palestine.[20] Once at the front, Iraqi units were placed under Glubb Pasha (John Glubb), the British commander of Jordan's Arab Legion, the best trained of the Arab armies. Despite a number of successes against Zionist forces, the Iraqi army lacked the ability to carry out a coordinated military campaign with other Arab armies. The ill-equipped Iraqi force, which did not even possess tanks or land mines, was no match for the Zionist Haganah, which enjoyed superior organization and shorter supply lines.[21]

The army's chagrin was compounded upon learning that Glubb Pasha actually sought to prevent Arab forces from making any significant military progress against Zionist units. In light of the recently documented collusion between King ʿAbdallah and Zionist leaders to divide Palestine, these perceptions were legitimate.[22] The disastrous Arab campaign not only added to the army's bitterness that resulted from the unsuccessful 1941 uprising, but it also bolstered the conspiratorial worldview to which many Pan-Arabist officers subscribed and which was a core component of Pan-Arabist historical memory.

By intensifying sectarian feelings, the Arab defeat in Palestine undermined efforts to develop a more pluralist and open political culture. It also undermined the Iraqist nationalist movement just as it was making great strides in mobilizing support. The fact that the ICP included Jews, Shiʿis,

Kurds, and representatives of virtually all Iraq's minority populations made its commitment to Arab issues suspect to Pan-Arabists. The Pan-Arabists considered their suspicions justified when the ICP, after initially condemning Zionism as an ally of imperialism, reversed its policy, albeit very reluctantly, in response to Soviet pressure to support the November 1947 United Nations' resolution partitioning Palestine into an Arab and Jewish state.[23]

For many Arabs and Iraqis, the establishment of Israel represented the continuation of European colonial influence and the further fragmentation of Arab society. In Iraq, the Palestine issue became a convenient weapon for the state and Pan-Arabist forces, such as the Independence Party, to attack the ICP, which had Jewish members, and the National Democratic Party, which did not actively promote Pan-Arab unity. Anti-Jewish feeling intensified as Iraqi Jews began to be deprived of their citizenship and the entire Jewish community, one of the oldest in the world, was placed under a cloud of suspicion. Iraqi Jews became the new al-ʿAjam, the modern reincarnation of the al-Shuʿubiya movement, as a purported fifth column for British colonial influence in Iraq. That many Iraqi Jews had requested British citizenship following World War I and the wealth of some urban Jewish families created resentment among parts of the populace, particularly the middle classes. However, by all objective criteria, the Iraqi Jews were thoroughly integrated into Iraqi society and considered themselves to be fully Iraqi. Already during the late 1930s, Pan-Arabist pressures had led certain positions in the Iraqi bureaucracy to be considered off-limits to Jews.[24] Thus the state used anti-Jewish hostility, stemming from the Iraqi Jewish community's identification with the British and then with Zionism, to divert attention away from social and economic problems and toward the issues of "authenticity" and "ethnic purity" promoted by Pan-Arabists.

While Iraqist nationalists intensified calls in 1948 for social reforms in light of a record high rate of inflation,[25] the populace's attention, especially that of the middle classes, was diverted away from economic issues to the Arab defeat in Palestine. In the southern port city of Basra, for example, the local press and Pan-Arabists affiliated with the Independence Party accused the local Jewish community of collusion with Zionism.[26] As the British consul general noted in September 1948, the martial law courts imposed after the Wathba used the issue of Palestine and alleged Zionist sympathies among Basra Jews to mete out unjust sentences in trials devoid of due process. The most egregious sentence was given to Shafiq Ades, a prominent merchant and head of the Basra Jewish community, who was alleged to have smuggled arms to Palestine and was sentenced to death by a local military court and hanged on September 23, 1948.[27]

As the partition of Palestine moved toward reality, Pan-Arabists increasingly were associated with anti-Jewish sentiments while Iraqist nationalists supported Jews against Pan-Arabist and government attacks. In Basra, British consular reports described a press that, with the exception of one newspaper, tried to incite hostility against the large Jewish community. During the spring of 1948, the demonstrations of the local Independence Party had a distinctly anti-Jewish tone. The left-leaning NDP, on the other hand, attracted Jewish support. As the British consul general pointed out, cries of "Long live Stalin," "Long live the Iraqi Jews," and "Down with the regent" were heard at NDP rallies.

However, the consul general also pointed to the "traditionally good relations between all the communities living in Basra [that] have so far survived the strain of the political feeling aroused by the partition of Palestine."[28] For example, during the fall of 1948, Christians, Jews, and Shi'is made speeches at a party to commemorate the forty-day anniversary of the death of a local Sunni notable, Shaykh Ahmad Nuri Bashayan, which was attended by the heads of all four communities. The local notables—whom the British referred to as "the better class Moslems"—were relieved when, shortly after Ades's execution, the Courts Martial in Basra were closed and anti-Jewish agitation subsided. Subsequently, many notables admitted to British officials that numerous injustices had been committed, even though none spoke out against them.[29]

Events in Basra in 1948 corresponded to behavior that occurred soon after the Ba'th Party came to power in 1968, namely the fabrication of spurious espionage charges against some of Iraq's remaining Jews, leading to a public spectacle designed to divert attention from social ills and intimidate citizens not to challenge the state. The prejudicial behavior of the harshest judges—the president of the Basra Law Courts, 'Abd al-Nadir Kamil, and the president of the Third District Court-Martial, 'Abdallah al-Nahani, were overheard at parties deciding sentences for Jews yet to be arrested—is not the main issue. Rather, the same timidity of the educated and notable classes in not protesting what many would later admit was a travesty of justice occurred in 1948 as in 1969. In 1969, there would be no public response to public hangings of Baghdadi Jews at a time when the new regime of Ahmad Hasan al-Bakr and Saddam Husayn still rested on a weak social base. The lack of active protest by the citizenry in both instances created a political vacuum that facilitated authoritarian rule. As in 1948, events in 1969 promoted a historical memory centered around notions of conspiracy and xenophobia (for example, the idea that Jews were responsible for the nation's ills) that the authoritarian state could mobilize at a later time for even more pernicious ends, such as torture and executions. This state-generated memory was used as a counterpoint to the more inclusionary and participatory memory stemming from the Wathba and the 1952 and 1956 *intifadas*.

Although reformist parties such as the NDP, and especially the ICP, were able to attract the sympathies of an ever-larger number of supporters, the NDP was never able to develop a truly mass following, and the ICP swerved ideologically, in a self-destructive fashion, from coalitional to radical politics. Despite these problems, at no point during the 1950s did Iraqist nationalists support sectarianism, ethnic exclusivity, or xenophobic nationalism. Questions of Pan-Arab unity and ethnic identity were not central to their concerns.[30] Even if the Iraqist nationalist leadership did not always practice what it preached, its message of social reform and ethnic inclusion elicited a positive response from large numbers of Iraqis.

The ability of the Iraqist nationalist movement to mobilize many supporters during the period leading to the 1958 Revolution was a sign of hope for the future. This is especially true considering the state's constant repression, especially of the ICP; the escalation of attacks by Pan-Arabists; and, following President Jamal ʿAbd al-Nasir's embrace of Pan-Arabism in 1956, an increase in attacks by the Egyptian government. The Iraqist nationalist vision was based on the idea of mutual respect among Iraq's ethnic groups, social justice through redistributive policies such as land reform and progressive labor laws, and permeable cultural boundaries that facilitated rather than restricted discourse about social difference. In short, Iraqist nationalism offered a vision of the Iraqi political community as a "big tent" in which all but the very rich and the "merchants of politics" *(tujjar al-siyasa)* could find a home.[31]

Pan-Arabism, especially strong in the so-called Sunni Arab triangle of north-central Iraq, provided an entirely different set of symbols by which to mobilize the Iraqi populace. Pan-Arabism's vision of making Arab society whole again following World War II with the anticipated end of British and French colonial control was shattered by the creation of a Jewish state in Palestine. The establishment of Israel, which was viewed as an alien Other, reinforced a worldview according to which the Arab world was besieged and betrayed from within by imperialists and their allies, namely local political elites and minorities. According to the Pan-Arabist view, the Arab world could only regain its strength by hermetically sealing itself from the "impurities" of the external world.[32]

The Palestine debacle fostered the creation of a set of cleavages that crosscut the symbolic universe of social reform. In this political vision, it was not redistributive social justice that would address the Arab world's problems, but instead political solidarity based on "cultural authenticity" *(al-asala)*. Despite largely ignoring social issues, Pan-Arabists faced their own internal cleavages. The Independence Party, for example, was no friend of the ex-Sharifian officers, such as Nuri al-Sa'id, who still dominated the Iraqi political elite. Although Independence Party members were drawn from the relatively well-to-do members of the white-collar middle class and small merchants and did not compare in social status with members of the traditional political elite, certainly they were distinguished from the Ba'thist Pan-Arabists, who were members of the lower middle class and had rural origins.

The third cleavage mentioned earlier raises questions about the role of intellectuals in social and political change. Did poets, novelists, and short story writers, artists, journalists, and student and labor leaders act as "organic intellectuals" and engage in a "war of position"? The new intellectual movements that developed during the late 1940s and 1950s and appealed largely to an educated audience were highly subversive in content, but they failed to provide well-articulated counterhegemonic models to challenge existing forms of political praxis. The focus on critique rather than on concrete alternative visions of society and strategies to enact those visions explains in large measure why intellectuals were initially so uncritical of the new military regime that came to power after the July 1958 Revolution. As Gramsci notes, a truly revolutionary strategy involves not only a critique of existing social conditions, but also a vision of the formation of a new, postrevolutionary society. Although the intelligentsia played a critical role in eroding the monarchy's legitimacy, it stood conceptually and ideologically naked when the monarchy was finally overthrown, and it was unable to encourage a transition to democratic politics and an ethnically inclusive political system. Instead, Qasim was given almost free rein to run society, which quickly produced an authoritarian rather than a democratic form of politics. Only NDP leader Kamil al-Chadirji, having learned from cooperating with the 1936 Sidqi-Sulayman government, pressed Qasim for immediate elections and a transition to civilian and democratic rule.

Nevertheless, many of the cultural and aesthetic contributions of Iraqi intellectuals during the postwar period proffered an implicit vision of a society in which all ethnic groups would enjoy cultural expression and be active agents in all facets of Iraqi society. The Free Verse Movement, for example, offered a critique of tradition that went far beyond poetry. As Terry DeYoung has so effectively argued, al-Sayyab's poetry challenged many prevalent assumptions. First, it rejected the romanticism that had dominated Arab poetry and the relationship between the individual and the nation implied in that tradition. As such, it contested the notion that "cultural authenticity," ethnic purity, and a unitary Pan-Arab nation were the "natural" components of Iraqi collective identity and political community. Second, the Free Verse Movement challenged the assumed unity between the poet and nation. The intensity of the moment of contact between poet and demonstrators—for example, during the Wathba —could neither be sustained nor provide effective measures for changing the political order. As one keen observer has noted, the Free Verse Movement was much more than a revolutionizing of poetic form. It rejected the "platform poetry" of the prewar romantics who simply asserted the unity of the exhortative poet and the crowd that was moved to political action, but who failed to theorize means of sustaining this decisive moment, such as that which brought about the Wathba.[33] In this context, intellectuals were clearly moving away from the catchphrases and sloganeering of both radical Pan-Arabism and the ICP's more dogmatic ideological pronouncements. Although this broadening of political and intellectual culture was not organized around abstract criteria but rather viewed as a mechanism for more effectively challenging colonial rule in Iraq, it nevertheless suggested a greater pluralism in cultural expression through the incorporation of a much broader symbolic nexus than had heretofore been part of the Iraqi intelligentsia's universe. Third, the increasing economic deprivation and consequent rise in social class (as well as nationalist) consciousness, especially clear after the Wathba, threatened to encourage greater fragmentation of Iraqi society. The Wathba and the partitioning of Palestine that followed the breakdown of the agrarian sector, as well as the intensification of conflict within the nationalist movement itself, stimulated Iraqi intellectuals to investigate aesthetics and new symbolic universes that took account of the new political and social reality implied by these events. For al-Sayyab and al-Mala'ika, this questioning led them to reject Iraqist nationalism and embrace Pan-Arabism.[34] Thus the Free Verse Movement, as well as all new literary, cultural, and artistic movements, must be seen in political as well as aesthetic terms.

The new directions in postwar Iraqi cultural production resulted in not only great works of poetry, but also advances in many genres of literature, the arts, archaeology, film, and music. The sharp disparities in income among social classes and the intensification of violence between the state and the nationalist movement stimulated intellectuals to explore the interstices of the growing social and political contradictions of Iraqi society. Rather than make reformist concessions that might have ameliorated these social disparities, the state became even less responsive to demands for change. Rich new intellectual explorations such as the poetry of al-Sayyab, al-Malaʾika, al-Bayati, al-Yusif, al-ʿAmara, and others constituted critical resources for building a new society and political community. However, the vituperative and ideologically rigid day-to-day politics under the monarchical state was still far removed from a complex and nuanced Iraq intellectual discourse. Much intellectual production during this period was politically contentious because it challenged and "reconstructed" or renegotiated tradition. Even if its goal was to create new forms of social, cultural, and political identity, this process initially resulted in further fragmentation through analyzing and rejecting much of what was derived from the past. As intellectuals grappled with such questions as the tension between individual rights and social responsibilities, the ability of tradition *(al-turath)* to address problems of "modernity," and the type of political and cultural identity needed to provide Iraq with societal unity, they likewise asked what types of historical memory were optimal in addressing these questions. This is one reason why writers, historians, and archaeologists not only searched deeply in Iraq's Arab heritage, particularly the ʿAbbasid period, but also looked for inspiration to Iraq's pre-Islamic Mesopotamian heritage. This activity was immensely complex and, in the Wittgensteinian sense, involved many different "private languages."[35] That is, much of the discourse surrounding intellectual production was not readily accessible to the populace at large, both because a large percentage of Iraqis were illiterate in the 1950s and because the discourse encompassed concepts and conceptual frameworks understood only by the specialists who discussed them. The poetry of al-Sayyab, the sculpture of Jawad al-Salim, and the significance of new archaeological findings from the pre-Islamic period were far removed from the masses, even as the intelligentsia created an ever more intricate aesthetic and symbolic universe in order to unravel a wide range of complex questions.

Despite these shortcomings, intellectuals did create important ties to the public. One example was the institution of the coffeehouse. The development of the coffeehouse as a center of nationalist politics was an indicator of the institutionalization of the Iraqi intelligentsia during the postwar era. This institutionalization can be seen in the intelligentsia's growth in size, the broadening of its cultural production by challenging tradition and opening new areas of expression, and its increasing role in challenging the state. The association of specific coffeehouses with individual poets or literary groups was not a new phenomenon in the postwar era. For example, famous poets such as Jamal Sidqi al-Zahawi, Maʿruf al-Rusafi, and Muhammad Mahdi al-Jawahiri had already lent their names to coffeehouses that they frequented, such as the Maqha al-Zahawi, the Haydarkhana (al-Rusafi),

Hasan al-ʿAjmi (al-Jawahiri), and the Parliament (Husayn Mirdan and ʿAbd al-Amir al-Husayri). Since a poet or group of writers that frequented a coffeehouse was usually associated with a particular political tendency, coffeehouses became quasi-public institutions in which the clientele was inculcated with political views and information. They helped expand the public sphere because people went to coffeehouses not just to drink coffee, chat with friends, read a newspaper, or play a game of backgammon, but also to discuss politics. Of course, politically active coffeehouses were also frequented by government informers, which required poets to develop finely honed skills of double entendre. Indeed, al-Sayyab and Buland al-Haydari each wrote a well-known poem about the persona of the informer. During the 1950s, the intelligentsia's experimental orientation led to the creation of new types of coffeehouses not directly connected to traditional literary themes and subject matter. The Swiss and Brazilian coffeehouses, for example, became focal points for the discussion of new intellectual currents such as existentialist thought.[36]

The coffeehouse linked intellectuals to the masses in other important ways. The coffeehouse provided illiterate Iraqis the opportunity to hear newspapers read aloud. For the literate poor, the coffeehouse provided access to newspapers, which were a luxury that they could not afford. Information shared within the coffeehouse helped spread nationalist and republican sentiments. Poetic themes, which often were coded in double entendres, fostered aesthetic sensitivities not just among the poets who had to hide their messages, but also among the audience that had to decipher the multiple levels of meaning in the poetry. For both the poet and audience, new cultural production and interpretive sophistication were necessary outcomes of the political atmosphere in which the coffeehouse functioned. Form and content acquired an increasingly sophisticated structure as poet and audience sought to conduct their intellectual and political business. In this sense, the coffeehouse became an important component of Iraqi civil society because it promoted not only opposition to the monarchical state, but also a greater appreciation of nuance, double entendre, and ambiguity in literary discourse. The coffeehouse became the public space par excellence for developing the "hidden transcripts" used to resist the state. Not surprisingly, demonstrators often retired to a specific coffeehouse after taking to the streets to protest government policies.[37]

The coffeehouse could not have expanded its cultural and political importance in the postwar era were it not for the increasing importance of the intelligentsia itself, which resulted from three interrelated factors. As noted earlier, the breakdown of the agrarian sector, which led to the growth of urban areas; the expansion of the educational system; and the increase in white-collar employment (civil servants, teachers, clerks, and so on) led to the rise of an effendi class.[38] Facing economic uncertainty, rapid social change, and a sense of dislocation as they moved to urban areas, and cognizant of the political system's pervasive corruption, this group was in the vanguard of nationalist protest. Although the military ultimately deposed the monarchy, it was the Iraqi intelligentsia's constant critique and laying bare the inequities of the political and social system that progressively chipped away at the monarchical state's legitimacy and authority. The expansion of the intelligentsia during the 1950s would lay the foundations for efforts undertaken by the Ba'th Party in the 1970s to restructure political and social memory as part of its project to rewrite history.

The political socialization that occurred in the coffeehouse represented only a small part of the intelligentsia's role in the expansion of civil society and the erosion of the monarchical state's authority during the postwar era. The proliferation of newspapers that invariably featured a literary and culture page and whose journalists were frequently short story writers, novelists, and poets provided another vehicle by which the intelligentsia could influence Iraqi society. Newspapers also reflected the growing cleavage that had developed around defining the future of Iraqi political community. *Sawt al-Ahali*, the NDP organ, and *al-Qa'ida, Ra'yat al-Shaghila, Kifah al-Sha'b*—and, later, *Ittihad al-Sha'b*—the ICP's newspapers (in some instances representing party factions), reflected Iraqist nationalist views, while *al-Istiqlal*, the Independence Party's paper, and the Ba'th Party's newspapers, *al-Afkar (Ideas)* and *al-Hurriya (Freedom)*, and a subsidiary newspaper, *al-'Amal (Labor)*, which began publication in 1954, represented Pan-Arabist thinking.[39] Because resources for publishing books were limited, newspapers were critical not only for disseminating political views but also for literary expression. The large number of newspapers and journals established during the postwar era is an indicator of the level of cultural production in Iraqi society during this period. Although the number of newspapers was no doubt exaggerated because many were forced by the police to close and then reappeared under new names, the resumption of the publication of newspapers itself demonstrated the tenacity of nationalist intellectuals in assuring their message's dissemination.

One of the most active organization in journalistic production was the Iraqi Communist Party. The ICP had its greatest journalistic successes in southern Iraq, where it launched a group of newspapers directed at the party's traditional constituencies, including *Sawt al-Kifah (The Voice of Struggle)* in 1951 and *Ittihad al-'Ummal (The Workers' Union)* and *Nidal al-Fallah (The Peasant's Struggle)* in 1952, whose purpose was to help create a peasant's organization, Jam'iyat Tahrir al-Fallahin (Society for the Liberation of the Peasantry). Two years later, *Sawt al-Furat (The Voice of the Euphrates)* began publication. Two of these newspapers continued publishing until June 1958. Both were repressed by Qasim, then reappeared clandestinely. In November 1962 *The Workers' Union* began publishing again as *Wahdat al-'Ummal (Workers' Unity)*, and in January 1963 *Sawt al-Furat* reappeared. The party also established newspapers to represent the interests of women *(Huquq al-Mar'a / Women's Rights)* and students *(Kifah al-Talaba / The Student's Struggle)*, as well as two papers in Armenian to represent the Armenian community.[40] In light of the numerous strikes, student demonstrations, and rural challenges to landowner prerogatives, all of which the British asserted were the work of the ICP, the distribution of these newspapers undoubtedly contributed to the party's success in mobilizing protest against the state.

Intellectuals were also active in professional syndicates and cultural organizations. Teachers, lawyers, journalists, and artists all belonged to professional syndicates and their attendant clubs, where members could meet to discuss professional, cultural, and political matters. These organizations frequently became involved in politics.[41] There were also many student organizations at the university level. Complementing the syndicates were many intellectual associations formed during the postwar years, such as the Society for Modern Art, the Iraqi Writers Association, and the group of communist intellectuals associated with *al-Thaqafa al-Jadida (New Culture)*, which first appeared in 1953. Considering the wide range of institutions and organizations within which the Iraqi intelligentsia functioned during the postwar era, the Iraqi intelligentsia acquired a more corporate sense of identity, which enhanced its impact on social and political affairs. Thus the ICP's *The Workers' Union* referred to radical intellectuals as *"al-Muthaqqifun al-Ahrar"* (free intellectuals) who would join the alliance of workers, peasants, *"kadihun"* (literally "toilers," i.e., the leaders of the ICP), and the masses to overthrow the existing system. The reference to intellectuals in group terms—as "free intellectuals"—was an indicator that a significant portion of the intelligentsia was indeed assuming a greater corporate identity.

Of particular importance was the short-lived journal *al-Thaqafa al-Jadida*, which published two issues in 1953 and 1954 before being closed by the government of Fadil al-Jamali. Although it later became affiliated with the ICP, the list of its founding members read like a veritable who's who of the Iraqi intelligentsia, such as the short story writers 'Abd al-Malik Nuri and Fu'ad al-Takarli, the poets Badr Shakir al-Sayyab, 'Abd al-Wahhab al-Bayati, and Kadhim al-Samawi, the novelist Gha'ib Tu'ama Farman, the critic Muhammad Sharara, the playwright Yusif al-'Ani, and, from the university, leftist professors such as Faysal al-Samir, Salah Khalis, and Ibrahim Kubba. The title of the journal, which first appeared in November 1953, indicated a desire to break with the past and its founders' belief in the central role of culture in bringing about political and social change. Its inaugural issue stated that its aim was to provide "a journal of scientific thought and free culture."[42] Although the journal's emphasis on publishing writings of practical value was commendable, a difficulty that plagued Iraqist nationalist politicians and intellectuals was their rejection of the past, which resulted in the continued neglect of traditional Arab culture. Although al-Thaqafa al-Jadida played a critical role in intellectual discourse when it reappeared after the July 1958 Revolution, its editorial board and contributors never seemed to realize that tradition remained important to the lives of many Iraqis, especially those of the politically active middle class.

Despite its rejection of the existing social and political system, it is difficult to characterize the postwar Iraqi intelligentsia as composed of "organic intellectuals" in the Gramscian sense. A key problem was the lack of intellectuals who were also active politicians and who could thus act as a bridge between intellectual creativity and political action. There were important exceptions. One was the famous communist leader Fahd (Yusif Salman Yusif), one of the founders of the ICP. Another was Kamil al-Chadirji, one of the founding members of the Ahali Group and founder of the NDP. Interestingly, both had backgrounds as journalists. Originally from the southern Iraqi city of al-Nasiriya, Fahd served as a journalist for the National Party newspaper prior to becoming a communist. Although his execution in February 1949 cut his life short, Fahd nevertheless left behind extensive writings on political and social affairs. He was especially sensitive to Iraq's multiethnic composition and was in the forefront of (male) writers who called for women's rights.[43]

One of Fahd's most important legacies for the 1950s was the introduction of the idea of the national front into Iraqi politics, which was pursued with great vigor by the communist movement both before and especially following Fahd's death. Because the communists could not openly participate in politics, the NDP under Kamil al-Chadirji's leadership dominated the two important national fronts formed during the 1950s. The first was the United Electoral Front, formed to contest the June 1954 elections. The second, the United National Front, was formed in February 1957 and aimed to rid Iraq of Nuri al-Sa'id, dissolve the National Assembly, withdraw Iraq from the

Baghdad Pact, commit the country to positive neutrality, implement democratic freedoms, end martial law, and release all political prisoners.[44]

The ICP achieved prominence by the late 1940s in large measure because of Fahd's organizing skills and his tireless efforts to expand its cadres. Following Fahd's execution in 1949, none of his successors matched his stature, as either an intellectual or a party leader, and constant police repression combined with the lack of an effective leader led to the ICP's fragmentation. By the mid-1950s a number of factions had developed within the party, the Qaʾida and Raʾyat al-Shaghila being the most prominent.

Another important intellectual and political activist was Kamil al-Chadirji, founder and head of the NDP. When he was a young man, al-Chadirji's reformist impulses led him to join the National Party. He subsequently joined the Ahali Group, and then accepted a ministerial portfolio in the Sidqi-Sulayman government in 1936. Despite the failure of the Sidqi regime, al-Chadirji's commitment to reform only intensified. As a result of his unceasing activities on behalf of a more politically participatory society and greater equity in the distribution of wealth, he was twice imprisoned during the 1950s.

Apart from his political activities, al-Chadirji was an accomplished photographer, as evidenced in *The Photography of Kamil Chadirji*, which was published posthumously by his son, Rifat.[45] He was likewise very interested in architecture, which could be seen in his house in Baghdad, which incorporated modern Western styles, including Bauhaus. al-Chadirji was well versed in literature and art as well as Western political philosophy. The newspapers he edited, *al-Ahali* and *Sawt al-Ahali*, both concentrated on Western and Soviet literature almost to the exclusion of Arab literature.

Few intellectuals were simultaneously politically active and efficacious, and those who were, such as Fahd and al-Chadirji, faced attacks not only from the state, but also from other quarters. For example, the credentials of the ICP and the NDP in supporting Arab causes were constantly being impugned. However, a careful analysis of the postwar era demonstrates that both Fahd and al-Chadirji were sympathetic to Pan-Arab concerns, although not according to the romantic, nostalgic, and corporatist model that traced its lineage to al-Husari, al-Sabʿawi, and al-Sabbagh. For Fahd, support for the Palestinian Arabs had less to do with ethnicity than with the ICP's view of Zionism as a tool of imperialism. The party's formation in 1946 of the League for Combating Zionism (ʿAsabat Mukafahat al-Sahyuniya) reflected this logic through its inclusion of both Arabs and Jews, among other groups. Nevertheless, the ICP remained suspicious of nationalism and only admitted insensitivity to Pan-Arab concerns in 1957, when it joined the

United National Front. The party's ambiguity toward Pan-Arabism and its continued inclusion of Jewish members during the late 1940s, after the founding of Israel, would later be used to great effect by the Baʿth Party to create a historical memory that impugned the ICP's patriotism by associating the party with sympathy for Zionism.[46]

For his part, al-Chadirji opposed the establishment of a Jewish state in Palestine and strongly supported strengthening the Arab League.[47] Already in 1946, *Sawt al-Ahali* was publishing editorials attacking Anglo-American pressures for the partition of Palestine and the creation of a Jewish state. Members of the NDP joined with other parties, particularly the Independence Party, in forming the Committee for the Defense of Palestine (Lajnat al-Difaʿ ʿan Filistin), which sent protests to the American and British ambassadors in Iraq and called, in May 1946, for a general strike to express Iraqi discontent with Western policy toward Palestine. When the 1948 Arab-Israeli War broke out, al-Chadirji published a front-page editorial in *Sawt al-Ahali* entitled "Palestine," in which he called for a vigorous defense of Palestinian rights, including military intervention by the Arab states.[48]

Perhaps al-Chadirji's major accomplishment during the postwar era was his effort in the 1950s to unite various political parties and organizations into a national front to oppose the monarchical state's dictatorial policies. al-Chadirji realized after the 1948 Wathba and the 1952 Intifada that a single party could not bring about significant change.[49] Already having joined with the Independence Party in 1946 to promote the Palestinian cause, al-Chadirji was the central actor in organizing a national front, which contested the parliamentary elections of June 1954, probably the closest approximation to free elections in modern Iraqi history.[50] Despite constant police coercion, the National Electoral Front (al-Jabha al-Intikhabiya al-Wataniya) was able to win 10 of the 135 seats.

The 1954 elections highlighted the growing tensions within the political elite. The relative freedom under which the elections were held was largely the result of the crown prince ʿAbd al-Ilah's resentment of Nuri al-Saʿid because of his control of parliament through the Constitutional Union Party (Hizb al-Ittihad al-Dusturi).[51] ʿAbd al-Ilah believed that by exploiting an opportunity when Nuri was out of office and abroad he could increase the number of independent candidates in the new parliament, thereby eliminating the party's absolute majority. The elections were the result of not only ʿAbd al-Ilah and Nuri's personal rivalry, but also their policy differences over whether Iraq should form a union with Syria. Although Nuri warned ʿAbd al-Ilah from London that his party needed to retain between seventy-two and eighty seats if serious political instability were to be avoided, the crown prince ignored the advice.

The parliamentary elections of June 1954, during which the monarchy relaxed its control over the electoral process, allowed opposition parties able to form the National Front and win ten seats in the elections.[52] What particularly unnerved Nuri and the traditional political elite was the vigor of the National Front's campaign and the fact that the seats it won were in Baghdad and Mosul, Iraq's two most important cities. Further, Nuri's party lost its parliamentary majority. The new parliament only met once, in July 1954, and was promptly dissolved. August elections created a new parliament, which Nuri's party once again dominated.

The National Front's strong showing in urban areas, where the state was least able to rig voting results, had the ironic consequence of forcing ʿAbd al-Ilah to dissolve the new parliament and turn to Nuri to form a new government, as the monarchy had repeatedly done during past crises. The flagrant manipulations of the new elections stripped whatever legitimacy the parliamentary system had maintained, especially following the arrest during the June campaign of several National Front candidates who were not released until the elections were over.

The June 1954 elections demonstrated that, under the appropriate conditions, the democratic election of civic-minded representatives in Iraq could occur. Further, the coalition that formed the National Front included political parties whose agendas and interests were divergent. The participants included the NDP, the Independence Party, the ICP, and the Peace Partisans, a front organization for the communists. The NDP and the Independence Party were the only declared political parties because the ICP was still an illegal organization.

A detailed analysis of the 1954 elections points to a number of important conclusions about prerevolution Iraqi politics. First, despite the continuity of authoritarian politics since the Bakr Sidqi coup of 1936 (except for the brief interregnum of the 1946 Tawfiq al-Suwaydi ministry), once repression abated in 1954, the politically active urban populace was able to quickly organize a campaign and engage in sophisticated political discourse and activities. Second, opposition parties were able to mount an effective campaign and win seats in strategic districts in Iraq's major urban centers. Third, the National Front included both Iraqist nationalists and Pan-Arabists who maintained their solidarity despite efforts by Pan-Arabists both within and outside the political elite to split the organization. Not only do these facts belie the idea that prerevolution Iraq was bereft of any democratic political process, but they also point to the development of the foundations of civil society among sectors of the urban middle class. The elections challenge the notion promoted by the Qasim regime and especially the Baʿthist regimes that political disorder and decay caused by imperialist domination necessitated military regimes and/or one-party rule to "protect the people."

The election results were all the more impressive because the authorities tried vigorously to suppress the National Front's campaign, which enjoyed widespread support not only in Baghdad and Mosul, but in cities in the south such as al-Najaf and al-Hilla and in Kurdish areas such as Sulaymaniya in the north. Large and spirited crowds appeared at campaign rallies, making the elections not only the freest but also the most spirited in modern Iraqi history. Banners appeared on houses in support of the National Front's candidates, and cars with megaphones patrolled city streets calling for voters to vote for the organization's candidates. Calls for an end to "feudalism" *(al-iqtaʿ)* and for distribution of land to the peasantry were profoundly frightening to the monarchy's supporters.[53]

Promonarchy newspapers criticized the National Front as unconcerned with Arab affairs and cited as evidence the absence of any reference to the liberation of Palestine in its charter. The hidden text was that the National Front's candidates were Iraqist nationalists (and comprised primarily of Shiʿis and other minorities) and therefore not true Iraqi patriots. This point underscores the manner in which the traditional political elite (like the Baʿth Party after it) was quick to provoke sectarianism as a way of dividing the political opposition. Second, it is important to note that the Independence Party joined the National Front despite the predominance of Iraqist nationalist forces, and did not withdraw under attacks designed to cast aspersions on its Pan-Arab credentials. In light of the party's strong Pan-Arabism, its position demonstrated that its primary commitment was to democratic reforms. In short, the 1954 elections indicate that ideologically diverse forces could cooperate, even under stressful conditions.

The electoral success of the National Front encouraged additional attempts at cooperative political action.[54] An important stimulus for creating a new national front stemmed from nationalist opposition to the Baghdad Pact, which was signed in 1955. The Tripartite Invasion of Egypt by Great Britain, France, and Israel following the 1956 nationalization of the Suez Canal was the catalyst that brought the idea to fruition. Armed uprisings in 1956 in the hotbed of revolution, al-Najaf and its nearby suburb al-Hayy, which accompanied demonstrations in support of Egypt throughout Iraq but which failed to effect any change in national policy, made the necessity of joint action even more urgent. The army's reticence in suppressing the al-

Najaf and al-Hayy revolts was, at the same time, a positive development in the eyes of the opposition political parties. Soon contact between the National Front and opposition elements within the military was established.

Once again Kamil al-Chadirji played a central role in opposing Nuri and the political elite. First, because it was a legal political party, the NDP was able to lead a national front. As the weakest opposition party, the Independence Party could not play a leadership role, while the ICP and the Ba'th Party were still illegal. Second, al-Chadirji made it clear that the NDP would only participate in a national front directed by a truly collective leadership. His insistence that no party try to subordinate the front to its own interests was intended as a message to the communists who had first approached him about creating it. Third, he emphasized that the front should be as inclusive as possible and not reach out only to parties on the left. Finally, and very significantly, in light of later attempts to characterize Iraqist nationalists as insensitive to Pan-Arabism, al-Chadirji stressed that the front should recognize the legitimacy of such concerns.[55]

The announcement of the front's creation, secretly printed by the ICP, was enthusiastically welcomed throughout Iraq.[56] At al-Chadirji's insistence, the front was led by a "Supreme Committee" (al-Lajna al-ʿUlya) consisting of the four main parties—the NDP, the ICP, and the Independence and Ba'th parties—and an executive committee, which included not only the National Front's four main parties, but also representatives of smaller parties and independents whose responsibility was to forge links with local organizations and disseminate information to affiliated groups throughout the country.[57]

It has been argued that given the failure of electoral politics and the persistence of police repression, the only alternative to the monarchy was military intervention. This argument makes it seem as though the nationalist movement had, by the late 1950s, reached its apogee in terms of strength and that the army was, in effect, forced to seize power. Taken to its logical extension, this model becomes a self-fulfilling prophecy for authoritarian rule in Iraq. In other words, the military interventions of 1936, 1941, and 1958 all demonstrated, to those who supported these interventions, that the fractious nature of Iraqi politics necessitated authoritarian rule by the military.

What this model neglects is that the nationalist movement's constant chipping away at the monarchy's legitimacy paved the way for the military's seizure of power in July 1958, and that its constant challenges to state prerogatives provided the military with the idea of seizing power itself. In 1936 and in 1941, the army opposed certain factions of the political elite but still envisioned itself as conceptually distinct from the machinery of the state. It was only after the failed campaign in Palestine in 1948 that the army began to envision a complete restructuring of the state, that is, the creation of a republic. However, it was the Wathba, which was organized by nationalist forces and forced the Salih Jabr government from power, that spread the idea among army officers that they could overthrow the monarchy. This issue is not just one of historical detail, but it is linked to a broader argument about whether military, and hence authoritarian, rule was preordained for the modern Iraqi state.

Materials that have come to light since the revolution point to the manner in which the constant street demonstrations eroded the political will of the monarchy and its supporters. Even the head of the secret police, Bahjat ʿAtiya, indicated in a secret report just prior to the revolution that the state faced a tenacious enemy.[58] By 1956, Nuri al-Saʿid was completely discredited along with most of the political elite. Reports prior to the revolution indicate that ʿAbd al-Ilah was resigned to the impending overthrow of the monarchy.[59] Indeed, on the morning of July 14, as the Rihab Palace was being shelled by rebellious army units, ʿAbd al-Ilah refused to order the palace guard to return fire, opting instead to surrender immediately and to sue for safe passage for the royal family from Iraq.[60]

The constant pressure by nationalist forces, combined with the divisions within the political elite between reformers such as Fadil al-Jamali and authoritarians such as Nuri and ʿAbd al-Ilah, undermined political authority to such an extent that the *ancien régime* fell with hardly a shot fired on July 14, 1958. Clearly, the nationalist movement established the necessary, if not sufficient, conditions for the revolution. Although the nationalist movement did not speak with one voice, the formation of a national front by its moderate core, namely the NDP and the Independence Party, indicated the possibility of reconciling competing interpretations of Iraqi political community. However, it was the more radical extremes of the two competing models of political community—the communists and especially the Baʿthists—that created the strident politics that later produced such violence and suffering for the Iraqi people. Likewise, much of the state-sponsored violence that characterized the Baʿth Party in 1963 and again after 1968 could already be seen in embryonic form during the late 1940s and 1950s. Public hangings, torture of political dissidents, the stripping of citizenship from opposition figures, the promotion of political divisions through sectarianism, censorship, the public licensing of typewriters, "good conduct" certificates for entering the university, and rule by decree instead of through established constitutional laws and regulations were all policies later perfected by the Baʿth Party.[61]

Despite the steady decline into authoritarianism, resulting in an increase of political violence and abuse of human rights, there were also developments that pointed in the opposite direction. The tremendous strides in innovative cultural production, which, for the most part, promoted tolerance, cultural diversity, and humanistic values, did not produce a correspondingly tolerant, participatory, and democratic politics prior to 1958. However, this cultural production did provide a historical memory that democratic forces could draw upon in their efforts to change the course of future Iraqi politics. It also set the stage for further advances in cultural production following the 1958 Revolution. That this legacy represented and continues to represent such an implicit threat helps explain why Saddam Husayn and the Ba'th Party were so keen to erase this historical memory.

The state's institutions had virtually atrophied by the 1958 Revolution. Apart from the crown prince, 'Abd al-Ilah, Nuri, and a small circle of supporters and the secret police, the institutions of the state did not comprise a coherent structure. The political elite was divided between reformers and hard-liners who refused to consider any political change. The army could not be trusted to support the monarchy and thus was denied access to ammunition for tanks, cannons, and small arms without the explicit permission of Nuri and 'Abd al-Ilah. Although there were many outstanding lawyers in prerevolution Iraq, the law was not applied in a consistent or equitable fashion. This was especially true in political cases, which were decided by the palace and Nuri.

Despite the loss of what Gramsci called the "trenches of civil society," by which he meant the support of the state's inner core by its outer defenses such as the educational, legal, and religious systems, the monarchy did make some tentative steps toward structuring political consciousness and historical memory. In this respect, it demonstrated some sensitivity to the need to spread hegemonic forms of thought. The official description of Iraq produced by the monarchy in 1939 is one example. By May 1953, a directorate-general of propaganda was active in the Ministry of the Interior.[62] The *Army Journal* was founded in 1939 to extol the military's virtues and its role in Iraq's social development and defense, and the army established its own press to disseminate information "on military subjects."[63] Stephen Hemsley Longrigg states that the monarchy briefly experimented with a Ministry of Guidance during the 1950s, which officially became the Ministry of Guidance and Information in 1958.[64]

The creation of institutions and media to structure the way in which the populace viewed history, culture, and politics was another indicator of the nationalist movement's impact. The use of propaganda reflected less an innovative strategy by the state than a response to nationalist challenges to its prerogatives. The enactment of the Labor Law of 1936, even though it excluded agricultural workers, was a tacit recognition of the increased strength of the labor movement, and particularly the power of unions and syndicates, which were first formed in 1924.[65] The law's amendment in 1944 to permit workers to organize, and in 1954 to settle worker-management disputes and create a minimum wage, which was raised again in 1957, also demonstrated a recognition of workers' increased political power in certain sectors of industry. Creation of the Social Security Law in 1956, which applied to government departments and, in the private sector, the oil industry, no doubt reflecting the law's strategic importance and the power of labor to influence it, reflected the same dynamics, namely an attempt to co-opt nationalist forces that posed a significant threat to the state.[66]

What were the structural impediments to the creation of a democratic polity on the eve of the 1958 Revolution? First, the tremendous disjuncture between urban and rural life represented a serious constraint. The conditions of rural society, where peasants lived almost as serfs and tribal shaykhs ruled semi-autonomous regions, offset the impact of the dynamic and progressive developments that were occurring in urban areas, especially Baghdad, Mosul, and Basra.[67] Realization of the fact that fewer than 1 percent of the populace owned more than 46 percent of the total cultivable land was a serious impediment to change led all reform-minded groups to call for land reform as a sine qua non for social change. Complementing the rural landowning class was the small elite of urban merchants and even smaller industrial bourgeoisie. Members of this social stratum were often extremely wealthy and loath to endorse any reforms that might undermine their economic and political power.

However, to attribute the problems of social change solely to the power of landowners and the urban mercantile and industrial bourgeoisie to impede such change ignores a number of important considerations. Focusing solely on the social class issue ignores the continuity of sectarianism as a core component of the political process. Although parties such as the NDP and ICP fought to overcome sectarian divisions, the major institutions of the state such as the parliament, the army, and the post of prime minister remained firmly under Sunni Arab domination and control. It was not until 1948 that Iraq finally appointed a Shi'i, Salih Jabr, prime minister. His appointment had less to do with redressing sectarian differences than with the political calculation that his pro-British sentiments combined with his confessional status would facilitate reformulation of the 1930 Anglo-Iraqi Treaty in a manner that would satisfy the political elite. The appointment in

1952 of another Shiʻi, Muhammad al-Sadr, a respected religious figure whose government lasted only four and a half months, was simply a response to that year's Intifada, a tacit recognition of large-scale Shiʻi dissatisfaction with political and social conditions. Put differently, Shiʻis were called upon to serve as prime ministers only when it suited the needs of the Sunni-dominated elite. Manipulation of sectarianism was not limited to the Shiʻa but also affected the Kurds. After the creation of the Arab Union with Jordan in response to Egypt and Syria forming the United Arab Republic, Jamal Baban was appointed prime minister to assuage the fears of his fellow Kurds that they would be submerged in the new union.

Two additional lessons from the postwar period help explain why authoritarian rule triumphed over a participatory model of political community. Since the onset of World War I in 1914, Iraq had been characterized by almost continuous periods of conflict and disorder. It is not difficult to comprehend how the urban middle classes could yearn for order and stability. In other words, certain sectors of the populace, the middle classes in particular, were increasingly prone to support authoritarian movements because of the strong desire for some sort of predictability in daily life. This attitude would be even more prevalent in 1968, when the second Baʻthist regime came to power after a decade of unparalleled turmoil.

A second factor influencing postwar political development was the increasing resort to conspiracy theories to explain the travails of Iraqi politics. The foundations of this thinking can be found in Satiʻ al-Husari's educational philosophy during the 1920s. The Sunni Arab middle class's interpretation (particularly in Baghdad) of the 1933 Assyrian uprising as a British conspiracy to divide Iraq and the view of the Bakr Sidqi's coup d'état as a Kurdish plot to appropriate Sunni Arab political prerogatives exemplified the development of this thinking. The al-Muthanna Club's promotion of anti-Jewish feelings was not just a manifestation of a racially oriented ideology, but also an effort to find simple explanations for complex problems. The lack of trust among different sectors of the political elite, economic deprivation, and the failure of political institutions, especially those insuring fair and free elections, continued to exist after 1958. Thus Saddam Husayn and the Baʻth Party were not the progenitors of a conspiratorial and bunker mentality, but rather were the heirs to that tradition who refined it to new heights of paranoia and xenophobia.

Nevertheless, the period between 1945 and 1958 witnessed an incredible outburst of organizational and cultural activity. Developments in literature and the arts were to place Iraq in the forefront of much intellectual development in the Arab world. Iraqis had demonstrated that they were politically sophisticated and able to participate in democratic elections. The proliferation of political parties, clubs, and civic and artistic associations was impressive in light of the state's hostility to any organization beyond its control. In newspapers, journals, and monographs, Iraqis expressed a strong sense of nationalism, indicating a commitment to the nation and a desire for political community. Although authoritarian rule was to triumph once again after the overthrow of the monarchy, a powerful historical memory of the post–World War II years remained that democratic forces opposed to the Ba'th Party could draw upon to mobilize in their attempt to remove it from power after the Iran-Iraq and Gulf wars and 1991 Intifada had dissipated support for the regime.

5 The Crucible

The July 14, 1958 Revolution and the Struggle over Historical Memory

> If the army and the Ministry of Defense were the mother of the Revolution, then the Ministry of Guidance and the Iraqi State Broadcasting System constitute the infant Revolution's nursery.
>
> *Committee for the Celebration of the July 14th Revolution*

Early on the morning of July 14, 1958, tanks of the Iraqi army's Twentieth Brigade rolled into Baghdad and surrounded the royal family at Rihab Palace. Despite the royal guard's desire to resist, the crown prince, 'Abd al-Ilah, quickly decided to surrender and sue for safe passage out of the country. As the royal family emerged from the palace, a captain in the attacking party opened fire with his machine gun, causing other troops to fire as well, and everyone in the royal family except the crown prince's sister was killed. An urban mob subsequently seized the bodies of the crown prince and King Faysal II and dragged them through the streets of Baghdad. The following day, the hated Nuri al-Sa'id was discovered trying to escape the city disguised as a woman. Whether he was immediately shot or shot himself is disputed. Following a secret burial, Nuri's body was disinterred by those in control of the street and paraded through the capital as well. After two days of urban unrest, the army intervened to reestablish public order. In a matter of hours and with hardly any struggle, the Hashimite Monarchy had come to an end. The ease with which the monarchy slipped in the annals of history was indicative of the complete lack of support it had come to enjoy by that fateful morning in July of 1958.

The July 14, 1958 Revolution created great expectations among the Iraqi people, the bloody events of the first day notwithstanding. Yet within a few months, the new regime was beset by internal struggles and dissension that spread to the populace at large. Why did the revolution experience so much internal conflict? Why did the revolution fail to adopt a more democratic character? Why, after entering the new government as cabinet ministers, were the nationalist politicians who had fought the monarchy so tenaciously unable to force the new military regime to hold open elections?

One problem in addressing these questions is that the existing "narratives of revolution" have placed excessive emphasis on the two main coconspirators of the July 1958 Revolution, Staff Brigadier ʿAbd al-Karim Qasim and Colonel ʿAbd al-Salam ʿArif. But focusing on these two central personalities causes us to lose sight of the many important changes that took place under the revolutionary regime, especially at the level of intellectual thought, and the extent to which the revolution reflected struggles that existed prior to it. Qasim's injection of the state into the realm of reassessing culture and the past represented the first systematic effort in modern Iraq to officially restructure historical memory. The state's extensive involvement in cultural production not only represented a new role for the state, but it also established a model for Saddam Husayn and the Baʿth Party to follow after the 1968 putsch that brought them to power. The impact of the July 1958 Revolution on this important aspect of political change has yet to be recognized. Of course, the state's efforts to appropriate culture under Qasim were directed at ameliorating, not intensifying, sectarian discrimination and thus stand as a major counterpoint to the intent of the post-1968 Baʿthist regime's so-called Project for the Rewriting of History (Mashruʿ Iʿadat Kitabat al-Tarikh), about which more will be said later.

The importance of emphasizing a framework that transcends struggles between competing personalities and elites lies in the conceptual links created between state and civil society, a relationship that has been portrayed to date almost entirely in negative terms.[1] The state had never before systematically attempted to appropriate folklore and structure cultural production and interpretations of the past for political ends.[2] Its efforts represented less an innovative policy on Qasim's part and more a continuation of the Iraqi intelligentsia's thought and activity that emerged, especially among those on the left, following World War II. Put differently, the processes that had achieved a critical mass following the war's end were now incorporated into the state.

Whether Qasim appropriated the intellectuals or the intellectuals appropriated the state apparatus is a difficult question to answer. Certainly, both the state and the intelligentsia benefited from their symbiotic relationship. The regime's focus on history and folklore was the result of several factors, but particularly the conjuncture of two important forces. First, the inclusion of many intellectuals in the state apparatus after the July 1958 Revolution perforce dramatically increased the influence of the left on cultural matters because a large percentage of the Iraqi intelligentsia were, as argued earlier, leftist or even communist in orientation. Because Qasim needed intellectuals to legitimate his new regime, and leftist intellectuals in particular to combat his Pan-Arabist rivals, he established the Ministry of Guidance, which, in turn, developed its own infrastructure, including an extensive radio and television network and a new Directorate of Folklore.[3] The power that the Iraqi Communist Party had acquired by 1959 led many of the state's intellectuals to focus on "history from below." In other words, to enhance the state's revolutionary credentials and in accordance with the orientation of many state intellectuals, strong emphasis was placed on the experiences of the lower classes, which could best be accomplished by stressing folklore.[4] Because this was less an innovative policy of the new state than an extension of the left's influence, the July 1958 Revolution did not represent an institutional break with the past in the area of cultural production, but rather a continuation and intensification of a growing interest in national heritage *(al-turath)*, which now assumed the added dimension of official state sponsorship, namely through the Ministry of Guidance.

Second, the state's efforts to organize cultural production were intended to offset Pan-Arabist challenges that were both domestic (especially from hostile elements in the army) and international (from the United Arab Republic and its Nasirist supporters in Iraq). Both of these threats were very real in light of 'Arif's challenge to Qasim in September 1958;[5] the Pan-Arabist Mosul uprising, which was supported by Egypt during March 1959; and the attempted assassination of Qasim by Ba'thist forces in October 1959. Through an emphasis on Iraq's pre-Arab and pre-Islamic heritage—which was symbolized by the choice of the Akkadian sun for the revolution's flag and the use of ancient Mesopotamian designs for its official symbol—the July 1958 Revolution eschewed the symbols of Pan-Arabism such as the red, green, and black tricolor with its eagle insignia. The twin motifs of folklore and ancient Mesopotamian heritage served as counterweights to Pan-Arabist designs by underlining Iraq's position as the "cradle of civilization," which obviously preceded Arab Semitic civilization.[6] Further, folklore served to bridge the ethnic gap between Sunni and Shi'i Arabs and Kurds because it emphasized their cultural commonalities, such as food, rituals, sports, and other leisure activities, rather than differences. Even Kurds could relate more to Iraq as symbolized through its ancient civilizations than to Pan-Arabist ideology, according to which Iraq was merely a region *(qutr)* of a larger Pan-Arab state dominated by Sunni Arabs.

The July 1958 Revolution has generally been viewed as a failure, attributable in particular to 'Abd al-Karim Qasim's "defective" character and personality and the revolution's supposed deviation from its Pan-Arab goals. Within this overall negative perspective, several narratives that purport to explain the revolution's rise and fall have emerged. Although some of these narratives have scholarly credentials, having been based upon significant research, all possess a hidden text. Viewed through its own conceptual prism, each narrative seeks to impose a particular form of historical memory on the revolution. The goal of each narrative is to influence the type of political community it normatively desires in contemporary Iraq and to prevent certain forces from gaining access to power. Each incorporates a strong counterfactual, or "what if," assumption. In other words, if the revolution had not occurred, or if it had followed a different course, the political development of Iraq after 1958 would not only have been different, but it would have proceeded along more positive lines.

As the continued intensity of debates indicates, the struggle over the interpretation of the July 1958 Revolution, more than any other event in twentieth-century Iraq, represents a continuing struggle over the definition of political community and the direction of political and social change in contemporary Iraq. One goal of this chapter is to assess what policies and achievements of the revolution were downplayed by the Baʿth Party in order to better understand what elements it viewed as threatening. If the Revolution did, in fact, encompass processes that potentially challenged Baʿth Party authoritarianism, such as the attempt to combat sectarianism, then to what extent might these processes assist forces that now seek to move post-Baʿthist Iraq toward a more open, participatory, and democratic political system?

In the "ethnic narrative," the would-be revolutionaries are accused of failing to appreciate the ethnic and cultural tolerance—and particularly the state's attitude toward minorities—that characterized Iraq under the monarchy. The effort of revolutionaries, and Pan-Arabists in particular, to homogenize Iraqi society through insisting that it conform to a unitary cultural model is seen as the key mechanism that undermined this tolerance. By invoking conspiracy theories to challenge the loyalty of minorities, who were portrayed as agents of foreign interests intent on socially and politically dividing Iraq, Pan-Arab (largely Sunni Arab) revolutionaries encouraged violence by denying the majority of the populace, especially the Shiʿa and Kurds, political and cultural participation. Although the monarchical state's repressive qualities are largely ignored, this model's assertion that Iraqis were unprepared for democracy in 1958 allows the narrative to avoid confronting the monarchy's role in causing the revolution by refusing to allow even moderate reforms.[7]

The ethnic narrative advances additional hypotheses, particularly the view that the revolution was doomed from the start. This view is based on the assumption that Iraq's three main ethnic groups, the Sunnis, the Shiʿa, and the Kurds, are unable to coexist in a unified political community. These

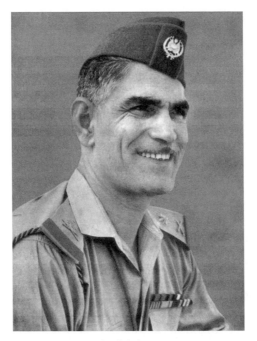

FIGURE 3. General ʿAbd al-Karim Qasim, founder of the Iraqi Republic. *al-Mawsim* 32 (1997): cover photograph.

cleavages, Iraq's lack of a democratic tradition, and the existence in 1958 of strong radical groups such as the ICP and the Baʿth Party, which did not support a participatory political system, are cited as impediments to any meaningful political development. According to this narrative, Iraqis seem destined to eternal political conflict and social decay.

Certainly the Pan-Arabist narrative of the revolution has been dominant. It was most systematically developed by the Takriti Baʿth after 1968. Similar to the other models, it too incorporates an important counterfactual assumption. If only Qasim had shared political power with the Free Officers and opted for immediate political unity *(al-wahda al-fawriya)* with Egypt, the revolution would have been spared internal turmoil. Pan-Arabists argue that instead Qasim seized dictatorial powers and prevented the revolution from achieving its original goal, namely establishing Pan-Arab unity. As one Pan-Arabist stated, Qasim caused the revolution to deviate from "the path that was prescribed for it" *(ʿan tariqihi allati kana marsuman laha).*[8] Instead of leading Iraq to immediate unity with Egypt, Qasim pursued a local nationalist vision according to which Iraq remained outside the Arab fold. Still worse, Qasim relied heavily on the Iraqi Communist Party and its sympathizers, who occupied many posts in his government, such as Municipalities Minister Naziha al-Dulaymi, the first Arab woman to assume a ministerial post. In short, Pan-Arabists accused Qasim of promoting social fragmentation rather than unity, thereby undermining Iraq's power as a nation-state and, by extension, the larger Arab world's ability to resist imperialism. This interpretation of the revolution, however, completely ignores Iraq's status as a multiethnic society and its need to confront a plurality of social interests.

The Pan-Arabist narrative attributes the revolution's "deviance" (al-inhiraf), with all the religious overtones of the word, to Qasim's cult of personality and his unwillingness to share power. Qasim's efforts to prevent military officers who had helped him seize power from holding political office and his failure to establish a Revolution Command Council, as had purportedly been agreed upon prior to the revolution, are cited as two examples of his exclusionary style that alienated many of his initial supporters. The Pan-Arabist model's silence on the champion of immediate unity with Egypt, ʿAbd al-Salam ʿArif, and his collaboration with Qasim to exclude the Free Officers through refusing to create a Revolution Command Council is indicative of its selective reading of the July 14 Revolution.

The communist narrative, not surprisingly, emphasizes external rather than internal factors—and especially the role of imperialism—as forces that undermined the revolution. According to this model, the revolution—which terminated the Arab Union with Jordan, severed Iraq's ties with the Baghdad Pact, supported a foreign policy based on "positive neutrality," imposed land reform, and called for the nationalization of the Iraq Petroleum Company—presented a major challenge to imperial, and particularly American, interests in the region. Western oil interests were threatened not only in Iraq, but also in neighboring allies of the United States such as Saudi Arabia and Kuwait. In favoring closer ties with the Soviet Union, Iraq likewise posed a threat to Western strategic interests in the Levant, Iran, and the Persian Gulf. The revolution failed because imperialism could not allow an Iraq independent of Western control to provide a role model for other states in the region. The CIA is asserted to have played a central role in the February 1963 coup that overthrew Qasim.[9] However, the ICP still has not addressed its own contribution to the revolution's demise through its opposition to democratic political reforms and its unqualified support for Qasim as sole leader, even when his policies were detrimental to the party's interests.

A recently developed narrative, which focuses on the lack of civil society in modern Iraq, explains the revolution's failure as a result of the Qasim regime's unwillingness to institutionalize a participatory and democratic form of government.[10] This model, which was often posited in a circuitous manner because it was formulated in part by scholars still in Iraq, came to the fore largely as the result of the excesses of Saddam Husayn's regime and, more generally, as a result of increased interest in the concept of civil society throughout the Arab world. In other words, scholars sought the origins of Ba'thist authoritarianism in the excesses of the prerevolution era, and then in the new revolutionary regime's unwillingness to nurture those democratic forces that participated in the first postmonarchy cabinet. The hypothesis is advanced that the revolutionary regime alienated its supporters in the democratic movement by failing to delegate to them any meaningful decision-making power, thereby progressively narrowing the regime's political and social base, which ultimately facilitated its overthrow.[11] Of course, it is possible to read into this critique of the July 1958 Revolution a similar critique of the Ba'thist regime under Saddam Husayn, which likewise increasingly alienated itself from the Iraqi populace. However, apart from the work of Hasan al-'Alawi and a few others, no model has seriously confronted the issue of sectarianism and its role in impeding democratic politics in Iraq.[12]

As each of these narratives demonstrates, the memory of the July 1958 Revolution remains highly contested. The revolution is, without doubt, the signal event in twentieth-century Iraqi history, encompassing in microcosm all the contradictions and potential for democratic change and social reform that had developed to that point in Iraqi society. Because the revolution represents such a critical juncture in modern Iraqi history, it is necessary to understand the reasons for its ultimate failure. Each of the above narratives makes a contribution to that end. However, each seems less interested in developing a comprehensive explanation for the revolution than in promoting its own political and conceptual agenda. Except for the narrative espoused by the left, none of the narratives transcends a focus on the state and political elites in its conceptualization of the revolution. In other words, the revolution's social impact, such as its mobilization of the masses and its promotion of artistic and literary creativity, is largely ignored. The critical role of culture in political change, both in terms of social revolution and democratic politics, is ignored. A focus solely on either Qasim as political leader or his regime allows no space for those who might use the July 1958 Revolution more broadly to challenge state authoritarianism. In their haste to explain political failure, those who propound the aforementioned narratives of revolution have neglected the revolution's positive legacy and the way it assisted opponents of the Ba'thist regime in their war of position. This legacy included a flourishing of artistic and literary creativity, a dramatic increase in the political and social mobilization of the populace, especially members of the lower classes, an intensification of the process of reexamining Iraq's history and folklore in an open fashion, land reform, the enactment of greater gender equality, and a heretofore unparalleled effort to overcome sectarianism in public life. Indeed, this legacy haunted Iraq's Ba'th Party, which sought to prevent the Iraqi populace from understanding the revolution's social and political contributions.

The historiography of the July 1958 Revolution needs to be rescued from the excessive emphasis placed by both its detractors and its proponents on the role and personality of 'Abd al-Karim Qasim. Nevertheless, a study of the leader of the July 1958 Revolution, if situated in a broader structural perspective, does provide critical insights into why Iraqist nationalism and its more inclusive vision of political community and cultural expression failed to sustain itself against a much more restrictive and chauvinist understanding of Pan-Arab nationalism provided by the Ba'thists who overthrew him.

The forces that unleashed the July 14, 1958 Revolution and that influenced its development and ultimate demise went far beyond Qasim's personality.[13] The lack of political institutions that could ameliorate the mistrust that existed among Iraq's different ethnic groups—a mistrust structured by economic and political differences that historically had privileged Sunni Arabs—tended to promote authoritarian and personalistic rule. Although Qasim assiduously tried to implement far-reaching social and economic reforms, his failure to institutionalize the revolution and promote widespread political participation beyond the symbolic level, as deemed necessary by the civil society narrative, represented a key shortcoming that led to his regime's collapse in 1963. However, this argument still begs the question: why has no political leader been able to bring about any significant political institutionalization and overcome ethnic cleavages in twentieth-century Iraq?

Qasim's overthrow and execution, and the calumny to which he was subjected after his demise, reflects the fate of most losers in history. Despite his increasingly autocratic rule as he became more isolated and withdrawn after 1961, Qasim provided a role model that differed from all of his predecessors and successors who have ruled modern Iraq. Qasim was essentially a simple man who sought little in the form of personal wealth. As his appellation *za'im* (leader) indicated, he was the first modern Iraqi leader to have been drawn from the Iraqi masses and to have enjoyed popular support. Unlike other rulers, he never used his positions as prime minister and defense minister to acquire property or wealth. Qasim worked in a small and simply furnished office in the Ministry of Defense.[14] After his execution, it was discovered that he was virtually penniless and had in fact been donating his government paychecks (as prime minister and defense minister) and his military pension to the poor.[15] Qasim never even acquired civilian clothes, having ruled and died in his military uniform. Although some analysts have attributed Qasim's popularity among the urban and rural poor to the fact that he was half Shi'i on his mother's side, it is probably more accurate to say that Qasim was beloved by the landless peasants and urban *sarifa* dwellers (known in colloquial Iraqi Arabic as *shargawiya*, literally "Easterners") because they believed that he truly represented their interests apart from any ethnic considerations.[16] Qasim's lack of corruption stands in sharp contrast to the venality of Nuri and the monarchical era's "political merchants" *(tujjar al-siyassa)*,[17] and to Saddam Husayn and his Ba'thist supporters after 1968. Indeed, it is striking that, despite the many efforts to vilify Qasim, few accusations of corruption have been directed at his regime, and none, besides a critique of his brother for having used nepotistic ties to accumulate wealth, has received any credence.[18]

Qasim's background is typical of that of many of the prominent actors in the second wave of Iraqist and Pan-Arab nationalism, which was dominated by the middle classes. Unlike the wealthy landlords and merchants who, from the turn of the century, had renegotiated political relations with their colonial overlords, the nationalists from more humble backgrounds such as Qasim and al-Nasir, who appeared on the political stage following World War II, argued that political independence was insufficient if the "social question" *(al-qadiya al-ijtima'iya)* were not addressed simultaneously. Another quality of many "second wave" nationalists was their status as recent immigrants from the countryside and the marginal position their families assumed in the city. Qasim's father, for example, was a tribesman with a respected background who lived in a little-known quarter of Baghdad inhabited by residents of modest means. The family's small house "pointed to its owners being situated between the middle class and the poor but [in reality] closer to the poor."[19]

Second, the revolutionary regime attempted to implement an ambitious program of land reform, urban development (the most prominent example being Madinat al-Thawra, or Revolution City, in Baghdad), and cultural innovations in addition to enacting the first legislation to ensure women's rights. Qasim was truly concerned with the plight of the masses and committed to a more egalitarian society, and even his opponents conceded his commitment was sincere.[20] This concern for the populace can be said to characterize only a few Iraqi leaders of the modern era. The opening up of government institutions to groups that were traditionally excluded, especially the Shiʿa, represented a radical break with past state behavior. The promulgation of a new and liberal personal status law was particularly disquieting to social conservatives, who were already anxious about Qasim's ties to the communists and his proposed reform programs.

Third, the Qasim regime was characterized by a relative lack of state-sponsored political violence. Compared to the record of Nuri Saʿid's regime, the Baʿthist regime that overthrew Qasim in 1963, or the second or Takriti Baʿthist regime after 1968, the Qasim regime was extremely benign in its treatment of opponents. Of the members of the *ancien régime* brought to trial, only four were executed, including Saʿid Qazzaz, the minister of the interior, and Bahjat ʿAtiyya, the hated head of the secret police, both of whom had been responsible for implementing many political executions during the postwar era and for the arbitrary imprisonment and torture of opponents of the monarchy. These executions, however, were only carried out after the March 1959 Mosul uprising, during which Pan-Arabists, supported by the United Arab Republic, and members of the *ancien régime* joined forces to overthrow the regime. Several members of the Mosul military units that attempted to overthrow Qasim during December 1959, including one of the two pilots who had flown their aircraft from Mosul to bomb Baghdad, were also executed. With the exception of these executions, Qasim was relatively lenient. His coconspirator and nemesis, ʿAbd al-Salam ʿArif, was neither imprisoned nor executed despite having been implicated in a plot to overthrow and even assassinate Qasim. Instead, he was sent abroad in November 1959 as ambassador to West Germany. When the ICP called for politicians associated with the monarchy—and even opponents of the monarchy such as Kamil al-Chadirji—to be executed, Qasim had them arrested and announced that dire fates awaited them, only to release them once public passions had calmed. As Fadil al-Jamali noted, these arrests were often protective rather than punitive.[21]

Fourth, the Qasim era was characterized by great cultural output despite efforts to censor the press, including the closure of the ICP's newspaper, *Ittihad al-Shaʿb*, in 1961. Poets, essayists, short story writers, and playwrights produced an enormous outpouring of innovative writing. Important advances were made in the plastic arts, including great sculpture such as Jawad Salim's *Nusb al-Hurriya* (Freedom Monument) in central Baghdad's Liberation Square.[22]

Finally, and most important, Qasim was the only twentieth-century Iraqi

FIGURE 4. Jawad Salim, detail of the Freedom Monument. *International Magazine of Arab Culture* (April 1985): 12. Ministry of Culture and Information, Republic of Iraq.

leader to seriously combat sectarianism in public life. For the first time, excluded groups such as the Shi'a, Kurds, women, and other minorities finally found themselves represented in government in a significant fashion. Even though the lower echelons of the bureaucracy and police largely remained in the hands of those who had served under the monarchy, the appointment of Shi'is and Kurds to important government posts provided the first hope for heretofore excluded groups that meaningful political participation would become available to them. The new attitude toward minorities seemed especially promising for the Kurds. The provisional constitution formulated immediately after the revolution stated that Arabs and Kurds were "partners" *(shuraka')* within the Iraqi nation-state. The Kurdish leader Mulla Mustafa al-Barzani was invited to return from exile in the Soviet Union, as were other Kurdish dissidents living abroad. Kurds responded by sending numerous telegrams welcoming the success of the revolution.[23]

Why, with these positive developments, was Qasim not a more effective ruler? In answering this question the problematic aspects of his personality cannot be ignored, even if they have been over emphasized in explaining the July 1958 Revolution. First, Qasim did not have an extensive background in party politics. He was a latecomer to the Free Officers Organization, which he may not have joined until 1956.[24] In Iraq as in other non-Western countries, being a highly respected military commander did not necessarily translate into becoming an effective political leader. Despite his sophisticated juggling act while prime minister, Qasim never acquired a sophisticated understanding of the machinery of state. Second, Qasim, like most of his fellow military conspirators, lacked a well-defined ideology with which to guide the actions of the state. Although the state promoted efforts to mobilize the populace behind populist policies and a attempted to propagate a general anti-imperialist message, these efforts seem less to have reflected Qasim's views than those of the leftists and communists who predominated in the Ministry of Guidance and the state radio and television. Third, Qasim never institutionalized his power in any systematic fashion. Instead, he tried to balance one political bloc against another. When ʿArif tried to mobilize Pan-Arabist sentiment against Qasim during the fall of 1958, the new Iraqi leader promoted the ICP. This became even more evident after the abortive Pan-Arabist uprising in Mosul in March 1959 led by ʿAbd al-Wahhab al-Shawwaf. When the communists became too powerful after 1959 and appeared to be challenging his rule, Qasim turned to the right, allowing groups hostile to the ICP, including Pan-Arabists, to attack party members. When he finally allowed political parties to organize in 1961, Qasim created a competing communist party under Daʾud Sayigh, which further undermined the ICP's traditional social base.

Because the two events highlight the shortcomings of paradigms that focus on the role of the revolutionary leader, it is instructive to compare the political trajectory of the 1952 Egyptian Revolution under al-Nasir with that of the July 1958 Revolution under Qasim. Unlike al-Nasir, Qasim did not move to institutionalize his leadership. Qasim never proposed a mass-based political party, such as the Liberation Rally that al-Nasir formed in 1954, or the subsequent National Union (1956) and Arab Socialist Union (1961). Instead, Qasim consistently argued that he was above the political fray ("above all tendencies," according to his formulation). Certainly the adulation heaped on him by the ICP ("maku zaʿim ila Karim," "there is no leader except ʿAbd al-Karim") and the genuine affection for him by the people gave him a false sense of security. Nevertheless, whereas al-Nasir steadily took greater control over society during the 1950s and then over the economy during the 1960s, Qasim relied on a small circle of advisors and became increasingly isolated from society at large.

On the one hand, it may be argued that al-Nasir was simply shrewder than Qasim. On the other hand, the juxtaposition of the two leaders points to the very different structural constraints faced by each. Although Qasim never had to experience an invasion such as the one that Egypt faced in

1956, al-Nasir represented an ethnically homogenous rural middle class that gave the July 1952 Revolution a relatively unified social base that extended far beyond the military.[25] Qasim, on the other hand, could never rely upon any type of unified social base, whether ethnic or ideological. Although the Iraqi Free Officers came from the same rural and relatively humble social origins as their compatriots in Egypt, ethnicity, regionalism, and tribal identities crosscut any homogeneity based on social class. In other words, the Iraqi Free Officers were never able to develop the social cohesion that bound together the Egyptian Free Officers. Undoubtedly Qasim feared forming a mass-based party in accordance with the Egyptian model because such a party would have been torn by the Pan-Arab–Iraqist nationalist cleavage, and because it would have been subject to attempts by the ICP to dominate it.

Perhaps the only opportunity for Qasim to institutionalize his rule occurred during a brief window after the revolution, when 'Arif and he were able to exclude the original Free Officers group from power and establish ties with the civilian oppositional leadership under the monarchy, specifically the parties that had united in the United National Front of 1957, such as the National Democratic and Independence parties and, sub rosa, the ICP and the emerging Ba'th Party. In reaching out to respected nationalists, Qasim initially pursued a much more democratic and participatory approach than had al-Nasir, who had nothing but scorn for Egypt's prerevolution politicians. Had Qasim sustained this approach and developed his regime on a base of the respected oppositional leaders who joined his first cabinet—such as Muhammad Mahdi al-Kubba, Sadiq Shanshal, Muhammad Hadid, Fa'iq al-Sammara'i and others—perhaps a workable coalition could have been formed.[26] However, once 'Arif had been removed from the political scene in November 1958, Qasim apparently felt strong enough to dispense with civilian support. Rather than publicly air the issues surrounding the definition of political community and redressing ethnic as well as class differences, even if only in a tentative and preliminary manner, Qasim chose the route taken by prior Iraqi rulers, namely the suppression of the opposition.

An analysis of Qasim's rule does not demonstrate the validity of focusing on his leadership qualities, but rather indicates the importance of structural constraints. First, Qasim inherited a state that lacked functioning political institutions. Second, existing ethnic tensions were obviously beyond Qasim's (or anyone else's) ability to solve.[27] Further, these tensions were highly correlated with power and social class differentials. For example, the higher echelons of the army continued to be dominated by Sunni Arab officers who did not want Shi'i and Kurdish officers acquiring any significant power in the officer corps. Indeed, this issue had already flared up during Bakr Sidqi's regime in 1936–37. Third, ideological tensions continued to intensify as Pan-Arabists accused communists and those they referred to as al-Shu'ubiyun (a reference to the Arabized Persian members of the 'Abbasid bureaucracy who supposedly worked to bring about the empire's collapse from within) of undermining the July 1958 Revolution's true mission of Arab unity. The radical Pan-Arabists' refusal to allow communists, Shi'is, and minorities any meaningful political participation constituted a major impediment to any working coalition within the new revolutionary regime. All of these matters represented structural constraints that transcended the ability of any one leader to solve.

Another shortcoming of focusing exclusively on Qasim and the debates that swirled around him is that it limits the analysis to both personalities and elites, for example Qasim versus 'Arif, or communists versus Ba'thists. The problem with this approach is that it fails to capture much of the political activity that was transpiring beyond elite circles. A focus on Qasim, shared even by a work such as Hanna Batatu's *The Old Social Classes,* which emphasizes social structure, yields an understanding that state and civil society during the 1958–63 period was lacking in institutional development. In terms of political parties, the judiciary, and political decision-making at the highest levels of government, this perception is correct. However, in other areas of the state, significant institutional development was taking place. Perhaps most important, such an approach fails to encourage the study of *why,* as an ideology, local Iraqist nationalism was so vulnerable during the early 1960s as compared to the much stronger Pan-Arabist movement.

In light of the ideological vacuum following the monarchy's fall and the aggressive attacks by Pan-Arabists, it was understandable why the Qasim regime initiated the first systematic efforts by the state to structure historical memory by documenting Iraqi culture, especially Iraqi folklore, in a methodical fashion.[28] Institutionally, perhaps the most significant change occurred at the level of intellectual production, which represented an extension and continuation of the postwar innovations and creativity discussed in chapter 4. Using sectors of the state apparatus such as the newly created Ministry of Guidance—formerly known as the Ministry of Information (Wizarat al-Anba')[29]—and the Directorate-General of Folklore, the Qasim regime began to systematically document Iraqi culture. The ministry was active in documenting folklore throughout the country, organizing the screening of films in rural areas, and in establishing regional libraries and museums. The ministry's activities were documented in the annual publication of the Committee for the Celebration of the July 14th Revolution (Lajnat Ihtifalat Thawrat 14 Tammuz).[30]

The Qasim regime's attempts to control historical memory are significant not only because it was the first regime to systematically engage in this activity, but also because it established a model that the Baʿth Party later adopted. The difference between the two, of course, was that whereas the Qasim regime sought to use culture and historical memory to overcome ethnic cleavages, the Baʿth Party used it to disguise and even promote ethnic differentials in access to political power and wealth. Thus the initiation of the restructuring of historical memory usually attributed to Saddam and the Baʿth really belongs to Qasim.

The monarchy had taken tentative steps to influence how the Iraqi populace viewed the state and its relationship to the past. Recognizing the British role in assuring his victory in the August 1921 Referendum, the hostility he faced from sectors of the Sunni elite who had aspired to control of the new state, his lack of support among the Shiʿa and the Kurds, and the general lack of enthusiasm for the monarchy among Iraqi nationalists, Faysal I attempted to draw attention to the Hashimites' links to the Meccan Quraysh tribe and hence to the family of the Prophet himself. Through creating new museums and renovating important historical monuments such as the Khan Murjan market, Faysal hoped to convince his new subjects that they shared not just a common heritage but also a common future. In the case of the Museum of Costumes, Faysal clearly sought to link Iraqi tribal identity to Hijazi tribal identity by pointing to the commonalities in their respective cultures.[31] Of course, throughout the 1920s Faysal's director-general of education, Khaldun Satiʿ al-Husari, continued to vigorously promote the idea of Pan-Arabism and its attendant historical memory in the curriculum of the public education system. Faysal developed ties to prominent poets such as Maʿruf al-Rusafi and Muhammad Mahdi al-Jawahiri.[32]

Faysal's attempt to structure Iraqi historical memory in ways that would create favorable opinions of the Hashimites in part reflected his family's recent involvement in internal Iraqi politics. It was also a response to nationalist concerns, on the increase during the 1920s, that the British controlled the state. Following Faysal's death in 1933, efforts to structure historical memory took a different form. First, Faysal's son, Ghazi I, attempted to mobilize popular support for the monarchy by championing the Palestinian cause, arguing that Kuwait should be part of Iraq and implicitly criticizing Great Britain's policies and presence in the Middle East. Many Iraqis today argue that Ghazi's death in an automobile accident in April 1939 was actually engineered by the British, who feared his increasingly anti-British rhetoric. Second, the nationalist movement expanded in scope and size as Pan-Arabist forces established an important forum through the al-Muthanna Club and its affiliated youth movements, the Ahali Group expanded its influence by joining the Sidqi-Sulayman cabinet in 1936, and various groups of Marxists came together to form the Iraqi Communist Party in 1934. Third, the army became more politicized and, after Bakr Sidqi's assassination, more active in the Pan-Arabist cause.

Nevertheless, despite Ghazi's efforts to more closely tie Iraq's identity to Pan-Arab affairs through his active involvement in the Palestinian cause, he was too preoccupied with political instability and British alarm over his criticisms of their Palestine policy to devote much time to expanding his father's efforts to mobilize historical memory on behalf of the Hashimite state. Following Ghazi's death the regent, Prince ʿAbd Il-Ilah, soon became identified with British interests after British forces restored him to power following the abortive May 1941 movement. The blatant efforts of the British to assure ʿAbd Il-Ilah's hold on power and the subsequent purging of the army of Pan-Arabists rendered ineffective any efforts by him to manipulate historical memory in ways favorable to the monarchical state. It is true that just prior to and following World War II, short texts extolling the virtues of the Hashimite state began to appear under the supervision of a newly created Directorate of Propaganda. However, these volumes were published in English in the United States, indicating that their audience was not Iraqis but rather Western elites, particularly Americans, who were perceived to be able to positively affect Iraqi interests abroad.[33]

Unlike the monarchical state, which did not organize its own organic intellectuals, the Qasim regime encouraged intellectuals, many of whom were leftists and even communists, to actively promote the revolution. In addition to encouraging the publishing of its ideas in the mass media, the state also attempted to strengthen sympathetic intellectual organizations. One such organization was the Iraqi Writers Union (Ittihad al-Udabaʾ al-ʿIraqiyin), which adopted as its motto "Literature in the service of the People and the Republic." The organization noted in the beginning of proceedings of its second conference, in 1960, that its two goals were "supporting the Republic and its foundations in all areas, especially the intellectual realm," and "developing the national literary heritage for the Iraqi people, [including] Arab, Kurdish, and all minority groups." The more comprehensive list of organizational goals listed later in the proceedings makes clear that the Union's main purpose was to defend the nascent revolution as stated in its first clause and to fight against "imperialist organizations," as stated in clause 6.[34]

It is significant that the Iraqi Writers Union, beyond its obvious commitment to defending the Qasim regime and promoting its interests, clearly sought to use literature to overcome sectarian differences and to play an important educational function in Iraqi society. In light of the extensive and diverse intellectual production that characterized the Qasim years, which included literature, film, theater, television, folklore, and the arts, the state was not able to control all this output. This production created genres of cultural production, for example, the extensive literature on folklore, that transcended the 1958 to 1963 period because they could not be erased by the violence that characterized the first Baʿthist regime that overthrew Qasim. For example, in the television and film industries, which had become dominated by communists and leftists, the same individuals who had worked under Qasim continued to occupy their positions under subsequent governments simply because there were no trained personnel to replace them.[35]

The importance of television is indicated by the prominent role it plays in the various volumes published by the Committee for the Celebration of the July 14th Revolution. Except for the first year, each annual produced by the committee was divided by ministry, with the Ministry of Defense appearing at the beginning of the text, indicating the army's central role in the state. The section on the Ministry of Guidance always begins with a discussion of advances in the communications sector, particularly television. Clearly, then, television had become a medium upon which the revolutionary regime relied heavily in its attempts to mobilize support. An obvious consequence of this new strategy was the increased significance of visual imagery in the process of ideological socialization. Through the broadcast of parades, Qasim's speeches, and other state-sponsored events, television also served the symbolic function of a substitute for the lack of participatory political institutions.

Early television broadcasts, which began in 1955, were confined to Baghdad and seen only by wealthy families. Programs catered to the interests and tastes of the upper class and were imported almost exclusively from the United States and Great Britain. Prior to July 1958, television had little or no relation to politics. As one observer notes, the monarchy's resort to sectarianism as a vehicle for political control limited "the effectiveness of the mass media for improving the political and social conditions of the people."[36] However, even during the pre-1958 period, television broadcasts carried political overtones. One regular program aired by the monarchy

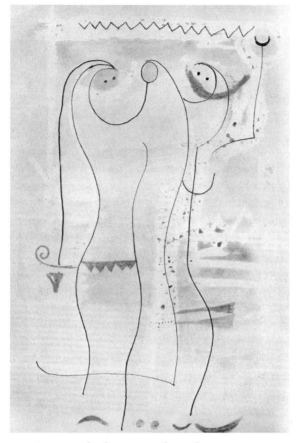

FIGURE 5. Jawad Salim, watercolor with wax crayon,
1953. *International Magazine of Arab Culture* (April
1985): 16. Ministry of Culture and Information, Republic
of Iraq.

presented films of King Faysal II attending the inauguration of important
public works projects such as the Wadi al-Tharthar irrigation project.[37] In
1956, a television broadcast of a play at a Baghdad theater at which King
Faysal and Crown Prince ʿAbd al-Ilah were present was abruptly interrupted when negative comments about the monarchy were made.[38] More
significantly for its impact on the middle and lower classes, televisions
began to appear in Baghdad coffeehouses. This was especially important to
illiterate and poorer customers, who could neither read daily newspapers
nor afford their own televisions.

Economic factors also influenced the Qasim regime's decision to use television as a means of reaching the Iraqi populace and transmitting the revolution's message. An economic factor that would become even more significant after the 1968 Ba'thist coup was the rise in oil prices during the late 1950s and early 1960s. Not only did the Qasim regime have more funds at its disposal, but more Iraqis were able to afford televisions. While Iraqi state television continued to follow its traditional mode of broadcasting, it also began to add programs that reflected its own ideological bent. Because communists were so central to the broadcasting industry, programming adopted a leftist slant.[39]

In addition to adding more transmitters and introducing new programming with political content, Iraqi State Television's most important activity was to broadcast the trials of members of the monarchical regime and subsequently the trials of 'Abd al-Salam 'Arif, the al-Shawwaf conspirators who attempted Mosul putsch in March 1959, and the Ba'thists who attempted to assassinate Qasim in Baghdad in December 1959. The first revolutionary court, which was established by Republican decree on July 21 to try the elite of the old regime, was designated a military court and headed by Qasim's cousin, Colonel Fadil 'Abbas al-Mahdawi, who served as chief judge. The legal status of the court was highly problematic. To begin, defendants were tried after the fact because the laws used to prosecute them were passed only after the purported offenses had been committed. Mahdawi himself had no legal training. Only one of the five associate judges, a member of the military engineering corps, had attended law school. The decree establishing the court was issued in a haphazard manner.[40] One observer noted that the trials circumvented the Ministry of Justice, which probably had little or no input in their proceedings.[41]

Although the trials of former supporters of the monarchy such as Fadil al-Jamali were initially conducted in a dignified manner, the court assumed an increasingly political character as tensions between Qasim and Pan-Arabists intensified. The early proceedings were replaced by what was by all accounts a circuslike atmosphere. Mahdawi frequently interrupted trial proceedings to mock defendants or to recite poetry, often composed by himself.[42] Broadcast live on Iraqi television between August 1958 and December 1959, the trials were initially seen in a positive light. However, it soon became clear that many Iraqis felt uneasy that the proceedings had little or no relationship to due process. Although political trials had been a staple of the monarchical system, Iraq had many excellent lawyers who had argued cases with great finesse. With the exception of the public hangings of Fahd and his comrades in 1949, the prerevolution legal system had avoided spectacle.

Gradually, the trials were transformed from an indictment of the monarchy through the trial of its main supporters to a competition between Iraqist nationalists and Pan-Arabists as Iraq's relationship to Jamal ʿAbd al-Nasir and the Pan-Arabist movement was increasingly put on trial through the appearance of Pan-Arabist defendants and their lawyers.

Significantly, the trials were interpreted differently according to the ideological leanings of the observer. Thus a leftist Iraqi expatriate intellectual has interpreted the trials as an important blow to reactionary forces in Iraq that was welcomed by the masses who observed the trial proceedings in Iraqi coffeehouses, while another intellectual, whose feelings were clearly Pan-Arabist, argues that the show trial and circuslike atmosphere helped turn the Iraqi viewing audience against the Qasim regime.[43] It is impossible to determine the trials' precise impact. Undoubtedly, the lower classes and communists were more supportive of the trials than were the middle and upper classes. Certainly the social and political cleavages changed as the trials shifted from *ancien régime* politicians to Qasim's opponents, who were from the same social background as the revolution's leader and his supporters, that is, the middle and lower middle classes. It was more jarring to see the "people" *(al-shaʿb)* being tried than the upper classes *(al-ahd al-baʾid)* of the *ancien régime*. In other words, as the social backgrounds of the defendants came to more closely resemble that of the viewing audience, and as Pan-Arabist defendants argued that their only crime was agitating for Arab unity, many viewers came to perceive the trials in much more ambiguous terms. Many defendants, such as the female poet Yusra Saʿid Thabit, mounted eloquent defenses, and the tables were sometimes turned on the People's Court, which became a forum, if only for brief interludes, for propagating Pan-Arabist thought.[44] Undoubtedly, those Iraqis who were sympathetic to efforts to unite Iraq with Egypt saw the trials as an effort to persecute Iraq's "true" revolutionaries and patriots.

Apart from the legitimate need to protect the state from counterrevolutionary forces, the courts were designed to settle accounts with the old elites and to intimidate dissenters rather than to serve as properly functioning legal institutions. In its haste to punish the "traitors" of the old regime, the new regime inadvertently created conditions that were even more dangerous to an emerging concept of civil society than conditions under the monarchy. Law 7 of 1958, which appeared in the official state gazette, *al-Waqaʾiʿ al-ʿIraqiya*, on August 8, was so broadly cast that almost anything the state choose to perceive as a "conspiracy" *(al-taʾamur)* could be so defined. In this sense it differed little from the laws passed under the monarchy. However, trials under the old regime had been held *in camera*, whereas the People's Court (or Mahdawi Court, as it came to be popularly known) consciously transformed itself into a spectacle intended to titillate the audience beyond the courtroom in an effort to both mobilize support and send a message that humiliation and defeat awaited those who challenged the new regime. In effect, Qasim opened the door to almost anyone becoming subject to accusations and trials. The use of spectacle to both mobilize the populace (for example, through poetry, often expressed in the colloquial vernacular, and *hawsat*, or rallying chants)[45] and intimidate people (seen in the treatment of defendants) was not lost on the emerging Baʿthists such as Saddam Husayn and Ahmad Hasan al-Bakr, who would also resort to spectacle in a much more vicious form through the public hanging of hapless Zionist "spies" in 1969.

At the same time, Pan-Arabist organizations appeared that challenged those who sought to defend Qasim's regime. Such organizations and their publications were in fact promoted by Qasim, who loosened constraints on Pan-Arabist activity in May 1959 after the apex of communist influence during the two "red months" of March and April 1959. One Pan-Arabist group was the Organization of Iraqi Authors and Writers (Jamʿiyat al-Muʾallifin wa-l-Kuttab al-ʿIraqiyin), which was formed to oppose the Iraqi Writers Union. Comparing the organizations' publications, the leftist Iraqi Writers' Union, headed by the famous poet Muhammad Mahdi al-Jawahiri, was clearly much more tolerant than the Society of Iraqi Authors and Writers, which promoted sectarianism through its attacks on the contemporary al-Shuʿubiyun, whom it associated with communists and the Qasim regime.[46] Pan-Arabist intellectuals opposed to Qasim used communism as a vehicle to attack him and his leftist supporters by linking this concept to a much broader framework that juxtaposed cultural authenticity to Otherness. Already during the 1950s, Syrian opponents of indigenous communists had begun to dub the Syrian communists *"shuʿubiyun."*[47] The inherent intolerance of this approach was evident from its stance that leftists who placed internal social reform before Pan-Arab unity on the political agenda were not loyal members of the political community. Pan-Arabists resurrected historical debates about the al-Shuʿubiya movement during the Umayyad and ʿAbbasid empires to equate communist activities with those of the earlier non-Arab Shuʿubiyun, both of whom were accused of intentionally fragmenting the political community, thereby preventing it from accomplishing its historical mission. In other words, the term *shuʿubi* became a synonym for communist, particularly a Shiʿi communist or one from a minority group. Like the al-Shuʿubiyun during the Umayyad and ʿAbbasid empires, communists were considered treacherous and disloyal.

On the surface, they appeared to be Arabs—or Arabized, if they were drawn from minorities, such as the Kurds—and committed to the good of Arab society by promoting social reforms. In their heart of hearts, however, their main goal was to deliver Arab society to the enemy. If the Shu'ubiyun in Iraq under the 'Abbasids sought to impose Persian culture on the Arabs, communists sought to place Iraq politically and culturally in the Soviet orbit.

Explaining the hatred of Qasim that developed requires a return to the theme of social and political fragmentation. The collapse of the agrarian sector and the resulting growth of urban centers, the fragmentation of society into rival political camps pitting nationalists against communists, the loss of Palestine to the Zionists who were viewed as the agents of Western colonialism, the army's humiliation in 1941 and in Palestine were all traced back to a larger conspiracy to prevent the Arabs from developing strength through unity. Employing a twisted logic, Sati' al-Husari argues that the communists were never strong in Iraq. Their purported strength was a result of, first, British efforts to build them up as a counterweight to the Pan-Arabists following the unsuccessful 1941 uprising and, second, the monarchy referring to all social protest and disturbances as "communist" in origin, thereby creating the illusion of communist strength. In al-Husari's work, monarchists, communists, the British, Zionists, and the Russians are all conflated, considered part of a single conspiracy to prevent Iraq from achieving its rightful place in the Pan-Arab fold. Communism is therefore "unnatural" in Iraq and "part of the oppressive legacy *(al-tarika al-thaqila)* which we inherited from the *ancien régime.*"[48]

Perhaps al-Husari's greatest insight was his argument that the struggle in Iraq between Pan-Arab nationalists and communists would determine the fate of the Arab nationalist movement in its entirety.[49] Indeed he refers to it as a "life-and-death struggle." Here another critical dimension of the communist-Ba'thist conflict can be understood in terms of the struggle of both groups over what was largely the same social base.[50] Even if the ICP sought to mobilize workers and peasants, party members were largely drawn from the lower-middle and middle classes. Ba'thist ferocity toward Iraqi communists and their supporters in 1963 reflected a deep-seated fear of the communist message's ability to mobilize the populace through advocating a political community that encompassed all "progressive forces," no matter what their ethnic background. Even a cursory survey of the ICP's main organ, *Ittihad al-Sha'b,* indicates that hundreds of labor unions, professional syndicates, and student organizations openly organized after July 1958. Almost all placed demands on the state, petitioning individual ministries, local municipalities (especially Baghdad), and Qasim himself for higher wages, better working conditions, and the curtailment or elimination of "the agents of imperialism," that is, the monarchy's supporters.[51]

As the struggle between Iraqist nationalism and Pan-Arabism intensified during the early 1960s, two small volumes published in 1962 highlight the role of historical memory in efforts to both undermine and enhance state power. One of these studies, *al-Judhur al-Tarikhiya li-l-Shu'ubiya [The Historical Roots of the Shu'ubiya Movement]*, written by the prominent Iraqi historian and Baghdad University professor 'Abd al-'Aziz al-Duri, represented a thinly veiled critique of the Qasim regime's Iraqist nationalist orientation.[52] Although the book ostensibly focuses on the decline of the 'Abbasid Empire and never mentions the Qasim regime directly, the tone and style of the volume and al-Duri's conservative and Pan-Arab orientation clearly indicate its political character, especially considering the year in which the volume was written, 1962. The year of its publication coincided with Qasim's increasing isolation from and disaffection with his regime. With quotations from popular 'Abbasid intellectuals such as al-Jahiz and al-Masu'di, and its publication as an inexpensive paperback edition, this work with 98 pages of text was polemical rather than scholarly. The commentary on its rear cover, stating that "this enemy," that is, the Shu'ubiya movement, represented "a literary, cultural, historical *[turathi]*, ethnic, linguistic, and religious attack" on (Sunni) Arab society that appears in different forms throughout history, both underlines al-Duri's arguments that the threat of the al-Shu'ubiyun is ever-present and links the author's historical analysis to the contemporary era. The fact that there was an eighteen-year hiatus between the initial publication and the second and third printings of the volume (1980 and 1981, respectively) points to the "remobilization" of the volume following the Islamic Revolution of 1978–79 in neighboring Iran and the efforts of the Ba'thist regime to amplify the threat that the revolution presented to Iraq and the larger Arab world. The rear cover note by the publisher, Dar al-Tali'a, claiming that this "comprehensive, scientific study" is presented to the "sons of Arabism *[abna' al-'uruba]* in every region *[qutr]*" of the Arab nation, further underlines the volume's Pan-Arabist orientation.

In stating his intention to avoid analyzing the direct attacks by Persian forces that resulted in the creation of small kingdoms within the 'Abbasid Empire at various points in time, al-Duri underlines that the danger to the Arab community under the 'Abbasids was less external than internal. Rather, al-Duri feels that the al-Shu'ubiya movement's cultural and religious influences were most effective and pernicious in functioning as a "fifth column" to undermine the empire's Arab character and unity. A lack of understanding and attention to internal subversion resulted in the ʿAbbasid Empire's collapse, with the corollary lesson that the same fate awaits modern Arab society unless it develops greater vigilance in counteracting the efforts of those who seek to erode its political, social, and cultural unity.

A key component of al-Duri's approach is an emphasis on conspiracy, which was to assume an omnipresent role in Iraqi political discourse once the Baʿth Party took power in 1968. Of course, such an approach is difficult to disprove precisely because it argues for subterfuges, hidden motives, and processes that are never made explicit by those with malicious intentions.

In asserting that the Persian intelligentsia (al-ʿAjam) sought to revive a pre-Islamic culture *(al-thaqafa al-qadima)* to erode Arabism and Islam, al-Duri's Arabs of Persian heritage, who were purported to be disloyal, tarnishes, in the modern context, the Iraqi Shiʿa who are often identified with their Persian coreligionists in the minds of Iraq's Sunni Arab minority. Politically, al-Duri's approach set the stage for questioning the loyalty of Iraqi citizens based strictly on a state of mind, namely their adherence to a purported historical memory that rejects Arabism.

Placing conspiracy at the center of the explanation of the ʿAbbasid Empire's decline presents critical empirical and methodological problems. It has been effectively argued that there is no evidence that the Arabized Persian members of the ʿAbbasid bureaucracy bore Arab culture any ill will, or that there were efforts made to undermine the empire politically. al-Duri's arguments are less about facts and historiography than about mythologizing the past for political ends. His work serves to reinforce the idea of Arab culture as permanently under siege and the need for Arabs to remain vigilant in relation to the Other, whether Arabs of Persian ethnic origins, Shiʿis, Kurds, Christians, or other minorities. Interestingly, ʿAbd al-Salam ʿArif, Qasim's co-conspirator and, following the revolution, his main rival, stated in July 1958 that the three groups that threatened the revolution were the "Kurds, Shiʿa, and Christians." ʿArif's comments, which underlined his distrust of Iraq's non–Sunni Arab communities, reflected the continuation of the tradition of his fellow colonel, Salah al-Din al-Sabbagh, who sought to differentiate authentic *(asil)* members of the Iraqi political community from those who were not.[53] al-Duri's approach, which promoted the view that non-Sunnis and non-Arabs were of questionable loyalty and harbored malicious intentions toward Sunni Arab culture, helps explain the insular quality of much Iraqi Baʿthist culture. Why would Sunni Arabs, the main supporters of the Baʿth Party, want to borrow culturally from groups that were purportedly hostile toward them? This type of siege mentality also explains, in part, the predisposition of Iraqi rulers to resort to authoritarian rule, which presumably provides the best defense against the alleged subversive threat. If this hypothesis is correct, then the Qasim regime's de-emphasis of sectarianism and its policy of more equitably distributing government posts among Iraq's multiethnic population constituted a great threat to the type of historical memory and identity politics stressed by al-Duri and Sunni sectarians. The persistence of a regime in which sectarianism was not the dominant norm, or at least was much less pronounced in comparison to prior regimes, provided a "demonstration effect" that could not be allowed to persist.[54]

al-Duri's polemic was intended to undermine Qasim's legitimacy by equating his regime with foreigners whom he asserts are culturally alien and maintain no loyalty to Pan-Arabism and Iraq. If doubts could be cast on the "real intentions" of Qasim's government, then citizens might begin to question whether he deserved their support. Because the al-Shuʿubiya controversy ultimately led to disorder and chaos as a result of the ʿAbbasid Empire's collapse, an important subtext of al-Duri's arguments is that Qasim's support of Iraqist nationalism would likewise lead to social turmoil. Of course, this argument became a self-fulfilling prophecy. It would reappear on a number of future occasions, such as in a series of articles in *al-Thawra* that Saddam published in April 1991 criticizing those who were involved in the March–April Intifada.

Dhu al-Nun Ayyub's *Li-l-Haqiqa wa-l-Tarikh: Jumhuriyat 14 Tammuz fi-l-ʿIraq wa Mufajjir Thawratiha Ibn al-Shaʿb al-Barr al-Zaʿim ʿAbd al-Karim Qasim [In Support of Reason and History: The July 14 Republic and the Creator of its Revolution, the Devoted Son of the People, the Leader ʿAbd al-Karim Qasim]* appeared at about the same time as al-Duri's volume.[55] This equally small book represented a vigorous defense of the July 1958 Revolution and, in particular, of Qasim's leadership by arguing that the revolutionary government had made considerable efforts to advance the well-being of the Iraqi populace through land reform, expansion of education, urban renewal, and promulgating laws to insure women's rights. Ayyub, Qasim's director-general of the Ministry of Guidance, was keen, in particular, to counter accusations that the revolution was not sensitive to Pan-Arabist concerns. He argues again and again that the main issue with which all Iraqis should be concerned was Western imperialism, which was behind efforts to undermine the revolution and ʿAbd al-Karim Qasim, an argument that, in retrospect, seems to have had merit.[56]

Ayyub's historical periodization differs markedly from that of al-Duri, reflecting the contending conceptual approaches that each author adopts toward Iraqi historical memory. Whereas history "begins" for al-Duri with the rise of Islam and especially the establishment of the ʿAbbasid Empire in Iraq, for Ayyub Iraqi history extends back "tens of centuries" (ʿasharat al-qarun) to the ancient Mesopotamian civilizations. Although Ayyub emphatically affirms Iraq's Arab and Islamic character, he also argues that Iraq is unique among Arab nations because of its civilizational heritage. Thus an asymmetry is introduced into the historical equation by Ayyub, who defines at least two Iraqi cultures, one that emerges from its own unique pre-Semitic historical experience in the Fertile Crescent, and another that links it to the Arab world. No such asymmetry exists for al-Duri, who simply ignores Iraq's pre-Islamic past and conflates Iraqis and Arabs by defining them all through the expansion of Islam.

A careful reading of Ayyub reveals his emphasis on Iraq's agrarian heritage and the extent to which Iraq's ancient civilizations were built through the efforts of the peasantry. Mesopotamian society's complex history created distinctive cultural practices and norms that make Iraq differ from other Arab societies. Here Ayyub is clearly trying to develop the intellectual foundations for the Qasim regime's policy that called for "federation, not unity" among Arab states. As Qasim consistently argued, it was necessary to recognize and support Arab brotherhood but also to respect the different characteristics and hence different internal problems that each Arab state faced.[57] By foregrounding the peasantry, the author also incorporated a social class component that reflected Ayyub's underlying commitment to a Marxist interpretation of Iraqi society, even though he had left the ICP by the time this work was published. Stressing the peasantry's central historical role reflected the Qasim regime's concern with the less fortunate members of society, expressed most concretely in the government's efforts at land reform.

Ayyub's emphasis on the peasantry is important in another, less obvious way. Many associated Pan-Arabist ideology with tribal Arabs such as the Hashimites, who mobilized this particular type of historical memory to convince Iraqis that, even though they originated in the Hijaz, tribal factors and Islam united Hashimites and Iraqis. In stressing Iraqi society's historical agrarian nature and the peasant's central role in creating "the first human civilization" and the first society to produce recorded laws, Ayyub fails to culturally or intellectually valorize a historical memory based in tribalism and Arabism.

By grounding Iraqi historical memory in Mesopotamian rather than Arab or Islamic heritage, Ayyub provides the foundation for his argument that Iraqi society has always been comprised of many diverse ethnic groups

FIGURE 6. Fa'iq Hasan, *Celebration. International Magazine of Arab Culture* (April 1985): 13. Ministry of Culture and Information, Republic of Iraq.

that have contributed foundational ideas of legal systems and justice. Ayyub's focus on law and justice can also be seen as an oblique criticism of Qasim, whose regime had become very dictatorial by this point. Ayyub's argument that the rise of Islam created a society similar to contemporary society by giving the oppressed an ideological weapon to use against its oppressors represented an effort to appropriate a radical interpretation of Iraq's dominant religion. This differs from the understanding of Islam of al-Duri, who is not sympathetic to efforts to mobilize Islam for revolutionary ends, such as those of the Qaramita and the Zanj movements. Ayyub's historical interpretation, in which he asserts that Iraq's historical instability can be related to the unceasing efforts of the peasantry and other oppressed groups to achieve a just society, constitutes an effort both to divert attention from the Pan-Arabist attempt to appropriate the discourse of a romanticized and nostalgic view of the Golden Age of Arab-Islamic empires. Instead, Ayyub substitutes a "history from below" for a focus on elite politics, high culture, and viewing the Arab-Islamic empires as prototypes of modern nation-states. While extolling the ʿAbbasid Empire's prodigious cultural production, especially in literature, the author is keen to show that the empire was caught in a struggle between the populace at large and the Arabized Persian elite that sought to transform it into a Roman Empire, by which he meant a highly stratified and hierarchically organized political and social system. According to Ayyub, in contrast with al-Duri, the Shuʿubiyun had less to do with cultural issues than with imposing a social class system that created common, not different, interests that linked them to Arab political and military elites. Ayyub's narrative is one of the Iraqi people constantly struggling for social justice, whether in ancient Mesopotamia or under the Arab-Islamic empires, and thus reflects the general conception of Iraqi history held by leftist intellectuals during this time.

At the same time, Ayyub also criticized "leftist sectarianism" (al-tatarruf al-yasari). Here he was referring to the causalities caused by the ICP attacks on those who had supported the al-Shawwaf Revolt in Mosul in March 1959, and the subsequent deliberate provocation of the largely conservative Turkoman population in Kirkuk on Revolution Day, 1959, during which Kurds loyal to the Kurdish Democratic Party (KDP), which was aligned with the ICP, purposely fostered riots leading to many more killed and wounded.[58] Unlike many other leftists and communists, Ayyub condemned the ICP for sending its cadres into Kirkuk during a politically sensitive period.

The different historical memories propounded by al-Duri and Ayyub are not just the result of differences over whether Iraq conforms to an Arab model or it possesses unique characteristics among Arab states. Rather, these differences also have important implications for whether Iraqi culture can be reduced to a narrow Pan-Arab dimension or must be seen in pluralistic terms. Clearly Ayyub's broad historical tableau makes it difficult to conceptualize Iraq as having a monolithic culture, which is a prerequisite for Pan-Arab thought.[59] If any unitary themes emerge from his historical overview, they are the existence of proto-classes from the dawn of civilization until the present and the continuous revolutionary character of Iraqi society.

The implicit debate between al-Duri and Ayyub represented much more than a simple attempt to appropriate historical memory. Despite its highly logical and rational perspective, Ayyub's work is a good indicator of the struggle of Iraqist nationalism to sustain itself before the onslaught of Pan-

Arabism during the early 1960s. Certainly the author was aware of Qasim's declining political fortunes. The volume's highly defensive tone and attempts to defend the revolution against accusations that it was unconcerned with Pan-Arab affairs can be seen in the discussion of the regime's commitment to the Palestinians, his critique of "leftist sectarianism" *(al-tatarruf al-yasari)*, and his defense of Qasim's positions on Kuwait and the Kurds.[60] In contrast to al-Duri's self-confident tone and forceful arguments, Ayyub's arguments contain numerous qualifications. These qualifications divert the reader away from Ayyub's central theme of the threat that Western imperialism poses to the July 1958 Revolution and its leader, ʿAbd al-Karim Qasim. al-Duri's arguments, on the other hand, which are meant to question the loyalty and ethnic purity of all but the Arab (here meaning Sunni) portion of Iraqi society, never waver or concede anything to the sociopolitical and cultural forces they oppose.

ʿAbd al-ʿAziz al-Duri and Dhu al-Nun Ayyub represented organic intellectuals in the strict Gramscian understanding of the term. Both mobilized their analytic and polemical skills to convince the Iraqi populace during the early 1960s of the validity of their particular model of political community by invoking an ideological reading of Iraqi history. Ethnicity stands opposed to social class. The ethnic purity of Arabness in constant struggle with forces that subjugate it, on the one hand, competes with the proto–class struggle of the oppressed peasantry in ancient Mesopotamia and under the ʿAbbasid Empire, and the very real class struggle of workers and peasants against imperialism before and after the July 1958 Revolution, on the other. Two narratives compete to appropriate historical memory and cultural authenticity. Why was one able to triumph over the other?

To answer this question requires a prior question: Why were Pan-Arabists so hostile to ʿAbd al-Karim Qasim? The fact that his executioners left him lying in a pool of blood in a Baghdad television studio for the entire country to witness and, in a play on the ninety-nine names of God, gave him the appellation "Adu al-Karim," the enemy of God, rather than ʿAbd al-Karim, the servant of God, indicates the depth of the Pan-Arabists' hatred toward him. Yet the subsequent imprisonment, torture, and execution of what some have estimated to be as many as three thousand communists and leftist sympathizers indicate that Qasim was only a symbol of a larger target that those who overthrew him sought to destroy.

It is important to remember that only the communists had engaged in a thoroughgoing "war of position." As Satiʿ al-Husari bitterly remarked in his polemic against the communists and their role in the 1958 Revolution, the ICP attempted to impose its political program on Iraq and seize control of the revolution during its very first day in power. The Pan-Arabists, on the other hand, had relatively little to offer beyond the slogan of immediate unity *(al-wahda al-fawriya)* with Egypt. No systematic program had been developed to confront Iraq's internal problems, such as sectarianism and the abysmal poverty that characterized the peasantry, urban workers, and slum dwellers. Pan-Arabists found themselves ideologically overwhelmed by the much more sophisticated communist movement, which had been debating social issues for well over two decades and had developed coherent policies for dealing with them. The split between Qasim, ʿArif, and the Free Officers over creation of a Revolution Command Council, on the one hand, and ʿArif and Qasim's power struggle, on the other, politically fragmented the Pan-Arab forces in the first days of the revolution as they tried to face a much more cohesive communist movement.

At the same time, the Pan-Arabists, many of whom were either current or retired officers, were still recovering from the sectarianism of the 1936 Bakr Sidqi coup and the humiliations of 1941 and 1948 discussed earlier. Pan-Arabists' initial euphoria at the monarchy's overthrow quickly gave way to the realization that, once again, their hopes and expectations were not to be realized. This was an especially bitter situation given Iraqi Pan-Arabists' perception of real progress by their colleagues in Syria and in Egypt who had created the United Arab Republic. While the Arab world was headed toward greater unity, which many Pan-Arabists thought would magically solve all the Arab world's problems, Iraq was being diverted from that goal by ʿAbd al-Karim Qasim. Even worse, the Pan-Arabists found themselves faced with new political cleavages and social fragmentation, which they blamed on the communists rather than on the *ancien régime*'s supporters who no longer controlled political power. The ability of Pan-Arabists, and particularly army officers, to avenge the humiliations of the past was snatched away yet again.

It is this context of humiliation, defeat, social fragmentation, and denied hopes and expectations that explains the hostility directed toward Qasim. Yet beyond these issues was the fear of what Iraqist nationalism meant for the long-term power structure of Iraqi society. Clearly Pan-Arabists were fearful that the influence that the ICP and other Iraqist nationalists assumed in the new revolutionary government represented a zero-sum game in which minorities would use their newly acquired power to settle scores with the Sunni Arabs who had dominated the army and the state bureaucracy. Pan-Arabists, who were disproportionately Sunni, feared that they would be more vulnerable than prior to the revolution. The specter of the of Bakr Sidqi nightmare loomed once again, suggesting the possibility of political assassinations and Pan-Arabists being forced to take refuge outside the country.

In addition, Pan-Arabists feared internal subversion by the Soviet Union. Had not the Iraqi Communist Party turned from active opposition to the Zionist movement (evident in its creation of the League for the Struggle Against Zionism in 1946) to support for the United Nations Partition Resolution of November 1947 under pressure from the USSR? If the communists seized control of the revolution, either directly or indirectly, would not the Soviets become the real power in Iraq? Further, the large street demonstrations the ICP mobilized during 1958 and 1959, the many labor unions and professional syndicates that it controlled, the party's ability to create regional organizations such as the League for the Defense of the Peasantry, and the ability of its daily, *Ittihad al-Sha'b*, to dramatically surpass the circulation of any other Iraqi newspaper were indicators of the communist movement's strong and growing roots among the Iraqi populace. That Qasim's air force commander, Jalal al-ʿAwqati, was a known communist, as was his chief of intelligence, Taha al-Shaykh Ahmad, and that many junior officers were either members of or sympathetic to the party, further unnerved Pan-Arabists.

The events leading up to ʿAbd al-Karim Qasim's overthrow and execution during the so-called Ramadan Revolution of February 8 and 9, 1963, have been extensively discussed.[61] All observers agree that the attempted assassination of Qasim in October 1959 deeply affected him, leading him to withdraw from public life and inspiring his belief that he had been spared death by divine providence in order to lead the 1958 Iraqi Revolution. His ill-conceived efforts in 1961 to suppress Kurdish demands for autonomy and his increasing resort to the suppression of social freedoms in response to challenges to his regime undermined his regime's development plans. A drop in oil prices during the early 1960s further constrained the regime's ability to implement reform policies. Qasim's foolhardy response to Great Britain's 1961 decision to give Kuwait complete independence by declaring the Kuwaiti amir a *qaʾimqam* (governor) of the Basra provincial administration garnered little or no Arab or international support. Having declared Kuwait part of Iraq and mobilized troops on the Iraqi-Kuwaiti border, the regime's backing down in the subsequent confrontation with the British humiliated the regime and the military, creating further disaffection with Qasim.

However, it was the decision to respond to Kurdish demands with force that was undoubtedly Qasim's most disadvantageous choice. Although the army was able to hold tentatively certain cities in Kurdistan as well as to exploit intertribal rivalries, it balked at attacking the Kurdish irregular forces or *peshmerga* in their mountain strongholds, leading to a stalemate. As the conflict became more protracted, Mustafa Barzani's forces became susceptible to the idea of working with Ba'thists, both civilian and military, to overthrow Qasim. By stationing a large portion of the military in Kurdistan, Qasim placed military units in the north that might have intervened to rescue him in 1963. By the time of the coup, Qasim had isolated himself from virtually all his politically significant supporters. When the revolt came, it surprised no one.

What was the effect of the Qasim regime on the development of a nascent civil society in Iraq? Part of the answer can be obtained by comparing Qasim's regime with Bakr Sidqi's ten-month regime of 1936–37. Indeed, many Iraqis made precisely this comparison, especially when it became known after the July 1958 Revolution that Qasim was related to Sidqi's air force chief of staff, Muhammad 'Ali Jawad, who was assassinated with Sidqi in August 1937. Both regimes came to be characterized as Iraqist nationalist in orientation. In both 1936 and 1958, a military regime sought to bolster its legitimacy by incorporating reformist civilian elements drawn from the left. In both cases, civilian cabinet ministers became disillusioned, leading them to resign from and isolate the government. The leaders of both regimes were originally assumed to have been sympathetic to Pan-Arabism. In 1933, Bakr Sidqi was cheered in the streets of Baghdad after the Assyrian massacre because of the assumption that he and the Iraqi army had affirmed not only the unity of Iraq, but also its Sunni Arab character.[62] Qasim's courageous and skillful military activities in Palestine in 1948 were likewise viewed as having established his Pan-Arab credentials. Once in power, both regimes greatly disappointed Pan-Arabists. Each was characterized as hostile to Pan-Arabism, especially Bakr Sidqi, who looked to Reza Shah in Iran and especially Mustafa Kemal in Turkey as role models for Iraq's social and economic development. Qasim's relationship to his cousin, Muhammad 'Ali Jawad, linked these two regimes in yet another way because his bitterness over Jawad's assassination was held to be the cause of his purported hostility to Pan-Arabism.

Both leaders became more isolated as their regimes progressed and they became (at least superficially) more powerful and secure in their respective leadership roles. Neither tried to develop a strong civilian base as part of an effort to lay the roots for a nascent civil society. Both moved away from and indeed tried to suppress reformist and leftist supporters once they aroused hostility from more conservative elements in society. Sidqi's speeches attacking "communism" and Qasim's efforts to circumscribe the power of the

FIGURE 7. Fa'iq Hasan, *Portrait of a Kurdish Man.*
International Magazine of Arab Culture (April 1985): 13.
Ministry of Culture and Information, Republic of Iraq.

ICP beginning in 1960 both reflected efforts to appease conservative forces in Iraqi society.

Yet here the parallels end. Sidqi was a committed sectarian who self-consciously tried to promote Kurdish officers at the expense of Sunni Arabs, the traditional power base of the army. Unlike Qasim, who supported federated ties among Arab states and consistently expressed support for the Palestinians, Sidqi totally ignored Arab nationalist concerns. Sidqi was bloodthirsty, having achieved his fame through the brutal repression of tribal revolts in the Middle Euphrates earlier in the 1930s and his infamous suppression of the Assyrian community in north-central Iraq in 1933. Qasim sought to avoid bloodshed at all costs, never even executing the conspirators convicted of trying to assassinate him in October 1959. Sidqi was well known for his corruption and loose morals, while Qasim was known to live an ascetic life devoted almost exclusively to his work as head of state.

But what most significantly distinguishes Sidqi's 1936 coup d'état from the July 1958 Revolution is not the differences in the characters of the two leaders, but the different relationship of the state to the populace. The consistent challenges to state authority reflected in the 1948 Wathba, the 1952 Intifada, and the demonstration against the Baghdad Pact in 1956 did not exist during the 1930s. It was only after World War II that the Iraqi populace experienced rapid social and political mobilization.[63] Ja'far Abu Timman and the Ahali Group were completely at the mercy of Bakr Sidqi, having had no significant social base in 1936. Qasim, on the other hand, spent most of his regime trying to outmaneuver the communists and, toward the end, the Ba'thists and Nasirists to prevent them from challenging his rule. The more extensive mobilization of the populace in 1958 compared to 1936 helps us to understand both the fear and anger of the Pan-Arabist forces and the problems of focusing on elites or personalities when analyzing Iraqi political development. In 1937 Pan-Arabists were able to dispense with Bakr Sidqi with relative ease, due in large measure to the lack of any popular reaction to the assassination of Sidqi and the air force commander Muhammad 'Ali Jawad, Qasim's cousin. In 1963, after capturing Qasim, the Ba'thist conspirators hastened to execute him, fearing that the masses who had taken to the street to support their leader might try to free him from his captors.[64]

The extensive mobilization of the Iraqi populace, large numbers of which became officially organized in a myriad of organizations after the 1958 Revolution, confronted the state with an emerging civil society. Organizations such as labor unions, professional associations, and student groups demanded not only the right to be officially recognized by the state, but also the right to publish their own newspapers, to establish offices or clubs where members could meet, to hold demonstrations, and to have their views considered in the state's decision-making process.

The 1963 coup d'état that overthrew Qasim has been referred to by one observer as the most important event in modern Iraqi history.[65] In one sense this is correct. The revolution broke the back, at least temporarily, of the ICP, cut down many of Iraq's intellectuals, rolled back many of the social reforms made under the revolution (such as the personal status law giving equal rights to men and women), and restructured Iraqi politics along the sectarian lines that Qasim's policies had sought to ameliorate. The February 1963 coup also set the stage for some of the brutal strategies and policies enacted by the Takriti Ba'th after 1968 because it set in motion a state-sponsored violence on a scale that had heretofore never been seen.

However, the coup that overthrew Qasim should not be given excessive importance. Even its own proponents did not refer to it as a revolution but rather as an *intifada*, designed to place the July 1958 Revolution back on course.[66] Instead, the events of 1963 need to be seen as part of an ongoing process and as a struggle or dialectic between those who have viewed Iraq in culturally and politically monolithic terms and those who continue to fight for a multiethnic and pluralist nation-state. Contra the implications of the view that 1963 represented the culmination of twentieth-century Iraqi political history, Qasim's overthrow and its aftermath did not constitute an end to the struggle to define Iraqi political community.

What, then, was the legacy of the July 1958 Revolution? First, it demonstrated that a nonsectarian state could be formed in Iraq. Within the state apparatus, there was no discrimination by Qasim or other high-level officials against particular ethnic groups, even if the lower echelons continued to reflect patterns of recruitment from the monarchical era. Indeed, Qasim's regime made a conscious effort to increase the representation of groups that had heretofore been discriminated against and to downplay tribal and sectarian criteria in political recruitment. Even Qasim's half-hearted military campaign in Kurdistan that began in 1961 and lasted until the February 1963 coup did not reflect ethnic sensitivities but rather a power struggle between Qasim and Mustafa al-Barzani. Second, the Qasim era allowed much of the intellectual and political ferment of the late 1940s and 1950s to become institutionalized in a nascent civil society. Even if this civil society was constrained, especially after 1961, in the form of press restrictions, limitations on the right to form political parties, and the removal of communists from many nongovernmental associations, there was nevertheless a tremendous burst of associational activity, especially during the first two years of the revolution. The extensive proliferation of cultural, social, and political organizations gave many sectors of the populace their first taste of power. Even where constraints were imposed, it is noteworthy that the testimony of trials of newspaper editors accused of threatening state security was allowed to be published on a daily basis. Such activity would have been unthinkable under the monarchy, much less under Saddam and the Baʻth.[67] Much of this organizational power was destroyed after 1963 as the Baʻth Party sought to root out all communist-dominated groups and their leftist supporters. However, the suppression of these organizations by the Baʻth could not eliminate the historical memory of what was achieved between 1958 and 1963.

Third, the regime allowed an environment to develop in which considerable intellectual ferment took place. Perhaps the most significant aspect of this environment was that alternative views about Iraqi political community were allowed to be expressed publicly for the first time. Neither Pan-Arabists nor communists had to publish through front organizations or via the underground press. The fact that dialogue and debate could occur, even if it were highly contentious, created a legacy that Iraqi intellectuals began to reexamine following the 1991 Gulf War and the subsequent Intifada. Placed in comparative perspective, the Qasim era has come to be seen by many intellectuals as a lost opportunity for tolerance and the relatively free expression of ideas. The relative benevolence of Qasim stands in sharp contrast to the brutality and even genocide of the Takriti Ba'th during its reign.

Fourth, one of Qasim's greatest legacies was his social reform policies. The passage of Law 80 in December 1961 created a framework that would constrain negotiations by all subsequent Iraqi governments, which were forced to adopt a nationalistic stance toward the Iraq Petroleum Company. Qasim thus set in motion the process that would lead to the full nationalization of oil in 1972. Although Law 30 of September 30, 1958, sought to implement land reform, the law itself was extremely contradictory in content and only affected a small percentage of extremely wealthy landowners who had provided the bulwark of support for the monarchy in the countryside.[68] Nevertheless, the appropriation of the rhetoric of expropriation by the ICP, whose members came to dominate the Ministry of Agrarian Reform, at least in the early years of the revolution, created the image of a radical agrarian land policy under Qasim. In the revolution's historical memory, land reform continues to inspire the theme of social justice articulated by the ICP and other leftist organizations.

Finally, there are the questions of ideology and power that emerge from the Qasim era. The events surrounding Qasim's defeat, capture, and execution indicated that, similar to events in 1958 and subsequently in 1968, political power changed hands through the activity of only a small handful of political activists. During the struggle between the Ba'thists and Qasim loyalists on February 8 and 9, army units around Baghdad remained largely inactive, waiting to see the outcome of the struggle. This indicates that large numbers of army officers were still not committed to a fixed ideological position in 1963, or, cynically, they wanted to throw their lot in with the winning side.[69] Had Qasim been able to convince a majority of the officer corps that an Iraq-first policy was best for the country, perhaps units that remained neutral might have come to his defense. Two cassettes recorded by Qasim in the Ministry of Defense on the evening of February 8 that he attempted to have delivered to radio stations for broadcast to the nation, and particularly to the army, never reached their destination. These tapes, which called upon the military to protect the revolution from imperialist forces, point to the Qasim regime's inability to appropriate the discourse of revolution. Ultimately, Qasim's inability to effectively wage a war of position did in his regime, as the military failed to come to his rescue.

Both Qasim and his adversaries sought to dominate the field of battle against imperialism by situating themselves as the true guardians of Iraq against imperialist aims. However, Qasim never organized a cadre of "organic intellectuals" that could have helped form what Gramsci calls a "historical bloc." Although they were relatively small in number, the Iraqist nationalist politicians who had served in the interim government immediately after the revolution but who had resigned to protest Qasim's failure to implement democratic reforms, particularly the licensing of political parties and the holding of free elections could have formed the core of such a bloc. They could have provided an important link to the many student, professional, and working-class organizations that proliferated after 1958. A number of observers, noting the small size of the NDP and the Istiqlal Party, have argued that Qasim could not have built a strong social base on these two parties, especially the NDP, which was ideologically closer to his positions than the Pan-Arabist Istiqlal Party. This perspective loses sight of the critical role of intellectuals in the process of state formation and the development of civil society. Although the democratic parties of the monarchical period were relatively small, their leaders maintained a prestige that far exceeded the size of the parties because of their sustained resistance to the political repression of Nuri Sa'id and others. The leadership of the NDP also could have provided links to less radical elements of the Iraqi left. Considering that many Iraqis were drawn to the ICP less because of its commitment to Marxism, of which few party members had a sophisticated understanding, than because of its message of social reform and ethnic and cultural inclusion, there were many communists who would have participated in a coalition government with the NDP. A good example was Dhu al-Nun Ayyub, mentioned earlier, who vigorously defended Qasim at the end of his regime. Once Qasim moved decisively away from democratic elections and began to offer greater political latitude to Pan-Arabists as a counterweight to the communists, he effectively cut himself off from creating a strong historical bloc. By October 1959, when the Ba'th attempted to assassinate him, the die had been cast and no group of Pan-Arabists, no matter how favorably they were treated by Qasim, would support him. Instead of moving to institutionalize the revolution, Qasim, like Saddam Husayn after him, ultimately relied upon a cult of personality.

In light of the structural constraints surrounding the Qasim regime and the July 14, 1958 Revolution more broadly defined, the question is less why

Qasim was such an incompetent leader, but rather how he managed to remain in power for more than four years. Consider the enemies of the July 14 Revolution. First, there were the Pan-Arabists in Iraq, both Nasirists and Ba'thists, who hated Qasim for failing to pursue immediate unity with Egypt after the overthrow of the monarchy and who organized coups and an attempted assassination. Second, there were the landowning and mercantile elites of the *ancien régime* who sought to sabotage any reforms such as redistribution of land to the peasantry, and who joined the 1959 Mosul uprising. Third, there was Egypt, which saw the Iraqi revolution as a challenge to its aspirations to dominate Pan-Arab politics. Because 'Abd al-Nasir viewed Qasim as both threatening his prestige and widening the scope of communist influence in the Arab east, the Iraqi regime was subjected to vituperative attacks by Cairo's powerful radio station, Sawt al-'Arab. Fourth, the United States opposed Qasim because of his termination of alliances that had promoted American interests, such as the Baghdad Pact and the Arab Union with Jordan. Conversely, Iraq's close military, political, and cultural ties with the Soviet Union were perceived as allowing it to gain a stronger foothold in the Middle East. Fifth, there were the Shi'i clerics of Karbala', al-Najaf and al-Kathimayn, who initially welcomed the revolution because unity with Egypt, which would have made the Shi'a a minority in a larger Pan-Arab state, was rejected by the new Iraqi regime. However, Qasim's reform of the personal status laws, especially giving women more rights over inheritance and divorce, was bitterly opposed by the clergy, who turned from a position of support to one of implacable hostility.[70] Sixth, there were the Kurds, which the regime alienated following the army's offensive in 1961 against Mulla Mustafa al-Barzani's forces. Kurdish support for the 1963 coup emboldened the Ba'th to move decisively to overthrow Qasim. Finally, and most important of all, the fact that the Pan-Arabists, and particularly army officers of middle- and lower-middle-class background, perceived the cleavage with Iraqist nationalists in zero-sum terms meant that Qasim was confronted with a fifth column in the most important organization, the army, throughout his rule. Undoubtedly, the dispatch of the army to Kurdistan in 1961 and to the Kuwaiti border in 1962 were both attempts to divert the army's attention away from an attempted coup d'état.

Ultimately, the political passions surrounding the July 1958 Revolution and the violence and brutality that characterized the overthrow of the Qasim regime in 1963 and subsequent persecution of communists and the Iraqist nationalist left involved a complex mix of factors that makes any effort to reduce the regime's 1963 demise to a simple dynamic of class conflict or ethnic strife untenable. The intense anger directed at Qasim telescoped onto his leadership a desire for revenge for past injustices that related not just to his purported deviation from Pan-Arabism, but also to the Iraqi army's humiliation in 1941, the subsequent execution of the Four Colonels, and the army's ignominious performance in Palestine. Qasim embodied for many Iraqis aspirations for social and political change that were either partially implemented (for the left, the Shiʿa, and minorities) or were not implemented (for the Pan-Arabists). For the Pan-Arabists who felt weak and humiliated, the accession to power by communists, Shiʿis, and other minorities such as the Kurds placed the state under the control of forces whose loyalty to the idea of Iraq as a core component of a Pan-Arab nation was dubious, and also presaged their further eclipse from power. In addition, it suggested the prospective dominance of a cultural idiom considered alien by the tribal inhabitants of the Sunni Arab triangle of north-central Iraq.

Certainly social class played a role in these processes. If we add to the equation Batatu's observation that the Sunni triangle comprised a section of Iraq where middling elements such as small merchants and landowners had suffered from the collapse of the Ottoman Empire and the loss of markets in the Levant through the creation of what were viewed as colonially imposed boundaries, it is possible to began to comprehend the depth of anger with which with Pan-Arabists, especially those in the officer corps who were largely drawn from this area, viewed Qasim's move toward an Iraqist nationalist model of political community.

Qasim died a failed leader. However, as many recent conferences and publications have shown, there is an intense interest in many quarters concerning the person and policies of ʿAbd al-Karim Qasim. Much of this questioning and reflection stems from the human rights abuses of the former Baʿthist regime of Saddam Husayn. Qasim continues to be admired as a leader who never forgot his humble roots and was honest, strongly antisectarian, and wholeheartedly committed to Iraq's welfare and progress. Whatever the historical verdict on Qasim and his rule, what this revisionist historical memory demonstrates is the potential power of symbols from the past to haunt the autocrats of the present.

6 Memories of State Ascendant, 1968–1979

> It is incorrect to view history as if it were a void or something
> to be ashamed of before Islam, just as it is incorrect, on the other
> hand, to analyze it as if it were based in class struggle because
> both perspectives do not accord with the facts of history. What
> is required is that our analysis of historical events apply our
> specifically Baʿthist perspective in building the Arab nation.
>
> SADDAM HUSAYN, *On the Writing of History*

> Folklore is at the service of the Arab struggle.
>
> Motto of the Arab Folklore Conference, Baghdad, 1977

The core of Baʿthist attempts to restructure historical memory is the so-called Project for the Rewriting of History (Mashruʿ Iʿadat Kitabat al-Tarikh). Although it was not officially articulated until 1979, the Baʿth Party began implementing the project shortly after taking power in 1968.[1] The scope and scale of this project was unprecedented in Iraq and elsewhere in the Arab world. More than simple political indoctrination, the project represented an attempt to construct a new public sphere, including the reconstitution of political identity, the relationship of the citizen to the state, and public understandings of national heritage. Simultaneously, it sought to negate Iraqist nationalism's inclusive legacy precisely while trying to appropriate it to build a "new Iraqi man and society." What were the project's origins, how successful was it, and what can it tell us about state-society relations, and particularly about the continuing struggle over the definition of political community, in Iraq under the Takriti Baʿth?[2]

If the July 1958 Revolution inspired a spontaneous outburst of political and civic activity, then the Revolution of July 15–30, 1968, severely curtailed it. Whereas the Qasim regime avoided sectarianism in staffing the state, the Takriti Baʿthist regime used sectarian criteria to fill all important posts, placing token Shiʿis and Christians in only a few prominent but powerless positions.[3] If the Qasim regime was more inclusive, why was it unsuccessful, especially compared to the July 17, 1968, putsch, which created one of the longest-lasting regimes in the Arab world? How was a regime that enjoyed little support when it seized power in 1968 able to become so firmly entrenched, while a regime that enjoyed such great popularity in 1958 fell in 1963?

After an initial period of instability, which ended with the failed coup attempt by security chief Nazim al-Kazzar in 1973, the Baʿthist regime consolidated its power over the next five years, supported by a historically unparalleled influx of oil wealth. Between 1973 and 1979, the regime developed a fairly widespread level of support, especially among Sunni Arabs, Christians, and many educated, secular Shiʿis. This was due in large measure to a deceptive political calm; the creation of a generous welfare state; massive infrastructural development, including roads, electrification of villages, and new housing complexes; and the nationalization of foreign oil. Many Iraqis believed that the new Baʿthist regime might actually confront sectarianism, given the appointment of a number of Shiʿis during the 1970s to positions within the Baʿth Party and the state. The regime's strident anti-imperialist rhetoric, especially before nationalizing the Iraq Petroleum Company in 1972, led many leftist Iraqist nationalists to believe that the Baʿth Party might pursue progressive economic policies based on a broad social coalition. State-sponsored cultural production during this period struck a number of receptive chords, especially state support for reviving folklore and popular culture *(al-turath al-shaʿbi)*, including extensive radio and television programming devoted to folkloric themes.

The origins of the 1968 coup d'état can be traced to 1958. By undermining the tentative institutional development that had occurred following World War II, the Free Officers, ʿAbd al-Karim Qasim, the Iraqi Communist Party, Pan-Arabist forces, and Qasim's successors paved the way for the success of the 1968 putsch. All post-1958 regimes weakened the fragile political institutions that already existed by combining executive and legislative authority in one body, whether in Qasim's Sovereignty Council (Majlis Siyadat al-Thawra), the first Baʿthist regime's National Council for the Revolutionary Command (al-Majlis al-Watani li Qiyadat al-Thawra), or the post-1968 regime's Revolution Command Council (Majlis Qiyadat al-Thawra).[4] Although the two Baʿthist regimes were the most prone to using violence, the second Baʿthist regime resorted to an additional strategy to elicit political consent, namely an extensive state-sponsored effort to rewrite and restructure the country's history and understandings of national heritage, in both its high and popular cultural forms.

The new regime also benefited from the weakness of civil society. By 1968, traditional democratic parties, such as the Independence and the National Democratic parties, were moribund, labor unions, which had formed an impressive national federation during the summer of 1959, had been reduced to appendages of the state, intellectual organizations had lost their autonomy, and peasant organizations, the most vulnerable of all, were increasingly subject to intimidation by landed interests.[5] Beginning in 1959, the Qasim regime sought to demobilize organizations that might challenge its prerogatives and to reconstitute them as extensions of the state. Labor unions controlled by official functionaries, intellectual organizations and publications controlled by the Ministry of Guidance (later the Ministry of Culture and Information), state-run youth organizations,[6] and government-controlled peasant organizations progressively curtailed independent initiatives by the citizenry. After 1968, the intelligentsia, which had formulated new understandings of political community during the 1950s and the early years of the Qasim regime, was mobilized by the Takriti Baʿth to implement its goals and enhance the power of the state. The intelligentsia's tasks were defined as disguising the persistence of power relations based on tribalism, sectarianism, and social class; expunging the Iraqist nationalist legacy from the historical record; strictly limiting religion to the private sphere; and enshrining a new Iraqi-centered concept of Pan-Arabism.[7] This model can be summarized as secular corporatism overlaid with a repressive authoritarianism.

Although some analysts noted a shift in the Baʿth's ideological approach to political community and historical memory away from Pan-Arabism to "Mesopotamianism," especially during the late 1970s, what differentiated the Takriti Baʿth from prior Pan-Arabist regimes, whether the 1941 Rashid ʿAli al-Gaylani regime, the first Baʿthist regime, or the ʿAbd al-Salam ʿArif regime, was its penchant for *integrating* Pan-Arabism with an Iraq-centered nationalism.[8] Juxtaposing a Pan-Arab Baʿth to one inclined toward "Mesopotamianism" fails to capture the complexities of the ideological and political forces at work after 1968. Only by taking Iraq's ancient civilizations seriously could the new regime argue that Iraq was uniquely suited to assume the role of *primus inter pares* among Arab states in creating a Pan-Arab nation. Further, Iraq's Mesopotamian heritage was the only heritage to which all Iraqis—Sunni and Shiʿi Arabs, Kurds, and other minorities alike—could unambiguously relate.[9]

However, there was a third reason why "Mesopotamianism" was so central to Baʿthist thought. In trying to minimize support for the ICP, the Baʿth moved to appropriate folk culture and establish itself as the true representative of mass interests. To accomplish this, the regime used folklore to demonstrate values, norms, and cultural preferences that were distinctly Iraqi. Here Pan-Arabism fell short in providing the regime's cultural commissars with an adequate palette of symbols with which to paint a vision of the "new Iraq." Like the Qasim regime, the state sought to demonstrate a continuity in Iraqi civilization by appropriating folk culture. Iraqis could feel as proud identifying with a heritage that was several thousand years old as they could with Iraq's more recent Arab roots. Further, a historical memory tied exclusively to the ʿAbbasid Empire, Iraq's greatest Arab legacy, was problematic. First, it represented an era of ethnic diversity in which Arabized Persians purportedly worked to undermine the empire's cohesion, leading to the al-Shuʿubiya controversy, which continues to color contemporary Iraqi politics. Second, the empire's collapse, caused by the Mongols' sacking of Iraq in 1258, demonstrates Arab weakness.[10] Had the Baʿth promoted a narrow Pan-Arabism, its ability to appropriate the past would have been circumscribed by a more limited "symbolic field."

The Takriti Baʿth differentiated itself from prior regimes through an important conjuncture of events. Central to this process was its ability to manipulate a strong yearning, especially among the urban middle classes, for political stability after more than thirty years of continuous turmoil. Equally significant, the new regime tapped a desire, again most pronounced among the urban middle classes, to establish stronger ties to the past. Nevertheless, the attempt to rewrite history entailed the negation of the culture and history of all but a small number of Iraqis. The Shiʿa, Kurds, other minorities, workers, and even urban Sunni Arabs received little social or cultural valorization. Inevitably, this attempt, which initially resonated with much of the educated urban middle classes, especially during the high-water mark of oil prices, ultimately proved unsuccessful following the severe deprivations that accompanied the Iran-Iraq and Gulf wars.

The 1963 coup that overthrew the Qasim regime represents a critical juncture in modern Iraqi history comparable to the 1920 and 1958 revolutions and the 1941 Movement. Whereas the 1920 and 1958 revolutions emphasized political and cultural inclusion, the 1941 uprising and 1963 coup were based upon a narrow Pan-Arabist definition of Iraqi political community that severely curtailed freedom of association and expression. The coup dealt a particularly serious blow to Iraqist nationalist forces by suppressing the ICP, its most powerful constituent. The ICP leadership's ties to the working class, students, and intellectuals were severely disrupted by the killing and imprisonment of much of the ICP's leadership. The party was forced to rely upon its Kurdish allies, particularly the Kurdish Democratic Party, and use Kurdistan as its primary base from which to oppose the Baʿthist regime. Because the ICP lost much of its Arab leadership in 1963, and moved its base of operations to Kurdistan, the 1963 coup intensified sectarianism as the communists became more closely identified in some Arab quarters with the Kurds. Although the overthrow of the first Ba'thist regime by 'Abd al-Salam 'Arif in November 1963 created a somewhat less restrictive political environment, the multiparty system of the late 1940s and 1950s never reappeared in Iraq. After 1963, intellectuals who supported democratic processes could no longer operate as a group, and the print media was increasingly subordinated to the state.

Following the 1963 coup, army officers, security operatives, and state bureaucrats increasingly dominated public life and discourse, continuing a trend begun under Qasim, especially after the attempt to assassinate him in 1959. The period between 1959 (and especially after 1963) and 1968 saw a progressive marginalization of those corporate groups and organizations that could have provided a check on state power. Despite a thaw in authoritarian policies during 1965 and 1966 under prime minister 'Abd al-Rahman al-Bazzaz, Iraqi politics between 1963 and 1968 was dominated by a small elite of army officers, technocrats, and Pan-Arabist ideologues. Although the Qasim regime avoided sectarian policies, it and not the Ba'th first placed labor unions under state control.[11] In the second provisional constitution promulgated by the first Ba'thist regime in 1963, support for women's equality that the Qasim regime had included its own provisional constitutional was eliminated in deference to religious interests.[12]

Political life became more sectarian after the 1963 coup.[13] Shi'is and Kurds were increasingly marginalized. 'Abd al-Salam 'Arif was well known as an extremely sectarian Sunni who reportedly refused to receive any medical treatment from Shi'i physicians.[14] Naji Talib, a respected former Free Officer and the one Shi'i who achieved prominence between 1963 and 1968, hesitated to initiate any new policies during his brief tenure as prime minister between April 1966, and May 1967. British sources note that Talib expressed fear that adopting any policies that antagonized the Sunni Arab elite could lead to the *sahl*, the colloquial Arabic term for being dragged through the streets, an allusion to the fate of Faysal II and 'Abd al-Ilah in July 1958.[15] As Hasan al-'Alawi notes, the pattern of turning to prominent Shi'is as prime ministers during crises—such as Salih Jabr to implement the Portsmouth Treaty in 1948, Sayyid Muhammad Sadr after the 1948 Wathba, Fadil al-Jamali in 1954, who provided the monarchy with a reformist veneer following the 1952 Intifada, and Naji Talib during the power struggle following 'Abd al-Salam 'Arif's death in 1965—represented no change in the dominant pattern of power.[16] Indeed, no Shi'i prime minister has implemented any long-standing policies since the founding of the modern Iraqi state.

Iraq's political instability, especially following 'Abd al-Salam 'Arif's unexpected death in a helicopter crash in April 1965, further undermined public confidence in the political system. The ineffectual rule of his brother, ʿAbd al-Rahman ʿArif, was underscored by Iraq's continued economic decline and its humiliating performance in the June 1967 Arab-Israeli War. The state's unwillingness to implement al-Bazzaz's thirteen-point plan in 1966 to definitively solve the Kurdish problem added to the sense of political malaise that enveloped the country. During the July 1968 coup, ʿArif and his prime minister, Taha Yahya, were as effortlessly overthrown as the triumvirate of Nuri al-Saʿid, ʿAbd Il-Ilah, and Faysal II in 1958, and without a shot being fired.

In sum, the 1968 putsch's success reflected more the ʿArif-Yahya regime's institutional weakness than popular support for the Baʿth.[17] At the pinnacle of power, Iraqi politics remained personalistic. Whether led by Faysal I, Bakr Sidqi, the Four Colonels, Nuri al-Saʿid, ʿAbd al-Karim Qasim, ʿAli Salih al-Saʿdi, the leader of the 1963 coup, or the ʿArif brothers, the Iraqi political system failed to develop enduring political institutions that transcended specific leaders and regimes. Without political institutionalization, politics reverted back to subnational groups based on tribal, ethnic or regional identities. These particularistic tendencies, which produced a constant reorganization of coalitions, provided a recipe for political instability. Thus the same Kurds who had supported the Pan-Arab Baʿthists in overthrowing Qasim in 1963 were by 1968 involved in a full-scale war with the Pan-Arab ʿArif-Yahya regime. No coalition had any staying power. Only the Iraqist nationalist model offered any hope for political stability by refusing to define political community according to religion or ethnicity. Its inclusive vision actively opposed the elitist cliques that dominated Iraqi politics throughout much of the twentieth century. It is within this context of the Baʿth Party's domestic and regional weakness in 1968 that the party's emphasis on the rewriting of history as an important component of its efforts to achieve hegemony must be understood.

The Baʿthist regime evolved through a number of phases. The first phase, from 1968 to 1973, was characterized by a belligerent anti-imperialist and anti-Zionist rhetoric, support for Arab unity, and overtures to the Iraqi Communist Party to form a united front. After the successful 1972 nationalization of the Iraq Petroleum Company, the oil price rises of the early 1970s, and the elimination of any credible rivals, the regime increasingly harassed its erstwhile ICP coalition partners and moved toward closer ties with the West. By 1979, when Saddam Husayn eliminated Ahmad Hasan al-Bakr, assumed the role of president, and eliminated all major opposition within the Baʿth Party, including a number of prominent Shiʿis, the Takriti

Ba'th was at the pinnacle of its power. Despite the Iran-Iraq War, there was a slight opening of cultural expression during the early 1980s, during which some nongovernment presses were allowed to function and publish material that had previously been forbidden, such as works exhibiting a more benign perspective on Qasim and a more open discussion of Iraqi tribes. This development was accompanied by an economic liberalization in which the agricultural and commercial sectors and some public sector enterprises were privatized. By the war's end in 1988, the regime entered a third phase, during which its credibility began to be challenged. Economic pressures caused by falling oil prices and war debts fueled public discontent at the regime's inability to enact the new policies that it had promised would follow the war's end. The invasion of Kuwait represented a deepening of the regime's postwar crisis, which was compounded by Iraq's horrendous defeat and the February–April 1991 Intifada, during which the Ba'th was almost overthrown.

Political conditions in July 1968 did not augur well for the new regime. Only the regime's leader, General Ahmad Hasan al-Bakr, who played a central role in 'Abd al-Karim Qasim's overthrow and execution, was nationally known. The regime was severely divided. Less than two weeks after seizing power, a conflict developed between the younger, non-Ba'thist members, represented by Lieutenant Colonel 'Abd al-Razzaq Nayif and Lieutenant Colonel Ibrahim Da'ud, and the more established officers, represented by al-Bakr and his two vice-premiers, generals Hardan al-Takriti and Salih Mahdi 'Ammash. Nayif and Da'ud's ouster on July 30, which the Ba'th characterized as a "second revolution," was the opening scene in a lengthy drama of continuous intrigues and shifting alliances during the new regime's first five years.

With Nayif and Da'ud in exile, a new rivalry immediately surfaced between the two vice-premiers, generals Hardan al-Takriti and Salih Mahdi 'Ammash.[18] Hardan al-Takriti was not a committed Ba'thist and fought efforts to give the new regime an exclusively Ba'thist stamp. His power rested on his control of the air force and derived from a certain popularity that he enjoyed among the urban middle classes as a result of his having curbed the excesses of the National Guard (al-Haras al-Qawmi) in 1963.[19] 'Ammash, who represented the Ba'th Party's left wing, was keen to assert ideological control over the new regime. The conflict between the two vice-premiers took form in a dispute over whether Ba'th Party founder Michel 'Aflaq would be allowed to visit Baghdad. al-Takriti opposed the visit, fearing that it would strengthen Ba'th Party control of the government. 'Aflaq did not in fact visit Baghdad until December 1968, six months after the coup.[20]

In addition to personal rivalries and ideological conflict, the regime faced serious domestic problems. During the late 1960s, the state suffered from serious budget deficits caused by stagnating oil prices exacerbated by the ʿArif-Yahya regime's arms spending designed to placate the military. Throughout the decade, the state became increasingly dependent on oil revenues as the agrarian sector continued to stagnate.[21] The Kurdish problem had still not been resolved, and neither the Kurds nor the Iraqi army could achieve military victory. The Shiʿa resented the state, feeling that they had been excluded from power since the 1963 coup. The civil service suffered from poor pay and extensive corruption. Distrustful of the new regime, entrepreneurs looked back nostalgically to the al-Bazzaz cabinet's liberal reforms. Foreign investors avoided the Iraqi market, uncertain of the new regime's economic policies. The ICP remained popular among intellectuals, students, and urban workers, making the prospect of its attempting to seize power always a possibility.

Internationally, the new regime was isolated. Its repression of the Nasirites who had participated in the July 17 coup placed it at odds with Egypt. Instead of the communists, its traditional enemy, the Takriti Baʿth now directed its hostility toward its Arab nationalist rivals, who were perceived as a greater threat. Thus, when Baʿthist cadres visited the notorious Abu Ghurayb prison after the coup, it was Nasirites and non-Baʿthist Arab nationalists, that is, the Harakiyun, whom they sought out, not communist prisoners.[22] To the west, relations with the regime's Syrian Baʿthist counterparts were strained due to the Damascus regime's leftist complexion. The Takriti Baʿth felt more comfortable with the more traditional, centrist party leadership of Michel ʿAflaq, Shibli al-ʿAysami, and Ilyas Farah, all of whom ultimately took refuge in Iraq. To the east, the Shah continued to support Iraq's Kurds, who also received assistance from Israel and the United States. Only in the Persian Gulf, where the Takriti Baʿth presented itself as the defender of Arab rights against an expansionist Iranian state, was the regime able to break out of its isolation.

To counter these problems, the new regime made a number of decisions. First, al-Bakr assured Iraqis that the dreaded National Guard, whose excesses following the February 1963 coup were still fresh in the minds of the populace, would not be allowed to reorganize. Second, the regime promised to release all political prisoners and invited all state employees who had been dismissed for political reasons to reapply for their former positions at the Presidential Palace.[23] Third, the regime offered a thorough reform of the civil service to mobilize urban middle-class support. Fourth, to attract foreign investment, the regime avoided a radical restructuring of the economy.

Finally, in an implicit acknowledgment of its weakness, the regime pressed for a popular front that would include other Arab nationalist groups and communists, despite al-Bakr's extreme distaste for the latter.

Many observers gave the regime, fraught with internal strife and enjoying little public support, a limited life expectancy. However, the Takriti Ba'th quickly differentiated itself from former regimes. During the fall of 1968, the regime reported the "discovery" of numerous conspiracies, comprised of "spy cells" allegedly working for Israel and the CIA, that included former prime minister 'Abd al-Rahman al-Bazzaz. To British observers, the trials were designed to both terrorize the populace and to make clear what policies the new regime found acceptable. al-Bazzaz's trial, for example, was an indicator that the regime would not allow a return to his liberal economic and political reforms.[24]

While Ahmad Hasan al-Bakr presided over the regime's competing factions, a new political actor was beginning to make his presence felt. Originally from 'Awja, a village just to the southeast of Takrit, Saddam Husayn al-Takriti was known for his activism, and especially his participation in the Ba'thist squad that attempted to assassinate 'Abd al-Karim Qasim in Baghdad in October 1959. Wounded and forced to flee through the desert to Jordan after the abortive assassination attempt, and later jailed from 1963 to 1965 by the 'Arif regime, Saddam had learned to be secretive.[25] Related to al-Bakr by marriage, Saddam was a young party deputy secretary at the time of the coup. By October 1968, British diplomats were already commenting on his increasing power within the party and state apparatus.[26] Behind the scenes, Saddam placed allies in strategic positions in the security and party apparatus.

The regime's fortunes improved not just as a result of Saddam's consummate skills at intrigue and infighting, but also because of the rapid rise in state oil revenues, from $1 billion dollars in 1972 to $33 billion in 1980. Although the bulk of these revenues were devoted to military procurement, expanding the security services, infrastructural development, and social welfare, a substantial portion of the money was devoted to developing a "culture production" industry. Although only government-sponsored newspapers were allowed to publish,[27] the number of new official publications, especially journals, expanded dramatically. International conferences and festivals became part of everyday cultural life. With the benefit of state largesse, new museums were established and archaeological activity significantly increased.

Why, after consolidating power in 1973, did the Ba'th feel the need to promote the massive undertaking of rewriting the nation's history and restructuring understandings of its cultural heritage? Opposition within the party had been eliminated, oil prices were on the rise, and the ICP had been subordinated through the arrest and harassment of its members and by the terms of the 1973 National Front that circumscribed the party's activities. Yet even with relative elite stability and the communist threat minimized, Saddam and the Baʿth still felt the need to appropriate historical memory. In answering why, three factors must be taken into account.

First, many Baʿthists felt the need to overcome the infighting within the political elite that had produced a decade of almost continuous political instability following the monarchy's overthrow. By positing a definition of political community that ostensibly incorporated all elements of Iraqi society, the Baʿth sought to eliminate political dissension by symbolically offering everyone limited political and cultural space. The effort to restructure historical memory through a synthesis of Pan-Arabism, "Mesopotamianism," and folk culture was intended both to provide a definition of political community around which everyone could rally and to strengthen the state.

Internal dissent and at least two coup attempts plagued the regime in its early years. The alleged January 1969 plot, which was purportedly connected to an Israeli spy ring operated by Iraqi Jews, was fabricated to intimidate potential opponents. However, coups in 1970 and 1973 were very real. The January 1970 coup attempt by Major-General ʿAbd al-Ghani al-Rawi and Colonel Salih Mahdi al-Samarraʾi was easily suppressed. In October 1971, Hardan al-Takriti was relieved of his post, reflecting concern with military influence in the new regime, only to be assassinated while in exile in Kuwait in March 1972. Although the last serious challenge to the new regime in 1973 by the chief of intelligence, Nazim al-Kazzar, was quickly suppressed, it was clear that internal opposition was still a possibility, either from the military or the intelligence services. Creating a hegemonic worldview that would provide a broader and more cohesive political identity for the Iraqi elite and populace would lessen the need to rely exclusively on the state's extensive security apparatus. Saddam and the Baʿth felt that overt repression alone could not sustain the regime in the long run.

Second, Saddam and the Baʿth sought to expunge the Iraqist nationalist model of political community from the historical record, especially for Iraqi youth. Through fostering negative associations with Iraqist nationalism and juxtaposing competing categories of thought to those it articulated, the Baʿth sought to eliminate the threat of its main rival, the communists, as well as cast aspersions on the large number of Shiʿis who saw Pan-Arabism as an attempt to relegate them to a minority status in a Sunni-dominated Pan-Arab state. If the regime could convince Iraqi youth to view communists and other Iraqist nationalists as alien, disloyal, and intent on harming Iraq, and it could simultaneously shape the categories through which they viewed the past, present, and future, then the Baʻth's rivals would find it extremely difficult to mobilize the younger generation. To further undermine Iraqist nationalism, which drew upon Iraq's ancient civilizations for many of its political cultural symbols, the Baʻth created its own "Mesopotamian" memory as a complement to the party's Pan-Arabism.

Third, Baʻthist efforts at rewriting history need to be understood in an international context since they were designed to promote not just the Baʻth's domestic agenda but its foreign policy objectives as well. State-sponsored conferences, professional associations, and journals invariably included intellectuals from other Arab countries, ostensibly demonstrating Iraq's commitment to Pan-Arabism, while the state's focus on its Mesopotamian and Arab-Islamic heritages underscored Iraq's cultural superiority over its main rivals, Egypt and Syria, for Pan-Arab leadership. Until the late 1980s, Iraq's oil wealth allowed it to bring large numbers of Arab and foreign intellectuals to the country, where they were lavishly treated, highlighting its status as arriviste leader of the Arab world.[28]

Within the vectors of the ideological forces operating in Iraq in 1968, both Pan-Arab and Iraqist nationalist concerns had to be addressed. Among Pan-Arabists and the urban middle classes more broadly defined, the inaction of the ʻArif regime during the June 1967 Arab-Israeli War created public displeasure with its weak and ineffectual rule. By adopting a radical stance toward Israel, the Baʻth was able to both garner popular support, especially among the officer corps and the urban middle classes, and distinguish itself from the ʻArif regime. Conflict with its Baʻthist rivals in neighboring Syria, especially with the "leftist" faction that had come to power under Salah Jadid in 1966, also required the Takriti Baʻth to prove that its own Baʻthist credentials were more authentic.[29] Clearly, the struggles with Israel and the Syrian Baʻth needed to be couched in Pan-Arab terms.

On the other hand, the regime could not afford to alienate the non-Sunni Arab population, especially Shiʻis and Kurds, in the face of hostile neighbors such as Syria, Iran, and Turkey. In this context, a rigid Pan-Arabism was counterproductive, especially in light of the disillusionment with Pan-Arabism following the 1967 defeat of Egypt, the main axis of Arab unity.[30] The regime's need to expand its social base, which led to a "progressive national front" with the ICP, worked against an exclusive Pan-Arabist position as well, since it would have prevented the new regime from attracting the left. Despite Saddam's assertion that he had been strongly influenced by Salah al-Din al-Sabbagh's memoirs, *The Knights of Arabism in Iraq*, Takriti

FIGURE 8. Pioneer Youth Organization members at a training camp. *The Talae on the March* (Ministry of Information and Culture, Republic of Iraq, 1980), p. 21.

Baʿthism clearly differed from the Pan-Arabism of al-Sabbagh and the participants in the 1941 Movement.[31]

The new regime faced a profound ideological contradiction. On the one hand, it could not adopt an exclusively Pan-Arabist ideology for fear of further alienating Shiʿis, Kurds, and the communists. On the other hand, it could not embrace Iraqist nationalism, which negated its own ideological tradition, which emphasized Pan-Arab unity. If it moved too far to the right, the Baʿth would undermine its "revolutionary" credentials. If it moved too far to the left, it could lose the support of the professional middle classes, the bulk of the army officers, merchants, and conservative sectors of society such as the Shiʿi *marjaʿiya*. Shrewdly, the regime made vague and highly abstract ideological pronouncements. Instead of focusing on ideology, its new cultural model proffered a subtler means of mobilizing consent and popular support. To be sure, shrill statements about the "Zionist entity" and the evils of imperialism continued to emanate from the government-controlled press. However, such pronouncements belied any serious efforts to combat either Israel or Western interests in the Arab world. Traditional Baʿthist ideology, and particularly its Pan-Arabist component, remained a veneer for the Takriti Baʿth. It was increasingly subordinated to a new national identity that looked less to the Ba'th Party's intellectual progenitors in the Levant, such as Michel 'Aflaq and Salah al-Din al-Bitar, for its inspiration than to Iraq's own national past.

The massive effort to reconstruct historical memory was also a reaction to the July 1958 Revolution and the fear of Iraqist nationalism, which, if not an immediate political threat, always lurked as an alternative to the Ba'thist project. Iraqist nationalism, especially as articulated by the ICP, leftist intellectuals, and the successors of the NDP, offered the Shi'a and Iraq's minorities integration into Iraq's political community. Pan-Arab nationalism, on the other hand, especially in its chauvinistic and conspiratorial Ba'thist form, constructed a sectarian state that, while offering subservient Shi'is, Kurds, and other minorities some political and cultural space, would remain under Sunni Arab control. The cry of the Iraqi democratic opposition and expatriate intellectuals during the 1990s that "democracy is the only answer" meant that political stability in Iraq depends upon redressing the grievances of those excluded from power.[32] The Ba'th's violence and terror, and its reliance on kinship in the form of tribe, clan, and family structure to build the state infrastructure, represented precisely the type of narrow political vision that the ICP's ideology and the Iraqist nationalist vision more broadly defined opposed.[33] The ICP's focus on social justice stood in sharp contrast to the Takriti Ba'th's nepotism and the internal corruption by which the party elite accumulated wealth.[34]

Pan-Arabism helped the Ba'th create a subterfuge to hide this infrastructure from the populace. It not only provided the conceptual prisms through which to view the past, but it also allowed the Ba'th to batter the left for its narrow Iraqi focus. In addition, it served to divert attention away from domestic problems and allowed the regime to emphasize the Palestinian problem, Western imperialism, and the threat from Iran. However, as the Takriti Ba'th felt more secure, especially as a result of rising oil prices and the accommodation with the Shah of Iran in 1975 over the Shatt al-'Arab in return for Iran's end of support for Iraq's Kurds, a focus on Iraq's ancient civilizations or "Mesopotamianism," rather than Pan-Arabism, became more prominent.

Efforts to structure a "Mesopotamian" historical memory traced their origins to the leftist intelligentsia of the 1940s and 1950s. Here, the Takriti Ba'th was influenced by the systematic effort of Iraqist nationalist intellectuals under Qasim, both within the state and within quasi-official organizations such as the Iraqi Writer's Union, to involve the state in cultural production. Their emphasis on folk culture, symbols derived from Iraq's ancient history, and the privileging of social class as an analytic unit could be seen in

Jawad Salim's sculpture, ʿAbd al-Wahhab al-Bayati's poetry, and Faysal al-Samir's history writing, to give just a few examples. Further, the model for subsuming public memory under state control was derived as much from the efforts of leftist intellectuals during the Qasim regime as it was from the inspiration of the writings of ʿAflaq, Salah al-Din al-Bitar and other Baʿth Party ideologues who were also concerned with history. However, Takriti Baʿthist historical memory had a much more parochial and exclusionary cast than the historical memory promoted by the state under Qasim. Efforts to impose a Baʿthist stamp on Iraqi history and culture attempted to exclude Iraqist nationalists once and for all from the nation's historical memory, and hence from its political agenda.

A second goal of the state's efforts to appropriate the past was linked to the weakness and contradictions of Baʿthist ideology. As a mechanism for eliciting consent, ideological tracts and exhortations were much less effective than creating a national political culture that would symbolically and materially co-opt the populace. The state's appropriation of the past dovetailed with the strong yearnings of many Iraqis for a greater sense of connection with time and place. The nation-state was still young and maintained uneasy relations with its neighbors. Many Iraqis had been uprooted from rural areas. A reexamination of the past therefore appealed not only to the Baʿth Party members themselves, but also to the Iraqi people at large, who desired a stronger connection with their historical origins and cultural heritage.

A third goal was the Baʿth's desire to restructure the younger generation's understandings of the past. During my first visit to Iraq in May 1980, I was struck by my Ministry of Culture and Information hosts' keen desire to arrange meetings with youth organizations sponsored by the Ministry of Youth, such as the Pioneers and Vanguard organizations and sports clubs.[35] The founding during the Iran-Iraq War of the literary journal *al-Taliʿa al-Adabiya (The Literary Vanguard)*, specifically devoted to young writers, was another indicator of the regime's concern to co-opt Iraqi youth.[36] With political participation and expression severely restricted, new journals, poetry festivals, and publications series provided outlets for the younger generation to express itself in ways that did not challenge Baʿthist control of the state and society. History writing, literary criticism, and folkloric studies became important outlets for emerging Iraqi intellectuals to make their mark on cultural production. By establishing explicit and implicit parameters regarding what could and could not be published, the Baʿth was socializing Iraqi youth into its own worldview. Intellectuals, by being required to write on subjects that conformed to the state's understandings of culture and the past, would develop "politically correct" ways of approaching their topics of inquiry. As we shall see in chapter 8, the outcomes were not always what the state intended.

If the Takriti Ba'th subordinated the development of a systematic ideology to the appropriation of historical memory through cultural production, what forms did this effort take? First, the regime increased the number of journals and magazines for various constituencies. Intellectuals saw a dramatic increase in the number of academic and scholarly publications by the Ministry of Culture and Information. Prominent examples include *The Journal of Popular Culture (Majallat al-Turath al-Sha'bi)*, which was first published privately in September 1963 and intermittently thereafter until it was placed under the ministry's control in 1969, *The Arab Intellectual (al-Muthaqqaf al-'Arabi)* (1969), *al-Mawrid (The Source)* (1971), *The Arab Gulf (al-Khalij al-'Arabi)* (1971), *Arab Perspectives (Afaq 'Arabiya)* (1975), and *The Arab Historian (al-Mu'arrikh al-'Arabi)* (1975).[37] Other government agencies published important journals such as *Cinema and Theater (al-Sinama' wa-l-Masrah)*, issued by the Film and Theater Authority. Universities published more specialized journals that, while not directly under the Ministry of Culture and Information's control, were certainly subject to its censorship. *Arab Scientific Heritage (al-Turath al-'Ilmi al-'Arabi)* (1977) was published by the Center for the Revival of Arab Scientific Heritage at Baghdad University, *University Perspectives (Afaq Jam'iya)* (1977) was published in Arabic and Kurdish by Sulaymaniya University, and *The Journal of the Faculty of Arts (Majallat Kulliyat al-Adab)* was published by Baghdad University. The budgets of these journals were often quite extensive. *Arab Perspectives*, for example, was established with a budget of ID250,000 ($833,000).[38]

Professional associations, women's organizations, labor unions, and peasant cooperatives were represented by government publications as well. Lawyers' interests were articulated in *The Arab Lawyer (al-Haquqi al-'Arabi)* (1976). The industrial sector was represented by *Industry and Agriculture (al-Sina'a wa-l-Zira'a)* (1977), which was published by the Iraqi Federation of Industry. *The [Iraqi] Woman (al-Mar'a)* (1970) was published by the Iraqi Federation of Women. Workers were represented by *Workers' Consciousness (Wa'i al-'Ummal)* (1969), published by the General Federation of Labor Unions, students by *Youth Consciousness (Wa'i al-Shabab)* (1974), which was published by the General Federation of Iraqi Youth, and peasants by a weekly newspaper, *The Peasant's Voice (Sawt al-Fallah)* (1968), published by the General Federation of Peasant Cooperatives. In some instances professional organs, such as *Majallat al-Ajyal (The*

FIGURE 9. Cover of the *Journal of Popular Culture* (Winter 1987).

Journal of the Generations), published by the Teachers Union, ceased publication.[39]

Significantly, the two publications that appeared almost immediately after the 1968 coup concerned workers and peasants, whereas intellectual and professional journals did not begin publication until the early and mid-1970s. Many of the regime's new publications demonstrated the influence of the Iraqi left, seen in titles such as *Workers' Consciousness.* New publications sought to co-opt journals that had appeared during the 1950s and the Qasim era. *The Arab Intellectual,* for example, appropriated the highly respected leftist journal, *The Intellectual,* first published in 1954. *The [Iraqi] Woman* appropriated the name of the journal published by the communist-leaning League of Iraqi Women between 1958 and 1963. The promotion of popular culture likewise demonstrated the left's influence on Baʿthist efforts to appropriate historical memory. Associating these journals with Pan-Arabism rather than an Iraqist nationalism was indicative of the regime's efforts to substitute a corporatist Arab identity for a class-based or social democratic understanding of Iraq society.

The Baʿth's appropriation of intellectual and cultural production included the publication of English-language works, also issued by the Ministry of Culture and Information. *Gilgamesh* appeared in 1990 under the editorship of one of the main commissars of Iraqi cultural production, Naji Hadithi.[40] *Ur,* subtitled "The International Magazine of Arab Culture," was an equally glossy publication. Distributed by the former Iraqi Cultural Center in London, both journals contained articles by prominent Iraqi and Arab intellectuals on literature, painting, architecture and the plastic arts, poetry, short stories, art, and photography. These and other periodic journals, such as those on Islamic sites in Iraq or Iraqi fashion, were designed to emulate, at least in form, associations with Western publications, such as including letters to the editor. Another English-language publication, *The Iraqi Woman,* which was published by the Iraqi Federation of Women, was obviously designed to project a Western modernist image of Iraqi society. Its fall 1982 issue indicated that its main market was Great Britain and France. Following the obligatory article promoting Saddam's cult of personality, the issue featured articles on fashion, cooking, women in the military, and women in the Iraqi film industry, to name a few themes. Other publications included sophisticated, glossy publications from the Iraqi Fashion House (Dar al-Azya' al-ʿIraqiya) in Arabic and English.[41] The stylish models and clothing became a vehicle for drawing the Western reader's attention to Iraq's civilizational heritage and Saddam's importance as a leader. On the first page, for example, we learn that "Iraq, the cradle of the sun and civilisation, the page on which was written the first letter of the first alphabet known to man . . . is the home of Nebuchadnezzar, Ashur Banipal, Hammurabi, Haroun al-Rashid, Salladin and *Saddam Hussein*" (italics added). Perhaps the Baʿthist regime's most important English-language publication was *Iraq Today,* which provided general interest stories to Western audiences. Even the Ministry of Oil issued publications for foreign consumption.[42]

In an effort to extend the appropriation of historical memory and culture to the international arena, the Takriti Baʿth employed foreign, and particularly Western, intellectuals. One of the most prominent was Pierre Rossi, a well-known Arabist who founded the French Cultural Center in Upper Egypt and later in Baghdad, where he served as French cultural attaché dur-

FIGURE 10. Iraqi fashion model with historical backdrop. Ministry of Culture and Information, Republic of Iraq, *Women's Fashion* (Baghdad: Dar al-ʿAzyaʾ al-ʿIraqiya, 1981), 3.

ing the 1970s. Another author close to the regime was Christine Moss Helms, whose *Iraq: Eastern Flank of the Arab World* sought to foster the Baʿthist image of a beleaguered nation-state defending the Arab nation's borders from those, such as the Iranians, intent on undermining its unity.[43] Lesser-known Western authors and photographers were employed to produce texts and images romanticizing Iraqi folklore and society and to translate literature that supported Baʿthist perspectives on Iraqi society.[44]

The structure of Baʿthist cultural production corresponded to that of other corporatist Arab nationalist regimes such as the Nasirist and Syrian Baʿthist regimes. The press was placed under direct government control and censorship. Some prestigious journals, such as *Sumer*, which began publication in 1945, were overtly political. Others, such as the *Journal of Popular Culture*, were less so. Prior to the Takriti Ba'thist regime, state involvement in journals devoted to high culture had been limited to a single publication, the prestigious literary and philosophical journal *al-Aqlam (Pens)*. Beginning with a print run of 1,500 copies at its inception in 1964, the journal's publication increased to 3,000 in 1968, to 6,000 in 1975, and to 15,000 by 1977.[45]

The expansion of state publication efforts can be seen in the increase in paper consumption by the government's main publishing house, Dar al-Hurriya Press. Consumption increased from 3,654 tons in 1974 to 11,211 tons just two years later. Part of this increase was the result of Dar al-Hurriya assuming publication of elementary and secondary school texts. Whereas in 1973 Dar al-Hurriya employed a staff of 650, by 1978 the number had increased to 1,600. Although the number of Iraqi printing presses in 1960 numbered 160, of which 65 were in Baghdad, this number had increased to 165 by 1965.[46] However, under the Ba'th this number shrank, indicating further contraction of civil society. As a state publication boasted, by 1977 Dar al-Hurriya was printing 95 percent of the works printed by the Directorate-General of Culture, 50 percent of the Ministry of Education publications, 80 percent of works printed by other government departments, and all "cultural programs of the Arab Socialist Ba'th Party."[47]

Sumer's politicization was particularly obvious because, throughout its history, it deviated from its strict scholarly tone only once, when it enthusiastically welcomed the July 1958 Revolution. On the revolution's first anniversary, chief archaeologist Tahir Baqir wrote an editorial entitled "Ila al-Imam: Jumhuriya Dimuqratiya Hurra ila-l-Abad" (Forward: A Free Democratic Republic Forever), which presented an Iraqist nationalist and leftist interpretation of the revolution, citing foreign capital's exploitation of Iraqi labor and emphasizing Qasim's role and democratic processes in building a new Iraq. He stressed the inspiration Iraqis derived from their illustrious ancient past in combating oppressive regimes. In the ecumenical tradition of all his scholarship, Baqir cites the works of a foreign scholar, Samuel Noah Kramer, to support his arguments.[48] In the July 1958 issue of *Sumer*, photographs of floats from the revolution's first anniversary parade extolled Iraq's Mesopotamian past.[49]

Sumer's Iraqist nationalist inclination can be explained in part by the political orientation of its staff, which was led for many years by Baqir, Iraq's most prestigious archaeologist and a member of Baghdad University's Department of Antiquities. It can also be explained by the mixed social class and ethnic composition of *Sumer's* editorial board, which was headed by an

FIGURE 11. Cover of *al-Riwaq* 15 (1985). Ministry of
Culture and Information, Republic of Iraq.

upper-class Sunni Arab, Naji Asil (a former minister in the Bakr Sidqi gov-
ernment), and included Baqir (a Shiʻi), Fuʼad Safar, Jirgis ʻAwad, and Francis
Bashir (all of whom were Christian), and Fuʼad Basmachi, a Turkoman or
Kurd who was director of the Iraq Museum.

A second way in which the Takriti Baʻth attempted to appropriate cultural production was by organizing in Iraq international conferences and
festivals that included large numbers of Arab and foreign intellectuals. The
regime also continued to pursue its more overtly political interests by making Baghdad the venue for meetings of organizations important to its foreign policy objectives, such as the Arab League, OPEC, the Non-Aligned
Movement, and the Palestinian Liberation Organization. However, the dramatic expansion after 1970 of conferences and festivals specifically devoted
to culture, particularly popular culture and archaeology, was striking. Most

prominent was the Mirbad Poetry Festival, which was held each fall in the southern port city of Basra beginning in 1979. Commemorating an ancient camel market (whose actual site is unknown) where poets gathered to recite their poetry, the festival assembled an impressive guest list from Iraq, the Arab world, and the global Arab studies community. Adding to its luster was the Saddam Literary Prize, which, in 1989, was awarded to six authors, poets, and writers.[50]

Prominent poetry, folklore, music, and film festivals were held in Baghdad, Mosul, and other Iraqi cities that possessed historical-cultural significance.[51] The Mosul Festival was used to introduce Mesopotamian themes into cultural production. Most prominent in this regard was the reconstruction of the ancient city of Babylon as a backdrop for intellectual and artistic gatherings. Although the Directorate of Antiquities referred to pre–World War I German archaeological plans of the ancient city, the Ishtar Temple was ultimately completed in a hasty fashion so the "city" could be used for a series of Babylon Festivals scheduled in 1987.[52] That each of the temple's bricks was inscribed with Saddam's name was indicative of its lack of archaeological authenticity.

In the new regime's cultural production industry, conferences and festivals highlighted the Ba'th Party's efforts to integrate traditional Pan-Arabism with its own "Mesopotamianism." Although integrating two different spatial referents—a Pan-Arab state as opposed to the Iraqi nation-state—presented difficulties, the Takriti Ba'th effectively manipulated this potential contradiction. On the one hand, to an extent unprecedented in any Arab country, including Egypt under Nasir, Ba'thist-controlled organizations such as the Union of Arab Historians, the Center for Arab Gulf Studies, and the Union of Arab Writers sought to position Iraq in the vanguard of Pan-Arabism by giving voice to Arab intellectuals who supported its corporatist worldview. On the other hand, hosting Arab intellectuals at conferences and festivals situated at sites that foregrounded Iraq's unique civilizational heritage emphasized Iraq's cultural superiority to other Arab countries. By holding conferences and festivals at sites that predated Iraq's Islamic heritage, the regime also sought to undermine the authority of the Shi'i *marja'iya*, who took umbrage at the Mirbad Festival, the Abu Tammam Festival in Mosul, and festivals in Babylon that commemorated not only the pre-Islamic era but also secular and pagan symbols.

Archaeology was the third area that the Ba'th used to create its own variant of Iraqist nationalism. Efforts to link Saddam to Mesopotamian rulers such as Nebuchadnezzar[53] and to Iraq's ancient civilizational heritage led to generous subsidies for new archaeological excavations. Despite its long and scholarly record, to read *Sumer* after the Baʿthist coup gave the impression that no significant archaeological activity had occurred prior to 1968.[54] Once *Sumer* was subordinated to the Baʿth's ideological dictates, Taha Baqir was removed from its editorial board and relegated to Baghdad University, where he remained until his retirement. Reflecting Saddam's influence, the first issues of *Sumer* in 1969 discussed new excavations in the town of Takrit and its environs.[55] Clearly members of the new regime hoped that the state's archaeologists would discover ruins that would add luster to their rural origins. Efforts to privilege Takrit as an urban area would assume even greater importance after Saddam seized total power in 1979.

State-sponsored artisan and "folkloric" crafts represented a particularly important area of Baʿthist cultural production. Although production by individual artisans certainly continued at the village level, the state no longer allowed the organized private production of traditional handicrafts. The most prominent state-controlled institution was the Institute of Popular Handicrafts, established in July 1970 to commemorate the second anniversary of the 1968 coup. In July 1972, the Baʿth replaced the existing Center for Handicraft Training with a new Institute of Popular Arts and Handicrafts. A Revolution Command Council decree moved the new institute from the Ministry of Education to the Ministry of Culture and Information, indicating the political importance that the Baʿth attached to cultural production in all its variants.[56]

During visits to Iraq during the 1980s, I was struck by the blatant integration of Baʿthist slogans and images into what were purported to be authentic craft products. Because these products were more expensive than rurally produced crafts and were often inscribed with state-sponsored propaganda, the audience was certainly the middle classes, especially Baʿthists and would-be party members who were often of rural origins. The center's message was that the state would preserve Iraq's folklore, but in a way that would inscribe in that heritage a clear linkage to contemporary politics and would continue to valorize rural life.

A final area of state activity involved establishing new museums and monuments that would become important political tools. In differentiating "tradition" from "modernity," museum exhibits represented a form of political and social control by suggesting what aspects of culture should be discarded, or rather relegated to "tradition," and what elements were considered "modern," and hence acceptable. Not only were new provincial museums devoted to folklore built, but older museums such as the Khan Murjan and the Museum of Costumes were renovated. A new Museum of the Arab Socialist Baʿth Party, established in Ahmad Hasan al-Bakr's home, which he donated for that purpose, had five halls that displayed "souvenirs," "instruments," and "party literature" related to the party's pre-1968 activities.[57] Monuments became particularly important during the Iran-Iraq War.

Even a cursory review indicates that the new Ba'thist regime devoted much more time and resources to Ministry of Culture and Information publications (for example, *al-Mawrid* and *al-Aqlam*), organizing conferences on folklore, sponsoring poetry conferences, funding new architectural projects, establishing museums, and creating professional organizations such as the Union of Arab Historians than publishing texts on Ba'thist ideology. State-sponsored cultural production sought to create a new definition of the citizen as subject, based on corporatist ties to the Iraqi nation-state. The fiction that Iraq was but a region *(qutr)* of a larger Pan-Arab political entity was retained, but it became progressively less important in the actual decisions taken by the state. Returning to Iraq in 1984 after an initial visit just prior to the Iran-Iraq War, I was struck that a neon sign near the Baghdad Hotel's entrance displaying the Ba'thist slogan "One Arab nation with an eternal mission" *(Umma 'Arabiya wahida dhat risala khalida),* which had been brightly lit in 1980, was now dark and in disrepair. Although the Ba'thist state, like many Arab states, paid lip service to Arab unity, national interests dominated policy making. What differed was that the Ba'th no longer articulated as vigorous a Pan-Arabism as it had when it first came to power in 1968.

State-sponsored cultural production under the Takriti Ba'th may be divided into three analytic categories. First, there were ideological tracts, such as the speeches and essays by Saddam and works by Ba'thist ideologues such as Michel 'Aflaq, Ilyas Farah, Shibli al-'Aysami, and Fadil Barak, to name a few. A second category encompassed works explicitly designed to use culture to promote the state's political and ideological objectives. In this instance, the author was fully conscious of the text's ideological and political objectives and was writing to achieve certain ends. A third category, however, included intellectuals who produced scholarly texts. The state often published the writings of these intellectuals because their themes were consistent with its own interests. This third category can provide important insights into the tensions involved in state-sponsored cultural production, which seeks to create a historical memory that erases, distorts, or simply minimizes important elements of Iraq's cultural heritage. Such works can also provide important insights into resistance to the state, especially where the author's literary or artistic efforts are ostensibly designed to promote state interests. Thus the study of the state's efforts to appropriate historical memory can itself, when appropriately conceptualized, provide critical understandings of the nature and role of political change.

The framework for the state's intervention in history writing and cultural production is codified in *On the Writing of History;* in an intellectual biography written by the Egyptian author Amin Iskandar, *Saddam Husayn: Struggler, Thinker and Human Being;* and in a much larger volume, *Saddam Husayn on the Writing of History.*[58] Published in 1979, *On the Writing of History* is comprised of an anonymous preface written by the Ministry of Culture and the Arts,[59] four speeches by Saddam, and twenty-three accompanying essays by prominent Iraqi scholars. As argued in the preface, history writing is intrinsically linked to "authenticity" *(al-asala),* which is indicative of this issue's continued salience in Iraqi Pan-Arab thought. For the Ba'th, authenticity is first and foremost about creating and policing cultural boundaries.[60] Thus the concept is almost always deployed in opposition to forces purportedly hostile to Arab-Iraqi heritage. Those who are culturally authentic *(asil)* are part of the Iraqi political community and those who are not reside outside it, with Saddam and the Takriti Ba'th the arbiters of what criteria determine inclusion.

Saddam's interviews with Amin Iskandar are more comprehensive than his speeches published in *On the Writing of History.* In these interviews, Saddam refers not only to sections of his "book," but also to other writings, such as those of Michel 'Aflaq, Marx, and even Schopenhauer. Clearly, he intended the Iskandar volume to reach an audience beyond Iraq, as evidenced by its English and French editions. Saddam's extensive critique of the communists is indicative of the continuing threat that the Ba'th perceived as emanating not from the ICP per se, but from the continuing resonance of the Iraqist nationalist model with large sectors of the Iraqi populace. Unlike *On the Writing of History,* Iskandar's work provides a broad tableau of Ba'thist thinking and social and political objectives. What is obvious, especially in Iskandar's study, is that Iraqi Ba'thism has never developed its own intellectual center of gravity and that much of its thinking has evolved in reaction to Iraqist nationalist ideas, and particularly those of its arch rival, the ICP.

In light of the implicit victimology inherent in *On the Writing of History* and the Iskandar biography—namely, the idea that the Arabs have been besieged throughout their history by hostile forces—it is tempting to speculate that Saddam's negative worldview was influenced by the terrible family dislocations and the general emotional instability that he faced during his childhood.[61] Although these factors no doubt helped shape Saddam's conspiratorial worldview, personality variables alone would not explain the attractiveness of his vision to other Baʿth Party members. Baʿthist historical and cultural verities—the Arab nation's unity and unbreakable ties to a unified culture and strong state, and the notion of a linear and unchanging Arab history that moves toward ever-higher levels of achievement and glory—reflected the need to socially and culturally reconstruct Iraqi society in response to the severe dislocations that occurred after the Ottoman Empire's collapse. That the large majority of Takriti Baʿthists were Sunni Arabs drawn from the Sunni triangle, which is situated in a rural and ethnically diverse area that has been associated with ethnic conflict, provides the second hypothesis to explain the Baʿthist model's exclusionary nature. As Hanna Batatu has argued, the Ottoman Empire's collapse disrupted the Sunni triangle's commercial and cultural ties to the Arab Levant, leading to a long period of decline for the small towns of the area such as Takrit, al-ʿAna, al-Ramadi, al- Haditha, and others.[62] In other words, economic decline exacerbated ethnic conflict. Traditional Sunni Arab domination of the state and the Takriti Baʿth's desire to sustain that domination also constitutes a core reason for the regime's ideological and cultural policies. This explains much of the hatred toward the Qasim regime, which was perceived as challenging the traditional access of lower-middle-class Sunni Arabs to positions within the state.[63]

The Baʿth party's claim to revolutionary status is based in large measure on its deep concern for the history of the "Arab nation" *(al-umma al-ʿArabiya)*. History writing provides a weapon against imperialist forces, which in this case not only occupied Iraq but also sought to extend their power by destroying Iraq's heritage (and therefore historical memory) and that of the Arab nation as a whole, as was particularly evident in the loss of Palestine. This concern with the past and rectifying a historical record that numerous (often unspecified) forces have attempted to distort is central to the civilizational struggle *(al-siraʿa al-hidari)* in which the Arab nation is engaged.

For Saddam, history writing is instrumental, as indicated by the question that he poses at the beginning of *On the Writing of History:* "For whom is history written?" *(Li-Man Yuktab al-Tarikh?),* which points again to the setting of cultural and political boundaries. If history writing is instrumental, then it is designed to serve certain groups or nations. Those who are not part of these groups or nations are excluded from the historical narrative. History writing must affirm the facts of the past and the linear trajectory of the future. This understanding of the world as ordered and subject to affirmation through the appropriate scientific methodology represents a very positivist perspective. The Arab world is assumed to have a fixed and unchanging structure that the history writer or folklorist discovers and elucidates through his or her research. History writing is in no way considered a creative process designed to open new theoretical and conceptual perspectives, but rather is meant to strengthen the individual's ties to the larger Arab nation. Since cultural production, paralleling society at large, is organized along corporatist lines, the intellectual represents an extension of group behavior and consciousness. All intellectuals are tied to a common agenda, which is to promote social consciousness of certain historical givens that are centered on the unity and glory of the Arab nation. The ultimate expression of this view was the initial and core volume of an ambitious series on Iraqi society, *al-ʿIraq fi-l-Tarikh (Iraq in History)*, which had no formal editor. Although the president of the Iraqi Academy, Dr. Salih Ahmad al-ʿAli, wrote the introduction, the volume's articles, which are not written by Iraq's most prominent historians, offer no footnotes and frequently contain erroneous information.[64]

Leadership was a major subject of interest to Saddam. On the one hand, Saddam was keen to promote the idea of strong leader who is characterized by his heroism *(al-butula)*. However, he was just as keen to insure that his position was not confused with that of a leader of a specific tribe or confessional group. Instead, Saddam promoted the idea of his leadership as an extension of the role of paramount shaykh. Just as the paramount shaykh guards the well-being of his tribal confederation and mediates tribal disputes, so Saddam assumed this benevolent and stabilizing role for the Iraqi nation (and in his not-to-be-realized dream, perhaps for the Arab nation as well).

Even though he sought to play down public consciousness and discussions of tribalism and confessionalism in Iraqi politics and society, Saddam simultaneously promoted himself as paramount shaykh of the Iraqi nation. As a category of thought, tribes began to reenter public discourse during the 1980s. First, after assuming sole power after ousting Ahmad Hasan al-Bakr, Saddam hoped to portray himself as paramount shaykh and to further differentiate himself from any remaining political opponents. Second, tribalism was a value to which all Iraq's ethnic groups—Sunnis, Shiʿs, and Kurds alike, especially those in rural areas—could relate. Third, tribalism assumed still greater importance after the onset of the Iran-Iraq War because Saddam used tribal images centered around the Battle of Qadisiya to mobilize the populace. Murals, for example, appeared throughout Iraq depicting seventh-century Arab forces attacking the Sasanian armies. Nevertheless, ʿAbbas al-ʿAzzawi's four-volume ʿAshaʾir al-ʿIraq *(The Tribes of Iraq)*, which contains extensive data on histories of individual Iraqi tribes, continued to be banned and remained unavailable to the Iraqi public. Because al-ʿAzzawi's incredibly detailed study points to conflict among tribes, which was not in keeping with the Baʿth Party's corporatist vision of Iraqi society, and because it foregrounds certain tribes viewed unfavorably by the regime, this study was deemed unacceptable. Instead, the notion of tribalism was confined to Iraq's origins and thus posited as an idealized, transhistorical category. In other words, tribe and tribalism became abstract historical concepts whose political implications for the present could not be openly discussed. Nevertheless, all sensitive observers realized that tribalism was being enshrined in the regime's political iconography to enhance Saddam's cult of personality.

By the end of the 1970s, the Takriti Baʿth, under Saddam's leadership, had achieved a level of power never before enjoyed by any modern Iraqi political elite. Oil revenues were at an all-time high. The ICP was a shell of its former self. In 1975, Saddam negotiated an end to the dispute with Iran over the Shatt al-ʿArab waterway in return for Iran's agreement to end military aid to Iraq's Kurds. In 1978, Saddam personally supervised the execution of twelve communist ministers. Reaching a new level of brutality, Baʿth Party officials were forced to carry out the executions themselves, thereby formally ending the already moribund National Front government. In July of 1979, after removing Ahmad Hasan al-Bakr and assuming the presidency, Saddam eliminated all potential opposition within the Baʿth Party. Alleging that some party members had conspired with Syria to form a united Syrian-Iraqi state under Hafiz al-Asad's control, Saddam called a meeting of party leaders to inform them of the "plot."[65] With feigned emotion, Saddam slowly and deliberately read out the names of fifty-five purported conspirators, who were immediately removed from the audience. A special court was hastily established and, after a brief trial, death sentences were handed down. Party members from each of the Baʿth's regional offices were forced to carry out the executions of the purported conspirators, which included one of Saddam's closest friends, ʿAdnan al-Hamdani. Because two of the five main party leaders put on trial, Hamdani and Muhi ʿAbd al-Husayn al-Mashhadi, were Shiʿis, Saddam appointed another Shiʿi and future parliament speaker, Naʿim Haddad, as court president. A now-famous videotape of the proceedings was circulated to party offices throughout the country to send a message about the consequences of challenging Saddam's authority.[66] Having eliminated all immediate opposition,

Saddam and the Baʻth felt secure enough to allow elections for a new parliament (Majlis Watani) to be held during the spring of 1980, even though candidates were limited to Baʻth Party members and independents sympathetic to the party. [67] By the summer of 1980, Saddam and the Baʻth seemed at the pinnacle of power.

7   Memories of State in Decline, 1979–1990

On September 22, 1980, Saddam Husayn launched the eight-year-long Iran-Iraq War, the deadliest of the twentieth century.[1] Although large oil reserves allowed the regime to maintain the appearance of normalcy early in the war, the conflict gradually began to unravel the gains made by the Ba'thist regime. With the economy devastated following the 1988 truce with Iran, the Ba'thist regime was unable to compensate the war-ravished population for its sacrifices, which led to widespread discontent. How did the Iran-Iraq War affect the state's attempt to control cultural production? What role did historical memory play in the war? Why did Saddam, having eliminated all major opposition and consolidated his power, begin such a foolhardy war? Was the war merely the ruinous miscalculation of an egotistic leader, or was it representative of something deeper and structural in the Ba'thist state? Answers to these questions are critical because Iraq's invasion of Iran set in motion forces that steadily eroded the Ba'thist state's power, provoking it to invade Kuwait in 1990 and almost leading to its collapse during the March–April 1991 Intifada.[2]

The second period of Ba'thist rule from 1979 to 1990, during which Saddam deposed Ahmad Hasan al-Bakr as president, and which ended with the August 1990 invasion of Kuwait, squandered whatever popular support the regime had amassed during the 1970s. Saddam's extended family replaced the Takriti Ba'th as the key decision makers in the party and state apparatus. The *hizb al-usra* (family party) included Saddam's three half-brothers, Barzan, Watban, and Sab'awi, his stepfather, Ibrahim Hasan al-Majid, and his cousin 'Ali Hasan al-Majid. It was later expanded to include Saddam's nephews, Husayn and Saddam Kamil, who married Saddam's two eldest daughters, Raghad and Rana respectively.[3] During the late 1980s, a further change occurred as Saddam's sons, 'Uday and Qusay, gained political influence, creating new cleavages within the regime. The rising influence and power of Saddam's sons marked the beginning of the third and final phase of Ba'thist rule.

As president, Ahmad Hasan al-Bakr was largely viewed as a benign leader.[4] He was commonly perceived as a national father figure, a reassuring image for many Iraqis during the first decade of Ba'thist rule. The respect al-Bakr enjoyed, which stemmed from his status as a senior army officer and his lack of higher political ambition, allowed him to play an important role as mediator among Ba'th Party factions. Once al-Bakr was eliminated, the party's internal stability and structure were disrupted. During the Takriti phase of Ba'thist rule, party members were drawn from a number of clans of the Al bu Nasir and related tribes. Examples included Hardan al-Takriti, Taha Yahya, Fadil Barak al-Takriti, and Salah 'Umar al-'Ali, Saddam's cousin and former Iraqi ambassador to the United Nations.[5] Ahmad Hasan al-Bakr and 'Adnan Khayrallah Tulfah, the Iraqi defense minister during the Iran-Iraq War, came from the section of the Al bu Nasir known as the Beyjat.[6] Husayn and Saddam Kamil came from the al-Majid clan and were Saddam's cousins on his deceased father's side.[7] An undistinguished tribe, the Al bu Nasir, like many Iraqi tribes, traced its origins to the Arabian peninsula.[8] In settling around Takrit, it developed ties with other tribes from the Sunni Arab towns of north-central Iraq such as the al-Dur, the al-Dulaym, the al-Jubur, the al-Rawi, and the al-Shammar. After 1979, these clans and families found their power and influence greatly reduced as power became more narrowly controlled by Saddam's immediate family members.[9]

The narrowing of the circle of political power after Saddam took power in 1979 is ironic, because Saddam and the Takriti Ba'th had been the target in 1973 of a coup attempt by security chief Nazim al-Kazzar, who is said to have resented Takriti domination of the state. The coup attempt prompted Saddam to rely on family members in building his own power base in the party and the state. Thus the changes that occurred in 1979 represented more of a culmination of a trend already in progress than a break with the past.

How did changes in the structure of the political elite and the political economy during the second period of Ba'thist rule affect the state's attempts to appropriate historical memory? With the Iran-Iraq War's enormous human and material losses, and the Ba'th Party's transformation into an organ of Saddam's extended family that was characterized by infighting, corruption, and degenerate behavior, the increasingly shrill quality of the state's efforts to use historical memory to elicit consent began to undermine the credibility the regime had gained during the 1970s. The state's attempt to appropriate historical memory was undermined by its subordination by Saddam's family members and the privatization policies enacted between 1979 and 1990 that reflected the regime's continued move to the right. These two policies combined to replace the regime's former corporate sense of identity with one grounded in the individualistic and materialistic interests of a small number of political actors, none of whom, besides Saddam, had much interest in historical memory or the cultural politics of the 1970s. Links between the state and the public began to be attenuated, thereby undermining the viability of the Ba'th's hegemonic project.

Saddam's replacement of Ba'th Party control of the state with control by his family members *(dawlat hizb al-usra)* was intended to increase his security, but his privatization policies had different ends. First, the Ba'th sought to improve the technology it was able to employ by reducing its dependence on Soviet and East bloc technology of poor quality. Second, by employing Western firms in large infrastructural projects, the Ba'th created incentives for the West to support the party, which was especially crucial during the war with Iran.[10] Third, privatization policies benefited members of the regime. Husayn Kamil, who rose from being a driver in Saddam's motorcade to being lieutenant-general in the Republican Guard and, ultimately, minister of military industries, became very wealthy through developing weapons projects.[11] Thus changes in the political economy that downplayed the state's "socialist" orientation served both international and domestic ends. Western technological assistance helped Iraq economically and militarily by allowing sophisticated infrastructural projects to move ahead, American agricultural credits freed other funds for use in the war, and credits that could be used to purchase dual-use machinery, such as helicopters and trucks, were converted to military use. This dual-use technology was critical during the 1980s in Iraq's efforts to develop and manufacture nuclear, chemical, and biological weapons. Western support simultaneously promoted the fortunes of a new state bourgeoisie, which, having already made great strides during the 1970s, implemented these projects.[12]

Perhaps nowhere was the shift away from "socialist" or state control of the economy as evident as in agriculture. Although trumpeted as one of the main achievements of the July 1958 Revolution, the Qasim regime's agrarian reform had always been ambiguous, less in its intent than in its application.[13] While the assets of the largest landowners and supporters of the monarchy had been expropriated, middle-level owners were only marginally affected. Further, limited state resources, especially the scarcity of trained officials to implement agrarian reform, meant that throughout the 1960s much appropriated land was never redistributed.

After coming to power in 1968, the Ba'th intensified land-reform policies, most likely to outflank the ICP, which had vociferously supported radical land reform under Qasim. Rather than redistributing land to small owners as the Qasim regime had intended, the Ba'th Party emphasized public ownership. The number of collective farms increased from six in 1972 to seventy-nine in 1976, and in the 1976–80 Five Year Plan the number was projected to increase to more than three hundred by 1980. More than 1.3 million *dunums* of agricultural land were converted to state ownership.[14] Saddam's reversal after 1979 of the collectivist policies of the 1970s represented a major policy change. Rather than increasing, the number of collective farms declined sharply, from seventy-seven in 1979 to only ten in 1983. Investment and credit policies benefited private investors. Law 35 of 1983 gave preferential treatment to private owners, who were often allowed to hold large amounts of land that exceeded the limits set by Law 117, enacted in 1970.[15]

Rather than benefiting small farmers, ostensibly the intended recipients, by increasing agricultural productivity, the state gave priority to capital-intensive crops. A new class of urban investors comprised of government employees, small businessmen, and party officials made considerable profits, often in niche farming ventures, by exploiting their ties to the Ba'th Party.[16] Contractors in rural towns who formed partnerships with local landowners also benefited. For urban consumers, the increase in the diversity of crops was offset by significant price increases.

In explaining Saddam's motives for pursuing privatization of the economy, it is necessary to realize that the Iraqi leader was never seriously committed to socialist policies. A 1977 commentary on the 1972 decree that nationalized Iraqi oil production, for example, demonstrates little concern with socialism.[17] Although Saddam relied upon the Leninist "vanguard party" as a model for the Ba'th Party and structured many youth and other organizations on the Soviet model, the economic dimensions of socialist thought never engaged his thinking. Among Saddam's huge body of writings (whether actually written by him or by others), there is very little on socialism per se or on socialist economics as it applies to Iraq.

The transition from the radical policies of the 1970s to the partial privatization of the economy during the 1980s was intended to create a new class of Iraqis for whom economic prosperity, not ideology, would insure its loyalty to Saddam and not the party. The goal of privatization was less increasing agricultural output than insuring the continued support of important Baʿth Party members and senior bureaucrats who benefited financially from it. This represented a shift in the regime's social base. The cry of "Folklore in the service of the Arab struggle," which had been printed on the dedication page of a 1976 Ministry of Information volume on the ʿAbbasid satirist and writer al-Jahiz, and which represented continuity with an older populist tradition begun by the ICP and leftist intelligentsia during the 1950s, now became redundant.[18] The Baʿthism of the 1970s sought to mobilize left-leaning members of the middle and lower-middle classes as well as workers and peasants, even if the party remained ideologically centrist. The Baʿth Party's radical veneer and the creation of a National Front with the ICP led many leftist intellectuals to feel that they could work with the party. After 1979, the regime's social base shifted to a middle class increasingly interested in consumerism and enjoying the prosperity created by oil wealth.[19] Having neutralized the party's upper echelons through executions in 1979, Saddam used privatization as part of his strategy for building a new power base during the 1980s. In building this new power base, Saddam relied not only on his enormous ego, privatizing the economy and eliminating the traditional Baʿthist cadres as a political threat, but he also relied on a class of urban and town-based nouveaux riches with ties to the state, the core of which was comprised of his extended family. As power and wealth increasingly gravitated into the hands of a small elite, the gap between the Baʿth Party's "socialist" rhetoric and its everyday policies became increasingly apparent. The regime's ability to manipulate historical memory began to be undermined, as it was no longer seen as pursuing the populace's interests.

This is not to argue that the Baʿth Party became irrelevant to Iraqi politics. In certain respects, the opposite was true. Numbering only a few hundred members in 1968, the party had reached one and a half million members (one of every ten Iraqis) by 1981.[20] Ties to the party remained important for anyone seeking to achieve important political or economic goals. Despite being more tightly controlled under Saddam, the Baʿth Party showed no signs that its domination of the state apparatus and the organizations of civil society was lessening. All aspects of public life continued to be strictly controlled through one of seven state bureaus.[21]

What actually transpired was the party's restructuring as a completely pliant element in Saddam's hands. Whereas during the 1970s upper echelon party members, at least, had been able to express opinions contrary to those of Saddam, and, in the case of al-Bakr, even try to reduce Saddam's power, now the party became a one-way transmission belt of power and influence. Through restructuring the party's highest organ, the Revolution Command

Council, and the Regional Command (al-Qiyada al-Qutriya), Saddam was intent on assuring that there would be no challenges to his authority. His intimate knowledge of conspiracies, stemming from his own activities in 1959 and 1968, and his awareness of the tenuous balance between the military and civilian political actors throughout the 1960s, made him determined to prevent the seizure of the state by "three officers and four tanks."[22]

During the 1970s, the Ba'th constantly rejected calls for a move toward democracy, characterizing such calls as "bourgeois," and instead advocated an ill-defined "third path" *(al-tariq al-thalith)* of "popular democracy," which purportedly stood between Western liberalism and Soviet communism. Prior to 1975, the regime cited the Kurdish uprising in the north as a reason to postpone democracy. Between 1975 and 1979, Saddam argued that the Iraqi Communist Party's threat, and then the Islamic Revolution in Iran, precluded any move toward a democratic form of government. Thus many were surprised in January 1980 by Saddam's call for the creation of a national parliament (al-Majlis al-Watani).

What were the motivations behind the abrupt decision to create an elected parliament? The parliament itself enjoyed no legislative power. Membership was confined to Ba'th Party members and party sympathizers, although the electoral lists in three polling stations I visited just prior to the parliamentary elections on June 20, 1980, listed Kurdish candidates supposedly allied with the Kurdish Democratic Party and "independents," in addition to Ba'th Party members.[23] Its deliberations and voting were strictly controlled. Nevertheless, the creation of the first parliament since the monarchy's fall gave some Iraqis hope that a gradual liberalization might be in the offing. However, the war with Iran that followed shortly after the parliament's creation provided yet another convenient excuse not to implement even a limited form of democracy.

The real motive behind the formation of the Majlis was Saddam's desire to further eclipse the Revolution Command Council (RCC) by creating a parallel decision-making body while simultaneously creating the impression that Iraq was moving toward a more popular form of government. As an institution empowered to pass laws, the Majlis Watani was a useful forum for bypassing, if necessary, the RCC. The *majlis* also provided a foil to Saddam's cult of personality. For those who thought the Iraqi regime was becoming too personalistic, it could be argued that Iraq was finally experiencing political institutionalization. The public had, for the first time since the July 1958 Revolution, a popularly elected assembly through which to express its views. The appointment of Shi'is (Na'im Haddad and Sa'dun

Hammadi) as speakers of the first two parliaments was intended to offset Shi'i discontent and Iranian propaganda intended to create sectarian dissension.[24] The rubber-stamp parliament could serve foreign policy objectives as well by leading the international community to believe that the regime was moving toward democratization. Despite the parliament's inability to initiate laws, its deliberations received extensive coverage in the press.[25]

The Ba'thist state found it increasingly difficult to follow a policy of "guns and butter" once it depleted its initial reserves and faced a recession in 1983. Even Western, Saudi, and Kuwaiti credits and loans, which were intended to offset Iraq's financial crisis and reduced oil production, could not prevent an economic downturn. These changes were paralleled by a reduced focus on the populist dimension of state-sponsored cultural production, which was replaced by the Qadisiyat Saddam campaign. As a sop to the educated middle classes, there was a slight opening in political and social expression, as topics formerly banned or dealt with in a strict party-line fashion were now allowed to be discussed in a more forthright manner.[26] Religion began to creep into Ba'thist pronouncements, culminating in the addition of "Allahu Akbar!" (God is great) to the Iraqi flag in 1990 following the mobilization of an international military coalition in the wake of Iraq's seizure of Kuwait.[27] Even aspects of the Hashimite Monarchy were revived, such as Saddam's rebuilding of Faysal I's statue, which had been torn down by demonstrators on July 14, 1958. Continuing the rapprochement with the West, Iraq and the United States reestablished diplomatic relations in 1984. Anti-imperialist and socialist rhetoric declined. Quietly, hostility to Israel was downplayed and support for radical Palestinian factions declined. The new emphasis on Saddam's contribution to Iraqi and Arab history, and on the hostile intentions of Iran and its agents within Iraq, fit well with the war effort and eclipsed populist and "socialist" themes in favor of the Iraqi president's personality cult.

Unable to deliver on promises of a return to prosperity following the Iran-Iraq War and faced with increasing discontent within the military,[28] Saddam's regime, in an act of desperation, seized Kuwait in 1990. With Saddam's son 'Uday playing a central role, Kuwait was methodically stripped of its valuables, from expensive automobiles to national treasures. The Ba'thist state's seizure of Kuwait suggested the increasing lawlessness and unpredictability of its behavior, which was based on an amalgam of the values of tribalism and organized crime. With Saddam's two sons, 'Uday and Qusay, emerging as key political actors during the early 1990s, more cleavages developed, leading to Saddam's three half brothers losing power and, in 1996, the murder of his two sons-in-law, Husayn and Saddam Kamil. Under the sanctions imposed on the regime by the United Nations after the Gulf War, the state's ability to appropriate historical memory was severely truncated.

The main contradiction that bedeviled the Baʻth in its efforts to appropriate historical memory as the basis of a new Iraqi collective identity finally manifested itself during the 1980s. Initially, the Baʻthist regime placed great emphasis on creating a political culture that could accommodate all sectors of Iraqi society, albeit in a hierarchical form. During the period of the Takriti Baʻth, that is, the years of the al-Bakr-Husayn condominium (1968–79), every Iraqi was relegated to a position in the sociopolitical pecking order, with Sunni Arabs (particularly those of nonurban tribal backgrounds) enjoying the greatest privileges, and the Shiʻa, Kurds, and minorities, who were willing to forgo asserting their ethnic identities, granted more limited privileges reflecting their lower social and political status. Care was taken to hide from Iraqis, other Arabs, and the non-Arab world generally the extent to which tribal and familial connections determined political and economic influence and power.[29] However, perceptive Iraqis were aware of the tremendous gap between the regime's rhetoric about using cultural production to create an egalitarian and socialist society, on the one hand, and political, social, and economic reality, on the other. Nevertheless, in areas such as the promotion of national folklore and popular culture through journals, magazines, newspapers, television programming, theater, films, art, and dance troupes, Iraqis took varying degrees of pride in what appeared to them to be the formation of a national culture and an emerging sense of national identity. Where the "rewriting of history" was not overtly political and resonated with the populace's cultural predispositions, it began to make inroads among the educated middle classes during the late 1970s, some of whom returned from abroad.[30]

The removal of al-Bakr, the liquidation of Saddam's potential challengers within the Baʻth Party, the Iraqi president's vision of replacing Iran as the major Gulf power, his ambition of becoming the Arab world's leader, and his desire to reshape Iraqi politics and society changed the direction and impact of the attempt to appropriate historical memory.[31] The state's promotion of a narrower definition of cultural production and its blatant attempt to link the past with the present—through posters and murals comparing Saddam with the Arab commander at al-Qadisiya, Saʻd Ibn Abi al-Waqqas, and the production of a genealogy that purported to trace the Iraqi president's lineage to ʻAli ibn Abi Talib—did not resonate effectively with the populace compared to the state-sponsored memory of the 1970s.[32] For many educated and secular Iraqis, it was difficult to reconcile the Baʻth's increasingly Islamic overtones with the fiercely secular policies of its early years. This antireligious orientation (directed especially against the Shi'i *marja'iya*) had been evident in the privileging of al-Jahiliya, or pre-Islamic, poetry, the focus on ancient Iraq, and on artistic representation, such as that of al-Wasiti, which stressed human imagery prohibited by Islam.[33] Many found developments such as the establishment in 1989 of a theological seminary named after Saddam bizarre to say the least.[34]

Another problematic aspect of the state's efforts to appropriate historical memory in the war with Iran and to link it to Saddam's persona was its increasingly negative tone. From the outset, state-sponsored cultural production under the Ba'th had emphasized the historical victimization of Iraq as a target of hostile forces. First and foremost, this perspective allowed the Ba'th to transfer blame for many of society's ills onto "external conspiracies," thereby exonerating the party of responsibility for them. Second, the notion of Iraq as a victim of hostile attacks implicitly justified Ba'thist authoritarianism because any democratic opening would compromise the regime's ability to defend Iraq against its enemies by allowing the proliferation of potentially subversive political groups and opinions. Third, playing the role of the victim became an important tool in forging a sense of national identity, particularly among the regime's rural tribal social base. As a superior society, Saddam argued, Iraq created envy and jealously among its enemies, who wanted to seize the country's wealth and civilizational heritage for themselves.[35]

Nowhere did this negative perspective manifest itself as clearly as in the continued emphasis on the al-Shu'ubiya movement. Extending back at least to the 1930s, this controversy was originally directed against the ancient al-'Ajam or Arabized Persian courtly class of scribes, clerks, and belletrists under the 'Abbasid Empire.[36] As noted earlier, the modern intellectual charge against the al-Shu'ubiya movement was led by the conservative (Sunni Arab) historian 'Abd al-'Aziz al-Duri. Despite his scholarly credentials as one of the deans of the modern Iraqi historical school, al-Duri's writing on the Shu'ubiya is distinctly polemical and directed at a lay rather than a scholarly audience.[37] For al-Duri, and other conservative Pan-Arabists such as Sati' al-Husari and 'Abd al-Rahman al-Bazzaz, the al-Shu'ubiyun represent a metaphor for the real enemy, the Iraqi communists and their leftist and Iraqist nationalist supporters, whose cultural pluralism and emphasis on social class cleavages downplayed Iraq's Arab character and threatened Iraqi unity.[38] In a 1983 volume, *al-Tayyar al-Qawmi fi-l-Shi'r al-'Iraqi al-Hadith, Munthu al-Harb al-'Alamiya al-Thaniya, 1939, Hatta Naksat Khuzayran 1967 (The Pan-Arabist Tendency in Modern Iraqi Poetry, From the Second World War, 1939, to the Setback of June,*

1967), Majid Ahmad al-Samarra'i likewise associates the Shu'ubiyun with leftists and Iraqist nationalists who, he argues, lack commitment to Arab unity. The ICP's support of Jewish-Arab solidarity against imperialism in Palestine is attacked as an indicator of the left's lack of patriotism, and its suspect loyalty to Iraq and the larger Arab nation. al-Samarra'i emphasizes the need to remain vigilant against a loss of confidence in Arab cultural heritage.[39]

During the Iran-Iraq War, the state's emphasis on the al-Shu'ubiya movement not only became much more prominent, but the interpretation of the movement underwent a metamorphosis. In a lengthy 1983 Ministry of Culture and Information volume, *Tarikh al-Munaza'at wa-l-Hurub Bayn al-'Iraq wa-l-Iran, (History of the Struggles between Iraq and Iran)*, Shakir Sabir al-Dabit, one of the founders of *The Journal of Popular Culture*, extends the al-Shu'ubiya framework to include the entire history of Iraqi-Persian relations.[40] Historically, the al-Shu'ubiya controversy was no longer confined to the 'Abbasid period or, politically, specifically directed against the left, but now became part of a much larger narrative linked to the Iran-Iraq War. In positing an unwavering Iranian hostility toward Iraq throughout history, al-Dabit essentializes Iraqi-Persian relations. Here again we confront the paradox of a state-sponsored historical analysis that negates history. This is particularly striking in light of al-Dabit's earlier, more scholarly, study on the boundaries between Iraq and Iran published in 1966. One of the results of the state appropriation of cultural production was the systematic transformation and degradation of Iraqi scholarship.

The al-Shu'ubiya controversy appeared in a new state-sponsored series on Iraqi history and culture that began with a large and carelessly argued volume, *al-'Iraq fi-l-Tarikh (Iraq and History)*, published in 1983.[41] Each volume of the series begins with a saying of Saddam Husayn and is distinguished by a brown or blue cover with a date palm in the cover's upper center, and many lack a formal editor.[42] One of the most important publications in this series was a 1983 volume on Iraqi-Iranian relations, *al-Sira'a al-'Iraqi al-Farisi (The Iraqi-Persian Conflict)*. In the introduction, 'Abd al-Salam Ra'uf extends the debate over the al-Shu'ubiyun to include all of Iraqi history.[43] However, Ra'uf presents a different and very significant argument, one that mirrors the Ba'th's fears about maintaining its power and control of the Iraqi state. Paralleling al-Dabit, Ra'uf claims that Iran covets Iraq because of its more innovative and hence culturally superior civilization. However, Ra'uf argues that the Persians (al-Furs) are a minority who have continually tried to physically suppress Iran's many minorities whose ethnic ties have historically extended beyond the state's boundaries. Only

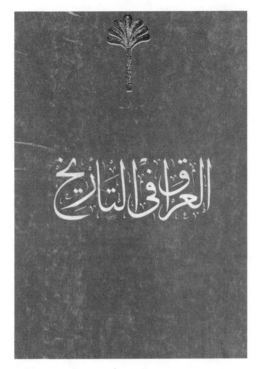

FIGURE 12. Cover of *Iraq in History* (1983),
first volume of a new Ba'thist series on Iraqi
history and culture during the 1980s.

through deceit and physical force has the Persian minority been able to sustain an artificial nation-state. Because Iran's minorities have never been able to express their true opinions, the Persians have engaged in continuous aggression against their neighbors as a means of suppressing internal dissent and creating a false sense of national unity. Of course, the unqualified transposing of modern concepts of nationalism and nationhood onto the distant past underlines the irony of all Ba'thist-sponsored history writing, which, although ostensibly deeply concerned with history, is profoundly antihistorical, conceptually, methodologically, and theoretically.

In the ultimate narrative on the al-Shu'ubiyun, Saddam gives his own views of the controversy in a 1989 volume, *Saddam Husayn wa Haqa'iq al-Tarikh al-'Arabi (Saddam Husayn and the Truth About Arab History).*[44] For Saddam, the al-Shu'ubiya controversy was not limited to the 'Abbasid period, but it extended back to the era of King Nebuchadnezzar, who faced a dual conspiracy, by the ancient Persians on the one hand, and by the Jews,

FIGURE 13. Cover of *The Iranian-Iraqi Conflict* (1983), early volume of a new Ba'thist series on Iraqi history and culture during the 1980s.

whom he had just defeated in Palestine and brought back to captivity in Babylon, on the other. In his portrayal of the al-Shu'ubiya controversy, Saddam augments the traditional narrative of the Semitic Arab Muslims pitted against the Zoroastrian Persians by adding that the Persians were aided by the Jews. Although he offers no details, Saddam asserts that the conspiracy in ancient Mesopotamia was identical to the Jewish conspiracy against the Palestinian Arabs in 1948 and after. The Iraqi Jewish community thus becomes a symbol for the aspersions that Saddam casts not just on the Shi'a for their hidden loyalty to Iran, but on all Iraq's minorities. This assertion is reinforced by his characterization of the leader of the Zanj Revolt as a Persian and Shu'ubi, a historical inaccuracy. For Saddam, only Sunni Arabs have the right to be considered culturally authentic *(asil)*. Saddam considers as a given the Arabs' superiority to all other cultures, which is enhanced by their strong ties to the land and the traditions such ties have engendered, and he uses spatial notions to reinforce the idea of Arab culture as unique, self-contained, and having developed using its own resources rather than borrowing from neighboring or foreign cultures.[45]

In emphasizing the al-Shuʿubiya controversy, Saddam lays down the gauntlet for the Iraqi Shiʿa. Although Saddam's target was first and foremost the Iranian enemy, he likewise sought to divide the Shiʿi marjaʿiya, for whom Khumayni's message would have the greatest affinity, from secular Shiʿis. In reality, Saddam's arguments go much deeper and challenge the Shiʿi community as a whole. Above all, the al-Shuʿubiya controversy is about deception and false loyalties. The Arabized Persians who called themselves Shuʿubiyun used their criticisms of the Arabs, particularly their culture and ethnic pride, as a subterfuge for their secret desires to bring about the latter's downfall. In effect, Saddam is arguing that, first, Iraq's major historical problem has been internal conspiracies or threats from within and, second, that the main source of these conspiracies has been the (Shiʿi) Persians to the east. When analyzed, these threats to Arab culture and society were by no means all based in religious ideology. In fact, most represented power politics pure and simple. By reformulating the al-Shuʿubiya controversy to include all Persians across time, Saddam casts a pall of suspicion over Iraq's entire Shiʿi community, secular and religious, throughout all of history because they are alleged to harbor continuous feelings of disloyalty and evil intent toward the Iraqi nation-state. For the Shiʿa, the only escape from these allegations is to become more Baʿthist than the Baʿthists to prove their loyalty to Iraq. In light of Saddam's attack, the defense of Iraq by the Iraqi army, whose infantry is predominantly Shiʿi, during the Iran-Iraq War was all the more remarkable, not as an indicator of support for Saddam and the Baʿth, but as an indicator of the Shiʿa's nationalism, which the Baʿth has constantly impugned.

As the war intensified, the Iraqi president was transformed into a latter-day "Arab knight" (faris al-ʿArab) who would defend the honor of the Arab nation from its Persian foes. This historical symbol was indicative of the attempt to tie the Baʿth Party more closely to its tribal base. Television programs "reenacted" the Battle of Qadisiya, and al-Diwaniya province, where the battle occurred, was renamed al-Qadisiya province.[46] In 1980, a new newspaper representing the armed forces, al-Qadisiya, was established.[47] To make this exploitation of the past more salient, Saddam extended his propaganda war to other Arab states, where his message was more warmly received than it was domestically. Egypt, Saudi Arabia, and Kuwait liked the idea of Iraq as defender of the Arab world's "eastern front, especially when Iraqi troops were conducting the defense."[48] With the Baʿth Party subordinated to Saddam's extended clan, his cult of personality represented not just a vainglorious ruler's attempt to become a historical figure, but also a new symbol that could substitute for the Baʿth Party's declining influence in the state's upper echelons. The invasion of Iran thus had profound implications for the state's efforts to shape a new definition of political community. Anticipating a lightning victory over Iran, Saddam expected to use the large "cultural sector" *(al-qitaʿ al-thaqafi)* to extol his virtues as a deft military commander, thereby facilitating his consolidation of power.

When the war did not follow his predictions and the Iraqi army was forced to retreat to the Iran-Iraq border in 1982, the cultural production industry began to appear as a propaganda vehicle for promoting the regime's interests and became less effective than it was before the war.[49] In contrast to the 1970s, when there were no social or political forces to effectively pose alternatives to the Baʿth's reinterpretation of the past, Iranian military victories posed the first real challenges to state-sponsored historical memory. How could the Iran-Iraq War be viewed as a modern-day Qadisiya if the Arabs won in 637 C.E. but were losing in the 1980s? For the regime, inspiring hatred of Iran was essential because it appeared that the war would be long and drawn out. Cultural boundaries had to be policed to insure that Iraq's Shiʿa would not side with Iran. Of course, the great irony was that Iraq's Shiʿa demonstrated great patriotism, and, without their military support, Iraq would have lost the war.

As state-sponsored cultural production became excessively focused on Saddam's persona, its credibility was further undermined. By the Gulf War, Saddam had become the fount of all knowledge and the only subject worth speaking about. His honorific titles proliferated. Whereas in a 1979 issue of the weekly journal *al-Funun (The Arts)* Saddam was referred to as *"al-Qaïd"* (The Leader), by the thirtieth anniversary of the July 1968 Revolution *al-Qadisiya* was portraying Saddam as a leader who was victorious according to God's will *(al-Sayyid al-Raïs al-Qaïd bi Mansur Allah).*[50] Not only did these pronouncements appear increasingly absurd to politically sophisticated Iraqis, but they also indicated that the Iraqi leader was becoming increasingly distant and seduced by his own rhetoric. By any objective indicators, his invasions of Iran and Kuwait were two of the worst foreign policy miscalculations by any state during the twentieth century.

No rewriting of history, no matter how widespread or how well supported by state largesse, could hide the reality that, by the end of the 1980s, the Baʿthist regime was built on a sectarian and social class base that privileged an increasingly lawless and rapacious elite.[51] When I first visited Iraq in the spring of 1980, many Iraqis disparaged the regime's authoritarianism. The regime's repressive quality could be seen in meetings with Iraqis, during which two individuals were always required to be present so that, if someone were accused of having made an unacceptable remark, the companion could confirm the conversation's content. Nevertheless, Iraqis frequently rationalized authoritarian rule by commenting that at least Saddam was not corrupt and maintained an honest government. By the end of the Iran-Iraq War, all illusions about how the regime functioned, including the belief in Saddam's honesty, had disappeared. Damage to Iraq's oil industry and lower crude oil prices at the end of the 1980s meant that state largesse, characteristic of the 1970s and the first years of the war, was sharply curtailed. This contrasted sharply with the development of a wealthy elite, many of whom were members of Saddam's immediate family, which benefited from ties to the regime, and sharpened perceptions of Iraq as a class-based society. Saddam himself had become involved in a well-publicized affair with Samira al-Shahbandar, wife of Nur al-Din al-Safi, general manager of Iraqi Airways, whom he married and with whom he had another son, ʿAli.[52] Once ʿUday acquired political influence during the 1990s, he used his power not only to enrich himself, but also to settle political scores and seduce young women. Authoritarian rule could no longer be explained away by invoking Saddam's clean hands or the prosperity created by oil wealth. Sectarian resentment spread. Sunni Arab hostility toward the Shiʿa was encouraged by the Qadisiyat Saddam campaign, while the Shiʿa's resentment increased because of the state's failure to valorize their contributions to the war effort.

Shiʿis, Kurds, other minorities, and non-Baʿthist Sunni Arabs continued to be excluded from power despite a dramatic growth in the Baʿth Party during the early 1980s. Throughout the 1970s there had been sporadic problems between the Baʿth and the Shiʿa. Already in June 1970, while marching in the funeral procession of Grand Ayatallah Muhsin al-Hakim in al-Najaf, President Ahmad Hasan al-Bakr was subject to chants by mourners that al-Hakim was not a spy.[53] Shiʿi riots in Karbala' and al-Najaf in 1977, assassination attempts of Baʿthist figures such as Foreign Minister Tariq ʿAziz on April 1, 1980, at Baghdad's al-Mustansariya University, and the attack on the funeral procession of those killed at the university five days later, as well as the rise of the shadowy Shiʿi radical religious organization Hizb al-Daʿwa al-Islamiya (Party of the Islamic Call), pointed to Shiʿa discontent.[54] Clearly the state's efforts to restructure historical memory had not fallen on receptive ears among the Shiʿa.

The regime responded vigorously to the threat it perceived from the Islamic Revolution in neighboring Iran by arresting and even executing prominent Iraqi Shiʿi clerics and organizing assassinations of Shiʿi leaders abroad who were presumed to be affiliated with al-Daʿwa. One of the most prominent executions was that of the highly respected cleric Ayatallah Muhammad Baqir al-Sadr and his sister, Bint al-Huda, in Baghdad in April 1980.[55] Large numbers of Iraqis of Persian ethnic origins were unceremoniously driven to the Iran-Iraq border and deported to Iran. Nevertheless, viewing the Iranian Revolution as the sole cause of the Iran-Iraq War leads one to lose sight of the impact of the changes that occurred in Iraq during the late 1970s. There were heightened fears not only about a Shiʿi threat, but also about continued Kurdish opposition to the Baʿth. The relocation of the ICP to Kurdistan, where it engaged in armed struggle, placed another opponent in a historically rebellious area. Whether the alleged Syrian involvement in the 1977 demonstrations in Iraq's Shiʿi shrine cities was real or imagined, Saddam did not feel comfortable with his neighbor to the west. His fears would soon prove to be justified when Syria sided with Iran during the Iran-Iraq War.

The unexpected demonstrations against the Baʿth in 1977 by two thousand Shiʿis in Karbalaʾ and al-Najaf during the ʿAshura demonstrations in the holy month of Muharram deeply shook the regime. Thus the Iranian Revolution was less the immediate cause of the Shiʿa's repression than an extension of the repression that had already occurred between 1977 and 1980, namely the suppression of the Ashura demonstrations, the struggle to crush the al-Daʿwa Party, and Muhammad Baqir al-Sadr's execution. It was not that organizations such as al-Daʿwa were that powerful (most observers feel that few Iraqi Shiʿis supported it), but rather that they represented oppositional poles around which discontented Shiʿis could potentially organize. To placate the Shiʿa and offset Khumayni's message, the regime toned down its secularism and strong antireligious orientation. While Shiʿi dissidents were being repressed, Saddam adopted the role of the Shiʿa's patron by lavishing funds on restoring holy sites in Karbalaʾ and al-Najaf, a policy that Iraqis have called "the carrot and the stick" *(al-taghrib wa-l-taghib)*. During the war, Saddam made the pilgrimage *(al-hajj)* to Mecca.[56] Long-range missiles designed to strike Teheran and other Iranian cities were called ʿAli and Husayn, honoring the founders of Shiʿism.

The resort to tribalism constituted more an indirect effort to overcome Shiʿi discontent and develop a sense of political community that transcended ethnicity than overt repression. This was also part of the continuing process of marginalizing the Baʿth Party and replacing it with the "family party" *(hizb al-usra)*. War posters and murals portrayed Arab tribal forces attacking the Sasanians and Saddam as a latter-day Saʿd Ibn Abi al-Waqqas, the Arab commander who defeated Sasanian armies at Qadisiya in 637 C.E.[57] Of course, the cleavage emphasized here was not intraethnic (because the Battle of Qadisiya preceded the Sunni-Shiʻi split in Islam) but rather interethnic, pitting Muslim Arab armies against Persian infidels, suggesting the unity of Iraq's Sunni and Shiʻi Arabs. Constant references to the historical struggle between the Arabs and the Persians also suggested tribalism's salience for the present. Arab solidarity was based on tribal origins that, under the ʻAbbasids, the Persians had sought to undermine. The Qadisiyat Saddam campaign's implicit tribal underpinnings represented an extension of the tribal dress Saddam had adopted even before deposing Ahmad Hasan al-Bakr. Photographs of Saddam bearing a conventional rifle were examples of the iconography aimed at encouraging the perception of him as the paramount shaykh of the Iraqi people.[58] The regime's focus on al-Qadisiya suggested religious in addition to tribal symbolism because the Sasanians' defeat was decisive in opening Mesopotamia and Persia to Islamization.

The Iran-Iraq War soon highlighted two contradictory facts. On the one hand, the Iraqi army quickly became bogged down in Iranian territory, demonstrating little enthusiasm for the war. Despite Iraq's material and air superiority, the army's overly cautious tactics, stemming from outmoded Soviet strategy and a desire to minimize casualties, made it ill suited to exploit its initial gains. Iran's tenacious opposition to the invasion offset its military disadvantages and a stalemate soon ensued. As the war progressed, Iran began launching missile attacks against Iraq's oil production facilities and industrial infrastructure and sending "human wave" assaults against Iraqi ground positions, increasing losses on both sides.

Predictions that the war would fragment Iraq along sectarian lines failed to materialize.[59] The Iraqi Shiʻa seem not to have been impressed by the Iranian Revolution. The division within the army between a Sunni-dominated officer corps and a Shiʻi-dominated infantry led few soldiers to defect to the Iranian side. Once the war shifted to Iraqi territory in 1985 and 1986—when Iran seized the abandoned city of Faw and the surrounding peninsula and threatened Basra, Iraq's main southern city—the Iraqi army fought vigorously and skillfully against Iranian forces. Realizing that defeat was a distinct possibility, especially if Basra fell, Saddam finally relinquished running the war to his generals. Under General Mahir ʻAbd al-Rashid, a fellow Takriti, the army pushed Iranian troops back across the Iran-Iraq border. Iraq's skillful use of long-range missiles against Iranian cities and its threat to use chemical weapons against population centers finally forced Iran to sign a truce in 1988. However, Iraq had accumulated more than 100,000 deaths and 300,000 casualties, had suffered more than $452.6 billion in material losses, and was deeply in debt to Kuwait and Saudi Arabia, which had bankrolled Iraq in the war's later years to prevent an Iranian victory.[60] Having committed the sin of becoming popular with his troops, General ʿAbd al-Rashid was called to Baghdad, ostensibly to be honored, but instead was placed under house arrest. His daughter's marriage to Saddam's son Qusay was annulled. However, his fate could have been worse. Saddam's cousin and childhood playmate, Defense Minister ʿAdnan Khayrallah Tulfah, who had also become popular as a result of his prosecution of the war, died in a helicopter crash that most observers believe was caused by a bomb placed in his helicopter on Saddam's orders.[61]

The Iran-Iraq War led to an intensified and narrowly focused state-sponsored historical memory based on the expectation of a lengthy conflict.[62] Fusing two symbols, Saddam's cult of personality and ethnic hatred, Qadisiyat Saddam conceptualized the conflict as the natural outcome of an essentialized and transhistorical enmity between Arabs and Persians. Although tied to distinct political objectives, the Project for the Rewriting of History at least maintained a thematically diverse quality during the 1970s, treating subjects ranging from pre-Islamic poetry, al-Wasiti's art, ʿAbbasid architecture, Jahiz's satirical writings, and the *1001 Nights*, to the glories of ancient Mesopotamia.[63] Although al-Bakr and Saddam's portraits often adorned the introductory pages of monographs and journals, the appropriation of historical memory was not linked to any one individual. Under Qadisiyat Saddam, cultural production gravitated toward a tedious uniformity designed to foster hatred toward Iran and greater support for Saddam, who increasingly was portrayed as a quasi-deity responsible for everything good in Iraqi society. In 1984, for example, the inhabitants of al-Diwaniya, in the newly created al-Qadisiya province in southwestern Iraq, were still said to be in awe of Saddam's visit two years before. The Iraqi president's visit was said to have inspired local residents to join the People's Army and renew their sacrifices for the glory of the state.[64] Nevertheless, aside from one photograph that shows a smiling resident (an anonymous *"fulan al-fulani,"* or "so-and-so," whom the reporter interviewed, perhaps the local Baʿth Party leader or provincial governor), the sullen faces in the remaining photographs suggest a very different narrative that belies the article's cheery tone.

As the war continued, there was a direct correlation between its intensification and Saddam's enhanced role in Iraqi society. By the mid- and late 1980s, volumes of his speeches, interviews, and essays proliferated. Unlike *On the Writing of History, Saddam Husayn on Political Affairs,*[65] or the numerous pamphlets of his speeches during the 1970s, these volumes reached three hundred, four hundred, and even five hundred pages in length. Most ambitious was a nineteen-volume work on his thinking published by a new government publishing house created during the 1980s, Dar al-Shu'un al-Thaqafiya al-ʿAmma, under the aegis of the Ministry of Culture and Information.[66] The length of these volumes must have tried the patience of even the most loyal and dedicated state and party officials.

The state's most grandiose mobilization of cultural symbols during the Iran-Iraq War was the construction of three monuments during the 1980s. The Unknown Soldier Monument, conceived by the well-known Iraqi sculptor Khalid al-Rahhal, was completed in 1982. It was followed in 1983 by a much more impressive monument known as Nusb Shuhada' Qadisiyat Saddam (The Monument to the Martyrs of Saddam's Qadisiya), or al-Shahid (The Martyrs' Monument) for short. This latter monument, "created by slicing vertically through a traditional onion-profile dome clad in turquoise-blue ceramic tile," and surrounding a twisted three-dimensional metal Iraqi flag, was conceived by the artist Ismaʿil al-Fattah. Both The Martyrs' and the Unknown Soldier monuments captured international attention.[67] In addition to these two Baghdad monuments, architects created a series of eighty life-size statues in Basra representing soldiers killed during the war, which faced out over the Shatt al-ʿArab, pointing accusingly at Iran for responsibility for the Iran-Iraq War.

These monuments can be contrasted to the Freedom Monument (Nusb al-Hurriya), constructed in 1961 by the famous Iraqi artist and architect Jawad al-Salim. As noted earlier, when Salim refused to put Qasim's likeness on his memorial, there was no retribution. When technical problems beyond his control confronted the consulting engineer on the Martyrs' Monument, Hisham al-Madfaʿi, in 1983, he was imprisoned. These two incidents indicate a sharp contrast between Qasim's rule and Saddam's oppressive dictatorship.

Of all the monuments inaugurated during the Iran-Iraq War, the most significant was the so-called Victory Arch (Qaws al-Nasr), an architectural project that highlighted Saddam's megalomaniac attempts to appropriate historical memory. Completed in 1985, the arch consisted of the supposed exact replicas of Saddam's arms below the elbows, his hands holding two enormous stainless-steel swords that crossed at the apex of the arch, to which was attached an Iraqi flag. Two huge duplicate arches bracket the ends of an enormous parade ground in downtown Baghdad. At the base of the two arches lie nets, each filled with 2,500 Iranian helmets taken from casualties, attached to the base of the "Swords of Qadisiya." The huge swords, supposedly cast from the melted-down weaponry of Iraqi war martyrs, rise as high as the Eiffel Tower, weigh more than forty-two tons, and were cast by a specially designed Iraqi foundry. The bronze forearms and sword grips

FIGURE 14. Nusb Shuhada' Qadisiyat Saddam (The Monument to the Martyrs of Saddam's Qadisiya), Baghdad, Iraq. Associated Press Photo. AP/Worldwide rights.

FIGURE 15. Unknown Soldier Monument, Baghdad, Iraq. Associated Press Photo, January 6, 2003. AP/Worldwide rights.

had to be sent to the world's largest bronze foundry in Great Britain and then transported back to Iraq by truck convoy.

In a provocative essay on the Victory Arch, Kanan Makiya (Samir al-Khalil) demolishes the idea of any inherent aesthetic in this monument to the Iraqi triumph over its purported historic enemy according to the Ba'th, Iran. Demonstrating that the arch has no ties to tradition *(al-turath)* despite its pretension to represent artistically the purportedly timeless conflict between Arab and Persian culture, Makiya argues that the monument, in its lack of sculptural integration—such as the awkward placement of the arms, which are out of scale compared to the rest of Saddam's body—possesses no aesthetic value. In contrast to Jawad Salim's Freedom Monument, Saddam's Victory Arch caricatures art. Whereas the Freedom Monument embodied the hopes and desires of the July 1958 Revolution, the Victory Arch underlines politics' complete superficiality in an era characterized by increasing private fortunes, sectarianism, and the populace's suffering.

The increased reliance on visual imagery to glorify Saddam and his regime during the 1980s, as represented by the construction of imposing monuments, was also reflected in film by an extravaganza devoted to the Battle of al-Qadisiya called *Saddam's Qadisiya (Qadisiyat Saddam)*. Directed by the highly respected Egyptian Salah Abu Sayf, the film enjoyed a budget of more than ID15 million ($45 million), making it the most expensive Arab film ever produced. The actors and staff were drawn from throughout the Arab world, including Lebanon, Syria, Tunisia, Egypt, and Morocco. To create a true spectacle, live elephants were used on scene and Iraqi army units helped create military verisimilitude. Despite an unlimited budget and a highly proficient director, the film received poor reviews. Heavy-handed, slow-moving, and unidimensional in its portrayal of the Arab and Persian commanders Sa'd Ibn Abi al-Waqqas and Rustum, the film failed to impress audiences. Critics argued that it was the worst of Abu Sayf's many films.[68] This film, as well as Saddam's monuments, proved that money alone could not purchase hegemony, which, if it is to crystallize, must emerge from a much more organic social and cultural interaction between the state and the populace at large.

By the end of the Iran-Iraq War, paralleling other dictators who relied on a cult of personality, Saddam had seduced himself through his attempt to appropriate historical memory. By constructing a genealogy that traced his origins to the Prophet Muhammad, claiming he was a descendant of the Prophet's son-in-law and fourth caliph, 'Ali, by continually increasing the number of texts, monuments, and other forms of cultural production that ascribed to him godlike qualities, Saddam lost touch with his own capabilities, which led him to believe that he could prosecute the war with Iran on his own. No longer allowing government officials and visitors to address him as "Mr. President," he now insisted on being called "Hero-President" or "Master."[69] Although Saddam's efforts to link his family to the Prophet Muhammad and his claims to be 'Ali's "grandson" were preposterous, he apparently took them seriously.

By 1990, the regime seems to have lost its sense of purpose and direction. Pan-Arab, Mesopotamian, and Islamic symbols had been mixed together in an intellectual stew that satisfied no one. This conflation of symbols confused the populace rather than providing them with any meaningful mediation of political reality or sense of political community. Resentment characterized Iraqi society. Civilians resented that the war's end failed to bring a return to prosperity, the military resented the treatment of senior officers and the lack of recognition of its contributions to the war, and the regime resented the lack of gratitude exhibited by other Arab states for having defended the Arab nation from the spread of radical Islam. In fact, Saddam was furious at the refusal of Saudi Arabia and Kuwait to forgive the tremendous debts that Iraq had incurred during the war. Their increased oil production, which continued to push oil prices down, angered Saddam and the Ba'th still further.

FIGURE 16. Martyr's Monument along the Shatt al-ʿArab, Basra, Iraq. Associated Press Photo, February 13, 2003. AP/Worldwide rights.

As is now well known, Iraq had set out during the 1970s and 1980s to develop a sophisticated arsenal of nuclear, chemical, and biological weapons. The Israeli air force had destroyed Iraq's initial nuclear reactor, Osiris, in 1981 and had assassinated some of the scientists who were considered part of Iraq's nuclear weapons program.[70] Nevertheless, in November 1988 the Baʿth's "weapons of mass destruction" program was tested on Iraq's own population as Kurds in the town of Halabja were subject to bombing with Tabin and Sarin gases, leading to an estimated three thousand to five thousand civilian deaths.

Most analysts have viewed the 1980s as period of decline in Iraq. Former supporters of the regime speak of great opportunities lost due to the blunder in invading Iran. Opponents of the Baʿthist regime see the period as one of great human suffering and material destruction. Without denying the validity of both of these perspectives, there were developments during the Iran-Iraq War that had important implications for the creation of a civil society in Iraq. First, the war effort, which was not hampered by ethnic or sectarian tensions, demonstrated once and for all the shortcomings of viewing Iraq exclusively through the conceptual prism of ethnic cleavages. Iraqis of all ethnicities worked together under extreme duress to successfully prosecute what was by all accounts the largest and most brutal war of the twentieth century. Second, the war elicited a deep sense of nationalism among all sectors of Iraqi society. The half-hearted pursuit of the invasion of Iran stands in sharp contrast to the vigor with which Iraq's army fought once the war moved to Iraqi territory. The army did not fight well because of Qadisiyat Saddam, but because soldiers were loyal to the nation-state of Iraq, whose existence was threatened by another nation-state. These two elements—the ability of Iraqis from all ethnic groups to work together in what is probably the most complex of human activities, war making, and the demonstration of their commitment to Iraqi nationalism—should dispel the idea that Iraq is an artificial nation-state. Third, the war eliminated the prevailing assumption of the 1970s that prosperity and the social welfare state were givens of the Iraqi political system. The great sacrifices that Iraqis were forced to make during the war with Iran made many realize that, although the regime could offer extensive material benefits, as it had done until 1983, it could also cause tremendous human and material suffering. The negative impact of the great concentration of power in the hands of Saddam and his family led many Iraqis to begin to contemplate alternatives to Ba'thist authoritarianism.

8 Memories of State and the Arts of Resistance

> The greater the disparity in power between dominant and subordinate and the more arbitrarily it is exercised, the more the public transcript of subordinates will take on a stereotyped, ritualistic cast. In other words, the more menacing the power, the thicker the mask.
>
> JAMES C. SCOTT, *Domination and the Arts of Resistance*

How did Iraqi intellectuals respond to the Baʿthist state's attempt to appropriate historical memory? How did they approach issues of historical beginnings, locality, social differentiation, and cultural heritage? In what ways did specific works that reconstructed standard historical approaches to these topics resonate with society at large? Perhaps of greatest interest, in what ways did studies intended to foster state power actually promote resistance, or at least provide readers with the tools to develop such resistance?

In answering these questions, ideological tracts would seem a logical starting point because the Baʿth Party has published much in the way of ideology.[1] However, using ideological tracts as an indicator of the state's appropriation of cultural production conflates traditional Levantine Baʿthism, heavily influenced by its main ideologue, Michel ʿAflaq, with Iraqi Baʿthism, which has been subject to many vicissitudes. The initial Shiʿi-dominated party of Fuʾad al-Rikabi during the 1950s, the ʿAli Salih al-Saʿdi faction, which overthrew Qasim in 1963, and the Takriti Baʿth all adopted the same party name, but they differ in important respects. Although al-Rikabi's writings emulated ʿAflaq's highly polemical, idealist, and abstract tone and structure, the al-Salih faction failed to produce any memorable texts, perhaps reflecting the petty criminal background of many of its members. Saddam Husayn has dominated writings by the Takriti Baʿth, but his arguments, while often vague and containing double entendres, always relate specifically to Iraqi interests rather than an abstract Pan-Arabism.

Not surprisingly, I found volumes on Baʿthist ideology gathering dust in bookstores both in Iraq and elsewhere during the late 1970s, 1980s, and 1990s. In addition to Ahmad Hasan al-Bakr's speeches and numerous collections of Saddam's speeches and writings, I often found ideological tracts that were written by non-Iraqi Baʿthists such as Ilyas Farah, Shibli al-ʿAysami, and, of course, Michel ʿAflaq, all of whom took refuge in Iraq after the split in the Syrian Baʿth Party. Even ʿAflaq's most important writings, *Fi Sabil al-Baʿth al-ʿArabi (For the Sake of the Arab Baʿth)* and *Nidal al-Baʿth (The Baʿthist Struggle)*, a compendium of his speeches and newspaper articles, were not conspicuously displayed in Baghdad bookstores during the 1980s.[2] Although the failure to foreground texts by the traditional party fathers could be ascribed to their Syrian and often Christian origins, a more fundamental reason is that these highly abstract texts did not resonate with Iraqis. During the late 1960s, Iraqi Pan-Arabists were much more concerned with Arab unity than in Baʿthism per se. These rarified texts did not address issues specific to Iraq. Even the new Baʿthist regime seemed to find them of little help in its efforts to consolidate power.

A far greater number of books focused on historical, social, and cultural analyses designed to foster a specific national identity supportive of Baʿthist power and policies. The regime, unlike in its use of torture and executions to suppress overt dissent, was subtler in using culture to elicit consent, preferring indirect means to inform Iraqis of accepted modes of understanding the public sphere, political practices, and a state-defined hierarchy of social groups. This approach reflected the regime's awareness of Shiʿi and Kurdish resentment at being excluded from power and culturally marginalized, and the continued resonance of the Iraqi Communist Party's message of ethnic inclusion.

The Ministry of Culture and Information began publishing studies even before the Baʿth took power in 1968, some of which constituted serious scholarship. Under the Baʿth, the ministry's publications list increased dramatically.[3] Despite efforts by some intellectuals to separate the organization into two ministries, which occurred briefly during the late 1970s, most ministers opposed this separation.[4] For reasons of prestige, status, and control, they preferred that the ministries remain combined. The prestige suggested by the term "culture" offset the heavy-handedness implied by "information." Because the minister of culture and information was an important Baʿthist with strong ties to the intelligence apparatus, this explains why studies that enjoyed official sponsorship came under serious state scrutiny. Many ministry-sponsored studies, especially those of better quality, were master's theses and doctoral dissertations suggested by faculty at Baghdad University and other schools.[5] A small number of studies were even sponsored by Baghdad University, although they were still subject to ministry control.[6]

Works the ministry chose for publication were not always the best studies available. For example, a number of master theses completed during the late 1970s under the supervision of Dr. Yusif al-Takriti at Baghdad University's Department of Sociology and Anthropology received the mark of *jayyid jiddan* (superior), yet remained unpublished.[7] However, one thesis on the southern village of al-Sharsh, which was supervised by the prominent Iraqi anthropologist Dr. Shakir Mustafa Salim, had far fewer political overtones and was the least interesting of all the theses, conceptually and in content. It received the lowest evaluation, *jayyid* (good). This work, by 'Abd 'Ali Salman 'Abdallah, was published by the Ministry of Culture and Information in 1980. Written by a Shi'i and conceptualizing rural life in terms of Western modernization theory, the study represented the type of patronizing and Westernized view of the Iraqi village of which Ba'thist political and cultural commissars approved. Although the volume's front page cites the report of the Ba'th Party's Eighth Party Congress (1974), which stressed the need to rid Iraq of "feudalism," this issue is not systematically treated in the study. [8] The other studies touched on much more sensitive political issues, such as the reverse migration of peasants from Baghdad to the countryside, working conditions in factories near Baghdad, and family problems in a Baghdad quarter. It seems probable that the thesis supervisor, Dr. Yusif al-Takriti, would have preferred to recommend these three theses for publication because they received a better evaluation than Salman's study. However, politics obviously prevailed over intellectual quality, as the reputation of Shakir Mustafa Salim prevailed over that of Yusif al-Takriti.[9] Clearly, then, the process by which a text came to be published was influenced by political considerations.

When considering state-sponsored cultural production, it is important to make a distinction between book-length studies and shorter articles. The Ministry of Culture and Information was likely to subject periodicals that achieved relatively wide circulation, such as *Afaq 'Arabiya (Arab Perspectives)* or *Majallat al-Turath al-Sha'bi (The Journal of Popular Culture)*, to greater scrutiny than book-length manuscripts on the assumption that the articles would be more widely read.[10] Because books treat topics in more depth than articles, I concentrate on the former. I have also chosen to focus on texts that were either written by powerful intellectuals, widely disseminated, or particularly able to subvert the purposes for which they were ostensibly published.

One of the most prominent studies by a senior intellectual is Dr. Nuri 'Ali Hammudi al-Qaysi's *al-Shi'r wa-l-Tarikh (Poetry and History)*, which was widely displayed in Iraqi bookstores and kiosks during the 1980s.[11] The book's author and its content make this an especially important work. First, like many converts to the Baʿthist project for rewriting history, al-Qaysi, a Baghdad Sunni from the al-ʿAdhamiya quarter, had been briefly associated with leftist politics, and possibly with the ICP. Second, his prior scholarly output was substantial and included a number of works on early Arabic poetry. Thus *Poetry and History* not only achieved considerable stature, but it also represented a marked deviation, one might say decline, from the academic standards of his previous works.[12] Third, despite his leftist background, al-Qaysi became dean of Baghdad University's Faculty of Arts and subsequently headed the Iraqi Academy (al-Majmaʿ al-ʿIlmi al-ʿIraqi), the country's most prestigious intellectual organization.[13] In studying the lineages of the Baʿthist state's efforts to control cultural production, it should be remembered that many leftist and communist intellectuals, some of whom worked under Qasim, later cooperated with if not actively assisted the Baʿth.[14] Finally, before passing away during the late 1990s, al-Qaysi served from the early 1980s to the mid-1990s as the regime's spokesman in a wide variety of intellectual forums throughout the Arab world.[15]

The title of al-Qaysi's work suggests a dialogue between poetry and history. However, his opening remarks make clear that this study is intended to assist authors to correctly reinterpret history according to Baʿthist thinking. In other words, poetry becomes a vehicle for elucidating the correct approach to writing about and understanding history rather than a literary or aesthetic end in itself. Because poetry represents the Arab world's historical cultural contribution par excellence, and because it has such a lengthy historical tradition, al-Qaysi argues for its centrality in history writing. It is culturally authentic because it speaks to the issue of cultural origins or beginnings, and it thus yields the best insights into Arab history. Poetry is also central to history writing because it is closely tied to popular culture. Thus a focus on poetry meets Saddam's criterion that history writing must be revolutionary in focus, thereby fulfilling its political and social mission. Poets are not only close to the masses but also help define social values and point to society's future values. Poets help celebrate and commemorate victories and a society's ability to overcome adversity. Poets have a better understanding of feelings and emotions than modern historians, who are usually temporally removed from the events they study. Further, early Arab historians such as al-Tabari relied heavily on poetry, thereby underscoring poetry's importance to historical analysis.[16] For all these reasons, al-Qaysi's text represents a critique of traditional history writing and an argument that history should be the purview of poets, literary specialists, and folklorists, who are history's most legitimate interpreters.

One of al-Qaysi's most important arguments concerns the pre-Islamic

Arab poets' closeness *(al-sila al-wathiqa)* to the land.[17] When al-Qaysi wrote his manuscript during the late 1970s, the Ba'thist regime considered religion an extremely sensitive topic, largely because the one group in Iraqi society that the Ba'th could restrict but never eliminate was the Shi'i *marja'iya*. A subtler method used in the Project for the Rewriting of History for marginalizing Islam was to attribute historical precedence to Arabism over Islam. While Islam is a critical component of Arab culture, Arabism provided the political and social framework that enabled Islam to expand, rather than the reverse. In demonstrating the pre-Islamic Arab poets' strong love of and commitment to the land, al-Qaysi argues that Arab tribes already possessed a well-developed sense of locality prior to Islam. Further, this tribal value, developed in early Arab culture, provides the prototype of modern Pan-Arab nationalism, which is said to prove Arab society's inherent tendency to think in nationalist terms.

The author's privileging of tribalism appears in his foregrounding of *al-butula* (heroism) and his emphasis on blood and ethnic ties as the basis of cooperation and egalitarianism. These arguments provide the basis for Saddam's image of himself as paramount shaykh *(shaykh al-mashayikh)* of the Iraqis after deposing Ahmad Hasan al-Bakr. It also privileges ethnicity over religion because the foundational values of Arab Iraqi society are to be found in the tribal culture of pre-Islamic Iraq. The patriarchal roots of Iraqi culture can also be found here in the emphasis on building social ties on blood relations, because such ties connect social solidarity to reproduction, the control of which becomes critical to the tribe.

al-Qaysi's emphasis on the centrality of early Arab culture in defining modern Iraqi history and the tribe as its fundamental social unit is significant given the Ba'th's banning of discussions of tribes during the 1970s. The Revolution Command Council issued a decree in 1978 that forbade Iraqis from using surnames that referred to their tribal or regional backgrounds in its efforts to hide the continued use of sectarian criteria in filling positions within the state apparatus and Ba'th Party itself.[18] Indeed, the most comprehensive study of Iraqi tribes, 'Abbas al-'Azzawi's four-volume *'Asha'ir al-'Iraq (The Tribes of Iraq)*, was banned during the 1970s and 1980s.[19]

al-Qaysi subtly reintroduces tribalism in his work, foreshadowing its increased political salience during the 1980s. As the faintly visible tribesmen on horseback on the volume's cover symbolically indicate, the poet's spatial locus is not the large city but the countryside and desert. By 1980, when this text was published, the notion of the tribe was slowly reentering public discourse as the Ba'thist regime, now firmly under Saddam's control, felt much more self-confident about its control of Iraqi society. In al-Qaysi's vision, the poets who inform us of Iraqi society's authentic values have tribal roots, especially those of the pre-Islamic era. ʿImru al-Qays rather than al-Mutanabbi stands out in this text. Interestingly, the term *al-jahiliya* (ignorance), used by al-Qaysi in his 1964 master's thesis on *al-furusiya* (chivalry) and in his subsequent monograph, is completely absent from *Poetry and History*, in which poetry that was formerly called *jahili* is now referred to nondisparagingly as "Arab poetry prior to Islam."[20] It was not lost on Iraqi intellectuals and the educated readership that al-Qaysi, in stressing cultural authenticity's rural and desert origins, was valorizing tribal groupings such as Saddam's own, the Al bu Nasir. Even though overt discussion of the role of tribalism in Iraqi public life, such as its importance in determining who obtained positions within the state bureaucracy, the army, or security services, was strictly forbidden in 1980, al-Qaysi's monograph directly links the values of Arab society to the tribe. Pan-Arabism, more than just legitimizing Arab unity or suggesting Iraq's role as primus inter pares among Arab nations, strengthened the Baʿthist regime's tribal base by privileging Arab tribal values as the basis for Iraqi culture and society.

With the Baʿth Party's emphasis on a revolutionary approach to history writing and its desire to challenge tradition, it is logical to assume that it would valorize revolutionary movements. In Arab society prior to and during the early Islamic period, which is al-Qaysi's focus, one revolutionary movement, namely the Zanj Revolt, stands out. The Zanj were black slaves brought from eastern Africa to southern Iraq to work in the rice fields during the ʿAbbasid Empire. In 869 C.E. the Zanj revolted, spreading a message of social justice throughout southern Iraq that threatened the empire's very survival. Like the insurgents during the 1991 Intifada, they used Iraq's southern marshes to prevent ʿAbbasid forces from suppressing them until 883.[21]

al-Qaysi devotes two lengthy appendices to the Zanj Revolt (pp. 141–209). Ideologically, the Zanj Revolt would presumably be attractive to the Baʿth since the revolt pressed for social justice, was secular, opposed a nonrevolutionary state, and was indigenous to Iraq. However, despite recognizing the terrible conditions under which the Zanj lived, al-Qaysi expresses no sympathy for the movement. He argues that the forces that have sought to appropriate the Zanj for political ends (by which he means the communists and the Iraqist nationalist left) have attempted to make it fit a preconceived contemporary conceptual framework.[22] Thus al-Qaysi's extensive analysis of the Zanj Revolt constitutes, in large measure, a response to the residual strength of leftist and Iraqist nationalist ideas. The author hints at this when he asserts that modern interest in the Zanj dates to the 1940s, when the left resurrected the movement, a fact of which sophisticated and especially older Iraqi intellectuals would be aware.[23] Among these leftist intellectuals, Dr. Faysal al-Samir, who was the most important of Qasim's ministers of guidance, was most prominent. Although he mentions al-Samir, al-Qaysi never cites al-Samir's study, which most Iraqi intellectuals consider the definitive study of the revolt.[24] Instead, al-Qaysi attacks less-well-known students of the Zanj Revolt as he seeks to relegate the movement to a politically acceptable historical niche.

al-Qaysi disputes the assertion in one article that the oppression of the Zanj in southern Iraq in the third-century *hijri* parallels oppression in that region today. He argues that the movement's contemporaries, such as al-Tabari and Ibn al-Rumi, had a much better sense of the movement than modern authors (namely leftists), who, he asserts, have exaggerated its political sophistication. Departing from his volume's key methodological premise, which emphasizes poetry and interpretative materials, al-Qaysi argues that without more factual data on the movement's political and social program it is impossible to know what type of state and social organization the Zanj would have imposed had they been victorious. Although poetry provides the informational base with which to measure the political sophistication of the pre-Islamic poets and their tribes, here al-Qaysi's argument can only be satisfied by more traditional historiography. However, at the beginning of *Poetry and History*, he asserts that traditional historiography, which claims to be detached and objective, is nonrevolutionary and anti-Ba'thist because it is individualistic and fails to link its intellectual production directly to the needs of the masses.[25] When it serves al-Qaysi's political objectives, poetry is the subject matter of choice for analyzing the past. When other concerns predominate, poetry is subordinated to the traditional historiography of historians such as al-Tabari.

al-Qaysi's antipathy toward the Zanj involves multiple levels. First, the Zanj were alien to Iraqi society and hence not culturally authentic *(asil)*. In this sense, they could function as a metaphor for the Shi'a, or even the Kurds, because the Zanj challenged the 'Abbasids, a state dominated by Sunni Arabs. Valorizing the Zanj would open Iraqi historical memory to greater political and cultural inclusion by the Shi'a, Kurds, and minorities rather than the Arab tribes whose values al-Qaysi seeks to privilege in his monograph. Second, valorizing the Zanj would challenge the Ba'th's corporatist model of social and political organization. In arguing that the Zanj was a radical impulse, perhaps analogous to the Vendée or the Jacquerie in France, rather than a sophisticated political movement, al-Qaysi argues for an elitist model of Iraqi politics that plays down social class. In contemporary Iraq, it is only the Ba'th Party, as a vanguard party in the Leninist sense, that has the political sophistication to run a modern society (analogous to the 'Abbasids' ability to run an empire that was beyond the capacity of the Zanj). Further, al-Qaysi realizes that the interest Iraqi leftists and communists began to show in the Zanj during the 1940s represented an attempt to create a historical memory for Iraqi society that privileges social class consciousness over time. For the left, the struggle of workers and peasants during the twentieth century is but a continuation of the historical struggle in Iraq of oppressed groups to eradicate social injustice.[26] By denigrating the Zanj and disputing the claim that inequality exists in modern Iraq, al-Qaysi attempts to marginalize social class's relevance as an analytic tool for contemporary Iraqi society.

In sum, al-Qaysi's volume is a handbook that instructs intellectuals how to interpret the state's visions of cultural production when it comes to history writing. History writing cannot follow its traditional path as a detached, contemplative, and dispassionate exercise that emphasizes sources and data. Instead, it must be instrumental and serve the masses.[27] *Poetry and History* shifts the locus of history writing away from professional historians to literary specialists and poets, thereby fostering much greater subjectivity in the study of history. History is understood in a much more profound manner if studied through folk culture, such as the poetry of the pre-Islamic Arabs who were close to the masses. History writing must be interpretive and in keeping with the Ba'th Party's revolutionary goals. Because al-Qaysi privileges Arab tribal culture in defining the origins of Iraqi society, *Poetry and History* helped legitimate Takriti rule. Saddam's use of a white horse during parades commemorating important national events, in addition to suggesting a parallel with Faysal I, who also rode a white horse during public events, can be seen as part of an effort to link him and the Takritis to the core tribal values of honor, love of land, bravery, and steadfastness in the face of adversity.[28]

Poetry and History was part of a process whereby the Ba'thist regime used literary texts and analyses to codify a new set of values. In addition to the greater interpretative opportunities that poetry provides compared to traditional history texts, a literary medium also becomes a much more effective way for educated sectors of society to identify with the Ba'th. In addition to serving a didactic function, literary texts such as a *diwan* of poetry, a short story, or the retelling of a folktale provide entertainment in a way that traditional historical scholarship often cannot.[29] Literary texts and folklore also provide a more emotive link to the past. In making literature and folk culture a primary focus of officially sponsored cultural production, the Ba'thist state attempted to promote itself as the guardian of cultural authenticity, enhance its populist image, and legitimate its revolutionary credentials.

Despite al-Qaysi's support of the Ba'th, his leftist background is still evident in his analytic framework. In his treatment of the Zanj, al-Qaysi makes reference to the "general laws" of history and the importance of the material bases of everyday life. He also argues for the notion of praxis, or the idea that history can only be understood if it is applied to general problems of life.[30] Despite the overall transhistorical quality of al-Qaysi's arguments, that is, his description of an Arab culture that has not changed from the pre-Islamic era to the present, the ability of the former leftist to integrate intellectually with the Ba'th stems from the superficial similarity between the ideologies of the ICP and the Ba'th Party. Both emphasized a vanguard party and claim revolutionary credentials in attempting to liberate the oppressed segments of Iraqi society from imperialism, feudalism, and the cultural hegemony of reactionary forces. An Islamist would have much greater difficulty making the transition to Ba'thism. Both the ICP and the Ba'th shared similar insecurities, in part because they recruited their leadership from the same social strata, which made their competition all the more intense and hence violent. Because intellectuals like al-Qaysi could easily move from the left to Ba'thism, the Ba'th has always feared the left's potential, due to its greater "historical depth" and inclusive message, to recruit Iraqi intellectuals and youth to its cause.

Dr. Majid Ahmad al-Samarra'i's study *al-Tayyar al-Qawmi fi-l-Shir al-'Iraqi al-Hadith, Munthu al-Harb al-'Alamiya al-Thaniya, 1939, Hatta Naksat Khuzayran 1967 (The Pan-Arabist Tendency in Modern Iraqi Poetry From The Second World War, 1939, Until the Setback of June 1967)* represents a prominent attempt to use poetry as a vehicle for understanding Iraq's modern historical development. The study's main concern is to demonstrate modern Iraqi poets' support for Pan-Arabism. The text's thesis is that, as the twentieth century progressed, especially after the beginning of World War II, the idea of Pan-Arabism crystallized among Iraqi poets and became the dominant form of political expression in their poetry.

This study originated as a doctoral dissertation completed under Nuri al-Qaysi at Baghdad University's Faculty of Arts. al-Samarra'i, who began his career in 1969 writing articles for the Ba'th Party newspaper *al-Thawra,* went on to become editor in chief of the magazine *Sawt al-Fallah (Voice of the Peasant).* When Latif Nusayyif Jasim became minister of culture and information during the 1980s, al-Samarra'i was appointed director of television and broadcasting. Between 1990 and 1997 he served as Iraqi ambassador to Venezuela, only to subsequently leave his post amid controversy over ʿUday Saddam Husayn's cocaine-smuggling activities between Venezuela and Great Britain.[31]

As the title of his work and the period that it covers make clear, al-Samarraʾi privileges Pan-Arabism over Iraqist nationalism. Although poets—many of them Shiʿi and Iraqist nationalist in outlook—played a central role in the June–October 1920 Revolution, the largest uprising in modern Iraq, the author avoids any discussion of their critical role. By ignoring the revolt and beginning his analysis in 1939, al-Samarraʾi can downplay the role of the poets in politics and political thought. Nevertheless, it was impossible for al-Samarraʾi to exclude the large body of political poetry that existed prior to 1939. Forced to confront this body of work, al-Samarraʾi assigned some of Iraq's most famous poets, such as al-Zahawi, al-Kathimi, and al-Shabibi, to the realm of "proto–Pan Arabism." Although he recognizes that these poets supported Iraq's independence from the British and thus played an important role in the anti-imperialist struggle, he nevertheless argues that consciousness of Arabism *(al-ʿUruba)* was not adequately developed before the 1940s.[32] These early modern poets, analogous to the treatment of pre-Islamic Arabs in Islamic thought, are relegated to their own politically defined *al-jahiliya* because they lacked the "true" consciousness of their politically mature colleagues who composed Pan-Arabist poetry after 1939.

al-Samarraʾi must also confront poets, such as Maʿruf al-Rusafi, who promoted Pan-Islamic themes in support of the Ottoman Turks and the fight against the British. For the author, intellectual support for the Ottomans, both during and after World War I, constituted residual and misplaced support for the 1908 Constitutional (Young Turk) Revolt, rendered irrelevant by the Ottoman Empire's collapse. All such poetry is thereby considered marginal. The Ottomans are blamed for having caused Iraq's backwardness and inability to confront British imperial domination. In this manner, religiously based poetry that supported the Ottomans is dismissed. Instead, al-Samarraʾi conflates both secular and religiously oriented poetry as formative parts of a political trajectory that emerges as a unified poetic field in the Pan-Arab hostility to the British that culminated in the 1941 Movement.

al-Samarraʾi's periodization seeks to establish new historical markers delineating the origins of "modern Iraq." For the Baʿth, modern Iraq does not begin with the 1920 Revolt or the state's founding in 1921 but rather with the 1941 Movement. In confronting Iraq's vibrant and deeply political modern poetic tradition prior to 1939, al-Samarraʾi subsumes all poetry under

Pan-Arabism. The author subtly criticizes the Shiʿa by arguing that Islamically oriented poetry that supported the Ottomans in World War I, most of which was written by Shiʿis, ran counter to the political will of the populace, which he asserts was uniformly anti-Ottoman. Pan-Islamism, which was mobilized by Shiʿi poets and clergy against the British, is transformed from an oppositional political ideology to one that is historically anachronistic and subordinated to Pan-Arabism, which has largely been the discourse of the Sunni Arab community.

Unlike al-Qaysi, al-Samarraʾi is less concerned with cultural history than with politics. Poetry becomes a vehicle for forcing twentieth-century political thought to fit a unitary mold. The author repeats al-Qaysi's argument that Pan-Arab nationalism (al-Qawmiya al-ʿArabiya) was evident from the time of the ancient Arab tribes who expressed it through the term *"asabiya"* (communal solidarity).[33] Because he is dealing with the modern and not the pre-Islamic period, al-Samarraʾi injects sectarianism into his discussion, linking it to authoritarianism and communism. He argues that dictatorial rule in Iraq alienated poets, producing a tremendous sense of depression and gloom *(talabbat samaʾ biladihim bi-ghuyum al-kaʾaba wa-l-huzn)*. Using the example of one of Iraq's most famous poets, Badr Shakir al-Sayyab, who, as is well known, rejected his early Marxism in favor of Pan-Arabism, al-Samarraʾi links authoritarian rule to the rejection of the al-Shuʿubiyun and communists. He cites al-Sayyab's 472-line poem "al-Mumis al-ʿAmyaʾ " (The Blind Whore), a poem that al-Samarraʾi claims was intended to overcome the prevalent sense of alienation and gloom at the time, to demonstrate the poet's move toward Pan-Arabism in 1954. al-Samarraʾi goes on to mention al-Sayyab's memoirs, *When I Was a Communist (ʾIndama Kuntu Shuyuʿiyan)*, which were serialized in 1959 in the Baʿthist newspaper *al-Hurriya*, saying that the poet acknowledged his realization that the most important Arab issue, solidarity with Palestine, stood in sharp contradiction to the concerns of his ICP comrades, who chanted "we are the brothers of the Jews."[34]

Although al-Sayyab broke with the ICP in June 1954, causing, al-Samarraʾi argues, strong reactions by Iraqi communists, the poem that al-Samarraʾi cites in conjunction with this rejection does not fit at all with a strict Pan-Arabism, and especially not with the chauvinist version propounded by the Takriti Baʿth. In her excellent study of al-Sayyab, Terri DeYoung demonstrates that "The Blind Whore" is a complex work filled with stylistic and political ambiguities, such as the shifting use of the second and third persons in relation to Salima, the protagonist who alternatively moves between subject and object.[35] While attacking the corruption and moral decay brought on by colonial rule, and particularly the sexually transmitted diseases Salima contracts and her desire for revenge, "The Blind Whore" self-consciously challenges the viability of binary oppositions as vehicles for enhancing an understanding of Iraq's colonial predicament and the human condition more broadly defined. Although al-Samarra'i views this poem in strictly nationalist terms—the Iraqis against the British—al-Sayyab also explores sexual oppression, which is caused by domestic culture and society and not just colonial rule. The poem also challenges the adequacy of the linear narrative as an appropriate vehicle for conveying the poet's message. "The Blind Whore" is overlaid with Qur'anic and other symbolism that is not congruent with Ba'thist ideology and historical memory. In light of "Sayyab's concern with the problematic nature of boundaries," and the fact that this poem "uses epic allusion to critique the false teleology of narrative assumptions about linear progression and change," al-Samarra'i's efforts to subsume al-Sayyab's complex work under a parochial Pan-Arabism represents a reductionism and vulgarization that belie his study's intellectual veneer. al-Sayyab does not see his poem as the culmination of hope in a (nationalist) future. Rather, the poem represented Iraqi intellectuals' deep frustration with the difficulty of escaping the clutches of the monarchy and the British.

While attempting to reduce Iraqi poetry's political content to a Pan-Arab narrative, al-Samarra'i simultaneously rewrites history in several ways. First, he commits numerous sins of omission. The voices of many Iraqi poets, such as Muhammad Mahdi al-Jawahiri, are not heard in his volume. Second, leftist and Iraqist nationalist poets are transformed into Pan-Arabists. For example, al-Samarra'i mobilizes one of the most famous leftist poets, Muhammad Salih Bahr al-'Ulum, who came from a prominent family of Shi'i *marja'iya*, in support of the Pan-Arab cause by reproducing his poem "Glory Belongs to You, Palestine."[36] He also cites a section of Bahr al-'Ulum's *Diwan* in which the poet rejects Iraq's alliance with Great Britain during World War II.[37] Bahr al-'Ulum's close ties to the Iraqi Communist Party, which was more concerned than Pan-Arabism with social class oppression, is totally ignored. Third, the author distorts the political events that were purportedly the source of inspiration for the poets he cites. For example, the ICP is accused of having supported the creation of a Jewish state in Palestine. The author cites a small pamphlet issued by the party called *Observations on the Question for Palestine (Adwa' 'ala al-Qadiya al-Filistiniya)*, in which the party called for intercommunal worker solidarity against "imperialist and reactionary plans."[38] In addition to ignoring the complexities implied by this political formulation and the erroneous as-

sumption that the ICP supported a Zionist state that would be an outpost of
Western interests, al-Samarra'i fails to mention that the ICP also esta-
blished the League for Combating Zionism ('Asaba li Mukafahat al-
Sahyuniya) in 1946, before submitting to Soviet pressure to support the
United Nations partition of Palestine into Arab and Jewish states. Finally, al-
Samarra'i distorts Iraqi cultural production. The complexities, ambiguities,
and subtleties of major poets such as al-Sayyab, al-Bayati, al-Jawahiri, and
the Kurdish poet Buland al-Haydari are either given short shrift or ignored.
Instead, lesser-known poets are cited as representative of the major trends
in Iraqi poetry. Shafiq al-Kamali (later to become one of the Takriti Ba'th's
cultural commissars), 'Ali al-Sharqi, 'Adnan al-Rawi, and 'Abd al-Ghani al-
Khadari, among others, are analyzed in detail, not because of the quality of
their poetry, but because they define Iraqi political community in Pan-Arab
terms.

al-Samarra'i attempts to culturally atomize the populace. Uniformity becomes the watchword as Iraqi cultural production moves toward an ever
more integrated thematic unity. While the Takriti Ba'th atomized all organizations in the private and public spheres, undermining any potentially subversive autonomous action by the citizenry, authors like al-Samarra'i
worked to intellectually denude the populace, and particularly the educated
middle classes who constitute this text's audience, of any sense of historical
diversity, tension between competing definitions of political community,
and struggle among indigenous social classes.

The third response to the Ba'thist effort to structure historical memory—a response that attempts to turn the rewriting of history on its head—
is certainly the most complex. To argue that all state-sponsored publications
during Ba'thist rule were ideologically biased and instrumental is simplistic
and shortchanges much serious scholarship. A very interesting example of
this third genre is a lengthy monograph by Baqir Jawad al-Zujaji, an employee of the Iraqi Ministry of Education in charge of its secondary school
curriculum, entitled *al-Riwaya al-'Iraqiya wa Qadiyat al-Rif (The Iraqi
Novel and the Agrarian Question).*[39] The study was originally a master's
thesis written under the supervision of 'Abd al-Ilah Ahmad, an expert on
the Iraqi short story at Baghdad University's Faculty of Arts, and recommended by Ahmad to the Ministry of Culture and Information for publication. A superficial reading of this text explains why the ministry chose to
publish it. It includes an extensive critique of pre-1958 Iraqi authors, both
novelists and short story writers, who used the countryside as their thematic venue. al-Zujaji criticizes these authors who, in their zeal to promote
social reform, are didactic, stereotype their subject matter, and fail to see any

positive aspects of the countryside. A complex treatment of rural values—whether positive, such as honor, hospitality, and social solidarity, or negative, such as revenge *(al-thar)*, arranged marriages, and lack of education—is largely absent in the works al-Zujaji surveys. The result is a patronizing representation that gives the peasantry no voice of its own.[40]

Because the vast majority of novels and short stories on the subject of the Iraqi countryside have been written by leftists and Iraqist nationalists, al-Zujaji's critique serves to discredit their attempt to act as the voice of the rural oppressed. Indirectly, his critique appears to strengthen the Ba'th Party's claim that Pan-Arabists can better represent and protect the masses' interests.[41] If Iraqist nationalists have inaccurately portrayed social and cultural relations in the village, then this casts doubt on the authenticity of their writings. al-Zujaji concedes that conditions under the monarchy, particularly the despotic control of tribal shaykh-landlords, prevented would-be authors from spending time in villages and thus being able to comprehend their dynamics. Nevertheless, al-Zujaji argues that most writings on the village are superficial and caricature rural life. In particular, he criticizes writers who view peasants as lacking the political consciousness required to bring about meaningful social change.[42] How can literary works help alter the oppressive conditions of rural life, he asks, if the peasantry is portrayed as lacking an understanding of current conditions and the means to change them?

For al-Zujaji, this approach is not only condescending but also inaccurate since peasants are much more sophisticated than they are portrayed in novels such as *Jalal Khalid, Dr. Ibrahim, al-Khala 'Atiya, Fi-L-Tariq, Qalat al-Ayyam, Shamkhi,* and *Runayn al-Qayyid.*[43] Rural life in novels and short stories is portrayed as static, which belies the change that has occurred in the countryside. For example, since the mid-1930s, many peasant uprisings *(intifadat)* have challenged shaykhly authority, village traditions have been openly questioned, and many peasants have opposed oppressive conditions by "voting with their feet" and migrating to urban areas.[44] To be fair, the author admits that some authors, particularly Dhu al-Nun Ayyub in his *al-Yadd wa-l-Ard wa-l-Ma' (The Hand, Earth, and Water),* demonstrated sensitivity to peasant attempts to bring about change and to the complex dynamics of gender oppression in the Iraqi village.[45] However, these limited insights do not vitiate the author's argument for the need for a more positive representation of rural values and his crediting of peasants with the potential to become active agents in bringing about change.

al-Zujaji's critique casts doubt on the quality and authenticity of writings on rural life, which were intended to draw urban readers' attention to the peasantry's oppression. Because he focuses on authors concerned with social reform, the author undermines the credibility of the left, which has portrayed itself as the champion of downtrodden workers and peasantry. al-Zujaji also transfers the focus of writing on the peasantry to the present. If past writings are inadequate, then obviously a new generation of writers is needed and the historical memory of the old generation of writers must be rejected. Since the Ba'th Party presents itself as guardian of the people's interests, then this implies that it represents peasant interests as well. al-Zujaji's critique facilitates the transfer of writing on the peasantry to the present and hence to Ba'th Party control.

Although the Ministry of Culture and Information chose al-Zujaji's study for political reasons, the author himself avoids polemics in favor of a study that is scholarly in tone and content. This lengthy work reflects extensive research and reveals al-Zujaji's obvious interest in an authentic portrayal of rural society, to which he undoubtedly traces his own social and cultural roots. A closer analysis indicates that this study, far from supporting the state, is actually subversive in content. Whether the author's double entendre is self-conscious or not is difficult to tell. A former academic mentor, Dr. Muhsin al-Musawi, portrays the author less as someone who is concerned with politics than as someone who is sincerely interested in questions of representation of the countryside in literary texts.[46]

The reader is struck by al-Zujaji's failure to invoke the requisite code words in a study that ostensibly supports the Ba'thist project for appropriating historical memory. The volume is devoid of obsequious references to Saddam Husayn, Pan-Arabism, and the Ba'th Party. Although the lack of references to Pan-Arabism might seem understandable in light of the text's subject matter, al-Zujaji's avoidance of the concept of al-Shu'ubiya is striking, especially given his critique of the left and his emphasis on cultural authenticity. al-Zujaji seems less concerned with intellectually marginalizing the leftist authors whose works he finds deficient than in promoting a more genuine understanding of rural life. By refusing to "Ba'thize" his text, and in viewing the countryside dynamically, al-Zujaji contradicts Ba'thist historiography, which embodies a static, essentialist, and transhistorical view of Arab culture and society, perhaps best captured in the party's slogan, "One Arab nation with an eternal mission" *(Umma 'Arabiya wahida dhat risala khalida)*.

al-Zujaji's own leftist sympathies become apparent when he cites one of the main reasons writings on the peasantry proliferated between World War II and the July 1958 Revolution, namely intensified class conflict in Iraqi society. A close reading of this text points to an author with Iraqist nationalist sympathies and an analytic framework grounded in an incipient Marxism, tinged with Gramscian overtones. For the author, material conditions matter and social class is a legitimate analytic category, but consciousness, and political activists taking their cues from peasants themselves, constitute the real stuff of meaningful social and political change.[47] Despite al-Zujaji's focus on the pre-1958 era, a period of increased tensions in the countryside, several of the studies he critiques were published during the mid- and late 1960s and early 1970s, that is, when Pan-Arabists controlled the state. Because of his inclusion of studies published shortly before his own in 1980, the reader could conclude that little had changed in the Iraqi countryside despite the July 1958 Revolution and the so-called Ba'thist revolutions of 1963 and 1968.

al-Zujaji's study is clearly relevant in light of the economic reductionism that characterized much writing on the countryside prior to 1958, writing that often ignored all other facets of rural life. Beyond creating a simplistic portrayal of the peasantry, such writing produced a deformed aesthetic as well. al-Zujaji indicts these works as distorted representations and bad art. The alienation *(al-ghurba)* of urban writers from rural life precluded high-quality literature describing the countryside. Whether romantic or realist, Iraqi novels and short stories have never penetrated the social psychology and culture of village life, and therefore have avoided the "thick description" that a rich and nuanced literary genre would need in order to flower. al-Zujaji's critique of the left for not developing a proper aesthetic, however, can also be interpreted as a subterfuge for a larger critique of Ba'thist approaches to the peasantry.

The author's attack on the leftist intelligentsia for its lack of understanding of the countryside, on the monarchy for supporting the tribal shaykhs' oppression, and on the abominable conditions of rural life were all charges that could be directed against the former Ba'thist regime. Despite their overwhelmingly rural origins, Ba'thist intellectuals were as urban in outlook as was the intelligentsia prior to the July 1958 Revolution. Few if any members of the Ba'thist regime made serious efforts to learn about the peasantry's culture and values. The urban intelligentsia is no more able to conduct open and frank discussions with peasants about the conditions of their lives today than were urban intellectuals under the monarchy. Interestingly, the only instance I have discovered of literary figures initiating contact with the peasantry and tribes and being able to move freely among them was under the Qasim regime.[48] It is unclear whether al-Zujaji is aware of these contacts.

The charge that Iraqi authors have failed to attribute agency to the peasantry is one that any educated and politically conscious Iraqi would realize was equally applicable to the Ba'thist regime. In one sense al-Zujaji's work was particularly subversive because the Baʿth Party, unlike the monarchy, which never pretended to solve the "rural question," claimed to be a vanguard party seeking revolutionary change. al-Zujaji, by attacking the leftist and Iraqist nationalists who wrote the first works on rural society, mounted an implicit critique of the Baʿth Party, whose "top-down" decision making, in which peasants enjoy little or no input, was just as condescending. Despite introducing schools and electricity to villages, the Baʿth Party has used television, illiteracy classes, and youth organizations such as the Vanguards (al-Talaʾiʿ) to indoctrinate peasants and weaken the ability of rural families to socialize their offspring. At the time al-Zujaji's study was published, land reform had not led to any serious redistribution of land. Peasants thus remained dependent on landlords, but were now dependent on the Baʿth Party as well. Throughout the 1980s, rural inequities became even more pronounced as the Baʿth privatized much of the agrarian sector. Interpreting al-Zujaji's work as critique of the Baʿth, then, became even more salient in the years following its publication.

One reading of al-Zujaji's study is that the authors he criticizes for their condescending and didactic approach to rural problems became a metaphor for the Baʿth's Leninism. The author's message is that conditions have changed very little. Urban ideologues and policy makers (like the monarchy and its rural agents, the shaykh-landlords, *sirkals,* and religious clergy before them) make decisions affecting the countryside without consulting the peasantry on what social change they desire. al-Zujaji does what many other authors of state-sponsored historical texts have also done, namely discuss current politics through focusing on the past. In this context, al-Zujaji's study was not only part of the state's effort to appropriate historical memory, but it also provided a potentially subversive space for political, social, and cultural discourse among educated Iraqis. Through their "hidden texts," such studies also served as a vehicle for opposing educated Iraqis' ostensible patron, the state.

A fourth type of state-sponsored publication is one that challenged the Baʿthist project for appropriating historical memory. A prominent example is Kamal Mazhar Ahmad's study *al-Tabaqa al-ʿAmila al-ʿIraqiya: al-Takkawun wa Badiyat al-Taharruk (The Iraqi Working Class: Its Formation and Early Activities).*[49] Ahmad, an emeritus professor of Kurdish extraction in Baghdad University's Department of Philosophy and a well-known leftist, treated an extremely sensitive topic without conforming to Baʿthist precepts. Ahmad's text raises a number of interesting questions. Because the text diverged from Baʿthist historiography, how far was the author able to stretch the limits of authoritarian rule by creating a counterhistorical memory? Why did the Ministry of Culture and Information permit the publication by a well-known and respected leftist of a sensitive text that challenged its own interpretation of the past?

As in other corporatist authoritarian Arab regimes, such as Nasirist Egypt, Ba'thist Syria, and Algeria under the National Liberation Front (FLN), in Iraq studies that avoid contemporary politics, and especially studies critical of the prerevolutionary past, were often permitted. This policy allowed the state to maintain the pretense of openness by allowing publications on topics that do not challenge its authority. Covering the period from the late nineteenth century until 1932, Ahmad's study would seem to fit into this category, especially because it is replete with criticisms of British colonial rule and the monarchy. However, any study of the working class in Iraq confronted the Ba'th Party with difficult problems.[50] First, the Iraqi working class was well organized and had developed close ties to the ICP long before the Ba'th Party was founded in Iraq. Second, after its formation in Iraq in 1952, the Ba'th Party was able to cite few examples where it directly served worker interests. Because the Takriti Ba'th intensified state control of labor unions, even appointing intelligence officers as union leaders, many workers were aware that the Ba'th Party sharply circumscribed their ability to act independently of the state.[51] Ahmad's study therefore presented the Ministry of Culture and Information's cultural commissars with a dilemma. If the Ba'th Party curtailed the working class, which, as this study so meticulously documents, played a central role in challenging the monarchy and the British, how could it represent itself as a "socialist" party interested in the conditions of the working class?

Periodization is as sensitive an issue in this study as in other volumes that were sponsored by the Ministry of Culture and Information. By bracketing his study from the late nineteenth century to 1932, Ahmad avoided discussing the Ba'th Party's nemesis, the ICP, which formally organized only in 1934. Ahmad also avoids relying on ICP members or party sympathizers as sources. There are only two references in his book to ICP publications, and those are to issues of the party's theoretical journal, *al-Thaqafa al-Jadida (New Culture)*, which were published in Baghdad in 1971 and 1975, when the Ba'thist regime was actively courting the ICP to join a national front government (1971) and when the ICP was officially part of the National Front (1975).[52] Obviously these particular references would have had the regime's approval and therefore could not be disavowed after the fact. A number of Soviet sources are also cited, reflecting the author's higher education in the Soviet Union. Leftist sources are balanced by reference to Ba'thist sources, such as the magazine *Wa'y al-'Ummal (Worker Conscious-*

ness), the journal *Afaq ʿArabiya (Arab Perspectives)*, and the writings of the main Baʿthist interpreter of the working class, a former worker and Shiʿi from al-Nasiriya in southern Iraq named Razzaq Ibrahim Hasan.[53] However, most of Ahmad's sources are drawn from the period under study, including the major newspapers of the period, worker newspapers, and files from the Iraqi National Archives (al-Markaz al-Watani li-l-Wathaʾiq).

One of the most important and sensitive sections of Ahmad's study is his introduction. The author laments the lack of studies on the Iraqi working class, noting the existence of only one doctoral dissertation on the topic, which was completed at the University of Cairo.[54] Ahmad points out that the historical study of the working class is much more developed in Egypt, Syria, Lebanon, and Iran and calls for more attention to be given to the central role played by workers in opposing imperialism in Iraq. By calling for greater study of a social and political movement that was only marginally influenced by the Baʿth Party, Ahmad advocates a genre of studies that cannot be neatly fitted into Baʿthist historiography's social, political, and cultural categories. His study also points to a diverse political coalition in the anticolonial struggle, certain not to please the Baʿth Party, which sought to claim responsibility for all political opposition to imperialism. In underlining the paucity of studies of the Iraqi working class, Ahmad implicitly denigrates the Baʿthist claim to be a party of the masses. Ahmad also implicitly criticizes the Baʿth by noting that, although other Middle Eastern countries have seen an increase in historical studies of their respective working classes, the study of the working class in Iraq has been relegated primarily to nonhistorians and limited to such themes as the role of the worker in the Iraqi short story and in the Iraqi press.[55] Ahmad is saying in effect that these studies, which were almost all written by a single government employee, are no substitute for serious historical scholarship. For Ahmad, the Baʿthist culture industry comes up wanting in representing worker interests in state-sponsored publications.

Ahmad claims that if one includes oil wealth and a wide variety of other productive activities, including artisan production, workers account for roughly 90 percent of Iraq's gross domestic product. In privileging workers, Ahmad subtly introduces a historical materialist perspective. Invoking the need for a "holistic objective approach" *(uslub mawduʿi shamil)* and the inability to understand change without a focus on "effort" *(juhud)*, by which he really means labor, Ahmad implicitly criticizes idealist theories. Referring to the pyramids of Giza, Ahmad argues that this architectural complex, although made possible in part by engineering genius, would never have been realized without "the sweat of the slaves" who "constructed these edifices on their shoulders." Like al-Zujaji, Ahmad eschews any reference to Pan-Arabism and the Ba'th Party. Indeed, his study exhibits Iraqist nationalism in its most blatant form.

At one level, Ahmad's lack of reference to the ICP, and his study of workers who organized themselves into labor associations and unions that challenged British and monarchical authority in a self-reliant manner, could be viewed as a criticism of the communists because workers demonstrated that they did not need the party to pursue their own interests. At another level, Ahmad's study is deeply subversive precisely because it does not incorporate the ICP. What Ahmad details, following al-Fahd's unpublished doctoral dissertation, is that workers early in this century were able, without external assistance, to create a wide range of organizations that represented their interests in virtually every sector of industry and artisan production.[56] Further, these organizations forced the British, who tried to increase municipal fees in 1931, to rescind the proposed increases in urban electricity rates, and forced the monarchy and the British to improve working conditions for laborers in a number of sectors of the economy such as the Iraqi State Railways, the Basra Port, and the oil industry.

Ahmad demonstrates that workers with little and sometimes no formal education were able to establish a counterhegemonic view of society. Labor unions fostered egalitarian feelings and challenged the sectarianism that dominated the state and other public and private organizations by avoiding reference to ethnicity in recruiting new members and eschewing sectarianism in the everyday running of their affairs. This all occurred among society's lower strata without the assistance of any political party and under the hostile eye of the state. Because workers were able to organize, defend their interests, and conduct their affairs without the sectarianism that has characterized the Iraqi state and certainly the Ba'th Party, the working-class organizations that Ahmad cites from the late 1920s and early 1930s constituted a proto-civil society and demonstrated that sectarianism need not dominate public space. The idea of the lower classes taking control of their own interests challenged the hierarchical quality built into all Ba'thist concepts of politics and society. It also challenged the allied concept of Ba'thist corporatism because workers clearly constituted a distinct corporate entity organized along social class lines whose interests frequently do not correspond to those of society as a whole.

Despite my focus on book-length studies, it would be inappropriate to neglect the most prominent journal that was published by the Ministry of Culture and Information, the *Journal of Popular Culture*. This journal was by far the most popular among educated readers, boasted the largest number of Iraqi intellectuals who contributed articles, and maintained the most extensive ties with Arab intellectuals outside Iraq. While in Baghdad, I was struck by the rapidity with which it disappeared from kiosks and bookstore shelves. Obviously the *Journal of Popular Culture* had a large and enthusiastic readership. Although it began to be published regularly under the auspices of the Ministry of Culture and Information in 1969, the journal first appeared in 1963, when four intellectuals, Lutfi al-Khuri, Ibrahim al-Daquqi, ʿAbd al-Hamid al-ʿAlwaji, and Shakir Sabir al-Dabit, applied for permission to begin a journal with the same title.[57] Between 1963 and 1964 several issues were published. In 1968, an attempt was made to reissue the journal. However, only in 1969 did the minister of culture and information, ʿAbdallah Sallum al-Samarraʾi, offer to have the state publish the journal with the promise that the ministry would not interfere with its editorial authority. Once the state became its publisher, the journal not only appeared on a regular basis, but it was also able to offer its contributors honoraria. It was published not only in Arabic, but in Turkish, Persian, French, English, and Italian as well.

The *Journal of Popular Culture*'s editorial statement, published in its first issue, in September 1963, is significant. The statement emphasized that the journal's goal was to improve understanding of the period "prior to scientific history" and the "unfathomable roots" of ancient history, suggesting that the editors conceived the journal as a vehicle for fostering greater integration between Iraq's ancient and more recent Arab heritage.[58] The fact that the journal began as a private venture and retained one of its founders as editor in chief after 1969 perhaps explains why it differed from other official journals in not assuming a didactic and overtly political quality once it acquired official state sponsorship. The Baʿthist regime's offer to finance the *Journal of Popular Culture*, which stemmed from its realization of the popularity of the journal's themes, was meant to enhance its populist credentials.

The *Journal of Popular Culture* was also important for the intellectual link that it maintained to the Qasim era. Lutfi al-Khuri, Ibrahim al-Daquqi, and ʿAbd al-Hamid al-ʿAlwaji, the dean of folkloric studies under the Qasim regime who produced both scholarly studies and small pamphlets on folklore designed for mass consumption, were all associated with the Ministry of Guidance under Faysal al-Samir.[59] Because of al-ʿAlwaji's status, and al-Khuri's considerable efforts in publishing the journal, including subsidizing it with his personal funds prior to 1969, the journal was able to attract many excellent articles. Between 1969 and 1983, when al-Khuri resigned, the journal was largely able to avoid direct commentary on political affairs. Only during the Iran-Iraq War did politics begin to intrude on the journal. Although editorial policies were still officially under the control of al-Khuri, who remained editor in chief, the editorial secretary, ʿAbd al-Sahib al-ʿAqabi, increasingly exercised control over the journal, adding an ever-greater political tone. The state credited the tremendous success of the *Journal of Popular Culture* for the development of various folkloric centers and workshops, and the journal was much celebrated on its tenth anniversary as a Ministry of Culture and Information publication in 1979.[60]

Even though it avoided adopting political stances during the 1970s, the journal supported the state in a variety of ways. First, the journal's many articles on all aspects of urban and rural folklore, ranging from music to tribal poetry to forms of dress, delighted its readers by feeding their nostalgia for the past. Second, these articles dealt with themes such as cuisine, dress, marriage rituals, music, dance, and tribal values, themes that, although they varied somewhat, were common to all major ethnic groups and thereby fostered a sense of common national identity. By publishing the journal, the state was credited with patronizing popular culture. Third, the many articles on the hero *(al-batal)* and the " male tough" *(qabaday* or *shaqi)* valorized strong and decisive leadership qualities. With Saddam seeking to portray a strong image of himself, both in visual imagery (photographs, murals, television programs, and even a film about his participation in the 1959 attempt to assassinate ʿAbd al-Karim Qasim)[61] and in his writings, there was a dovetailing of interests between these many articles and the Iraqi leader's larger political project.[62]

Having analyzed state-sponsored cultural production intended for Baʿth Party members, regime officials, the educated middle classes, and Arab intellectuals outside Iraq, how did the Project for the Rewriting of History affect the educational system, and specifically university- and secondary school–level texts? In 1980, the Baghdad University Department of Political Science was a sophisticated academic unit with a well-developed curriculum similar to that found in Western universities.[63] Of interest in terms of the presentation of its subject matter was a comparative politics text, *al-Mushkilat al-Siyasiya fi-l-ʿAlim al-Thalith (Political Problems in the Third World)*, written by the chair of the Political Science Department, Dr. Riyad ʿAziz Hadi.[64] The approach of the text, which surveys several non-Western political systems outside the Middle East, parallels most introductory comparative politics texts while adding a focus on political economy in its treatment of state intervention in the economy and formation of development policies.

Most significant is Hadi's use of academic sources in analyzing foreign political systems, which would make this text acceptable in most open universities. However, his eight-page chapter on Iraq, "The Arab Road to Socialism in Light of the Thought of the Arab Socialist Baʿth Party and the Experiment in the Iraqi Region," relies exclusively on Baʿthist documents, almost all of which are speeches by Saddam Husayn.[65] These speeches, which stress the Baʿth's purported implementation of Iraq's transition to socialism, lack supporting data. The juxtaposition of lengthy quotes from Saddam's speeches to the thoughts of other prominent scholars, such as Yves Lacoste, Raymond Aron, Pierre Jalée, Rodolfo Stavenhagen, Maurice Duverger, Joseph Schumpeter, and Charles Bettelheim, placed the Iraqi president at a distinct intellectual disadvantage. Although ideologically mixed, Hadi's sources favor leftist interpretations of third world development, probably reflecting his own political preferences.

Any serious political science student at Baghdad University or other Iraqi schools would recognize the discrepancy between the author's analysis of Iraq and his analysis of other non-Western political systems. The student would also certainly notice Hadi's implicit critique of the Baʿthist regime through his failure to cite any substantive sources when analyzing Iraqi political development and his use of Saddam's speeches instead. The constant references to Saddam's speeches sent a message that the analysis of Iraqi politics must be subordinated to the state's intellectual dictates. This text is intriguing because any Ministry of Higher Education or Baʿth Party official would have found it difficult to criticize it. Because the author relies so heavily on Saddam's speeches, anyone who criticized his chapter on Iraq would have risked being accused of denigrating Saddam's thought, a danger to be avoided at all costs.[66] Professor Hadi subtly but assuredly provoked questioning by his students by making clear his own distaste for Baʿthist intellectual production.

Two other university texts that are of interest were used in the Department of Sociology and Anthropology and the Department of Archaeology and Antiquities, respectively. The first is an ethnography, *al-Binaʾ al-Ijtimaʿi wa-l-Taghir fi-l-Mujtamaʿ al-Rifi: al-Rashidiya, Dirasa Anthrubulujiya Ijtimaʿiya (Social Structure and Change in Rural Society: al-Rashidiya, a Social Anthropological Study)*, written by a young and upcoming Shiʿi anthropologist, Alaʾ al-Din Jasim al-Bayati, whom I met at Baghdad University in May 1980.[67] The text, which adopts a Western structural-functionalist and modernization theory approach, lacks any references to Baʿthist ideology or rural social policies. Even the bibliography only contains one reference to a Baʿthist publication, the *Journal of Popular Culture*. Most of the works cited are by well-known Arab anthropologists, and no books by either Saddam or the Baʿth Party are cited.

This text, al-Bayati informed me, was used in his courses. Although not subversive in content, neither did it promote the state's interests. However, al-Bayati's discussion of parochialism and tribal disputes, including revenge *(al-thar)* exacted in the event of physical harm and even the murder of members of one tribe by another, presents an unflattering portrayal of tribal life.[68] Thus al-Bayati's ethnography ran counter to the idealized view of tribal culture expressed in many articles on rural folklore and Saddam's explicit valorization of tribalism during the 1980s. al-Bayati was probably able to avoid political interference when he published his text for two reasons. First, the Ba'th Party showed much less interest in anthropology than in the treatment of political issues in political science texts. Second, the modernization theory approach adopted by al-Bayati fit well with Ba'th Party officials' views of rural society.

The second text, *Turuq al-Bahth al-'Ilmi fi Tarikh al-Athar (Methods of Scientific Research in History and Archaeology)*, by the well-known and highly respected Iraqi archaeologist Taha Baqir and his assistant, Dr. 'Abd al-'Aziz Humayd, was also intended for use in university classes.[69] This text, which carried the imprimatur of the Ministry of Higher Education and Scientific Research, not only includes detailed procedures for archaeological excavations but also contains a chapter on theories of history, including a discussion of hermeneutics.[70] In light of the emphasis that Saddam and the Ba'th Party had already placed on Mesopotamianism during the 1970s, including festivals and the "reconstruction" of Babylon, it is significant that this text, which was used to train Iraqi archaeologists, did nothing to prepare them politically from a Ba'thist perspective. The authors state in their introduction that their task is to explain to students how "the science of history" differs from other sciences, particularly the natural sciences. The sophisticated presentation of different historiographies was completely opposed to the Ba'thist conception of history, which firmly states that there is only one instrumentally defined approach. Thus future archaeologists studying at Baghdad, Mosul, and other universities were being trained to think in ways that ran counter to the Ba'thist approach to history, such as that articulated in Nuri al-Qaysi's *Poetry and History*. That this text's senior author was the renowned Taha Baqir not only strengthened its academic credentials, but it also probably warded off academic censors. Indeed, it was remarkable that in 1986, at the Iran-Iraq War's most critical moment, when Iraqi forces were fighting to prevent the fall of Basra, Dar al-Shu'un al-Thaqafiya al-'Amma, under Dr. Muhsin Jasim al-Musawi's directorship, chose to republish Baqir's 1975 volume, *Muqaddima fi Tarikh al-Hidara al-Qadima (An Introduction to the History of Ancient Civilization)*. This reissue was startling because of Baqir's numerous arguments demonstrating Persian and Meso-potamian cultural intermingling throughout history, arguments that directly opposed those of Saddam and other Baʿthists in their discussion of the al-Shuʿubiya controversy. It is equally striking that Baqir states that the origins of the name "Iraq" can be traced to an Arabized Persian term.[71]

The Baʿthist project seems to have only superficially entered the educational curriculum at the secondary school level. In a sixth-level history text of the modern Arab world, the Qadisiyat Saddam campaign seems to have been hastily added onto the next to last page.[72] Elsewhere, a cursory effort was made to insert Saddam's Qadisiya into the text in making a comparison between the 1920 Revolution and the Iran-Iraq War by arguing that both conflicts involved efforts to protect Iraq from external aggression.[73] However, this argument is brief and unelaborated, making it difficult for the student to understand the (spurious) comparison.[74]

Turning to the study of Islam, there are no references at all to Qadisiyat Saddam in a textbook of Arab Islamic history.[75] Although, amazingly, the text in question, *The History of Arab-Islamic Civilization*, does not even mention the dispute over the succession to the caliphate in 661 C.E. that led to a split between Sunnis and Shiʿis, one would assume that the Qadisiyat Saddam campaign would be a pronounced theme in such a text given the campaign's heavy Islamic symbolism. Apart from this major lacunae, the text presents a straightforward account of Islamic history. Either the Ministry of Education was so understaffed that it was unable to change its textbooks or, probably closer to the truth, ministry officials sought to maintain what they considered the integrity of their texts and made minimal efforts to include information that, from their perspective, had no historical validity.

Perhaps the best study with which to conclude this survey of texts that were connected to the Project for the Rewriting of History is Nuri al-Qaysi's *al-Adib wa-l-Iltizam (The Writer and Commitment)*.[76] Of particular interest is the last chapter, "Commitment and Alienation," in which we find important clues to the motivation behind state efforts to appropriate historical memory. Although al-Qaysi quotes the Prophet Muhammad to show that alienation existed even when Islam had few adherents, he dates modern alienation from Hulagu's invasion of Iraq during the thirteenth century and destruction of the ʿAbbasid Empire. Following the empire's collapse, intellectuals felt cut off from their past as they struggled to sustain a sense of intellectual life. Arguing against the view that intellectual life stagnated between the fall of the ʿAbbasid Empire and Napoleon's invasion of

Egypt in 1798, al-Qaysi asserts that Arab intellectuals maintained continuity with the past as they developed new areas of creativity. In his view, the real problem was the multiple conspiracies directed against the Arabs, which sought to obfuscate the continuity of Arab culture and tradition.

In referring to post-ʿAbbasid Iraq as the "Iraqi region" *(al-Quṭr al-ʿIraqi)*, al-Qaysi hints at the unease that the Arab Sunni community feels because of its minority status. As long as Iraq remains a *region*, Sunni Arabs can surmount this unease by envisioning an Arab nation that transcends Iraq's borders and in which they are no longer a minority. Alienation, as al-Qaysi uses the term, seems to refer, in large measure, to the problems that the Sunni Arab triangle of north-central Iraq has faced over time, beginning with the destruction of the ʿAbbasid Empire. Indeed, Hulagu's invasion seems to have caused the greatest destruction and left its deepest social imprint in northern Iraq. Unlike Saddam, who argued after the 1991 Intifada that the uprising reflected the residue of the destruction caused by the Mongol invasion, al-Qaysi considered that intellectuals helped Iraq sustain the unity and continuity of Arab culture in the face of this destruction between 1258 and 1798, a period that did not, in his view, constitute the Arab "Dark Ages."

For al-Qaysi, and Sunni Arab Iraqis who share his mindset, the unity of Arab culture and history represents the highest good, although many forces seek to destroy it. This perspective does not seem to be as widely shared in the more ethnically homogeneous southern part of the country dominated by the Shiʿa. al-Qaysi's task, as he sees it, is to overcome alienation by creating a uniform and unchanging Arab individual, people, nation, history, and culture. For him there can be no change and no periodization. The only tension that exists is between the Arabs, who are naturally inclined toward a uniform culture and community, and those who conspire to create disunity in Arab ranks. In light of the Sunni Arab historical memory of dislocation and suffering, and continued communal tensions with Kurds, Turkomans, Assyrians, and Christians in Iraq's ethnically diverse north-central region, the bases of Sunni Arab sectarianism become clearer. If we add to this equation the economic decline and deprivation of the rural Sunni Arabs of the north-central river towns such as Takrit, and the fear of rural Sunni Arabs that they may lose control of their positions in the state apparatus to other ethnic groups, then the transformation of this alienation or insecurity into hatred and violence is not difficult to understand.

This survey should underscore the always open-ended quality and intellectual ambiguity of state efforts to impose hegemonic thinking through appropriating historical memory and national heritage. It should also serve as an antidote to notions such as the "republic of fear" or the "silence of the intellectuals." Although some intellectuals subordinated their creative interests and sold their souls to the state, others, following James Scott's analysis, developed new and subtle forms of resistance that kept alive the spark of opposition until the final fall of Saddam and the Ba'th, and the possibility of building civil society and democracy.[77]

9 Memories of State or Memories of the People?

Iraq Following the Gulf War

Having failed to learn its lesson from the first Gulf War, the Ba'thist regime embarked on a disastrous invasion of Kuwait on August 20, 1990. Saddam Husayn seriously miscalculated Arab and Western opposition to Iraq's annexation of Kuwait. Soon the Iraqi regime faced an international military coalition led by the United States, which attacked Iraqi forces in January 1991, overwhelmingly defeating them and driving them from Kuwait. In a few short weeks, allied bombing destroyed a significant portion of Iraq's industry, military capacity, and power and transportation infrastructure, sending industrial production back to the level of the early 1960s. With electric power, potable water, and sewage treatment severely damaged, food distribution suffered and disease spread. Reacting to this social breakdown, Iraqi army units mutinied in Basra on February 28, 1991. Soon sixteen of Iraq's eighteen provinces were engaged in a massive *intifada* that sought to overthrow the Iraqi regime. By April, this uprising had been crushed. Only the three northern provinces comprising Kurdistan remained free of Ba'thist control. How did the Ba'thist state survive the Gulf War and the subsequent *intifada*? How did these events affect the balance of power between the state and opposition forces, and sectarian feelings in Iraq? What changes occurred in state cultural production after the Gulf War? What role did the counter-hegemonic memory developed by the Iraqi opposition play in the Ba'th's collapse, and what role can it play in the ongoing transition to democracy?

The 1991 Intifada left great physical and emotional scars on Iraqi society. Not only was Iraq's infrastructure further damaged, but at least a hundred thousand Iraqis were killed or wounded, in addition to those already killed during the Gulf War.[1] The sanctions and reparations the United Nations imposed after the war created further domestic suffering. However, the Intifada initiated an intense discussion of Iraqi politics and society in which many fundamental issues were frankly confronted for the first time. Sectarian feelings expressed during the Intifada, manifest in graffiti on Republican Guard tanks that declared "No more Shiʿa after today" *(La shiʿa baʿd al-yawm)*, and the invoking of religious symbolism by some Shiʿi insurgents, intensified fears and further undermined trust on both sides of the Sunni-Shiʿi divide. At the same time, historically separated opposition political groups met to discuss a common plan of action for the first time. Meanwhile, the state's subordination to tribalism and control by Saddam's family intensified. The impoverishment of the urban working class and large segments of the urban middle class made the growth of a wealthy elite comprised of black marketeers, contractors, and Baʿth Party officials all the more egregious. Innovations in state-sponsored cultural production ground to a halt, indicating the regime's lack of direction. The only new idea was Saddam's designation of the Gulf War, which he claimed to have won, as "the Mother of all Battles" (Umm al-Maʿarik). The regime's continued hold on power was based more on the opposition's military weakness than on the regime's own strength.

Ideologically and culturally, the most important impact of the second Gulf War and the 1991 Intifada was to transform Iraqi political discourse. During the 1970s, few questioned the Baʿth's hold on power. The Gulf War and Intifada raised questions for the first time about the Iraqi regime's longevity and indicated that alternatives to Baʿthist rule were beginning to be taken seriously. An Iraqi opposition that was broader than the Baʿth's traditional foes, the ICP and the Kurds, began to coalesce. Iraqi activists and intellectuals belonging to a large expatriate community that ultimately reached an estimated two to three million Iraqis, or 10 to 15 percent of the population, addressed not only alternatives to Baʿthist rule, but also more fundamental problems such as how Iraq's different ethnic groups could peacefully and democratically coexist.[2] Most significantly, sectarianism was seriously confronted for the first time in the modern state's history. The word "Shiʿi," which had been almost totally absent from political discourse, entered the vocabulary of Iraqi politics.[3]

One of the problems with post–Gulf War interpretations of Iraqi politics has been their negative and pessimistic tone. No one would disagree that the war and its aftermath wreaked havoc on Iraq or that the United Nations sanctions caused great suffering and many needless deaths, especially those of children.[4] Unfortunately, the analytic discourse engendered by the war and the sanctions regime, not to mention the Baʿth Party's continued brutality, belied any positive developments in Iraqi politics. In unintended ways, notions such as "the republic of fear," "cruelty and silence," "endless torture," and the "resurrection of Saddam Hussein" reinforced the idea of an unchanging authoritarianism, and the idea that only old age would lead to Saddam's demise.[5] This analysis offered little hope for the future. Without a "politics of hope and tolerance" to offset the "politics of repression and fear," the Takriti Baʿthist regime was inadvertently attributed more power than warranted, belying the ease with which the regime collapsed in 2003.

The outpouring of detailed studies of Iraqi politics and society during the 1990s, the opposition's re-examination of modern historical memory, and the formulation of policies designed to create a post-Baʿthist democratic society reflected important developments following the Gulf War. Although a comprehensive history of the Gulf War and 1991 Intifada has yet to be written, the general outlines are well known. Iraq's seizure of Kuwait was stimulated by its severe economic straits in 1988 and 1989 as a result of large war debts and depressed oil prices.[6] Saddam and the Baʿth faced the problem of integrating a million-man standing army back into Iraqi society. After 200,000 soldiers were demobilized in 1989, riots broke out in Baghdad between returning soldiers and Egyptian workers. Many former soldiers were placed in Iraq's burgeoning military industrial complex, which, with 100,000 Iraqi employees by 1989, placed a tremendous strain on the state budget.[7] Food shortages, unemployment, and onerous debt repayments placed the regime in a precarious position. In 1988, a reported 178 officers were arrested for plotting a coup.[8]

For the Baʿth, seizing Kuwait would solve Iraq's economic problems, allow Iraq to dominate Gulf oil production, deliver the decisive victory that had eluded Saddam in the war with Iran, and distract Iraqis from domestic political discontent. Although some have blamed Iraq's invasion on the ambiguous signals that the United States gave to Iraq, it is difficult to believe that a rational leader would fail to comprehend that seizing Kuwait would evoke international condemnation.[9] This is especially true because control of Kuwait, a major oil producer, would have allowed Saddam to dominate neighboring Saudi Arabia and the other Gulf states as well. Blaming the invasion solely on ambiguous American cues overlooks the fact that Saddam's understanding of international relations in 1990 was highly simplistic. Although Qasim had been humiliated in an attempt to annex Kuwait in 1962, Saddam's own institutional memory was short. Kuwait's seizure was a case study in how the process of appropriating historical memory can create barriers between the regime and the populace as much as it can integrate state and society. Saddam seemed to have been seduced by his own rhetoric about Iraq's military capabilities, with obvious disastrous consequences.

Unlike the invasion of Iran, the seizure of Kuwait was a sign of political weakness and domestic malaise. Far from achieving Saddam's goals, the war led to Iraq's defeat and thwarted Saddam's foreign policy objectives, especially his goal of becoming the Arab world's dominant leader. The war led to the first serious challenge to Ba'thist rule and the death of many party officials by insurgents; curtailed Iraq's nuclear, chemical, and biological weapons programs; opened the captured files of Saddam's security services to international scrutiny; and drastically reduced the state's ability to promote cultural production to enhance its power.[10] Because the privations that followed the war created tremendous discontent, the state was required to devote enormous resources to repressive measures. Meanwhile, dissent within the regime itself had increasingly narrowed the number of decision makers, and power became centralized in the hands of Saddam and his two sons, 'Uday and Qusay.

Why did the Intifada, following the devastating Gulf War defeat, fail? According to one argument, the Intifada failed because the United States allowed Iraq to deploy helicopter gunships that turned the tide against the rebel forces. It is also argued that, had allied troops inside Iraq supported the insurgents, antiregime forces would have been victorious. Unfortunately, these counterfactual arguments do not account for the fact that if Saddam's Republican Guard units had been defeated, disorder would have reigned because the Intifada lacked a unified program and political leadership. Only the Kurds were able to establish a functioning political system following the Intifada, one facilitated by the allied no-fly zone established above the 36th parallel. However, the Kurds' long historical struggle to establish a semiautonomous cultural and political region had already inspired an extensive dialogue regarding the strategies needed to achieve their objectives.[11] Having negotiated numerous unimplemented accords with various Baghdad regimes, the Kurds had been forced to think carefully about their relationship to the larger Iraqi nation-state.

The Iraqi Shi'a and Sunni Arabs who supported the Intifada had no oppositional history comparable to the Kurds and little idea of what to put in place of the collapsing regime. Many Sunni Arabs, although they opposed Saddam, were fearful that an overthrow of the Ba'th would lead to disorder or a sectarian Shi'i regime, possibly supported by the Kurds, which would marginalize them politically and economically. Among the Shi'a, the only well-developed alternative was the idea of an Islamic state, although it was advocated only by a very small segment of the *marja'iya* and a few religious radicals. Neither group represented the larger Shi'i community, much of which was secular and inclined toward the left, and the group certainly did not represent the rest of the Iraqi populace. The ICP's only organized base of operations was in Kurdistan, where it was weaker than either of the two dominant Kurdish parties, the Kurdish Democratic Party (KDP), dominated by the al-Barzani family, and the smaller Patriotic Union of Kurdistan (PUK), led by Jalal Talabani.[12]

The Intifada was brutally repressed, especially in the south, where an estimated 20,000 to 100,000 people were killed. SCUD missiles and artillery shells were fired into the city of Karbala', and many young Shi'i men were arrested and never seen again.[13] Following the Intifada, the Iraqi regime began to drain the southern marshlands, one of the world's most pristine ecological preserves, to prevent its use as a guerilla haven. By the late 1990s, in one of the twentieth century's most serious ecological crimes, this area had been all but totally destroyed.[14] Meanwhile, Ba'thist repression intensified, with repeated executions of army officers accused of plotting against the regime. With prisons filled beyond capacity, Qusay Saddam Husayn, who controlled the state security apparatus, began a series of prison "cleansing campaigns" in 1997, executing all prisoners with sentences of fifteen or more years to reduce overcrowding.[15]

Because the groups involved in the Intifada realized that none of them could topple the Ba'th alone, the opposition was forced to interact politically. The struggle to find common political ground soon led to a much broader discourse that transcended the immediate goal of overthrowing the Ba'th. How would communists and Islamists develop a common vocabulary with which to discuss Iraq's political future? How could Shi'is feel confident that Sunnis were taking their political interests seriously? How could Sunnis be reassured that Shi'is who acquired power in a post-Saddam Iraq would not seek revenge for historical injustices? How could the Kurds be assured that they would finally control their own politics, education, culture, and economy? Would members of the ICP and former Ba'thist officers now in opposition respect democratic norms in a post-Saddam Iraq?[16] While these were difficult questions, the fact that opposition groups confronted issues such as sectarianism, democracy, cultural pluralism, federalism, and demilitarization of the state, not to mention issues of social justice, represented a sea change in Iraqi political discourse. Because a large percentage of expatriate Iraqis, representing some of the country's best minds, were involved in the discourse of transcending the current regime, a "war of position" was in full swing by the mid-1990s.[17]

Before we turn to a discussion of the Iraqi opposition's countermemory and policy prescriptions in greater detail, what transpired inside Iraq after the suppression of the Intifada? Iraq was placed under some of the most severe sanctions ever imposed on a country by the international community. The sanctions had a disastrous effect on Iraq's civilian population, especially the salaried urban population and the Shi'a in the south. With the spiraling devaluation of the Iraqi dinar, salaries were totally inadequate to support middle- and working-class families. Because government rations only covered one-half to two-thirds of a typical family's monthly nutritional requirements, most white-collar employees and workers were forced to find additional employment. Many families sold their possessions to buy enough food to survive. Medicines were in short supply, which meant that even simple illnesses often became serious. Before the Gulf War, Iraq had one of the most advanced medical systems in the Middle East. Soon smallpox and cholera, which had previously all but disappeared, spread. Infant mortality rose. Many schoolchildren lacked books and pencils (banned because lead was a prohibited item), and computers were unknown to the vast majority of Iraqi youth. Only the Kurds, who remained free of Baghdad's control, prospered.[18]

Far from suffering, Saddam and his elite benefited from the sanctions regime. During the 1990s Saddam built at least twenty-six new palaces throughout Iraq, using imported marble and other expensive building materials.[19] Ba'thist officials established an extensive black market import-export trade, primarily through Jordan but also through Kurdistan to Turkey and the Levant, and imported luxury items for the elite. Often paying heavy tolls, the regime secretly exported oil through Iranian coastal waters and through Kurdistan to Eastern Turkey and Iran. Military technology for rebuilding Iraqi weapons programs, such as new missile systems, was also smuggled into the country.[20] Lavish parties thrown by the regime highlighted the tremendous disparity between the political elite and the populace at large. While the elite enjoyed the high life, the increasingly desperate middle class turned increasingly to religion. Aware of this disparity between elite and middle-class behavior, Saddam increased the use of Islamic symbols to bolster his image. In 1995, he closed all nightclubs and discotheques and banned the public sale of alcohol. To combat the rising crime rate the regime imposed "Islamic punishments," including amputations for theft.[21]

Whereas the morale of post–Gulf War military personnel suffered because of low salaries and poor equipment, new military units that enjoyed high salaries and extensive privileges were created to protect the regime. The elite Republican Guard was replaced in 1992 by the Golden Division, or Special Republican Guard, and a special unit called Fida'iyu Saddam (Saddam's Fida'iyun or Fedayeen) was established to protect the Iraqi president.[22] A unit of young children, called Ashbal Saddam (Saddam's Cubs), was trained in weapons usage and to be fiercely loyal to Saddam and the Ba'th.[23] After an attempted assassination of 'Uday in December 1996, the se-

FIGURE 17. "Saddam's Cubs" (Ashbal Saddam), Baghdad, Iraq. Associated Press Photo, August 11, 2002. AP/Worldwide rights.

curity services came under the control of Saddam's youngest son, Qusay, making him Saddam's heir apparent.

The continued consolidation of power within Saddam's immediate family intensified cleavages within the regime. After Saddam had ousted and executed all potential opponents within the Baʿth Party in 1979, he relied on his half brothers, Barzan, who became head of intelligence (Daʾirat al-Mukhabarat al-ʿAmma), Sabʿawi, who became head of General Security (al-ʿAmn al-ʿAmm), and Watban, who became minister of the interior. Husayn Kamil's marriage to Saddam's daughter, Raghad, in 1984 caused severe strain between Saddam and his half brothers since Barzan had wanted Raghad to marry one of his own sons and feared that the marriage would diminish his power. The rift grew until finally Saddam dismissed Barzan as head of General Security and sent him into exile.[24] Meanwhile, Kamil, who began as an army recruit and then a driver in Saddam's motorcade, was promoted by Saddam to lieutenant in 1979, captain in 1982, and then minister of the new combined Ministry of Industry and Military Industrialization Organization.[25] Kamil, who insisted on commissions for all armament contracts, acquired the reputation of being extremely greedy.[26]

By the mid-1990s, it was 'Uday's turn to expand his power at the expense of other members of the "family party state" *(dawlat hizb al-usra)*. Serious dissent spread during 1994–95, as evidenced by a number of bomb explosions in Baghdad. Previously loyal tribes reacted against the economy's continued deterioration. General Muhammad Mazlum al-Dulaymi, one of the most respected members of the powerful al-Dulaym tribe centered in al-Ramadi on the western Euphrates, was arrested in early 1995 and accused of plotting against the regime. When his body was returned to his family in May 1995 exhibiting clear signs of torture, rioting broke out and special army units were needed to suppress the rebellion.[27] 'Uday exploited the incident to criticize Watban and Sab'awi for failing to anticipate the uprising. The same month, Watban was dismissed as minister of the interior. Barzan, who had led the investigation and prosecution of the alleged plotters against Saddam in 1979, had already lost influence through his transfer to Geneva in 1993, where he incongruously became Iraq's representative to the United Nations Human Rights Organization. In August 1995, 'Uday, angered that his uncle Watban had been speaking ill of him, burst into a party, spraying the room with bullets. Watban was seriously injured in the leg, which had to be amputated, and several Gypsy dancers were killed.[28] In 1998, not content to allow Barzan to retain a high-profile ambassadorial position, 'Uday abruptly replaced him by one of his minions, a minor official in the Baghdad presidential office.[29]

During this period, Saddam, despite his regime's supposed Islamic orientation (which was evident in the 1995 ban on serving alcohol in public), began emulating 'Uday's decadent behavior. His public affair during the 1980s with a noted ophthalmologist, Samira al-Shahbandar, led to angry protests from his wife Sajida after he married al-Shahbandar and had a third son, 'Ali. During a November 1988 party, 'Uday burst into a dinner party honoring Suzanne Mubarak, the wife of Egyptian president Husni Mubarak, and killed Saddam's trusted personal bodyguard Kamil Hanna Jaju.[30] 'Uday was furious that Jaju had arranged many of Saddam's sexual liaisons with Samira al-Shahbandar and other women, and he feared that Saddam's second marriage might threaten his own position within the regime. These feelings were intensified because al-Shahbandar came from an old and prominent Baghdad family with which Saddam's family maintained a love-hate relationship.

Violence was followed by melodrama as 'Uday subsequently took an overdose of sleeping pills. Confronting 'Uday in the hospital, Saddam threatened to try him for murder. 'Uday was relieved of his government duties and exiled to Switzerland. After a 1989 press campaign on his behalf,

'Uday was reinstated as head of Iraq's Olympic Committee, an organization he continued to use to build his political and especially economic power. He also became head of the Iraqi Journalists Union, a prelude to the founding of his own newspaper, *Babil*, in 1990. His erratic behavior, which included seizing young women at clubs and restaurants and raping them, continued. He made particular efforts to humiliate and economically undermine Iraq's traditional families.[31] 'Uday's behavior, which verged on the pathological, created countless enemies of the regime and was an indicator of the extent to which the Iraqi political system had, by the mid-1990s, become even more personalistic and less subject to any shared "rules of the game" than in the 1970s and 1980s. Another indicator of the pathology of power in post–Gulf War Iraq was 'Uday's behavior in the sports and the intellectual arenas. Appointed head of al-Rashid, Iraq's premier soccer club, 'Uday humiliated or even tortured players who failed to perform well.[32] Intellectually, 'Uday fancied himself a scholar of international affairs. His newspapers, *Babil* and the weekly *al-Musawwar al-ʿArabi*, were, together with his position as head of the Iraqi Journalists Union, intended to give him intellectual stature. In 1998, he completed a Ph.D. dissertation at Baghdad University's Faculty of Law and Political Science on globalization's future impact on the international political system.[33] Awarded highest honors, the thesis purportedly presented an analytically innovative discussion of contemporary world politics and was posted on the Internet so non-Iraqis could benefit from its supposed insights.[34] By all accounts, 'Uday was an unaccomplished student and the thesis undistinguished.[35] The details of 'Uday's erratic and egocentric behavior are not the critical element. However, as one of the regime's most powerful men, he was, together with Qusay, a possible successor to Saddam, which boded ill for the future of the Baʿthist regime.

During the mid-1990s, tensions mounted between 'Uday and Saddam's nephew, Husayn Kamil, whom 'Uday resented because of his power and economic influence on Iraq's military industrial complex. Kamil's appointment to the sensitive position of minister of military industries demonstrated extremely poor judgment by Saddam, since Kamil had a limited education, no economic training, and no political background apart from creating the General Security (al-ʾAmn al-ʿAmm), designed to protect Saddam after a mid-1980s assassination attempt. Kamil was responsible for expanding the Republican Guard during the Iran-Iraq War and was promoted to lieutenant-general in 1988. During the Intifada, he led the successful counterattack against Karbalaʾ. Resented because of his rapid climb to power, in large part due to his marriage to Saddam's favorite daughter, Raghad, he was known to be extremely corrupt. Angered by and afraid of 'Uday's at-

FIGURE 18. Photograph of 'Uday Saddam
Husayn, receiving his political science doctoral
degree, and Saddam Husayn. *al-Ittihad,*
December 1, 1998.

tacks, especially after 'Uday shot Watban Ibrahim, Husayn, his brother Saddam, and their two wives, Raghad and Rana, defected to Jordan in August 1995. Kamil seemed to have expected his defection to provoke a coup that would result in his assuming leadership of the country.

Kamil's defection heightened anticipation of a possible coup attempt against Saddam. Once Kamil divulged significant information on Iraq's continued covert weapons program to UNSCOM, the special commission designated to monitor Iraq's destruction of its weapons of mass destruction, many observers thought the Ba'th faced imminent collapse. No coup attempts materialized, despite Kamil's calls for Saddam's overthrow. After Kamil had lived in Amman for several months, his erratic behavior increasingly becoming a political problem for the Jordanian government, he and his entourage, supposedly at their wives' urging and with Saddam's assurances of a lack of reprisals, returned to Iraq in February 1996. Although Saddam kept his word, the patriarch of the al-Majid clan, 'Ali Hasan al-Majid, demanded revenge to clear his family's honor. According to tribal custom, weapons were sent to Husayn and Saddam Kamil's villa on the edge of Baghdad to ensure a "fair fight" and, with clan and Ba'th Party members taken in minibuses to the villa as observers, the attack began just after dawn. After a thirteen-hour firefight, both were killed. Saddam had the entire event videotaped as a warning to others who might entertain thoughts of betraying the regime. In keeping with tribal protocol, 'Ali Hasan al-Majid declared that the clan's honor had been avenged.[36]

Sometime in 1982, an al-Da'wa assassination squad attacked Saddam's motorcade as it passed through the village of Dujayl in the Balad district, killing a number of security officers. The perpetrators who escaped were never apprehended, but Dujayl was razed and its inhabitants removed to a different town. That was the last time that Saddam rode through the streets in public.[37] Other assassination attempts were reported in 1992 and 1993.[38] However, a brazen attack on 'Uday Saddam Husayn in 1996 caused the greatest concern. While driving to an evening party on December 12, 1996, in Baghdad's exclusive al-Mansur district, home to many top Ba'thist officials, 'Uday was attacked at a major intersection by two assailants with machine guns while riding in a cortege of three white Mercedes limousines. The attack left him partially paralyzed and able to walk only with a cane. Although the perpetrators were never found, the assailants were thought to be 'Uday's rivals who resented his economic empire and rising political fortunes. In reality, a group known as al-Nahda (Renaissance), comprised of young Iraqi professionals who had studied Latin American urban guerrilla tactics, were responsible for the assassination attempt.[39]

As violence proliferated, Saddam withdrew from public appearances. Obsessed with safety, he recruited as many as eight doubles, which meant that, bizarrely, he could seem to be in more than one place at a time. The building of many new palaces was not simply egomania, but it reflected security concerns, because no one knew in which palace he slept.[40] Saddam would constantly change his plans at the last minute so that few, if any, officials knew his daily itinerary. In one instance he told his cabinet ministers to pack heavy coats because they were going to the north on state business, only to actually have them travel to the south instead. This is very different from the Saddam whom I saw on Iraqi television on the evening of June 20, 1980, when he spontaneously visited the homes of poor elderly women dressed in their black 'abbat to inquire whether they had voted in that day's parliamentary elections. Obviously, assassination attempts came to be uppermost in the minds of Saddam and other prominent officials in a way that they were not before the Iran-Iraq War.

These developments provided the backdrop to the structure of the Iraqi state during the post–Gulf War era. A state ruled by poorly qualified and psychologically handicapped leaders, the squandering of state resources, and the placing of the privy purse in the hands of corrupt officials were compounded by Saddam's divide-and-conquer tactics that intensified cleavages within the regime. The state's failure to develop any institutional mechanisms to cope with personal and policy disagreements, and its placement of Saddam's sons above the law, represented a political strategy manqué with an inherent tendency toward destabilization. The proliferation of new security agencies with overlapping jurisdictions and ill-defined mandates created less, rather than greater, efficiency in suppressing dissent. Indeed, supplying false testimony to one or more of these agencies became a standard mechanism for eliminating opponents or taking revenge for even the smallest personal slight.[41] The use of gratuitous violence, including assassination and the execution of anyone suspected of disloyalty or disliked by Saddam, his sons, or their immediate relatives, eliminated many dedicated and competent officials.[42] As Aburish has perceptively noted, Takritis suffered disproportionately at the hands of Saddam's regime because so many occupied sensitive political or military positions.[43] The skills of many excellent officers were lost, undermining the military's effectiveness. Since many of those killed were from large tribes, Saddam and his sons created many powerful enemies.

Perhaps the regime's decline was most evident in the reintroduction of tribalism as the basis for Ba'thist rule. When it first seized power, the Ba'th vowed to eradicate tribalism, which it condemned as a reactionary vestige of imperialism.[44] Still, tribalism was always a core component of Ba'thist rule. The state's harsh reaction to any public discussion of the issue during the 1970s was an indication of its sensitivity. 'Abbas al-'Azzawi's four-volume, 'Asha'ir al-'Iraq (The Tribes of Iraq) was banned. Nevertheless, themes relating to tribalism were always part of state cultural production, whether in the emphasis on al-butula (heroism), al-furusiya (chivalry), or al-shaqawa (toughness) seen in journals such as Majallat al-Turath al-Sha'bi (The Journal of Popular Culture), or in texts such as Nuri al-Qaysi's study of pre-Islamic Arab tribal culture in al-Shi'r wa-l-Tarikh (Poetry and History). By the mid-1980s, books on tribes were readily available in Baghdad bookstores.[45]

The Ba'th has always considered tribal values useful in bridging the divide between Iraq's different ethnic groups, especially because both the Arab Shi'i (who were recent converts to Shi'ism, as Nakash has shown) and Arab Sunnis could relate to them.[46] During the Intifada, many Ba'thist officials were killed, especially in the south. Harking back to the monarchical state, Saddam rehabilitated tribalism during the early 1990s by inviting tribal shaykhs to serve as rural government officials in lieu of Ba'th Party members. Where tribal leaders no longer existed, Saddam invited offspring and relatives to become tribal shaykhs, thereby re-creating forms of social organization that had all but disappeared. Rural life had come full circle as tribal shaykhs were given carte blanche to treat local peasants as they had under the monarchy. Although he had discouraged the use of tribal surnames during the 1970s, Saddam now encouraged their reintroduction, asking members of army units their tribal affiliation when visiting military bases.[47]

The reintroduction of tribalism paralleled the transformation of the Ba'th Party in the 1970s and 1980s from an organization dominated by army officers, veteran party members, and intellectuals into one dominated, at the top, by Saddam's family and, in the ranks, by the rural and tribally based lower middle class. Saddam had never felt comfortable with the Ba'th's left wing or its traditional (urban) ideologues. A pliant party and military not only served Saddam's goals, but it also reflected a political configuration with which he felt culturally akin since the Ba'th Party and regime now mirrored his own rural and tribal background.[48] The urban middle classes, who considered tribes and tribalism vestigial forms of political and social organization, frowned upon these developments. Further, the regime's fostering of tribal power led to increased violence, precisely what the prominent Iraqi sociologist Dr. 'Ali al-Wardi strongly cautioned against shortly before his death in 1995.[49]

How did the state use the appropriation of historical memory to offset these contradictions? Paradoxically, despite the regime's efforts to hide both its increased brutality during and after the Intifada and its obsession with secrecy, its inner workings were open to public scrutiny as never before. Intensified infighting, including Saddam's disputes with his half brothers, Sajida's public protestations at Saddam's affair and marriage to Samira al-Shahbandar, 'Uday's killing of Kamil Jaju and wounding of Watban Ibrahim, 'Uday's imprisonment, brief exile to Switzerland, and public chastisement in the press in 1988, Husayn and Saddam Kamil's defection to Jordan and their murders after their return to Iraq, and 'Uday's escape from death in 1996 all conveyed images of uncontrolled tribal and gang warfare rather than a modern functioning nation-state. These events impeded the state's efforts to restructure historical memory after the Gulf War and the Intifada. Any lofty ideals that the state attempted to formulate flew in the face of sordid political realities. Thus Saddam's decision to build his power base on nepotism, tribalism, and sectarianism entailed a high price.

Even if the Ba'thist regime had not been prone to violent and erratic behavior, manipulating cultural production for political ends during the 1990s would have been difficult. First, international sanctions prevented the regime from sustaining the level of cultural production of the 1970s and 1980s. In 1993, for example, I received a set of publications from an Iraqi colleague in Baghdad. The stamps on the package were almost illegible, and the publications themselves, of inferior quality and limited in size—especially compared to the large, glossy publications prior to the Gulf War—were not likely to impress the target audience. The shortage of paper also limited the size and quality of newspapers. Iraqi dinar notes were thin, poorly printed, and easy to counterfeit. The state's inability to pursue its former policies of cultural production after 1991 underlined the extent to which its power was based on oil wealth.[50] Although the quality of publications had improved somewhat by 2002, the state's cultural infrastructure was still a shell of its former self.

An article titled "The Impact of the Embargo on Culture and Education in Iraq and How It Is Being Confronted," published in the July–August 1994 issue of *Afaq 'Arabiya (Arab Perspectives)*, highlighted the sanctions' impact on the state's ability to appropriate historical memory. Riyad Hamid al-Dabbagh, a faculty member at al-Mustansiriya University, provided data indicating that, by 1994, the number of issues published annually of all state-sponsored publications had been reduced by between a half and two-thirds. The number of copies and pages of each issue had likewise been drastically reduced, also approximately by half. *al-Tal'ia al-Adabiya (The Literary Vanguard)*, a journal devoted to publishing young writers, ceased publication altogether. The highly popular *Journal of Popular Culture (Majallat al-Turath al-Sha'bi)* declined from a monthly circulation of 15,000 in 1977, or an aggregate publication of 180,000 issues per year, to a quarterly publication in 1990 of 7,000 issues, or 28,000 issues per year. By 1994, its circulation had dropped to 3,000 copies semiannually, or 6,000 per year.

Book publication likewise declined dramatically. From an aggregate of 8,568 books in 1977 (almost all published by the government printing house, Dar al-Hurriya li-l-Tiba'a), the number of books published dropped to 1,904 in 1990 and 312 in 1994, a decline in less than twenty years of more than 275 percent. al-Dabbagh pointed out that, prior to the embargo, Iraq had exported more than ID1.5 million ($4.5 million at the official pre–Iran-Iraq War exchange rate) of books and ID500,000 of newspapers and journals, and had participated in twelve international book fairs annually in cooperation with a number of Arab publishing houses. According to the article, more than 315 publishing houses, printing presses, and affiliated companies were closed as a result of the embargo.[51]

The state's limited cultural production after the Gulf War underscored its weakened position both domestically and internationally. Isolated and no longer in the good graces of the Arab community, Saddam was faced with limited options. The Kurds were beyond the central government's control for the first time in the modern state's history, the military and Ba'th Party officials dared not circulate in many areas of the south after dark, and guerrilla groups continued to use the Shatt al-ʿArab marshlands for hit-and-run attacks against Iraqi troops.[52] Although a 1996 CIA-sponsored coup attempt by the Iraqi National Accord (al-Wifaq al-Watani al-ʿIraqi), an opposition group comprised of army and security officers and former Ba'thists, had failed due to infiltration by Saddam's agents, and the United States had turned its back on the main opposition group, the Iraqi National Congress (INC), when Saddam, with the Kurdish Democratic Party's connivance, invaded Kurdistan, capturing many INC members in August 1996, these events belied the opposition's potential. An attack on northern Iraq by INC forces from Kurdistan earlier that same year had led hundreds of regular army Iraqi troops to defect, underscoring the army's unreliability.[53]

How did cultural production after the 1991 Intifada affect the Ba'thist state's ability to confront its problems? Ba'thist cultural production during the 1990s differed from that of the 1970s, which focused on marginalizing the ICP, Iraqist nationalists, and the Shi'i *marjaʿiya*. It also did not display the degree of xenophobia that had characterized the 1980s Qadisiyat Saddam campaign. The aggressive effort to appropriate historical memory was replaced by a defensive program that was less self-confident in outlook and tone, more reactive than proactive, and lacking in focus. In retrospect, the sharp focus and discipline of the 1970s stemmed from the Takriti Ba'th's need to build its power base and state apparatus, as well as its reaction to the forces of the "cultural market," namely competition with leftist Iraqist nationalism. With state-sponsored cultural production in the 1980s focused on Qadisiyat Saddam, the absence of any "counterhegemonic" forces, and hence the lack of any "cultural market" opposed to state-sponsored memory, allowed Saddam the freedom to develop a view of the past, present, and future that was sharply sectarian, devoid of any program that addressed social welfare (particularly egregious given the great material sacrifices required by the war with Iran), and out of touch with the realities of Iraqi society. Placed in the context of the tremendous suffering caused by the Iran-Iraq War, this state-sponsored memory failed to resonate with the Iraqi populace.

These problems were evident in the regime's first major effort to confront the outcomes of the Gulf War. Immediately after the Intifada's suppression, a series of seven articles issued in the name of the Arab Socialist Ba'th Party, but which most analysts believe were authored by Saddam, appeared in the party's newspaper, *al-Thawra*.[54] These articles, published between April 3 and April 14, 1991 under the awkward title "What Happened During the Final Months of 1990 and the (Initial) Months of 1991—Why Did What Happened Happen?" *(Madha Hasal fi Awakhir 'Amm 1990 wa Hadhihi al-Ashhur min 'Amm 1991—wa Limadha Hasal alladhi Hasal?),* dealt with a wide variety of themes.[55]

The *al-Thawra* series constituted an inquiry, however confused and illogical, into the nature of Iraqi collective identity. These articles were a response to the hostility directed toward the Ba'th during the Intifada.[56] This series was at the same time both extraordinary in the annals of Iraqi politics—extraordinary because Saddam discusses issues publicly that had never before been confronted in such an open fashion—and extremely trite and banal. For the first time of which I am aware, a state document intended for public consumption uses the word "Shi'a" in a political sense. That issues heretofore prohibited and confined to private circles were now being discussed publicly constituted a major change in Iraqi political discourse.

The articles span an enormous time frame and discuss many of Iraq's different ethnic groups. Themes range from ancient Mesopotamia to Hulagu's invasion of Iraq in 1258 C.E. to King Faysal I's Arabism, to the Shi'a, the southern marsh Arabs, the Kurds, and the attributes of the petty merchant class and the women of Baghdad. The articles suggest that the author was thinking out loud about a momentous event that he had not yet entirely digested or comprehended. They also suggest that Saddam was still in shock over the Intifada. Rather than following a logical progression, the articles range across many topics in a rambling fashion. This was in marked contrast to Saddam's previous writings, which follow a more well defined trajectory. In the *al-Thawra* series, the transitions are often disjointed and the ideas do not seem logically connected, especially in the historically oriented articles, such as the one published on April 14.

Saddam's first article (April 3) begins by recognizing Iraq's ethnic diversity. He admits that, throughout its history, Iraq experienced invasions, occupation, and contact with foreign communities. Its amalgam of cultures is reflected in the difficulty that Iraqis have in understanding some indigenous dialects because of their incorporation of foreign vocabulary. In delving into the details of the Shi'a, such as how they learn about Islam and the manner in which certain communities earn their living, Saddam demonstrates a concern for the particularities of contemporary Iraqi society that was lacking in his earlier writings.[57] Although the Kurds are initially referred to as either "mountain people" or "inhabitants of the north," later, especially in his last article (April 14), the term "Kurd" is actually used. Likewise, the term "Shi'i" only appears in his third article (April 5). That Saddam begins with implicit references to different ethnic groups and ends with explicit references indicates an awareness that the old circuitous and hidden political discourse was no longer functional. This awareness demonstrates that, in the post–Gulf War political economy, efforts to appropriate historical memory required a new discourse.

Under the title "Criticism of the Iraqi People—The Impact of Iranian Sectarianism" (April 5), Saddam blames the Intifada's chaos and destruction on the Iraqi people, whose lack of unity and discipline allowed Iranian sectarianism to take hold in Iraq. Paralleling Western analysts who view Iraq through an ethnic lens, Saddam's articles were primarily directed at the Shi'a, whom he viewed as the cornerstone of this sectarianism. Emulating the Qadisiyat Saddam strategy, the Iraqi leader tries to divide and conquer. Whereas during the 1980s Saddam sought to separate the Shi'i *marja'iya* from secular Shi'is by linking the former with the clerics who led the Iranian Revolution, here he tries to divide the Shi'a into respectable religious Shi'is, on the one hand, and lower-class, even déclassé, elements, on the other, who do not conform to societal standards "as understood by the inhabitants of Baghdad, al-Najaf, al-Qadisiya, or al-Muthanna."[58] This latter group, which Saddam asserts originated in the al-Ahwar, the Shatt al-'Arab marshlands, suffer from deviant values that stem from their origins in India, where they raised water buffalo. In pointing out that the southern marshes extend to the Iranian border, he clearly implies that this is an area through which Iranian culture infiltrates Iraqi society. The members of the latter group fail to behave according to the standards of Islam *(ma'ayir al-halal wa-l-haram)*, are misogynists, engage in deviant sexual behavior, and are dishonest in their business dealings. Saddam argued that these people are much in evidence in Baghdad, as itinerant peddlers, street vendors, and petty merchants who sell their wares in open-air markets or near the gates of the city. Saddam emphasizes that the roots of the petty merchant's dishonest business practices were not economic, since they enjoy a decent standard of living compared to other segments of Iraqi society. Rather, their behavior is the result of the moral shortcomings of their culture, as evidenced, for example, by parents who demand of their children that they return each evening with a set amount of money or goods, often illicitly obtained, which in turn corrupts these youth.

At first glance, it seems strange that Saddam would subtitle his third article (April 5) "Shi'i Fanaticism—The Moral Corruption of the People of the Ahwar" *(al-Ta'assub al-Shi'i—Fasad Ikhlaq Ahl al-Ahwar)*. Here the southern marsh dwellers, a minuscule percentage of the Iraqi populace, serve as a metaphor for those Shi'is who refuse to conform to Ba'thist rule. Geographical isolation, which precludes contact with urban life, has made this group insular and backward and prevented their integration into the larger society's value system. Saddam argues that, to a lesser degree, this model also characterizes the Kurds, who suffer from geographical isolation as well. Not only does Saddam try to create another cleavage based on social class within the Shi'i community, but he also tries to frighten his Sunni Arab base by portraying the Intifada leaders not only as "criminals," but also as irrational, uneducated, morally decadent, and devious. Because this group is culturally primitive, allowing it to gain political power would represent a tremendous step backward for Iraq. In discussing the chaos that this eventuality would bring, Saddam is sure to remind his readers of Hulagu's invasion in 1258 C.E. that wreaked such devastation on 'Abbasid Iraq.

An important legacy of the Intifada was to force Saddam and the Ba'th to finally confront sectarianism in a direct and public fashion. Heretofore, ethnic discourse had been largely confined to the symbolic realm, such as the appointment of prominent Shi'is as prime minister following periods of major crisis, which was intended to convey the message that the state valued the Shi'a as citizens.[59] It is likewise significant that, although Saddam's articles blame foreigners (using the generic *ajnabi*)—and Iranians and Ottomans in particular—for many of Iraq's current ills, the difference between these articles and his commentaries during Qadisiyat Saddam (the original battle in 637 C.E. now referred to as "the first Qadisiya," or *"al-Qadisiya al-Uwla"*) is that his comments were no longer structured by a conceptually exogenous analysis but by one that had become endogenous. To be sure, Saddam blames the 1991 Intifada on a "foreign conspiracy" intended to undermine Iraq's national identity *(hawiya wa jinsiya)*, as well as its collective mind, conscience, and sensitivities *(al-'aql wa-l-damir wa-l-ahsas)*. Nevertheless, the problems that led to the "recent criminal events" are not rooted in corruption caused by foreigners, even if those foreigners play a central role, but rather in the structural characteristics of Iraqi society itself, characteristics that are inherently cultural and moral in origin.

Saddam's political "coming out of the closet," as it were, was remarkable in terms of the issues that were publicly addressed for the first time. Although his articles contain some truths, the reality that Saddam portrays is largely fabricated. The argument that the southern marsh Arabs (al-Ma'din) had caused many of Iraq's current problems, and their use as representatives for the entire Shi'i community, was absurd. First, the inhabitants of the al-Ahwar have never been known as a violent and unruly people. This role would be much more appropriately assigned to the Middle Euphrates tribes who revolted on numerous occasions during the twentieth century. However, because tribalism became an even more important building block of Ba'thist power during the 1990s, criticizing tribes and tribalism would have been counterproductive. Indeed, Saddam praised the tribes of the Middle Euphrates for maintaining the noble values of authentic Arab culture.

My own contact with the al-Ahwar's inhabitants during the spring of 1980 suggested a people much closer to the portrait painted by Wilfred Thesiger in *The Marsh Arabs*.[60] Although they were poor, they were also dignified, were reserved but friendly, and seemed to mind their own affairs. Second, the idea of this group as primitive and cut off from the outside world contradicts my own experiences. Having been able to evade my Ministry of Information minder *(rafiq)* while near the village of al-Shabayyish by going off in a canoe with a young fisherman, I was able to learn how the Ba'th oppressed the local populace. As we passed numerous houses on stilts, the young man pointed out several households that had lost family members who were accused of working for the al-Da'wa Party or, more often, the ICP. All these families had been forbidden to demonstrate any signs of mourning when the bodies of deceased family members had been returned. A much more knowledgeable account of al-Shabayyish by the noted Iraqi anthropologist Shakir Mustafa Salim details the fallacies of Saddam's arguments.[61] Saddam's real reason for selecting the marsh Arabs to receive the brunt of his criticism was not only because they lacked national political influence, but also because the remaining Intifada insurgents in the south had withdrawn into the marshes to continue guerrilla attacks against the Iraqi army.

A significant, albeit implicit, admission in the articles is that Iraq is characterized by an authoritarian and repressive state (April 7). Saddam justifies this authoritarianism by arguing that any nation-state undergoing a material and cultural renaissance *(al-nahda al-madi wa-l-ma'ani)* must pass through a transitional period characterized by violence and ill-defined citizen rights. According to Saddam, Western countries confronted this situation during their own development into prosperous and stable nation-states. Following the July 1968 Revolution, the Ba'th Party started from zero in many areas, including the state budget. Power and wealth were limited to a small elite, and rural areas were backward and without electricity. Not only did the state electrify rural areas, Saddam argues, but it also improved agriculture through new irrigation projects. Nevertheless, much of the state's efforts at improving the citizenry's standard of living was under-mined by continuous broadcasts from foreign countries, including "the sec-tarian state in Syria," which spread lies about Iraq's internal situation and, later, its war with Iran.

The fifth article (April 9) mentions the word *"intifada"* for the first time. Whereas all the other articles are three to four pages in length, this article is only two and, despite being entitled "The Causes of the Intifada" (Asbab al-Intifada), offers no serious explanation for the uprising. Instead, Saddam as-serts that the uprising was caused by the weaknesses and deficiencies of cer-tain groups that allowed them to be exploited by foreign influences and agents. These groups were degraded by their treating politics as a commod-ity from which they could benefit rather than comprehending its eternal message *(imtahanu al-siyasa ka sila' wa laysa ka risala)*. Internal treason combined with external threats led to both Qadisiyat Saddam and Umm al-Ma'arak (The Mother of All Battles). Saddam's use of these two constructs suggests that he believed that the fictions he created were real. Despite Sad-dam's attention to the details of everyday life in Iraq, all the articles demon-strate that the Iraqi leader was out of touch with Iraqi society. The invoca-tion "God is great!" throughout this article was intended either to exploit Islamic symbolism or to reinforce the idea that Saddam was a quasi-deity looked upon with special favor by God, a view he sought to spread during the Iran-Iraq War.[62]

In his last article, "The Kurds, Turkomans, and the Struggle for Su-premacy—the March 11 Declaration" (April 14), Saddam portrays Iraq's minorities as the vehicles for Ottoman Turkish and Iranian interference in the nation's internal affairs.[63] Despite ethnic differentiation, he argues, the peoples of ancient Iraq were never divided. This unity continued when Baghdad became the capital of the 'Abbasid Empire. Only in modern times did sectarianism spread, as Iraq became a battleground between the Turks to the west and the Persians to the east. By arguing that the Iranians used the city of Khanaqin as a base from which to attack Baghdad, and that the Ot-toman sultans used the Khanaqin-Mandali-Kirkuk axis to create a "human barrier" *(hajiz bashari)* between themselves and Iran, Saddam casts further doubt on the loyalty of both the Shi'a and the Kurds. Because Khanaqin and Mandali are two northern cities with large Shi'i populations, and Kirkuk is largely inhabited by Kurds, he implies that the local inhabitants of the three cities conspired with foreign forces at Iraq's expense.

Saddam implicates the Turkomans as well. Despite choosing to remain in Iraq after World War I rather than emigrate to republican Turkey, the Turkomans, due to their geographical position between the Kurds to the north and the Arabs to the south and west, developed a superiority complex that prevented them from integrating into the Iraqi nation-state. Even though the Turkomans were part of Iraq, Saddam argues, their retention of a Pan-Turanic ideology and their development of a *dhimmi* mentality hindered Iraq's attempts at nation building.

Saddam gives great credit to Faysal I for building a society in which Kurds and Arabs worked together and in which Kurds occupied some of the highest positions in government. It was only after Faysal's death that this cooperation was disrupted, when the British used Bakr Sidqi's coup as a Kurdish Trojan horse to change certain Iraqi policies with which they were dissatisfied. More serious was Mulla Mustafa al-Barzani's revolt in 1945. Rather than continue fighting when the military situation deteriorated, al-Barzani fled in a cowardly fashion to the Soviet Union and did not return to Iraq until invited back by Qasim after the 1958 Revolution. Saddam points out that the al-Barzanis are not a tribe *('ashira)*, and that the family only settled in Iraq in recent times. Establishing a form of religious or Sufi brotherhood, actually more akin to a gang *('asaba)*, as a means of fostering a sense of solidarity, the al-Barzanis cast the family patriarch, Mustafa, as a religious leader *(mulla)*.

Finally, treating the most important event that split the country, 'Abd al-Karim Qasim's rule, Saddam asserts that Iraq's present problems can be traced to the inclusion of the Kurds in the Qasim regime's provisional constitution (by which he means the clause that stated that Arabs and Kurds share an equal partnership in Iraq). With the communists' help, Qasim promoted *shu'ubi* (anti-Arab nationalist) thinking and behavior, thereby undermining Iraq's unity. When Qasim turned against his former allies, the communists established a base of operations in Kurdistan under al-Barzani family control. The ICP's dependence on the Kurdish Democratic Party increased after the 1963 Ba'thist revolution. Thus the Kurds were successively agents for the British (Bakr Sidqi), Iraqist nationalists (the *shu'ubi* Qasim and his supporters), and communists (after 1963), all of whom sought to divide Iraq and create disunity. Saddam goes on to discuss the well-known assistance that Mustafa al-Barzani received during the 1970s from the United States and Israel, both of whom coveted control of Iraq's oil production and tried to disrupt Pan-Arab unity. Saddam concludes by rejecting an independent Kurdish state, which the West has been trying to establish since the end of World War I.

In referring to "the enemies of Iraq and the Arabs," Saddam pits urban Sunni and tribal Arabs against the Shi'a and non-Arabs. In using the Sunni Arab community's values and history as a standard by which to measure all other ethnic groups, Saddam asserts that, at its core, Iraq is a Sunni Arab state. When the day is done, Iraq's problems stem from those groups that are not culturally authentic *(asil)*, including the Shi'a of the southern marshes and the Kurds and Turkomans in the north. Saddam barely mentions the Sunni Arab population of Iraq in these seven articles, except to note in passing the nobility and cultural authenticity of Arab tribes. In a supreme irony, Saddam asserts that family rule, such as that pursued by the al-Barzanis, and violence cannot be tolerated and must be replaced by democracy built on dialogue. Saddam's message is ultimately a banal one. The state had done nothing but try to build a unified political community and prosperous nation-state. Groups marginal to Iraq's core culture had, by relying on backward values and forms of behavior, facilitated the influx of ideas foreign to Iraqi society, thereby creating discontent and disorder. Having chastised almost all elements of Iraqi society and having refused to accept responsibility for any of Iraq's problems, Saddam offered little hope in this series to those seeking political change.

If Saddam's articles were based on specious arguments and attacked the very communities that were at the Intifada's core, what, exactly, was he trying to accomplish?[64] Did he believe his own arguments? Why did he intensify sectarianism by casting still further aspersions on the Shi'a, the majority community in Iraq? Who was the target audience of these articles? First, this series was intended above all to reassure Saddam's Sunni Arab base that the Intifada was not caused by a flawed system, but rather by deviant Iraqi elements who allowed foreign interests—Iran, the United States and Israel—to create disorder and political chaos. Despite the preposterousness of these arguments, there is little doubt that they resonated with the poorer inhabitants of the Sunni Arab triangle, whom Saddam tried to woo with flattering comments about Iraq's tribes and tribal values. Second, the Iraqi leader's arguments were intended to reinforce fears that Iraq could break apart if marginal groups acquired political power. Although this message would resonate first and foremost with Iraq's Sunni Arab community, it could also find adherents among the Shi'i and Kurdish middle classes, who would have much to lose from political disorder and the country's possible breakup. Third, Saddam's comments were intended to provide Ba'th Party members with a "party line" explanation of the Intifada that they could present to friends, relatives, government officials, and party sympathizers. Saddam's arguments were also designed to strengthen the resolve of party members to prevent marginal groups from gaining control of the state. Fourth, the articles were directed at members of the Shi'i urban middle classes, whom Saddam reminded that he was a close relative, claiming that he was a descendant *(hafid)* of Imam ʿAli ibn Abi Talib.[65] Unlike the many criminals that Saddam mentioned, educated Shiʿis who rejected mixing religion and politics and who showed the appropriate deference to the regime had nothing to fear in the post-Intifada era.

Perhaps the most interesting aspect of this preposterous interpretation of Iraqi society was the insights that it yields into the thinking of Saddam and the "family party" *(hizb al-usra)* that surrounded him. Almost all the qualities that Saddam attributes to the marsh dwellers (and the Kurds) were a mirror image of those of his own childhood village of al-ʿAwja, near Takrit. Saddam came from an extremely dysfunctional family. His father, Husayn, whose background is largely unknown and never made any mark on life, disappeared before he was born. When his mother, Subha, married her cousin, Hasan Ibrahim al-Majid (known in al-ʿAwja as "Hasan the Liar" because he had adopted the title of *al-hajj* despite never having made the pilgrimage to Mecca), Saddam acquired a lazy stepfather who beat him. Those who have studied Saddam's family support his assertion that they were very poor. Commenting on Saddam's home, Saïd Aburish states:

> The house appeared [from photographs] to be a one-room affair similar to many in al Awja. The room would have been occupied by Subha, Hassan, Saddam and his [three] brothers, while the animals inhabited the shed attached to it. There was no lavatory, running water, electricity, kitchen, or anything which we normally associate with the term 'house'. Those who lived in such huts were known as the people who ate with all five *(ili baklyu bi al khamsah)*, because they had no utensils and ate rice-based, largely meatless food with their hands from a communal pot. The whole family slept on the mud floor in cramped, unhygienic quarters.[66]

Saddam became a "son of the alley" *(ibn aziqa)* who played along dirty alleyways and stole chickens or eggs for his family's meals while his stepfather whiled away the days in the local coffeehouse. Saddam was known as a street tough *(shaqi)* and is said to have sold watermelon to passengers on the train from Mosul to Baghdad when it stopped in Takrit. Saddam told his official biographer, Amin Iskandar, that he never enjoyed a normal, happy childhood. As a young man, Saddam fell under the influence of his uncle, Khayrallah Tulfah, who, dismissed from the army after the failed May 1941 Movement, taught Saddam to hate not only the monarchy, the British, and the Sunni upper classes, but also the Shiʿa, whom Tulfah, like many Takritis, did not consider true Arabs but culturally Persian.[67] Like many Iraqis during the 1940s and 1950s, Saddam migrated to Baghdad, where he encountered his first Shiʿis in the lower-middle-class al-Karkh district, whose mixed population was more than half Shi'i. Saddam's family, like many in al-Karkh, aspired to upward mobility and, as Aburish observes, hostility often developed between competing lower-middle-class ethnic groups.[68]

Saddam's description of the marsh Arabs in the *al-Thawra* series parallels in many ways his own childhood experiences. He too was poor, from a dysfunctional family, and forced to earn money for the family, often in a dishonest manner. He was neither taught proper values nor given a good education, but was taken to an urban area where he was left to rely on himself. Saddam's experience differs from that of the marsh Arabs, however, in that he remained close to his uncle, Khayrallah Tulfah, who, because of his army connections dating back to 1941, met frequently with other Takriti officers such as Ahmad Hasan al-Bakr, whom Saddam came to know. Later, when Saddam was thirty-one, these officers would help promote him to Ba'th Party assistant secretary, and shortly thereafter to vice-president of Iraq.

If Saddam's defiant arguments had little chance of engaging large numbers of Iraqis because of their specious cultural, historical, and sociological perspectives, neither did they provide much direction to the Iraqi intelligentsia in its own cultural production. Hindered in part by the shortage of funds for extensive publications and projects, neither the state, represented by the Ministry of Culture and Information, nor the intelligentsia showed much innovation during the 1990s. Prior to the Gulf War, Iraq sponsored a wide range of conferences both inside Iraq and abroad. Indeed, the Mirbad Poetry Festival continued throughout the Iran-Iraq War. With the embargo, limited state funds and the lack of air service into Iraq made it difficult for intellectuals to travel abroad. Thus a conference entitled "The Challenges of Arab Culture," cosponsored by the Lebanon-based Center for Arab Unity Studies and the Iraqi Academy, was held on April 19 and 20, 1994, at the Iraqi Academy in Baghdad rather than in Beirut.[69] The center had been the venue of a number of Iraqi-sponsored conferences in the past through the Ba'th Party's ties with its director, Khayr al-Din al-Hasib, who was best known for advocating the nationalization of industries to build the public sector in the mid-1960s.

The five main conference papers are indicative of the lack of innovation and dynamism in state-sponsored political, cultural, and historical analysis in the wake of the Gulf War. The conference began with opening remarks by one of Iraq's most distinguished historians, Iraqi Academy president Dr. Salih 'Ahmad al-'Ali, whose Pan-Arab lineage can be traced to the anti-Qasim Organization of Iraqi Authors and Writers in the 1960s.[70] In an apologia thoroughly at variance with his intellectual acumen, al-'Ali criticized those who have been dazzled by Western culture. Conversely, he argued, these same individuals have failed to appreciate the much greater historical depth of Arab and Islamic culture, which has always valorized the progressive contributions of Western culture, science, and knowledge. The difference between the two cultures is that, unlike Western culture, which views science and technology as ends in themselves, Arab-Islamic culture attempts to use advancements in these fields to better people's lives. al-ʿAli concludes by arguing that Arab intellectuals need to return to the past to rediscover the power of Arab culture. This type of unconvincing apologia, which has characterized one form of Arab response to the West since the nineteenth century, began the conference on a very undistinguished note.[71]

The first paper, "Pan-Arab Nationalism and Representation: A Discussion of the Subject, I and We," was delivered by the longtime Baʿthist, Shiʿi economist, and sometime foreign minister and prime minister, Dr. Saʿdun Hammadi.[72] This piece contains the usual critiques of Marxism and the local nationalist state *(al-dawla al-qutriya)*. Marxism is criticized for its mechanistic view of history, its lack of analysis of man's ethical development, and its failure to recognize, in the Hegelian sense, the state's positive role in providing a context for human development. Contradicting the reality of Iraq's repressive state, which was dominated by Saddam's family, tribalism, and sectarianism, Hammadi disingenuously argued that the Pan-Arab state represents the opposite of the dark ages, when society was under the control of the tribe, religious doctrine *(al-madhhab)*, sect, city, or even family.[73] Because it does not benefit from the strength of being part of a unified Pan-Arab state, Hammadi argued that the local nationalist state is unable to oppose Western imperialism either in maintaining fair prices for oil or confronting the "Zionist entity." Hammadi's arguments about Pan-Arab unity and a strong state entailed an attack on Iraqist nationalism, which he views as promoting the centrifugal forces that emerged during the 1991 Intifada that called for Iraq's transformation into a federal and more decentralized state.

Despite a fifteen-year hiatus between *al-Shiʿr wa-l-Tarikh (Poetry and History)* and his contribution to the conference, Nuri al-Qaysi's essay "The Place of the Highest Ideal in Arab Culture in the Jahiliya Period" demonstrated little new thinking on pre-Islamic Arab society.[74] Perhaps the only innovation is al-Qaysi's use of the term "al-Jahiliya."[75] In earlier writings he strongly advocated dispensing with the term "Jahiliya" in favor of the more neutral *"al-ʿArab qabla al-Islam"* (the Arabs prior to Islam). In keeping with the regime's post-1991 efforts to adopt a more "Islamic" orientation, this concession to traditional Muslim scholarship's view of this period as one of "ignorance" (al-Jahiliya) helps explain his change of focus. As in his prior work, al-Qaysi is keen to erect cultural boundaries between Arab and other cultures through reference to "Semitic values" and by idealizing tribal society. al-Qaysi was fully aware of the extent to which tribalism had intensified under Ba'thist rule during the 1990s. He argued that the tribal knight *(al-faris)* pursued violence not for violence's sake, but rather for noble ideals such as defending one's tribe and the tribal domain *(al-dira)*. Indeed, the pre-Islamic tribal warrior approaches the Western medieval chivalric knight in al-Qaysi's portrayal. He observed that the pre-Islamic Arab tribes "never recognized any political authority except the honest authority that is what characterized them, the truth toward which they were naturally predisposed, and the loyalty to which they were committed."[76] Throughout their lives, the Jahili Arabs never left their tribal domain.[77] In terms of historical memory, al-Qaysi's analysis complements Hammadi's because it argued that the ancient Arab value system provides the basis for the modern Pan-Arab state, even if the mechanisms of cultural transmission are left unspecified. In light of political developments following the Gulf War, this analysis must have struck the conference participants as much more specious in 1994 than in 1980, when similar arguments were made in *Poetry and History* and Iraqis aspired to progressive change. It undoubtedly pleased Saddam by providing further justification for the ongoing retribalization of Iraqi politics during the 1990s.

The two final essays, by Hussam Muhyi al-Din al-Alusi and 'Abd al-Sittar 'Izz al-Din al-Rawi, were also unimaginative. Both were members of Baghdad University's Department of Philosophy; al-Alusi served as chair and government advisor in 1994 and was also a mentor to al-Rawi, who was formerly his student and was now an assistant professor. A highly respected philosophy professor, al-Alusi demonstrates in his lengthy essay his strong command of the thought of William James and Charles Pierce. However, his concluding section, in which he links pragmatism to American imperial interests in the Arab world and Iraq, is superficial. Surely few of his colleagues would find convincing his reductionist argument that the moral relativism inherent in pragmatism has been the key element in shaping a United States foreign policy based exclusively on realpolitik. al-Rawi's disjointed essay on Islamic rationalism adds little new to traditional discussions of Mu'tazilite doctrine and its role in the 'Abbasid Empire, except perhaps to underscore the regime's preferred view of Islamic doctrine.

A survey of other state-sponsored studies of the 1990s reveals that little innovative work was produced. During the 1970s, *Afaq 'Arabiya*, under the editorship of Dr. Muhsin Jasim al-Musawi, had presented some scholarly articles on the pre-1958 era and had served as a forum for some important debates, such as a lengthy discussion of the concept of Orientalism contained in three consecutive issues.[78] However, in July–August 1995, under the editorship of Trad Kubaysi, a former communist turned Baʻthist, much of the journal was taken up with sycophantic praises of Saddam. A singularly unimpressive article summarizing a seminar on Saddam Husayn held in honor of his birthday (April 30) was written by the seminar convener, Hasan Tuwalba, one of the regime's hack ideologues.[79] To Kubaysi's credit, the issue did contain a very flattering obituary of the great Iraqi sociologist ʻAli al-Wardi, a story that had political overtones because many Baghdadis had feared marching in his funeral procession in view of the sensitive nature of his life-long research on the impact of tribes, sects, and ethnic groups on the Iraqi character.[80] Another prominent journal, *al-Aqlam*, had likewise shrunk to a shell of its former self by 1995.[81]

By 1999, the Iraqi cultural scene seemed to be regaining some strength. Five new journals with ambitious publishing agendas were founded that year: *Dirasat Ijtimaʻiya (Social Studies), Dirasat Tarikhiya (Historical Studies), al-Zahaf al-Kabir (The Long March), Dirasat Siyasiya (Political Studies)*, and *Dirasat Falsafiya (Philosophical Studies)*. Despite the fact that they were somewhat larger and of better quality than journals published earlier in the decade, their contents, such as an uninspiring interview with Ilyas Farah, a former Syrian Baʻthist ideologue, on the state of Pan-Arabism after the "Mother of All Battles" (Umm al-Maʻarik), were still uninteresting.[82]

Why were these journals founded while others were closed (e.g., *al-Taliʻa al-Adabiya [The Literary Vanguard]*) or drastically cut in size, number of issues, and runs (e.g., *Majallat al-Turath al-Shaʻbi [The Journal of Popular Culture]*)? The pernicious influence on the state by Saddam's immediate family was evident in cultural production. ʻUday's influence, which spread throughout the 1990s, did not extend only to business, politics, and sports, but to cultural production as well. No new publication could be established without ʻUday's permission. Following the virtual destruction of much of the original Baʻthist intellectual elite, cultural production followed a random trajectory, with new journals and newspapers reflecting the whims of powerful individuals with close ties to ʻUday. For example, *Shuʼun Siyasiya (Political Affairs)*, which appeared in 1995, was the idea of Salah al-Mukhtar, a former leftist who, after a short but difficult prison stay, became a Baʻthist. Rising from press attaché at the Iraqi Mission to the United Nations in 1980 to become an important Ministry of Foreign Affairs official, he held various ambassadorial posts, including Iraqi ambassador to India. In a self-congratulatory and promotional editorial in the spring 1995 issue, al-

Mukhtar noted that his new journal had been met with tremendous interest.[83] Since his earlier days, when he published articles in *Dirasat 'Arabiya (Arab Studies)*, al-Mukhtar had fancied himself a foreign policy analyst.[84] Having acquired the necessary power and influence, he now established his own journal.

A more sophisticated policy studies journal, *Umm al-Ma'arik (Mother of All Battles)*, appeared in 1995. The April 1999 issue of the journal, a quarterly published by the Umm al-Ma'arik Research Center in al-Salhiya, an upscale district of Baghdad, was 167 pages and printed on good paper stock. Edited by Dr. Mazin Isma'il al-Ramadani, a Baghdad University political science professor with close ties to the state security apparatus, the journal contained a number of Shi'is on its board of directors. The English table of contents, instructions in Arabic and English for ordering foreign subscriptions both within and outside the Arab world, and the professional criteria required for the submission of articles indicated that the journal was intended more for foreign than domestic consumption. This journal was part of the Ba'thist regime's efforts to reenter the international intellectual community. Topics such as globalization's impact on Arab culture, sources of American power in the Arab world, and the Asian financial crisis were designed to appeal to a wide variety of Arab intellectuals outside Iraq, while the scholarly tone and documentation of articles, including leftist sources such as the Lebanese Communist Party's theoretical journal *al-Tariq (The Path)*, lent the journal an aura of academic respectability. The founding of two strategic policy journals in 1995, both requiring 'Uday's imprimatur, and the decline of several traditional Ba'thist journals pointed to a move away from journals concerned with cultural production toward a greater focus on contemporary Arab politics and the global political economy. This new focus reflected 'Uday's concerns in his purported doctoral dissertation.[85]

Of the five journals founded in 1999, four, *Dirasat Ijtima'iya, Dirasat Tarikhiya, Dirasat Falsafiya*, and *Dirasat Siyasiya*, were affiliated with a new publishing house, Bayt al-Hikma (literally, "the House of Wisdom"), which evoked the extensive research library that the 'Abbasid caliph Ma'mun established in 830 C.E.[86] The patron of these new publications was Saddam's longtime personal secretary and fellow Takriti, Hamad Hammadi, who had begun his political life as a communist and had been imprisoned and beaten in 1963. A former army lieutenant, he later became editor of the armed forces newspaper *al-Qadisiya*. His wife, a college sports instructor during the late 1960s, had taught Saddam tennis and etiquette during the 1970s. These new journals were less concerned with intellectual production than with keeping a group of older and respected scholars content by assigning them jobs as editors and giving them an additional salary. Yet another new journal that appeared in 1999 was *al-Zahaf al-Kabir (The Long March)*, which was published by the newspaper *al-Qadisiya*, reflecting the military elite's interests. The founding of this journal, which duplicated the strategic policy focus of Salah al-Mukhtar's *Political Affairs*, the Mother of All Battles Research Center's *Mother of All Battles*, and Bayt al-Hikma's *Political Studies*, pointed to competing intellectual foci that did not exist during the 1970s. Returning to al-Dabbagh's article in *Afaq ʿArabiya*, it was not just the embargo that negatively affected cultural production, but also the desire of powerful political actors such as ʿUday and Hamad Hammadi to put their own stamp on state-sponsored intellectual activity. Because newsprint was scarce, older journals were sacrificed as resources were shifted to new publications, which represented the new constellation of power in post–Gulf War Iraq.

Another traditional venue for cultural production was the daily press. During the 1990s, a number of new newspapers appeared, of which the most important was *Babil (Babylon)*, published by ʿUday Saddam Husayn. Newspapers could no longer publish the lengthy cultural commentaries that they had in the 1970s and early to mid-1980s, however, because of their greatly reduced size. The November 29 and December 2, 1998, issues of *Babil*, for example, were small eight-page tabloids with short articles and only a few small photographs (interestingly, without the front-page photograph of Saddam that was de rigueur for *al-Thawra (The Revolution)*, the Baʿth Party's newspaper, and *al-Jumhuriya (The Republic)*, the government's main daily, which were not published by ʿUday). Although some of ʿUday's publications, such as his weekly *al-Musawwar al-ʿArabi (The Arab Photographer)*, were larger and had more pages, much of their space was devoted to ʿUday's signature articles—namely his attacks on bureaucratic inefficiency and corruption—than to articles on history and cultural heritage.[87] Attempting to create a chic image, and reflecting its appeal to the regime elite, *al-Musawwar al-ʿArabi* devoted considerable space to photographs of attractive women, fashion, and advertisements. It also conveyed an image that business in Iraq went on as usual, and that the country was not suffering any serious material deprivation.[88]

The effect of the sanctions regime on cultural production was the elimination of some publications, especially those associated with the Takriti Baʿth of the 1970s, and the promotion of new ones that were intended to enhance the power of key new political actors such as ʿUday and his allies. State-sponsored cultural production during the 1990s, which reflected the fragmentation of the Baʿthist consensus on historical memory, suggests a number of observations. First, there was little coordination of cultural production from a long-term policy perspective. Instead, cultural production mirrored narrow individual political agendas. Although individual political concerns were also expressed during the 1970s, Ba'thist cultural production exhibited at least some thematic unity, which was reflected in a number of core journals. Only three newspapers published material that mattered in the 1970s: the party's *al-Thawra* and the government newspapers *al-Jumhuriya* and *al-'Iraq*.[89] During the 1990s, newspapers and journals with differing thematic emphases and widely divergent topics were established. *Afaq 'Arabiya*, for example, a journal that formerly focused on historical and cultural topics, published articles on OPEC and the global demand for Iraqi oil.[90] Second, the fragmentation of cultural production indicated the lack of a more cohesive cultural elite such as had existed during the 1970s. With the execution of some prominent intellectuals, such as Shafiq al-Kamali, founder of *Afaq 'Arabiya* and head of the Iraqi Writer's Union (Ittihad al-Udaba' al-'Iraqiyin), and the self-imposed exile of many others, such as Dr. Muhsin Jasim al-Musawi, the literary critic, former editor in chief of *Afaq 'Arabiya*, and head of the board of directors of the state publishing house Dar al-Shu'un al-Thaqafiya al-'Amma, the state lacked intellectuals of stature, particularly those whom it could trust, to replace them. Third, 'Uday's political agenda undermined state appropriation of historical memory. Under his influence, state-sponsored publications became more explicitly ideological and "presentist," *Babil*'s historical symbolism notwithstanding. 'Uday, reflecting the uncultured younger elite that surrounded him, was uninterested in the past. Born into wealth, a product of urban centers rather than the rural Sunni Arab triangle, and not influenced by the 1970s struggles with the ICP and the Iraqist nationalists, this new generation was concerned above all with power and material gain.

In a political irony, the eradication of the left actually undermined the Ba'thist regime. Because the organized left inside Iraq, and particularly the ICP, was no longer considered a serious threat, many of the populist links that formerly tied the regime to the populace, such as folklore and popular culture, became attenuated or were even dispensed with. Through a diminution of the themes stressed during the 1970s and early 1980s, and the intellectual schizophrenia that characterized state-sponsored cultural production during the 1980s, the regime was much less effective in using such production for political ends. About the only constant in state-sponsored cultural production was Saddam's quasi-deification, which proceeded unabated. During the spring of 2002, Saddam was seen again in Iraqi newspapers reviewing plans for yet another extensive monument to his personage and his military prowess in the Gulf War. Singularly undistinguished, and created by a relatively unknown Iraqi artist, the Nusb Milhamat Saddam (Monument to Saddam's Epic Struggle) was sure to impress no one and underlined the cultural bankruptcy of the regime's hegemonic project.[91] Saddam's efforts to build a series of huge mosques as part of his legacy likewise seems not to have had the desired effects, as few Iraqis prayed in these new structures. Although ʿUday desperately sought such adulation himself, he was universally despised and possessed none of Saddam's historical depth or leadership qualities[92] ʿUday's ongoing struggle with his brother Qusay, reflected in the criticisms published in *Babil* of the security services that Qusay controlled, suggested not only that ʿUday and Qusay lacked Saddam's leadership qualities (here meaning his political cunning and ability to instill fear), but also that the lines of succession were deeply contested.

Now that the Baʿthist regime has been deposed, what are the prospects for the democratic opposition to build a new, democratic Iraq? A comprehensive history of the Iraqi opposition, like the Intifada, has yet to be written. In both Arab and Western political and military circles, the democratic opposition has been denigrated as fractious, ideologically diverse, and unable to rule Iraq.[93] This view loses sight of the powerful political discourse that the Iraqi opposition, which includes members of formal groups and independent intellectuals, fashioned during the 1990s. This discourse, which centered on the problem of sectarianism *(al-taʾifiya)*, broke the "politics of silence" on this subject, making it impossible for any serious Iraqi intellectual to ignore it. Based on this discourse, what has the opposition accomplished to date?

First, the opposition that coalesced following the 1991 Intifada represented the first broad coalition of political organizations with divergent ideologies to fashion a common agenda to overthrow the Baʿthist regime. The main groups included the Iraqi National Congress (INC), which was formed in Kurdistan in October 1992 when the two main Kurdish organizations, the KDP and PUK, agreed to form a coalition with Arab opposition groups. Although the role of the INC was diminished somewhat in the late 1990s because of disenchantment with its leader, Ahmad Chalabi, a London-trained economist and secular Shiʿi who formerly headed the Petra Bank in Jordan, it continued to play a central role in organizing anti-Saddam activities. Second, the Iraqi Communist Party continued to attract strong support among significant sectors of the Iraqi intelligentsia. The ICP's message of antisectarianism, cultural inclusion, and social justice has given it great legitimacy throughout its seventy-year struggle against a series of repressive regimes. The ICP maintained a clandestine organization inside Iraq under the Baʿth, as evident in the constant stream of information that it provided on attacks

FIGURE 19. Saddam Husayn viewing a model of the Monument to Saddam's Epic Struggle (Nusb Milhamat Saddam). *al-Jumhuriya*, April 16, 2002.

on regime officials, political executions, and other human rights abuses. A third set of organizations comprised the Islamist groups, the most important of which was the Supreme Council for the Islamic Revolution in Iraq (SCIRI), but which also contained the smaller Hizb al-Daʿwa (The Islamic Call) and related groups. Despite the Islamist orientation of these groups, none called for imposing an Islamic republic on Iraq or creating a separate Shiʿi state. A fourth opposition group was the Iraqi National Accord (al-Wifaq al-Watani al-ʿIraqi), comprised of former Baʿthists, disgruntled military officers, and former members of the state security services. Its secretary-general, ʿIyad ʿAllawi, was reported to have participated in the Baʿthist violence against the left following the February 1963 coup that overthrew the Qasim regime. Finally, there were smaller groups such as the Iraqi Constitutional Monarchy Movement, led by Sharif Husayn Bin ʿAli, a member of the Iraqi wing of the Hashimite family that was spared during the killings of the royal family on the morning of July 14, 1958, and the Union of Iraqi Democrats, which publishes *al-Dimuqrati* in London and has organized intellectuals and politicians who seek to establish a democratic government in Iraq.

Although it had been argued that the Iraqi opposition would never be able to form a governing coalition should the Ba'thist regime collapse, it did, by bringing divergent groups together in a wide variety of forums, establish new forms of communication and mutual understanding that bode well for the future of Iraqi democracy and civil society. During the 1990s, a number of the important opposition groups altered their ideological perspectives, making it easier for them to interact with other groups. The Iraqi Communist Party, for example, no longer considers itself a Leninist party and does not insist that its members rigidly conform to a "party line."[94] Likewise, the Islamist movement, represented most forcefully in SCIRI, has eschewed a sectarian platform. Representatives of the ICP and SCIRI appeared together at conferences where each made favorable remarks about the other's organization. At a Los Angeles conference in February 2000 organized by the Iraqi Forum for Democracy, the ICP representative, Dr. Hassan Akif Hammoudi, and the noted scholar Dr. Hamid al-Bayati observed that only SCIRI and the ICP were actively working against the current regime inside Iraq.[95]

After the 1991 Intifada, the Iraqi opposition had already established an alternative political system in three liberated provinces in Kurdistan, representing roughly 15 percent of Iraq's population, before the Takriti Ba'th's collapse. With Kurds having developed a flourishing press and broadcasting system (there are currently thirteen different television channels), and with non-Kurdish Iraqis having organized conferences on democracy and civil society in Kurdistan and Iraq, a "demonstration effect" occurred. Despite the fact that Kurdistan was landlocked, devoid of any major industries besides the nonfunctioning oil industry, and suffering from an embargo by the Ba'thist regime, its inhabitants enjoyed a much higher standard of living than Iraqis under Ba'thist control.[96] Food was plentiful, infant mortality was lower, and diseases less prevalent than in the government-controlled areas of Iraq. Because there was a considerable movement of people and smuggling across the porous borders, much of what occurred in Kurdistan was known to Iraqis to the south.

Iraqi opposition groups were extremely effective in using the Internet to publicize human rights abuses by the Iraqi state, detail the regime's political infighting, and promote alternative models of political community. These web sites and listservs were important vehicles for expatriate Iraqis and opposition groups to communicate with one another. By detailing the constant executions, political assassinations, and "prison cleansings" on the Internet, the Iraqi opposition made it difficult for Saddam to break out of his isolation. This was especially important in the Arab world where, prior to the Gulf War, many Arabs still maintained a positive image of Saddam and his regime. The fact that the only strong foreign alliance that Saddam and the Ba'th were able to form after the Gulf War was with the former Yugoslavian regime of Slobodan Milosevic, who has been tried for international human rights abuses, was a telling commentary on Iraq's international isolation.[97]

Perhaps the Iraqi opposition's most important achievement, which has yet to be fully recognized, is the extensive amount of high-quality writing that was produced by Iraqi exiles and anti-Ba'thist groups. Not only did these studies document the regime's inner workings, but, unlike many earlier studies, which focused almost exclusively on the details of repression, they self-consciously related to larger discourses centered around sectarianism, the roots of authoritarianism in Iraq, and the notion of an Iraqi civil society. In the process, these studies fostered a historical countermemory by reexamining important historical events and separating them from many of the Ba'thist-generated myths that surround them.

One of the most important components of this countermemory was the beginning of a reexamination of 'Abd al-Karim Qasim and the July 1958 Revolution. Comparisons of Qasim's regime with the first and second Ba'thist regimes and consideration of his reformist policies and sincere interest in the Iraqi populace's well-being have led to a reevaluation of Qasim's contribution to modern Iraq. His honesty, distaste for violence, antisectarianism, pragmatic and nonideological approach to politics, and enactment of reforms designed to help peasants, women, and the poor have been reexamined, causing many to reconsider the dominant perspective, which has portrayed him as a traitor to Pan-Arabism and responsible for the failure of the July 1958 Revolution.[98] However, this reevaluation, which demonstrates that Qasim was concerned with Pan-Arab issues such as the Palestinian and Algerian revolutions, has avoided romanticizing him. A number of articles in the ICP's theoretical journal, *al-Thaqafa al-Jadida*, have recently reassessed the July 1958 Revolution, suggesting an effort to ground it in a new historical memory. Although these articles still suffer from the ICP's unwillingness to admit its own role in the revolution's failure, the party's recognition of the lack of any serious political participation or meaningful democracy under Qasim, and the need to create mechanisms to prevent the military from dominating the state represent positive developments. They are crucial components of a new conceptual framework that eschews rigid ideological formulations in favor of recognizing civil society as the basis of any progress in Iraq. Naziha al-Dulaymi, who enjoys the status as the first Arab woman to have become a government minister, in 1959, argues that despite Qasim's formation of the Sovereignty Council (Majlis Siyadat al-Thawra) and cabinet, he and a few aides controlled all decision making. Even as minister of municipalities, al-Dulaymi found that the real power to influence municipal affairs resided outside her office.[99]

Perhaps the most interesting development, because of its sensitivity, is the emergence of a substantial literature on sectarianism in Iraq. One of the most important works on this theme is Dr. Sa'id al-Samarra'i's *al-Ta'ifiya fi-l-'Iraq: al-Waqi'wa-l-Hall* (Sectarianism in Iraq: The Reality and the Solution), which was published by a Shi'i press, Mu'assasat al-Fajr, in London. Although a Sunni, the author states that Saddam's attack on the Shi'a in the April 1991 al-Thawra series was without parallel in Iraq's history and was the main stimulus for his study.[100] al-Samarra'i argued that the problem of sectarianism can only be solved if confronted honestly and directly. He cited examples of elite behavior during the 1960s that set the stage for Ba'thist sectarianism, such as President 'Abd al-Salam 'Arif's refusal in 1965 to visit the offices of the National Insurance Company after he discovered that its directors were all Shi'i or Christian.[101]

This work is significant because the author did not only place the onus of sectarianism on the Sunni community, but he shows that Shi'i sectarian feelings exist as well.[102] Unlike the Ba'th, who tried, in tribal fashion, to establish cultural boundaries according to blood relations (for example, by asserting that there is "Semitic blood"), al-Samarra'i demonstrates sectarianism's political roots. He shows that many Sunni Arabs were terrified in 1991 that the Intifada would be successful. This fear was exactly what Sunni Arab intellectuals and politicians, such as 'Abd al-'Aziz al-Duri and 'Abd al-Salam 'Arif, who had been emphasizing the al-Shu'ubiya theme for years, intended to evoke. One Sunni Arab exclaimed to the author that "They want to bring an *'Ajami*—an Iranian—to rule Iraq," indicating his fear that the Intifada might lead to Iranian control of Iraq.[103] Echoing Wamidh 'Umar al-Nazmi's study cited earlier, al-Samarra'i points out that this differed from 1920, when Sunni Arabs joined Shi'i Arabs and other ethnic groups to make the Great Iraqi Revolution.[104] However, no state-sponsored texts, whether schoolbooks, Ministry of Culture and Information publications, or state-run newspapers, have detailed the intercommunal cooperation exhibited during the 1920 Revolution, making it difficult to gain access to this countermemory.[105]

al-Samarra'i argues that sectarianism is not a cultural given but is socially and politically constructed. Terms like "al-'Ajam" and "al-Shu'ubiyun" are intended to identify Iraq's Shi'a with Iranians. If they are really foreigners, then logically they do not deserve to hold political power.[106] One of al-Samarra'i's examples is indicative of sectarianism's political origins. When Saddam invaded Kuwait, former minister of the interior and United Nations

262 / Iraq Following the Gulf War

ambassador Salah 'Umar al-'Ali criticized the invasion and broke with the regime. When the Iraqi National Accord (al-Withaq al-Watani al-'Iraqi) was established after the 1991 Intifada, al-'Ali, now in exile, assumed that because of his former positions in the Iraqi government he would head the organization. When the accord elected 'Iyad 'Allawi, a Shi'i, as president instead, al-'Ali objected, even though the elections were fairly held. When his opposition to 'Allawi was not heeded, al-'Ali left the organization to form his own political organization and newspaper.

Superficially, it would seem that al-'Ali, a Takriti and Saddam's cousin, was expressing inbred Sunni sectarian feelings toward the Shi'a. Although al-'Ali may indeed hold such feelings, al-Samarra'i notes that al-'Ali's opposition to 'Allawi was in fact an attempt to please his patrons in Saudi Arabia, where his organization was headquartered, who vigorously opposed any increase in Shi'i political influence in Iraq, fearing that the creation of a neighboring Shi'i state would encourage their own Shi'i populace to demand more rights. In other words, politics rather than instinctual feelings colored al-'Ali's reaction to 'Allawi's election as head of the accord.[107] The impact of external forces on sectarian dynamics in Iraq needs to be seriously considered, because neither Saudi Arabia, Kuwait, nor Jordan wants to see the Iraqi Shi'a gain more political power.

In the summer of 1995, Iraq's most prominent sociologist, Dr. 'Ali al-Wardi, author of thirty-one books on Iraqi society, died at age eighty-two. Despite fear of the regime, thousands of mourners joined his funeral procession. Why would the state find an aged sociologist so threatening? Responding to the 1991 Intifada, the former editor in chief of *al-Jumhuriya*, Sa'd al-Bazzaz, had interviewed al-Wardi in Jordan shortly before his death on a number of themes relating to Iraqi society. These interviews were published in Jordan as a book a year after al-Wardi's death. This volume's discussions of tribal values, the "crisis of the Iraqi woman" (*ma'zaq al-mar'a al-'Iraqiya*), the Iraqi character, and the ideal of "chivalry" or valor (*al-furusiya*) make it clear why al-Wardi's writings threatened the regime. Although a liberal sociologist who eschewed politics, al-Wardi strongly condemned tribalism at a time when it was becoming a more important component of the regime's ideological structure, and the regime was increasing the tribal shaykhs' power. al-Wardi's discussion of the status of women in Iraqi society is also a critique of tribalism. al-Wardi noted that although women have made tremendous advances in the public sphere, such as in employment and education, residual tribal values continued to lead to violence against women suspected of dishonoring their extended family and tribe.[108] He cited a 1989 Baghdad Police conference he attended that was organized to contain this problem. When he discussed *al-furusiya* and its conflict with Islam at the end of the al-Jahiliya era, al-Wardi argued that tribalism and Islamic values are incompatible, directly contradicting Saddam's efforts to use both as new foundations for his faltering regime.

According to al-Wardi, the rapid change in population distribution caused by rural-to-urban migration has led, especially because of the impact of oil wealth, to great material changes that have not been accompanied by changes in the dominant value system. Because the Ba'thist state and its organ, the General Federation of Iraqi Women, have done little to change male attitudes toward women, instead painting a rosy picture of women's status in contemporary Iraqi society, al-Wardi provided a countermemory to this simplistic view. The Ba'thist regime's real intention in fostering women's rights was to disrupt male control of the family—an important institution with oppositional potential—by encouraging women to enter the workforce, which likewise helped alleviate Iraq's perennial labor shortage. Certainly Saddam's personal treatment of women did not indicate any enlightened view of gender relations.

Although the Ba'th Party, and Saddam in particular, emphasized the central role of women in Iraqi society, and the Revolution Command Council passed various decrees designed to improve women's status,[109] at least one study of urban women from all social classes and regional backgrounds made clear that they were extremely dissatisfied with their lives in both the private and the public spheres and that there has been relatively little change in male control of women's lives over the past two decades. The depth of their dissatisfaction was revealed in a series of lengthy interviews with fifty married women in Baghdad conducted over several months in 1982.[110]

Counterintuitively, a study conducted by a Baghdad University sociologist during the late 1980s among 768 married rural women from all regions of Iraq demonstrated a sense that gender relations in the countryside were improving. Unlike urban women, who complained that their husbands allowed them little decision-making power and made little effort to consult them or to understand their feelings, rural women pointed to the breakdown of tribal and extended family control over their immediate families, suggesting that it resulted in improved communication and cooperation in their marriages.[111]

What these two studies suggest is that, while patriarchal values stemming from a tribal culture had not undergone the type of transformation that might be expected given Ba'thist rhetoric and material changes in urban areas during the 1960s and 1970s, urban married women still experienced tight control over their public and private lives. This control was intensified by the retribalization of society underway during the 1990s. Rural women seemed happier with what they felt were positive changes occurring in the countryside. With the process of retribalization, it would seem that urban women's dissatisfaction in their marriages only increased, and that their ability to pursue employment in the public sphere became even more strictly controlled, especially as the state moved to either reverse laws and regulations designed to loosen patriarchal controls or to simply ignore them. In 1990, for example, a law was passed requiring a woman who travels outside Iraq to be accompanied by a male on the paternal side of her immediate family. Rural women no doubt experienced the sharpest disaffection when they witnessed positive trends of the 1980s being reversed. The issue of gender relations and its impact on broader social and political trends in society still waits for serious analysis by Iraqi intellectuals.

Another important intervention by opposition writers was the "rediscovery" of the 1930s, 1940s, and 1950s, especially the years between 1945 and 1961, when cultural life and political opposition flourished until they were disrupted by the problems affecting the Qasim regime. Building on the study of Ja'far 'Abbas Humaydi, *al-Tatawwurat wa-l-Ittijahat al-Siyasiya al-Dakhiliya fi-l-'Iraq, 1953–1958*, there was a renewed focus in political analysis on coalitional activities during the 1950s and political figures who fought the monarchy's repressive policies. One such study is Ibrahim al-Juburi's *Sanawat min Tarikh al-'Iraq: al-Nishat al-Siyasi al-Mushtarak li Hizbay al-Istiqlal wa-l-Watani al-Dimuqrati fi-l-'Iraq, 1952–1959 (Historical Years in Iraq: The Joint Political Activity of the Independence and National Democratic Parties in Iraq, 1952–1959).*[112] In his book published by an old independent press, al-Maktaba al-'Alamiya, al-Juburi argues that only by creating a national front could these two parties effectively confront the monarchy. Despite divergent ideologies related to either Pan-Arabism or Iraqist nationalism, the parties were able to work together and respect each other's perspectives. The author emphasizes his debt to Iraqi historians in the liberal tradition, such as the late 'Abd al-Razzaq al-Hasani, author of the sixteen-volume *Tarikh al-Wizarat al-'Iraqiya (The History of Iraqi Ministries)*, who gave him access to his private papers; Fadil Husayn, author of an important study of the National Democratic Party; the expatriate historian Majid al-Khadduri, who wrote many studies of modern Iraqi politics; and Ja'far Humaydi, for his study mentioned above.

Although this study probably had limited distribution in Iraq, if only because its printing in England made it prohibitively expensive, it nevertheless suggests a number of critical considerations for Iraqi intellectuals who support democratic change in Iraq. First, political cooperation is essential in combating authoritarian rule. Second, there are important examples in the past of political parties cooperating despite their different ideological perspectives, such as during the 1950s. Third, Iraqis have demonstrated sustained commitment to democratic principles, as seen in several efforts by political parties to create national front organizations. The implications of al-Juburi's observations on the 1950s for the current post-Baʿthist transition to democracy would not be lost on any intelligent Iraqi reader.

The rich innovations in cultural production during the 1950s have led a number of Iraqis to reconstruct these developments for contemporary readers. The well-known Iraqi architect Rifat Chadirji, son of NDP head Kamil al-Chadirji and former architecture and urban planning consultant to the city of Baghdad during the early 1980s, has written a comprehensive study, *Ukhaydar*, that documents the lives and work of numerous Iraqi artists and architects during the 1950s and early 1960s.[113] The fact that these intellectuals and artists were inspired by richly diverse historical symbols makes ridiculous any effort to describe Iraqi cultural production as limited to the narrow confines defined by Baʿthist Pan-Arabism. It is precisely the use and mixture of symbols from various periods of Iraqi and Mesopotamian history in diverse pieces of art, as well as much borrowing from foreign cultures, that gives these works their beauty and vitality. Chadirji's message is that Iraq can reach great cultural heights when intellectuals are left to pursue their own interests free from state interference.[114]

Another interesting example of the reexamination of the pre-1958 era has been the renewed interest in the Iraqi Jewish community. The Baʿthist view was always that Iraqi Jews were traitors, uniformly pro-Zionist, and opposed to Iraq's unification with other Arab countries because it would strengthen the Arab world in its confrontation with Israel. In his 1998 memoir *Baghdad, Dhalika al-Zaman (Baghdad, Those Were the Days)*, ʿAziz al-Hajj Haydar, a Fayli (Shiʿi) Kurd, former Iraqi Communist Party member, and Iraqi representative to UNESCO, describes his Baghdad childhood during the 1940s. Although his family resided in the Shiʿi suburb of Baghdad, al-Kathimiya, and his father was very religious, the family maintained contact with Jews in the neighborhood, including one who performed circumcisions, as well as Sunni Kurds and other ethnic groups. al-Hajj notes that among his secondary school teachers was a Jewish teacher of mathematics, and his literature instructor was Sadiq al-Malaʾika, the father of the famous poet Nazik al-Malaʾika, an ardent Pan-Arabist. In other words, through his description of daily life, including children's play, family rituals, and schooling, al-Hajj documents as he did in his earlier memoir, *Dafatir al-*

Shakhs al-Akhir (Notebooks of Another Person), a relaxed and tolerant Iraqi society where citizens did not have to fear what they said or who they interacted with, and where they engaged in civil personal interactions despite differing political views.[115]

Most striking about *Baghdad, Those Were the Days* is chapter 7, "The Ethnic Groups of Baghdad: The Jews of Baghdad," in which al-Hajj challenges Pan-Arab views about the Iraqi Jewish community. Arguing that Jews have historically been mistreated, al-Hajj points out that Jews made tremendous contributions to Iraqi society in the field of commerce (they were a majority in the Baghdad Chamber of Commerce in 1936), education, the professions, and the arts. Jews served in the armed forces after Iraqi independence in 1932 and were fully integrated into Iraqi society. The idea that they uniformly supported Zionism is belied by the League for Combating Zionism, which the ICP formed in 1946 and which contained many Jewish members. al-Hajj's father, despite being a religious Shi'i, chose a Jewish instructor to help him improve his English in 1942, providing yet another example of Iraqis' ability to separate the public and private spheres.[116]

Recently, the Iraqi Communist Party has also begun reexamining modern Iraq's Jewish heritage. Its theoretical journal, *al-Thaqafa al-Jadida*, published a lengthy interview with Samir al-Naqqash in its May–June 2000 issue entitled "Indeed, I Lived All My Life in Baghdad." The journal points out that Nobel laureate Najib Mahfuz (Naguib Mahfouz) has characterized al-Naqqash as the best Israeli author writing in Arabic. Like al-Hajj, al-Naqqash discusses his boyhood in Baghdad, stressing that ethnic conflict in Iraq was driven by the elite, especially Nuri al-Sa'id, whom he claims cooperated with David Ben-Gurion to force the Iraqi Jewish community to emigrate to Israel.[117] The interview emphasizes that ordinary citizens among Iraq's different ethnic groups had no inherent dislike of each other. Rather, social class factors underlay ethnic tensions that the political elite manipulated to mask its own corrupt and morally bankrupt policies.

This era of social tolerance contrasts sharply with the ethnic intolerance of the post-1968 era. 'Aziz al-Hajj notes that between 1971 and 1982 more than thirty thousand Fayli (Shi'i) Kurds were forcibly transferred from Baghdad and other urban centers in the central and southern part of the country, causing many deaths, especially among the elderly. The regime feared that they would act as a "fifth column" for Iran.[118] Like the Jews, the Kurdish community, with a long and distinguished history and culture in Baghdad, was destroyed. al-Hajj's message, like that of other opposition figures, is that ethnic discrimination not only harms particular groups, but is destructive in a much broader way because it deprives Iraq of rich cultural heritages and contributions.

These studies are significant because they have stimulated scholars to transform their studies of sectarianism and the denial of cultural difference into more sophisticated political analyses. A number of studies have analyzed the political and legal institutionalization of sectarianism and the type of political transformation necessary to transcend these structural barriers to democracy and civil society. In 1991, ʿAbd al-Karim al-Izri, a member of the NDP during the 1950s and subsequently minister of education under the monarchy, published an important study, *Mushkilat al-Hukm fi-l-ʿIraq (The Problem of Political Rule in Iraq)*. In his outline of the conceptual foundations of a liberal civil society, legal structures play a central role. al-Izri argues that the Baʿthist criminal code did not correspond to Iraq's Basic Law (al-Qanun al-Assasi) or the 1925 Constitution. Although citizens could be penalized with prison sentences of up to seven years for inciting ethnic conflict, government officials who used their position to incite such feelings were not subject to the law. Because the state in Iraq has been the major source of ethnic tensions, it is imperative that the law institutionalize penalties for officials who exploit their positions to promote ethnic tensions.[119] The author also argues that the armed forces need to be restructured to reflect the percentages of ethnic groups in society. An ombudsman would insure that the laws of the newly constructed state were strictly enforced.

Two books by Hasan al-ʿAlawi, whose study of the Shiʿa and the nationalist state was cited earlier, call for a total restructuring of Iraqi political life. Reacting to the horrors inflicted on Iraq by Saddam and the Baʿth, al-ʿAlawi blames many of Iraq's problems on the imported nature of its state, or what he calls "the transplanted nationalist state" *(dawlat al-istaʿara al-qawmiya)*.[120] Iraqis have never participated in the construction of the state, whether during the British-manipulated referendum of 1921, the fraudulent elections under the monarchy, or the imposition of military and one-party rule after 1958. Although his call for creating a constitutional monarchy along British lines with Sharif Husayn Bin ʿAli as a new Iraqi monarch has generated only limited support, al-ʿAlawi's books nevertheless highlight the extent to which political thinkers have been attempting to develop liberal democratic theory that would apply to post-Baʿthist Iraq.[121]

If studies by opposition intellectuals challenged the myths of xenophobic and chauvinistic Pan-Arab thought in Iraq, then a number of important publications nurtured these efforts on a daily basis. Perhaps most important is the London-based *al-Hayat*, the daily Arabic newspaper of record. Hardly a day passes without a major political analysis, poem, or cultural article on Iraq. When two of Iraq's most important modern poets, Muhammad Mahdi al-Jawahiri and ʿAbd al-Wahhab al-Bayati, whose work had important political overtones, passed away, *al-Hayat* covered their lives and work extensively. Occasionally, *al-Hayat* elicited responses from Iraq while it was still under Baʿthist rule, such as the critique by Baghdad University political scientist Dr. Saʿd Naji Jawad of ʿAziz al-Hajj's defense of the ICP in its efforts to promote democracy in Iraq during the 1950s.

Other newspapers and journals, such as the London-based *al-Zaman* (now in Baghdad), edited by Saʿd al-Bazzaz, the Saudi-sponsored *al-Sharq al-Awsat,* and the weekly magazine *al-Watan al-ʿArabi,* have extensively covered Iraq as well. In addition, a number of listservs and web sites have produced a continuous flow of articles on political, social, and cultural developments inside Iraq and have provided a venue for the exchange of opinions on the future of Iraqi society and politics. One of the most active listservs is Iraq List, which was established in 1997 and is based in San José, Costa Rica. Operated by Dr. Anwar al-Ghassani, an Iraqi expatriate professor of journalism, communications, and the Internet at the University of San José, Iraq List has described in detail political persecution in Iraq and the negative impact of sanctions, and it has provided a forum for numerous discussions on Iraq. A poet, Dr. al-Ghassani, has offered Iraq List subscribers access to his literary works and his reflections on Iraqi society and culture prior to the Baʿth, reflections that point once again to an era of rich cultural production.

All major Iraqi opposition groups have maintained web sites, many of which contain important documents, policy statements, and links to other related web sites. The Iraqi Forum for Democracy was in the forefront of attempts to try Saddam Husayn and other members of his regime for human rights abuses and war crimes through its INDICT campaign. The group has also provided venues for representatives of Iraqi opposition groups with differing political agendas to appear together and attempt to move toward a common approach to overthrowing the Baʿthist regime.[122]

Many documents were formulated as a result of the discussion of issues through conferences, informal meetings and Internet contacts. One of the most important was Charter 91, which emerged from a meeting of opposition groups in the city of Salahuddin in Kurdistan, and was signed by a large number of Iraqis in mid-1991.[123] The charter is concise but decisive in its emphasis on democracy, human rights, and civil society. It begins by stating that:

Civil society in Iraq has been continuously violated by the state in the name of ideology. As a consequence the networks through which civility is normally produced and reproduced have been destroyed. A collapse of values in Iraq has therefore coincided with the destruction of the public realm for uncoerced human association. In these conditions, the first task of a new politics is to reject barbarism and reconstitute civility.[124]

Charter 91 is an extraordinary document. Many of the repressive policies pursued by the Ba'th actually preceded its rule. Under the monarchy, Nuri al-Sa'id deprived Iraqi citizens who were politically undesirable of their citizenship. Political dissidents were tortured in notorious prisons and even hanged in public. Political violence was committed by semiofficial militias during both the 1941 Farhud and the National Guard's violence against the left in 1963. Sectarianism was the order of the day, and the gap in wealth between the rich and poor was enormous, as it became once again under Saddam's regime. Nevertheless, there was only a limited response from the international community, which was largely unaware of the state's repression. At present, with the Ba'th Party's collapse, Iraq is in the eye of the international community, and even nondemocratic organizations in the former opposition, such as the Iraqi National Accord, feel the need to emphasize their commitment to democracy. In the "war of position," opposition forces that advocated democracy have acquired the upper hand. The signing of Charter 91 by so many divergent groups in the Iraqi opposition represented a recognition that "democracy requires coordinating the representation of differences among many people on three levels: within civil society; between civil society and the state; and between the executive, legislative and judicial realm of government."[125]

Beyond Charter 91, opposition groups began an international campaign to establish an international criminal tribunal known as INDICT to try Saddam's regime "for crimes of war and genocide." Organized by the Iraqi Forum for Democracy and supported by more than forty Iraqi organizations worldwide, the campaign, which received legal support from the detention of former Chilean president Augusto Pinochet in the United Kingdom, led Iraqi vice-president and Saddam confidant 'Izzat Ibrahim al-Duri to flee Vienna, where he had gone for treatment of leukemia, when a city council member went to serve him with an international arrest warrant. [126] This campaign publicized missing persons and detailed descriptions of torture and executions (such as "prison cleansings") inside Iraq on its web site. The campaign's effectiveness was evident from the Ba'thist regime's creation of a Special Information Branch, which, with an enormous budget, was responsible for culling and rebutting articles that accused the Iraqi dictator of war crimes.[127]

The Iraqi opposition accomplished much more than its critics are aware since the 1991 Intifada. The scrutiny Iraq received after the Gulf War helped publicize Ba'thist repression, which heretofore had largely been ignored by the international community. The continued crises engendered by the Ba'thist regime precluded the United States and its allies from concluding any deal with Saddam that might have helped extend his life in power. Indeed, at the time of this writing, the United States has forcibly overthrown Saddam's regime, an interim constitution has been signed, and most Iraqis look to a democratic future. The Iraqi intelligentsia's writings on the need for democracy, the elimination of sectarianism, and the contours of a future Iraqi civil society have influenced other Arab intellectuals to write on themes they have raised. Global pressures for democratization and the creation of legal structures to try political leaders if they commit crimes against their own people place the Iraqi opposition within an international political process that is gaining ever-greater momentum.

10 Conclusion

al-ʿabd hurrun ma qunīʾa. (The slave is as free as he believes himself to be.)   *Arab proverb*

Mu kull m'dabl joz. (Not everything that is round is a walnut.)
                                                 Iraqi colloquial saying

All states require the consent of the governed to rule and insure public order. Likewise, the state is invariably controlled by elites who seek to use it to enhance their own political and economic power and status. Because the use of force represents an inefficient means of rule, and because elites strive to enhance their power and material interests, all states seek to establish hegemony or engage in what I prefer to call the "hegemonic project."[1]

There are several motives for attempting to establish hegemony. First, to elicit consent and ensure more efficient rule, the state seeks to generalize its interests to the populace. If those who control the state can convince large segments of the population that elite and mass interests coincide, then the state's policies will be widely accepted. Second, and closely related, the hegemonic project involves the state's attempt to convince the populace that its definition of political community and the public good constitutes the "natural order of things." This process represents less an effort to instill a "false consciousness" among subaltern groups than an attempt to create parameters that define acceptable political thought. By creating boundaries of thought that specify the "natural" political order while stigmatizing political constructs beyond these boundaries as deviant and opposed to the "will of the people," the state seeks to minimize counterhegemonic thinking, and particularly models of political community that challenge its own.[2] Third, in constructing its hegemonic project, the state seeks to reduce the costs of social control by maximizing consent based on self-imposed norms of behavior and minimizing the need to use force. If subaltern groups are disinclined to challenge the state, then the state can direct its energies elsewhere.

The hegemonic project's potential for success will depend not only on the messages it disseminates, but also on the extent to which it can materially and psychologically integrate subaltern groups. If the state excludes large segments of the populace from its hegemonic project, the project will fail. As Gramsci notes, subaltern groups must receive some material benefits to motivate them to embrace the state's hegemonic messages. In societies such as Iraq that have sharply drawn ethnic and regional cleavages (which usually also subsume social class cleavages), not only must the state offer material benefits, but it must culturally valorize groups as well.

Ideology plays a critical role in all hegemonic projects. However, referencing the past—creating "memories of state"—is an integral part of all ideological formulations. This is because all states contend that they represent and uphold the continuity of core myths and traditions of a society or, conversely, that they represent a "new order" that seeks to transcend the past, which is denigrated as contrary to the people's interests. In Iraq, the hegemonic project of the Ba'thist state entailed extensive efforts to restructure understandings of the past. Because of the tremendous political instability that the Iraqi nation-state has experienced since its founding, the Ba'thist state sought to reduce the need for force as a mechanism for eliciting the consent of the populace over which it rules. The Iraqi case suggests that in societies with sharply drawn ethnic and regional cleavages, the hegemonic project will eschew detailed and overt ideological statements in favor of greater reliance on the manipulation of historical memory to achieve its ends. This is especially true in states controlled by an ethnic minority.[3]

Clearly, when the Ba'th first articulated its would-be hegemonic view of history and culture, its formulations were designed to combat and appropriate oppositional views, particularly those of Iraqist nationalists (comprised primarily of communists, party sympathizers, and the non-Marxist left), and to politically marginalize ethnic groups it considered threatening, especially the majority Shi'i community and the Kurds. However, a frontal assault on the Shi'a and the Kurds would have elicited severe reactions that might have toppled the regime.

In organizing its hegemonic project around the appropriation and restructuring of historical memory—what came to be known as the Project for the Rewriting of History—the Ba'th tried to atomize groups it considered hostile through a divide-and-conquer strategy. During the 1970s, the hegemonic project resonated even with marginalized groups to a limited degree because Ba'thist policies seemed to offer the possibility of political stability and a new national identity. For the left, the Ba'th's anti-imperialist rhetoric, its National Front with the ICP, and the nationalization of the Iraq Petroleum Company created the aura of a regime committed to social justice. However, leftists had to renounce all autonomous political activity and totally subordinate their activity to Ba'thist dictates. If members of non-elite groups implicitly renounced those aspects of their ethnicity or ideology that the Baʿth found objectionable, such as Marxism or traditional Shiʿi religion and culture, and if they approached the state as individuals rather than members of corporate entities, they often received material rewards and enhanced status as well.

In terms of the Shiʿa, efforts to restructure understandings of the past were designed to sharply contrast secular and religious outlooks. Shiʿis who continued to adhere to their religion and culture were linked to movements and symbols that the Baʿth portrayed as unpatriotic, such as the al-Shuʿubiyun and the al-ʿAjam, who were symbolic not just of Persians but outsiders generally. The Baʿth branded the communists, whom they also viewed as threatening, as unpatriotic by associating them with stigmatized minorities, particularly Iraq's Jewish population. They did this by manipulating the historical memory of the Jewish community's activities in Iraq prior to the founding of Israel and by portraying the ICP as dominated by Jews, pro-Zionist and hostile to Pan-Arab unity.

The Baʿth likewise sought to undermine its opponents by appropriating the Mesopotamian symbols used in Iraqist political discourse. Unlike earlier Iraqi Pan-Arabists, Saddam and the Takriti Baʿth actively promoted archaeology and historical studies on ancient Mesopotamia to give Iraqis a sense that they were the most "civilized" Arab people. In treatises that argued that the inhabitants of ancient Mesopotamia were "Semitic," the Baʿth attempted to appropriate Iraqist nationalism and integrate it into Pan-Arab political discourse.

Through the Qadisiyat Saddam campaign, the state's cultural policies were designed to negate the impact on Iraqi society of Khumayni's ideology of an Islamic republic and to redirect the focus of political discourse onto Saddam Husayn.[4] Here the Baʿth's hegemonic project was less successful because material rewards became scarcer as the Iran-Iraq War progressed and the party under Saddam's exclusive leadership after 1979 became more overtly sectarian. In the wake of the disastrous Iran-Iraq and Gulf wars and the February–April 1991 Intifada, Baʿthist efforts to manipulate the past fell on less receptive ears. The regime found it increasingly necessary to rely on torture and violence, and human rights abuses proliferated. Because this physical intimidation was associated in large measure with Saddam's two sons, 'Uday and Qusay, the possibility of these self-designated heirs enjoying widespread support after their father's demise was greatly diminished. The regime found itself relying on an ever-smaller circle of supporters and shorn of any support provided by even a limited impact of its hegemonic project to rewrite the past.[5]

What can we learn about efforts to impose hegemony from the case of Ba'thist Iraq? I would offer six hypotheses. First, assuming a relatively unified political elite, state efforts to impose hegemonic modes of thinking will most likely appear in an overt fashion in societies undergoing rapid social change in which the "taken-for-grantedness" of life is fundamentally challenged. Second, state appropriation of public memory will fall on sympathetic ears not only in societies undergoing rapid change, but also in those that, like Iraq, that conform to the "new states / old societies" configuration. Unless a newly formed nation-state has a substantial historical memory to draw upon, the development of an effective hegemonic project will encounter difficulty.[6] Third, state efforts to appropriate historical memory must be syncretic. That is, they will be widely accepted only if they build on "organic" processes—those not generated and imposed by the state—already underway. Thus the Ba'th was successful in its efforts to appropriate popular culture (al-turath al-sha'bi) and use it for political ends because of widespread public interest in it prior to the Ba'th coming to power.

Fourth, historical memory cannot be appropriated and disseminated in a thoroughly authoritarian fashion. If historical memory affords a particular group symbolic participation but offers the members of that group few or no material benefits, such as increased opportunities or political power, then the new configuration of memory will not penetrate very deeply into those segments of society. For Saddam to speak approvingly of pre-Islamic Arab tribal culture, and to claim that he is a descendent of 'Ali ibn Abi Talib, valorizes the heritage of both Sunni and Shi'i Arabs. However, the relationship of this valorization to the two communities' access to political power and economic benefits is very different. Sunni Arab Iraqis, particularly those drawn from the rural tribal nexus upon which the Takriti Ba'th based its power, enjoyed privileged access to the state—including its administrative arm, the cultural bureaucracy, the diplomatic corps, the military, the police, and the security services—by virtue of being a member of this ethnic group. Shi'is, however, enjoyed no such privileged status under the Ba'th. Although many Shi'is acquired status and power within the state, they always did so as *individuals* rather than as Shi'is, and they were dependent on their Sunni Arab compatriots in order to maintain their positions or be promoted. This often produced disaffection, for example as seen in the attempt by Shi'i security chief Nazim al-Kazzar's to seize power in 1973 because of his resentment of Takritis and the influence of Saddam's family within the state. Ba'thist rule, increasingly based on tribalism and nepotism after 1979, was so blatantly at odds with party ideology that it alienated many party members and ideologically motivated candidates for membership. Thus the prospects for imposing cultural (and hence political) hegemony became even less feasible during the 1980s, given the Ba'th's self-inflicted wounds that were caused by the two Gulf wars and increased sectarianism, which circumscribed still further Kurdish, minority, and especially Shi'i access to the state. Such access was critical given the state's overwhelming control of a myriad of political, social, economic, and cultural institutions and hence its role as the distributor of material largesse, political power, and social status. This control is especially true in nonmarket societies such as Iraq, where the state is responsible for distributing material rewards.

The Ba'th's Project for the Rewriting of History suggests that, in order to be effective, an effort to promote hegemony must not only be organically linked to the experiences, interests, and needs of key constituencies in a body politic, but must also be accompanied by institutional developments that will allow target audiences to achieve practical benefits by adopting a state-sponsored worldview. The material prosperity and relative political stability that Iraqis enjoyed during the 1970s attracted significant support among urban and rural Sunni Arabs and many urban Shi'is despite the regime's authoritarianism and human rights abuses. Although the Ba'th Party's significant growth and the establishment of a national parliament inspired hope that meaningful political participation might be a future option, such institutional development never materialized, thereby blunting support for the Ba'th.

Fifth, states divided along ethnic lines will encounter greater difficulty constructing a national historical memory, and hence an effective hegemonic project, than societies that do not suffer from such cleavages, even if the state possesses the necessary material and human resources. The vertical cleavages that characterize ethnically divided societies create boundaries that are often difficult to transcend. Paradoxically, those states most in need of a shared political culture are often the ones that find it most difficult to achieve. Only through the development of transethnic institutions, such as a mass party whose ideology and daily functioning is based on nonsectarian and culturally inclusive criteria, can such cleavages be addressed. Ironically, it was the Iraqi Communist Party, and to a lesser extent the National Democratic Party, that helped create a distinctly Iraqi nationalism that crossed ethnic lines, thereby establishing the counterpoint against which the Ba'th launched its own Project for the Rewriting of History.[7]

Sixth, the success of a hegemonic project will be directly linked to the strength of counterhegemonic narratives. Despite the decline of Iraqist nationalism after the 1963 Ba'thist coup d'état, its message of cultural inclusion and social justice has continued to resonate with many Iraqis, especially the huge expatriate population of intellectuals and professionals. Many Iraqist nationalist intellectuals did concern themselves with history and historical memory. Before 1963, the archaeologists organized around the journal *Sumer*, and many Iraqist intellectuals, such as poets and short story writers, took Iraqi *national* historical memory seriously. The two main political organizations in the Iraqist nationalist camp, however, did not. The ICP was more concerned with Soviet history and culture, and the NDP with Western European and Russian history and culture, with the result that neither sought to engage Iraq's past, whether ancient Mesopotamia, the pre-Islamic Arab past, or ʿAbbassid history, in any systematic way. This neglect of indigenous historical memory played into the hands of the Pan-Arabists, who were more effective in engaging the nation-state's collective desire to overcome decades of social fragmentation and political turmoil. Further, in failing to engage Iraqi historical memory, the Iraqist nationalist political parties ceded much of the intellectual terrain centered on the nation to Pan-Arabists. In other words, Pan-Arabists were able to dominate the discourse of nation more effectively by positioning themselves as the bearer of important national traditions in a way that neither the ICP nor the NDP was capable of doing. This does not mean that Iraqi Pan-Arabists possessed a more realistic sense of political community. Pan-Arabism has never been able to meaningfully address the questions of ethnic and cultural diversity and social inequality that Iraq still suffers from today.

Despite the enormous expenditure of energy and revenues during the 1970s, the state's efforts to establish itself as a hegemonic force in Iraqi society ultimately failed. The 1991 Intifada and the tremendous exodus from the country of the Iraqi middle class (and anyone else who had the financial means to leave) created one of the largest expatriate communities in the world. Similar to prior regimes, the Baʿth Party was unable to establish a political culture shared by large segments of the populace, causing a problem that has led some observers to label Iraq an "artificial state," particularly because of its ethnic divisions.[8] This study rejects that view, which confuses the state's lack of hegemonic control with the populace's feelings toward Iraq as a nation-state.

First, Iraq's three main ethnic groups have never indicated anything but a desire to remain an integral part of the Iraqi nation-state. During the Intifada, no Shiʿi organization called for an independent Shiʿi state. This is also true of the Kurds, who have enjoyed autonomy from Baghdad since 1991 and who want federalism, not independence. Second, two of the most bloody and materially devastating wars of the twentieth century failed to destroy

Iraq's cohesion as a nation-state. As I argued earlier, the Iran-Iraq War was won by Iraq's Shi'i-dominated infantry fighting against fellow Shi'is from Iran. Indeed, this was the first war of Shi'a fighting Shi'a.

Because the Ba'th Party failed in its efforts to impose a hegemonic view of culture and history on Iraq, and it became captive of its own historical memory—namely one of cruelty, torture, war, and economic degradation—there was little or no possibility that the current regime would rehabilitate itself after 1991. The Ba'thist regime was able to prolong its hold on power through acquiring additional funds by concluding contracts with foreign oil firms and manipulating the sale of oil under the United Nation's Oil for Food Program, thereby largely circumventing United Nations sanctions. Through a combination of increased brutality, venality, corruption, and nepotism, and the thoroughly disjointed nature of cultural production, the regime after the 1991 Gulf War and Intifada resembled a mob that exploited the state for personal ends more than a government concerned with the public good. This is true not only of Saddam, who became increasingly remote from the people, but even more so of the main political actors standing in the wing: 'Uday, whose violent outbursts and quixotic behavior verged on the unstable, and Qusay, who was despised for his brutality in suppressing dissent, and especially his so-called "prison cleansing" campaigns. In Gramscian terms, the state denuded itself of the "inner fortresses and earthworks" that it had attempted to provide by its hegemonic project. Force and bribery became its only protection. Politics ultimately comes down to choices. To use Gramscian terms, when a political situation changes from a "war of position" to a "war of maneuver," that is, to a situation when a state is directly challenged, citizens need reasons to choose to defend the state from such challenges. If the populace does not identify its own interests with those of the state, the state will never be able to withstand a serious challenge.

What, then, are the prospects for a more participatory form of politics and cultural pluralism now that Saddam and the Ba'thist regime have been removed from power? The transition to democracy in Iraq will not be easy. The social and political toll of twenty years of war and sanctions cannot be overcome overnight. Many of Iraq's professionals and intellectuals, having established roots abroad, will not return to Iraq, even now that Saddam and the Ba'th have been overthrown.[9] Many have argued that the Kurds, with no economic base of their own and generous United Nations assistance at the present, did not want to see the Ba'thist regime collapse. The extent to which the Kurds will help the Arab democratic forces now that the Ba'thist order is gone is not entirely clear. Surrounding states, especially Syria,

Saudi Arabia, Kuwait, and, to a lesser extent, Jordan, do not want an Iraqi regime that encourages political participation and cultural pluralism because it will reflect negatively on their own authoritarian regimes. Their support of the new Iraqi government, especially if it contains a significant Shi'i presence as it must, cannot be counted on. Turkey fears the formation of a breakaway Kurdish state in the north of Iraq, and it may intervene in Iraq's domestic politics should such a state appear to be a possibility. Finally, the tensions caused by the retribalization of Iraq will also place a great burden on any democratically minded government. Although the tribal system was moribund by the early 1950s, and the Qasim regime seemingly sealed its fate through reformist laws passed after the 1958 revolution, Saddam's revival of the system during the 1990s, even if based on "invented tradition," created new interests, centers of power, and cleavages between tribal leaders and peasants.

In this context, the forces of globalization have exerted a salutary effect on political change in Iraq. A global culture of democracy and the rejection of state-sponsored human rights abuses, as seen in the greater integration of communications networks and the development of international legal institutions and precedents, makes it more difficult for states like Iraq, which depend heavily on the world market for their economic success, to avoid adhering to international political norms. The Iraqi democratic opposition's discussion and practice of democracy abroad after the Gulf War and Intifada of 1991 developed important skills, including the ability to negotiate and compromise, a new political vocabulary of participation and cultural pluralism, and new levels of trust and tolerance. These skills will serve the opposition well as it tries to establish a democratic system and promote the development of civil society.

What are the implications for state theory of Ba'thist efforts to establish a hegemonic view of politics through manipulating Iraqis' sense of the past? Much has been made of the notion of the "rentier state" as the foundation of power for political elites in oil-producing states such as Iraq through the creation of their relative autonomy from the populace at large.[10] Without a doubt, the tremendous increase in oil revenues was critical to the Ba'thist state's development of a massive cultural production infrastructure. Conversely, as indicated in chapter 9, once these revenues declined, the state's cultural production shrunk by more than 50 percent. Despite being almost an archetypical rentier state during the 1970s, the Ba'thist state lost its power and influence during the 1980s and 1990s, finally collapsing in 2003. It would seem that only when efforts are made to translate the wealth available to the rentier state into the development of a shared political culture and effective political institutions does this concept do anything more than provide a temporally bounded description of state power. In limiting their theorizing to the structural components of the "rentier state," the proponents of this theory have failed to theorize the components of agency whereby access to externally derived rents is translated into effective and lasting political power. Under what conditions do elites who control rentier states succeed in reproducing themselves over time, and under what conditions do they fail to do so? This study of the initial success and ultimate failure of the Baʿth Party's hegemonic project in Iraq represents an attempt to answer this question.

It can be hypothesized from the Iraqi case (and the neighboring Iranian case as well) that the mechanisms for extracting rents from the international economy, which purportedly increased state autonomy and power through a decreased economic dependence on domestic society, can actually produce a concomitant political cultural distancing of political elites from that society, which undermines their power and control. When the Takriti Baʿth felt challenged by opposition groups during the 1970s, state-sponsored cultural production focused on marginalizing that opposition. Populism, folklore, al-Bakr's paternal rule, and photographs depicting Saddam's humble origins, which made him one of the people *(ibn al-balad)*, highlighted this effort to sustain strong ties to the populace. During the 1980s and 1990s, the state, dominated by Saddam and the "family party" *(hizb al-usra)*, lost touch with political and social reality. The regime was seriously threatened by Iran's invasion of southern Iraq in 1986, and was almost overthrown in March 1991.[11]

Recent studies have challenged the agentic assumptions of many structural theories. These studies' argument that agency cannot necessarily be deduced from structural determinants is a powerful one.[12] They assert instead that the study of choice and decision making at the microanalytic level is necessary before any meaningful statements about political behavior can be made. Although differing ontologically and epistemologically, both the rational choice and neo-Marxist paradigms argue that choice is central to any political equation.[13] Only by making choices (or failing to do so, which is, in effect, a form of choice) do citizens either support or challenge the state. Neither the Iraqi nor the Egyptian army—both having retained a powerful memory of the humiliation each suffered at British hands in 1941 and 1942, respectively, and chagrined by their poor performance in the 1948 Palestine campaign because of defective equipment and poor training— defended their respective monarchies when the Free Officer movements in each country moved to overthrow them in 1952 and 1958. Likewise, the army chose not to defend ʿAbd al-Karim Qasim in 1963 or to come to the aid of the Shah of Iran in the face of massive street demonstrations in 1978. In each instance, the military's choice not to act was a critical factor in the collapse of the state. By detailing state efforts to impose hegemonic modes of thought and the responses of subaltern groups to these efforts, the concept of hegemony can help us better understand choices, and the structural nexus within which these choices are made. Hence the concept of hegemony offers the possibility of bridging the methodological divide between structure and agency, thereby integrating theoretical approaches derived from both political culture and political economy. Because hegemony has many affinities with legitimacy, a concept that is at the core of much political science research not just on Western democracies but on the Arab and non-Western world as well, what is the advantage of constructing the analysis of state-sponsored efforts to appropriate historical memory around hegemony rather than legitimacy?[14]

Legitimacy, understood in Weber's formulation as support for rational-legal authority, suggests a democratic polity with a developed civil society. Only in a political setting where citizens enjoy organizational rights (political parties, professional groups, civic associations) and institutional rights (laws, individual rights, constraints on executive authority) can the governed freely decide whether or not to attribute legitimacy to those who control the state. In the context of the modern nation-state, legitimacy actually denotes legitimate authority and the citizen's freedom to decide whether to bestow legitimacy on a particular form of political authority. Although the concept of legitimacy suggests different analytic levels, especially between the political leadership that controls the state and seeks to make its authority legitimate, on the one hand, and the citizenry, which must decide whether to bestow legitimacy on a particular form of authority, on the other, the concept of hegemony is broader because it is applicable to both authoritarian and democratic societies. The concept of hegemony likewise offers a more dynamic notion of political process than the concept of legitimacy.

Unlike the Weberian notion of legitimacy, hegemony, at least in its Gramscian construction, implies a dialectical approach to political process, because hegemony always entails counterhegemony.[15] Because hegemony, unlike legitimacy, assumes that elites or ruling classes will invariably seek to skew the distribution of political and economic resources in their favor, subaltern groups will oppose such policies, as reflected in the development of counterhegemonic worldviews. The concept of legitimacy in its modern formulation, that is, defined in relation to rational-legal authority, seems more applicable to democratic political systems, in which citizens enjoy a greater ability to make choices.[16]

During the 1980s, however, the Ba'th Party's influence was increasingly subordinated to the "family party," and it quickly became apparent that the Iraqi parliament would not be delegated any meaningful legislative power. The Iran-Iraq War, coupled with intensified corruption and nepotism within the regime, increasingly circumscribed opportunities for upward mobility and undermined the material gains of the 1970s. As Gramsci argues, hegemony never resides solely in the cultural realm. Unless the hegemonic ideology proposed by the state is accompanied by material benefits for the targeted social strata, efforts to inculcate the populace with the notion that its interests are synonymous with those of the ruling elite will fall on deaf ears. By restricting state-sponsored memory to the cult of personality surrounding Saddam, and by narrowing political and especially economic opportunities to a relatively small elite, the regime moved away from the populism of the 1970s and constrained rather than expanded the institutional development that was necessary to promote acceptance of its own worldview. When the Iran-Iraq War ended and the state was unable to fulfill its promises of a return to the prosperity of the status quo ante, serious discontent quickly surfaced, providing one of the stimuli for invading Kuwait.

Because war making proved to be so counterproductive for the Ba'th Party, the question arises whether initiating wars was a function of Saddam's aggressive personality or a deeper structural characteristic of sectarian states. I have argued that there was a direct relationship between the Ba'thist state's efforts to promote a hegemonic worldview and its efforts to institutionalize sectarianism in the Iraqi political system. Likewise, I would argue that sectarian states maintain aggressive tendencies because they are inherently unstable. In Iraq, the Ba'thist state's aggressive and violent character was fostered not only by sectarianism, but by reliance on tribalism as well.

The Iraqi case demonstrates the difficulty of theorizing "stateness" in the abstract. It provides strong support for developing theories of the modern state from detailed case studies that later may be compared within and across regions. One particularly salient question is how to measure the strength of an individual state. If, in the Iraqi case, we are to conclude that the Ba'thist state was strong, then the prospects for the development of civil society are limited. If, as I maintain, the state ultimately lacked ideological direction and came to rest on a narrow social base, then this indicates that its hold on power was always more tenuous than recognized.

In the final analysis, Iraq did not possess a strong state under the Ba'th. It undermined its future prospects by allowing little meaningful political in-stitutionalization and the dissipation of whatever political capital the Baʿthist regime had accumulated during the 1970s. To counter those who point to the widespread security and military apparatus the regime devel-oped under the "republic of fear," I would ask whether a gang holding hostages whom it terrorizes is exhibiting strength or power in any mean-ingful sense for any duration of time. Increasingly the Iraqi state came to be seen by both Iraqis and Westerners as "rule by the mob," invoking the no-tion of a criminal or rogue state.[17] Once this occurred, the days of the "fam-ily party" were clearly numbered.

Hopefully, this study demonstrates the fallacy that states can impose a hegemonic view of politics on a society through financial co-optation and physical intimidation. Hegemony can only be successful if it finds its origins in society, not in the state apparatus.[18] Although the Baʿthist state did build upon cultural sentiments already extant in Iraqi society when it came to power, its attempt to appropriate these sentiments in an authoritarian fash-ion ultimately served to undermine that process. The state came to believe that it was the fount of history and culture rather than deriving its cues from the populace. The ultimate rejection of the Baʿthist Project for the Rewriting of History stands in marked contrast to the reaction to similar cultural policies followed by the Qasim regime, policies that were pursued in a much more culturally authentic manner and attracted significant intel-lectual and popular support. All regimes must convince their citizens that they rule in their interests, and hence that the citizenry should identify its interests with those of the state. What the Iraqi case underlines is that dem-ocratic rule is not just an ethical imperative, but it is ultimately the best way for the ruler and the ruled to achieve a shared sense of political community. However, forces that support democracy and culturally inclusive policies, especially important in ethnically diverse societies, need to heed another lesson of the Baʿthist experience. Democratic forces that fail to engage the past in newly developed states, such as the Iraqist nationalists failed to do in Iraq, risk alienating themselves from the populace. Unfortunately, one of the most difficult tasks for future Iraqi governments will be to face a com-plex public memory and answer the question of how the terror and cruelty of the Baʿth was able to dominate Iraqi society for so long.

In summary, I have argued that a conceptual framework that allows the study of the interrelationship between historical memory, collective identity, and political community introduces an emphasis on contingency and change that is often missing from the models that have heretofore been used to conceptualize Iraqi politics and society. A focus on memory avoids the essentialist tendencies and static quality of the "ethnic model," and the model that characterizes Iraq as a "republic of fear." By drawing our attention to intellectual production, it reinserts the saliency of ideas into political analysis. By stressing the dialectic of memory and countermemory, it forces any model that utilizes the concept to focus on the constant process of the renegotiation of repression and the resistance by subaltern groups to the state. The concept of historical memory also calls attention to the concept of agency and the microanalytic level of politics by focusing on individual behavior, namely, the process by which intellectuals engage in cultural production and ordinary citizens go about creating their understandings of the past in the face of the intrusiveness of the state. An approach that incorporates historical memory offers an antidote to the poverty of agency that plagues much structural analysis, especially reductionist Marxist models that continue to insist upon the links between political consciousness and "objective conditions." Historical memory also offers a means to refine the concept of hegemony, understood not as the top-down imposition of "false consciousness," but rather as a domain of struggle that can open numerous analytic vistas on political processes. Understood politically, the concept of historical memory can yield great insights into nation-states undergoing rapid change. It can be especially useful in understanding societies that are politically fragmented along ethnic or social class lines, in which the use of an explicit ideology may only threaten to exacerbate those cleavages. Yet any model that uses historical memory needs to be conscious of its own uses of history. Unless situated within a systematic approach that draws upon political economy and political culture, the analytic potential of historical memory to help us better understand political change will not be realized.

Charter 91

Civil society in Iraq has been continuously violated by the state in the name of ideology. As a consequence the networks through which civility is normally produced and reproduced have been destroyed. A collapse of values in Iraq has therefore coincided with the destruction of the public realm for uncoerced human association. In these conditions, the first task of a new politics is to reject barbarism and reconstitute civility.

With this in mind, we the undersigned, a group of men and women from Iraq comprised of different nationalities, religious denominations, ideological and political convictions, hereby declare:

1. PEOPLE HAVE RIGHTS FOR NO OTHER REASON THAN THAT THEY EXIST AS INDIVIDUAL HUMAN BEINGS.

These rights can only be secured by the rule of law and due process as set out in a written constitution. Such a document comes prior to the formation of legitimate political authority. Political legitimacy must be grounded in a constitution which sets out the principles and constraints of that foundation. Any political authority arising prior to the adoption of a constitution founded on human rights is either transitory, transitional or illegitimate.

2. FREEDOM FROM FEAR IS THE ESSENTIAL PREREQUISITE FOR REALIZING THE INHERENT DIGNITY OF THE HUMAN PERSON.

Specifically, freedom from fear requires that a new Iraqi constitution provide that:

Taken from "Charter 91," 2nd ed. (Washington, D.C.: Iraq Foundation, November 1993).

The quality of being an Iraqi shall never again be held in doubt because of faith, belief or presumed loyalty.

Citizenship become the irrevocable right of every individual born in Iraq, or to an Iraqi parent, or naturalized by an Iraqi state.

No Iraqi be subjected to arbitrary arrest or detention or deportation.

No Iraqi be subjected to cruel, inhuman or degrading treatment or punishment.

No confession of guilt, however obtained, be considered admissible in an Iraqi court of law.

A moratorium on capital punishment be promulgated for a period of not less than ten years.

Liability for punishment be always individual, never collective.

Unrestricted freedom of travel within and outside the boundaries of Iraq be an absolute and inalienable right of every citizen.

The villages, towns, cities, water sources, forests and historic and religious sites of Iraq be declared a National Trust which no political authority can capriciously destroy, disfigure or relocate.

The Universal Declaration of Human rights, adopted and proclaimed by the United Nations General Assembly resolution 217A (III) of 10 December 1948, be considered binding and constitutive of the legal system of Iraq.

Any Iraqi official found to have violated the above be dismissed and prosecuted to the fullest extent of the law.

3. REBUILDING CIVIL SOCIETY MEANS ELEVATING THE PRINCIPLE OF TOLERATION INTO A NEW PUBLIC NORM SOARING ABOVE ALL IDEOLOGIES.

Toleration in matters of politics, religion, and ethnic feeling is the only true alternative to violence and the rule of fear. The full creative potential of Iraqis, in which we deeply believe, will only be realized when toleration burns as fiercely in individual hearts and minds as it does in the new constitution of Iraq.

The only acceptable constraints upon toleration are those imposed by the rule of law as secured by a constitution founded on human rights. Toleration will not be extended to those who would abolish its rule through violence.

And toleration does not mean that gross violations of human rights from the past will be forgotten.

Toleration is a solution to the fact of ethnic, religious, political, and human differentiation. At bottom, it entails finding ways of accommodating or putting up with such differences. It involves putting up with things that one does not actually like, and may even consider immoral. No one "tolerates" what they actually enjoy or positively approve of. We choose to tolerate other individuals, organizations, religions, ideas, sects or ethnic groups. because we realize that there is a much higher value in forbearance than there is in trying to eradicate difference.

Toleration is a value superior to loyalty of blood or common heritage. It is superior to ritual nationalist affirmation. Toleration celebrates the human condition because it places the highest possible premium on human life in all its forms. Toleration is the supreme civic virtue.

4. REPRESENTATIVE PARLIAMENTARY DEMOCRACY IS THE RULE IN THE REPUBLIC OF TOLERANCE.

Democracy requires coordinating the representation of differences among people on three levels: within civil society; between civil society and that state; and between the executive, legislative and judicial realms of governments. Democracy is not only ruling in the name of people, nor is it simply majority rule. Central to democracy is the constitutionally guaranteed set of rights which protect the part from the tyranny of the whole. The fundamental idea is that the majority rules only because it is a majority, not because it has a monopoly on the truth.

In a democracy, freedom is always the right to think, work, and express oneself—as an individual or as a group—differently. It is the right to live differently, or to speak and learn in a different language. The only acceptable constraint upon freedom is that its exercise must not bring harm upon others.

The protected part may be a whole ethnic group, a minority religion, or sect, or it may be a group of individuals who want to voice or organize around a particular political opinion. At the limit the part may be a single human being; and democracy becomes protecting the solitary person's right to be different from everyone else.

Democracy involves securing the freedom of everyone to participate equally in the determination of a shared political destiny. Human beings best realize themselves as individuals who propose, debate and decide. The institutionally structured activity of politics accounts for more than any final results.

5. THE NOTION THAT STRENGTH RESIDES IN LARGE STANDING ARMIES AND UP-TO-DATE WEAPONS OF DESTRUCTION HAS PROVED BANKRUPT.

Real strength is always internal, in the creative, cultural and wealth-producing capabilities of a people. It is found in civil society, not in the army or in the state. Armies often threaten democracy; the larger they grow the more they weaken civil society. This is what happened in Iraq. Therefore, conditional upon international and regional guarantees which secure the territorial integrity of Iraq, preferably within the framework of an overall reduction in the levels of militarization of the whole Middle East, a new Iraqi constitution should:

> Abolish conscription and reorganize the army into a professional, small and purely defensive force which will never be used for internal repression.

> Set an absolute upper limit on expenditure on this new force equal to 2% of Iraqi National Income.

> Have as its first article the following: "Aspiring sincerely to an international peace based on justice and order, the Iraqi people forever renounce war as a sovereign right of the nation and the threat or use of force as a means of settling international disputes. The right of belligerency of the Iraqi states will not be recognized."

6. CHARTER 91 IS A SIGNATURE-GATHERING CAMPAIGN CALLING FOR A WRITTEN CONSTITUTION FOR IRAQ THAT ARISES OUT OF A COLLECTIVE EXPERIENCE OF DEBATE AND DISCUSSION.

Charter 91 is not an organization; it has no rules or formal membership. The campaign embraces everyone who is willing to put his or her name to the words in this document.

All signatories must use their full and real names. Nothing in this charter should be taken as binding on a future constitutional convention for Iraq. Each signatory gives permission that his or her name may be freely publicized as part of the effort to promote the Charter.

Finally, Charter 91 derives its name symbolically from a terrible year in the history of Iraq. 1991 is the year of a wantonly destructive war which laid waste of the infrastructure of the country, giving rise to famine and disease unprecedented in the country's modern history. 1991 is also the year when large numbers of Iraqis rose up against the evil which had become the norm inside their country and which they held responsible for that war. And it is the year when that uprising was crushed by the brutal razing of cities and massive loss of life. No Iraqi will ever forget 1991.

Charter 91 is a different reason for remembering the year 1991. By its existence this charter is proof that the barrier of fear has been broken: Never again will we Iraqis hang our heads in shame and let violence rule in our name.

Notes

PREFACE

1. The results of the SSRC project were published in a volume I coedited with Nicolas Gavrielides, *Statecraft in the Middle East: Oil, Historical Memory, and Popular Culture* (Miami: Florida International University Press/University Presses of Florida, 1991). One of the findings of this project was that oil wealth more often than not led to social and political instability, thereby weakening rather than strengthening the state. Thus oil wealth by itself was not a good predictor of political stability and state power. This counterintuitive finding paralleled earlier research on Arab oil-producing states that I conducted during the late 1970s. This research demonstrated that, far from opposing Western interests, as implied by interpretations of the 1975 Arab oil boycott of the West, the interests of Arab oil states complemented those of the West. See my "The Political Economy of the Arab Oil-Producing Countries: Convergence with Western Interests," *Studies in Comparative International Development* 14, no. 2 (1979): 75–94.

2. For the principles underlying this project, see Saddam Husayn, *Hawla Kitabat al-Tarikh [On the Writing of History]* (Baghdad: Dar al-Hurriya li-l-Tibaʿa, 1978). Although authorship is attributed to Saddam, the volume consists of four speeches by Saddam on history writing followed by twenty-three essays by prominent Iraqi intellectuals elucidating the need for the project.

CHAPTER 1. INTRODUCTION

1. Antonio Gramsci, *Selections from the Prison Notebooks* (London: Lawrence & Wishart, 1971), 57–58. An often-cited example of hegemonic rule is medieval Christendom, where church and state combined to dominate economics, politics, and culture.

2. Here I am referring to Weber's well-known definition of the state as that institution that enjoys the legitimate monopolization of force in society.

3. For details of the putsch, see the series in *al-Hayat*, especially Mar. 8, 2003, by Salah ʿUmar al-ʿAli, Saddam's cousin and former Revolution Command Council member, now in exile.

4. Craig Calhoun, "The Politics of Identity and Recognition," in his *Critical Social Theory: Culture, History, and the Challenge of Difference* (Oxford: Blackwell, 1995), 220.

5. Surprisingly, the modern literature on historical memory does not generally treat its relationship to politics. For some of the more prominent texts on historical memory, see Maurice Halbwachs, *Les cadres sociaux de la mémoire [The Social Frameworks of Memory]* (New York: Arno Press, 1975 [1952]); David Lowenthal, *The Past is a Foreign Country* (Cambridge: Cambridge University Press, 1985); Jacques Le Goff, *History and Memory* (New York: Columbia University Press, 1992); Paul Connorton, *How Societies Remember* (Cambridge: Cambridge University Press, 1989); and James Fentress and Chris Wickham, *Social Memory* (Oxford: Blackwell, 1992).

6. In Iraq, a number of prominent Shiʿi religious figures were assassinated under obscure circumstances during 1998 and 1999. Their sole transgression seems to have been their refusal to alter their Friday sermon *(khutba)* to accord with Baʿthist dictates.

7. For a discussion of this process, see my "The Museum and the Politics of Social Control in Modern Iraq," in *Commemorations: The Politics of Memory and Identity*, ed. John Gillis (Princeton, N.J.: Princeton University Press, 1994), 90–104.

8. In differentiating between historical and historical-cultural narratives, I distinguish cultural production that focuses on specific historical events such as military battles, e.g., the Battle of Qadisiya, in which Arab-Islamic forces defeated the Sasanians, who ruled Persia, in 637 C.E., from that which focuses on the historical continuity of certain traditions, e.g., the Baʿthist emphasis on the continuity between music, sports, and marriage rituals in ancient Mesopotamia and in contemporary Iraq. See, for example, Subhi Anwar Rashid, *al-Musiqa fi-l-ʿIraq al-Qadim [Music in Ancient Iraq]* (Baghdad: Dar al-Shuʾun al-Thaqafiya al-ʿAmma, 1988).

9. The irony of the Hammurabi Brigade and other Special Republican Guard units that bear names drawn from ancient Mesopotamia is that their members were drawn exclusively from the Sunni Arab tribal groupings near Saddam's hometown of Takrit and allied neighboring tribes. Clearly, the state's "Mesopotamianism" made no concessions to an Iraqist definition of society.

10. Amatzia Baram, *Culture and Ideology in the Making of Baʿthist Iraq, 1968–1989* (New York: St. Martin's Press, 1989). The argument that there is ethnic continuity between the peoples of ancient Mesopotamian civilizations and modern Iraqis reflects the Baʿthist effort to categorize all Iraqis as belonging to a unitary Arab culture. This differs from the Iraqist view, whose focus on ancient Mesopotamia is part of an effort to emphasize cultural diversity rather than an artificial and fictive unity.

11. Eric Davis, "State-Building in Iraq During the Iran-Iraq and Gulf Wars,"

in *The Internationalization of Communal Strife,* ed. M. Midlarsky (New York: Routledge, 1992), 68–91.

12. Syria is ruled by a rival wing of the Baʿth Party that ousted Michel ʿAflaq and other leaders of the original party organization in 1966 who later fled to Iraq. The Iraqi Baʿth considers Syria a traitor to the Arab cause because it has fostered divisions among Pan-Arabists by creating a "nonauthentic" wing of the party.

13. Perhaps Marx's notion of the individual as a "carrier" *(Träger)* of ideas suggests a more dynamic understanding of human agency and hence would be preferable to "perceiver."

14. For example, the many posters and murals that depicted Saddam Husayn embodying the legacy of Saʿd Ibn Abi al-Waqqas, the Arab general who defeated the Persians at al-Qadisiya in 637 C.E., require some understanding of the battle's historical significance. See Samir al-Khalil [Kanan Makiya], *The Monument: Art, Vulgarity and Responsibility in Iraq* (Berkeley: University of California Press, 1991).

15. Samir al-Khalil [Kanan Makiya], *Republic of Fear: The Degradation of Politics in Modern Iraq* (Berkeley: University of California Press, 1989), esp. chapter 1, "The Institutions of Violence," and chapter 2, "A World of Fear." Nazih Ayubi, *Overstating the Arab State: Politics and Society in the Middle East* (London: I. B. Tauris, 1995), 424, has noted that al-Khalil [Makiya] "has given a vivid, if *nightmarish,* picture of the reign of terror in Iraq" (emphasis added). Of course, this perspective includes a wide variety of authors, e.g., Hamid al-Bayati, *al-Tarikh al-Damawi li Saddam al-Takriti fi Dawʾ al-Wathaʾiq al-Sirriya al-Britaniya, 1937–1966 [The Bloody History of Saddam al-Takriti in Light of Secret British Documents, 1937–1966]* (London: Muʾassasat al-Rafid li-l-Nashr wa-l-Tawziʿa, 1998), and Baqir Yasin, *Tarikh al-ʿUnf al-Damawi fi-l-ʿIraq: al-Waqaʾiʿ, al-Dawafiʿ, al-Hulul [The History of Violence in Iraq: The Events, Motivations and Solutions]* (Damascus: Dar al-Kunuz al-Adabiya, 1999).

16. It might be argued that there is a third, or Islamist, vision of political community. However, those Shiʿi mujtahids who supported such a perspective were largely marginalized by the Hashimites and the British during the 1920s, and by the increasingly secular nature of the Iraqi Shiʿi community itself. See ʿAbd al-Halim al-Rahimi, *Tarikh al-Haraka al-Islamiya fi-l-ʿIraq: al-Judhur al-Fikriya wa-l-Waqiʿ al-Tarikhi, 1900–1924 [The History of the Islamic Movement in Iraq: The Intellectual Roots and the Historical Reality, 1900–1924]* (Beirut: al-Dar al-ʿAlamiya li-l-Tibaʿa wa-l-Nashr wa-l-Tawziʿ, 1985), 235–83; and Yitzhak Nakash, *The Shiʿis of Iraq* (Princeton, N.J.: Princeton University Press, 1994), 94–108.

17. See al-Khalil [Kanan Makiya], *Republic of Fear,* and Kanan Makiya, *Cruelty and Silence: War, Tyranny, Uprising, and the Arab World* (New York: W. W. Norton, 1993).

18. Eric Hobsbawm and Terence Ranger, *The Invention of Tradition* (Cambridge: Cambridge University Press, 1982), esp. pp. 1–14.

19. See, for example, Baram, *Culture and Ideology in the Making of Baʿthist*

Iraq; Davis and Gavrielides, "Statecraft, Historical Memory and Popular Culture in Iraq and Kuwait," in *Statecraft in the Middle East,* 116–48; and Davis, "The Museum and the Politics of Social Control," 90–104.

20. On the notion of "imagined community," see Benedict Anderson, *Imagined Communities: Reflections on the Origins of Nationalism* (London: Verso, 1983).

21. This formulation was developed by the Committee on New Nations at the University of Chicago during the 1960s. See Clifford Geertz, ed., *Old Societies and New States* (New York: The Free Press, 1964).

22. See David Fromkin, *A Peace to End All Peace: The Fall of the Ottoman Empire and the Creation of the Modern Middle East* (New York: Avon Books, 1989).

23. Many older Iraqis informed me that it was considered very impolite to ask someone their ethnic affiliation or discuss ethnic relations in public. Only after the 1991 Gulf War and subsequent Intifada did the subject of ethnicity and sectarianism become part of public discourse.

24. The Marquis Massimo d'Azeglio, *I miei ricordi [My Memoirs]* (Florence: Barbera, 1867), as cited in *Fare gli Italiani: Scuola e cultura nell'Italia contemporanea [Making Italians: Schooling and Culture in Contemporary Italy],* ed. Simonetta Soldani and Gabrielle Turin (Bologna: Il Mulino, 1993), 1: 17. A "top-down" approach to Ba'thist attempts to create hegemony is one of the conceptual problems that characterizes in Amatzia Baram's otherwise excellent study, *Culture and Ideology in the Making of Ba'thist Iraq.*

25. For a discussion of the conceptual problems associated with viewing individuals as passive recipients of knowledge, see Paulo Freire's discussion of the "banking theory" as opposed to the "problem posing" approach to education in *Pedagogy of the Oppressed* (New York: Continuum, 1970), esp. chapter 2, 57–74.

26. For a critique of Gramsci's conceptualization of hegemony, see Perry Anderson, "The Antinomies of Antonio Gramsci," *New Left Review* 100 (1976–77): 5–80.

27. See, for example, Elie Kedourie, *Arabic Political Memoirs and Other Studies* (London: Frank Cass, 1974), *The Chatham House Version and Other Middle Eastern Studies* (New York: Praeger, 1970), and *Democracy and Arab Political Culture* (Washington, D.C.: Washington Institute for Near East Policy, 1992), esp. 25–35. For a British colonial perspective, see Gertrude Bell, *The Letters of Gertrude Bell,* 2 vols. (New York: Liveright / Liveright and Boni, 1927); and British Foreign Office documents, e.g., FO 371/110089/990. For an American diplomatic perspective, see the memoirs of the ambassador just prior to the 1958 Revolution, Waldemar Gallman, *Iraq Under General Nuri: My Recollections of Nuri al-Said, 1954–1958* (Baltimore, Md.: Johns Hopkins Press, 1964).

28. H. Mahdavy, "The Patterns and Problems of Development in Rentier States: The Case of Iran," in *Studies in the Economic History of the Middle East,* ed. Michael Cook (Oxford: Oxford University Press, 1970), 466–67. See also Hazem Beblawi, "The Rentier State in the Arab World," in *The Rentier State,*

ed. Hazem Beblawi and Giacomo Luciani (London: Croom Helm, 1987), 52; Davis and Gavrielides, "Statecraft, Historical Memory and Popular Culture in Iraq and Kuwait," 143. See also Jacques Delacroix, "The Distributive State in the World System," *Studies in Comparative International Development* 15, no. 3 (1980): 3–21

29. Falih ʿAbd al-Jabbar, *al-Dawla, al-Mujtamaʿ al-Madani wa-l-Tahawwul al-Dimuqrati fi-l-ʿIraq* [*The State, Civil Society and the Future of Democratic Transition in Iraq*] (Cairo: Ibn Khaldun Center and Dar al-Amin li-l-Nashr wa-l-Tawziʿ, 1995), 139–42.

30. Giacomo Luciani, "Allocation vs. Production States: A Theoretical Framework," in *The Rentier State*, ed. Beblawi and Luciani, 63–82.

31. See, for example, Saʿd al-Din Ibrahim's lengthy introduction to ʿAbd al-Jabbar, *al-Dawla*, 5–40. Ibrahim, the former director of the Ibn Khaldun Center, was tried, imprisoned, and later released by the Egyptian government as a result of his center's political activities in trying to explain to peasants and workers how to vote.

32. In his writings, Gramsci emphasizes the notion of the "war of position" in which the state or counterhegemonic forces attempt to mobilize support for their ideology, worldview, and vision of the future prior to the outbreak of overt struggle (what Gramsci call the "war of maneuver"). I suspect that, far from being offended by Khalil and ʿAbd al-Jabbar's characterizations of the Iraqi state, Saddam Husayn and his fellow Baʿthists would have found them to provide ideological sustenance in their attribution of greater power to the state than it actually possessed.

33. Diane Singerman, *Avenues of Participation: Family, Politics and Networks in Urban Quarters of Cairo* (Princeton, N.J.: Princeton University Press, 1995), esp. 173–268.

34. The only area that was not directly affected by the uprising was Baghdad, the nerve center of the state. Three factors made Baghdad's participation in the uprising problematic. First, Saddam had retained some of his best Republican Guard units around the city during the Gulf War; second, the city was infested with secret police agents; and third, the regime is said to have evacuated at least two million people from the city following the end of the Gulf War to minimize the possibility of an uprising.

35. An excellent antidote to the notion of the omnipotent authoritarian state is Ayubi, *Overstating the Arab State*, 447, in which he states, "That the Arab state is an authoritarian state, and that it is so averse to democracy and resistant to its pressures should not, of course, be taken as a measure of the strength of that state—indeed, quite the reverse."

36. ʿAbd al-Jabbar, *al-Dawla*, 137–39.

37. For a discussion of these new trends, see Makiya, *Cruelty and Silence*, and the numerous articles in the London based daily *al-Hayat*.

38. The glorification of the Gulf War is particularly evident in the proliferation of the name that Saddam gave to it, Umm al-Maʿarik (Mother of All Battles), which has been applied even to Mother of All Battles Research Center in

Baghdad and a quarterly strategic studies journal by the same name. During the nightly Baʻthist television news broadcast from Baghdad, the words "Umm al-Maʻarik al-Khalida" (the Immortal Mother of all Battles) served as a backdrop to the news announcer in case the viewer forgot the importance of this event. This issue is discussed further in chapter 9.

CHAPTER 2. THE FORMATION OF THE IRAQI
INTELLIGENTSIA AND MODERN HISTORICAL MEMORY

1. The *sada* claim to be descendants of the Prophet Muhammad. See Hanna Batatu, *The Old Social Classes and Revolutionary Movements of Iraq* (Princeton, N.J.: Princeton University Press, 1978), 153–210.

2. Ibid., 75. In their efforts to undermine the power of the tribes, the Ottomans resettled tribes in areas already under the control of another tribe, thereby setting off conflict between them. They also used *tapu* rights to promote sedentization as well as tribal fragmentation by encouraging tribal shaykhs to develop greater loyalty to their individual landholdings than to their tribe or tribal federation.

3. For a detailed discussion of this process in Egypt and its parallels with Iraq, see my *Challenging Colonialism: Bank Misr and Egyptian Industrialization, 1920–1941* (Princeton, N.J.: Princeton University Press, 1941), esp. 12–79.

4. Ibrahim Khalil Ahmad, *Tatawwur al-Taʻlim al-Watani fi-l-ʻIraq, 1869–1932* [*The Development of National Education in Iraq, 1869–1932*] (Basra: Center for Arab Gulf Studies and Basra University Press, 1982), 26–29; W. J. O. Nadhmi, "The Political, Intellectual and Social Roots of the Iraqi Independence Movement, 1920," Ph.D. diss., School of Oriental Studies, Durham University, 1974, 59, n. 6.

5. This condition was part of the legacy of the sacking of the country by the Mongols in 1258 C.E., which included the destruction of the irrigation system.

6. Batatu, *The Old Social Classes*, 24, 78.

7. Exports increased from 147,000 pounds for the period between 1864 and 1871 to 2,960,000 pounds in 1912–13. Mohammad Salman Hasan, "The Role of Foreign Trade in the Economic Development of Iraq, 1864–1964: A Study in the Growth of a Dependent Economy," in *Studies in the Economic History of the Middle East*, ed. M. A. Cook (London: Oxford University Press, 1970), 348. There was a twelvefold increase in imports to Iraq between 1864 and 1913. Ibid., 353. At the onset of World War I, 70 percent of Iraq's imports were from Western industrialized countries.

8. Ibid., 348. The restructuring of trade was facilitated in particular by improvements in transportation. Most important was the beginning of steam transport on the Tigris River in 1857 and the establishment of the first navigation company, the British-owned Euphrates and Tigris Steamship Navigation Company, in 1861. This company facilitated the expansion of internal trade as well as British commercial and political influence The opening of the Suez Canal in 1869 was equally important since it significantly expanded Iraq's ability to

trade with Europe. Trade was also enhanced by the establishment of telegraph communications that linked Iraq with Europe and India during the 1860s. Nadhmi, "The Political, Intellectual and Social Roots," 13.

9. Hasan, "The Role of Foreign Trade," 349.

10. Batatu, *The Old Social Classes*, 77.

11. Perhaps the impact of steam navigation is most evident when comparing the Euphrates, where such navigation was not feasible, with the Tigris. The Ottomans were able to subjugate tribes along the Tigris much earlier than those along the Euphrates. Nadhmi, "The Political, Intellectual and Social Roots," 14.

12. Barrington Moore, Jr., *Social Origins of Dictatorship and Democracy* (Boston: Beacon Press, 1966), 197.

13. Batatu, *The Old Social Classes*, 53, 55; Roger Owen, *The Middle East in the World Economy, 1800–1914* (London: Methuen, 1981), 185–86.

14. Nadhmi, "The Political, Intellectual and Social Roots."

15. Ahmad, *Tatawwur al-Taʿlim*, 36–37. In 1869 he founded a military school, known as al-Madrasa al-Rushdiya al-ʿAskariya, which was followed in 1870 by a civilian counterpart, al-Madrasa al-Rushdiya al-Malakiya.

16. This school, al-Maktab al-Nisiya, was opened in 1871 with 144 students. Students worked in spinning, metalwork, and shoe production using European implements. Ahmad, *Tatawwur al-Taʿlim*, 38.

17. Batatu, *The Old Social Classes*, 320.

18. Ibid., 169.

19. Midhat's successor, Radif Pasha, was able to found a preparatory school in 1873. The press's role in the expansion of Iraq's education system should also be noted. The newspaper *al-Zawra*' (reestablished by Saddam Husayn's son, ʿUday, in the 1990s) produced a steady stream of articles arguing for the need for more schools, including those teaching specialized subjects and, in a radical position for the late nineteenth century, schools for girls. See Ahmad, *Tatawwur al-Taʿlim*, 40–41.

20. The first such school was established by the Carmelite Mission in Baghdad in 1728. The Dominican order, which opened its first mission in 1750 and offered education on a nonsectarian basis, was especially successful since it received financial support from the French and offered specialized training such as medical training. Christian and Jewish schools also offered education for girls, which was neglected by the state schools. Ibid., 43. Abbas Shiblak, *The Lure of Zion: The Case of the Iraqi Jews* (London: al-Saqi Books, 1986), 23.

21. Ahmad, *Tatawwur al-Taʿlim*, 48.

22. Ibid., 48–49.

23. This school was established by a transplanted Mosul lawyer, Sulayman Faydi. The role of the middle classes in the development of early nationalist institutions is obvious.

24. Ahmad, *Tatawwur al-Taʿlim*, 49.

25. For Abu Timman's influence on interwar Iraqi politics, see al-ʿAbd al-Razzaq ʿAbd al-Darraji, *Jaʿfar Abu Timman: Dawruhu fi-l-Haraka al-Wataniya fi-l-ʿIraq [Jaʿfar Abu Timman and His Role in the Iraqi Nationalist Movement]*

(Baghdad: Ministry of Culture and Arts, 1978). It is interesting to note that during this period when the Ministry of Culture and Arts was separated from the Ministry of Information, the former set up its own publications series and published a text on a noted Iraqist nationalist and Shiʿi who was not part of the Pan-Arab pantheon of modern Iraqi political figures.

26. In the attempt to create an Arabic language education system, one can see the beginnings of intercommunal tensions. Although the desire to have all students share one language of instruction was logical if the goal was nation building, the attempt to impose Arabic as the only instruction language was resented by the minority communities.

27. Salih J. Altoma, "America, the Gulf War and Arabic Poetry," *al-Jadid* 3, no. 21 (Fall 1997): 17–19.

28. Ibrahim al-Waʾili, *al-Shiʿr al-Siyassi al-ʿIraqi fi-l-Qarn al-Tasiʿ ʿAshar [Iraqi Political Poetry During the Nineteenth Century]* (Baghdad: Matbaʿat al-Maʿrif, 1978), 102–3.

29. Joyce N. Wiley, *The Islamic Movement of Iraqi Shiʿas* (Boulder, Colo.: Lynne Rienner, 1992), 22.

30. During the crisis of January–February 1998, Iraqi intellectuals continually invoked a historical memory situated in ancient Sumeria and Babylonia to argue for the indivisible unity of Iraq. See *al-Hayat*, Feb. 5, 15, 1998.

31. Zahida Ibrahim, *Kashshaf bi al-Jaraʾid wa-l-Majallat al-ʿIraqiya, 1869–1978 [Index of Iraqi Newspapers and Journals, 1869–1978]* (Kuwait: Dar al-Nashr wa-l-Matbuʿat al-Kuwaytiya, 1982), 452–53.

32. Faʾiq Butti, *al-Sihafa al-Yasariya fi-l-ʿIraq [Left-wing Journalism in Iraq]* (London: n.p., 1985), 5–6.

33. The Egyptian periodicals *al-Muqtataf, al-Hilal, al-Mustaqbal,* and *al-Musawwar* were four of the most influential among educated Iraqis. Ibid., 16.

34. Batatu, *The Old Social Classes,* 172–73; Mudhaffar al-Amin, "Jamaat al-Ahali: Its Origin, Ideology, and Role in Iraqi Politics, 1932–1946," Ph.D. diss., School of Oriental Studies, Durham University, 1980, 44 ff.

35. al-Waʾili, *al-Shiʿr al-Siyassi al-ʿIraqi,* 108.

36. Although the tribal shaykhs of the Middle Euphrates made many charitable contributions to the Shiʿi ʿulamaʾ, their goal seems to have been to garner status for themselves rather than to represent their control over men of religion. See Batatu, *The Old Social Classes,* 149–50.

37. Abdul-Salaam Yacoob Yousif, "Vanguardist Cultural Practices: The Formation of an Alternative Cultural Hegemony in Iraq and Chile, 1930s–1970s," Ph.D. diss., University of Iowa, 1988, 110.

38. Unfortunately, a focus on the intellectual necessitates a somewhat "elitist" approach because the study of written texts and visual imagery such as paintings, sculpture, drawings, or photographs emphasizes the more formal aspects of culture, which are usually produced by the more privileged, who have had access to education. By concentrating on intellectuals who produced physical objects in the form of books or visual materials, I do not want to deny the important contributions of the oral tradition to the debate over national identity.

However, it is the codified forms of production such as written texts that provided the cultural milieu for the development of explicit ideologies such as Pan-Arabism, local variants of communism, and the "populism" *(al-sha'biya)* of the al-Ahali group, as well as the delegitimation of other ideologies such as the ersatz liberalism that characterized Iraq under the monarchy.

39. The concept of "organic intellectual" is discussed by Gramsci in *Selections from the Prison Notebooks* (London: Lawrence & Wishart, 1971), 6.

40. Hala Fattah, *The Politics of Regional Trade in Iraq, Arabia, and the Gulf, 1745–1900* (Albany: State University of New York Press, 1997), 28–41, 69–72, 79–82, 185–91, 195–97, 201–5.

41. No attempt is being made here to pose a rigid dichotomy between "secular" and "religious" or "modern" and "traditional." In their political thinking, many *'ulama'* themselves moved conceptually from a local to a national perspective. Examples are those who participated in the 1918 al-Najaf uprising and those who participated in the nationally oriented 1920 Revolution.

42. al-Wa'ili, *al-Shi'r al-Siyassi al-'Iraqi*, 127, 129–30, 319–20.

43. 'Abd al-Hamid al-'Alwaji, "al-Turath al-Sha'bi" (Popular Heritage/Culture), in *Hidarat al-'Iraq: al-'Iraq al-Mu'asir [Iraq's Civilization: Modern Iraq]*, ed. "An Elite Group of Iraqi Researchers" (Baghdad: Dar al-Hurriya li-l-Tiba'a, 1985), 13: 34. al-'Alwaji, former director of Iraq's National Library, told me that the study of Iraqi folklore was greatly influenced by German folkloric studies as transmitted to Iraq early in the twentieth century through the Ottoman Empire. Interview, Iraqi National Library (al-Maktaba al-Wataniya al-'Iraqiya), June 14, 1984.

44. Yousif, "Vanguardist Cultural Practices," 107.

45. Yousif Izzidien ('Izz al-Din), "Poetry in the Social and Political Development of 20th-Century Iraq," Ph.D. diss., School of Oriental and African Studies, University of London, 1956, 15.

46. Izzidien, "Poetry in the Social and Political Development," 95.

47. Yousif, "Vanguardist Cultural Practices," 115.

48. Izzidien, "Poetry in the Social and Political Development," 47–64.

49. Mahmoud Haddad, "Iraq Before World War I," in *The Origins of Arab Nationalism*, ed. Rashid Khalidi et al. (New York: Columbia University Press, 1991), 133, 138.

50. Ibid., 130–32.

51. Ibid., 135–36, 140–41.

52. Izzidien, "Poetry in the Social and Political Development," 92. This action by Jamal Pasha created a strong reaction throughout the Arab world and was one of the stimuli for the founding of the al-'Ahd (Covenant) Party.

53. Ibid., 53. In some of his poems on the Italian invasion, especially after the Ottomans had been defeated and the resistance was being carried on by the Sanusi, al-Rusafi makes no references to the sultan at all. Here the emphasis on the role of Arab forces further sharpened the distinction between Turk and Iraqi Arab in the mind of the reader.

54. Batatu, *The Old Social Classes*, Appendix B, 1141, notes that the most

politicized of the 'ulama' were the lesser mujtahids and the sons of the most prominent mujtahids, e.g., Sayyid Muhammad al-Sadr (son of Sayyid Hasan al-Sadr), Muhammad al-Khalisi (son of Shaykh Mahdi al-Khalisi), and Mirza Muhammad Rida (son of Mirza Muhammad Taqi al-Shirazi).

55. Izzidien, "Poetry in the Social and Political Development," 77–80.

56. Particularly influential in this regard was General Maude's declaration of British intentions upon entering Baghdad in 1917 that, "our Armies have not come . . . as conquerors . . . but as Liberators . . . the people . . . shall flourish . . . under institutions which are in consonance with their sacred laws and their racial ideals." Nadhmi, "The Political, Intellectual and Social Roots," 316.

57. A. F. al Nafesi, "The Role of the Shi'ah in the Political Development of Modern Iraq, 1914–1921," Ph.D. diss., Cambridge University, 1972, 249, 318.

58. The founding of Kemalist Turkey, the Najaf uprising of 1918, and the 1919 Egyptian Revolution also served to heighten nationalist feelings.

59. Nadhmi, "The Political, Intellectual and Social Roots," 120.

60. Batatu, *The Old Social Classes*, 19–20.

61. al-Nafesi, "The Role of the Shi'ah," 249, 320. After initially welcoming the British as liberators, many notables in Karbala' and al-Najaf came to resent their new overlords, who sought to dominate the political and economic scene. This led to strong British reaction, including trials, exile, and even executions of Iraqi opponents. Nadhmi, "The Political, Intellectual and Social Roots," 339–40.

62. 'Abd al-Halim al-Rahimi, *Tarikh al-Haraka al-Islamiya fi-l-'Iraq: al-Judhur al-Fikriya wa-l-Waqi' al-Tarikhi, 1900–1924 [The History of the Islamic Movement in Iraq: The Intellectual Roots and the Historical Reality, 1900–1924]* (Beirut: al-Dar al-'Alamiya li-l-Tiba'a wa-l-Nashr wa-l-Tawzi', 1985), 238.

63. This was the view of the notable Sulayman Faydi, who described Shi'i domination of the political scene as an "unthinkable disaster." Nadhmi, "The Social, Intellectual and Political Roots," 353.

64. Ibid., 367.

65. Izzidien, "Poetry in the Political and Social Development," 125, 128. Thus Shi'i poets read poetry in the al-Haydarkhana mosque and Sunnis read poetry in mosques in the Shi'i quarters of Baghdad.

66. Nadhmi, "The Social, Intellectual and Political Roots," 362–63.

67. Ibid., 369.

68. Ibid.

69. Gertrude Bell, *The Letters of Gertrude Bell* (New York: Liveright / Liveright and Boni, 1927), 2: 585.

70. Ibrahim Khalil Ahmad, "al-Sihafa al-'Iraqiya, 1914–1958" (The Iraqi Press, 1914–1958), in *Hidarat al-'Iraq*, 209–10.

71. Ibrahim, *Kashshaf al-Jara'id wa-l-Majallat*, 73, 123, 158, 272. Among these was *Dijla [Tigris]*, which was purportedly the first Iraqi newspaper to openly discuss socialism, *al-'Alam al-'Arabi [the Arab World]*, *al-Misbah [The Light]*, and the journal *al-Sahifa* (literally, *The Newspaper*). These periodicals were first issued in 1921, 1924, 1924, and 1927, respectively.

72. Butti, *al-Sihafa al-Yasariya*, 212; Ibrahim, *Kashshaf al-Jara'id wa-l-Majallat*, 158.

73. Batatu, *The Old Social Classes*, 394–95; Butti, *al-Sihafa al-Yasariya*, 18–22.

74. In this sense, the number of periodicals established during the 1920s and indeed throughout the period of the monarchy is somewhat exaggerated. Many newspapers and journals that were closed by the government simply reorganized under a new name and editor while still representing the same political interests.

75. See Batatu, *The Old Social Classes*, 398–400, for details of these incidents.

76. A survey in 1934 indicated that Baghdad alone had six hundred coffee shops. al-'Alwaji, "al-Turath al-Sha'bi," 38. For a wonderful discussion of Baghdad coffeehouses during the 1920s, see 'Abbas Baghdadi, *Li-alla Nansa: Baghdad fi-l-'Ashriniyat [Lest We Not Forget: Baghdad During the 1920s]* (Beirut: al-Mu'assasa al-'Arabiya li-l-Dirasat wa-l-Nashr, 1998), 119–31.

77. 'Abd al-Razzaq al-Hasani, *al-Thawra al-'Iraqiya al-Kubra* (Sidon: Matba'at al-'Irfan, 1952), 53.

78. The leadership of the Haras is discussed in ibid., 51–53. Batatu (*The Old Social Classes*, 220–21) uses the terms "bureaucrat-*mallak*" and "administrator-*mallak*" to refer to members of this social stratum.

79. al-Hasani, *al-Thawra al-'Iraqiya*, 53. This quote is taken from point 7 of the Haras charter.

80. Izzidien, "Poetry in the Political and Social Development," 171, 172, 173, 174. These opposition newspapers included *al-Mufid, Shatt al-'Arab, al-'Amal, al-Falah,* and *Lisan al-'Arab.*

81. "*Shurugi*" is the colloquial Iraqi equivalent of the classical Arabic "*sharqawi.*"

82. Khaldun Sati' al-Husari, *Mudhakkarti fi-l-'Iraq [My Memoirs of Iraq]* (Beirut: Dar al-Tali'a, 1967), 1: 173.

83. Of the one hundred delegates to the assembly, only sixty-three turned out for the discussion of the treaty, and only thirty-seven signed their names to it. Ibid., 1: 180.

84. Mohammad A. Tarbush, *The Role of the Military in Politics: A Case Study of Iraq to 1941* (London: Kegan Paul International, 1982), 184–85.

CHAPTER 3. NATIONALISM, MEMORY, AND THE DECLINE
OF THE MONARCHICAL STATE

1. The reasons for this greater sensitivity may have to do with the greater ethnic and social homogeneity of the Pan-Arabists, who were largely Sunni and Arab, which was reinforced by their domination of the state bureaucracy and military under the Ottomans.

2. Of course, World War II, the 1948 Wathba, the *intifadas* of 1952 and 1956, and the 1958 Revolution, which are discussed later, were as significant as the

302 / Notes to Pages 56–63

prewar crises for the period between 1946 and the overthrow of the Hashimite Monarchy. These crises are discussed in subsequent chapters.

3. Hasan al-ʿAlawi provides a comprehensive overview of the manner in which ministries under the monarchy consistently excluded Shiʿis, who were only given political authority during crises, when the state invariably appointed a Shiʿi prime minister who would serve only until the crisis had subsided. Because this pattern persisted under all twentieth-century Iraqi regimes except that of ʿAbd al-Karim Qasim, we may refer to al-ʿAlawi's "law of sectarian responses to crises" as a law that hopefully will no longer hold in post Baʿthist Iraq. See Hasan al-ʿAlawi, al-Shiʿa wa-l-Dawla al-Qawmiya fi-l-ʿIraq [The Shiʿa and the National State in Iraq] (Paris: CEDI Press, 1989).

4. Majid Khadduri, Independent Iraq (Oxford: Oxford University Press, 1960).

5. al-ʿAlawi, al-Shiʿa wa-l-Dawla al-Qawmiya, 163–90. For the concept of "path dependence," see Douglass North, Institutions, Institutional Change and Economic Performance (Cambridge: Cambridge University Press, 1990), 112, and Robert Putnam, Making Democracy Work: Civic Traditions in Modern Italy (Princeton, N.J.: Princeton University Press, 1993), 179–81.

6. Dhu al-Nun Ayyub, al-Yadd wa-l-Ard wa-l-Maʾ [The Hand, Earth, and Water] (Baghdad: Matbaʿat al-Shafiq, 1970 [1939]).

7. Hanna Batatu, The Old Social Classes and Revolutionary Movements of Iraq (Princeton, N.J.: Princeton University Press, 1978), 326.

8. Faleh Abdel Jabar aptly refers to the tribes during this period as "mobile mini-states commanding military might, substantial pastures, and the ability to extract tribute from settled areas." "Shaykhs and Ideologues: Detribalization and Retribalization in Iraq, 1968–1998," Middle East Report 215, vol. 30, no. 2 (Summer 2000): 28.

9. For an excellent analysis of the crisis, see Sami Zubaida, "Contested Nations: Iraq and the Assyrians," Nations & Nationalism 6, no. 3 (Summer 2000): 363–82.

10. Albert Hourani, Minorities in the Arab World (Oxford: Oxford University Press, 1947), 99.

11. Mohammed A. Tarbush, The Role of the Military in Politics: A Case Study of Iraq to 1941 (London: Kegan Paul International, 1982), 76.

12. Ibid., 83.

13. al-Shaʿbiya, which roughly translates as "populism," was meant to convey a political perspective grounded in the interests of the common people. See Mudhaffar Abdullah Amin, "Jamaat al-Ahali: Its Origin, Ideology, and Role in Iraqi Politics, 1932–1946," Ph.D. diss, School of Oriental Studies, Durham University, 1980, 116–23.

14. A key motivation for Sulayman's participation in the coup was his anger at Yasin al-Hashimi's failure to include him in his cabinet. Sulayman feared that al-Hashimi's boast that "he would remain in power ten years" meant that he would be excluded from politics for an extended period of time.

15. Batatu, The Old Social Classes, 439–40.

16. Amin, "Jamaat al-Ahali," 167.

17. Ibid., 171.

18. Tarbush, *The Role of the Military*, 138–39, 257–58 n. 72.

19. Ibid., 139.

20. Amin, "Jamaat al-Ahali," 190.

21. Ambassador Clark Kerr (Baghdad) to Secretary of State for Foreign Affairs, Apr. 1, 1936, FO 371/20014/E7147, as cited in Amin, "Jamaat al-Ahali," 184.

22. Amin, "Jamaat al-Ahali," 173.

23. The regime's four most prominent members were considered political outsiders by Pan-Arabists. Sidqi was of Kurdish origins, Sulayman was of Turkish extraction, Abu Timman was Shi'i, and Kamil al-Chadirji was from a very old Baghdadi family of Persian descent.

24. Khadduri, *Independent Iraq*, 141.

25. For the text of this reform program, see Tarbush, *The Role of the Military*, Appendix II, 191–95.

26. For a Ba'thist perspective, see Fadil Barak (al-Takriti), *Dawr al-Jaysh al-'Iraqi fi Hukumat al-Difa' al-Watani wa-l-Harb ma' Britaniya Sanat 1941 [The Role of the Iraqi Army in the National Defense Government and the 1941 War with Britain]* (Baghdad: al-Dar al-'Arabiya li-l-Tiba'a, 1979). See also Batatu, *The Old Social Classes*, 298–99, 453–62, and Khadduri, *Independent Iraq*, 221–35.

27. Batatu, *The Old Social Classes*, 345.

28. For a sympathetic portrait of al-Sab'awi, see Khaldun S. al-Husry (Sati' al-Husari's son), "The Political Ideas of Yunis Al-Sab'awi," in *Intellectual Life in the Arab East, 1890–1935*, ed. Marwan R. Buheiry (Beirut: American University of Beirut Press, 1981), 165–75.

29. Hayyim J. Cohen, "The Anti-Jewish *Farhûd* in Baghdad, 1941," *Middle Eastern Studies* 3, no. 1 (1966): 2–17.

30. Even al-Sabbagh criticizes his fellow colonels of the Golden Square for their lack of nerve in fighting the British to the end. See *Fursan al-'Uruba fi-l-'Iraq [The Knights of Arabism in Iraq]* (Damascus: al-Shabab al-'Arabi, 1956), 22. This book lists as its publisher "al-Shabab al-'Arabi," which simply means "the Arab youth."

31. Karl Deutsch, "Social Mobilization and Political Development," *American Political Science Review* 55 (Sept. 1961): 494; Benedict Anderson, *Imagined Communities: Reflections on the Origins of Nationalism* (London: Verso, 1983).

32. For an analysis of the new artisan organizations and the Union of Artisan Organizations, see Kamal Mazhar Ahmad, *al-Tabaqa al-'Amila al-'Iraqiya: al-Takkawun wa Bidayat al-Taharruk [The Iraqi Working Class: Its Formation and Early Activities]* (Baghdad: Dar al-Rashid li-l-Nashr, 1981), 127–54.

33. Fahim Qubain, *Education and Science in the Arab World* (Baltimore, Md.: Johns Hopkins Press, 1966), 258, 261, 273–74, 276.

34. Sati' al-Husari notes that one of the main agitators for al-Nusuli's dismissal was Ja'far al-Shabibi, the brother of Shaykh Rida al-Shabibi. *Mudhakkirati fi-l-'Iraq [My Memoirs of Iraq]* (Beirut: Dar al-Tal'ia, 1967), 1: 564.

35. This influence should not be exaggerated. The director-general of education, who was a civil servant and not a political appointee, represented the real power in the education system because he remained in office far longer than the various ministers of education, whose tenures were usually brief. Most of these civil servants, such as Satiʿ al-Husari, were Sunni Arabs.

36. Indeed, al-Husari includes passages from al-Nusuli's study *al-Dawla al-Umawiya fi-l-Sham [The Umayyad State in the Levant]*, which contain statements unfavorable to the Shiʿa. See *Mudhakkirati*, 560.

37. Dr. Mohammed Baqir Alwan notes that when he was growing up in Baghdad during the 1940s neither he nor his schoolmates were aware of sectarian differences. Personal conversation with the author, June 19, 1998.

38. al-Husari, *Mudhakkirati*, 566.

39. Amin, "Jamaat al-Ahali," 314–16.

40. These parties were the al-Hizb al-Watani al-Dimuqrati (National Democratic Party), Hizb al-Shaʿb (People's Party), and Hizb al-Ittihad al-Watani (National Unionist Party). Kamil al-Chadirji controlled the NDP, which became the most powerful of the three factions, while his rival within the Ahali Group, ʿAbd al-Fattah Ibrahim, controlled the People's Party. The most leftist was the National Unionist Party, which was controlled by ʿAziz al-Sharif, who later joined the ICP.

41. At this time, sectarian identities were still relatively fluid in relationship to the Iraqist nationalist–Pan-Arabist cleavage. One indicator was that al-Kubba was a Shiʿi and ardent Pan-Arabist. The Iraqi branch of the Pan-Arabist Baʿth Party, which would be formed in 1952, was dominated until 1961 by Shiʿis under Fuʾad al-Rikabi's leadership.

42. Faʾiq Butti, *al-Sihafa al-Yasariya fi-l-ʿIraq [Leftist Journalism in Iraq]* (London: n.p., 1985), 23, 52–53.

43. On the development of the short story, see ʿAbd al-Ilah Ahmad, *Nashʾat al-Qissa al-Qasira fi-l-ʿIraq [The Origins of the Short Story in Iraq]*, 2 vols. (Baghdad: Matbaʿat al-Shafiq, 1966); and Muhsin Jassim al-Musawi, "The Sociopolitical Context of the Iraqi Short Story, 1908–1968," in *Statecraft in the Middle East: Oil, Historical Memory and Popular Culture*, ed. Eric Davis and Nicolas Gavrielides (Miami: Florida International University Press / University Presses of Florida, 1991), 202–27.

44. For a more detailed discussion of this issue, see Eric Davis, "The Museum and the Politics of Social Control in Modern Iraq," in *Commemorations: The Politics of Memory and Identity*, ed. John Gillis (Princeton, N.J.: Princeton University Press, 1994), 89–110.

45. In *Fursan al-ʿUruba* (262), al-Sabbagh notes as he crossed into Republican Turkey when fleeing from the British that he envied the Turks that no foreign forces occupied their country.

46. al-Sabbagh, *Fursan al-ʿUruba*, 14–25.

47. Although they do not represent the origins of Pan-Arabist thinking in Iraq, al-Sabbagh's memoirs strongly influenced the particularly chauvinist form of Pan-Arabism that later characterized the Takriti Baʿth. Clearly Pan-Arabism

existed well before 1941. However, Faysal's Pan-Arabism maintained the possibility of political participation of most, if not all, of Iraqi society. This contrasts sharply with al-Sabbagh and the Takriti Ba'thists.

48. Nuri al-Sa'id, for example, knew five languages—Arabic Turkish, English, French, and German—as a result of his educational background and travels.

49. For the links between the Four Colonels and the al-Muthanna Club, see Batatu, *The Old Social Classes*, 299–300.

50. The first German mission to the Ottoman Empire arrived in Istanbul in 1872. In an interview in Baghdad on June 20, 1984, the late director of the Iraqi National Library and prominent folklorist 'Abd al-Hamid al-Alwaji emphasized the importance of German thought to the development of Pan-Arabist thought in Iraq.

51. See Kamil al-Chadirji, *Mudhakkirat Kamil al-Chadirji wa Tarikh al-Hizb al-Watani al-Dimuqrati [The Memoirs of Kamil al-Chadirji and the History of the National Democratic Party]* (Beirut: Dar al-Tal'ia, 1970), and *Min Awraq Kamil al-Chadirji [From the Private Papers of Kamil al-Chadirji]* (Beirut: Dar al-Tal'ia, 1971); and Rifat Chadirji, *The Photography of Kamil Chadirji* (Surrey: LAAM, 1991). Kamil al-Chadirji's son Rifat Chadirji, an internationally respected architect and Saddam Husayn's architectural consultant for Baghdad city planning in 1981–82, relates that his father was not interested in Arab history or Arabic literature but preferred instead reading anthropological, archaeological, and scientific studies. Interview, Surrey, England, Jan. 20, 2000. At the same time, it should be noted that al-Chadirji's sensitive and beautiful photographs as compiled by his son Rifat are of Iraq and the Mashriq.

52. See the writings of Yusif Salman Yusif (Fahd), *Kitabat al-Rafiq Fahd [The Writings of Comrade Fahd]* (Baghdad: al-Tariq al-Jadid; Beirut: Dar al-Farabi, 1976). None of the articles, including a short piece on cultural struggle ("al-Kifah al-Fikri," pp. 230–34), deals with literary or cultural developments inside Iraq.

53. Muhammad 'Awayd al-Dulaymi, *Kamil al-Chadirji wa Dawruhu fi-l-Siyasa al-'Iraqiya, 1898–1968 [Kamil al-Chadirji and His Role in Iraqi Politics, 1898–1968]* (Baghdad: al-Adib Press, 1997), 18–19.

54. See Qasim's director-general of the Ministry of Guidance and director of Broadcasting Dhu al-Nun Ayyub's vigorous defense of the Qasim regime in his polemical work *Li-l-Haqiqa wa-l-Tarikh [For Truth and History]* (Baghdad: al-Sharika al-Wataniya li-l-Tiba'a wa-l-'Alan, 1962). Ayyub argued that Qasim's support of the Palestinian, Algerian, and South Yemen causes were all indicators of his support for Pan-Arab concerns.

55. Gramsci defines "war of position" as the process that must precede any successful revolutionary change in which those who are needed to support the revolution become convinced of the legitimacy of the proposed new order. See Antonio Gramsci, *Selections from the Prison Notebooks* (London: Lawrence & Wishart, 1971), 238.

CHAPTER 4. MEMORY, THE INTELLIGENTSIA,
AND THE ANTINOMIES OF CIVIL SOCIETY, 1945–1958

1. Although workers had formally received this right in 1944, only in 1946 under the Tawfiq al-Suwaydi ministry were they able to exercise it effectively.

2. Rifat Chadirji, *al-Ukhaydir wa-l-Qasr al-Balluri: Nushu° al-Nathariya al-Jadiliya fi-l-°Amara [al-Ukhaydir and the Crystal Palace: The Development of a Dialectical Theory of Architecture]* (London: Riad El-Rayyes Books, 1991), 103.

3. On developments in Iraqi architecture, see ibid., esp. 248–64, 382–432.

4. Although there had been a number of excavations in Iraq prior to World War II, it was only after the war that these efforts assumed an institutionalized form in *Sumer*, which promoted increased contact with foreign archaeological missions and the study of Iraqi archaeology at Baghdad University under Professor Tahir Baqir's leadership.

5. Terry DeYoung, *Placing the Poet: Badr Shakir al-Sayyab and Post-Colonial Iraq* (Albany: State University of New York Press, 1998), 221–40.

6. A good indication of the loss of legitimacy was the resigned attitude that characterized °Abd al-Ilah's responses to reports by informers of military plots against the monarchy during the year before the July 1958 Revolution. Despite being described as having a personality that was "strong even to the point of being fierce" *(qasiyan ila hadd al-sharasa)*, °Abd al-Ilah refused to order his palace guard to defend the royal family on the morning of July 14th. Instead, he sued for safe passage from the country, indicating that he was well aware that the monarchy no longer possessed any institutional future in Iraq. See Sulayman al-Takriti, *al-Wasi °Abd al-Ilah bin °Ali Yabhathu °an °Arsh, 1939–1953 [The Regent °Abd al-Ilah in Search of a Throne, 1939–1953]* (Beirut: al-Dar al-°Arabiya li-l-Mawsu°at, 1988), 15; Elie Kedourie, *Arabic Political Memoirs and Other Studies* (London: Frank Cass, 1974), 179–81.

7. Indeed, in the aftermath of the 1963 overthrow of Qasim, the Ba°th Party's paramilitary unit, the National Guard (al-Haras al-Qawmi), went on a rampage that led to the death or imprisonment of more than three thousand communists and suspected leftist sympathizers. These events are discussed in greater detail in chapter 5.

8. One might compare the production of the 1950s to that of the late 1970s and 1980s, which directly served the state by vilifying Otherness, particularly those of Persian heritage (al-°Ajam). This was especially true of the short stories published in *al-Tali°a al-Adabiya [The Literary Vanguard]*, a journal published by the Ministry of Culture and Information, which focused on the Iran-Iraq War, which the Ba°thist regime referred to as "Saddam's Qadisiya" in an attempt to focus historical memory on the defeat of the Sasanians by Arab forces in Mesopotamia in 637 C.E.

9. DeYoung, *Placing the Poet*, 265–67.

10. Hanna Batatu, *The Old Social Classes and Revolutionary Movements of Iraq* (Princeton, N.J., Princeton University Press, 1978), 553.

11. The British Labor Advisor, reporting on May 14, 1948, to the Baghdad

Embassy on the strike of workers at the K3 (al-Haditha) and K2 (Baiji) pumping stations, remarked, "The view of the present strikes . . . held by Station Superintendents and Security Officers is that they are not genuine industrial dispute, but a disciplined subversive movement, planned and directed by the Iraqi Communist Party." The strike leaders included "a fanatic," "a communist Zionist," two Christians, and a Muslim. FO 371/68479.

12. Mahmud Shabib, *Wathba fi-l-ʿIraq wa Suqut Salih Jabr [The Wathba of 1948 and the Fall of Salih Jabr]* (Baghdad: Dar al-Thaqafa, 1988), 17.

13. Ibid., 13, 18–19.

14. Even in 1924, nationalist groups had demonstrated outside the Iraqi parliament against the British-inspired law creating the new Iraqi parliament and voting system.

15. Although Jabr led the Iraqi negotiating delegation as prime minister, he was accompanied by Nuri al-Saʿid and Fadil al-Jamali.

16. For the text of these discussions, see Shabib, *Wathba fi-l-ʿIraq*, 29–43.

17. The Arabic title of the organization was al-Dubbat al-Wataniyun. See Khalil Ibrahim Husayn, *ʿAbd al-Karim Qasim: al-Lughz al-Muhayyar [ʿAbd al-Karim Qasim: The Perplexing Riddle]*, vol. 6 of *Mawsuʿat Thawrat 14 Tammuz [Encyclopedia of the July 14th Revolution]* (Baghdad: Dar al-Hurriya li-l-Tibaʿa, 1989), 65.

18. Shabib, *Wathba fi-l-Iraq*, 8.

19. The statements of member of the Free Officers organizations in both Egypt and Iraq immediately following the successful overthrow of their respective monarchies indicate that the defeat in Palestine was one of the prime motivating factors behind the revolts.

20. Husayn, *ʿAbd al-Karim Qasim*, 32.

21. Ibid., 65.

22. On this issue, see Avi Schlaim, *Collusion Across the Jordan: King Abdullah, the Zionist Movement, and the Partition of Palestine* (Oxford: Clarendon Press, 1988).

23. Batatu, *The Old Social Classes*, 598–99.

24. Reeva S. Simon, *Iraq Between the Two World Wars* (New York: Columbia University Press, 1986), 192, n. 80; and Hayyim J. Cohen, "The Anti-Jewish *Farhûd* in Baghdad, 1941," *Middle Eastern Studies* 3, no. 1 (1966): 5.

25. FO 371/68482/6116, British Labor Advisor, "Provisional Recommendations: Cost of Living."

26. FO 371/68459/611714, Basra Consulate-General: Monthly Summary, Sept. 1948.

27. FO 371/68459/611714, Basra Consulate-General: Monthly Summary, Dec. 1947. It should be noted that the British considered the election of Ades by the Basra Jewish community as its head unwise because he was already under suspicion for having Zionist sympathies.

28. FO 371/68459/611714.

29. FO 371/68459/611714, Basra Consulate-General: Monthly Summary, Sept. 1948.

30. Indeed, Dr. Mohammed Baqir Alwan, an Iraqi scholar who teaches at Tufts University, informed me that during the 1950s, when he was attending secondary school in Baghdad, the terms Sunni and Shi'i were never used by students in any derogatory manner. Interview, Tufts University, June 19, 1998.

31. Baqir Muhammad Jawad al-Zujaji, *al-Riwaya al-'Iraqiya wa Qadiyat al-Rif [The Iraqi Novel and the Agrarian Question]* (Baghdad: Ministry of Culture and Information, Dar al-Rashid li-l-Nashr, 1983), 13.

32. It is interesting to note the similarities between the structure of Pan-Arabist thought and that of later Islamist thought developed by Sayyid Qutb and his followers in the so-called Islamic Groups (al-Jama'at al-Islamiya) in Egypt. In both contexts, the emphasis is on the besieged quality and cultural impurity caused by exogenous influences, particularly those of the West and non-Sunni groups, whether the Shi'a or minorities in the Iraqi case or minorities such as the Copts in the Egyptian case. See Qutb, *Mu'alim fi-l-Tariq [Signposts Along the Path]* (Cairo: n.p., 1965).

33. DeYoung, *Placing the Poet*, 194–95.

34. This concern with overcoming fragmentation perhaps helps to explain why al-Sayyab left the ICP. The imputation by other party members that he was unable to comprehend Marxism because of his "petty bourgeois" background no doubt added to his ultimate alienation from the party. See DeYoung, *Placing the Poet*, 196.

35. For his discussion of the social dimension of language, see Ludwig Wittgenstein, *Philosophical Investigations*, 3d ed. (London: MacMillan, 1953), sections 256–80, 91e–97e.

36. Abdul-Salaam Yacoob Yousif, "Vanguardist Cultural Practices: The Formation of an Alternative Cultural Hegemony in Iraq and Chile, 1930s–1970s," Ph.D. diss., University of Iowa, 1988, 126.

37. Ja'far 'Abbas Humaydi discusses the retreat of Ba'thist-led protestors against the May 1958 parliamentary elections to the al-Baladiya Coffeehouse following the end of their demonstrations. Humaydi, *al-Tatawwurat wa-l-Ittijahat al-Siyasiya al-Dhakhilya fi-l-'Iraq, 1953–1958 [The Development of Domestic Political Tendencies in Iraq, 1953–1958]* (Baghdad: Baghdad University Press, 1980), 265.

38. This term has generally been used in the twentieth century throughout the Arab world to refer to educated people of modest economic means. Becoming an effendi entailed shedding traditional rural clothing and becoming associated with white-collar employment rather than with manual labor. A good example of this persona is the character Muhammad Effendi in 'Abd al-Rahman al-Sharqawi's *al-Ard*, translated by Desmond Stewart as *The Egyptian Earth* (Austin: University of Texas Press, 1990).

39. Humaydi, *al-Tatawwurat wa-l-Ittijahat al-Siyassiya*, 194–210, 215.

40. Fa'iq Butti, *al-Sihafa al-Yasariya fi-l-'Iraq [Leftist Journalism in Iraq]* (London: n.p., 1985), 107–9.

41. Humaydi, *al-Tatawwurat wa-l-Ittijahat al-Siyassiya*, 144, 162, 164, 166, describes how the Iraqi Lawyers' Syndicate expressed support for the Al-

gerian Revolution, the Iraqi Women's Union (Ittihad al-Nisaʾ al-ʿIraqi) called for volunteers to fight for Egypt, and engineering, medical, pharmacy chemistry, and dental students organized large demonstrations against the Tripartite Invasion.

42. *"Majallat al-tafkir al-ʿilmi wa-l-thaqafa al-hurra"*; Butti, *al-Sihafa al-Yasariya*, 115.

43. See, for example, Republic of Iraq, "Yawm al-Nisaʾ al-ʿAlami, 8 Idhar" [International Women's Day, March 8], in *Min Kitabat al-Rafiq Fahd [From the Writings of Comrade Fahd]* (Baghdad: al-Tariq al-Jadid; Beirut: Dar al-Farabi, 1976), 407–13. This essay was originally published in *al-Qaʿida*, Aug. 9–11, 1944.

44. Humaydi, *al-Tatawwurat wa-l-Ittijahat al-Siyassiya*, 88.

45. Rifat Chadirji, *The Photography of Kamil Chadirji* (London: LAAM, 1991).

46. See Samir ʿAbd al-Karim, *Adwaʾ ʿala al-Haraka al-Shuyuʿiya fi-l-ʿIraq [Insights into the Communist Movement in Iraq]*, 5 vols. (Beirut: Dar al-Mirsad, 197?–1979). This volume was apparently secretly compiled by the Iraqi Baʿth Party and published in Beirut. One of the Baʿth's main ideologues and propagandists, Fadil al-Barak (al-Takriti), and former ICP member Malik Sayf provided al-Karim with documents for the volume. Interview with Isam al-Khafaji, New York University, Nov. 16, 1999.

47. Muhammad ʿAwayd al-Dulaymi, *Kamil al-Chadirji wa Dawruhu fi-l-Siyasa al-ʿIraqiya, 1898–1968 [Kamil al-Chadirji and His Role in Iraqi Politics, 1898–1968]* (Baghdad: al-Adib Press, 1997), 154. This study was originally a doctoral dissertation. al-Dulaymi studied for his B.A. and M.A. degrees at Baghdad University with Jaʿfar Humaydi, who wrote the introduction to his volume.

48. Ibid., 156.

49. Ibid., 190, 196.

50. Humaydi, *al-Tatawwurat wa-l-Ittijahat al-Siyassiya*, 94; FO 371/110989/80978, British Embassy, Bagdad, to P. S. Falla, Levant Department, Foreign Office, May 19, 1954.

51. Batatu notes that the party was based upon tribal shaykhs, whose control over the rural political economy was, by the late 1940s, in serious decline. That the system of tribal shaykh–landlords was already moribund during the late 1940s is interesting in light of Saddam Husayn's efforts to revive tribalism during the 1990s following the 1991 Gulf War and Intifada. Batatu, *The Old Social Classes*, 104.

52. Batatu and al-Dulaymi assert that the National Front won eleven seats, and the former United States ambassador Waldemar Gallman claims that it won fourteen seats, but al-Humaydi puts the total at ten, including Kamil al-Chadirji and Dhu al-Nun Ayyub. See Humaydi, *al- Tatawwurat wa-l-Ittijahat al-Siyassiya*, 93; Batatu, *The Old Social Classes*, 686; al-Dulaymi, *Kamil al-Chadirji*, 183; and Gallman, *Iraq Under General Nuri: My Recollections of Nuri al-Said, 1954–1958* (Baltimore, Md.: Johns Hopkins Press, 1964), 4.

53. Gallman, *Iraq Under General Nuri*, 4; Batatu, *The Old Social Classes*, 686.

54. Batatu, *The Old Social Classes*, 761.

55. Ibid., 759.

56. Humaydi, *al-Tatawwurat wa-l-Ittijahat al-Siyassiya*, 239.

57. For a discussion of the National Front and its platform, see Batatu, *The Old Social Classes*, 758–63; Humaydi, *al-Tatawwurat wa-l-Ittijahat al-Siyassiya*, 236–42; and al-Dulaymi, *Kamil al-Chadirji*, 179. Batatu, Humaydi, and al-Dulaymi agree that Muhammad Hadid and Fu'ad al-Rikabi represented the NDP and the Ba'th Party, respectively, but they disagree on who represented the ICP and the Independence Party. Batatu mentions 'Aziz al-Shaykh and Muhammad Mahdi al-Kubba as the representatives, while Humaydi and al-Dulaymi assert that Jamal al-Haydari and Sadiq Shanshal represented the ICP and the Independence Party. See Batatu, *The Old Social Classes*, 763; Humaydi, *al-Tatawwurat wa-l-Ittijahat al-Siyassiya*, 240; and al-Dulaymi, *Kamil Chadirji*, 180.

58. Humaydi, *al-Tatawwurat wa-l-Ittijahat al-Siyassiya*, 345–48.

59. For an analysis of 'Abd al-Ilah's final years as crown prince (his position after the investiture of King Faysal II in 1953), see al-Takriti, *al-Wasi 'Abd al-Ilah*.

60. Elie Kedourie, *Arabic Political Memoirs and Other Studies* (London: Frank Cass, 1974), 181.

61. Yousif, "Vanguardist Cultural Practices," 200–201; Humaydi, *al-Tatawwurat wa-l-Ittijahat al-Siyassiya*, 313.

62. Directorate-General of Propaganda, *Iraq Today* (Baghdad: Ministry of Interior, 1953).

63. Ibid., 47. The *Army Journal* was described as "a liberal source of military knowledge on a variety of service topics."

64. Stephen Hemsley Longrigg and Frank Stoakes, *Iraq* (London: Ernest Benn, 1958), 78.

65. Ibid., 168–69.

66. Numerous strikes in the oil fields, including an especially long and violent strike in Kirkuk in 1946, demonstrated both the power of labor solidarity and its potential to severely harm Iraq's oil industry, its main source of foreign revenue. See my "Utopia From Below: The Inclusionary Discourse of the Iraqi Working Class," paper delivered at the Rutgers Center for Historical Analysis, Rutgers University, Mar. 22, 2000.

67. For a sense of the tremendous power wielded by tribal shaykhs in their rural domains *(al-dira)*, see Dhu al-Nun Ayyub's novel, the first about Iraqi peasant life, *al-Yadd wa-l-Ard wa-l-Ma' [The Hand, Earth, and Water]*, 2d ed. (Baghdad: Matba'at al-Shafiq, 1970 [1939]). For a critique of Ayyub's approach to rural life, see al-Zujaji, *al-Riwaya al-'Iraqiya*, esp. 76–78.

CHAPTER 5. THE CRUCIBLE

1. For a recent study that adopts this perspective, see Malik Mufti, *Sovereign Creations: Pan-Arabism and Political Order in Syria and Iraq* (Ithaca, N.Y.:

Cornell University Press, 1996). For a government-sponsored study that focuses on the negative impact of the personalities of ʿAbd al-Karim Qasim and ʿAbd al-Salam ʿArif on the revolution, see Muhammad Husayn al-Zubaydi, *Thawrat 14 Tammuz 1958 fi-l-ʿIraq [The July 14, 1958 Revolution in Iraq]* (Baghdad: Ministry of Culture and Information, Daʾirat al-Shuʾun al-Thaqafiya wa-l-Nashr, 1983).

2. Satiʿ al-Husari's efforts in the 1920s to use the education system to instill in Iraqi youth a Pan-Arabist orientation and the tentative efforts of the Hashimite Monarchy to mobilize historical memory as a means of legitimating the new regime were of a different scale. First, al-Husari's activities were limited to the realm of education and often at odds with his supposed superior, the minister of education, who was customarily a Shiʿi. Second, Hashimite efforts at restructuring historical memory were largely limited to the reign of Faysal I and, to a lesser extent, that of his son Ghazi, and at any rate were sporadic at best. Finally, much of what was published on archaeology, music, and the arts after ʿAbd al-Ilah was appointed regent in 1941 was in English, not Arabic, indicating that its target audience was in the West rather than the Arab world.

3. In the government's annual publication celebrating the July 1958 Revolution, many of the Ministry of Guidance's activities described are in the broadcasting field. See, for example, Republic of Iraq, Ministry of Guidance, *al-Lajna al-ʿUlya li Ihtifalat Thawrat ʿArbaʿta ʿashara Tammuz fi ʿAmiha al-Awal, al-Thani wa-l-Thalith [Higher Committee for Celebrating the July 14th Revolution in its First, Second, and Third Years]* (Baghdad: Ministry of Guidance and al-Rabita Press, 1959, 1960, 1961). For a description of the Ministry of Guidance and its staff, see Directorate of Scientific Education, *Dalil al-Jumhuriya al-ʿIraqiya li Sanat 1960 [Guide to the Iraqi Republic for the Year 1960]* (Baghdad: Ministry of Guidance, 1960), 635–38. I would like to thank Dr. Salih J. Altoma for drawing my attention to this reference.

4. I would note that a number of Iraqi scholars, the most notable of whom was the noted Iraqi folklorist ʿAbd al-Hamid al-ʿAlwaji, former director of the Iraqi National Library (al-Maktaba al-Wataniya al-ʿIraqiya), emphasized the pre–World War I influence of German understandings of folklore on Iraqi conceptions. Undoubtedly, this influence was transmitted through the Ottoman Empire as a result of its ties with imperial Germany. The German uses of folklore in state building and similar efforts in Iraq still await a comparative study. Interview, Iraqi National Library, Baghdad, June 14, 1984.

5. It has been argued that ʿArif actually removed his revolver from its holster during a meeting with Qasim as part of an assassination attempt. ʿArif subsequently argued that this was just an emotional outburst that reflected no threat to Qasim.

6. Of course, the second Baʿthist regime of Saddam Husayn sought to argue that Iraq's ancient populations were in fact of Semitic origins as well.

7. The ethnic narrative is closely associated with the writings of the late Elie Kedourie, Uriel Dann, and the former United States ambassador to Iraq, Waldemar Gallman. See Elie Kedourie, *The Chatham House Version and Other*

Middle Eastern Studies (New York: Praeger, 1970), *Arabic Political Memoirs and Other Studies* (London: Frank Cass, 1974), *Democracy and Arab Political Culture* (Washington, D.C.: Washington Institute for Near East Policy, 1992), and *Politics in the Middle East* (Oxford: Oxford University Press, 1992), esp. 317–25; Uriel Dann, *Iraq Under Qassem* (New York: Praeger, 1969); and Waldemar Gallman, *Iraq Under General Nuri: My Recollections of Nuri al-Said, 1954–1958* (Baltimore, Md.: Johns Hopkins Press, 1964).

8. Khalil Ibrahim Husayn, *al-Sira'at Bayn 'Abd al-Karim Qasim wa-l-Shuyu'iyin wa Rifa't al-Hajj Sirri wa-l-Qawmiyin [The Conflicts Between 'Abd al-Karim Qasim, the Communists, Rifa't al-Hajj Sirri and the Pan-Arab Nationalists]*, vol. 3 of *Mawsu'at 14 Tammuz [Encyclopedia of the July 14th Revolution]* (Baghdad: Dar al-Hurriya li-l-Tiba'a, 1988).

9. Although United States support for the coup has never been definitively established, much circumstantial evidence lends weight to this assertion, not the least of which is the comment by the coup's leader, 'Ali Salih al-Sa'di, that "we arrived on an American train." 'Abd al-Khaliq Husayn, "al-Za'im 'Abd al-Karim Qasim wa-l-Mawdu'a al-Dimuqratiya" [The Leader 'Abd al-Karim Qasim and the Question of Democracy], *al-Mawsim* 32 (1997): 121.

10. See Falih 'Abd al-Jabbar, *al-Dawla al-Mujtama' al-Madani wa-l-Tahawwul al-Dimuqrati fi-l-'Iraq [The State, Civil Society and the Democratic Transition in Iraq]* (Cairo: Ibn al-Khaldun Center and Dar al-Amin li-l-Nashr wa-l-Tawzi', 1995).

11. Husayn, "al-Za'im 'Abd al-Karim Qasim," 105.

12. Hasan al-'Alawi, *al-Shi'a wa-l-Dawla al-Qawmiya fi-l-'Iraq [The Shi'a and the National State in Iraq]* (Paris: CEDI Press, 1989).

13. The focus on personalities dominated studies of Iraqi politics during the prerevolution period as well, when the most prominent and powerful leaders—Faysal I, the regent (and later crown prince) 'Abd al-Ilah, and especially Nuri al-Sa'id—became the focus of political analysis, in both Arabic and Western texts. Of course, the emphasis on personalities continued in the contemporary era in the form of excessive focus on Saddam Husayn. There are important exceptions to this generalization. Hanna Batatu's study, *The Old Social Classes and Revolutionary Movements of Iraq* (Princeton, N.J.: Princeton University Press, 1978), which covers modern Iraqi politics from the early 1900s to the late 1970s, and the study by Marion Farouk-Sluglett and Peter Sluglett, *Iraq Since 1958: From Revolution to Dictatorship* (London: I. B. Tauris, 1990), are among the most prominent examples of works that adopt a historical and conceptual approach.

14. Dalir Mustafa, "Milaff al-Za'im 'Abd al-Karim Qasim" [The File of the Leader 'Abd al-Karim Qasim], *al-Mawsim* 32 (1997): 48; Hamza al-Hasan, "Insafan li Rajil wa-l-Tarikh: Man Qatal al-Za'im?" [Justice for a Man and History: Who Killed the Leader?], *al-Mawsim* 32 (1997): 140.

15. Batatu, *The Old Social Classes*, 981; Dann, *Iraq Under Qassem*, 356.

16. Batatu, *The Old Social Classes*, 977–78, 981; interview with Dr. Isam al-Khafaji, New York University, Nov. 16, 1999.

17. This is a term used by Baqir Muhammad Jawad al-Zujaji, *al-Riwaya al-ʿIraqiya wa Qadiyat al-Rif [The Iraqi Novel and the Agrarian Question]* (Baghdad: Ministry of Culture and Information, 1980), 13.

18. ʿAlaʾ al-Din al-Thahir, "al-Jawanib al-Ijabiya fi ʿAhd wa Shakhsiyat al-Fariq al-Rukn ʿAbd al-Karim Qasim" [The Positive Dimensions of the Era and Personality of Staff Brigadier ʿAbd al-Karim Qasim], *al-Mawsim* 32 (1997): 82–84.

19. Dhu al-Nun Ayyub, *Li-l-Haqiqa wa-l-Tarikh: Jumhuriyat 14 Tammuz wa Mufajjir Thawratihi wa Ibn al-Shaʿb al-Barr ʿAbd al-Karim Qasim [For the Sake of Truth and History: The July 14ᵗʰ Republic and the Creator of its Revolution and Devoted Son of the People ʿAbd al-Karim Qasim]* (Baghdad: al-Sharika al-Wataniya li-l-Tibaʿa wa-l-ʿAlan, n.d.), 37. Although no official date of publication is given, the author states on p. 4 that the revolution is now into its fourth year, clearly establishing 1962 as the date of publication.

20. Mustafa, "Milaff al-Zaʿim," 49

21. Telephone conversation with the late Dr. Fadil al-Jamali in Tunis, June 20, 1995.

22. Qasim purportedly asked Salim to add his figure to the sculpture but the artist refused. The monarchy would not have tolerated such behavior, while under the Takriti Baʿth such refusal would have undoubtedly led the artist to prison or the execution chamber. Samir al-Khalil, *The Monument: Art, Vulgarity and Responsibility in Iraq* (Berkeley: University of California Press, 1991), 82.

23. Muhammad ʿAwayd al-Dulaymi, *Kamil al-Chadirji wa Dawruhu fi-l-Siyasa al-ʿIraqiya, 1898–1968 [Kamil al-Chadirji and His Role in Iraqi Politics, 1898–1968]* (Baghdad: al-Adib Press, 1997), 279.

24. The origins and development of the Free Officers Organization in Iraq is still shrouded in considerable mystery. What seems likely is that during the late 1940s a number of parallel organizations stimulated by the Arab defeat in Palestine, the unsuccessful attempt to conclude the Portsmouth Treaty, the 1948 Wathba, the 1952 Intifada, and especially the Egyptian Revolution of July 1952 began to develop, and that many of these groups maintained varying levels of contact and coordination. Qasim claims to have headed a separate organization formed in 1953 or 1954. The invitation to join the Free Officers officially extended to him in 1956 seems to have been inspired by his seniority within the officers corps and the reputation that he established as a forceful and competent general in the Iraqi army's campaign in Palestine. See Husayn, *al-Lughz al-Muhayyar*, 60–70.

25. Leonard Binder, "Political Recruitment and Participation in Egypt," in *Political Parties and Political Development*, ed. Joseph LaPalombara and Myron Weiner (Princeton, N.J.: Princeton University Press, 1966), esp. 234–40; and "Egypt: The Integrative Revolution," in *Political Culture and Political Development*, ed. Lucian W. Pye and Sidney Verba (Princeton, N.J.: Princeton University Press, 1965), 419–49.

26. Although it might be argued that Pan-Arabist ministers such as Faʾiq al-Samarrʾi and Sadiq Shanshal would have resigned in any event given Qasim's

refusal to unite with Egypt, there still would have remained a respected core of politicians that could have been used as a political bridge to prodemocratic forces (a small but influential group) in Iraqi society.

27. This assertion may seem to run counter to the argument just made that Qasim did not pursue the option of publicly airing grievances of the Shiʿa, Kurds, and other excluded groups. Undoubtedly such an effort would have been very risky and possibly opened a Pandora's box of complaints and demands on the state. It was probably precisely this fear that led Qasim instead to attempt to incrementally improve the status of heretofore excluded groups by giving them greater access to positions within the state. Nevertheless, a frontal assault on sectarianism always was and remains today an option theoretically open to the Iraqi state, especially now that the Baʿthist regime has been deposed.

28. Unlike the Takriti Baʿth after 1968, the Qasim regime did not demonstrate an interest in the rewriting of history because restructuring historical consciousness along well-defined lines was not part of the state's ideology. The leftist intellectuals who predominated in the various arms of the state concerned with cultural production seemed to have been more interested in folklore because it provided cultural and political links to the peasant masses and because it could enhance an Iraqist nationalist vision by tying together ethnic groups, all of whom could share folklore. Thus the different political strategies of the Qasim regime's Iraqist nationalism and concern with social reform and the Baʿth Party's concern with Pan-Arabism (at least in the 1970s) and the policy of ethnic exclusion help explain the different cultural focal point of each regime.

29. In Arabic, *anbaʾ* means news. Here, "information" represents a more accurate translation, given the propaganda purposes of the ministry.

30. This committee published four volumes commemorating the July 1958 Revolution. It is interesting that the first volumes, written when the Qasim regime was strong, had a strong leftist orientation, although the last volume, written in 1963, when the regime was very weak and enjoyed little public support, emphasized religious values. See Committee for the Celebration of the July 14th Revolution, *The July 14th Revolution in its First, Second, Third, and Fourth Years* (Baghdad: Matbaʿat al-Irshad and the Times Press, 1959–62).

31. For a broader discussion of the relationship of museums to historical memory, see E. Davis, "The Museum and the Politics of Social Control in Modern Iraq," in *Commemorations: The Politics of Memory and Identity,* ed. John Gillis (Princeton, N.J.: Princeton University Press, 1994), 90–104.

32. Abdul-Salaam Yousif, "The Struggle for Cultural Hegemony in Iraq," in *The Iraqi Revolution of 1958: The Old Social Classes Revisited,* ed. Robert Fernea and Wm. Roger Louis (London: I. B. Tauris, 1991), 173.

33. See, for example, Directorate General of Propaganda, *Iraq Today,* n.d., n.p.; and A Committee of Officials, *An Introduction to the Past and Present of the Kingdom of Iraq* (Baltimore, Md.: Lord Baltimore Press), 1946.

34. Ittihad al-Udabaʾ al-ʿIraqiyin, *al-Muʾtamar al-Thani li Ittihad al-Udabaʾ al-ʿIraqiyin, Huzayran, 1960 [The Second Conference of the Iraqi Writers Union, June 1960]* (Baghdad: Matbaʿat al-Nujum, 1960), 113.

35. Jabbar Audah Allawi, "Television and Film in Iraq: A Socio-Political and Cultural Study, 1946–1980," Ph.D. diss, University of Michigan, 1983, 124.

36. Ibid., 114.

37. Ibid., 115.

38. Ibid., 116.

39. Interview with Colonel Salim Fakhri, former director of broadcasting under Qasim, London, July 3, 1984.

40. For example, it did not refer for its legal basis to Qasim's July 21 declaration.

41. Khalil Ibrahim Husayn, *Thawrat al-Shawwaf fi-l-Mawsal* (Mosul) *1959: al-Siraʿat Bayn ʿAbd al-Karim Qasim wa ʿAbd al-Salam ʿArif [The Shawwaf Revolution in Mosul 1959: The Struggles Between ʿAbd al-Karim Qasim and ʿAbd al-Salam ʿArif]* (Baghdad: Dar al-Hurriya li-l-Tibaʿa, 1987), 280, vol. 1 of *Mawsuʿat 14 Tammuz [The July 14 Encyclopedia]*; Dann, *Iraq Under Qassem*, 48, notes the date of the decree as July 21.

42. Dann, *Iraq Under Qassem*, 135.

43. Yousif notes that, "So popular were the televised proceedings of the People's Court that some viewers at home or in coffee-houses would join the applause when al-Mahdawi (popularly known as *lisan al-Shaʿb*, the people's tongue) uttered a cutting epithet" ("The Struggle for Cultural Hegemony," 185). Allawi, on the other hand, notes that "The court's proceedings were fully televised and the people viewed them as if it were a theatrical performance. Others described the trials as a comedy or circus. In the end, when the young militants were put on trial, the audience's sympathies turned against the government because they could witness how unfair the court was to the accused. The program aroused bitter hatred for the Qassem regime among many viewers" ("Television and Film in Iraq," 120). It in interesting that neither Yousif nor Allawi experienced the period yet both hold strong opinions about the politics of the period. It is noteworthy that Batatu's comprehensive study of modern Iraq, which contains an extensive discussion of the Qasim era, ignores the People's Court, mentioning only in passing that Mahdawi was its head. See *The Old Social Classes*, 846.

44. Yousif, "The Struggle for Cultural Hegemony," 196, n. 34.

45. Ibid., 185; Dann, *Iraq Under Qassem*, 135.

46. Ittihad al-Udabaʾ al-ʿIraqiyin, *al-Muʾtamar al-Thani*, esp. al-Jawahiri's introductory comments, 21–26; Jamʿiyat al-Muʾallifin wa-l-Kuttab al-ʿIraqiyin, *Tafsir al-Tarikh [Historical Explanation]* (Baghdad: Maktabat al-Nahda, 1961[?]), esp. the essays by ʿAbd al-ʿAziz al-Duri, "al-Tarikh wa-l-Hadir" ("History and the Present"), 3–16; Salih Ahmad al-ʿAli, "Tafsir al-Tarikh" ("Historical Explanation"), 17–33; and Jaʿfar Husayn Khasbak, "al-Tafsir al-Marksi li-l-Tarikh" ("The Marxist Interpretation of History"), 34–55. It is noteworthy that al-Duri's arguments correspond to many of the parameters that defined Baʿthist historiography after 1968. He argues that the present cannot be comprehended without an understanding of history, that Arabs have their own unique history that separates them from other cultures and that can only be understood by

them alone, that despite the West's attempt to impose its historical narrative on the entire world there is no universal history, and that Marxists have emphasized economic factors while ignoring the importance of the past. The only area in which al-Duri differs from Ba'thist historiography is in his valorization of Islam as a critical component of Arab history and culture. However, the "rediscovery" of religion by Saddam Husayn and the Ba'th Party following the onset of the Iran-Iraq War in 1980 and especially after the 1991 Gulf War and Intifada would even vitiate this difference of interpretation.

47. Dann, *Iraq Under Qassem*, 162, n. 14.

48. Khaldun Sati' al-Husari, *Thawrat 14 Tammuz wa Haqiqat al-Shuyu'iyin fi-l-'Iraq [The July 14ᵗʰ Revolution and the Truth About the Communists in Iraq]* (Beirut: Dar al-Tal'ia li-l-Tiba'a wa-l-Nashr, 1960), 100.

49. Ibid., 101.

50. I am grateful to Dr. Isam al-Khafaji for making this point during discussions on this issue. Interview, New York University, Nov. 16, 1999.

51. See, for example, the August through October 1960 issues of *Ittihad al-Sha'b*.

52. Beirut: Dar al-Tal'ia, [1970] 1962.

53. I would like to thank Dr. Isam al-Khafaji for drawing my attention to this point. Interview, New York University, Nov. 16, 1999.

54. Although one author, Malik Mufti, has tried to argue that the Shi'a fared better in terms of political representation under Saddam and the Ba'th Party, the gradual transformation of the party into the almost exclusive domain of Saddam's tribal supporters and relatives from Takrit belies this assertion. Even when Shi'is had positions of authority in the Ba'thist regime—Sa'dun al-Hammadi, for example, was prime minister, and Na'im Haddad was speaker of the Iraqi parliament (al-Majlis al-Watani)—these positions never gave them any meaningful power. Like Tariq 'Aziz, a Chaldean Christian who was deputy prime minister, those outside Saddam's circle always played to his fiddle. This is as much a statement about the tribal and familial base of Saddam's regime as it is about sectarian discrimination. Trust did not transcend sectarian boundaries, not because of some fatal flaw in a primordial "Iraqi national character," but rather because the Takriti Ba'th self-consciously opted for a regime of political rule in which the institutions of civil society—institutions that would facilitate such cross-ethnic alliances as they have done in the past—were brutally repressed. See Falih 'Abd al-Jabbar, *al-Dawla, al-Mujtama' al-Madani wa-l-Tahawwul al-Dimuqrati fi-l-'Iraq*, and Hasan al-'Alawi, *al-Shi'a wa-l-Dawla al-Qawmiya fi-l-'Iraq*, esp. 156–63.

55. Baghdad: al-Sharika al-Wataniya li-l-Tiba'a wa-l-'Alan, 1962.

56. Although Allen Dulles's reference to the situation in Iraq in 1959 as the "most dangerous in the world today" reflected hyperbole, there is no question that the United States and Great Britain were extremely concerned with communist influence during the Qasim regime. See the *New York Times*, Apr. 29, 1959, as cited in Batatu, *The Old Social Classes*, 899.

57. See Qasim's speech to the Second Congress of the Peace Partisans, Bagh-

dad, April 14, 1959, in *Principles of the July 14 Revolution* (Baghdad: n.p., n.d.), 3–7; and *Messages and Greetings from Major-General Abdul Karim Qassim Prime Minister and Commander-in-Chief of the Armed Forces to the International Conferences* (Baghdad: Ministry of Guidance, n.d.), esp. his letters to the Seventh Arab Engineering Conference, Beirut, April 19, 1959, 22–24, and his letter to the Arabs Lawyers' Conference, Beirut, September 1, 1959, 24–26.

58. Ayyub, *Li-l-Haqiqa*, 45–47; see also, Batatu, *The Old Social Classes*, 864–89, 912–21; and, Dann, *Iraq Under Qassem*, 175–76, 223–24.

59. Later Saddam and the state intellectuals of the Ba'th Party would try and have it both ways by claiming Iraq's greater historical civilizational depth rooted in Mesopotamian antiquity and by arguing that the ancient Mesopotamians were Semites, just like the Arabs. See Baram, *Culture and Ideology in the Making of Ba'thist Iraq, 1968–1989* (New York: St. Martin's Press, 1991), 101–9.

60. Ayyub, *Li-l-Haqiqa*, 62.

61. See, for example, Batatu, *The Old Social Classes*, 966–94; Dann, *Iraq Under Qassem*, 362–72; and Phoebe Marr, *The Modern History of Iraq* (Boulder, Colo.: Westview Press, 1985), 184–85.

62. Because the Assyrian challenge to Iraqi sovereignty occurred within the north central Iraq or the so-called Sunni Arab triangle, it was the Sunni Arab population that rallied to sing the praises of Sidqi and the army following the massacre. See Sami Zubaida, "Contested Nations: Iraq and the Assyrians," *Nations & Nationalism* 6, no. 3 (Summer 2000); and Khaldun S. Husry, "The Assyrian Affair of 1933," parts 1 and 2, *International Journal of Middle Eastern Studies* 5, nos. 2 and 3: 161–76, 344–60.

63. One example of this rising mass consciousness was the General Strike of 1931 against British efforts to impose new municipal taxes *(rusum al-baladiyat)* on Iraq for electricity and other services. See Kamal Mazhar Ahmad, *al-Tabiqa al-'Amila al-'Iraqiya: al-Takkawun wa Bidayat al-Taharruk [The Iraqi Working Class: Its Formation and Early Activities]* (Baghdad: Dar al-Rashid li-l-Nashr, 1981), 202–24.

64. 'Aqil al-Nasiri, "Laylat al-Sa'ud ila Sama' al-Khalud: Qira'a Tahliliya li-l-Yawm al-Akhir min Hayat al-Za'im al-Rahil 'Abd al-Karim Qasim" [The Night of Ascension: An Analytic Reading of the Last Day in the Life of the Late Leader, 'Abd al-Karim Qasim], *al-Mawsim* 32 (1997): 178.

65. Peter Gran, *Beyond Eurocentrism: A New View of Modern World History* (Syracuse, N.Y.: Syracuse University Press, 1996), 70.

66. 'Ali Karim Sa'id, *'Iraq 8 Shabbat 1963: Min Hiwar al-Mafahim ila Hiwar al-Damm—Muraja't fi Dhakirat Talib Shabib [Iraq, February 8, 1963: From a Dialogue of Understanding to a Dialogue of Blood—Reflections on Talib Shabib's Memory]* (Beirut: Dar al-Kanuz al-'Arabiya, 1999), 12, n. 1; 67, n. 1.

67. See, for example, the testimony of 'Abd al-Qadir Isma'il, editor in chief of *Ittihad al-Sha'b*, before the Martial Law Court during the fall of 1960 as reported extensively by the ICP's paper, Sept. 28, 29, 1960.

68. Derek Hopwood et al., *Iraq: Power and Society* (London: Ithaca Press, 1993), 175–80.

69. It is interesting to note that during the 1941 Pan-Arabist struggle with the British many Iraqi army units likewise waited to see which group would gain the upper hand before choosing one side or the other .

70. al-ʿAlawi argues that the "religious movement" *(haraka diniya)* was greatly disturbed by Qasim's issuance of a new Personal Status Law, which it saw as promoting atheism and as part of an overall increase in communist influence in the country *(al-Shiʿa wa-l-Dawla al-Qawmiya*, 210).

CHAPTER 6. MEMORIES OF STATE ASCENDANT,
1968–1979

1. The official reference to this project appeared in the short volume attributed to Saddam Husayn, *Hawla Kitabat al-Tarikh [On the Writing of History]* (Baghdad: Dar al-Hurriya li-l-Tibaʿa, 1979), which includes four speeches by Saddam followed by twenty-three essays by some of the country's most prominent historians and cultural critics on the need to rewrite Iraq's history.

2. I use the term "Takriti Baʿth" to refer to the second Baʿthist regime, which came to power in 1968, because, as Batatu and others have shown, the party was dominated by Sunni Arab members drawn from the town of Takrit, sixty miles to the northwest of Baghdad in the so-called Sunni Arab triangle. However, that term is less accurate and less analytically useful when applied to the period after 1979, when Saddam Husayn deposed President Ahmad Hasan al-Bakr and began placing members of his immediate family in important positions within the state apparatus. See Hanna Batatu, *The Old Social Classes and Revolutionary Movements of Iraq* (Princeton, N.J.: Princeton University Press, 1978), 1071–1110; and Falih ʿAbd al-Jabbar, "Min Dawlat Hizb al-Wahid ila Dawlat al-Hizb/al-Usra" [From the One-Party State to the Family/Party State], *al-Thaqafa al-Jadida* 267 (Dec. 1995–Jan/Feb. 1996): 6–28.

3. Examples include the longtime foreign minister and deputy prime minister Tariq ʿAziz, a Christian who reportedly Arabized his name from Tariq Yuhanna Mikhaʾil ʿAziz; former economics professor and Shiʿi Saʿdun Hammadi, who has served as prime minister; and the former Shiʿi speaker of the Iraqi parliament, Naʿim Haddad. Among the Kurdish population, one can cite ʿUbayd Allah, one of the sons of the former Kurdish leader; and head of the Kurdish Democratic Party, Mulla Mustafa al-Barzani.

4. ʿAbd al-Jabbar notes this was first time since 1925 that executive and legislative authority were fused in one body ("Min Dawlat al-Hizb al-Wahid," 17).

5. For post-1963 efforts to force workers to conform to state policies, see "General Economic Affairs—Social and Industrial Policies and Labour Developments in the Arab States in the Middle East—Annual Report on Labour and Social Affairs," British Embassy, Beirut, R. L. Morris, June 27, 1967, FCO17/96.

6. These included the al-Talaʾiʿ (Vanguards) and al-Ruwwad (Pioneers) organizations modeled on Soviet youth organizations such as the Komsomol. For a comprehensive discussion of the Vanguards' activities, see The Vanguards Organization, *Waqaʾaʿ al-Mahrajan al-Awal li-l-Talaʾiʿ wa-l-Nashiʾa al-ʿArab, al-*

Qutr al-ʿIraqi li-l-Fatra min 17–27, Tammuz 1979 [Report on the First Festival of the Vanguards and Arab Youth, the Iraqi Region, July 17–27, 1979 (Baghdad: The Vanguards Organization, 1980).

7. It is important to note that, despite Saddam's acknowledgment of the impact of the 1941 Movement on his own political formation, and the Iraqi Baʿth's privileging of the movement in defining twentieth-century political community, there is no valorization of ancient Iraqi civilization in al-Sabbagh's memoirs. Nor did the al-Rikabi or al-Saʿdi factions of the Baʿth stress this perspective. In this sense, the Takriti Baʿth's "Mesopotamianism" represented a new departure for Iraqi Baʿthism, one that significantly modified its traditional Pan-Arab focus.

8. See, for example, Amatzia Baram, *Culture and Ideology in the Formation of Baʿthist Iraq, 1968–1989* (New York: St. Martin's Press, 1991), who focuses more on the competing rather than complementary nature of these two world views. See esp. 38–52, 53–57, 61–96.

9. This comment was valid when the Takriti Baʿth first came to power in 1968, because Sunni Arab domination as an ethnic group obviously did not relate to ancient Iraq. However, once the Baʿth began emphasizing that ancient Iraqis were also Semites, the ability of Iraq's Kurds to identity with Iraq's ancient civilizations was put in jeopardy.

10. Iraq's population prior to the Mongol invasion has been estimated as high as 30 million people, compared to the current population of 24 million.

11. For details of these efforts, see the lengthy file FO371/149996, "Labour Situation and Trade Unions, 1960."

12. For a discussion of the temporary constitutions promulgated in 1958, 1964, and 1970, see Husayn ʿAbd ʿAli, "al-Wadaʿiya al-Qanuniya li Muwattanay al-Jumhuriya al-ʿIraqiya, 1958–1979" [The Legal Status of Citizens of the Iraqi Republic, 1958–1979], *al-Thaqafa al-Jadida* 159, vols. 31–32 (1984): 52–62.

13. Batatu, *The Old Social Classes*, 982.

14. Dr. Isam al-Khafaji's uncle, who was Qasim's doctor, was the source of this information, having heard ʿArif state that he would only be treated by Sunni physicians. Interview, New York University, Nov. 16, 1999.

15. FCO17/416, "Iraq: Political Affairs—Internal: Naji Talib Administration 9th August 1966–10th May 1967." Writing to the Foreign Office on June 9, 1967, the British ambassador in Baghdad, Sir Richard Beaumont, commented, "[Talib's] trouble was that he was anxious to be on good terms with everyone. A revolutionary run to seed, a Shia unable to come to terms with his co-religionists but showing the streak of masochism which is common among Shias, his principle character was lack of public leadership and moral courage. To a quite remarkable degree he was motivated by fear, as he frequently said in his many talks with the Managing Director of the IPC [Iraq Petroleum Company] and occasionally with myself—fear of being dragged in the streets by the mob."

16. Hasan al-ʿAlawi, *al-Shiʿa wa-l-Dawla al-Qawmiya fi-l-ʿIraq [The Shiʿa and the National State in Iraq]* (Paris, CEDI Press, 1989), 192–94.

17. Although these events tend to substantiate Theda Skocpol's argument that revolutions are frequently caused by the state's weakness rather than by

the mobilization of the masses, what remains problematic is determining the conditions under which the seizure of the state by small groups of conspirators should be considered a revolution, as opposed to a coup d'état or a putsch. See *States and Social Revolutions* (Cambridge: Cambridge University Press, 1979), esp. 14–18.

18. Underlining the notion of ideological fluidity is a British Embassy, Baghdad, report that stated that Nayif, who went to Morocco after being deposed, was actually suspected of having Muslim Brotherhood sympathies. FCO17/418, Walker, Rabat, to Montgomery, Eastern Dept. Foreign Office, Aug. 2, 1968.

19. FCO17/418, Evans, Baghdad, to Foreign Office, Aug. 22, 1968.

20. FCO17/01, "Political Affairs Internal—Political Parties in the Middle East: Ba'thism," Saunders, Baghdad, to Makinson, Eastern Dept. Foreign Office, Sept. 27, 1968; FCO17/418, "Iraq: Political Affairs (Internal)—Internal Situation (After the Coup of 17 July)," Saunders, Beirut, to Saunders, Baghdad, Oct. 13, 1968; FCO17/871, Report of Baghdad Radio broadcast, Dec. 17, 1969.

21. Marion Farouk-Sluglett and Peter Sluglett, *Iraq Since 1958: From Revolution to Dictatorship* (London: I. B. Tauris, 1990), 242–46, 265–66, 273–82.

22. Interview with ʿAziz al-Hajj Haydar, Paris, Jan. 14, 2000. The most prominent casualty was Fuʾad al-Rikabi, the founder of the Baʿth Party in Iraq, who was executed in prison in 1970. Ousted from the party in 1961, he joined forces with the Nasirist movement, for which he was never forgiven by his former Baʿthist colleagues.

23. When the day was done, almost all the prisoners released turned out to be supporters of the regime. Some communists, however, were also released. See FCO17/418.

24. FCO17/869, Makinson, Near East Dept., to Budd, Foreign Office, Jan. 15, 1969; FCO17/871, "Iraq: Reports on the Internal Situation," Acland, Baghdad, to Stewart Near East Dept., Foreign Office, Aug. 25, 1969.

25. This event, and especially Saddam's role, was completely exaggerated by the Takriti Baʿth. A novel, *The Days*, a film, and a comic strip series were some of the many ways in which the assassination attempt and Saddam's role in it were commemorated. See Allen Douglass and Fedwa Malti-Douglas, "Machismo and Arabism: Saddâm Husayn as Lone Hero," in *Arab Comic Strips: Politics of an Emerging Mass Culture* (Bloomington: Indiana University Press, 1994), 46–59.

26. FCO17/869, Jenner, Baghdad, to Hincliffe, Near East Dept., Foreign Office, Mar. 8, 1969. Jenner notes that Britain's defense attaché in Baghdad was told by his Sudanese colleague that "Sadam [sic] al Tikriti was a 'very dangerous man' but did not specify why he thought so." FCO17/871, Iraq Political Report—Memo, Baghdad Embassy, Nov. 15, 1969, states that Saddam is a "presentable young man. Initially regarded as a party extremist, but responsibility may mellow him."

27. The main daily newspapers were the party organ *al-Thawra [The Revolution]* and the government papers *al-Jumhuriya [The Republic]*, *al-ʿIraq*, and the English-language *Baghdad Times*.

28. An engineering professor at Rutgers University relates how, during a visit of Arab-Americans to Iraq during the late 1970s, Iraqi officials climbed onto his tour bus and began throwing Iraqi dinar notes at the occupants.

29. For a discussion of the conflict between the Syrian and Iraqi wings of the Ba'th Party, see Farouk-Sluglett and Sluglett, *Iraq Since 1958*, 202–3.

30. Baram, *Culture and Ideology*, 13–17.

31. See Majid Khadduri's interview with Saddam as reported in his *Socialist Iraq: A Study of Iraqi Politics Since 1968* (Washington, D.C.: Middle East Institute, 1978), 73. Khadduri cites al-Sabbagh's memoirs as *Fursan al-'Uruba fi-l-Mizan* (Damascus, 1956), while the copy that I possess is entitled *Fursan al-'Uruba fi-l-'Iraq* (Damascus, 1956), with "Shabab al-'Arabi" listed as the publisher.

32. See, for example, the publication of the London-based Association of Iraqi Democrats, *al-Dimuqrati*, for this perspective: nos. 17 and 18 (Feb.–Mar. 1994), no. 28 (July 1996), and no. 33 (Apr. 1999). This organization was headed by the prominent Iraqi Kurdish poet Buland al-Haydari until his death in 1996 and was subsequently led by his wife, Dalal al-Haydari. The journal is published by Muhammad El-Dhahir, who was head of the Directorate of Oilfields during the Qasim period.

33. In this context, Ra'id Fahmi, the editor in chief of the ICP theoretical journal *al-Thaqafa al-Jadida*, noted the irony that, in contemporary Iraq, only the communists are true nationalists because they constitute the only political organization that represents all of Iraq rather than sectarian or regional interests. Interview, Paris, Jan. 12, 2000.

34. This accumulation process assumed a spatial dimension as well, since Ba'th Party members lived in exclusive quarters of Baghdad such as al-Mansur.

35. At one site I was given a mimeographed document that outlined the many activities available to youths participating in the Markaz al-Shabab fi Baghdad al-Karkh wa-l-Rasafa (Youth Center for the Baghdad Districts of al-Karkh and al-Rasafa). In addition to sports training, the schedule for the month from May 31 to June 30, 1980, included seminars on social research, the social psychology of elementary school instruction, tourism, logic, and social service and planning. Clearly these centers functioned not only as sports facilities, but as venues for intensive after-school learning and indoctrination as well.

36. Interview with Mundhir al-Juburi, editorial secretary, *al-Tali'a al-Adabiya*, June 8, 1984. The journal was first published in November 1974. See Zahida Ibrahim, *Kashshaf al-Jara'id wa-l-Majallat al-'Iraqiya, 1869–1978 [Index of Iraqi Newspapers and Journals, 1869–1978]*, 2d ed. (Kuwait: Dar al-Nashr wa-l-Matbu'at al-Kuwaytiya, 1982), 430.

37. For information on these publications, see Ibrahim, *Kashshaf al-Jara'id wa-l-Majallat*.

38. *al-Waqa'i' al-'Iraqiya [The Iraqi Official Gazette]*, Dec. 22, 1975, article 2b.

39. The journal was closed in October 1969. Another Iraqi Teachers Union publication, *Majallat Akhbar Niqabat al-Mu'allimin [Journal of Information of*

the Teachers Union], seems to have ceased publication in 1965. For more on this publication, see Ibrahim, *Kashshaf al-Jara'id wa-l-Majallat.*

40. al-Hadithi was head of the London Cultural Center and then director of publications for the Ministry of Information beginning in 1979. He has since held other diplomatic posts, including ambassador to Austria, which is an important post given OPEC's headquarters in Vienna. At the time of the fall of the Ba'th, he was Iraqi minister of foreign affairs.

41. Ministry of Culture and Information, *Dar al-Azya' al-'Iraqiya* (Baghdad, 1981).

42. See, for example, Ministry of Oil, Information and Public Relations Department, *Iraq Oil Procession* [sic] (Baghdad, n.d. [ca. 1980]). When in May 1980 I met with al-Hadithi, who was then director of publications for the Ministry of Information, he offered to purchase ten thousand copies of any book favorable to Iraq for distribution through Iraqi embassies throughout the world. Before making this offer, al-Hadithi had offered an extended justification for the hanging of fourteen Iraqi Jews in Liberation Square (Sahat al-Tahrir) in order to gauge my reaction. Needless to say, I did not avail myself of his offer.

43. Christine Moss Helms, *Iraq: Eastern Flank of the Arab World* (Washington, D.C.: The Brookings Institution, 1984).

44. See, for example, the illustrations on Iraqi society and soldiers during the Iran-Iraq War by Ken Sprague, *The Smoke at the End of the Road* (London: Iraqi Cultural Centre, 1981). Although I am getting a little ahead of our story, Iraqi efforts at influencing foreign audiences did not stop in Europe. I was struck by the cover of the Dallas-based Caltex Petroleum Corporation's journal, *Oil Progress,* for fall 1987, which had a photograph of an Assyrian wall relief on its cover and contained a lengthy article, "The Artists of Baghdad" (2–19), by Mary E. King, who was at the time executive director of the U.S.–Iraq Business Forum based in Washington, D.C. Interested that an American had such a sophisticated understanding of Iraqi painting and sculpture, I called Ms. King who, when reached by telephone, became very nervous at my questions as it quickly became obvious that she knew nothing about Iraqi art. Finally, she referred me to the Iraqi embassy's cultural attaché, whom I had the distinct impression wrote the article under Ms. King's name.

45. République Irakienne, Ministère de la Culture et des Arts, *La Culture et des Arts en Irak: Celebration du Xeme Anniversaire de la Révolution du 17–30 Juillet* (Baghdad: n.p., 1978), 144. Other journals also enjoyed relatively large runs, such as the *Journal of Popular Culture,* which reached ten thousand copies per issue by 1977, and *al-Tal'ia al-Adabiya,* which reached ten thousand copies per month. A children's magazine, *Majallati,* which began publication in February 1968 and was then taken over by the Ministry of Information, also had a wide circulation. See Ibrahim, *Kashshaf al-Jara'id wa-l-Majallat,* 492. Many Iraqi publications were published in multiple languages, including copies of Ahmad Hasan al-Bakr's speeches, which I discovered in Romanian and Chinese.

46. République Irakienne, Ministère de la Culture et des Arts, *La Culture et des Arts en Irak,* 141.

47. Ibid., 151.

48. *Sumer* 15, nos. 1 and 2 (July 1959): 3–6.

49. Ibid., 57, 59. The Qasim regime's Iraqist nationalist emphasis was evident in these floats, which carried Qasim's photograph and images of and references to Iraq's ancient civilizations, e.g., "Tamouz, the Good Son," and "Iraqi mathematicians preceded Euclid in his theory by 1,700 years (2000 B.C.)."

50. See "Mirbad Poetry Festival: Saddam Literary Prizes" in *Gilgamesh* (Spring 1990), where Dr. Nuri al-Qaysi, one of the main players in Baʿthist efforts to restructure historical memory, received an award for literary history. An award for linguistics studies went to Dr. Ahmad Mukhtar ʿUmar of Egypt, a poetry award to the Sudanese poet Muhammad al-Fayturi, a literary studies award to Dr. Muhammad Muftah of Morocco, and an award for short story and drama writing to the well-known Egyptian author Fathi Ghanim.

51. For a partial listing and discussion of the many festivals organized by the Baʿthist regime, see Baram, *Culture and Ideology,* 31–32, 36, 47–51, 53–60.

52. Ibid., 47.

53. For example, a large poster in downtown Baghdad portrays Nebuchadnezzar, with his eyes cast slightly downward, shaking hands with Saddam Husayn, who looks directly into his face, indicating who is the more powerful of the two leaders.

54. See, for example, the introduction to *Sumer* 25, nos. 1 and 2 (Winter/Spring 1969): a–p, by Dr. Isa (ʿIsa) Salman, director-general of antiquities, in which he describes the excavations of the organization for the previous year.

55. Ibid., l–m.

56. République Irakienne, Ministère de la Culture et des Arts, *La Culture et des Arts en Irak,* 157–58.

57. Ibid., 92. See also *al-Masira: Lamahat Mudayiʿa min Nidal Hizb al-Baʿth al-ʿArabi al-Ishtiraki / Images of the Struggle of the Arab Baʿath Socialist Party* (Baghdad: n.p., n.d. [ca. 1982]), 86–87, 91, 92, 93–94. This volume contains images of the Party Museum (Mathaf al-Hizb) and parallel texts in Arabic, English, and French.

58. *On the Writing of History [Hawla Kitabat al-Tarikh]* was published in Baghdad by Dar al-Hurriya li-l-Tibaʿa in 1979. Iskandar's work, *Saddam Husayn: Munadilan wa Mufakkiran wa Insanan,* was published by Hachette in French, English, and Arabic in Paris in 1980.

59. During this period, the Ministry of Culture and Information was divided into two separate ministries. The reasons for this are discussed in chapter 7.

60. I use the phrase "this point in time" because, during the 1980s and 1990s, Saddam and the Baʿth began to politically resurrect Faysal I, for example by reinstalling a statue of him in Baghdad, and Saddam appeared on a white horse in parades, reminiscent of Faysal. One of Saddam's speeches in *On the Writing of History* uses the martyrs of the May 1941 Movement to elucidate the need for individuals to endure sacrifice for the benefit of society. It should be remembered that the Baʿth Party viewed the 1941 Movement as demarcating the beginning of modern Iraqi history.

61. Saddam's psychological and emotional difficulties as a child have been dealt with extensively. See Iskandar, *Saddam Husayn*, 15–25, and Efraim Karsh and Inari Rautsi, *Saddam Hussein: A Political Biography* (New York: The Free Press, 1991), 6–10.

62. Batatu, *The Old Social Classes*, 29. Dr. Isam al-Khafaji, on the other hand, argues that the small river towns of the so-called Sunni Arab triangle were in decline well before the collapse of the Ottoman Empire. Interview, New York University, Nov. 16, 1999.

63. Batatu, *The Old Social Classes*, 1078–79, indicates that one reason so many Shi'is were arrested after the February 8, 1963, coup was that the police were predominantly Sunni Arabs from rural backgrounds who avoided arresting Sunni activists. This datum underscores Sunni domination of the state.

64. See *al-'Iraq fi-l-Tarikh [Iraq in History]* (Baghdad: Dar al-Hurriya li-l-Tiba'a, 1983).

65. The cover article in the Iraqi magazine *Alif Ba'* drove home Saddam's exclusion from the proposed new state. On the cover, al-Bakr and Asad were seated (without Saddam) discussing the new pact, while on the inside of the magazine they were shown signing the National Action Pact (Mithaq al-'Amal al-Qawmi) with Saddam standing in the background. See "Mithaq al-'Amal al-Qawmi: Bidaya li Marhala Tarikhiya Jadida" [The National Action Covenant: The Beginning of a New Historical Epoch], *Alif Ba'* (Nov. 1, 1978): 6–7.

66. For a discussion of these events, see Farouk-Sluglett and Sluglett, *Iraq Since 1958*, 208–9, and Karsh and Rautsi, *Saddam Hussein*, 112–18.

67. During the elections on June 20 I visited a number of polling sites where candidate lists were prominently displayed. Officials at these sites indicated that representatives of the Kurdish Democratic Party were also participating in the election. I later learned that many of the so-called Independents were actually former Ba'thists or party sympathizers. Certainly all candidates had to be approved by the party to assure their loyalty to the regime.

CHAPTER 7. MEMORIES OF STATE IN DECLINE, 1979–1990

1. The Ba'th claimed that Iran actually began the war on September 4, 1980, with attacks on Iraq. See Hadi Hasan 'Alaywi and Walid al-Hadithi, *Saddam Husayn wa Qadaya al-Thaqafa wa-l-'Alam [Saddam Husayn and Issues Regarding Culture and Information]*, (Baghdad: Ministry of Culture and Information, Dar al-Shu'un al-Thaqafiya al-'Amma, 1991), 192, 202. This book is volume 14 of 19 in the series *Saddam Husayn: Silsilat al-Fikr al-Riyadi [Saddam Husayn: The Pioneering Thought Series]*, which apparently became required reading for all top Ba'thist officials. See Saïd Aburish, *Saddam Husayn: The Politics of Revenge* (New York: Bloomsbury Press, 2000), 328.

2. In an article written shortly after the war began, I warned of the impending dangers that it presented for Iraq. See "The War's Economic, Political Damage to Iraq," *New York Times*, Oct. 7, 1980.

3. Because of the use of chemical weapons in the village of Halabja and surrounding areas in 1988 and the role that Saddam assigned al-Majid as military commander of Kurdistan to suppress the Kurds, al-Majid acquired the nickname "Chemical ʿAli."

4. Perhaps few Iraqis were aware that, among the 1963 putschists, al-Bakr had been in the forefront of those favoring Qasim's immediate execution after his surrender on February 9, 1963, fearing that his supporters would try to free him if they knew he were still alive. ʿAqil al-Nasiri, "Laylat al-Samʿud ila Samaʾ al-Khalud: Qiraʾt Tahliliya li-l-Yawm al-Akhir min Hiyat al-Zaʿim al-Rahil ʿAbd al-Karim Qasim" [The Night of Ascending to Immortality: An Analytic Reading of the Last Day in the Life of the Deceased Leader, ʿAbd al-Karim Qasim], *al-Mawsim* 32 (1997): 177–78.

5. Falih ʿAbd al-Jabbar, "Min Dawlat al-Hizb al-Wahid ila Dawlat al-Hizb / al-Usra" [From the One-Party State to the Family/Party State], *al-Thaqafa al-Jadida* 267 (Dec. 1995–Jan./Feb. 1996): 10, 14. Salah ʿUmar al-ʿAli's rural background is evident from the tattoo of a bird on his left wrist, which I recall seeing during a dinner at the Iraqi ambassador's residence at the United Nations in April 1980. As we dined in a sumptuous setting, the ambassador pointed out that "of course, we are all socialists," referring to the Baʿth's purported socialist orientation. This was the same person who currently is supposedly committed to a democratic transition in Iraq, despite his continued sectarian behavior, even in exile in Saudi Arabia (see chapter 9, n. 108). This is also the same person who gave speeches exhorting the crowds to support the January 1969 hanging of Iraqi Jews in Liberation Square in Baghdad.

6. Ibid., 14.

7. Saddam's father, Husayn al-Majid, died before Saddam was born. His mother remarried Hasan Ibrahim al-Majid, although the man who had the defining impact on him seems to have been his paternal uncle, Khayrallah Tulfah, the future mayor of Baghdad and a man known for his cruel disposition. See Aburish, *Saddam Husayn*, 18–25.

8. ʿAbd al-Jabbar notes that the most prominent work on Iraqi tribes (banned in Iraq during the 1970s and 1980s), ʿAbbas al-ʿAzzawi's four-volume, *ʿAshaʾir al-ʿIraq*, does not mention the Al bu Nasir tribe ("Min Dawlat al-Hizb al-Wahid," 14).

9. Ibid., 14–15.

10. During my first visit to Iraq, one of the sites on my Ministry of Information itinerary was the iron-and-steel plant near Zubayr in southern Iraq that was built by the San Francisco–based Bechtel Corporation and the French firm Creusot-Loire.

11. The Republican Guard was created by ʿAbd al-Salam ʿArif in 1964 to replace the al-Haras al-Qawmi (National Guard), which had been the power base of the first Baʿthist regime that ousted ʿAbd al-Karim Qasim in February 1963, and then had been overthrown in turn by ʿArif in November 1963. After the Gulf War, the Republican Guard, heretofore an elite unit within the Iraqi army, was in turn superseded in status and power by a new force, the Special Republican Guard.

12. For the best analysis of the growth of this sector, see Isam al-Khafaji, *al-Dawla wa Tatawwur al-Ra'smaliya fi-l-'Iraq, 1968–1978 [The State and Capitalist Development in Iraq, 1968–1978]* (Cairo: Dar al-Mustaqbal al-'Arabi, 1983), 67–86.

13. Rony Gabbay, *Communism and Agrarian Reform in Iraq* (London: Croom Helm, 1978).

14. Robert Springborg, "Infitah, Agrarian Transformation, and Elite Consolidation in Contemporary Iraq," *Middle East Journal* 40, no. 1 (Winter 1986): 36.

15. Ibid., 37.

16. Ibid., 40–41.

17. "al-Ustadh Saddam Husayn Na'ib Ra'is Majlis Qiyadat al-Thawra Yatahadath 'an Ma'rakat al-Ta'mim" [The Honorable Saddam Husayn, Vice-President of the Revolution Command Council, Discusses the Nationalization Struggle], in Khalid 'Abd al-Mun'im al-'Ani, *Mawsu'at al-'Iraq al-Hadith [The Encyclopedia of Modern Iraq]* (Baghdad: al-Dar al-'Arabiya li-l-Mawsu'at, 1977), 2: 583. It is significant that Saddam's remarks are omitted in the English section, which parallels the Arab section of the encyclopedia. It is also interesting to compare Saddam's designation as *"ustadh"* (teacher or professor) in 1977 with the honorifics used by the late 1980s, e.g., *"al-ra'is al-munadil al-khalid"* ("the immortal struggler president").

18. For the reasons why the Ba'th Party cultural commissars found al-Jahiz such a compelling historical figure, see Eric Davis and Nicolas Gavrielides, "Statecraft, Historical Memory and Popular Culture in Iraq and Kuwait," in E. Davis and N. Gavrielides, eds., *Statecraft in the Middle East: Oil, Memory and Popular Culture* (Miami: Florida International University Press / University Presses of Florida, 1991), 135–37.

19. Taking agricultural production as an indicator of this change, in 1980 Saddam abolished an important party organization, the Higher Agricultural Council (HAC), which had exercised oversight over reform, the conservative Ministry of Agriculture, and privately owned agricultural land. For a discussion of the HAC, see al-'Ani, *Mawsu'at*, 809.

20. 'Abd al-Jabbar, "Min Dawlat al-Hizb al-Wahid," 9.

21. These bureaus included the Military Bureau (al-Maktab al-'Askari), which oversaw the army, security services, police, and military intelligence; the Propaganda Bureau (al-Maktab al-'Alami), which controlled radio and television broadcasting and newspapers; the Labor Bureau (al-Maktab al-'Ummali), which was responsible for the General Federation of Labor Unions and all public and private-sector unions; the Peasant Bureau (al-Maktab al-Fallahi), which controlled peasant organizations and cooperatives; the Student Bureau (Maktab al-Tullab), which supervised the General Federation of Students, which included university, secondary, and institute students; the Bureau of Professional Organizations (Maktab al-Munazzamat al-Mihaniya), which was responsible for the General Federation of Iraqi Women and all professional associations; and the Bureau of State-Party Relations (Maktab 'Alaqat ma' al-Dawla) (ibid.).

22. Ibid., 8.

23. These candidates were likely those standing for election to the separate al-Majlis al-Tashri'i (Legislative Council) in the Kurdish Autonomous Region in the north, for which elections were held in September 1980.

24. It is not correct, as Falih 'Abd al-Jabbar asserts ("Min Dawlat al-Hizb al-Wahid," 21), that the first three speakers of the parliament were Shi'is. The third speaker, Sa'di Mahdi Salih, who assumed his post in 1989, was a Sunni from the Takrit area who died during the early 1990s while receiving medical treatment in Italy.

25. For information on the parliament, see the interview with Sa'di Mahdi Salih, "Istidafa al-Ajanib fi-l-'Iraq Ijra' Yafda ila al-Salam" [Foreigners Having Access to Iraq Will Lead to Peace], *al-Jumhuriya* (Oct. 6, 1990).

26. One study by Khalil Ibrahim Husayn, *'Abd al-Karim Qasim: al-Lughz al-Muhayyar ('Abd al-Karim Qasim: The Perplexing Riddle)* (Baghdad: Dar al-Hurriya li-l-Tiba'a, 1988), vol. 3 of *Mawsu'at 14 Tammuz [Encyclopedia of the July 14th Revolution]*, was particularly interesting because it contained many favorable references to 'Abd al-Karim Qasim, despite an overall unfavorable assessment. The partial rehabilitation of Qasim, through discussion of his excellence as an instructor in the Iraqi Military Academy, his valor in the 1948 Palestine campaign, and the respect with which he was held by his officers and infantry, contradicts the standard historiography of him as a brutal and self-centered military dictator.

27. The superficiality of this symbolism can be seen in the Iraqi flag that flies above the United Nations embassy and ambassador's residence on East 79th Street in New York City. For more than ten years, the pre–Gulf War flag continued to fly, devoid of the *"Allahu Akbar!"* inscription. Only in the spring of 2002 was the new flag finally raised over the Iraqi embassy.

28. In 1988 there was a reported attempt by 178 army officers to overthrow the regime. See Eric Davis, "State-Building in Iraq During the Iran-Iraq War and the Gulf Crisis," in *The Internationalization of Communal Strife*, ed. Manus I. Midlarsky (New York: Routledge, 1992), 85.

29. A law was passed in 1978 forbidding all Iraqis from using tribal or regional surnames. Saddam Husayn for example, dropped his surname, al-Takriti. This law was designed to protect Ba'th Party members, many of whom shared similar surnames such as al-Takriti, al-Rawi, al-Hadithi, and so on, from public scrutiny. I would like to thank Dr. Wadood Hamad for calling my attention to the date of this decree.

30. This was true, for example, of the male head of a Shi'i family who had been employed by the library of a major American university but who brought his family back to Iraq during the late 1970s.

31. For a discussion of the use of the Iran-Iraq War in Iraqi state building, see Eric Davis, "State Building in Iraq," 69–92.

32. For this genealogy, see Amin Iskandar, *Saddam Husayn: Munadilan wa Mufakkiran wa Insanan* (Paris: Hachette, 1980), 21.

33. For a discussion of al-Wasiti's art, see the special issue of the Iraqi art journal *al-Riwaq* 15 (1984).

34. The new seminary was named the Saddam Islamic Studies Academy. See *al-Waqa'i' al-'Iraqiya [The Official Gazette]* no. 3243, Feb. 20, 1989. In light of the many religious figures Saddam had executed, few Iraqis saw this as representative of a newfound support for religion on the part of the regime.

35. Saddam Husayn, *Saddam Husayn wa Haqa'iq al-Tarikh al-'Arabi [Saddam Husayn and the Facts of Arab History]* (Baghdad: Dar al-Hurriya li-l-Tiba'a, 1989), 14.

36. Interview with the late Dr. Wadia Juwaideh, Emeritus Professor of Near Eastern Studies, Indiana University, Nov. 10, 1999. Dr. Juwaideh recalls hearing discussions of the al-Shu'ubiya controversy early in his professional life, when he worked in the legal department of the Ministry of Defense (Nazirat al-Difa'a) during the mid- and late 1930s. This suggests that the issue was extant even earlier in Iraqi political discourse.

37. His *The Rise of Historical Writing Among the Arabs,* which was published by Princeton University Press in 1983, is the only work by a modern Iraq historian of which I am aware to be translated into English. Other members of what might be called the Iraqi Historical School include 'Abd al-Razzaq al-Hasani, Salih Ahmad al-'Ali, Fadil Husayn, Jawad 'Ali, Ahmad Susa, and Muhammad Mahdi al-Bashir. For a discussion of history writing in Iraq, see Reeva Simon, "The Teaching of History in Iraq Before the Rashid Ali Coup," *Middle Eastern Studies* 22, no. 1 (Jan. 1986): 37–51; and Peter Gran, *Beyond Eurocentrism: A New View of Modern World History* (Syracuse, N.Y.: Syracuse University Press, 1996), 78–87.

38. It should be recalled that the Shu'ubiyun refers to the Arabized Persian literary and bureaucratic elite during the 'Abbasid Empire, which was alleged to have conspired against the Arabs to weaken their self-confidence and hence their internal resolve.

39. *The Pan-Arabist Tendency in Modern Iraqi Poetry, 1939–1967* (Baghdad: Ministry of Culture and Information, 1983). I would hypothesize that this strong emphasis on the need to maintain self-confidence and social psychological steadfastness more broadly defined reflected the insecurities under Saddam of the rural tribal base of the Ba'th Party, which became increasingly important after 1979. Because members of this group came from very modest backgrounds and lacked significant formal education, this insecurity entailed hostility not just toward non-Sunni groups such as the Shi'a and Kurds, but also toward more established urban Sunni Arabs. This explains the extreme hostility of Saddam, his family, and his close confidants toward the established urban families that the Ba'th sought to destroy during the 1980s.

40. al-Dabit's association with the *Journal of Popular Culture* was purely instrumental and is discussed in greater detail in chapter 8.

41. Baghdad: Dar al-Hurriya li-l-Tiba'a, 1983. This volume reflects a new state strategy, an emphasis on collective authorship. The volume is not attributed to a single editor, but rather said to be written by "an elite group of researchers" *(Safwat al-Bahithin)* and, despite its length and broad range, there are no footnotes. Many of the volume's arguments run counter to traditional in-

terpretations of the subjects in question. One of the authors closely associated with this volume was Dr. Salih Ahmad al-ʿAli, former president of the Iraqi Academy and a distinguished historian, whom I interviewed in 1980 and 1984. Although in 1980 I sensed that Dr. al-ʿAli lent at least some support to state-sponsored cultural production, by 1984 he indicated, by gestures and double entendre, his rejection of this enterprise. I also had the distinct sense that he felt coerced to participate in the volume *Iraq and History*. Interviews, Baghdad, May 30, 1980, and June 21, 1984.

42. Saddam notes on the front page of *Iraq and History* that "History is the end result of what the nation itself determines it to be according to its own will," while in *The Iraqi-Persian Conflict*, Saddam notes that "When we face aggression, it is our right to return to history to find an explanation of the reasons for the aggression."

43. Baghdad: Dar al-Hurriya li-l-Tibaʿa, 1983. Raʾuf is listed as an assistant professor of modern Arab history at the Faculty of Education (a position equivalent to an associate professorship in the United States). Assigning the introduction of this widely distributed volume to an unknown historian drawn from the Faculty of Education rather than a history department is odd and would seem to indicate either a lack of interest in the volume by traditional historians, or the regime's need to resort to lesser lights who would argue its increasingly untenable intellectual positions.

44. Baghdad: Dar al-Hurriya li-l-Tibaʿa, 1989. Saddam's essay is entitled, "Arab History and the Destructive Role of the Shuʿubiya," 11–54.

45. In seeking to assess the strength of Iraqi Pan-Arabism as compared to Iraqist nationalism, it is noteworthy that Saddam and the Baʿth Party continually theorize space/location/nationhood in a way that the Iraqist nationalists, including the Iraqi left, have yet to successfully theorize themselves. Being more concrete, such notions are often easier to comprehend than the more abstract concept of social class, which the communists, for example, have privileged in their political discourse.

46. Aburish, *Saddam Husayn*, 201.

47. The newspaper's masthead describes it as "a political, military daily newspaper." Above the newspaper's title is Saddam's saying, "The pen and the rifle [come from] the same source " *(al-Qalam wa-l-Bunduqiya Fuha Wahida)*.

48. Aburish, *Saddam Husayn*, 203.

49. Ibid., 199.

50. "The Mr. President Leader Who Is Victorious by the Will of God."

51. For the best analysis of the changing Iraqi political economy and how it affected the fortunes of upper echelon members of the Baʿth Party and their allies in the private sector, see al-Khafaji, *al-Dawla wa Tatawwur al-Raʾsmaliya*.

52. Aburish, *Saddam Husayn*, 237.

53. The chant was *"as-Sayyid Mahdi mu jasus, ismaʿ ya raʾis"* (Listen, Mr. President, al-Sayyid Mahdi is not a spy). Robert Soeterik, *The Islamic Movement of Iraq, 1958–1980* (Amsterdam: Middle East Research Associates, Occasional Paper no. 12, 1980), 18.

54. Most observers agree that the Hizb al-Da'wa al-Islamiya (Party of the Islamic Call) was formed by religiously oriented Shi'is during the late 1960s in the Shi'i shrine cities of Karbala' and al-Najaf. However, the organization only became active during the late 1970s and 1980, at the time of the Islamic Revolution in neighboring Iran. See ibid., 21; and Joyce Wiley, *The Islamic Movements of Iraqi Shi'as* (Boulder, Colo.: Lynne Rienner, 1992), 53–66.

55. al-Sadr was a prolific writer. See, for example, one of his most famous works, *Iqtisaduna [Our Economy]*, 2d ed. (Beirut: Dar al-Fikr, 1970).

56. The state produced a glossy brochure of photographs of Saddam performing the pilgrimage. See Da'irat al-'Alam al-Dhakili, *Ziyarat al-Sayyid al-Ra'is al-Qa'id Saddam Husayn li-l-'Atabat al-Muqqadisa [The Visits of the Leader President Saddam Husayn to the Muslim Holy Sites]* (Baghdad: Dar al-Hurriya li-l-Tiba'a, n.d.).

57. Needless to say, no actual physical representation of Abu Waqqas exists.

58. For reproductions of these images, see Samir al-Khalil, *The Monument: Art, Vulgarity and Responsibility in Iraq* (Berkeley: University of California Press, 1991); for more information on this study, see my review in *The Middle East Journal* 46, no. 1 (Winter 1992): 102–3. See also the image in Aburish, *Saddam Husayn*, between pages 184 and 185.

59. In the piece that I wrote in the *New York Times* referred to above, I argued that predictions that Iraq's Shi'a would support Iran were ill founded.

60. On the economic costs and casualties of the war, see Abbas Alnasrawi, *The Economy of Iraq: Oil, Wars, Destruction of Development and Prospects, 1950–2010* (Westport, Conn.: Greenwood Press, 1994), 120; for Iraqi casualties during the Gulf War, see Geoff Simons, *Iraq: From Sumer to Saddam*, 2d ed. (New York: St. Martin's Press, 1996), 7. According to Sa'id Aburish, Iraq owed $35 billion to Western creditors, $40 billion to Saudi Arabia and Kuwait, and $11 billion to the USSR (*Saddam Husayn*, 259).

61. Aburish, *Saddam Husayn*, 263.

62. This would seem to be indicated by Saddam's comments regarding the war. His constant talk about sacrifice, patience, and developing greater national self-confidence all point to the regime's perception that it had to prepare the populace for an extended struggle with Iran. See Hadi Hasan 'Alaywi and Walid al-Hadithi, *Saddam Husayn wa Qadaya fi-l-Thaqafa wa-l-'Alam [Saddam Husayn and Issues Regarding Culture and Information]* (Baghdad: Ministry of Culture and Information, Dar al-Shu'un al-Thaqafiya al-'Amma, 1991), 180, 190–95. Saddam's objectives in starting the war and his perceptions of where it might lead have still not been satisfactorily explained. Did he feel that the invasion would embarrass Khumayni by forcing him to quickly sue for peace? Did he seek to annex Iranian territory? Did he not realize that, whatever the military outcome of the war, he might create a festering political crisis with Iran?

63. Davis and Gavrielides, "Statecraft, Historical Memory and Popular Culture in Iraq and Kuwait," in *Statecraft in the Middle East: Oil, Historical Memory and Popular Culture* (Miami: Florida International University Press / University Presses of Florida, 1991), ed. Davis and Gavrielides, 135–38.

64. "Bi-l-Dhikri al-Thaniya li Ziyarat al-Qaʾid fi Irwaʿ Mahrajan Jamahiri, Muhafizat al-Qadisiya Tuʿabbir ʿan Hubbiha wa Wifaʾiha li Qaʾid al-Nasr" [On the Anniversary of the Leader's Visit to the Most Wonderful Popular Festival, al-Qadisiya Province Expresses It Love and Loyalty to the Victorious Leader], *al-Jumhuriya*, Jan. 14, 1984.

65. *Saddam Hussein on Current Events in Iraq* (London: Longman Group, 1977); *Saddam Hussein on Social and Foreign Affairs in Iraq* (London: Croom Helm, 1979).

66. Aburish, *Saddam Husayn*, 328. According to Dr. Muhsin Jasim al-Musawi, the former president of the board of directors of al-Adib al-ʿArabi, the new publishing house, the reasons behind its creation were largely financial, reflecting the absorption of the private publishing house directed by Dr. al-Musawi, which had been very successful in terms of both the number of its publications (which far exceeded in one year what the Ministry of Culture and Information had published during the previous six years) and profits. The state's interest in absorbing this publishing venture reflected less its interest in its lists, which included many of the latest works of cultural criticism published in the West, than an interest in making profits. This again reflects the increasing subordination of cultural production to material incentives during the 1980s. Interview, Dr. al-Musawi, Tunis, July 19, 2000.

67. al-Khalil, *The Monument*, 25–29.

68. Jabbar Audah Allawi, "Television and Film in Iraq: A Socio-Political and Cultural Study, 1946–1980," Ph.D. diss., University of Michigan, 1983, 238–41.

69. Aburish, *Saddam Hussein*, 327.

70. Adel Darwish and Gregory Alexander, *Unholy Babylon: The Secret History of Saddam's War* (New York: St. Martin's Press, 1991), 124–25.

CHAPTER 8. MEMORIES OF STATE AND THE ARTS
OF RESISTANCE

1. Elizabeth Picard has argued that Baʿthist ideology, "functions [or acts] as a utopia and not as a program" (fonctionne comme une utopie et non comme un programme). Its ideology must remain vague and abstract because it is required to encompass so many divergent interests, "from the Persian Gulf to the Atlantic Ocean." See "Le régime irakien et la crise: les ressorts d'une politique," *Maghreb/Machrek* 130 (Oct.–Dec. 1990): 32.

2. *Fi Sabil al-Baʿth al-ʿArabi* (Beirut: Dar al-Taliʿa, 1963), and *Nidal al-Baʿth*, 11 vols. (Beirut: Dar al-Talʿia li-l-Tibaʿa wa-l-Nashr, 1976).

3. For publications statistics at the beginning of the Baʿthist regime, see chapter 6. For the dramatic decline in the number of publications after the Gulf War, see chapter 9.

4. Interview with Dr. Muhsin Jasim al-Musawi, former editor in chief of *Afaq ʿArabiya*, Tunis, Mar. 15, 2000.

5. Dr. Muhsin al-Musawi notes that numerous studies were recommended by Baghdad University faculty members. For example, Professor ʿAbd Il-Ilah

Ahmad at Baghdad University's Faculty of Arts, who, as a specialist on the Iraqi short story, supervised many theses on Iraqi literature, subsequently recommended his students' work to the ministry for publication. Interview, Tunis, Mar. 15, 2000.

6. Some studies, such as Ja°far °Abbas Humaydi's *al-Tatawwurat wa-l-Ittijahat al-Siyasiya al-Dhakhilya fi-l-°Iraq, 1953–1958,* cited in chapter 4, were in fact of high quality and based upon extensive research.

7. See, for example, Dia' °Abd al-Jalil al-Shaybani, "al-°A'ila bi-Hayy Jamila fi Madinat Baghdad" [The Family in the Jamila Quarter of Baghdad], Master's thesis, Department of Sociology, Baghdad University, 1974; Muhammad Harbi Hasan, "Aham al-Mushakil al-°Ummaliya fi Masani° Baghdad" [The Most Important Labor Problems in Baghdad Factories], Master's thesis, Department of Sociology, Baghdad University, 1974; Ibrahim Mushab al-Dulaymi, "al-Hijira al-Mu°akisa: Dirasa Ijtima°iya li Ahwal Muhajirin min Madinat Baghdad" [Reverse Migration: A Sociological Study of the Conditions of Migrants From Baghdad], Master's thesis, Department of Sociology, Baghdad University, 1976; and °Abd °Ali Salman °Abdallah, "Qaryat al-Sharsh" [al-Sharsh Village], Master's thesis, Department of Sociology, Baghdad University, 1976, which was supervised by the famous Iraqi anthropologist Dr. Shakir Mustafa Salim. Only Salman's study was later published by the Ministry of Culture and Information, under the title *al-Mujtama° al-Rifi fi-l-°Iraq* [*Rural Society in Iraq*] (Baghdad: Dar al-Rashid li-l-Nashr, 1980). I would like to thank Zahida Ibrahim, former director of Iraq's National Library, for having these theses photocopied for me.

8. The agrarian policies that Saddam and his "family party" began to implement in 1980 entirely contradicted the 1974 Eighth Party Congress's objectives with regards to rural society.

9. This reputation was based in large measure on his two-volume ethnography of a village in the southern marshes. See Shakir Mustafa Salim, *al-Shabayyish* (Baghdad: Matba°at al-Rabita, 1956, 1957).

10. Dr. Isam al-Khafaji, in a conversation at New York University on Apr. 12, 2000, pointed to a similar problem in Syria, where, until recently, he was editor in chief of *Jadal (Controversy)*. To avoid censorship, he informed Syrian authorities that, since it was often 200–330 pages in length, *Jadal* was in fact a book and not a journal.

11. Baghdad: Baghdad University Press, 1978.

12. See, for example, his M.A. thesis, which received the evaluation of *jayyid jiddan* from the Faculty of Arts at Cairo University in 1964 and was published the same year in Baghdad as *al-Furusiya fi-l-Shi°r al-Jahili* [*Chivalry in Pre-Islamic Poetry*] by Baghdad University and al-Nahda Press. This was followed by his two-volume *Shu°ara Umawiyin* [*Umayyad Poets*] in 1976, also published by Baghdad University Press. It is noteworthy that his publication of *Poetry and History* coincided with his rapid rise from assistant professor in 1976 to dean of the Faculty of Arts in 1980.

13. Dr. Muhsin al-Musawi notes that al-Qaysi, whatever the impact of his

earlier contact with the left, always had a sectarian edge to him. Interview, Tunis, May 16, 2000.

14. The prominent playwright Yusif al-ʿAni and the ICP activist-author ʿAziz al-Hajj, who became the Baʿthist regime's representative to UNESCO, are just two of many examples. Other intellectuals tried, sometimes unsuccessfully, to retain their integrity while continuing to work under the Baʿth. Examples include Wamidh ʿUmar al-Nazmi and Saʿd Naji al-Jawad of Baghdad University's Political Science Department and Kamal Mazhar Ahmad of the Department of Philosophy, who recently resigned from the Kurdish Institute in Baghdad.

15. See, for example, his prominent role in the conference "The Role of Literature in Arab Unity," sponsored by the Center for Arab Unity Studies (Markaz Dirassat al-Wahda al-ʿArabiya) in Beirut in 1978, and the published proceedings of the conference, *Dawr al Adab fil-Waʾi al-Qawmi al-ʿArabi [The Role of Literature in the Pan-Arab Nationalist Consciousness]*, 2d ed. (Beirut: Center for Arab Gulf Studies, 1982).

16. al-Qaysi, *al-Shiʿr wa-l-Tarikh*, 18, 20.

17. Ibid., 30.

18. The following incident indicates how sensitive the regime was to discussions of tribalism during the 1970s. A Baghdad University faculty member told me that he was imprisoned for three months upon returning from his studies in Europe because he had mentioned, during a talk before an Arab students organization in England, that tribal factors still influenced recruitment to posts in the Foreign Ministry. Upon leaving prison he was told that if he ever made the remark again he would return to prison and never come out.

19. *Ashaʾir al-ʿIraq [The Tribes of Iraq]*, 4 vols. (Baghdad: Matbaʿat al-Maʿarif, 1947).

20. al-Qaysi, *al-Shiʿr wa-l-Tarikh*, 29.

21. Marshall G. S. Hodgson, *The Venture of Islam: Conscience and History in a World Civilization*, vol. 1, *The Classical Age of Islam* (Chicago: University of Chicago Press, 1974), 487–88.

22. al-Qaysi, *al-Shiʿr wa-l-Tarikh*, 208–9.

23. Ibid., 197.

24. Faysal al-Samir, *Thawrat al-Zanj [The Zanj Rebellion]* (Baghdad: n.p., 1967).

25. al-Qaysi, *al-Shiʿr wa-l-Tarikh*, 13. The author makes the argument, which was shortly thereafter implemented by the Ministry of Culture and Information, that history writing should be collective rather than individual.

26. See the discussion of the debate between Dhu al-Nun Ayyub, who adopts this position, and ʿAbd al-ʿAziz al-Duri, who does not, in chapter 5. In *Li-l-Haqiqa wa-l-Tarikh [For Truth and History]* (Baghdad: al-Sharika al-Wataniya li-l-Tibaʿa wa-l-ʿAlan, 1962), Ayyub argues that the peasantry has retained a strong sense of social class consciousness, which began in ancient Mesopotamia.

27. Here it is important to recall the first question that Saddam poses about history writing on page 7 of *On the Writing of History* (Baghdad: Dar al-

Hurriya li-l-Tibaʿa, 1979): "Li Man Yuktab al-Tarikh?" (For Whom Is History Written?").

28. Indeed, the tribesman in the center of the cover of *Poetry and History* is riding a white horse.

29. al-Qaysi, *al-Shiʿr wa-l-Tarikh*, 20–21.

30. Ibid., 192.

31. In 1998 al-Samarraʾi provided information on ʿUday's international cocaine-smuggling ring in exchange for political asylum in the United Kingdom. See "Saddam's Son is a Cocaine Kingpin," *Times of London*, as reported by Tabloid News Service, Feb. 9, 1998, www.tabloid.net/1998/02/09/.

32. al-Samarraʾi, *al-Tayyar al-Qawmi*, 452.

33. Ibid., 5, 12.

34. Ibid., 146.

35. Terri DeYoung, *Placing the Poet: Badr Shakir al-Sayyab and Postcolonial Iraq* (Albany: State University of New York Press, 1998), 244–45.

36. al-Samarraʾi, *al-Tayyar al-Qawmi*, 62.

37. Ibid., 50.

38. al-Qaysi, *al-Shiʿr wa-l-Tarikh*, 65, n. 42. It is interesting to note the perhaps intentional parallel between the title of the cited ICP pamphlet and the main anti-ICP text distributed by the Baʿth Party during the late 1970s, *Adwaʾ ʿala al-Haraka al-Shuyuʿiya fi-l-ʿIraq [Shedding Light on the Communist Movement in Iraq]*, 5 vols. (Beirut: Dar al-Mirsad, 197?-1979). According to Dr. Isam al-Khafaji, former ICP member Malik Sayf and Baʿth Party ideologue Fadil al-Barak (al-Takriti) were central in providing the ostensible author of the series with information on the ICP. Interview with Isam al-Khafaji, Rutgers University, Apr. 14, 2000.

39. Baghdad: Ministry of Culture and Information, 1980. The use of the term "novel" *(riwaya)* in the title is somewhat ambiguous. Although at the outset al-Zujaji claims that the novel is but an extension of the short story, the more developed form of writing in Iraq, he seems to use *riwaya* to refer to both genres throughout the volume, applying it, for example, both to Dhu al-Nun Ayyub's two-hundred-page *The Hand, Earth, and Water [al-Yadd, wa-l-Ard, wa-l-Maʾ]* and to conventional short stories that are sometimes quite long.

40. This negativism is supported by many quotes from novels cited by al-Zujaji. Ahmad, the narrator in Ghalib ʿAbd al-Razzaq's novel *Qalat Ayyam*, for example, says, "in my village there is no difference between children and flies," given the many illnesses and short life span of the former. al-Zujaji, *al-Riwaya al-ʿIraqiya wa Qadiyat al-Rif*, 59.

41. To the extent that many of the authors that al-Zujaji criticizes are Shiʿi, and that much of the pre-1958 literature on the Iraqi countryside deals with the south, where the majority of the population is Shiʿi, this work could also be interpreted as intended to further marginalize Shiʿi intellectuals.

42. al-Zujaji, *al-Riwaya al-ʿIraqiya wa Qadiyat al-Rif*, 71.

43. These novels were written by Mahmud Ahmad al-Sayyid, Dhu al-Nun

Ayyub, Edmund Sabri, ʿAbd al-Majid Lutfi, ʿGhalib ʿAbd al-Razzaq, ʿAbd al-Wadud ʿIsa, and Husayn Waralkafali respectively. For a complete list of the texts analyzed by al-Zujaji, see ibid., 410–11.

44. al-Zujaji cites a number of peasants uprisings, such as that by the Al bu Mutayyat tribe in 1946 in Mosul, the Al Azyurij tribe in al-ʿAmara in 1952, the Duzhi peasants in Arbil in 1953, the al-Shamiya peasants in 1954, and the al-Diwaniya peasants in 1958. These uprisings have yet to receive serious study.

45. al-Zujaji, *al-Riwaya al-ʿIraqiya wa Qadiyat al-Rif,* 90–91.

46. Interview with Dr. Muhsin al-Musawi, Tunis, Feb. 16, 2000. According to Dr. al-Musawi, Baqir al-Zujaji was responsible for secondary school curriculum in the Ministry of Education (Wizarat al-Tarbiya).

47. This accords with Gramsci's opposition to the Leninist notion of the vanguard party because he believed that meaningful revolutionary change could only occur when a revolutionary leadership takes its cues from those it purports to lead. See Gramsci, *Selections from the Prison Notebooks* (London: Lawrence & Wishart, 1971), 418; and Anne Showstack Sassoon, *Gramsci's Politics* (New York: St. Martin's Press, 1980), 46–47.

48. During the summer of 1959, the left-leaning Union of Iraqi Writers sent a delegation of writers and poets to the al-ʿAmara region in southern Iraq to record tribal poetry and women's songs, the first example of any such effort to understand the folk culture of rural Iraqi women. According to the poet Saʿdi Yusif, one of the delegation's members, the al-ʿAmara region was chosen because "close ties had already been established with that area." This comment suggests that the efforts at organization that the ICP had already made in the area facilitated the contacts with local tribes such as the Al Fartus, Al bu Muhammad, Al bu ʿIsa, and al-Azyurij. See Union of Iraqi Writers, *al-Muʾtamar al-Thani li Ittihad al-Udabaʾ al-ʿIraqiyin, Khuzayran, 1960* (Baghdad: Matbaʿat al-Nujum, 1960), 69–76. Saʿdi Yusif's comments were contained in an email message from London dated March 13, 2000. I want to thank Faleh Abdel Jabar for forwarding this information to me.

49. Baghdad: Dar al-Rashid li-l-Nashr, 1981. When I organized a conference on Arab oil states under the auspices of the Social Science Research Council at Rutgers University in August 1985, I extended an invitation to Professor Ahmad, whom I later learned very much wanted to attend. However, Dr. Mustafa ʿAbd al-Qadir al-Najjar, general-secretary of the Union of Arab Historians at the time (and former director of the Center for Arab Gulf Studies at Basra University) and the state's "minder" of Iraqi intellectuals at the conference, failed to secure an exit visa for Professor Ahmad, whose leftism made him much too suspect to represent Iraq in international forums.

50. For a more detailed discussion of this issue, see my "History for the Many or History for the Few? The Historiography of the Iraqi Working Class," *Workers and Working Classes in the Middle East: Struggles, Histories, Historiographies,* ed. Zachary Lockman (Albany: State University of New York Press, 1994), 271–301.

51. It should be noted that the process of state control of labor unions began

under the Qasim regime. However, Qasim never subjected labor unions to the repressive policies followed by subsequent regimes.

52. Ahmad, al-Tabaqa al-ʿAmila, 279, 282.

53. Ibid., 277, 279, 282.

54. This almost six-hundred-page study, Tarikh al-Haraka al-ʿUmmaliya fi-l-ʿIraq, 1922–1958, written by ʿAbd al-Razzaq Mutlak al-Fahd and completed in 1977, is an extremely impressive study both analytically and in terms of its wide range. Ahmad's citation of this study is itself controversial because, first, it indicates that a student interested in the working class was obliged to study at Cairo University, and, second, the study was completed under one of the Arab world's most prominent Marxist historians, Dr. Muhammad Anis.

55. The three works that Ahmad is referring to are Hasan's al-Shakhsiya al-ʿUmmaliya fi-l-Qissa al-ʿIraqiya [The Worker's Character in the Iraqi Short Story] and al-Sihafa al-ʿUmmaliya fi-l-ʿIraq [The Labor Press in Iraq] and Raʾuf Hasan, al-ʿUmmal fil-l-Qissa al-Kurdiya [Workers in the Kurdish Short Story]. See Ahmad, al-Tabaqa al-ʿAmila, 6, n. 5.

56. See note 77 below.

57. Amatzia Baram is incorrect in stating in Culture and Ideology in the Making of Baʿthist Iraq, 1968–1989 (New York: St. Martin's Press, 1991), 31, that the journal began publication in 1969. See Zahida Ibrahim, Kashshaf al-Jaraʾid wa-l-Majallat al-ʿIraqiya, 1869–1978 [Index of Iraqi Newspapers and Journals, 1869–1978] (Kuwait: Dar al-Nashr wa-l-Matbuʿat al-Kuwaytiya, 1982), 328, where she gives the correct date as 1963. Faris Couri, the son of the journal's founder and longtime editor, Lutfi al-Khuri, also confirmed that the journal began publishing intermittently in 1963. Interview, London, July 24, 2000.

58. " 'Majallat ʿal-Turath al-Shaʿbi': Majallat al-Fulklur al-Uwla," ["Popular Heritage": The First Folklore Journal], al-Turath al-Shaʿbi 8, no. 2 (1977): 194.

59. al-Khuri worked in the censorship department, where he met Ibrahim al-Daquqi and also Shakir Sabir al-Dabit, who was to play an important role in the founding of the journal even though he was not particularly interested in folklore. Because Iraqi law required that any founder of a new journal have a university degree, which al-Khuri did not, al-Dabit, an officer and university graduate, was asked to sign the request to establish the new publication submitted to the Ministry of Guidance in November 1963. Interview with Faris Couri, London, July 28, 2000.

60. See the editorial introduction to the journal, vol. 11, no. 1 (1980): 5–6.

61. The star of this film was a Saddam look-alike and son-in-law, Saddam Kamil, who was killed with his brother Husayn in February 1996. See chapter 9 for details of this incident.

62. For a list of these articles from 1969 to 1982, see Center for Scientific Documentation of the Arab Gulf States, Kashshaf Majallat al-Turath al-Shaʿbi, Silsilat al-Kashshafat 4 li-l-Sanawat 1969–1982 [Index of Journals of Popular Culture, Series of Indexes 4, 1969–1982] (Baghdad: n.p., 1984), 10. For further

information on Saddam's use of visual imagery, see "Machismo and Arabism: Saddâm as Lone Hero," in Allen Douglass and Fedwa Malti-Douglas, *Arab Comic Strips: Politics of an Emerging Mass Culture* (Bloomington: Indiana University Press, 1994), 46–59.

63. See the forty-seven-page guide for the Faculty of Law and Politics in 1984, *Dalil Kuliyat al-Qanun wa-l-Siyasa, Jami'at Baghdad, 1984,* published by Baghdad University. In the politics section it lists thirty-six professors, ten specializing in nationalism and the third world, twelve in international relations, seven in political systems, and seven in political theory. Aside from a course on the Palestinian Question required in the first year (p. 42), the four-year curriculum differs little from those of political science departments in Western universities. The faculty's professionalism is further underlined by the issue of its journal *Majallat al-'Alum al-Qanuniya wa-l-Siyasiya [The Journal of Legal and Political Sciences]* celebrating its seventy-fifth jubilee in May 1984. Except for one article on the political status of the Arabs in the Ahwaz region of Iran along the Persian Gulf, all of the articles are scholarly and well documented, giving no hint of an ongoing war with Iran. On the other hand, that same month the faculty sponsored a study by various members of the faculty on Saddam's political and legal thought, Kuliyat al-Qanun wa-l-Siyasa [Faculty of Law and Politics], Baghdad University, *Fi-l-Fikr al-Siyasi w-al-Qanuni li-l-Ra'is al-Qa'id Saddam Husayn [On the Political and Legal Thought of the Leader President Saddam Husayn]* (Baghdad: Dar al-'Arabiya, 1984). Another indicator of the contradictory nature of much of the writing connected with the Ba'thist Project for the Rewriting of History is Dr. Sabbah Kubba's citation in his essay in this volume, "On Development," of Leonard Binder's study *The Ideological Revolution in the Middle East* in support of Ba'thist theory, 317. Certainly Leonard Binder is no supporter of Ba'thism.

64. Baghdad: Dar al-Hurriya li-l-Tiba'a, 1979.

65. "al-Tariq al-'Arabi fi Daw' Fikr Hizb al-Ba'th al-'Arabi al-Ishtiraki wa-l-Tajriba fi-l-Qutr al-'Iraqi," 97–104.

66. Hadi uses speeches written after 1979, namely after Ahmad Hasan al-Bakr was deposed as president.

67. Baghdad: Mu'assasat al-A'lami / Dar al-Tarbiya, 1975.

68. al-Bayati, *al-Bina' al-Ijtima'i,* 105–7.

69. Mosul: Mu'assasat Dar al-Kutub li-l-Tiba'a wa-l-Nashr, 1980.

70. Baqir and Humayd, *Turuq al-Bahth al-'Ilmi,* 77–81.

71. Baqir, *Muqaddima fi Tarikh al-Hidara al-Qadima* (Baghdad: Dar al-Shu'un al-Thaqafiya al-'Amma, 1986), 1: 9.

72. Republic of Iraq, Ministry of Education, *al-Tarikh al-Hadith wa-l-Mu'asir li-l-Watan al-'Arabi li-l-Saff al-Sadis al-Adabi [The Modern and Contemporary History of the Arab Nation for the Sixth Literary Level]* (Arbil: Ministry of Education Press, 1989), 337.

73. Textbooks published by the post–Islamic Revolution regime in Iran exhibit interesting parallels with Iraqi secondary school history textbooks. Despite the new Islamic Republic's claim to have implemented a thoroughgoing revolu-

tionary transformation of Iranian culture and society, secondary school history texts in fact demonstrate no real change from the Pahlavian vision of an "immemorial" Iranian nation. See Haggay Ram, "The Immemorial Iranian Nation? School Textbooks and Historical Memory in Post-Revolution Iran," *Nations & Nationalism* 6, no. 1 (Winter 2000): 67–90.

74. *al-Tarikh al-Hadith*, 175–76.

75. Republic of Iraq, Ministry of Education, *Tarikh al-Hidara al-ʿArabiya al-Islamiya [The History of Arab-Islamic Civilization]* (Baghdad: Sharika al-Sarmad li-l-Tibaʿa al-Mahduda, 1989).

76. Baghdad: Dar al-Hurriya li-l-Tibaʿa, 1979.

77. See James C. Scott, *Domination and the Arts of Resistance: Hidden Transcripts* (New Haven, Conn.: Yale University Press, 1990).

CHAPTER 9. MEMORIES OF STATE OR MEMORIES OF THE PEOPLE?

1. Abbas Alnasrawi estimates Iraqi losses during the six-week Gulf War at between 50,000 and 120,000 soldiers killed. If one takes Dilip Hiro's calculations of 82,000 soldiers killed, Alnasrawi argues that this amounts to between one-third and one-half of the casualties Iraq sustained during the entire (464-week) Iran-Iraq War. Alnasrawi goes on to estimate civilian deaths at between 5,000 and 15,000 during the Gulf War, and between 20,000 and 100,000 during the Intifada, especially in the south. He estimates another 15,000 to 30,000 Kurds died in refugee camps or while displaced from their homes, while an additional 4,000 to 16,000 non-Kurdish Iraqis died from disease and starvation. The combined totals of both the war and Intifada, according to Alnasrawi, was between 94,000 and 281,000 Iraqis. *The Economy of Iraq: Oil, Wars, Destruction of Development and Prospects, 1950–2010* (Westport, Conn.: Greenwood Press, 1994), 120.

2. Placed in comparative perspective, if the same percentage were applied to United States, it would result in an expatriate community of thirty-three million Americans.

3. An early work that openly confronts the issue of sectarianism in Iraqi society is Hasan al-ʿAlawi's *al-Shiʿa wa-l-Dawla al-Qawmiya fi-l-ʿIraq [The Shiʿa and the Nationalist State in Iraq]* (Paris: CEDI Press, 1989). More recent works include Dr. Saʿid al-Samarraʾi, *al-Taʾifiya fi-l-ʿIraq: al-Waqiʿ wa-l-Hall [Sectarianism in Iraq: The Reality and the Solution]* (London: Muʾassasat al-Fajr, 1993); the recent special issue of *al-Mawsim* 33 (1997) on ʿAbd al-Karim Qasim and the July 1958 Revolution; Falih ʿAbd al-Jabbar, *al-Dawla, al-Mujtamaʿ al-Madani wa-l-Tahawwul al-Dimuqrati fi-l-ʿIraq [The State, Civil Society, and the Democratic Transition in Iraq]* (Cairo: Ibn Khaldun Center and Dar al Amin li-l-Nashr wa-l-Tawziʿ, 1995); Dr. Farhad Ibrahim, *al-Taʾifiya wa-l-Siyasa fi-l-ʿAlam al-ʿArabi: Namudhij al-Shiʿa fi-l-ʿIraq, Ruʾya fi Mawduʿ al-Din wa-l-Siyasa fi-l-Mujtamaʿ al-ʿArabi al-Muʿasir [Sectarianism and Politics in the Arab World: The Case of the Shiʿa in Iraq, An Overview of Politics and Religion*

in Contemporary Arab Society] (Cairo: Maktabat Madbuli, 1996). Ibrahim is director of the Free University of Berlin's Middle East Center.

4. See A. Ascherio, T. Cote, et al., "Effects of the Gulf War on Infant and Child Mortality in Iraq," *New England Journal of Medicine* 327, no. 13 (1992); Sarah Graham-Brown, *Sanctioning Iraq: The Politics of Intervention in Iraq* (London: I. B. Tauris), 1999; and Richard Garfield, "The Public Health Impact of Sanctions: Contrasting Responses of Iraq and Cuba," *Middle East Report* 215, 30, no. 2 (Summer 2000): 16–19.

5. These terms are taken from the titles of the following works, respectively: Samir al-Khalil (Kanan Makiya), *The Republic of Fear: The Degradation of Politics in Modern Iraq* (Berkeley: University of California Press, 1989); Kanan Makiya, *Cruelty and Silence: War, Uprising, and the Arab World* (New York, W. W. Norton, 1993); Middle East Watch, *Endless Torture: The 1991 Uprising in Iraq and Its Aftermath* (New York: Human Rights Watch, 1992); Middle East Watch, *Bureaucracy of Repression: The Iraqi Government in Its Own Words* (New York: Middle East Watch, 1994); and Andrew Cockburn and Patrick Cockburn, *Out of the Ashes: The Resurrection of Saddam Hussein* (New York: Harper Collins, 1999).

6. In addition to the $452.6 billion that Iraq is estimated to have lost as a result of the war, Iraq owed Saudi and Kuwait $40 billion, Western states and banks $35 billion, and the Soviet Union $11 billion. Abbas Alnasrawi, *The Economy of Iraq*, 100, 109. As former chief of military intelligence (al-Istikhbarat al-ʿAskariya) Lieutenant-General Wafiq Samarraʾi points out, the regime considered oil prices to be at unacceptable levels in 1989. More than half of Iraq's profits from oil were consumed by interest on the debt it owed. See Samarraʾi, *Hattam al-Bawaba al-Sharqiya [The Destruction of the Eastern Gate]* (Kuwait City: Dar al-Qabas, 1997), 213.

7. Alnasrawi, *The Economy of Iraq*, 110.

8. Eric Davis, "State-Building in Iraq During the Iran-Iraq War and the Gulf Crisis," in Manus I. Midlarsky, ed., *The Internationalization of Communal Strife* (London: Routledge, 1992), 85.

9. For a discussion of some of the events leading up to the Gulf War, see Eric Davis, "The Persian Gulf War: Myths and Reality," in Hooshang Amirahmadi, ed., *The United States and the Middle East: The Search for New Perspectives* (Albany: State University of New York Press, 1993), esp. 258.

10. Because of this military defeat, for example, Saddam's promise to build the world's largest mosque, the Grand Saddam Mosque, in Baghdad, could not be fulfilled. After the foundation was laid and a tower built, construction ceased due to the state's inability to import the construction materials necessary to complete the project. Cockburn and Cockburn, *Out of the Ashes*, 129–30.

11. Most analysts agree that a crucial development was the almost whole-sale defection of the Baʿthist National Brigades (known locally as *jahsh*, Kurdish for "little donkey") who were responsible for law and order in the three Kurdish provinces to the rebels side. See Makiya, *Cruelty and Silence*, 83–84. For a more

detailed view of the Kurdish military role in the Intifada, see Samarra'i, *Hattam al-Bawaba,* 420–25.

12. Prior to 1991, the ICP had not been particularly active in mounting military operations against the Ba'thist regime. Although a breakaway faction of the ICP, the Central Command (al-Qiyada al-Markaziya), had attempted to organize an uprising in the southern marsh areas (al-Ahwar) near the confluence of the Tigris and Euphrates rivers during the late 1960s under the leadership of 'Aziz al-Hajj Haydar, a Fayli (Shi'i) Kurd, this uprising was crushed by the Iraqi army, and al-Hajj and other leaders were taken prisoner. al-Hajj, whom I interviewed in Paris on January 10, 2000, supplied his Ba'thist captors with information about his fellow conspirators subsequent to being arrested and appeared on Iraqi television to renounce his own activities. For these actions, he was later rewarded with the position of Iraq's representative to UNESCO in Paris.

13. I rely here on Michael Wood's video *Saddam's Latest War* (1993), which was produced after the Intifada and was the result of extensive travel by Wood through the Arab and Kurdish parts of Iraq. Wood claims that several SCUD missiles were fired into Karbala' while Republican Guard units were suppressing rebel forces.

14. For a detailed discussion of the Iraqi state's assault on the marshlands near the Shatt al-'Arab, see the Iraqi National Congress web site, www.INC.org.uk. Hans von Sponeck, who resigned as United Nations administrator of humanitarian aid in Iraq on March 31, 2000, indicated to me, at a Princeton University lecture on the effects of United Nations sanctions on Iraq on May 14, 2000, that the marshlands had been completely destroyed. However, there is some evidence that at least one-third of the marshlands may be able to be restored.

15. For details of this campaign, see the following postings on the web site for the Iraqi National Congress: "Mass Executions in Iraq," Dec. 12, 1997; "Over 800 Executions of Opposition Members in Iraq" and "More Names of Executed Prisoners," both Dec. 22, 1997. See also Iraq List (Iraqyahoogroups.com), a list serv that monitors political, social, and cultural developments in Iraq: Jan. 5, 1999, Mar. 22, 1999, and Apr. 13, 1999.

16. For details of past attempts by former Iraqi officers in exile to form their own opposition movement, see "With Potential in the Air, Iraqi Exiles Meet," *New York Times,* July 14, 2002.

17. This is by no means meant to downplay the important contributions of other opposition groups, especially the Iraqi Communist Party, prior to 1991. The ICP's theoretical journal, *al-Thaqafa al-Jadida,* consistently presented insightful critiques of all dimensions of Ba'thist policies throughout the period that the regime was in power. What is important, however, is that the Iraqi opposition after 1991 was much broader than the opposition that existed before the 1990 Gulf War.

18. See, for example, the article by David Aquila Lawrence in the *Christian Science Monitor,* May 3, 2000, which detailed the economic progress of the Kurds during the prior three years.

19. Saïd Aburish reports that blue marble was imported from Argentina at a cost of $3,000 to $4,000 a square meter in midst of the financial crisis. *Saddam Husayn and the Politics of Revenge* (London: Bloomsbury, 2000), 266.

20. The lead article in the July 1, 2000, edition of the *New York Times,* "Flight Tests Show Iraq Has Resumed a Missile Program," indicated that Iraq had developed its al-Samud (resistance) ballistic missile, which could carry conventional or chemical or nuclear payloads. Although its range was less than ninety-five miles, General Anthony Zinni claimed that the technology developed through this missile could easily be transferred to longer-range missiles.

21. For images of Iraqi army deserters and convicted thieves who received these punishments, see the web site of the Iraqi National Congress, www.INC.org.uk.

22. *Fidaʾi* (pl. *fidaʾiyun*) translates as "one who sacrifices," meaning one who would sacrifice his or her life for Saddam.

23. *Alif Ba',* July 15, 1999. See also "Dawra Jadida li ʿAshbal Saddam' " (A New Role for "Saddam's Cubs' "), *al-Hayat,* June 23, 2002.

24. Aburish, *Saddam Husayn,* 235.

25. Samarraʾi, *Hattam al-Bawaba,* 470.

26. Aburish, *Saddam Husayn,* 266.

27. Cockburn and Cockburn, *Out of the Ashes,* 192.

28. Ibid.

29. Jihad Salim, "Hall Yundim Barzan al-Takriti ila al-Muʿarida al-ʿIraqiya?" (Will Barzan al-Takriti Join the Iraqi Opposition?), *al-Watan al-ʿArabi,* Oct. 10, 1998, 24–26.

30. Cockburn, *Out of the Ashes,* 153–54.

31. Falih ʿAbd al-Jabbar, "Min Dawlat Hizb al-Wahid ila Dawlat al-Hizb/al-Usra" (From the One-Party State to the Family/Party State), *al-Thaqafa al-Jadida* 267 (Dec. 1995–Jan./Feb. 1996): 6–28

32. One of Iraq's most prominent players, Sharar Haydar Muhammad al-Hadithi, was imprisoned and had his feet beaten, then dragged over gravel and thrown into sewer water to make his wounds become infected, after Iraq lost an important soccer match. Jon Swain, "Foul Play—It's a Grim Life in Saddam United FC," *Sunday Times* (London), Aug. 15, 1999.

33. See the Iraqi newspaper *al-Ittihad,* Dec. 1, 1998, in which a photograph of ʿUday appeared with Saddam after his Ph.D. dissertation defense. The photograph's caption indicated that the defense continued for five hours due to the depth of ʿUday's thoughts and the audience's interest in his ideas. Needless to say, he received the highest ranking *(imtiyaz)* for his defense. It should be noted that ʿUday was the publisher of the newspaper.

34. The web site was formerly at www.index.com.jo/Iraqtoday/.

35. One of ʿUday's university instructors was tortured for not awarding him highest honors when he graduated in 1984. See Aburish, *Saddam Husayn,* 236.

36. Ibid., 339.

37. Ibid., 221. Aburish notes, "This was the end of Saddam the populist, for after Dujail he never made an impromptu visit anywhere. This must have come

as a blow to him—by all accounts he truly enjoyed doing so and engaging people in spontaneous conversation."

38. Ibid., 325.

39. Cockburn and Cockburn, Out of the Ashes, 251–53. Apparently, ʿUday escaped being killed because, unlike most evenings, he was not driving but rather sitting in the front passenger seat.

40. Aburish, Saddam Husayn, 266.

41. Such was the fate of Rifat Chadirji—son of Kamil al-Chadirji, former president of the NDP—who served as Saddam's counselor for urban planning between 1981 and 1982. Prior to assuming this position, Chadirji had been in the notorious Abu Ghurayb prison because of the resentment a former al-Muthanna Airport security guard, now a Baʿthist official, had felt toward his father. Because the security guard felt that Chadirji's father had slighted him by refusing to salute him at the airport, he concocted a story that resulted in Chadirji's imprisonment until Saddam had him released to help him enact a huge urban development project in Baghdad. Interview with Rifat Chadirji, Surrey, England, Jan. 20, 2000.

42. One such figure was the former head of General Security, Fadil Barak (al-Takriti), who distinguished himself in ferreting out al-Daʿwa members during the late 1980s. al-Samarraʾi, Hattam al-Bawaba, 192–93.

43. Aburish, Saddam Husayn, 328.

44. For a discussion of this development, see the excellent article by Amatzia Baram, "Neo-tribalism in Iraq: Saddam Hussein's Tribal Politics," International Journal of Middle Eastern Studies 29 (1997): 1–31; and also, more recently, the fine intervention by Faleh Abdel Jabbar, "Shaykhs and Ideologues: Detribalization and Retribalization in Iraq, 1968–1998," Middle East Report 215, 30, no. 2 (Summer 2000): 28–31, 48.

45. See, for example, the study by Farhan Ahmad Saʿid, Al Rabiʿ al-Taʾi (Beirut: al-Dar al-ʿArabiya li-l-Mawsuʿat, 1983). This study emphasizes the need to reexamine tribal history, which the author asserts precedes Islam and has been neglected (5, 7). Interestingly, the book's jacket emphasizes the author's extensive career as a lawyer and police official, indicating that the study was written by someone the Baʿth considered politically trustworthy.

46. On the development of Iraq's Shiʿi community during the nineteenth and twentieth centuries, see the excellent study by Yitzhak Nakash, The Shiʿis of Iraq (Princeton, N.J.: Princeton University Press, 1994).

47. Baram, "Neo-tribalism in Iraq," 6.

48. For an analysis of the transformation of the Revolution Command Council and the Baʿth Party from old-line party members, intellectuals, and army officers to rural lower-middle-class officials, see Amatzia Baram, "The Ruling Political Elite in Baʿthi Iraq, 1968–1986: The Changing Features of a Collective Profile," International Journal of Middle Eastern Studies 21 (1986): 447–93.

49. An analysis of al-Wardi's views is contained in ʿAli al-Wardi fi-l-Tabʿia al-Bashariya: Taqdim Saʿd al-Bazzaz [ʿAli al-Wardi on Human Nature: Pre-

sented by Sa'd al-Bazzaz] (Amman: al-Ahliya li-l-Nashr wa-l-Tawzi'a, 1996), which is discussed below.

50. In this sense, it makes sense to speak of the political economy of cultural production, because a state's effort to appropriate historical memory is clearly dependent on the resources at its disposal. The Nasir regime in Egypt after the 1952 Revolution established a Ministry of Guidance, which the Qasim regime undoubtedly used as a model for its own, and began efforts to restructure understandings of the past. One of the results of these efforts was *Ikhtarna Laka [We Have Chosen for You]*, a series of small books on historical and cultural topics, which the Ba'th seem to have copied in their own *al-Mawsu'a al-Saghira [The Little Encyclopedia]*, which had reached 129 volumes by 1983. However, Egypt did not have the same resources as Iraq, especially oil wealth, to establish the same system of cultural production.

51. For publication figures for 1977, see Ministry of Culture and Arts, Republic of Iraq, *Culture and Arts in Iraq* (Baghdad: n.p., 1978), 142; and al-Dabbagh, "Ta'thir al-Hussar 'ala al-Thaqafa wa-l-Ta'lim fi-l-'Iraq wa Majabituhu," *Afaq 'Arabiya* 20, nos. 7/8 (July–Aug. 1994): 31.

52. For some of the attacks on government forces and officials in Shi'i areas in the south, see the SCIRI web site, particularly http://ourworld.compuserve.com/homepages/sciri/news.htm#95.

53. Aburish, *Saddam Husayn*, 336.

54. Dr. Wadood Hamad believes that the style of the articles indicates that they may have been authored by Saddam's long-time confidant and intellectual mentor and the former editor in chief of *al-Thawra*, Tariq 'Aziz. Whoever the author was, there is no doubt that these articles reflected Saddam's views above all else. Interview with Dr. Hamad, Mahwah, New Jersey, July 18, 2000.

55. These articles were reprinted in *al-Milaff al-'Iraqi [The Iraq File]*, which is published by the Center for Iraqi Studies in Surrey, England. I am grateful to Ambassador Rend Rahim, former director of the Iraq Foundation, Washington, D.C., for providing me with a copy of these articles.

56. For details of the uprising, see Majid al-Majid, *Intifadat al-Sha'b fi-l-'Iraq [The Uprising of the Iraqi People]* (Beirut: Dar al-Wifaq, 1991); Muhammad al-'Abbasi, *Min al-Zakhu ila Karbala': Qissat al-Mu'amira 'ala al-Thawra al-Sha'biya fi-l-'Iraq [From Zakho to Karbala: The Story of the Conspiracy Against the People's Uprising in Iraq]* (Cairo: al-Zahara' li-l-'Alam al-'Arabi, 1992); and Kanan Makiya, *Cruelty and Silence*.

57. One can find references in Saddam's writings to specific issues relating to Iraqi culture, such as his reference to the different types of headdresses worn by Kurds and Arabs on holidays and at celebratory rituals. However, such references are invariably parenthetical to idealized claims about a culturally homogenous society. In the instance just cited, Saddam's reference to headdresses does not constitute a recognition and respect for difference but is rather a discourse on how culture should be manipulated to make Kurds and Arabs feel as though they are part of the same culture. See *Hawla Kitabat al-Tarikh* (Baghdad: Dar al-Hurriya li-l-Tiba'a, 1979), 7–9.

58. *al-Thawra*, Apr. 4, 17.

59. Following what we might call "al-ʿAlawi's law of sectarian response to crises," Saddam appointed a prominent Shiʿi, Saʿdun Hammadi, as prime minister immediately after the Intifada was suppressed. Hammadi only served until the following fall, when he was replaced by a less prominent Shiʿi, Muhammad Hamza al-Zubaydi. I refer here to Hasan al-ʿAlawi's observation that all major crises under the monarchy and after have led to the temporary appointments of Shiʿi prime ministers. See *al-Shiʿa wa-l-Dawla al-Qawmiya fi-l-ʿIraq* (Paris: CEDI, 1989).

60. London: Longmans, 1964.

61. Shakir Mustafa Salim, *al-Shabayyish*, 2 vols. (Baghdad: Matbaʿat al-Rabita, 1956, 1957).

62. The way in which Saddam was described in the Baʿthist press reflected this deified status. See, for example, his speech on July 17, 1999, in the newspaper *al-Qadisiya* on the twenty-first anniversary of the July 1968 Revolution, which is prefaced by reference to him as *"al-Qaʾid al-Mansur bi-Allah"* (the Leader who is victorious by the will of God).

63. By "March 11 Declaration," Saddam is referring to the agreement in the March 11, 1970 Manifesto giving the Kurds semiautonomous status in Kurdistan. The Baʿth never implemented the agreement, and fighting between the regime and Kurdish forces broke out again in 1974. See Edmund Ghareeb, *The Kurdish Question in Iraq* (Syracuse, N.Y.: Syracuse University Press, 1981), 113–15, and al-Khalil, *Republic of Fear*, 6.

64. In this regard, it is interesting that a secret report written by Saddam entitled "Plan of Action: A Top Secret Internal Memo," dated January 20, 1992, and distributed to "All Department Heads, Sector Officers, and Headquarters Branches" by the director of Taʾmim Governorate Security, states, "We in the Leadership and the Party consider the factions that took up arms against us during the rabble, as being irresponsible and as having failed to comprehend the Leader Party's principles. Our articles in the *al-Thawra* newspaper, in the aftermath of what they called their uprising, are sufficient for them, even if they did wound and scratch some of them and we have received some blame from the mothers (of lost sons)" (www.pbs.org/wgbh/frontline/shows/saddam/readings/action.html). In addition to showing that Saddam felt no remorse for the Iraqi regime's suppression of the Intifada, these comments show that he still took no responsibility for the uprising. The report was uncovered by the investigative reporters associated with the United States public television program *Frontline*.

65. For a genealogy that purports to trace Saddam's lineage to ʿAli, see Amin Iskandar, *Saddam Husayn: Munadilan wa Mufakkiran wa Insanan [Saddam Husayn: Fighter, Thinker and Human Being]* (Paris: Hachette, 1980), 21.

66. Aburish, *Saddam Husayn*, 15.

67. Tulfah is well known for his infamous "book," *Three Whom God Should Not Have Created: Persians, Jews and Flies*. The sociological reasons that many Takritis seem to have felt this way needs to be studied historically, since their

opinions differ dramatically from those expressed by other Sunni Arabs, Shiʿis, and minority groups who did not resent living in mixed ethnic neighborhoods. The writings of ʿAli al-Wardi represent one place to begin an analysis of ethnic relations in Iraq. See, for example, his *Dirasa fi Tabiʿat al-Mujtamaʿ al-ʿIraqi [A Study of the Nature of Iraqi Society]* (Baghdad: Matbaʿat al-ʿAni, 1965).

68. Aburish, *Saddam Husayn*, 21–22.

69. The conference papers were published the following year. See Nuri Hammudi al-Qaysi et al., *al-Thaqafa al-ʿArabiya wa-l-Tahaddi [The Challenge to Arab Culture]* (Beirut: Center for Arab Unity Studies, 1995).

70. Dr. al-ʿAli's purported Pan-Arabism raises a number of questions in light of his concern with Baʿthist cultural policies that he discussed with me at meetings at his home and at the Iraqi Academy in May 1980 and June 1984. Further, his emphasis on the impact of the prominent Egyptian historian Shafiq Ghurbal, with whom many Iraqi historians completed their advanced studies and who was not known for having a particular interest in Pan-Arabism, leads one to question the extent to which his adoption of Pan-Arab positions reflects sincere convictions or merely political expediency, or perhaps a combination of both. Originally from Mosul, a city known for its Pan-Arab sympathies, al-ʿAli probably felt most comfortable with the conservative Pan-Arabism of his former colleague and fellow Society of Iraqi Authors and Writers member, ʿAbd al-ʿAziz al-Duri.

71. al-Qaysi et al., *al-Thaqafa al-ʿArabiya*.

72. Hammadi still remained within the corridors of power as president of the Iraqi parliament as of April 2002. See *al-Jumhuriya*, Apr. 15, 2002.

73. al-Qaysi et al., *al-Thaqafa al-ʿArabiya*, 17.

74. In the 1980 conference "The Role of Literature in Pan-Arab Nationalism," al-Qaysi offered yet another lecture on this topic, "(Arab) Unity and the Role of Poetry Before Islam" [al-Wahda wa Dawr al-Shiʿr Qabla al-Islam], published in Center for Arab Gulf Studies, *Dawr al-Adab fi-l-Waʿi al-Qawmi al-ʿArabi [The Role of Literature in the Pan-Arab Nationalist Consciousness]*, 2d ed. (Beirut: Center for Arab Unity Studies, 1982), 59–90.

75. In using the term "al-Jahiliya" to refer to the pre-Islamic period, al-Qaysi was criticized by a young philosophy professor, ʿAli Husayn al-Jabiri.

76. al-Qaysi et al., *al-Thaqafa al-ʿArabiya*, 33.

77. Ibid., 36.

78. See *Afaq ʾArabiya* 3 (1989), for example, for the discussion of Orientalism.

79. When I first visited Iraq during the spring of 1980, everyone with whom I spoke had nothing but contempt for Tuwalba, who was at that time a propaganda czar.

80. ʿAli al-Wardi, *ʿAli al-Wardi fi al-Tabiʿa al-Bashariya*, 7.

81. The 81-page April–June 1995 issue should be compared to issues during the 1980s; the March 1980 issue had 432 pages.

82. See the interview by the editors of *Dirasat Ijtimaʿiya* with al-Farah under the title "al-Mashruʿ al-Nahdawi al-ʿArabi" [The Arab Renaissance Proj-

ect], which focused on the consequences of the Mother of All Battles for re-building Arab unity (2–7).

83. "Stratijiyat al-Hujum wa Mawqif al-Muthaqqafin" [The Strategy of Attack and the Position of the Intelligentsia], 4–6. While at the Iraqi Mission to the United Nations, al-Mukhtar was a key figure in organizing my first trip to Iraq during the spring of 1980.

84. See his article "Min al-Dawla al-Diniya ila al-Dawla al-Qawmiya" [From the Religious State to the Pan-Arab Nationalist State], *Dirasat ʿArabiya* 8 (June 1980): 24–33.

85. Iraqi informants assert that ʿUday did not write the dissertation but rather had others write it for him.

86. Marshall Hodgson, *The Venture of Islam: Conscience and History in a World Civilization*, vol. 1: *The Classical Age of Islam* (Chicago: University of Chicago Press, 1974), 298.

87. See, for example, Muhammad ʿAli Ibrahim, "al-Bitaqa al-Dawʾiya: Hall Wudiʿat Haddan li Tassarub al-Adwiya min al-ʿIyadat al-Shaʿbiya" [The Medi-cine Identity Card: Has It Placed a Limit on the Flight of Medicine from Gov-ernment Clinics?], *Babil*, Dec, 2, 1998; and ʿAbd al-Zahra al-Hindawi, "Tadris Khususi Bi Asar Khususi Jiddan!!!" [Private Lessons for a Very Private [Special] Price!!!], in the "Qadiyat al-Saʿa" (Issues of the Moment) section in the No-vember 29, 1998, issue of *al-Musawwar al-ʿArabi*, which concerns the efforts of schoolteachers to intimidate students—even very young children—into taking private lessons at a fee, even during normal school hours.

88. A number of members of the regime's inner circle apparently felt that conditions in Iraq were not that bad. Dr. Muhsin al-Musawi indicated to me that Salah al-Mukhtar, the Iraqi diplomat and editor in chief of *Political Affairs*, made this argument at a conference in Malaysia in the late 1990s. Such ostrich-like thinking was another indicator of the regime's failure to develop a long-term strategy for Iraq's future and of the Baʿthist state's inability to comprehend its position within a larger nexus of power. Interview with Dr. Muhsin Jasim al-Musawi, Toronto, July 19, 2000.

89. *al-ʿIraq* was founded in February 1976.

90. See, for example, Dr. Hamid al-Jumayli, "Tazayud al-Talab ʿala Naft Obik wa Namu al-Iqtisad al-ʿAlami Khilal al-Nisf al-Thani min ʿAqd al-Tisʿinat" [The Increased Demand for OPEC Oil During the Second Half of the 1990s], *Afaq ʿArabiya* 7/8 (July–Aug. 1995): 15–22. Politically, this article re-flects an effort to focus public thinking on the period beyond the embargo by stressing that the global market cannot survive without Iraqi oil production.

91. For front-page articles and photographs of Saddam's new monument, see "al-Qaʾid Yutalliʿa ʿala Namudhij Tasmim Nusb Milhamat Saddam" [The Leader Inspects a Model of the Design for Saddam's Epic Battle Monument], *al-ʿIraq*, Apr. 16, 2002; and "al-Qaʾid al-Mujahid Yutalliʿa ʿala Namudhij Tasmim Nusb Milhamat Saddam" [The Struggler Leader Inspects a Model of the Design for the Monument to Saddam's Epic Struggle], *al-Jumhuriya*, Apr. 16, 2002. The artist who designed the monument is Dr. ʿAlaʾ Bashir.

92. By this I mean that Saddam has a much more developed sense of the history of political struggle in Iraq than did 'Uday, and Saddam was much more calculating and hence effective in eliminating actual and potential opponents compared to his much less sophisticated and less intelligent son. These remarks are in no way meant to suggest that Saddam was a leader in any positive sense of the term.

93. For views during the 1990s on the possibility of using the opposition to bring down Saddam, see "Ousting Saddam Seen as a Long Shot," *Washington Post,* Feb. 20, 1998; Kenneth Katzman, "CRS Report: Iraq's Opposition Movements," www.fas.org/irp/crs/crs-iraq-op.htm; and "New Evidence of Clinton's Failure Update: Humiliation in Iraq," House Republican Policy Committee Policy Perspective, Oct. 22, 1996, http://policy.house.gov/Prspctvs/update2.htm.

94. Interview with Ghanim Hamdun al-Muri, former editor in chief of *al-Thaqafa al-Jadida,* London, May, 16, 2000.

95. See the proceedings of the conference at www.iraqifd.org/anaheim-Feb262000.html.

96. David Aquila Lawrence, "Iraqi Kurds Enjoy a De Facto State," *Christian Science Monitor,* May 3, 2000. Despite the embargo, it should be noted that the KDP cooperated with the Ba'thist regime to smuggle oil through Kurdistan to Turkey. In this instance, the embargo was not strictly enforced. In a play on words, this led to the satirical reference to the leadership of the Kurdish Democratic Party (KDP) and Patriotic Union of Kurdistan (PUK), which controlled the smuggling, as "Umm al-Gamarik," or the "Mother of all Customs," drawing a parallel with Saddam's title for the 1991 Gulf War as the "Mother of All Battles" (Umm al-Ma'arik).

97. See Stratfor Special Reports, "Yugoslavia and Iraq: The Alliance Reunites," Nov. 9, 1999, www.stratfor.com/MEAF/specialreports/special.8.htm.

98. See the seventeen essays in the special issue on Qasim, *al-Mawsim* 33 (1997), a journal that describes itself as a quarterly dedicated to archaeology and Islamic tradition and is published by the Kufa Academy in the Netherlands. The cover displays a photograph of Qasim under which is written "The Leader *[al-Za'im]* 'Abd al-Karim Qasim: Founder of the Iraqi Republic." Of special interest are: 'Ala' al-Din al-Thahir, "al-Jawanib al-Ijabiya fi 'Ahd wa Shakhsiyat al-Fariq al-Rukn 'Abd al-Karim Qasim" [The Positive Aspects of the Era and Personality of the Staff Brigadier 'Abd al-Karim Qasim], 58–93; 'Abd al-Khaliq Husayn, "al-Za'im 'Abd al-Karim Qasim wa Mawdu' al-Dimuqratiya" [The Leader 'Abd al-Karim Qasim and the Question of Democracy]; and 'Adnan Fadil, "Janib min Shakhsiyat Qa'id Thawrat 14 Tammuz fi-l-'Iraq: 'Abd al-Karim Qasim wa-l-Ta'ifiya" [An Aspect of the Personality of the July 14th Revolution in Iraq's Leader: 'Abd al-Karim Qasim and Sectarianism], 127–29. See also al-Samarra'i, *al-Ta'ifiya fi-l-'Iraq,* 78–81, where the author compares Qasim to his successors, 'Ali Sa'di al-Salih and 'Abd al-Salam 'Arif.

99. Naziha Jawdat al-Dulaymi, "Thawrat 14 Tammuz wa Ahdafuha" [The July 14th Revolution and Its Goals], *al-Thaqafa al-Jadida* 284 (1998): 7–24.

100. al-Samarra'i, *al-Ta'ifiya,* 17.

101. Ibid., 46.

102. Ibid., 84–93.

103. Ibid., 95.

104. Ibid., 103.

105. For example, in the sixth-level high school text on the modern history of the Arab nation, the 1920 Revolution is given short shrift and intercommunal cooperation is not mentioned. Indeed, the revolution is presented as a Pan-Arab movement, which, according to the text, explains British opposition to it. The 1920 Revolution is also seen as having parallels with Qadisiyat Saddam in its efforts to keep Iraq free of occupation. Republic of Iraq, Ministry of Education, *al-Tarikh al-Hadith wa-l-Muʿasir li-l-Watan al-ʿArabi li-l-Saff al-Sadis al-Adabi al-Awal* (Arbil: Ministry of Education Press, 1989), 171–76.

106. al-Samarraʾi, *al-Taʾifiya*, 108.

107. Ibid., 93–94.

108. ʿAli al-Wardi, *ʿAli al-Wardi fi al-Tabiʿa al-Bashariya*, 51.

109. See, for example, Law No. 191 of 1975, "Equality of Women with Men in Rights and Financial Advantages," *al-Waqaʾiʿ al-ʿIraqiya [The Official Gazette]*, no. 2500, Jan. 12, 1975. For an idealized view of Iraqi women see the study by Hala al-Badri, *al-Marʾa al-ʿIraqiya fi-l-Rif wa-l-Madina wa-l-Sahal wa-l-Jabal [The Iraqi Woman in the Countryside, the City, the Plains and the Mountain Regions]* (Beirut: Dar ʾAfaq and the General Federation of Iraqi Women, 1980).

110. Sana al-Khayyat, *Honour & Shame: Women in Modern Iraq* (London: al-Saqi Books, 1990). The author, a sociologist, ends her study by saying that, "In conclusion, the recent modernization system has had a negative impact on women. Their role has merely become more complicated and their lifestyle more stressful and anxiety-provoking."

111. Qais N. al-Nouri, "Iraqi Rural Women's Participation in Domestic Decision-Making," *Journal of Comparative Family Studies* 24, no. 1 (Spring 1993): 81–95.

112. Baghdad: al-Maktaba al-ʿAlamiya / Namsa Limited, n.d. (ca. 1999).

113. Rifat al-Chadirji, *al-Ukhaydar wa-l-Qasr al-Balluri: Nushuʾ al-Nathiriya al-Jadliya fi-l-ʿImara [al-Ukhaydar and the Crystal Palace: The Development of a Dialectical Theory in Architecture]* (London: Riad El-Rayyes, 1991). Chadirji has also published a study of his father's photography, which portrays the 1930s to 1960s in visual imagery. See *The Photography of Kamil Chadirji* (Surrey: LAAM, 1991).

114. Chadirji is not trying to argue that in the 1950s artists were never harassed. Nuri al-Saʿid did harass Jawad al-Salim for the political content of his art. However, what occurred during the 1950s cannot compare to the treatment of intellectuals and artists under the Baʿth.

115. See *Baghdad, Dhalika al-Zaman [Baghdad, Those Were the Days]* (Beirut: al-Muʾassasa al-ʿArabiya li-l-Dirasat wa-l-Nashr, 1998), 15–36. Here we should also note that, despite the static analysis inherent in the ethnic prism

through which Elie Kedourie views Iraqi society, he nevertheless made an important point in *Arabic Political Memoirs* about the greater tolerance among ethnic groups in Iraq prior to the rise of corporatist Pan-Arabism.

116. al-Hajj, *Baghdad,* 125–31.

117. Samrud ʿIzz al-Din, "Inna Ma ʿAshtuhu fi Baghdad Huwa Kull Hiyati" [Indeed, I Lived All My Life in Baghdad], *al-Thaqafa al-Jadida* 294 (May–June 2000): 139.

118. al-Hajj, *Baghdad,* 119.

119. ʿAbd al-Karim al-Izri, *Mushkilat al-Hukm fi-l-ʿIraq: Tahlil li-l-ʿAwamil al-Taʾifiya wa-l-ʿUnsuriya fi Taʿtil al-Hukm al-Dimuqrati fi-l-ʿIraq wa-l-Hulul al-Dururiya li-l-Taghallub ʿAlayha [The Problem of Political Rule in Iraq: An Analysis of the Ethnic and Sectarian Elements That Have Impaired Democratic Rule in Iraq and the Necessary Solutions to Surmount Them]* (London: n.p., 1991), 333–34.

120. Hasan al-ʿAlawi, *Dawlat al-Istiʿara al-Qawmiya: Min Faysal al-Awal ila Saddam Husayn [The Transplanted Nationalist State: From Faysal I to Saddam Husayn]* (London: Dar al-Zawraʾ, 1993).

121. Hasan al-ʿAlawi, *Aswar al-Tin fi ʿAqdat al-Kuwayt wa Idiyulujiyat al-Damm [Mud Walls in the Kuwayt Debacle and the Ideology of Expansionism]* (Beirut: Dar al-Kanuz al-Adabiya, 1995), esp. 252–60.

122. The Iraqi Forum for Democracy's web site is at www.iraqifd.org.

123. For a complete text of Charter 91, see the appendix.

124. www.iraqfoundation.org/forum/charter91.html.

125. Charter 91, Section 4, 2.

126. www.iraq.net/org/ifd/indict_saddam/indict-concern.html, 3; "US Pushes for War Crimes Indictment of Saddam Hussein," Agence France-Presse, Sept. 13, 1999, www.iraqifd.org/indict_saddam/indict-concern.html, which also discusses the al-Duri flight from Vienna.

127. See ʿAziz al-Hajj Haydar, "Baghdad Takhshi Ittiham Saddam bi Jaraʾim Tathir ʾIraqi" [Baghdad is Frightened Over the Accusations Against Saddam for Committing Genocide], *al-Hayat,* July 5, 1999.

CHAPTER 10. CONCLUSION

1. Because no state ever achieves absolute hegemony, I prefer to use the phrase "hegemonic project" to denote the continual and open-ended nature of this process.

2. This is the main contribution of the classic article by Peter Bachrach and Morton Baratz, "The Two Faces of Power," *American Political Science Review* 56, no. 4 (Dec. 1962): 947–52

3. Hitlerian Germany, for example, did not experience similar ethnic and regional cleavages because the Jews and other marginalized groups constituted a small percentage of the population. Nazi ideology was not only crude but explicit. Hitler never hid his hatred of the Jews, nor his desire to rid Germany and

Europe of them and other designated *"Untermenschen."* Nor did Lenin or Stalin feel any compunction about explicitly categorizing capitalists and the nobility as enemies of the Soviet proletarian revolution.

4. For a discussion of the subordination of Islamic doctrine to Western republican notions in the formulation of the constitution of the Islamic Republic of Iran, see Olivier Roy, *The Failure of Political Islam* (Cambridge, Mass.: Harvard University Press, 1994).

5. Despite undergoing a rapid period of industrial development between 1860 and 1914, the czarist state still found itself weakened after participating in World War I. Gramsci's comments on Russia suggest parallels with Ba'thist Iraq: "In Russia, the State was everything, civil society was primordial and gelatinous; in the West, there was a proper relationship between State and civil society, and when the State trembled a sturdy structure of civil society was at once revealed. The State was only an outer ditch, behind which there stood a powerful system of fortresses and earthworks: more or less numerous from one State to the next, it goes without saying—but this precisely necessitated an accurate reconnaissance of each individual country." Likewise in Iraq as in Russia, there was no strong civil society to provide support for the state, especially in times of crisis. *Selections from the Prison Notebooks* (London: Lawrence & Wishart, 1971), 238.

6. Some states, such as those of the Arab Gulf, do not enjoy a strong sense of historical memory. For a discussion of historical memory in relation to one Arab Gulf state, Kuwait, see Eric Davis and Nicolas Gavrielides, "Statecraft, Historical Memory and Popular Culture in Iraq and Kuwait," in *Statecraft in the Middle East: Oil, Historical Memory and Popular Culture*, ed. E. Davis and N. Gavrielides (Miami: Florida International University Press and University Presses of Florida, 1991).

7. Ra'id Fahmi, the editor of the ICP's theoretical journal *al-Thaqafa al-Jadida*, stated that the only nationalists in Iraq at present are the communists. By this he meant that only the ICP continues to operate with the concerns of the entire country in mind rather than answering to a particular political or ethnic constituency or region. Interview, Paris, Jan. 12, 2000.

8. See, for example, Daniel Byman's article with the disturbing title "Let Iraq Collapse," *The National Interest* (Fall 1996): 48–60, which underscores the superficiality of many Western policy analysts' knowledge of Iraqi politics.

9. An article in the Iraqi daily *al-Zawra'* indicated that more than three hundred of Iraq's most prominent literary figures were in exile. One of the reasons it cited for this fact was the inability of writers to make ends meet in Iraq. See the issue for July 10, 2000.

10. For a discussion of issues surrounding this concept, see, for example, Jacques Delacroix, "The Distributive State in the World System," *Studies in Comparative International Development* 15 (1980): 3–21; Hazem Beblawi and Giacomo Luciani, eds., *The Rentier State* (London: Croom Helm, 1987); and Theda Skocpol, "Rentier State and Shi'a Islam in the Iranian Revolution," *Theory & Society* 11 (1982): 265–83, which expresses less certainty that a state's

rentier status will produce "relative autonomy." More recently, see Falih 'Abd al-Jabbar, *al-Dawla, al-Mujtama' al-Madani wa-l-Tahawwul al-Dimuqrati fi-l-'Iraq [The State, Civil Society, and the Democratic Transition in Iraq]* (Cairo: Ibn Khaldun Center, 1995).

11. Wafiq al-Samarra'i, *Hattam al-Bawaba al-Sharqiya [The Destruction of the Eastern Gate]* (Kuwait City: Dar al-Qabas, 1997), 420.

12. On this issue, see Mustafa Amirbayer and Ann Mische, "What is Agency?" *American Journal of Sociology* 103, no. 4 (Jan. 1998): 962–1023.

13. In the Marxist case, this is clear from Marx's distinction between a class-in-itself *(Klasse-an-sich)* and a class-for-itself *(Klasse-für-sich).* In other words, revolutions only occur when classes are conscious of their corporate interests and then *choose* to challenge the prerogatives of the state and ruling class. Karl Marx, *The Eighteenth Brumaire of Louis Bonaparte* (New York: International Publishers, 1969), 124.

14. Among the many works that focus on legitimacy in Arab politics, see Michael Hudson, *Arab Politics: The Search for Legitimacy* (New Haven, Conn.: Yale University Press, 1977).

15. It might be argued that Weber's notion of legitimacy does suggest a dynamic and processual framework. For example, does not the notion of charismatic authority incorporate a *relational* dimension, namely, that a leader can only enjoy charismatic authority if he or she is viewed in such terms by the masses? Although this relation is true, apart from the lack of strong political institutions, the general conditions necessary for the rise of charismatic authority are not well defined. Further, Weber's other categories, traditional and rational-legal authority, are even more ambiguous in terms of the dynamics of the relationship between ruler and ruled. What accounts for the persistence of traditional authority? What are the dynamics behind what Weber sees as the inexorable development of rational-legal authority in Western industrialized societies? When the conceptual day is done, Weber's discussion of legitimacy offers a typology with important heuristic insights. However, its explanatory dimensions need further articulation.

16. The question of whether hegemony exists in advanced industrial societies is beyond the scope of this study. To the extent that a hegemonic ideology does exist, I would argue that it originates in civil society rather than being promoted directly by the state. The attempt during the Reagan administration to refocus American historical memory on the Puritan era as a means of promoting a more individualistic view of politics may be something of an exception to this observation.

17. See, for example, Michael Kelly, "Mob Town," *New York Times Magazine*, Feb. 14, 1993, 18–19, 40–42, 45–46, 50. Reports during the late 1990s of 'Uday Saddam Husayn attempting to assert control over the security services, traditionally his brother Qusay's area of control, suggested an intensification of struggle within the state apparatus. See the article in *al-Hayat*, May 16, 2000, "Saddam's Son Purges Intelligence Service."

18. It is worth recalling Foucault's comments: "I don't want to say that the

State isn't important; what I want to say is that relations of power, and hence the analysis that must be made of them, necessarily extend beyond the limits of the State. In two senses: first of all because the State, for all the omnipotence of its apparatuses, is far from being able to occupy the whole field of actual power relations, and further because the State can only operate on the basis of other, already existing power relations. The State is superstructural in relation to a whole series of power networks that invest the body, sexuality, the family, kinship, knowledge, technology and so forth. . . . I would say that the State consists of the codification of a whole number of power relations which render its functioning possible." *Power-Knowledge: Selected Interviews and Other Writings, 1972–1977* (New York: Pantheon Books, 1980), 122.

Glossary

ʿaba	cloak-like wrap, often black, worn by women of the poorer classes
al-ʿAjam	term used to refer to non-Arabs, especially those of Persian origins
ʿalim/pl. ʿulamaʾ	men of religious learning in Islam
amir	prince
ayatallah	a title bestowed on the most eminent of Shiʿi legal scholars
Bayt al-Hikma	a research institute founded by the ʿAbbasid Caliph al-Maʾmun in 832 C.E. that became famous for its translations of Greek philosophical texts into Arabic
dhimmi	protected non-Muslims, especially Christians and Jews, living under Islamic rule
dunum	a measurement of land equal to 0.618 acre
effendiya	educated white collar social stratum that emerged in the early twentieth century
fatwa/pl. fatawi	a formal religious edict on a point of Islamic law
Farhud	the attack by Pan-Arabists on the Jewish community in Baghdad on June 1–2, 1941
Free Officers	the group of military officers that overthrew the Hashimite monarchy in 1958
Harakiyun	a diminutive Pan-Arab nationalist movement linked to Nasirism
imam	leader of a congregational prayer

353

intifada	names given to the 1952, 1956 and 1991 uprisings in Iraq
al-Jahiliya	"the period of ignorance" that refers to the pre-Islamic era when the world had not yet received God's final revelation
jihad	to struggle on behalf of Islam, including engaging in Holy War
al-Khulafaʾ al-Rashidun	the four "rightly guided caliphs" who ruled after the Prophet Muhammad's death in 632 C.E.
marjaʿ al-taqlid/pl. al-majaʾiya	lit. the "source of emulation;" the reference in Shiʿism to a learned religious scholar whose legal decisions are considered as binding by his followers
al-Majlis al-Watani	Iraq's national assembly established in 1980
mawlid/pl. *mawalid*	Sunni ceremonial observance of the Prophet Muhammad's birthday
mujtahid	a Shiʿi man of religion who has the authority of making independent legal decisions
naqib	marshal of those who claim descent from the Prophet Muhammad
Republican Guard	military unit established by ʿAbd al-Salam ʿArif in 1965 that later became Saddam Husayn's Praetorian guard
Qadisiyat Saddam	lit. "Saddam's Qadisiya;" name given by Saddam Husayn to the Iran-Iraq War to commemorate the Arab defeat of the Sasanians in 637 C.E.
qutr	region in Pan-Arabist ideology, meaning the individual Arab countries that will become part of the Pan-Arab nation
sada	notables who claim descent from the Prophet Muhammad
al-Shuʿubiyun	those members of the bureaucracy of the ʿAbbasid Empire who were of Persian origins and who some Arab scholars claim were responsible for the Empire's ultimate collapse; this term became a metaphor in the twentieth century for minorities in Arab countries who supposedly sought to undermine Pan-Arab unity

shurugi/pl. *shargawiya*	lit. "Easterner;" term used to refer to immigrants from the rural south of Iraq to Baghdad where they often were unable to find employment and lived in poverty
shaykh	Arab tribal leader
shaykh al-mashayikh	paramount chief or chief of a tribal federation
Shi'a	Muslims who consider the fourth caliph 'Ali and his descendants who follow in the Prophet Muhammad's bloodline as the only legitimate successors to leadership of the Islamic community
sirkal	the landlord's representative who collected rents from the peasantry
sultan	lit. "one invested with power and authority;" a term used to refer, beginning in the tenth century, to Muslim leaders who exercised temporal authority
sunna	norm or customary practice referring to the sayings and behavior of the Prophet that became the exemplary precedent and model for all Muslims
Sunnis	the majority of the Muslim community who, unlike the Shi'a, accept the *sunna* of the Prophet Muhammad and the historical succession through election of the caliph
Tapu	a type of land ownership established in Iraq after 1858 that allowed for hereditary usufruct of land
ta'ziya/pl. *ta'azin*	Shi'i lamentation for the martyrdom of Husayn, the grandson of the Prophet Muhammad
al-turath	Arab heritage
al-turath al-sha'bi	popular culture or folklore
wali	the Ottoman ruler of Iraq
al-Wathba	the mass based uprising of 1948; lit., the "Great Leap"
za'im	lit. "leader;" term used to refer to the leader of the July 1958 Revolution, 'Abd al-Karim Qasim

Bibliography

ARABIC NEWSPAPERS

Babil
al-Hayat (London)
al-ʿIraq
Iraq Press (Damascus)
Ittihad al-Shaʿb
al-Jumhuriya (Baghdad)
al-Musawwar al-ʿArabi
al-Qadisiya
Sawt al-Ahali
al-Thawra (Baghdad)
al-Watan al-ʿArabi (Paris)
al-Zaman (London)
al-Zawraʾ (Baghdad)

ENGLISH-LANGUAGE NEWSPAPERS

Christian Science Monitor
The Guardian (London)
Los Angeles Times
New York Times
Sunday Times (London)
Times of London
Washington Post

WORKS IN ARABIC

al-ʿAbbasi, Muhammad. *Min al-Zakhu ila Karbalaʾ: Qissat al-Muʾamira ʿala al-Thawra al-Shaʿbiya fi-l-ʿIraq [From Zakho to Karbala: The Story of the Conspiracy Against the People's Uprising]*. Cairo: al-Zaharaʾ li-l-ʿAlam al-ʿArabi, 1992.

ʿAbd al-Darraji, ʿAbd al-Razzaq. *Jaʿfar Abu Timman: Dawruhu fi-l-Haraka al-Wataniya fi-l-ʿIraq [Jaʿfar Abu Timman and His Role in the Iraqi Nationalist Movement]*. Baghdad: Ministry of Culture and Arts, 1978.

Abd al-Jabbar, Ahmad Fawzi. *Ashhar al-Ightiyalat al-Siyasiya fi-l-ʿIraq [The Most Famous Political Assassinations in Iraq]*. Baghdad: Matbaʿat al-Diwani, 1987.

ʿAbd al-Jabbar, Falih. *al-Dawla, al-Mujtamaʿ al-Madani wa-l-Tahawwul al-Dimuqrati fi-l-ʿIraq [The State, Civil Society, and the Democratic Transition in Iraq]*. Cairo: Ibn Khaldun Center, 1995.

———. Min Dawlat al-Hizb al-Wahid ila Dawlat al-Hizb/al-Usra" [From the One-Party State to the Family/Party State]. *al-Thaqafa al-Jadida* 267 (Dec. 1995–Jan./Feb. 1996): 6–28.

ʿAbd al-Karim, Samir ʿAbd. *Adwaʾ ʿala al-Haraka al-Shuyuʿiya fi-l-ʿIraq [Insights into the Communist Movement in Iraq]*. 5 vols. Beirut: Dar al-Mirsad, 197?–1979.

Adwaʾ ʿala al-Haraka al-Shuyuʿiya fi-l-ʿIraq [Shedding Light on The Communist Movement in Iraq]. 5 vols. Beirut: Dar al-Mirsad, 197?–1979.

ʿAflaq, Michel. *Fi Sabil al-Baʿth al-ʿArabi [For the Sake of the Baʿth]*. Beirut: Dar al-Taliʿa, 1963.

———. *Nidal al-Baʿth [The Baʿthist Struggle]*. 11 vols. Beirut: Dar al-Taliʿa li-l-Tibaʿa wa-l-Nashr, 1976.

Ahmad, ʿAbd al-Ilah. *Nashʾat al-Qissa al-Qasira fi-l-ʿIraq [The Origins of the Short Story in Iraq]*. Baghdad: Matbaʿat al-Shafiq, 1966.

Ahmad, Ibrahim Khalil. "al-Sihafa al-ʿIraqiya, 1914–1958" [The Iraqi Press, 1914–1958]. In *Hidarat al ʿIraq: al ʿIraq al-Muʿasir [Iraq's Civilization: Modern Iraq]*, vol. 13, ed. "An Elite of Iraqi Researchers," 209–10. *Alif Baʾ*, July 15, 1999.

———. *Tatawwur al-Taʿlim al-Watani fi-l-ʿIraq, 1869–1932 [The Development of National Education in Iraq, 1869–1932]*. Basra: Center for Arab Gulf Studies and Basra University Press, 1982.

Ahmad, Kamal Mazhar. *al-Tabaqa al-ʿAmila al-ʿIraqiya: al-Takawwun wa Bidayat al-Taharruk [The Iraqi Working Class: Its Formation and Early Activities]*. Baghdad: Dar al-Rashid li-l-Nashr, 1981.

al-ʿAlawi, Hasan. *Aswar al-Tin fi ʿAqdat al-Kuwayt wa Idiyulujiyat al-Damm [Mud Walls in the Kuwait Debacle and the Ideology of Expansionism]*. Beirut: Dar al-Kunuz al-Adabiya, 1995.

———. *Dawlat al-Istiʿara al-Qawmiya: Min Faysal al-Awal ila Saddam Husayn [The Transplanted Nationalist State: From Faysal I to Saddam Husayn]*. London: Dar al-Zawraʾ, 1993.

———. *al-Shiʿa wa-l-Dawla al-Qawmiya fi-l-ʿIraq [The Shiʿa and the National State in Iraq]*. Paris: CEDI Press, 1989.

ʿAlaywi, Hadi Hasan, and Walid al-Hadithi. *Saddam Husayn wa Qadaya fi-l-Thaqafa wa-l-ʿAlam [Saddam Husayn and Issues Regarding Culture and Information]*. Baghdad: Ministry of Culture and Information, Dar al-Shuʾ un al-Thaqafiya al-ʿAmma, 1991.

ʿAli, Husayn ʿAbd. "al-Wadaʿiya al-Qanuniya li Muwattanay al-Jumhuriya al-

'Iraqiya, 1958–1979" [The Legal Status of Citizens of the Iraqi Republic, 1958–1979]. *al-Thaqafa al- Jadida* 159, vols. 31–32 (1984): 52–62.

al-ʿAli, Salih Ahmad. "Tafsir al-Tarikh" [Historical Explanation]. In Society of Iraqi Authors and Writers, *Tafsir al-Tarikh [Historical Explanation]*, 17–33. Baghdad: Maktabat al-Nahda, 1962?.

al-ʿAlwaji, ʿAbd al-Hamid. "al-Turath al-Shaʿbi" [Popular Heritage/Culture]. In *Hidarat al-ʿIraq: al-ʿIraq al-Muʿasir [Iraq's Civilization: Modern Iraq]*, vol. 13, ed. "An Elite Group of Iraqi Researchers," 33–120. Baghdad: Dar al-Hurriya li-l-Tibaʿa, 1985.

Ayyub, Dhu al-Nun. *Li-l-Haqiqa wa-l-Tarikh: Jumhuriyat 14 Tammuz wa Mufajjir Thawratihi wa Ibn al-Shaʿb al-Barr ʿAbd al-Karim Qasim [For Truth and History: The July 14th Republic and the Creator of its Revolution and Devoted Son of the People ʿAbd al-Karim Qasim]*. Baghdad: al-Sharika al-Wataniya li-l-Tibaʿa wa-l-ʿAlan, 1962.

———. *al-Yadd wa-l-Ard wa-l-Maʾ [The Hand, Earth, and Water]*. 2d ed. Baghdad: Matbaʿat al-Shafiq, 1970 (1939).

al-ʿAzzawi, ʿAbbas. *ʿAshaʾir al-ʿIraq [The Tribes of Iraq]*. 4 vols. Baghdad: Matbaʿat al-Maʿarif, 1947.

al-Badri, Hala. *al-Marʾa al-ʿIraqiya fi-l-Rif wa-l-Madina wa-l-Sahal wa-l-Jabal [The Iraqi Woman in the Countryside, the City, the Plains and the Mountain Regions]*. Beirut: Dar ʿAfaq and the General Federation of Iraqi Women, 1980.

Baghdadi, ʿAbbas. *Li-alla Nansa: Baghdad fi-l-ʿAshriniyat [Lest We Not Forget: Baghdad During the 1920s]*. Beirut: al-Muʾassasa al-ʿArabiya li-l-Dirasat wa-l-Nashr, 1998.

Baqir, Taha. *Muqaddima fi Tarikh al-Hidara al-Qadima [An Introduction to the History of Ancient Civilization]*. Baghdad: Dar al-Shuʾun al-Thaqafiya al-ʿAmma, 1986 (1975).

Baqir, Taha, and ʿAbd al-ʿAziz Humayd. *Turuq al-Baʿth al-ʿIlmi fi Tarikh al-Athar [Methods of Scientific Research in History and Archaeology]*. Mosul: Muʾassasat Dar al-Kutub li-l-Tibaʿa wa-l-Nashr, 1980.

al-Barak, Fadil (al-Takriti). *Dawr al-Jaysh al-ʿIraqi fi Hukumat al-Difaʿ al-Watani wa-l-Harb maʿ Britaniya Sanat 1941 [The Role of the Iraqi Army in the National Defense Government and the 1941 War with Britain]*. Baghdad: al-Dar al-ʿArabiya li-l-Tibaʿa, 1979.

al-Bayati, ʿAlaʾ al-Din Jasim. *al-Binaʾ al-Ijtimaʿi wa-l-Taghir fi-l-Mujtamaʿ al-Rifi: al-Rashidiya, Dirasa Anthrubulujiya Ijtimaʿiya [Social Structure and Change in Rural Society: al-Rashidiya, a Social Anthropological Study]*. Baghdad: Muʾassasat al-Aʿlami / Dar al-Tarbiya, 1975.

al-Bayati, Hamid. *al-Tarikh al-Damawi li Saddam al-Takriti fi Dawʾ al-Wathaʾiq al-Sirriya al-Britaniya, 1937–1966 [The Bloody History of Saddam al-Takriti in Light of Secret British Documents, 1937–1966]*. London: Muʾassasat al-Rafid li-l-Nashr wa-l-Tawziʿ, 1998.

"Bi-l-Dhikri al-Thaniya li Ziyarat al-Qaʾid fi Irwaʿ Mahrajan Jamahiri, Muhafizat al-Qadisiya Tuʿabbir ʿan Hubbiha wa Wifaʾiha li Qaʾid al-Nasr"

[On the Anniversary of the Leader's Visit to the Most Wonderful Popular Festival, al-Qadisiya Province Expresses Its Love and Loyalty to the Victorious Leader]. *al-Jumhuriya*, Jan. 14, 1984.

Butti, Fa'iq. *al-Sihafa al-Yasariya fi-l-ʿIraq [Left-wing Journalism in Iraq]*. London: n.p., 1985.

Center for Scientific Documentation of the Arab Gulf States. *Kashshaf Majallat al-Turath al-Shaʿbi, Silsilat al-Kashafat 4 li-l-Sanawat 1969–1982 [Index of Journals of Popular Culture, Series of Indexes 4, 1969–1982]*. Baghdad: n.p., 1984.

al-Chadirji, Kamil. *Min Awraq Kamil al-Chadirji [From the Private Papers of Kamil al-Chadirji]*. Beirut: Dar al-Taliʿa, 1971.

———. *Mudhakkirat Kamil al-Chadirji wa Tarikh al-Hizb al-Watani al-Dimuqrati [Memoirs of Kamil al-Chadirji and the History of the National Democratic Party]*. Beirut: Dar al-Taliʿa, 1970.

Chadirji, Rifat. *al-Ukhaydir wa-l-Qasr al-Balluri: Nushu' al-Nathariya al-Jadiliya fi-l-ʿImara [al-Ukhaydir and the Crystal Palace: The Development of a Dialectical Theory of Architecture]*. London: Riad El-Rayyes Books, 1991.

al-Dabbagh, Riyad Hamid. "Ta'thir al-Hussar ʿala al-Thaqafa wa-l-Taʿlim fi-l-Iraq wa Mujabahatuhu" [The Impact of the Embargo on Culture and Education in Iraq and How It Is Being Confronted]. *Afaq ʿArabiya* 20, nos. 7/8 (July–Aug. 1994): 31–35.

Da'irat al ʿAlam al-Dhakhili. *Ziyarat al-Sayyid al-Ra'is al-Qa'id Saddam Husayn li-l-ʿAtabat al Muqqadisa [The Visits of the Leader President Saddam Husayn to the Muslim Holy Sites]*. Baghdad: Dar al-Hurriya li-l-Tibaʿa, n.d.

Dalil Kuliyat al-Qanun wa-l-Siyasa, Jamiʿat Baghdad [Guide to the Faculty of Law and Politics, Baghdad University]. Baghdad: Baghdad University, 1984.

"Dawra Jadida li 'Ashbal Saddam" [A New Role for "Saddam's Cubs"]. *al-Hayat*, June 23, 2002.

Dia', ʿAbd al-Jalil al-Shaybani. "al-ʿA'ila bi-Hayy Jamila fi Madinat Baghdad" [The Family in the Jamila Quarter of Baghdad]. Master's thesis, Department of Sociology, Baghdad University, 1974.

al-Din, Samrud ʿIzz. "Inna Ma ʿAshtuhu fi Baghdad Huwa Kull Hiyati" [Indeed, I Lived All My Life in Baghdad]. *al-Thaqafa al-Jadida* 294 (May–June 2000): 139–45.

Directorate of Scientific Education. *Dalil al-Jumhuriya al-ʿIraqiya li Sanat 1960 [Guide to the Iraqi Republic for the Year 1960]*. Baghdad: Ministry of Guidance, 1960.

al-Dulaymi, Ibrahim Mushab. "al-Hijira al-Muʿakisa: Dirasa Ijtimaʿiya li Ahwal Muhajirin min Madinat Baghdad" [Reverse Migration: A Sociological Study of the Conditions of Migrants From Baghdad]. Master's thesis, Department of Sociology, Baghdad University, 1976.

al-Dulaymi, Muhammad ʿAwayd. *Kamil al-Chadirji wa Dawruhu fi-l-Siyasa al-ʿIraqiya, 1898–1968 [Kamil al Chadirji and His Role in Iraqi Politics, 1898–1968].* Baghdad: al-Adib Press, 1997.

al-Dulaymi, Naziha Jawdat. "Thawrat 14 Tammuz wa Ahdafuha" [The July 14th Revolution and Its Goals]. *al-Thaqafa al-Jadida* 284 (1998): 7–24.

al-Duri, ʿAbd al-ʿAziz. *al-Judhur al-Tarikhiya li-l-Shuʿubiya [The Historical Roots of the Shuʿubiya Movement].* 3d ed. Beirut: Dar al-Taliʿa, 1970 (1962).

———. "al Tarikh wa-l-Hadir" [History and the Present]. In Society of Iraqi Authors and Writers, *Tafsir al-Tarikh [Historical Explanation],* 3–16. Baghdad: Maktabat al-Nahda, 1962?.

"Equality of Women with Men in Rights and Financial Advantages." Law No. 191 of 1975. *al-Waqaʾiʿ al-ʿIraqiya [The Official Gazette]* no. 2500, Jan. 12, 1975.

Fadil, ʿAdnan. "Janib min Shakhsiyat Qaʾid Thawrat 14 Tammuz fi-l-ʿIraq: ʿAbd al-Karim Qasim wa-l-Taʾifiya" [An Aspect of the Personality of the July 14th Revolution in Iraq's Leader: ʿAbd al-Karim Qasim and Sectarianism]. *al-Mawsim* 32 (1997): 127–29.

al-Fahd, ʿAbd al-Razzaq Mutlak. "Tarikh al-Haraka al-ʿUmmaliya fi-l-ʿIraq, 1922–1958" [History of the Labor Movement in Iraq, 1922–1958]. Ph.D. diss., Faculty of Arts, Cairo University, 1977.

Hadi, Riyad ʿAziz. *al-Mushkilat al-Siyasiya fi-l-ʿAlim al-Thalith [Political Problems in the Third World].* Baghdad: Dar al-Hurriya li-l-Tibaʿa, 1979.

al-Hajj [Haydar], ʿAziz. *Baghdad, Dhalika al-Zaman [Baghdad, Those Were the Days].* Beirut: al-Muʾassasa al ʿArabiya li-l-Dirasat wa-l-Nashr, 1998.

Hammadi, Saʿdun, et al. *Dawr al-Adab fi al-Waʿi al Qawmi al-ʿArabi [The Role of Literature in Pan-Arab Nationalist Consciousness].* 2d ed. Beirut: Center for Arab Unity Studies, 1982.

al-Hasan, Hamza. "Insafan li Rajil wa-l-Tarikh: Man Qatal al-Zaʿim?" [Justice for a Man and History: Who Killed the Leader?]. *al-Mawsim* 32 (1997): 139–45.

Hasan, Muhammad Harbi. "Aham al-Mushakil al-ʿUmmaliya fi Masaniʿ Baghdad" [The Most Important Labor Problems in Baghdad Factories]. Master's thesis, Department of Sociology, Baghdad University, 1974.

Hasan, Muhammad Salman. *al-Tatawwur al-Iqtisadi fi-l-ʿIraq: al-Tijara al-Kharijiya wa-l-Tatawwur al-Iqtisadi, 1864–1958 [Economic Development in Iraq: Foreign Trade and Economic Development, 1864–1958],* vol. 1. Sidon: al-Maktaba al-ʿAsriya li-l-Tibaʿa wa-l-Nashr, 1965.

al-Hasani, ʿAbd al-Razzaq. *al-Thawra al-ʿIraqiya al-Kubra [The Great Iraqi Revolution].* Sidon: Matbaʿat al-ʿIrfan, 1952.

Haydar, ʿAziz al-Hajj. "Baghdad Takhshi Ittiham Saddam bi Jaraʾim Tathir ʿIraqi" [Baghdad is Frightened Over the Accusations Against Saddam for Committing Genocide]. *al-Hayat,* July 5, 1999.

al-Hindawi, ʿAbd al-Zahra. "Tadris Khususi Bi Asar Khususi Jiddan!!!" [Private Lessons for a Very Private (Special) Price!!!]. *al-Musawwar al-ʿArabi,* Nov. 29, 1998.

Humaydi, Jaʿfar ʿAbbas. *al-Tatawwurat wa-l-Ittijahat al-Siyasiya al-Dhakhilya fi-l-ʿIraq, 1953–1958, [The Development of Domestic Political Tendencies in Iraq, 1953–1958].* Baghdad: Baghdad University Press, 1980.

al-Husari, Khaldun Sati'. *Mudhakkirati fi-l-'Iraq [My Memoirs of Iraq]*, vol. 1 (1921–27). Beirut: Dar al-Tali'a, 1967.

———. *Thawrat 14 Tammuz wa Haqiqat al-Shuyu'iyin fi-l-'Iraq [The July 14th Revolution and the Truth About the Communists in Iraq]*. Beirut: Dar al-Tali'a li-l-Tiba'a wa-l-Nashr, 1960.

Husayn, 'Abd al-Khaliq. "al-Za'im 'Abd al-Karim Qasim wa Mawdu'a al-Dimuqratiya" [The Leader 'Abd al-Karim Qasim and the Question of Democracy]. *al-Mawsim* 32 (1997): 105–15.

Husayn, Khalil Ibrahim. *'Abd al-Karim Qasim: al-Lughz al-Muhayyar ['Abd al-Karim Qasim: The Perplexing Riddle]*, vol. 6, *Mawsu'at 14 Tammuz [Encyclopedia of the July 14th Revolution]*. Baghdad: Dar al-Hurriya li-l-Tiba'a, 1989.

———. *al-Sira'at Bayn 'Abd al-Karim Qasim wa-l-Shuyu'iyin wa Rifa't al-Hajj Sirri al-wa-l-Qawmiyin [The Conflicts Between 'Abd al-Karim Qasim, the Communists, Rifa't al-Hajj Sirri, and the Pan-Arab Nationalists]*, vol. 3, *Mawsu'at 14 Tammuz [Encyclopedia of the July 14th Revolution]*. Baghdad: Dar al-Hurriya li-l-Tiba'a, 1988.

———. *Thawrat al-Shawwaf fi-l-Mawsal 1959: al-Sira'at Bayn 'Abd al-Karim Qasim wa 'Abd al-Salam 'Arif [The Shawwaf Revolution in Mosul 1959: The Struggles Between 'Abd al-Karim Qasim and 'Abd al-Salam 'Arif]*, vol. 1. Baghdad: Dar al-Hurriya li-l-Tiba'a, 1987.

Husayn, Saddam. *Hawla Kitabat al-Tarikh [On the Writing of History]*. Baghdad: Dar al-Hurriya li-l-Tiba'a, 1979.

Ibrahim, Farhad. *al-Ta'ifiya wa-l-Siyasa fi-l-'Alam al-'Arabi: Namudhij al-Shi'a fi-l-'Iraq, Ru'ya fi Mawdu' al-Din wa-l-Siyasa fi-l-Mujtama' al-'Arabi al-Mu'asir [Sectarianism and Politics in the Arab World: The Case of the Shi'a in Iraq, An Overview of Politics and Religion in Contemporary Arab Society]*. Cairo: Maktabat Madbuli, 1996.

Ibrahim, Muhammad 'Ali. "al-Bitaqa al-Daw'iya: Hall Wudi'at Haddan li Tassarub al-Adwiya min al-'Iyadat al-Sha'biya" [The Medicine Identity Card: Has It Placed a Limit on the Flight of Medicine from Government Clinics?]. *Babil*, Dec. 2, 1998.

Ibrahim, Zahida. *Kashshaf bi al-Jara'id wa-l-Majallat al-'Iraqiya, 1869–1978 [Index of Iraqi Newspapers and Journals, 1869–1978]*. 2d ed. Kuwait: Dar al-Nashr wa-l-Matbu'at al-Kuwaytiya, 1982.

———. *Kashshaf bi al-Jara'id wa-l-Majallat al-'Iraqiya [Index to Iraqi Newspapers and Journals]*. Baghdad: Ministry of Information, 1976.

al-'Iraq fi-l-Tarikh [Iraq in History]. Baghdad: Dar al-Hurriya li-l-Tiba'a, 1983.

Iskandar, Amin. *Saddam Husayn: Munadilan wa Mufakkiran wa Insanan [Saddam Husayn: Fighter, Thinker, and Human Being]*. Paris: Hachette, 1980.

"Istidafa al-Ajanib fi-l-'Iraq Ijra Yafda ila al-Salam" [Foreigners Having Access to Iraq Will Lead to Peace]. *al-Jumhuriya*, Oct. 6, 1990.

"al-Istithmarat al-Ajnabiya fi-l-Duwal al-'Arabiya la Tata'addi 1 fi-l-Miya Min al-Ijmali al-'Alam" [Foreign Investments in the Arab States Do Not Exceed 1 Percent of the Global Total]. *al-Hayat*, Oct. 18, 1997.

Ittihad al-Udaba² al-ʿIraqiyin [Union of Iraqi Writers]. *al-Muʾtamar al-Thani li Ittihad al-Udaba² al-ʿIraqiyun, Huzayran, 1960 [The Second Conference of the Iraqi Writers Union, June 1960]*. Baghdad: Matbaʿat al-Nujum, 1960.

al-Izri, ʿAbd al-Karim. *Mushkilat al-Hukm fi-l-ʿIraq: Tahlil li-l-ʿAwamil al-Taʾifiya wa-l-ʿUnsuriya fi Taʾtil al-Hukm al-Dimuqrati fi-l-ʿIraq wa-l-Hulul al-Daruriya li-l-Taghallub ʿAlayha [The Problem of Political Rule in Iraq: An Analysis of the Ethnic and Sectarian Elements That Have Impaired Democratic Rule in Iraq and the Necessary Solutions to Surmount Them]*. London: n.p., 1991.

Jamʿiyat al-Muʾallifin wa-l-Kuttab al-ʿIraqiyin [Society of Iraqi Authors and Writers]. *Tafsir al-Tarikh [Historical Explanation]*. Baghdad: Maktabat al-Nahda, 1961[?].

al-Juburi, Ibrahim. *Sanawat min Tarikh al-ʿIraq: al-Nishat al-Siyasi al-Mushtarak li Hizbay al-Istiqlal wa-l-Watani al-Dimuqrati fi-l-ʿIraq, 1952–1959 [Years from the History of Iraq: The Joint Political Activity of the Independence and National Democratic Parties in Iraq, 1952–1959]*. Baghdad: al-Maktaba al-ʿAlamiya / Namsa Limited, n.d. (ca. 1999).

al-Jumayli, Hamid. "Tazayud al-Talab ʿala Naft Obik wa Namu al-Iqtisad al-ʿAlami Khilal al-Nisf al-Thani min ʿAqd al-Tisʿinat" [The Increased Demand for OPEC Oil During the Second Half of the 1990s]. *Afaq ʿArabiya* 7/8 (July–Aug. 1995): 15–22.

al-Khafaji, Isam. *al-Dawla wa Tatawwur al-Raʾsmaliya fi-l-ʿIraq, 1968–1978 [The State and Capitalist Development in Iraq, 1968–1978]*. Cairo: Dar al-Mustaqbal al-ʿArabi, 1983.

Khalidi, Zuhayr Sadiq Rida. *Saddam Husayn wa Haqaʾiq al-Tarikh al-ʿArabi [Saddam Husayn and the Truth About Arab History]*. Baghdad: Dar al-Hurriya li-l-Tibaʿa, 1989.

Khasbak, Jaʿfar Husayn. "al-Tafsir al-Marksi li-l-Tarikh" [The Marxist Interpretation of History]. In Society of Iraqi Authors and Writers, *Tafsir al-Tarikh [Historical Explanation]*, 34–55. Baghdad: Maktabat al-Nahda, 1961.

Kuliyat al-Qanun wa-l-Siyasa [Faculty of Law and Politics], Baghdad University. *Fi-l-Fikr al-Siyasi w-al-Qanuni li-l-Raʾis al-Qaʾid Saddam Husayn [On the Political and Legal Thought of the Leader President Saddam Husayn]*. Baghdad: Dar al-ʿArabiya, 1984.

" ʾMajallat ʾal-Turath al-Shaʿbi': Majallat al-Fulklur al-Uwla," ["Popular Heritage": The First Folklore Journal]. *al-Turath al-Shaʿbi* 8, no. 2 (1977): 194: 193–200.

al-Majid, Majid. *Intifadat al-Shaʿb fi-l-ʿIraq [The Uprising of the Iraqi People]*. Beirut: Dar al-Wifaq, 1991.

"al-Mashruʿ al-Nahdawi al-ʿArabi" [The Arab Renaissance Project]. *Dirasat Ijtimaʿiya [Social Studies]* 1, no. 1 (Spring 1999): 2–7.

al-Masira: Lamahat Mudayiʿa min Nidal Hizb al-Baʿth al-ʿArabi al-Ishtiraki / Images of the Struggle of the Arab Baʾath Socialist Party. Baghdad: n.p., n.d. (ca. 1982).

Mukhtar, Salah. "Min al-Dawla al-Diniya ila al-Dawla al-Qawmiya" [From the

Religious State to the Pan-Arab Nationalist State]. *Dirasat ʿArabiya* 8 (June 1980): 24–33.

Mustafa, Dalir. "Milaff al-Zaʿim ʿAbd al-Karim Qasim" [The File of the Leader ʿAbd al-Karim Qasim]. *al-Mawsim* 32 (1997): 47–50.

al-Nasiri, ʿAqil. "Laylat al-Saʿud ila Samaʾ al-Khalud: Qiraʾt Tahliliya li-l-Yawm al-Akhir min Hiyat al Zaʿim al-Rahil ʿAbd al-Karim Qasim" [The Night of Ascending to Immortality: An Analytic Reading of the Last Day in the Life of the Deceased Leader, ʿAbd al-Karim Qasim]. *al-Mawsim* 32 (1997): 51–56.

al-Qaysi, Nuri Hammudi. *al-Adib wa-l-Iltizam* [The Writer and Commit-ment]. Baghdad: Dar al-Hurriya li-l-Tibaʿa, 1979.

———. *al-Shiʿr wa-l-Tarikh* [Poetry and History]. Baghdad: Baghdad Univer-sity Press, 1979.

———. "al-Wahda wa Dawr al-Shiʿr Qabla al-Islam" [Unity and the Role of Poetry Prior to Islam]. In Saʿdun Hammadi et al., *Dawr al Adab fil-Waʿi al-Qawmi al-ʿArabi* [The Role of Literature in the Pan-Arab Nationalist Consciousness], 2d ed., 59–90. Beirut: Center for Arab Unity Studies, 1982.

al-Qaysi, Nuri Hammudi, et al. *al-Thaqafa al-ʿArabiya wa-l-Tahaddi* [The Challenge to Arab Culture]. Beirut: Center for Arab Unity Studies, 1995.

Qutb, Sayyid. *Muʿalim fi-l-Tariq* [Signposts Along the Path]. Cairo: n.p., 1965.

al-Rahimi, ʿAbd al-Halim. *Tarikh al-Haraka al-Islamiya fi-l-ʿIraq: al-Judhur al-Fikriya wa-l-Waqiʿ al-Tarikhi, 1900–1924* [The History of the Islamic Movement in Iraq: The Intellectual Roots and the Historical Reality, 1900–1924]. Beirut: al-Dar al-ʿAlamiya li-l-Tibaʿa wa-l-Nashr wa-l-Tawziʿ, 1985.

Rashid, Subhi Anwar. *al-Musiqa fi-l-ʿIraq al-Qadim* [Music in Ancient Iraq]. Baghdad: Dar al-Shuʾun al-Thaqafiya al-ʿAmma, 1988.

Republic of Iraq, Ministry of Education. *al-Tarikh al-Hadith wa-l-Muʿasir li-l-Watan al-ʿArabi li-l-Saff al-Sadis al-Adabi al-Awal* [The Modern and Contemporary History of the Arab Nation for the Sixth Literary Level]. Arbil: Ministry of Education Press, 1989.

———. *Tarikh al-Hidara al-ʿArabiya al-Islamiya* [The History of Arab-Islamic Civilization]. Baghdad: Shirkat al-Sarmad li-l-Tibaʿa al-Mahduda, 1989.

Republic of Iraq, Ministry of Guidance, Directorate of Scientific Education. *Dalil al-Jumhuriya al-ʿIraqiya li Sanat 1960* [Guide to the Iraqi Republic for 1960]. Baghdad: Ministry of Guidance, 1960.

———. *al-Lajna al-ʿUlya li Ihtifalat Thawrat ʿArbaʿta ʿashara Tammuz fi ʿAmiha al-Awal, al-Thani wa-l-Thalath* [Higher Committee for Celebrating the July 14th Revolution in its First, Second, and Third Years]. Baghdad: Ministry of Guidance and al-Rabita Press, 1959, 1960, 1961, 1962.

Republic of Iraq, Ministry of Oil, Public Relations Department. *Iraq Oil Proces-sion [sic]*. Baghdad: n.p., n.d. (ca. 1980).

al-Sabbagh, Salah al-Din. *Fursan al-ʿUruba fi-l-ʿIraq* [The Knights of Arabism in Iraq]. Damascus: al-Shabab al-ʿArabi, 1956.

"Ibn Saddam Yutahhir al-Mukhabarat." [Saddam's Son Purges Intelligence Service]. *al-Hayat*, May 16, 2000.

al-Sadr, Muhammad Baqir. *Iqtisaduna [Our Economy]*. 2d ed. Beirut: Dar al-Fikr, 1970.

Sa'id, 'Ali Karim. *'Iraq 8 Shabbat 1963: Min Hiwar al-Mafahim ila Hiwar al-Damn-Muraja'at fi Dhakirat Talib Shabib [Iraq, February 8, 1963: From a Dialogue of Understanding to a Dialogue of Blood—Reflections on Talib Shabib's Memory]*. Beirut: Dar al-Kanuz al-'Arabiya, 1999.

Sa'id, Farhan Ahmad. *Al Rabi' al-Ta'iyun [The Al Rabi' al-Ta'iyun Tribe]*. Beirut: al-Dar al-'Arabiya li-l-Mawsu'at, 1983.

Salim, Jihad. "Hall Yundim Barzan al-Takriti ila al-Mu'arida al 'Iraqiya?" [Will Barzan al-Takriti Join the Iraqi Opposition?]. *al-Watan al-'Arabi*, Oct. 10, 1998.

Salim, Shakir Mustafa. *al-Shabayyish [al-Shabayyish Village]*. 2 vols. Baghdad: Matba'at al-Rabita, 1956, 1957.

Salman, 'Abd al-'Ali. *al-Mujtama' al-Rifi fi-l-'Iraq [Rural Society in Iraq]*. Baghdad: Dar al-Rashid li-l-Nashr, 1980.

———. "Qaryat al-Sharsh" [al-Sharsh Village]. Master's thesis, Department of Sociology, Baghdad University, 1976.

al-Samarra'i, Majid Ahmad. *al-Tayyar al-Qawmi fi-l-Shi'r al-'Iraqi al-Hadith Munthu al-Harb al-'Alamiya al-Thaniya, 1939, Hatta Naksat Khuzayran 1967 [The Pan-Arabist Tendency in Modern Iraqi Poetry from the Second World War, 1939, to the Setback of June, 1967]*. Baghdad: Ministry of Culture and Information, 1983.

al-Samarra'i, Sa'id. *al-Ta'ifiya fi-l-'Iraq: al-Waqi' wa-l-Hall [Sectarianism in Iraq: The Reality and the Solution]*. London: Mu'assasat al-Fajr, 1993.

al-Samarra'i, Wafiq. *Hattam al-Bawaba al-Sharqiya [The Destruction of the Eastern Gate]*. Kuwait City: Dar al-Qabas, 1997.

al-Samir, Faysal. *Thawrat al-Zanj [The Zanj Rebellion]*. Baghdad: n.p., 1967.

Shabib, Mahmud. *Wathba fi-l-'Iraq wa Suqut Salih Jabr [The of 1948 and the Fall of Salih Jabr]*. Baghdad: Dar al-Thaqafa, 1988.

al-Shabibi, Ja'far. *Mudhakkirati fi-l-'Iraq [My Memoirs of Iraq]*, vol. 1 (1921–27). Beirut: Dar al-Tali'a, 1967.

al-Sira'a al-'Iraqi al-Farisi [The Iraqi-Persian Conflict]. Baghdad: Dar al-Hurriya li-l-Tiba'a, 1983.

al-Takriti, Sulayman. *al-Wasi 'Abd al-Ilah bin 'Ali Yabhathu 'an 'Arsh, 1939–1953 [The Regent 'Abd al-Ilah in Search of a Throne, 1939–1953]*. Beirut: al-Dar al-'Arabiya li-l-Mawsu'at, 1988.

al-Thahir, 'Ala' al-Din. "al-Jawanib al-Ijabiya fi 'Ahd wa Shakhisiyat al-Fariq al-Rukn 'Abd al-Karim Qasim" [The Positive Aspects of the Era and Personality of the Staff Brigadier 'Abd al-Karim Qasim]. *al-Mawsim* 32 (1997): 58–93.

"al-Ustadh Saddam Husayn Na'ib Ra'is Majlis Qiyadat al-Thawra Yatahadath 'an Ma'rakat al-Ta'mim" [The Honorable Saddam Husayn, Vice-President of the Revolution Command Council, Discusses the Nationalization Struggle]. In

Khalid ʿAbd al Munʿim al-ʿAni, *Mawsuʿat al-ʿIraq al-Hadith [The Encyclopedia of Modern Iraq]*, vol. 2. Baghdad: al-Dar al-ʿArabiya li-l-Mawsuʿat, 1977.

The Vanguards Organization [al-Talaʾiʿ]. *Waqaʿaʿ al-Mahrajan al-Awal li-l-Talaʾiʿ wa-l- Nashiʾa al-ʿArab, al-Qutr al-ʿIraqi li-l-Fatra min 17–27, Tammuz 1979 [Report on the First Festival of the Vanguards and Arab Youth, the Iraqi Region, July 17–27, 1979]*. Baghdad: The Vanguards Organization, 1980.

al-Waʾili, Ibrahim. *al-Shiʿr al-Siyasi al-ʿIraqi fi-l-Qarn al-TasiʿʿAshar [Iraqi Political Poetry During the Nineteenth Century]*. Baghdad: Matbaʿat al-Maʿrif, 1978.

al-Wardi, ʿAli. *ʿAli al-Wardi fi al-Tabiʿa al-Bashariya: Taqdim Saʿd al-Bazzaz [ʿAli al-Wardi on Human Nature: Presented by Saʿd al-Bazzaz]*. ʿAmman: al-Ahliya li-l-Nashr wa-l-Tawziʿa, 1996.

———. *Dirasa fi Tabiʿat al-Mujtamaʿ al-ʿIraqi [A Study of the Nature of Iraqi Society]*. Baghdad: Matbaʿat al-ʿAni, 1965.

Yasin, Baqir. *Tarikh al-ʿUnf al-Damawi fi-l-ʿIraq: al-Waqaʾiʿ, al-Dawafiʿ, al-Hulul [The History of Violence in Iraq: The Events, Motivations and Solutions]*. Damascus: Dar al- Kunuz al-Adabiya, 1999.

Yawm al-Nisaʾ al-ʿAlami, 8 Idhar" [International Women's Day, March 8]. In *Min Kitabat al-Rafiq Fahd [From the Writings of Comrade Fahd]*. Baghdad: al-Tariq al-Jadid; Beirut: Dar al-Farabi, 1976.

Yusif, Yusif Salman [Fahd]. *Kitabat al-Rafiq Fahd [The Writings of Comrade Fahd]*. Baghdad: al-Tariq al-Jadid; Beirut: Dar al-Farabi, 1976.

al-Zubaydi, Muhammad Husayn. *Thawrat 14 Tammuz 1958 fi-l-ʿIraq [The July 14, 1958, Revolution in Iraq]*. Baghdad: Ministry of Culture and Information, Daʾirat al-Shuʾun al-Thaqafiya wa-l-Nashr, 1983.

al-Zujaji, Baqir Muhammad Jawad. *al-Riwaya al-ʿIraqiya wa Qadiyat al-Rif [The Iraqi Novel and the Agrarian Question]*. Baghdad: Ministry of Culture and Information, 1980.

WORKS IN WESTERN LANGUAGES

Abercrombie, Nicholas, Stephen Hill, and Bryan S. Turner. *The Dominant Ideology Thesis.* London: George Allen & Unwin, 1980.

Aburish Saïd. *Saddam Husayn: The Politics of Revenge.* New York: Bloomsbury Press, 2000.

Allawi, Jabbar Audah. "Television and Film in Iraq: A Socio-Political and Cultural Study, 1946–1980." Ph.D. diss, University of Michigan, 1983.

Alnasrawi, Abbas. *The Economy of Iraq: Oil, Wars, Destruction of Development and Prospects, 1950–2010.* Westport, Conn.: Greenwood Press, 1994.

Altoma, Salih J. "America, the Gulf War and Arabic Poetry." *al-Jadid* 3, no. 21 (Fall 1997): 16.

al-Amin, Mudhaffar Abdullah. "Jamaat al-Ahali: Its Origin, Ideology, and Role in Iraqi Politics, 1932–1946." Ph.D. diss., School of Oriental Studies, Durham University, 1980.

Amirbayer, Mustafa, and Ann Mische. "What is Agency?" *American Journal of Sociology* 103, no. 4 (Jan. 1998): 962–1023.

Anderson, Benedict. *Imagined Communities: Reflections on the Origins of Nationalism.* London: Verso, 1983.

Anderson, Perry. "The Antinomies of Antonio Gramsci." *New Left Review* 100 (1976–77): 5–80.

Ascherio, A., T. Cote, et al. "Effects of the Gulf War on Infant and Child Mortality in Iraq." *New England Journal of Medicine* 327, no. 13 (1992): 931–36.

Ayubi, Nazih. *Overstating the Arab State: Politics and Society in the Middle East.* London: I. B. Tauris, 1995.

Bachrach, Peter, and Morton Baratz. "The Two Faces of Power." *American Political Science Review* 56, no. 4 (Dec. 1962): 947–52.

Baram, Amatzia. *Culture and Ideology in the Making of Ba'thist Iraq, 1968–1989.* New York: St. Martin's Press, 1991.

———. "Neo-Tribalism in Iraq: Saddam Hussein's Tribal Politics." *International Journal of Middle Eastern Studies* 29 (1997): 1–31.

———. "The Ruling Political Elite in Ba'thi Iraq, 1968–1986: The Changing Features of a Collective Profile." *International Journal of Middle Eastern Studies* 21 (1986): 447–93.

Batatu, Hanna. *The Old Social Classes and Revolutionary Movements of Iraq.* Princeton, N.J., Princeton University Press, 1978.

Beblawi, Hazem, and Giacomo Luciani, eds. *The Rentier State.* London: Croom Helm, 1987.

Bell, Gertrude. *The Letters of Gertrude Bell,* 2 vols. New York: Liveright / Liveright and Boni, 1927.

Bhabha, Homi. *Nation and Narration.* London: Routledge, 1990.

Binder, Leonard. "Egypt: The Integrative Revolution." In *Political Culture and Political Development,* ed. Lucian W. Pye and Sidney Verba, 419–49. Princeton, N.J.: Princeton University Press, 1965.

———. "Political Recruitment and Participation in Egypt." In *Political Parties and Political Development,* ed. Joseph LaPalombara and Myron Weiner, 234–40. Princeton, N.J.: Princeton University Press, 1966.

Burns, John F. "With Potential in the Air, Iraqi Exiles Meet." *New York Times,* July 14, 2002.

Byman, Daniel. "Let Iraq Collapse." *The National Interest* (Fall 1996): 48–60.

Calhoun, Craig, ed. *Critical Social Theory: Culture, History, and the Challenge of Difference.* Oxford: Blackwell, 1995.

Chadirji, Rifat. *The Photography of Kamil Chadirji: Social Life in the Middle East, 1920–1940.* Surrey: LAAM, 1991.

Cockburn, Andrew, and Patrick Cockburn. *Out of the Ashes: The Resurrection of Saddam Hussein.* New York: Harper Collins, 1999.

Cohen, Hayyim J. "The Anti-Jewish *Farhûd* in Baghdad, 1941." *Middle Eastern Studies* 3, no. 1 (Oct. 1966): 2–17.

Committee for the Celebration of the July 14th Revolution. *The July 14th Rev-*

olution in its First, Second, Third, and Fourth Years, vols. 1–4. Baghdad: Matba'at al-Irshad and the Times Press, 1959–62.

A Committee of Officials. *An Introduction to the Past and Present of the Kingdom of Iraq.* Baltimore, Md.: Lord Baltimore Press, 1946.

Connorton, Paul. *How Societies Remember.* Cambridge: Cambridge University Press, 1989.

Dann, Uriel. *Iraq Under Qassem.* New York: Praeger, 1969.

Darwish, Adel, and Gregory Alexander. *Unholy Babylon: The Secret History of Saddam's War.* New York: St. Martin's Press, 1991.

Davis, Eric M. *Challenging Colonialism: Bank Misr and Egyptian Industrialization, 1920–1941.* Princeton, N.J.: Princeton University Press, 1983.

———. "History for the Many or History for the Few? The Historiography of the Iraqi Working Class." In *Workers and Working Classes in the Middle East: Struggles, Histories, Historiographies,* ed. Zachary Lockman, 271–301. Albany: State University of New York Press, 1994.

———. "The Museum and the Politics of Social Control in Modern Iraq." In *Commemorations: The Politics of Memory and Identity,* ed. John Gillis, 90–104. Princeton, N.J.: Princeton University Press, 1994.

———. "The Persian Gulf War: Myths and Reality." In *The United States and the Middle East: The Search for New Perspectives,* ed. Hooshang Amirahmadi, 261–83. Albany: State University of New York Press, 1993.

———. "The Political Economy of the Arab Oil-Producing Countries: Convergence with Western Interests." *Studies in Comparative International Development* 14, no. 2 (1979): 75–94.

———. "State-Building in Iraq During the Iran-Iraq War and the Gulf Crisis." In *The Internationalization of Communal Strife,* ed. Manus I. Midlarsky, 68–91. London: Routledge, 1992.

———. " 'Utopia From Below': The Inclusionary Discourse of the Iraqi Working Class." Paper delivered at the Rutgers Center for Historical Analysis, Rutgers University, Mar. 22, 2000.

———. "The War's Economic, Political Damage to Iraq." *New York Times,* Oct. 7, 1980.

Davis, Eric M., and Nicolas Gavrielides. "Statecraft, Historical Memory and Popular Culture in Iraq and Kuwait." In *Statecraft in the Middle East: Oil, Historical Memory and Popular Culture,* ed. Eric Davis and Nicolas Gavrielides, 116–48. Miami: Florida International University Press / University Presses of Florida, 1991.

Delacroix, Jacques. "The Distributive State in the World System." *Studies in Comparative International Development* 15, no. 3 (1980): 3–21.

Deutsch, Karl. "Social Mobilization and Political Development." *American Political Science Review* 55, no. 3 (Sept. 1961): 493–514.

DeYoung, Terry. *Placing the Poet: Badr Shakir al-Sayyab and Postcolonial Iraq.* Albany: State University of New York Press, 1998.

Directorate-General of Propaganda. *Iraq Today.* Baghdad: Ministry of Interior, 1953.

Douglass, Allen, and Fedwa Malti-Douglas. *Arab Comic Strips: Politics of an Emerging Mass Culture.* Bloomington: Indiana University Press, 1994.

Eley, Geoff, and Ronald Grigor Suny, eds. *Becoming National.* Oxford: Oxford University Press, 1996.

Evans, Peter. "The Eclipse of the State: Reflections on Stateness in an Era of Globalization." *World Politics* 50 (Oct. 1997): 62–87.

Farouk-Sluglett, Marion, and Peter Sluglett. *Iraq Since 1958: From Revolution to Dictatorship.* London: I. B. Tauris, 1990.

Fattah, Hala. *The Politics of Regional Trade in Iraq, Arabia, and the Gulf, 1745–1900.* Albany: State University of New York Press, 1997.

Fentress, James, and Chris Wickham. *Social Memory.* Oxford: Blackwell, 1992.

Foucault, Michel. *Power-Knowledge: Selected Interviews and Other Writings, 1972–1977.* New York: Pantheon Books, 1980.

Freire, Paulo. *Pedagogy of the Oppressed.* New York: Continuum, 1970.

Fromkin, David. *A Peace to End All Peace: The Fall of the Ottoman Empire and the Creation of the Modern Middle East.* New York: Avon Books, 1989.

Gabbay, Rony. *Communism and Agrarian Reform in Iraq.* London: Croom Helm, 1978.

Gallman, Waldemar. *Iraq Under General Nuri: My Recollections of Nuri al-Said, 1954–1958.* Baltimore, Md.: Johns Hopkins Press, 1964.

Garfield, Richard. "The Public Health Impact of Sanctions: Contrasting Responses of Iraq and Cuba." *Middle East Report* 215, 30, no. 2 (Summer 2000): 16–19.

Geertz, Clifford, ed. *Old Societies and New States.* New York: The Free Press, 1964.

Gellner, Ernest. *Nations and Nationalism.* Ithaca, N.Y.: Cornell University Press, 1983.

Ghareeb, Edmund. *The Kurdish Question in Iraq.* Syracuse, N.Y.: Syracuse University Press, 1981.

Gordon, Colin, ed. *Power-Knowledge: Selected Interviews and Other Writings, 1972–1977.* New York: Pantheon Books, 1980.

Graham-Brown, Sarah. *Sanctioning Iraq: The Politics of Intervention in Iraq.* London: I. B. Tauris, 1999.

Gramsci, Antonio. *Selections from the Prison Notebooks.* London: Lawrence & Wishart, 1971.

Gran, Peter. *Beyond Eurocentrism: A New View of Modern World History.* Syracuse, N.Y.: Syracuse University Press, 1996.

Haddad, Mahmoud. "Iraq Before World War I." In *The Origins of Arab Nationalism,* ed. Rashid Khalidi et al., 130–41. New York: Columbia University Press, 1991.

Halbwachs, Maurice. *Les cadres sociaux de la mémoire [The Social Frameworks of Memory].* New York: Arno Press, 1975 (1952).

Hasan, Mohammad Salman. "The Role of Foreign Trade in the Economic Development of Iraq, 1864–1964: A Study in the Growth of a Dependent Economy." In *Studies in the Economic History of the Middle East*, ed. M. A. Cook, 346–72. London: Oxford University Press, 1970.

Helms, Christine Moss. *Iraq: Eastern Flank of the Arab World*. Washington, D.C.: The Brookings Institution, 1984.

Hobsbawm, Eric, and Terence Ranger. *The Invention of Tradition*. Cambridge: Cambridge University Press, 1982.

Hodgson, Marshall G. S. *The Venture of Islam: Conscience and History in a World Civilization*. 3 vols. Chicago: University of Chicago Press, 1974.

Hopwood, Derek, et al. *Iraq: Power and Society*. London: Ithaca Press, 1993.

Hourani, Albert. *Minorities in the Arab World*. Oxford: Oxford University Press, 1947.

House Republican Policy Committee. "New Evidence of Clinton's Failure Update: Humiliation in Iraq." http://policy.house.gov/Prspctvs/update2.htm. Oct. 22, 1996.

Hudson, Michael C. *Arab Politics: The Search for Legitimacy*. New Haven, Conn.: Yale University Press, 1977.

Huntington, Samuel. *The Clash of Civilizations and the Remaking of World Order*. New York: Simon & Schuster, 1996.

———. *Political Order in Changing Societies*. New Haven, Conn.: Yale University Press, 1968.

al-Husry, Khaldun S. "The Assyrian Affair of 1933," parts 1 and 2. *International Journal of Middle Eastern Studies* 5, nos. 2 and 3: 161–76 and 344–60.

———. "The Political Ideas of Yunis al-Sab'awi." In *Intellectual Life in the Arab East, 1890–1935*, ed. Marwan R. Buheiry, 165–75. Beirut: American University of Beirut Press, 1981.

Hussein, Saddam. *Saddam Hussein on Current Events in Iraq*, trans. Khalid Kishtainy. London: Longman, 1977.

Huxley, Aldous. *Brave New World*. New York: Harper and Brothers, 1946.

Iraq Forum for Democracy. www.iraqifd.org/anaheimFeb262000.html. Feb. 26, 2000.

Iraqi National Congress. "Over 800 Executions of Opposition Members in Iraq." www.INC.org.uk. Dec. 22, 1997.

Izzidien, Yousif. "Poetry in the Social and Political Development of 20th-Century Iraq." Ph.D. diss, School of Oriental and African Studies, University of London, 1956.

Jabar, Faleh Abdel. "Shaykhs and Ideologues: Detribalization and Retribalization in Iraq, 1968–1998." *Middle East Report* 215, vol. 30, no. 2 (Summer 2000): 28–31, 48.

Karsh, Efraim, and Inari Rautsi. *Saddam Hussein: A Political Biography*. New York: The Free Press, 1991.

Katzman, Kenneth. "CRS Report: Iraq's Opposition Movements." www.fas.org/irp/crs/crs-iraq-op.htm.

Kedourie, Elie. *Arabic Political Memoirs and Other Studies*. London: Frank Cass, 1974.

————. *The Chatham House Version and Other Middle Eastern Studies*. New York: Praeger, 1970.

————. *Democracy and Arab Political Culture*. Washington, D.C.: Washington Institute for Near East Policy, 1992.

————. *Politics in the Middle East*. Oxford: Oxford University Press, 1992.

Kelly, Michael. "Mob Town." *New York Times Magazine*, Feb. 14, 1993, 18–50.

al-Khadduri, Majid. *Independent Iraq*. Oxford: Oxford University Press, 1960.

————. *Republican Iraq: A Study in Iraqi Politics Since the Revolution of 1958*. London: Oxford University Press, 1969.

————. *Socialist Iraq: A Study of Iraqi Politics Since 1968*. Washington, D.C.: Middle East Institute, 1978.

al-Khalil, Samir [Kanan Makiya]. *The Republic of Fear: The Degradation of Politics in Modern Iraq*. Berkeley: University of California Press, 1989.

————. *The Monument: Art, Vulgarity and Responsibility in Iraq*. Berkeley: University of California Press, 1991.

al-Khayyat, Sana. *Honour and Shame: Women in Modern Iraq*. London: al-Saqi Books, 1990.

King, Mary E. "The Artists of Baghdad." *Oil Progress* (Fall 1987): 2–19.

Lawrence, David Aquila. "Iraqi Kurds Enjoy a De Facto State." *Christian Science Monitor*, May 3, 2000.

Le Goff, Jacques. *History and Memory*. New York: Columbia University Press, 1992 (1971).

Lefevbre, Henri. *The Production of Space*. Oxford: Blackwell Publishers, 1991 (1974).

Longrigg, Stephen Hemsley, and Frank Stoakes. *Iraq*. London: Ernest Benn, 1958.

Lowenthal, David. *The Past is a Foreign Country*. Cambridge: Cambridge University Press, 1985.

Mahdavy, H. "The Patterns and Problems of Economic Development in Rentier States: The Case of Iran." In *Studies in the Economic History of the Middle East*, ed. Michael Cook, 428–67. Oxford: Oxford University Press, 1970.

Makiya, Kanan. *Cruelty and Silence: War, Tyranny, Uprising, and the Arab World*. New York: W. W. Norton & Co., 1993.

Marr, Phebe. *The Modern History of Iraq*. Boulder, Colo: Westview Press, 1985.

Marx, Karl. *The Eighteenth Brumaire of Louis Bonaparte*. New York: International Publishers, 1969.

"Mass Executions in Iraq." www.INC.org.uk. Iraqi National Congress Internet site, Dec. 12, 1997.

Middle East Watch. *Bureaucracy of Repression: The Iraqi Government in Its Own Words*. New York: Middle East Watch, 1994.

————. *Endless Torture: The 1991 Uprising in Iraq and Its Aftermath*. New York: Human Rights Watch, 1992.

Meyer, Steven Lee. "Flight Tests Show Iraq Has Resumed a Missile Program." *New York Times,* July 1, 2000.

"Mirbad Poetry Festival: Saddam Literary Prizes." *Gilgamesh* (Spring 1990).

Moore, Barrington, Jr. *Social Origins of Dictatorship and Democracy.* Boston: Beacon Press, 1966.

"More Names of Executed Prisoners." www.INC.org.uk. Iraqi National Congress Internet site, Dec. 22, 1997.

Morris, Benny. *1948 and After: Israel and the Palestinians.* New York: Oxford University Press, 1990.

Mottahedeh, Roy. "The Shu'ubiyah Controversy and the Social History of Early Islamic Iran." *International Journal of Middle Eastern Studies* 7 (1976): 161–82.

Mufti, Malik. *Sovereign Creations: Pan-Arabism and Political Order in Syria and Iraq.* Ithaca, N.Y.: Cornell University Press, 1996.

al-Musawi, Muhsin Jassim. "The Sociopolitical Context of the Iraqi Short Story, 1908–1968." In *Statecraft in the Middle East: Oil, Historical Memory, and Popular Culture,* ed. Eric Davis and Nicolas Gavrielides, 202–27. Miami: Florida International University Press / University Presses of Florida, 1991.

Nadhmi, W. J. O. "The Political, Intellectual, and Social Roots of the Iraqi Independence Movement, 1920." Ph.D. diss, School of Oriental Studies, Durham University, 1974.

al Nafesi, A. F. "The Role of the Shi'ah in the Political Development of Modern Iraq, 1914–1921." Ph.D. diss, Cambridge University, 1972.

Nakash, Yitzhak. *The Shi'is of Iraq.* Princeton, N.J.: Princeton University Press, 1994.

North, Douglass. *Institutions, Institutional Change and Economic Performance.* Cambridge: Cambridge University Press, 1990.

al-Nouri, Qais N. "Iraqi Rural Women's Participation in Domestic Decision-Making." *Journal of Comparative Family Studies* 24, no. 1 (Spring 1993): 81–95.

"Ousting Saddam Seen as a Long Shot." *Washington Post,* Feb. 20, 1998.

Owen, Roger. *The Middle East in the World Economy, 1800–1914.* London: Methuen, 1981.

Putnam, Robert. *Making Democracy Work: Civic Traditions in Modern Italy.* Princeton, N.J.: Princeton University Press, 1993.

Qassim, Major-General Abdul Karim. *Messages and Greetings from Major-General Abdul Karim Qassim Prime Minister and Commander-in-Chief of the Armed Forces to the International Conferences.* Baghdad: Ministry of Guidance, n.d.

———. *Principles of the July 14 Revolution.* Baghdad: n.p., n.d.

Qubain, Fahim. *Education and Science in the Arab World.* Baltimore, Md.: Johns Hopkins Press, 1966.

Picard, Elizabeth. "Le régime irakien et la crise: les ressorts d'une politique." *Maghreb/Machrek* 130 (Oct.–Dec. 1990): 32–40.

Ram, Haggay. "The Immemorial Iranian Nation? School Textbooks and Historical Memory in Post-Revolution Iran." *Nations & Nationalism* 6, no. 1 (Winter 2000): 67–90.

Reich, Wilhelm. *Sex-Pol: Essays, 1929–1934.* New York: Vintage, 1972.

Republic of Iraq, Ministry of Culture and Arts. *Culture and Arts in Iraq.* Baghdad: n.p., 1978.

Republic of Iraq, Ministry of Culture and Information. *Women's Fashion.* Baghdad: Dar al-ʿAzyaʾ al-ʿIraqiya, 1981.

République Irakienne, Ministère de la Culture et des Arts [Republic of Iraq, Ministry of Culture and Arts]. *La Culture et des Arts en Irak: Celebration du Xeme Anniversaire de la Révolution du 17–30 Juillet* [Celebration of the 20th Anniversary of the Revolution of July 17–30]. Baghdad: n.p., 1978.

Roy, Olivier. *The Failure of Political Islam.* Cambridge, Mass.: Harvard University Press, 1994.

"Saddam Cancer Fear Spurs Rivals." *Times of London,* July 28, 2000.

"Saddam's Son is a Cocaine Kingpin." *Times of London.* As reported by Tabloid News Service, Feb. 9, 1998, www.tabloid.net/1998/02/09/.

Sassoon, Anne Showstack. *Gramsci's Politics.* New York: St. Martin's Press, 1980.

Schlaim, Avi. *Collusion Across the Jordan: King Abdullah, the Zionist Movement, and the Partition of Palestine.* Oxford: Clarendon Press, 1988.

Scott, James C. *Domination and the Arts of Resistance: Hidden Transcripts.* New Haven, Conn.: Yale University Press, 1990.

al-Sharqawi, Abdel Rahman. *The Egyptian Earth,* trans. Desmond Stewart. Austin: University of Texas Press, 1990.

Shiblak, Abbas. *The Lure of Zion: The Case of the Iraqi Jews.* London: al-Saqi Books, 1986.

Simon, Reeva S. *Iraq Between the Two World Wars.* New York: Columbia University Press, 1986.

———. "The Teaching of History in Iraq Before the Rashid Ali Coup." *Middle Eastern Studies* 22 (Jan. 1986): 37–51.

Simons, Geoff. *Iraq: From Sumer to Saddam.* 2d ed. New York: St. Martin's Press, 1996.

Singerman, Diane. *Avenues of Participation: Family, Politics and Networks in Urban Quarters of Cairo.* Princeton, N.J.: Princeton University Press, 1995.

Skocpol, Theda. "Rentier State and Shiʾa Islam in the Iranian Revolution." *Theory & Society* 11 (1982): 265–83.

———. *States and Social Revolutions.* Cambridge: Cambridge University Press, 1979.

Smith, Anthony D. *The Ethnic Origins of Nations.* Oxford: Blackwell Publishers, 1986.

Soeterik, Robert. *The Islamic Movement of Iraq, 1958–1980.* Amsterdam: Middle East Research Associates, Occasional Paper no. 12, 1980.

Soldani, Simonetta, and Gabrielle Turin. *Fare gli Italiani: Scuola e cultura nell' Italia contemporanea [Making Italians: Schooling and Culture in Contemporary Italy].* Bologna: Il Mulino, 1993.

Sprague, Ken. *The Smoke at the End of the Road.* London: Iraqi Cultural Centre, 1981.

Springborg, Robert. "Intifah, Agrarian Transformation, and Elite Consolidation in Contemporary Iraq." *Middle East Journal* 40, no. 1 (Winter 1986): 33–52.

Stratfor Special Reports. "Yugoslavia and Iraq: The Alliance Reunites." Nov. 9, 1999. www.stratfor.com/MEAF/specialreports/special118.htm.

Swain, Jon. "Foul Play—It's a Grim Life in Saddam United FC." *Sunday Times* (London), Aug. 15, 1999.

Tarbush, Mohammad A. *The Role of the Military in Politics: A Case Study of Iraq to 1941.* London: Kegan Paul International, 1982.

Thesiger, Wilfred. *The Marsh Arabs.* London: Longmans, 1964

"US Pushes for War Crimes Indictment of Saddam Hussein." *Agence France-Presse.* www.iraq.net/org/ird/indict_saddam/indict-concern.html. Sept. 13, 1999.

Wiley, Joyce N. *The Islamic Movement of Iraqi Shīʿas.* Boulder, Colo.: Lynne Rienner, 1992.Wittgenstein, Ludwig. *Philosophical Investigations.* 3d ed. London: MacMillan, 1953.

Yousif, Abdul-Salaam. "The Struggle for Cultural Hegemony in Iraq." In *The Iraqi Revolution of 1958: The Old Social Classes Revisited,* ed. Robert Fernea and Wm. Roger Louis, 173–96. London: I. B. Tauris, 1991.

Yousif, Abdul-Salaam Yacoob. "Vanguardist Cultural Practices: The Formation of an Alternative Cultural Hegemony in Iraq and Chile, 1930s–1970s." Ph.D. diss., University of Iowa, 1988.

Zeruvabel, Yael. *Recovered Roots: Collective Memory and the Making of Israeli National Tradition.* Chicago: University of Chicago Press, 1995.

Zubaida, Sami. "Contested Nations: Iraq and the Assyrians." *Nations & Nationalism* 6, no. 3 (Summer 2000): 363–82.

MANUSCRIPT COLLECTIONS

Great Britain, Foreign Office Drafts and Dispatches, Public Record Office, London Documents of the British Foreign Office, London. Extracts from the following series were used: FO371, 1947–60; FCO 1967–69.

INTERVIEWS

Dr. Salih Ahmad al-ʿAli, former President of the Iraqi Academy, Baghdad, May 30, 1980, and June 21, 1984.

Dr. ʿAbd al-Hamid al-ʿAlwaji, Iraqi National Library, Baghdad, June 14, 1984.

Dr. Mohammed Baqir Alwan, Tufts University, June 19, 1998.

Rifat Chadirji, Surrey, England, Jan. 20, 2000.

Faris Couri, London, July 24 and July 28, 2000. Telephone interview.

Raʾid Fahmi, Editor in Chief of *al-Thaqafa al-Jadida,* Paris, Jan. 12, 2000.

Colonel Salim Fakhri, former Director of Broadcasting under Qasim, London, July 3, 1984.

Dr. Wadood Hamad, Mahwah, New Jersey, July 18, 2000. Telephone interview.
'Aziz al-Hajj Haydar, Paris, Jan. 14, 2000.
Dr. Fadil al-Jamali, Tunis, June 20, 1995. Telephone interview.
Mundhir al-Juburi, Editorial Secretary, *al-Tali'a al-Adabiya*, June 8, 1984.
Dr. Wadia Juwaideh, late Emeritus Professor of Near Eastern Studies, Indiana University, Nov. 10, 1999. Telephone interview.
Dr. Isam al-Khafaji, New York and Rutgers Universities, Nov. 16, 1999, Apr. 12 and Apr. 14, 2000.
Ghanim Hamdun al-Muri, former editor in chief of *al-Thaqafa al-Jadida*, London, May 16, 2000. Telephone interview.
Dr. Muhsin Jasim al-Musawi, former editor in chief of *Afaq 'Arabiya*, Tunis, Feb. 16, Mar. 15, and May 16, 2000. Toronto, July 19, 2000. Telephone interview.

Index

Compositor	Binghamton Valley Composition, LLC
Text	10/13 Aldus
Display	Aldus
Printer and binder	Thomson-Shore, Inc.